ActiveX from the Ground Up

ActiveX from the Ground Up

John Paul Mueller

Osborne **McGraw-Hill**

Berkeley New York St. Louis San Francisco Auckland Bogotá Hamburg London Madrid Mexico City
Milan Montreal New Delhi Panama City Paris São Paulo Singapore Sydney Tokyo Toronto

Osborne **McGraw-Hill**
2600 Tenth Street
Berkeley, California 94710
U.S.A.

For information on translations or book distributors outside the U.S.A., or to arrange bulk purchase discounts for sales promotions, premiums, or fundraisers, please contact Osborne/**McGraw-Hill** at the above address.

ActiveX from the Ground Up

1234567890 DOC 9987

ISBN 0-07-882264-5

Publisher
Brandon A. Nordin

Acquisitions Editor
Wendy Rinaldi

Project Editor
Mark Karmendy

Copy Editor
Judith Brown

Proofreader
Stephany Otis

Computer Designer
Roberta Steele

Series Design
Marcela V. Hancik

Illustrator
Roberta Steele

Quality Control Specialist
Joe Scuderi

Cover Design
Ted Mader Associates

About the Author

John Mueller is a freelance author and technical editor. He has writing in his blood, having produced 29 books and almost 200 articles to date. The topics range from networking to artificial intelligence and from database management to heads down programming. Some of his current books include a Delphi programmers guide and a Windows NT advanced user tutorial. His technical editing skills have helped over 22 authors refine the content of their manuscripts. In addition to book projects, John has provided technical editing services to both *Data Based Advisor* and *Coast Compute* magazines.

When John isn't working at the computer, you can find him in his workshop. He's an avid woodworker and candlemaker. On any given afternoon you can find him working at a lathe or putting the finishing touches on a bookcase. One of his favorite projects is making candlesticks and the candles to go with them. You can reach John on CompuServe at 71570,641 or on the Internet at JMueller@pacbell.net.

This book is dedicated to my brothers and sisters: Mark, Lori, Christine, and Lee—who could ask for better companions on life's long road?

Contents at a Glance

I ▬▬ ActiveX Nuts & Bolts

1 ▬▬ Introducing ActiveX 3

2 ▬▬ Building a Basic Control 25

3 ▬▬ OLE and ActiveX 65

4 ▬▬ HTML and ActiveX 107

5 ▬▬ ActiveX Documents 143

II ▬▬ ActiveX and the Environment

6 ▬▬ Addressing Security Concerns 169

7 ▬▬ Scripting and ActiveX 223

8 ▬▬ The Internet Is Not Your Computer 261

III ▬▬ Real World ActiveX

9 ▬▬ Utilities and ActiveX 297

10 ▬▬ New Technologies and ActiveX 329

11 ▪▪▪ **Graphics and ActiveX** **367**

12 ▪▪▪ **Data Entry and ActiveX** **423**

13 ▪▪▪ **The Database Connection** **449**

14 ▪▪▪ **Multimedia and ActiveX** **491**

IV ▪▪▪ **Appendixes**

A ▪▪▪ **ActiveX Component Resources** **517**

B ▪▪▪ **Glossary** **535**

▪▪▪ **Index** **553**

Table
of Contents

Acknowledgments . . . . *xvii*
Introduction . . . . *xix*

I ■■■ ActiveX Nuts & Bolts

1 ■■■ Introducing ActiveX 3
ActiveX—The Historical View 6
    DDE—The Point of Origin 6
    OLE—The Next Step 7
    From OLE 1 to OLE 2 9
    Making OLE Easy Through OCXs 13
    Network OLE, Better Known as DCOM 14
    The ActiveX Connection 15
What Is ActiveX? 15
What Will ActiveX Do for You? 17
ActiveX Versus OCX Controls 18
Working with the JavaScript Language 19
Working with the VBScript Language 21
ActiveX from the User's Perspective 22

2 ■■■ Building a Basic Control 25
Defining a Project 26
    Writing the Code 28
    Modifying the Default About Box 30
    Adding Properties and Events 30
    Defining the Property Page 33

Adding Some Code 37
Breaking the Code into Pieces 46
Testing the Control 49
Internal Testing Phase 1—Use the Control in a
Standard Environment 50
Internal Testing Phase 2—Test Locally Within
a Browser 54
Internal Testing Phase 3—Use a Network
Connection to Test a Full Web Page 60
External Testing—Check Control
Functionality on an Uncontaminated
Machine 61

3 ▬▬ OLE and ActiveX **65**
A Quick Look at the Component Object Model (COM)
and OLE 67
OLE Control Hosting 69
Creating an Interface 71
Storing the Data 73
An Overview of the OLE Portion of the Windows
Registry 75
A Look at the Registry 76
Understanding Special Extension Subkeys 80
Understanding the OLE 1 Registry Entries 82
Understanding the OLE 2 Registry Entries 87
Using the OLEViewer Utility 87
Looking at Interfaces with OLEViewer 94
Freeing Memory Used by Object Instances 96
Seeing the Bigger Picture 96
Creating OLE Control Streams Using ODS_TOOL.EXE 98

4 ▬▬ HTML and ActiveX **107**
Quick Overview of HTML 109
Understanding the <HEAD> Tag 111
Adding Headings Using the <H*x*> Tag 111
Modifying the Default About Box 112
Adding Properites and Events 112
Links and Anchors 113

Creating a Simple HTML Document 114
    Working with Lists 116
    Adding Graphics 118
    Creating Tables 121
    Using Forms 124
Where Does ActiveX Fit In? 131
Downloading from the Internet 134
Building Component Download (CAB) Files Using
    DIANTZ.EXE 136

5 ■■ ActiveX Documents **143**
What Are ActiveX Documents
    (A.K.A. OLE Document Objects)? 145
    Creating the Connection 149
    Using the Web Publishing Wizard 150
An Overview of the ActiveX Document Architecture 155
    IOleDocument 159
    IOleDocumentView 160
    IOleCommandTarget 162
    IPrint 164

II ■■ ActiveX and the Environment

6 ■■ Addressing Security Concerns ....■■■ **169**
The Internet—Wild and Untamed 172
    The Business Perspective of the Internet 173
    Defining the Object of Protection—Data 175
    Creating Some Form of Protection 176
    Implementing a Solution 177
Internet Security Standards 178
    Who Is W^3C? 179
    Standard Methods of Handling Money 187
Making Windows NT Security Work for You 189
    Built-in Security Features 191
    Private Communication Technology (PCT) 201
    Using Digital Signatures 204
    Understanding the CryptoAPI 208

Ensuring the Safe Download of Internet Code 213
    Using the Windows Trust Verification API 214
    Understanding the Windows Software
      Publishing Trust Provider 217
    Mechanics of Downloading Internet
      Components 219
    Unregistering Your Control 219
    Signing Your Control 219
    Performing a Live Test 221

7 ▬ Scripting and ActiveX **223**
    Overview of ActiveX Scripting 225
    Overview of Visual Basic Scripting (VBScript) 229
    Overview of Java Scripting (JavaScript) 234
    The Basics of Working with Scripts 237
      Using VBScript 238
      Using JavaScript 243
    Working with ActiveX Controls 248
      Using VBScript 249
      Using JavaScript 254

8 ▬ The Internet Is Not Your Computer **261**
    Designing with the Internet in Mind 263
    Avoiding the Pixel Trap 266
    Using Tricks of the Trade to Reduce Processing Needs 269
    Creating an Animated GIF 276
    Getting Where You Want to Go 285
      Overview of URL Monikers 286
      Creating an URL Moniker 288
      Hyperlinking Basics 289
      Understanding the Hyperlink Interface 293

III ▬ Real World ActiveX

9 ▬ Utilities and ActiveX **297**
    Grabbing User Information 299
    Launching a Program 307
    Working a Color Change 314

10 ■■■ **New Technologies and ActiveX** **329**

 New Features of Visual C++ 4.2 331
  A Look at the ISAPI Wizard 332
  Application Enhancements 337
  ActiveX Control Improvements 337
 Creating an ActiveX Document 339
  Testing the Default Application—Step 1 342
  Fixing the ActiveX Document Server 345
  Testing the Default Application—Step 2 352
  Converting an Existing Application 352
 Working with URL Monikers 356
  Adding Library Support 357
  Creating the Required Resources 358
  Defining New Classes and Writing Code 360

11 ■■■ **Graphics and ActiveX** **367**

 Implementing an Icon and Text Button 369
  Adding Properties and Events 371
  Defining the Property Pages 371
  Defining a Message Map 375
  Adding Some Code 377
  Creating a Simple Test Program 388
  Using the New Control on a Web Page 391
  Adding Custom Icons 394
 Creating a Simple Drawing 397
  Building the DepictIt Control 397
  Testing the DepictIt Control 415

12 ■■■ **Data Entry and ActiveX** **423**

 The Basic Data Entry Form 425
  Form Aesthetics and Usability Considerations 425
  Working with Cookies 436
 Data Entry Forms with Scripts 441

13 ■■■ **The Database Connection** **449**

 Using the HREF Anchor Technique 451
 Understanding the Objects in Data Access Objects
  (DAO) 453
  Defining DAO 454

DAO Versus ODBC 456

Understanding Double Buffering 459

A Practical Example of Using DAO 461

Data Access in an HTML Layout 476

Using the Microsoft RemoteData Control 480

14 ■ **Multimedia and ActiveX** **491**

Using Windows' Built-in

Multimedia Capabilities 493

Using the ActiveMovie Control 498

Third-Party Multimedia Solutions 508

RealAudio for Great Sounds 509

IV ■ **Appendixes**

A ■ **ActiveX Component Resources** **517**

How to Get the Best Deal 518

Royalties 518

Source Code 519

Recommendations from Other Programmers 519

Demo or Shareware Versions 519

Money-Back Guarantee 520

Company Stability and Support 520

Cost per Component Versus Quality 521

Flexibility 521

Efficiency 521

OCXs—A Step Away from ActiveX 522

ActiveX Controls 526

Browser Plug-Ins Based on ActiveX Controls 531

B ■ **Glossary** **535**

■ **Index** **553**

Acknowledgments

Thanks to my wife Rebecca for her assistance and support in getting this book completed. I really don't know what I would have done without her help in researching and compiling some of the information that appears in the book. She also did a fine job of proofreading my rough draft.

Joe O'Neil did a superb job of technically editing the book. He did more than just check the facts by offering thoughtful input where needed to improve the book as a whole.

Matt Wagner, my agent, deserves credit for helping me get the contract in the first place and taking care of all the details that most authors really don't think about.

Finally, I would like to thank Wendy Rinaldi, Mark Karmendy, Nancy McLaughlin, Ann Sellers, Daniela Dell'Orco, and all the other people at Osborne/McGraw-Hill for their assistance in bringing this book to print.

Introduction

The idea that the Internet's going to be the next big deal in the computer industry is already well entrenched. Every on-line service out there touts Internet access as one of the reasons that you should subscribe. Look at a television screen and you're apt to see an Internet address (more commonly referred to as an *URL* or *uniform resource locator*) somewhere along the way. Take a look at Microsoft and Novell. They both moved their news groups from CompuServe to the Internet in order to serve a larger audience. (Obviously it doesn't hurt that both companies have a big stake in the Internet.)

One of the problems with using the Internet today is that the methods for implementing a Web page are often arcane and difficult to understand once you get past the idea of simply distributing information. In addition, people don't want to simply look at a static page when it comes to dazzling presentations. They want a page that allows them to actually interact with the information you want to present. If you want to interact with the user, then you'd normally have to resort to using all kinds of devious script languages that only a UNIX programmer would love. The idea of actually sending the user anything other than text was a foreign idea as late as a year ago. It's no wonder then that many companies are finding their first entry into Internet computing less than awe inspiring.

ActiveX is a new way of interacting with the user and distributing applications on the Internet. It also gives the webmaster a lot more in the way of tools to dazzle potential visitors. In many cases, you get all of these new capabilities without writing a single line of script. Obviously, the first question is, "Who cares?" The answer is all those companies who are trying to develop intranet or Internet sites. A recent survey showed that 48 percent of the companies they talked to are implementing applications on the Internet today. Another 14 percent said they planned to do so within the next six months and 16 percent planned to do so within a year (for a total of 78 percent). Obviously there's more than a little interest in Internet applications. These applications will allow the vendor to do a variety of things. In fact, you should expect applications that do anything from conducting a survey to providing you with the latest version of the spell checker for your on-line word processor.

The new capabilities provided by ActiveX aren't something that Microsoft simply hopes will work out. There are more than a few companies who are already getting their feet wet by providing some type of Internet enabled applications through ActiveX. For example, Lotus has recently decided to provide some types of ActiveX utilities that will enable access to Notes. Other companies like Quarterdeck plan to port their entire line of utility programs to the Internet. Just how the downloading of these programs will work is uncertain right now, but the idea of on-line shopping is appealing to a lot of people who need to keep their software updated.

The answers provided in the previous two paragraphs lead to a second question. Why is the Internet such a hot environment? Another survey asked businesses why they would use the Internet to provide some kind of value-added service or better access to information by employees. Seventy-nine percent of the people surveyed cited ease of use. All you need to access the vast quantity of information on the Internet is an ISP (Internet Service Provider) and a browser. Installing the browser is no more difficult than any other Windows application—sometimes even less. In addition, a number of ISPs supply installation programs that are so automatic the user doesn't have to do much more than supply a name, address, and some billing information like a credit card number. For example, the Pacific Bell installation program that I recently tried automatically created the connection I needed under Windows 95, dialed their local Web site to help me find the best access number, and performed a setup by checking another Web site.

Obviously, if ease of use was the only reason to use the Internet, many companies would have more than enough reason to do so. However, there are other reasons that came out of the survey including ease of availability (69 percent), use of existing infrastructure (65 percent), cost (51 percent), and ease of maintenance (36 percent)—the survey allowed the reader to select more than one answer in this area. The Internet provides a central repository of information and is probably the best way for most companies to provide ready access to company databases to distant employees.

Of course, this doesn't explain why ActiveX is an important consideration. ActiveX is Microsoft's answer to writing Internet applications. Looking at another survey shows that a whopping 59 percent of the people who intend to implement Internet applications plan to use a Microsoft product to do so.

Microsoft has also managed to garner a large following of third party support according to a recent PC Week article. A LAN Times article also mentioned a prominent Microsoft presence in the future plans of most network administrators that they talked with. The fact that ActiveX is based on OLE, an existing technology, only strengthens Microsoft's case. Obviously there are other players in the market, but no one can ignore Microsoft's role in Internet application development very easily. ActiveX is going to be one of the leading technologies out there in the near future.

What's in This Book

Now that I've piqued your curiosity a bit, let's look at what this book has to offer. I'm going to look at ActiveX programming from the intermediate programmer level. If you're a novice programmer, you may find some of the concepts a little too difficult to understand. However, some chapters, like Chapter 4 on HTML, will help just about anyone. Advanced programmers may want to skip some of the simpler chapters like Chapter 2 where we look at building a basic control. You'll still find plenty of information to use, especially in Part 3 where we take a real-world look at ActiveX programming.

To use this book you're going to have to know the C programming language. You won't find much novice-level material in this book, so it's best to learn C before you even begin to read it. In fact, a knowledge of C++ is highly recommended since all of the examples use C++ as their basis. Even though we go through a basic control programming example, a knowledge of writing OCXs or DLLs will also come in handy. You'll learn the information in this book a lot faster if you've gotten a little bit of lower level programming under your belt before you begin. Again, there are some "refresher course" style examples, but they don't provide a lot novice-level information.

So, now that you have some idea of who is supposed to read this book, let's take a look at what it will cover. Here's an overview of the book that tells the three areas where you can expect to spend the bulk of your time.

Part 1 is where you'll learn basic theory. For example, we'll build a basic control and see how it works. We'll also take a look at just what makes an ActiveX control different (and the same) as the OCXs that you used in the past. While we won't take an exhaustive look at things like OLE interfaces, we'll at least get an overview of the new interfaces that ActiveX controls add to the existing OLE specification. This is the place where we'll start taking a look at Internet issues. For example, you might have created a hundred OCXs already, but may not know the first thing about HTML. We'll take a look at that subject in Chapter 4. You'll also learn how common OLE features like in-place activation work on the Internet (see Chapter 5 for a discussion of Active Document that uses in-place activation).

In Part 2, we'll start looking at how ActiveX will affect the computing environment as a whole. For example, you'll definitely need to take a new look at security when using ActiveX controls on your Web page. We look at that issue in Chapter 6. ActiveX controls also require some level of scripting, but it's of a totally different sort than Internet programmers are used to. In Chapter 7 we'll look at both JavaScript and VBScript—the two languages of choice for working with ActiveX controls. Some of you may also have a problem moving from the local computer to the world wide view of the Internet. In Chapter 8, we'll look at some of those issues (along with some of the things you'll need to know to make that access easier for users).

Many of you won't want to spend any time at all learning theoretical information. That's why Part 3 of the book doesn't spend any time at all in this area. We're going to spend time looking at all kinds of real world applications. There's a chapter here for everyone. For example, if you need to work with databases, then take a look at Chapters 12 and 13. Chapter 12 looks at data entry screens. Chapter 13 looks at the mechanics of working with an actual database.

Of course, this is just an overview. You'll find that this book is packed with all kinds of useful tips and hints about using ActiveX to its fullest.

What You'll Need

ActiveX is a new technology so you won't find everything wrapped up in one easy-to-use package right now. Throughout the book you're going to find tips and notes that tell you where to find tools, information, utilities, or even helpful examples of how to create an ActiveX application. You'll always see a tip when the source of information is optional. In other words, you won't need that information to use this book but it'll come in handy somewhere along the way. Notes contain sources of information that you either need to use this book or to completely implement the examples it contains. You'll probably want to spend a little more time looking at the Web sites contained in a note.

Some of the other items you'll need for using this book include the ActiveX SDK, the ActiveX Control Pad utility (make sure you run all of the optional programs so that you end up with a complete installation), the latest Win32 SDK (available only through an MSDN subscription), a copy of Internet Explorer 3.0 (or Netscape Navigator 3.0 with an appropriate plug-in for using ActiveX controls), and a C++ compiler (preferably Microsoft Visual C++ 4.1

or 4.2). Some optional programming aids include the OLE 2 SDK and copies of the JavaScript or VBScript documentation (you'll find an URL for these in Chapter 7). Make certain you perform a full installation of all tools because we'll be stretching them to their fullest capacity in this book.

NOTE: Many of the concepts you'll learn in this book won't appear in your on-line documentation. Some of it is so new that it only appears on selected Web sites. You'll find either a tip or note alerting you to the location of such information throughout the book. In addition, Microsoft made some material available only through selected channels like an MSDN subscription. Other pieces of information are simply undocumented and you won't find them anywhere except within a news group when someone finds the feature accidentally.

You'll also need a computer running Windows 95 or Windows NT 4.0 to use as a workstation. A second machine acting as a local Web server is also important. This book assumes that you're using either Windows NT Server or Windows NT Workstation as an Internet server. The two pieces of tested software include Internet Information Server (IIS) and Peer Web Services (the version provided with Windows NT Workstation 4.0). Both computers will require enough RAM and other resources to fully support the tools you'll need throughout this book. In most cases that means you'll need a minimum of a 66 MHz 80486 computer with 32 MB of RAM and at least 1 GB of hard disk space. Even though you could potentially get by with less, you'll find that a lower-end computer will quickly bog down as you try to write code and test it.

Conventions Used in This Book

What we'll cover in this section is usage conventions. We'll discuss programming conventions a little later on when we look at Hungarian notation and how to use it. This book uses the following conventions:

| [<Filename>] | When you see square brackets around a value, switch, or command, it means that this is an optional component. You don't have to include it as part of the command line or dialog field unless you want the additional functionality that the value, switch, or command provides. |

<Filename>	A variable name between angle brackets is a value that you need to replace with something else. The variable name you'll see usually provides a clue as to what kind of information you need to supply. In this case, you'll need to provide a filename. Never type the angle brackets when you type the value.
ALL CAPS	There are three places you'll see ALL CAPS: commands, filenames, and case sensitive registry entries. Normally you'll type a command at the DOS prompt, within a PIF file field, or within the Run dialog field. If you see ALL CAPS somewhere else, it's safe to assume that the item is a case-sensitive registry entry or some other value like a filename.
File | Open	Menus and the selections on them appear with a vertical bar. "File | Open" means "Access the File menu and choose Open."
italic	There are three places you see *italic* text: new words, multi-value entries, and undefined values. You'll always see a value in *italic* whenever the actual value of something is unknown. The book also uses *italic* where more than one value might be correct. For example, you might see FILE*xxxx* in text. This means that the value could be anywhere between FILE0000 and FILE9999.
monospace	It's important to differentiate the text that you'll use in a macro or type at the command line from the text that explains it. This book uses monospace type to make this differentiation. Every time you see monospace text, you'll know that the information you see will appear in a macro, within a system file like CONFIG.SYS or AUTOEXEC.BAT, or as something you'll type at the command line. You'll even see the switches used with Windows commands in this text. There is another time you'll see monospace text. Every code listing uses monospaced code to make the text easier to read. Using monospaced text also makes it easier to add things like indentation to the coding example.

Icons

This book contains many icons that help you identify certain types of information. The following paragraphs describe the purpose of each icon.

NOTE: Notes tell you about interesting facts that don't necessarily affect your ability to use the other information in the book. I use note boxes to give you bits of information that I've picked up while using Delphi, Windows NT, or Windows 95.

TIP: Everyone likes tips because they tell you new ways of doing things that you might not have thought about before. Tip boxes also provide an alternative way of doing something that you might like better than the first approach I provided.

WARNING: This means watch out! Warnings almost always tell you about some kind of system or data damage that'll occur if you perform a certain action (or fail to perform others). Make sure you understand a warning thoroughly before you follow any instructions that come after it.

You'll also fine a variety of margin notes in the book. They describe some bit of information you should remember before starting a procedure or performing other kinds of work. Margin notes also contain useful tidbits of information like the location of a file or something you should look for in an example program. In most cases margin notes are simply helpful nuggets of information you can use to improve your programming as a whole.

An Overview of Hungarian Notation

Secret codes are the stuff of spy movies and a variety of other human endeavors. When you first see Hungarian Notation, you may view it as just another secret code. It contains all the elements of a secret code including an arcane series of letters that you have to decode and an almost indecipherable result when you do. However, it won't take long for you to realize that it is other programmers' code that is secret, not the Hungarian Notation used in this book.

Hungarian Notation can save you a lot of time and effort. Anyone who has spent enough time programming realizes the value of good documentation when you try to understand what you did in a previous coding session or interpret someone else's code. That's part of what Hungarian Notation will do for you; document your code.

An understanding of Hungarian Notion will also help you receive more information from the examples in this book and from the Microsoft (and other vendor) manuals in general. Just about every Windows programming language vendor uses some form of Hungarian Notation in their manuals. In addition, these same concepts are equally applicable to other languages like Visual FoxPro, Delphi, and Visual BASIC. The codes remain similar across a variety of programming languages, even when the language itself doesn't.

Don't think for a moment that this notation has remained static either. Many of the ideas presented in the original form of Hungarian Notation have been discussed by developers at conferences and on bulletin board systems (BBS). You'd be surprised at just how many forms of Hungarian Notation have evolved since its inception.

So what precisely is Hungarian Notation? It's a way of telling other people what you intend to do with a variable. Knowing what a variable is supposed to do can often help explain the code itself. For example, if I tell you that a particular variable contains a handle to a window, then you know a lot more about it than the fact that it is simply a variable. You can interpret the code surrounding that variable with the understanding that it's supposed to do something with a window.

The first stage of development for this variable naming system was started by Charles Simonyi of Microsoft Corporation. He called his system Hungarian Notation, so that's the name we'll use here. There are many places that you can obtain a copy of his work, including BBS and some of the Microsoft programming Web sites on the Internet. (Many on-line services like CompuServe also carry copies of Hungarian Notation in its various incarnations.) His work was further enhanced by other developers. For example, Xbase programmers use their own special version of Hungarian Notation. It takes the different types of variables that Xbase provides into account. An enhanced Xbase version of Hungarian Notation was published by Robert A. Difalco of Fresh Technologies. You can find his work on a few DBMS-specific BBSs as well as the Computer Associates Clipper forum on CompuServe.

The basis for the ideas presented in this section are found in one of the two previously mentioned documents in one form or another. The purpose in publishing them here is to make you aware of the exact nature of the conventions I use and how to use them to their best advantage in your own code. There are four reasons why you should use these naming conventions in your programs:

1. **Mnemonic Value** This allows you to remember the name of a variable more easily, an important consideration for team projects.

2. **Suggestive Value** You may not be the only one modifying your code. If you're working on a team project, others in the team will most likely at least look at the code you have written. Using these conventions will help others understand what you mean when using a specific convention.

3. **Consistency** A programmer's ability is often viewed as not only how efficiently they program, or how well the programs they create function, but how easily another programmer can read their code. Using these conventions will help you maintain uniform code from one project to another. Other programmers will be able to anticipate the value or function of a section of code simply by the conventions you use.

4. **Speed of Decision** In the business world, the speed at which you can create and modify code will often determine how successful a particular venture will be. Using consistent code will reduce the time you spend trying to decide what someone meant when creating a variable or function. This reduction in decision time will increase the amount of time you have available for productive work.

Now that I've told you why you should use Hungarian Notation, let's look at how I plan to implement it in this book. I'll use the following rules when naming variables. You'll also see me use them when naming database fields or other value related constructs. Some functions and procedures will use them as well, but only if Hungarian Notation will make the meaning of the function or procedure clearer.

1. Always prefix a variable with one or more lowercase letters indicating its type. In most cases this is the first letter of the variable type, so it's easy to remember what letter to use. The following examples show the most common prefixes for Visual BASIC, Delphi, and C. (There are literally hundreds of combinations used in Windows that don't appear here.) You'll also see a few database-specific identifiers provided here:

    a   Array
    c   Character
    d   Date

dbl	Double
dc	Device Context
dw	Double Word
f	Flag, Boolean, or Logical
h	Handle
I	Integer
inst	Instance
l	Long
li	Long Integer
lp	Long Pointer
msg	Message
n	Numeric
o	Object
pal	Palette
psz	Pointer to a Zero Terminated String
ptr	Pointer (or P when used with other variables like psz)
r	Real
rc	Rectangle
rgb	Red, Green, Blue (color variable)
rsrc	Resource
sgl	Single
si	Short Integer
sz	Zero Terminated String
u	Unsigned
ui	Unsigned Integer or Byte
w	Word
wnd	Window

2. Some variables represent the state of an object like a database, a field, or a control. They might even store the state of another variable. Telling other programmers that a variable monitors the current state of an object can help them see its significance within the program. You can identify state variables using one of the following three character qualifiers:

New	A New state
Sav	A Saved state
Tem	A Temporary state

3. A standard qualifier can help someone see the purpose of a variable almost instantly. This isn't the type of information that the variable contains, but how it reacts with other variables. For example, using the Clr qualifier tells the viewer that this variable is used in some way with color. You can even combine the qualifiers to amplify their effect and

describe how the variable is used. For example, cClrCrs is a character variable that determines the color of the cursor on the display. Using one to three of these qualifiers is usually sufficient to describe the purpose of a variable. The following standard qualifiers are examples of the more common types:

Ar	Array
Attr	Attribute
B	Bottom
Clr	Color
Col	Column
Crs	Cursor
Dbf	Database File
F	First
File	File
Fld	Field
L	Last/Left
Msg	Message
Name	Name
Ntx	Index File
R	Right
Rec	Record Number
Ret	Return Value
Scr	Screen
Str	String
T	Top
X	Row
Y	Column

4. Once you clearly define the variable's contents and purpose, you can further define it with some descriptive text. For example, you might have a long pointer to a string containing an employee's name that looks like this: lpszEmpName. The first two letters tell you that this is a long pointer. The second two letters tells you that this is a zero (or null) terminated string. The rest of the letters tell you that this is an employee name. (Notice that I used the standard qualifier, Name, for this example.) Seeing a variable name like this in a piece of code tells you what to expect from it at a glance.

5. There are times when you won't be able to satisfy every need in a particular module using a single variable. In those cases you might want to create more than one of that variable type and simply number them. You could also designate its function using some type of number indicator like those shown here:

1,2,3   State pointer references as in cSavClr1, cSavClr2, etc.
Max   Strict upper limit as in nFldMax, maximum number of Fields
Min   Strict lower limit as in nRecMin, minimum number of Records
Ord   An ordinal number of some type

PART

1

ActiveX Nuts & Bolts

Chapter

1

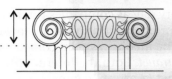

Introducing
ActiveX

You may wonder what all the hoopla is about when it comes to ActiveX controls (or any other new Internet technology for that matter). Just take a look at any trade press, and you'll find that you aren't alone. Every week sees the introduction of some new technology designed to make the Internet a breeze to use from both an administrator's and user's perspective. The bottom line is that many professionals aren't buying the ease-of-use stories that they read. The Internet is a complex environment and requires robust tools to get the job done. ActiveX is a tool that's at least built on time-proven, mature technology. That is why it's a good candidate for getting your Web applications up and running.

Any discussion of ActiveX begins with the Internet and ends with Microsoft. You must have at least a basic understanding of what the Internet is all about before you can understand the need for ActiveX. Once you understand the need for

3

ActiveX, you can begin to see how Microsoft has extended current OLE and OCX technology to meet that need.

The Internet is gaining more attention every day as companies try to use it to meet specific needs such as advertising products or providing a means for employees on the road to communicate. The media has even coined a new term for the second of these needs—the *Intranet*. Both the Internet (the public form of the network) and the Intranet (a private company's extension of a LAN or WAN) allow people from various locations to communicate using a local telephone call. (There are other, higher-speed connections such as ISDN as well, but the actual communication medium isn't important to the current discussion.) This is a lot different from the days when you had to dial a long-distance number every time you wanted access to the company's database from another area of the world. A single call can now connect you to the resources of your company as well as resources of others. In addition, it makes the resources of vendor companies and news services available to you. The Internet (or a company Intranet) could conceivably replace both BBSs and dial-in network connections.

NOTE: Throughout this book I'm going to refrain from distinguishing between the Internet and Intranet unless there is some significant difference you need to know about. While there are differences that affect a network administrator or a Webmaster, there aren't any appreciable differences for the programmer—at least not the ActiveX programmer. The idea of an Internet versus an Intranet is one of information exposure and the associated security concerns.

Information exchange is the reason that the Internet got started in the first place. The government needed a way to share information between research centers—the Internet originally served that purpose alone. Today the Internet contains a lot more than just government information. You'll find that the Internet gives you more opportunities to provide users with a vast array of information without forcing them to jump through hoops to get it. Just take a look at some of the search pages that the Internet currently provides, such as Lycos, Yahoo, and WebCrawler, and you'll see what kinds of resources are available.

The basic information container on the Internet is an HTML (hypertext markup language) page. At the lowest level of Internet information exchange, you'll see a page containing some combination of text, graphics, links, and commands. The text and graphic elements provide information. A link normally takes you to another page containing additional information. A command might tell the host computer to perform some kind of task like adding user input to a database.

Aside from the information exchange aspect, looking at a typical Web page also shows you something else. A standard Web page is static—the content doesn't change once you download the page unless it uses one of the newer technologies on the market. It doesn't take long to realize that your ability to present that information in a dynamic way is extremely limited with current HTML technology. We'll take a look at HTML in Chapter 4. The important idea to remember is that standard HTML pages are static.

Just displaying information isn't enough in today's computing environment. You'll want to get some feedback from the user as well in most cases. If you think HTML is limited, just try getting some information from the user with CGI (common gateway interface). You'll find yourself using new and not so exciting languages such as Perl to make the required connections. Most people find that any form of information exchange from the client to your server is an error-prone and time-consuming process. In fact, standard Web data exchange to date is more black art than science.

So, if you want to create a standard Web page today, you have to use an out-of-date, static interface for displaying information and an even more archaic method of getting information back from the user. It sounds like someone should probably update the technology used by the Internet to something more modern. The Internet Management Task Force (IMTF) is responsible for implementing new technologies on the Internet. The problem is that this group is mainly composed of volunteers. The wheels of progress grind slowly for the IMTF, just like any other standards organization. It's so slow, in fact, that many companies have come up with their own solutions for making the Internet a friendlier place to work. One of these technologies, the one covered in this book, is ActiveX.

Most of you reading this book haven't dealt with ActiveX before when it comes to Internet access. In fact, some of you might have only the slightest notion of what an ActiveX control is all about. Before we explore the actual elements of programming, let's take a few moments to look at ActiveX itself. You'll probably find that you know more about ActiveX than you thought you did. This chapter begins by showing you some of the history behind ActiveX, then tells you what ActiveX is all about. We're not going to look at a lot of theory; my purpose is to acquaint you with the technology from a very general perspective.

ActiveX—The Historical View

It's important to know the history of any technology you use as a programmer. For one thing, knowing history often helps explain those frustrating inconsistencies in implementation that most technologies suffer from. The longer the technology's history, the better your chance of running into some seemingly minor problem that no one can get rid of. The following sections will help you understand a bit of the history behind ActiveX. You'll find that it has a rather long history despite Microsoft's hype that it's a new technology. The best way to view ActiveX is as the reasonable outcome of previous decisions Microsoft made. It's an evolutionary step along the road to exchanging information more efficiently.

DDE—The Point of Origin

The history of ActiveX actually begins with DDE (dynamic data exchange). Microsoft was looking for some method of moving data from one place to another within Windows, and DDE was their first attempt. DDE allows Windows applications to exchange data through the Clipboard. DDE actually has two parts: data exchange and macro language. The data exchange part of the specification has been largely replaced by OLE (object linking and embedding). Only older applications still use DDE as their major form of data exchange in a manual data transfer. However, the macro portion of DDE is still alive and well. All you need to do is look at some of the entries in the registry or even scan some through the file associations you create using Windows 95 Explorer to see that DDE is still there.

One of the big things you need to remember about the data exchange portion of DDE is that it's static. Once you copy the data from one point to another, any changes in the source document don't get reflected in the destination. The data in the destination is independent of the source. In fact, this problem was one of the reasons that Microsoft started abandoning DDE in favor of OLE.

Another major problem with DDE was the way it handled the exchange. The client program had to know how to work with the kind of data provided by the server. In other words, you couldn't place a graphic image on the Clipboard into a text document unless the text editor also knew how to handle graphics.

There are two types of DDE implementation: clients and servers. (Most applications provide both.) The client is literally the user end of the DDE process. It's the part that a user will interact with when creating a DDE macro. A user provides macro steps that your application will read and act upon. The client starts a conversation with a server—which means starting it if necessary. One of the standard DDE macro commands tells what server the user wants the client to start a conversation with. You also need to pick a topic of discussion. In most cases this is a document of some sort. The next step is to send macro commands from the client to the server. A server accepts the macro input from the client and acts upon it. Once the macro is complete, the client ends the conversation. Besides documents, every server also supports the following topics:

- ◆ **SysItems** Requesting this item returns a list of all items in the SYSTEM topic. In other words, you'll still use the SYSTEM topic, but you can discuss other items within that topic.

- ◆ **Topics** Use this item to get a list of available topics. You would supply one of these other topics in place of the SYSTEM topic the next time you started a conversation with the DDE server.

- ◆ **Formats** Sometimes you need to know what kind of data the server supports before you make a PokeData or a PokeDataLines call. This item returns a list of all the Clipboard formats supported by the server application.

OLE—The Next Step

Now that you have a better idea of what DDE is all about, let's look at the next step in the process of creating the ultimate data connection (at least from Microsoft's perspective). Microsoft needed something better than DDE for data exchange, so they created OLE. The process of copying a piece of data to the Clipboard, then pasting it into a document, left users with a lot of documents that contained out-of-date information. OLE builds on the foundation created by DDE; it still uses the Clipboard as an intermediate data location. However, it has several advantages over DDE. For one thing, you can create a dynamic link with OLE. Changes in the source document are reflected in the destination. That's because you copy an object, not data, to the Clipboard. We'll look at what this means near the end of this section.

You can also create *compound documents* using OLE. These are documents that contain more than one data type. For example, you can use OLE to place a picture within a word processed document. Since the word processor doesn't understand the picture, it will call on the OLE server (a graphics program in this case) to handle any changes or display tasks.

OLE is also a lot more complex than DDE. You don't have the simple relationships DDE provides. For this reason, we need to look at a bit of terminology before going much further. You need to speak the language of OLE to really understand it. The following list defines some of the terms you'll see in this chapter (and those that follow).

♦ **Client** This term refers to the application that holds the linked or embedded object. For example, if you place a spreadsheet object in your word processed document, the word processor becomes the client.

♦ **Server** The server is the application that the client calls to manipulate an object. Embedded or linked objects are still in the native format of the application that created them. A client must call on the originating application to make any required changes to the object's content. What you really have is two applications working together to create a cohesive document.

♦ **Compound document** This is a document that contains one or more objects. Every OLE document is considered a compound document. We'll take a better look at what this means a little later in this chapter.

♦ **Object** An object is a piece of data that you move from one application to another in its native format. Objects also have properties. For example, an object includes the name of the application that created it and some specifics about its format. You can create objects from any data if the originating application supports OLE. This is the big difference between an object and the cutting and pasting capabilities provided by DDE. You can do a lot more with an object because it contains intelligence that a simple piece of text does not.

♦ **Object menu** This is the menu you use to change the contents of an OLE document, convert it, or perform any other operations that the object allows. For example, if you embed a wave file within a word processed document, the Object menu will contain an entry for playing that file.

♦ **Container** An object that holds other objects is called a container. Visualize a folder, like the ones used by Windows Explorer, and you'll have a good idea of what a container represents. However, instead of simply holding files like a folder does, an OLE container can hold any kind of OLE object.

Every application that supports OLE is either a client, a server, or a combination of both. A client always acts as a container for objects that it receives from a server. The client doesn't need to know what to do with those objects—that's the server's responsibility. It's the client's responsibility to store the objects in such a way that it can retrieve them intact later. The client establishes contact with the server and requests the data it needs. The server normally places this data on the Clipboard. We're not talking about data in the same sense as DDE offered here; we're talking about data objects. An object has properties, and you can interact with it in more than one way. That fact differentiates a dynamic data object from the static data offered by DDE.

OLE also provides two main methods for exchanging information: linking and embedding. Linking creates a pointer to the data contained in the source document. In other words, the destination document doesn't even contain a copy of the data. The main advantages to this method are that you save data storage space and the destination document always has a source for new information. Embedding places a copy of the data—actually the data object—in the destination document. The OLE server still manages the data, but there isn't any method for automatically updating it from the source. (The idea here is that you can create a compound document using the tool best designed to manipulate the data.) The advantage to this method of data exchange is that you won't lose your connection to the data when the container document gets moved.

From OLE 1 to OLE 2

Two versions of OLE exist right now. Microsoft introduced OLE 1 as part of Windows 3.*x*. It provided a basic set of linking and embedding features that users soon outgrew. One of the biggest problems was the huge amount of memory that OLE required to create more than one or two links with other applications. When using OLE 1, the client application loads every application required to service the objects contained in a document. In addition, the client loads the full application—not just the portion required to manipulate the data. Obviously, loading entire applications takes a lot of time, so speed is a major issue for OLE 1.

OLE 2 is supposed to remedy some of the problems associated with OLE 1 and provide much more functionality to boot. The following improvements give you an idea of what Microsoft did in the way of upgrading OLE 1. Some of these improvements are programmer specific; others affect both the programmer and the user.

T IP: Most of these new features require that both applications support OLE 2. At the very minimum, the client must support OLE 2 in order to make any of the features work. Unfortunately, it's not always easy to determine what level of support an older application provides. The Windows registry contains complete information on every OLE server on your machine. Newer versions of Windows, beginning with Windows 95, include separate registry sections for OLE 1 and OLE 2. OLE 1 entries usually appear as part of the file association information for the application. Basic OLE 2 information always appears under the HKEY_CLASSES_ROOT I CLSID registry key.

Visual Editing   One of the problems with OLE 1 was that the user's train of thought was disrupted every time he or she needed to make a change to an object. The reason is simple: OLE 1 loaded a copy of the server and displayed the object in the originating application's window for editing. OLE 2 allows visual (or in-place) editing. Instead of opening a new window, the host merely overlays its toolbar, menu structure, and controls with those of the client. The user simply sees a change in tools, not a change in applications. As a result, the transition between documents is less noticeable.

Nested Objects   OLE 1 allowed you to place one object at a time in the container document. An object couldn't become a container; all the objects existed as a single layer within the container. OLE 2 treats every potential container as just that—a container. It doesn't matter how many containers you place inside a container or how many ways you stack them. To get a better idea of how nesting will help you, look at the way Windows 95 implements folders within Explorer. You can treat OLE 2 container objects the same way.

Drag and Drop   You used to cut or copy an object in the server application and then place it in the client using the Paste Special command. This option still works. However, OLE 2 provides a new method of creating links to other documents. You can simply grab the object and move it wherever you want. It becomes linked wherever you decide to drop it.

Storage-Independent Links   OLE 2 allows you to create links to other documents, even if they aren't physically located on the local drive. It implements this using an LRPC (Light Remote Procedure Call) mechanism. Unfortunately, this linking mechanism has limitations. For example, you'll find that it works fine with some peer-to-peer networks, but it works only marginally with other network types. This is one of the major fixes provided by ActiveX.

Adaptable Links   Many users screamed for this feature. If you moved any of the files required to create a compound document under OLE 1, all the links were destroyed, and you had to re-create them. This older version stored the full path, including drive, to the linked data. OLE 2 stores only enough path information to maintain the link. If you create links between two files in the same directory, you can move these two files anywhere on the drive, and OLE 2 can maintain the link. The only criteria for maintaining a link under OLE 2 is that the relative path remains the same.

OLE Automation   Everyone knows about Visual Basic for Applications (VBA), right? This is the new programming language that Microsoft is trying to get everyone to support. OLE automation is part of VBA. VBA defines a standard interface for talking with the server application. This allows the client application to send commands to the server that will change the contents of an object indirectly. OLE automation is the direct descendent of the DDE macro language that many applications still use. The big difference from the user's perspective is that DDE macros were difficult to write and very prone to error. VBA is the native language of the application and is consistent across platforms. Quite a few applications now support the VBA interface as a server—you could send them VBA commands and get some kind of useful output. However, support for the VBA programming language (or something compatible) is still pretty difficult to find.

Version Management   Have you ever received a document from someone, only to find that part of it wouldn't work with your software? OLE 2 can store the application name and version number as part of the link. If an application developer implements this feature correctly, a server (or client, for that matter) will detect an old version of a file and ask if you want to update it. This means that you'll never have an old file sitting around just waiting to make life difficult. Unfortunately, except for a few Microsoft applications and one or two other vendors, this feature is largely unimplemented right now. We can only hope that more vendors will incorporate this feature as new versions of Windows, such as Windows 95, arrive on the scene.

Object Conversion   Your friend uses Excel and you use Lotus 1-2-3, yet you need to share OLE documents containing spreadsheets. One of you could go through the inconvenience and expense of changing to the other person's application and document format, but OLE 2 can probably solve this problem without such a change. Object conversion allows Excel to act as a server for a compound document containing a Lotus 1-2-3 object. All you need to do is select the Convert option from the Object menu in either program to convert it to that program's format. At least, that's how it's supposed to work. Real life is a bit different. Conversion will work only if the other application already supports that data format. Of course, when you think about it, this restriction makes sense.

Optimized Object Storage   Memory is a considerable problem when using OLE 1 since both applications have to run. Some users found this limitation so difficult to get around that they didn't use OLE at all. Optimized object storage is part of the cure. It allows the linked documents to stay on disk until needed. That way, Windows doesn't need to load every application and data file required to support the compound document. In most cases, Windows uses a buffer-zone technique. A word processor might keep the applications and objects required for the preceding, current, and next page in memory. The rest of the objects stay on disk, greatly reducing the memory footprint of a compound document in some cases. You'll find the functions for implementing this feature in the STORAGE.DLL file in your SYSTEM directory.

Component Object Model (COM)   This is a new standard interface that Windows provides for component objects. Essentially, this is Microsoft's way of making 16-bit and 32-bit application OLE conversations transparent. This is also the feature that's responsible for allowing OLE 1 and OLE 2 applications to live together. You'll find the calls for the component object module in COMPOBJ.DLL. Windows issues a pointer to a list of functions when you create an object using one of these DLL calls.

With all the changes to OLE 2, you might think that there would be compatibility problems. OLE 1 and OLE 2 can mix freely on your machine. Unfortunately, compatibility doesn't come without a price. You could encounter all kinds of problems when using OLE with various applications. The important thing to remember here is that OLE takes a least-common-denominator approach. Everything is tied to the application that has the fewest capabilities. This means that if you had four OLE 2 applications and one OLE 1 application, everything would be tied to the level of support provided by the OLE 1 application. Likewise, if you have two OLE 2 applications, the one with the least number of features will determine what you'll see within a document.

Making OLE Easy Through OCXs

Let's look at the programming end of OLE for a few minutes. If you want to exchange information between two applications, you have to figure out a way for them to communicate. In the past that meant loading both applications. What if you could simply load the pieces of the server application required to display and edit a data object? That's part of the impetus behind designing OCXs (OLE Control eXtension). An OCX is a DLL (dynamic link library) with an OLE twist. It's a piece of an application that allows for data transfer to take place.

There's more to the OCX picture than simply data exchange. OCXs are objects and DLLs combined. (Remember that a DLL is the equivalent of a library under DOS—a set of canned functions that are already debugged and ready for use.) When Microsoft first introduced OLE, you needed a college degree to implement it. In fact, the documentation for OLE continues to grow and daily threatens to exceed the bounds of the single CD used to hold it. Most developers couldn't figure out the basics of implementing OLE, much less how to get an OLE-enabled application to work. An OCX provides a canned set of object-handling routines that a programmer can use without worrying about the OLE specification.

You also need to look at one other piece of the puzzle. One of the biggest boons to programmer productivity occurred with the growth of RAD (rapid application development) programming environments. These platforms included the idea that developers should simply draw the controls that they wanted to implement, then define some behaviors for the controls. The only coding programmers had to do was to respond to specific events such as a keypress.

The 16-bit versions of most RAD programming environments provided controls that did the bare minimum required to get the job done. The VBX (Visual Basic eXtension) controls introduced by Microsoft allowed for code reuse and increased programming speed. Drawing a control, assigning some values to its properties, then adding some event code is a lot faster than designing a control from scratch. The 32-bit version of those same environments not only provided the controls, but made them OLE-enabled. Drawing an OCX control on a form still provides the same ease-of-use features that a VBX does, but adds OLE-specific features as well.

The introduction of OCXs is the second part of the ActiveX story. The OCX is the predecessor for the type of control we'll talk about in this book. However, before you can implement an ActiveX control, you still need something else. The next section introduces DCOM, the OLE extension needed to make ActiveX viable.

Network OLE, Better Known as DCOM

Just a few months ago no one had even heard of DCOM (distributed component object model) since Microsoft was still talking about it as network OLE. In the previous sections we have looked at OLE in quite a bit of detail. The explanation for DCOM is short and to the point—it's the version of OLE that allows you to exchange information over a network. The previous implementations of OLE were limited to the local machine—they needed path information to the linked file. Sure, you could create a link between your machine and someone else's machine on the same network, but the code for that link would execute on your local machine. DCOM is something more than that—it allows you to create OLE links that rely on code stored on other machines. In most cases that code will also execute remotely.

So, what's so good about this new technology? Think about it for a second. How does an Internet connection differ from those that you've worked with so far? Of course, the code is executed on a Web server, not your local machine. When you run a CGI script, the Internet server does all of the processing. Your machine acts as a dumb terminal that accepts information from the host, then displays it.

The problem with this approach is that the host can get overburdened. In addition, you need a high-speed communication link to get good performance because every piece of data has to travel to the host for processing. What if you could cut down network traffic by offloading some of the required processing onto the client? That's what network OLE is all about—smart data transfers and a combination of local and remote processing.

Using DCOM allows you to create links from your machine to a Web server without all the added baggage that you've had to contend with before. Gone are the days of endless scripts and archaic languages. ActiveX (and technologies like it) use a more modern method for exchanging information dynamically, one based on modern technology. In this case we're talking about OLE, but other technologies are available as well.

The ActiveX Connection

By now the connection between DDE, OLE, OCXs, network OLE (or DCOM), and ActiveX should be fairly apparent. If you can implement OLE on a local machine using OCX controls, what's to stop you from using those same controls over the Internet? Using extensions to the HTML scripting language (called tags) allows you to call ActiveX controls—essentially an application (or applet) version of the OCX that many of you have used within RAD environments such as Visual Basic and Delphi. In other words, controls that you've used in the past to create a special type of component like a button, display a spreadsheet, or add some type of connectivity between applications, will also work in the Internet environment. In addition, you'll find special controls here that are Internet-specific, like a special search applet for finding a special URL.

Here's how the connection works. A user looks at your Web page and downloads one or more ActiveX controls as a result. The ActiveX controls contain intelligence that allows them to work with the user locally. When the user does request some information, the control can request only the information the user actually needs. What you're really getting with ActiveX is an advanced OLE 2 connection over the Internet. This is a gross oversimplification, but it's where we'll start for now.

What Is ActiveX?

The simple answer to what ActiveX is appeared in the previous section— ActiveX is an advanced form of OCX (maybe a simpler form of OLE is a better way to look at it). However, that doesn't even begin to scratch the surface of what you'll actually find under the hood. OLE is the user's view of ActiveX. For the programmer, ActiveX is also a set of enabling technologies for the Internet. It provides a method for exchanging information that you didn't have in the past.

To really appreciate ActiveX as a programmer, you have to look at OLE from the programmer's perspective, and that means looking at OCXs. In the earlier sections, we talked about a user's perspective of all this technology. OCXs are a lot more than just data exchange. They include an idea called the component object model (COM). COM is a specification that defines a standard binary interface between object modules. This interface defines a function-calling methodology, standard structure-based data passing techniques, and even a few standard function calls. Using COM means that it doesn't matter which language you use to write an application module such as an OCX; the interface for that module is the same at the binary level.

TIP: Now may be a good time to check your ActiveX toolkit. You'll need an ActiveX-compatible browser such as Microsoft's Internet Explorer 3 that you can download at http://www.microsoft.com/ie/iedl.htm. You'll need the ActiveX SDK, which you can download at http://www.microsoft.com/IntDev/sdk/. Finally, since ActiveX is a work in progress, you'll need some additional help from Microsoft. They're rolling the completed portions of ActiveX into the Win32 SDK. (ISAPI—Internet Server API—recently joined the list of items you'll find here.) An MSDN (Microsoft Developer Network) subscription will keep you up-to-date with changes in the Win32 SDK. Go to http://www.microsoft.com/msdn/ to learn more about this product. Microsoft promises that future releases of the premiere version of MSDN will include the full ActiveX SDK.

NOTE: At the time of this writing, Microsoft was working on an integration technology between Internet Explorer and Windows 95's system Explorer called WebView. This new technology will make Web sites as easy to access as the drives and other resources listed in Explorer right now. You'll also see plain English names in place of the more familiar URLs that you need to know now.

So, how does COM affect applications you write? The answer is fairly complex because of the number of ways in which COM gets used, not because the technology itself is so overwhelming. When a user places a graphic image object within a container controlled by your application, what do you know about that object? The only thing you really know about it is who created the object in the first place. Knowing this information allows you to call on that application for a variety of services, such as displaying the graphic or allowing the user to edit it. In reality, what you're doing is sharing that application's code.

Programmers benefit from using COM as well. When you install an OCX into your programming environment, what have you really accomplished? In most cases you have a new control that you stick on a form somewhere.

You really don't need to know about the control's inner workings. The only important factors are what the control will do for your application and how you interact with it. Again, you're calling a particular module of code installed on your machine using a standard interface—that's what COM is all about.

ActiveX is an extension of this idea. You're still using a standard interface. However, instead of simply calling that code from the local machine environment or over the persistent connection of a LAN/WAN, you'll call it from the Internet. In addition, this new code can take the form of applets or mini-applications. We'll start to see how this works as the book progresses.

What Will ActiveX Do for You?

ActiveX will do for the Internet what OCXs have done for the desktop. However, you'll find ActiveX controls in places that you hadn't really thought about in the past. For example, NetManage, Inc. plans to create a new email client called Z-Mail Pro. This package supports ActiveX technology in a way that allows users to exchange, create, and view HTML documents directly in the message viewing window. What this means to users is that they now have the ability to create dynamic Web pages, something that you have to really work at today.

Remote connections will also benefit from the use of ActiveX. For example, Proginet Corporation is currently working on ActiveX technology that will bring mainframe data to the desktop. Their Fusion FTMS (File Transfer Management System) will work with any development language that supports OLE containers, such as Delphi, Visual C++, and PowerBuilder. Essentially you'll place an ActiveX control on a form, define where to find the data, then rely on the control to make the connection. No longer will remote access over the Internet require the user to jump through hoops. A special transfer server on the mainframe will complete the package by automating all transfer requests. No longer will an operator have to manually download a needed file to the company's Web site before a client can access it.

Even Microsoft Exchange will benefit from ActiveX. Wang Laboratories, Inc. and other companies are creating new add-ons that mix Exchange and ActiveX together. Wang's product is a client/server imaging add-on. It will allow users to scan, view, annotate, manipulate, or print graphic images no matter where they are located. This same product will include a hierarchical storage management ActiveX control. The two technologies will work together to make graphics easier to access and use in a large company.

They'll also make it easier to find a needed graphic—which should ultimately result in a storage savings to the company.

Microsoft itself has issued a whole slew of ActiveX controls. Some of these controls are free for downloading from their Internet site (http://www.microsoft.com). Examples of these new controls include Animation Player for PowerPoint and Internet Assistant for both Access and Schedule+. The Internet Assistant for Access will create a snapshot of a database table that gets uploaded as a static image. The snapshot automatically updates every time the user accesses the page. The Internet Assistant for Schedule+ will allow you to upload scheduling information to a Web page. Since the data gets updated every time a user accesses the site, you no longer have to worry about compute-at-home employees missing meetings. Finally, the PowerPoint Animation Player will allow you to play a PowerPoint presentation from within any ActiveX-compliant browser.

TIP: Microsoft isn't just sitting around and waiting for other people to develop tools. They've updated Microsoft C++ 4.1 to work with ISAPI (Internet Server API). This includes five new classes that implement the ActiveX Server Framework. In addition, you can download a free copy of Microsoft Frontpage (a general-purpose design tool for Web pages) and Control Pad (an ActiveX-specific design tool for Web pages) from their Web site.

Finally, if you think ActiveX won't help with security, think again. A lot of new firewall and certificate strategies are making the rounds these days. One of those new strategies is Net2000. It's a set of APIs that will allow developers to tie NetWare core services (including directory, security, and licensing) into their applications. You'll be able to tap this API through ActiveX controls over an Intranet. How will this help users and developers alike? It means that with the proper programming constructs, a network administrator will be able to track license usage throughout the entire network, even across Internet connections. This is going to become a much bigger issue as more people begin to compute from home rather than the office.

ActiveX Versus OCX Controls

For the most part, ActiveX and OCX controls are totally interchangeable. You'll see ads for ActiveX controls that have nothing to do with the Internet.

Look a little closer, and you'll find that those controls probably appeared in an OCX listing sometime in the not-too-distant past.

The Internet places some special challenges on the programming environment. For one thing, you don't have the luxury of high-speed loading anymore. The size of an OCX becomes a critical issue when used within the Internet environment. Downloading a 60 KB OCX may test a user's patience—trying to download a 200 KB OCX will probably result in the user stopping the download altogether. ActiveX controls are small versions of OCXs.

ActiveX controls also suffer from various machine-specific requirements. When you install an OCX on your machine, the installation program can check the machine and make allowances as needed. The same can't be said about an ActiveX control. You can't assume anything about the client machine at all. It could be anything from a new Pentium to yesterday's 80386.

Browser capabilities will eventually affect ActiveX controls as well. Consider a browser that doesn't quite implement ActiveX support as Microsoft sees it. You might create a control that works fine with most browsers but won't work in some instances due to browser limitations. Obviously, keeping a close watch on which browsers the users in your company use is going to be a big deal.

You'll also need to deal with some situations that an OCX programmer would never have to think about. For one thing, what happens if the browser doesn't support ActiveX at all? The current method of dealing with this is that the browser would simply ignore any HTML tags that it doesn't know how to work with. Dealing with a browser that is non-ActiveX-compliant is easy in this case—just leave a message telling the user that his browser won't work with the current page, and direct the user to an alternative.

Working with the JavaScript Language

To create any kind of a visual element on a Web page, you have to use a tag—essentially an instruction to the browser to do something. The World Wide Web Consortium (W3C) is the standards body responsible for defining these tags. Current browser technology states that if the browser doesn't support a particular tag, it simply ignores it. For the most part though, you'll find that the vast majority of browsers on the market will support the standard tags defined by the W3C as of the time of their introduction on the market.

HTML documents don't provide tags for ActiveX controls. That may change in the future since Microsoft is working with the W3C to add new tags (we'll talk about the basics of using these tags in Chapter 4), but for today there isn't any way to add an ActiveX control directly to your Web pages without help. One form of help is JavaScript—a scripting language add-on for some browsers on the market today. For example, if you're using Netscape or Internet Explorer 3.0, you have some limited form of JavaScript support.

NOTE: Changes to the current HTML tag list are inevitable as vendors try to move various technologies to the Internet. For example, Microsoft is currently trying to change the Windows help engine into something that's Internet friendly. They're working with W3C to add HTML tags that support searchable keywords. How will this help you as a programmer? It means that you'll have added capability to help users find specific information on a particular Web page fast. In addition, Microsoft wants to create a compressed Web page format. Again, this is a direct result of their desire to move the Windows help engine to the Internet. However, it will help programmers by reducing the burden of keeping Web pages small. The current uncompressed Web page format makes it difficult for anyone to include many graphics and also hinders technologies such as ActiveX since the size of the applets must be kept small.

Essentially what happens is that the browser will see a tag for JavaScript, then pass control to the JavaScript interpreter. JavaScript currently supports variables, conditional processing, loops, and event-driven program response. An ending tag tells the interpreter when it's time to pass control back to the browser. The actual process is a bit more complex than it looks, and we'll study it in detail in Chapter 3.

TIP: Don't confuse JavaScript and Java. JavaScript is a scripting language that you can include within HTML documents. It first appeared with Netscape 2.0. JavaScript is always interpreted as part of the Web page when you load it, and the number of things you can do with JavaScript are somewhat limited. The JavaScript language bears little resemblance to the syntax used by the Java language. Java, on the other hand, is a full-fledged programming language based on C. Sun Microsystems originally produced this language. Right now it's also interpreted, but that may change. You may eventually see Java compilers on the market that will greatly increase the execution speed of the applets you create with it.

The current twist with JavaScript is that it's starting to receive a lot of attention—most notably from Microsoft. Current plans are to include a JavaScript interpreter as part of future versions of Windows. This will accomplish two things: make browsers smaller and more efficient and standardize the JavaScript interface for Windows users.

How will this change affect VBScript users? For the time being Microsoft says that it plans to support a variety of scripting languages. However, if JavaScript does indeed become an implant in Windows, then the life expectancy for VBScript may be short indeed. Obviously, JavaScript will have to include all of the functionality required to implement new technologies such as ActiveX, but that shouldn't take too much time to happen.

Working with the VBScript Language

VBScript (Visual Basic Script) is a new product from Microsoft based on a very old one. In one way or another, Microsoft has promoted Basic from day one. Every version of DOS that ever shipped included Basic. You'll find that Microsoft spends a great deal of time promoting Basic and for good reason—it's where they started.

From a programmer's perspective you'll find that VBScript will probably have fewer bugs when released than some of the other products on the market. It will also have a more mature feature set. Unlike JavaScript, VBScript will probably provide everything that a full-fledged programming language would, except the ability to compile it. You can't compile something like a Web page scripting language and still maintain cross-platform compatibility. The only real way to make sure the language will run on everything is to keep it interpreted.

 T IP: If you want to find out more about VBScript, take a look at the working description Microsoft has provided at http://www.microsoft.com/intdev/vbs/vbscript.htm. You'll find that this page changes content on a fairly regular basis as Microsoft irons out all of the details. It's one of the best places to keep track of where VBScript is going in layperson's terms.

All of this extra functionality won't come without a price tag though. Using VBScript will probably require a bit more work on the part of the programmer. Some people are already saying that JavaScript will have a lower learning curve than VBScript. What you'll probably find is that most serious programmers will use VBScript to write complex applications. Its flexibility will be a strong selling point in this situation. JavaScript will be the language for the rest of us. Its ease of use will be a major selling point in an environment where ease of use is key.

The fact that Microsoft seems to be providing equal support for both JavaScript and VBScript says a lot too. You'll probably find that they position each language for specific purposes (at least from the Microsoft point of view) somewhere along the way. The bottom line is that you'll want to at least try VBScript before you head off in the direction of JavaScript.

ActiveX from the User's Perspective

As a programmer, you always have to take the user's perspective into account when thinking about a new technology. Just what will a user gain from ActiveX? Users are going to benefit greatly from ActiveX and other technologies like it in a number of ways:

Increased Capabilities   Users will find that they have more features to choose from on a typical Web page implementing ActiveX. That's because a lot of the programming constraints that you used to have with standard HTML are gone. Just about anything you can do with an OCX, you can do with an ActiveX control. This means you could add specialized forms features such as a spelling checker, graphics, or even live data to your repertoire.

Decreased Response Time   Right now users must rely on CGI scripts to get any kind of interactive feedback from a Web server. Every request is handled separately. Adding a new piece of information to a field requires another call to the server. Using ActiveX will allow programmers to maintain a live data connection that requires a minimum of network traffic and therefore increases perceived performance.

Application Integration   A lot of vendors are coming out with ActiveX-type controls that you can include with local applications just as you can include an OCX. For example, you could include an ActiveX control that automatically creates a connection to a Web site as needed to get remote information. As far as the user is concerned, that data might be coming from a local hard drive or the LAN; only the programmer knows that it's really coming from the Internet somewhere. This is only the tip of the iceberg. We'll look at some of these controls in Appendix A. The bottom line is that an application such as a word processor or database manager could become a browser as well—it's simply a matter of including the right ActiveX controls with your application.

1

Enhanced Security   Right now there are a lot of problems with maintaining security on the Internet. A good portion of that problem is because of the way the Internet currently implements IP (Internet protocol). There are a ton of very "messy" solutions to fix the problem, but most of them are going to require a lot of work on the part of the user. Consider something as simple as certificates that require users to perform a lot of additional setup on their machines. An ActiveX control may not provide the ultimate in security, but there are ways of writing these controls so that they do provide a modicum of security in a totally seamless manner. We'll look at this issue in Chapter 6.

Reduced Waiting for Application Updates   Using ActiveX to provide canned modules for common application pieces will reduce the workload on you as a programmer. Think about it this way: you'll let someone else write and debug pieces of your application for you. The only thing you really need to worry about is putting the modules together and adding any custom code. What users will see are faster updates—something everyone wants and needs in today's competitive environment.

There's one major consideration when viewing ActiveX from the user's perspective—the user will have to use an ActiveX-compatible browser. You can control this particular criteria in a corporate environment, but how about in the world at large? It's for this reason that most programmers will use ActiveX as an Intranet rather than an Internet technology at first. In an Intranet scenario you can control which browsers are used to access a Web site; not so within the Internet environment. Trying to maintain a Web site is already difficult enough. Keeping the pages up-to-date can really try the resources available to a typical Webmaster. Trying to maintain two sets of pages, one for ActiveX users and another for other users, would be even more difficult. For the time being, the cost of ActiveX may just be too high for the Internet, but it is definitely the choice to consider for the Intranet.

Another problem from a user's perspective will be the time required to download ActiveX controls from the Internet. Remember that users won't be installing these controls as part of an application—they'll most likely download them in real time from the Internet sites they visit. If your site uses five or six moderately sized controls, you may find a less than receptive audience. We'll cover some guidelines for making your ActiveX controls user friendly in Chapter 4. For now though, it's important to know that download size versus perceived benefit is going to be a major issue from the user's point of view. As programmers learn how to get more functionality from a smaller ActiveX control package, the impact of this problem should decrease.

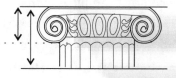

Building a Basic Control

Some people hate the idea of learning anything new, especially when it looks hard or complicated. OCXs fall into that category for many people. The idea of writing an OLE control fits into the same category as writing device drivers under DOS. Now that Microsoft has changed the name for what amounts to a new version of the OCX to ActiveX, many people will find even more excuses for not trying out this technology.

Since you're already reading this book, I have to assume that you're at least mildly interested in the technology behind ActiveX controls. We're not going to do anything in this chapter that will dazzle your buddies. In fact, the programming example I've created (while very useful) falls into the category of the mundane. The main example we'll look at is a new type of pushbutton—an on/off switch.

The reason for choosing this example is easy to figure out: most people find that working with something familiar eases the burden of learning something new. In addition, this particular coding example is extremely easy to implement. You'll find that learning how it works only takes a modicum of time.

NOTE: The examples in this chapter were developed using Microsoft Visual C++ version 4.0. The code shown won't work with Borland C++ or any previous version of the Microsoft C++ product without at least some modifications. Unfortunately, developing OCXs is a relatively new process, and trying to create a generic example that works with everyone's product didn't prove viable. The examples in this chapter will provide you with valuable hints and tips on developing your own OCXs no matter which programming language product you decide to use.

Once the example is written, you'll learn several ways to test your new ActiveX control. Some people may want to rush the control out the door and onto the nearest HTML page. That really isn't the best way to do things. A three-step approach usually works best for in-house testing with a step added during actual implementation.

This chapter will also spend some time looking at the two APIs that begin to define an ActiveX control versus its counterpart, the OCX. You'll find that the vast majority of your OCXs already work great as ActiveX controls. About the only thing that will hold you back from using them is the way the vendor licensed the control for use. The public nature of the Internet makes it more difficult to use the current set of controls you may have—most vendors allow you to include them with applications you create, not as part of a Web page.

Defining a Project

We looked at some of the criteria for developing an ActiveX control from the user's perspective in Chapter 1. Now it's time to take a more in-depth look from the programmer's perspective. Before you start looking at the first programming example, let's take a quick look at some of the criteria you need to keep in mind when defining a specific ActiveX control. The following advice should provide some insights into the special constraints you'll have to observe for ActiveX controls.

T **IP:** Although you can create an ActiveX control using just about any compiler that will produce OCXs, you'll find that using Microsoft's Visual C++ 4.2 product will save you considerable time. You'll see in this chapter that some extra steps are needed to make an OCX work properly as an ActiveX control even in the best of circumstances. Using an older compiler means that you'll need to rely on DOS command line tools to perform the extra steps. The newer 4.2 version of the Microsoft Visual C++ compiler includes these tools as part of the package and automates their use.

2

Keep Code Small   A good rule of thumb is to keep your ActiveX controls to 40 KB or less. The average user won't want to download a huge control that animates some graphic on the page. If at all possible, break a large component into smaller, functional pieces.

T **IP:**   You can also reduce the download size of a control by compressing it into a CAB file. We'll look at the process for doing this in Chapter 4.

Use a Minimum of Persistent Data   Some OCXs require a huge amount of persistent data to accomplish their task. For example, you might stick a spreadsheet control on a form and not think twice about the amount of persistent data that it contains. ActiveX controls don't have this luxury since you can't assume much about the client machine. Not only does persistent data increase load time and memory requirements, it also boosts the size of the control itself.

Keep Bells and Whistles to a Minimum   Bells and whistles can really make an onscreen presentation sparkle. When you're writing an OCX for local machine use, a few bells and whistles don't really create any problems. In fact, most programmers would be surprised if you didn't include them. Transfer time is a really big issue on the Internet. Every time you add graphics that you really don't need to a control, or some special sound effect, you're increasing load time and decreasing the value of your control. An ActiveX control can't even assume that some special effects will work correctly on the client machine (it may not include a sound board, for example).

Single Function Is Key One of the original purposes for libraries was to store a large number of function calls in a precompiled and easily accessible form. DLLs, one of the predecessors to OCXs, exist for this very reason. You'll find that many OCXs on the market, like DLLs, contain more than one object, such as a pushbutton. In fact, some of them contain a whole family of objects. This strategy works fine on the desktop, but won't work well on the Internet. Make sure you maintain one object in each ActiveX control. Doing so modularizes the controls and ensures that users don't download any more functionality than they absolutely need.

NOTE: We're going to talk about objects quite a bit in this chapter. Every object in this chapter is a Windows object (or a special form of it used by COM). Some C++ programmers might get the idea that a Windows object is precisely the same as a C++ object. Since the COM uses a special form of Windows object, these same programmers might think that they won't run into any problems using any C++ object on hand to write an OCX. Nothing could be further from the truth. Although you can use a C++ object to create a Windows object, there are limitations. There isn't space in this chapter to get into a full discourse on the intricacies of C++ programming—that's a topic that some authors take an entire chapter (or two) to cover as an overview—but it's important to know that there are limits to what you can and should do when writing an OCX using C++. Following the example in this chapter is the best way to get started writing OCXs without running into problems. As the book progresses, we'll refine this example and add a few unique twists to it.

Test, Test, Test It isn't enough to test an ActiveX control locally or on the network. You've got to test in a variety of situations using different connections. We'll eventually look at three levels of local testing and one level of Internet-specific testing in this chapter. You may want to add more levels than this. The bottom line is that you can't test an ActiveX control too much. (It's important that you test before releasing the control, but invariably you'll also have to do some bug hunting after the fact. Keeping accurate problem logs is essential in making your ActiveX control work properly.)

Writing the Code

It's time to take a look at a simple coding example. This chapter uses Microsoft Visual C++, as mentioned earlier. Let's begin with a new C++

project. However, unlike other projects you may have created, you'll want to start with the OLE Control Wizard to create your workspace. To do that, use the File | New command to display the New dialog. Select the Project Workspace option, and you'll see a dialog like the one shown in Figure 2-1. Notice the OLE Control Wizard entry in this dialog. That's the one you'll need to start the project. The Wizard provides you with an OCX framework that you can build on to create the final version of this example.

NOTE: I used the new Microsoft Developer Studio setup for this example. All the screen shots you see will reflect the Windows 95 orientation of that setup. If you choose to use the older interface, your screen shots won't match mine at all. There may be subtle differences even if you do use the Developer Studio interface due to the variety of configuration options that this product provides.

2

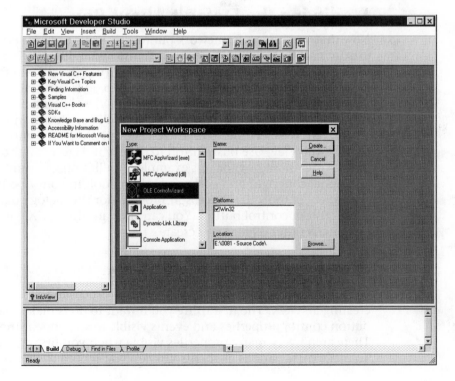

Microsoft Visual C++ 4.0 offers several new workspace project types, including the one you'll need to create an OCX.

Figure 2-1.

To get the project started, you'll have to type something in the Name field. This example uses OCXExmpl for a project name. You'll also need to click on the OLE Control Wizard entry in the Type field, then on the Create button. Microsoft Visual C++ automatically selects the Win32 option for you. It also creates a project directory.

What you'll see next are two dialogs worth of OLE Control Wizard screens. I accepted the defaults on both screens except for the subclass entry on the second page. You'll want to select the BUTTON class here if you want to create an example like this one. Otherwise, look through the list of available classes to determine what you want to use as a basis for your control. Notice that Visual C++ allows you to create your own basic class.

Once you click on the Finish button in the second Wizard screen, you'll see a New Project Information dialog. You'll want to look through the list of features presented here just to make certain the project contains everything you need. After you verify that the project setup is correct, click on OK to get the project started. Visual C++ will churn your disk for a few moments, and then you'll see the project framework.

Modifying the Default About Box

Now that you have a framework put together, it's time to start filling it out. I usually start by tackling the easy stuff first—who doesn't. The first thing you'll want to do is modify the About box. Yes, Visual C++ creates one of those for you automatically—all you need to do is customize it. Getting access to the About box is easy. Just use the View | Resource Symbols command to display the Resource Symbols dialog shown in Figure 2-2. You'll want to select the IDD_ABOUTBOX_OCXEXMPL entry, and then click on the View Use pushbutton to display it. Figure 2-3 shows one way to modify the About box for this example. You'll probably want to include additional copyright and company information in your About box. Notice the variety of tools that Microsoft provides for the dialog box. One of them is the custom control button. You can stick another OCX within the About box or any other dialogs you create.

Adding Properties and Events

Customizing the About box is fun, but let's get down to the business of creating an OCX. The first thing you'll want to do is make some of the button control properties and events visible to someone using the OCX. There aren't very many properties visible when you first create a button. To make these various elements visibles, you'll need to use the Class Wizard.

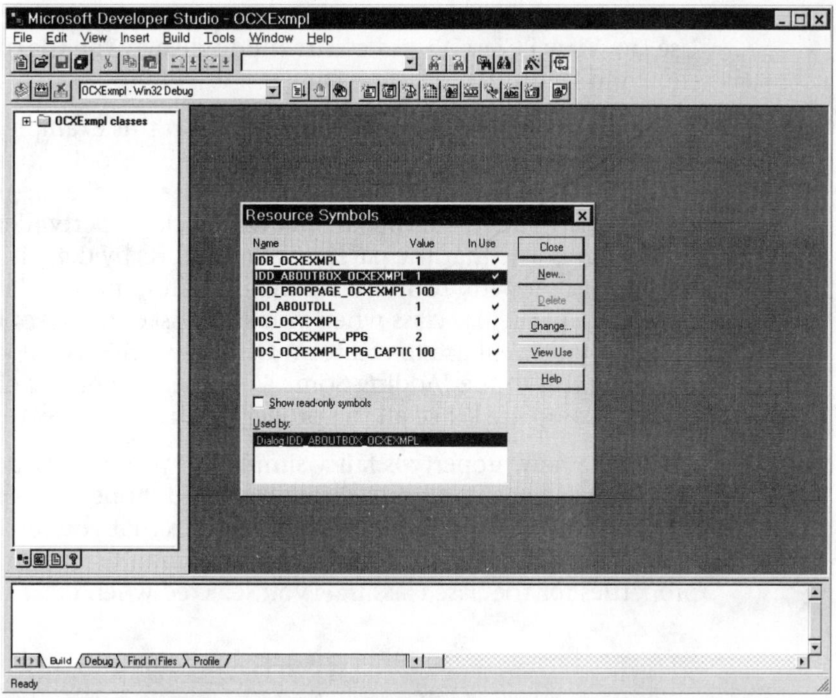

2

The Resource Symbols dialog displays a list of all the symbol resources in your project.
Figure 2-2.

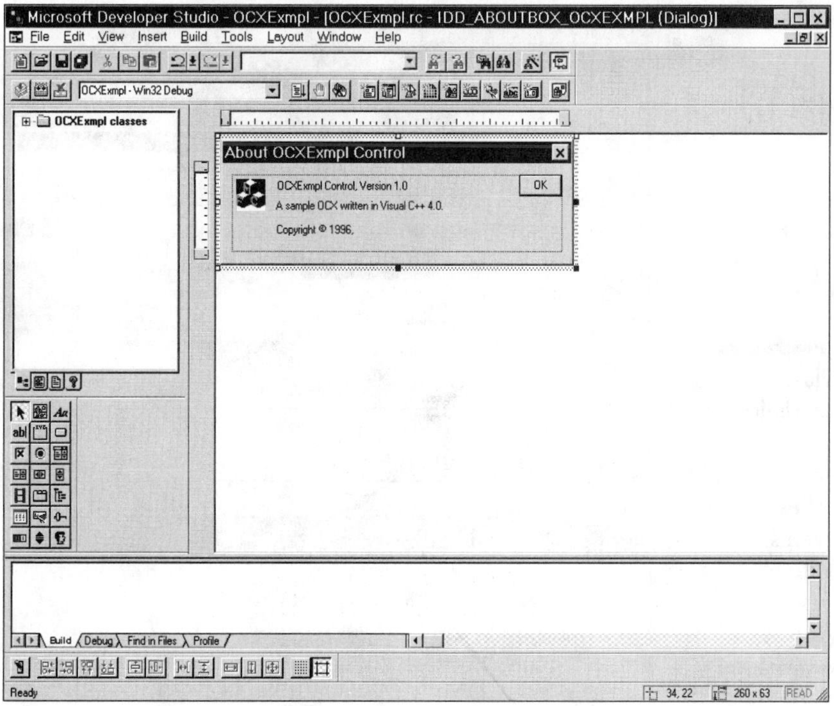

The dialog editor looks like the one provided with Visual Basic—the difference is that you have to access it separately from the main editor screen.
Figure 2-3.

Use the View | ClassWizard command to display the Class Wizard dialog shown in Figure 2-4.

We'll use two different kinds of properties in this example—Microsoft provides access to a lot more. The first type is a stock property. You'll find that things like the Caption property that we all take for granted aren't visible when you first create an OCX. A stock property (denoted by an *S* in the figure) is one that the parent class supports by default. The second type is a custom property (*C* in the figure). A custom property is one that you've added to a particular class when you subclassed it. One of them is the OnOff property that we'll use to create an OnOff switch. We'll look at the process for doing this in the "Adding Some Code" section of this chapter. Figure 2-4 shows a complete list of all the properties that we'll create in this example.

Creating a new property is fairly simple. All you need to do is click on the Add Property pushbutton to display the Add Property dialog shown in Figure 2-5. This dialog has some important features that you might not see at first. The External Name combo box contains a complete list of the default properties for the base class that you selected when creating the OCX.

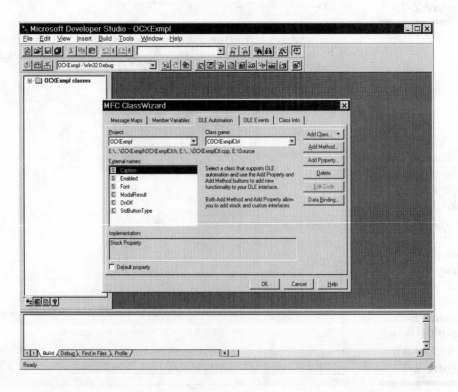

The Class Wizard dialog allows you to make properties and events visible to the OCX user.

Figure 2-4.

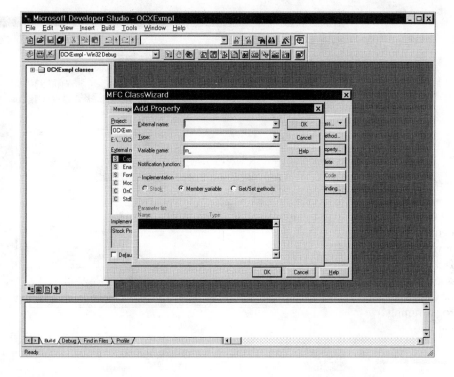

The Add
Property
dialog allows
you to
create new
properties for
your OCX or
make existing
ones visible to
the user.

Figure 2-5.

2

In this case you'll see things like the Caption property. To create a stock property, just select one of the items from this list and click on OK. Visual C++ will take care of the details for you in this case. We'll also need three custom properties: ModalResult, OnOff, and StdButtonType. To create these properties, type the names I've just mentioned into the External Name field. You'll need to select a type as well. In this case the ModalResult and StdButtonType properties are the long type, while OnOff is a BOOL.

All of the events we'll use in this example are stock—they come as part of the button base class. All you need to do is click on the OLE Events page to display the dialog shown in Figure 2-6. Adding a stock event is about the same as adding a stock property. Just click on the Add Event button to display the Add Event dialog. Select a stock name from the External Name combo box, and click on OK to complete the process. Figure 2-6 shows all of the stock events you'll need for this example.

Defining the Property Page

Now it's time to add some functionality to the property page. You access it the same way that you did the About box, using the View I Resource Symbols

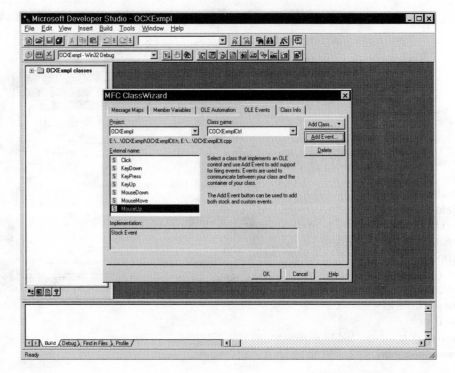

The OLE Events page shows all the stock events added to our OCX programming example.

Figure 2-6.

command. In this case you'll select the IDD_PROPPAGE_OCXEXMPL entry in the Resource Symbols dialog. The property page is used for a wide variety of purposes—most of them configuration oriented. What we'll do now is add a method for defining standard button types to the page, as shown in Figure 2-7. These are radio buttons. You'll need ten of them. Each radio button should have a different ID so that you can detect which one the user clicks (see the ID field on the General page of the Radio Button Properties dialog).

Double-clicking on a radio button displays the Radio Button Properties dialog shown in Figure 2-8. You'll need to make a few subtle changes to your radio buttons before they look like the one in Figure 2-8. First, select the Styles page of the Radio Button Properties dialog, and select the push-like check box for each button. You'll also need to place the radio buttons into a group. To do that select the Group and the Tabstop check boxes on the first radio button in the group. Only check the Tabstop check box for all of the other radio buttons, or you'll end up with ten groups of one button instead of one group of ten buttons. Visual C++ starts with the first button it sees that has the Group check box selected as the starting point for the group.

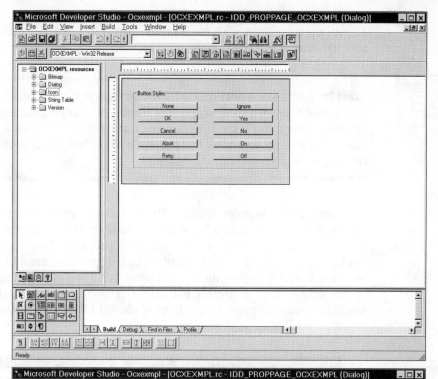

The Property Page dialog allows the user to create standard button types in addition to the on/off button.
Figure 2-7.

2

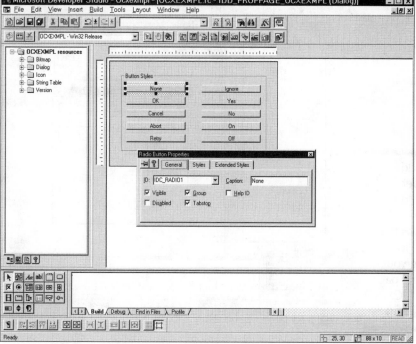

The Radio Button Properties dialog allows you to change the visual presentation of the radio button as well as place the radio button in a group.
Figure 2-8.

The group continues with each radio button in tab order until Visual C++
sees the next one with the Group check box selected.

T IP: Most Microsoft products prefer that you use a property page size of
250 X 62 or 250 X 110 dialog units. However, you can use any size you need.
The only thing you'll see is a message stating that you used a nonstandard
size when you try to access the property page. Simply clear the message, and
the property page will appear as usual.

We have to do one more thing with the radio buttons in this dialog. To
create an OLE connection between the radio buttons and the OCX control,
you have to assign their output to an OLE property. Press CTRL as you
double-click on the first radio button in the group to display the Add
Member Variable dialog shown in Figure 2-9. (You can also access this dialog
by pressing CTRL-W to display the MFC ClassWizard dialog, selecting the
Member Variables page, then clicking the Add Variable button.) The entries

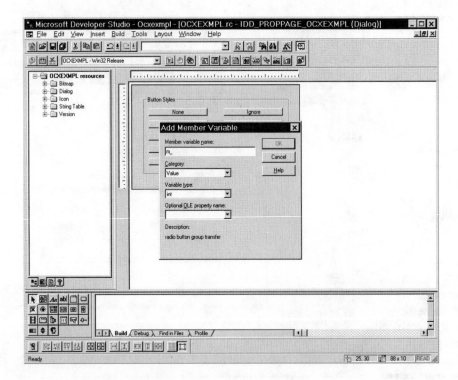

The Add
Member
Variable
dialog
provides the
means for
linking your
property page
to the OCX.

Figure 2-9.

2

you make here are crucial because Visual C++ doesn't check them for errors, and there isn't any way to select them from a list. In the Member Variable Name field, type **m_stdButtonType**. That's the internal name for one of the custom properties that we created earlier. Leave the Category and Variable Type fields alone. Type **StdButtonType** in the Optional OLE Property Name field. This is the entry that links the property page to your OCX control. Remember that C++ is case sensitive—capitalization is important.

Adding Some Code

Up to this point we haven't added a single line of code to our application. That's because we've been building a framework for the code. Now it's time to start adding code to the OCX. Listings 2-1 and 2-2 show you how to flesh out the OCXEXMPLCtl.CPP and OCXEXMPLCtl.H files. Pay special attention to the BOOL m_SetOn entry in Listing 2-2—it keeps track of the on/off button state for you.

Listing 2-1

```
// OCXEXMPLCtl.cpp : Implementation of the COCXEXMPLCtrl OLE control class.

#include "stdafx.h"
#include "OCXEXMPL.h"
#include "OCXEXMPLCtl.h"
#include "OCXEXMPLPpg.h"

#ifdef _DEBUG
#define new DEBUG_NEW
#undef THIS_FILE
static char THIS_FILE[] = __FILE__;
#endif

IMPLEMENT_DYNCREATE(COCXEXMPLCtrl, COleControl)

/////////////////////////////////////////////////////////////////////////////
// Message map

BEGIN_MESSAGE_MAP(COCXEXMPLCtrl, COleControl)
    //{{AFX_MSG_MAP(COCXEXMPLCtrl)
    // NOTE - ClassWizard will add and remove message map entries
    //    DO NOT EDIT what you see in these blocks of generated code !
    //}}AFX_MSG_MAP
    ON_MESSAGE(OCM_COMMAND, OnOcmCommand)
    ON_OLEVERB(AFX_IDS_VERB_PROPERTIES, OnProperties)
END_MESSAGE_MAP()
```

```
/////////////////////////////////////////////////////////////////////////
// Dispatch map

BEGIN_DISPATCH_MAP(COCXEXMPLCtrl, COleControl)
    //{{AFX_DISPATCH_MAP(COCXEXMPLCtrl)
    DISP_PROPERTY_NOTIFY(COCXEXMPLCtrl, "OnOff", m_onOff, OnOnOffChanged,
VT_BOOL)
    DISP_PROPERTY_NOTIFY(COCXEXMPLCtrl, "ModalResult", m_modalResult,
OnModalResultChanged, VT_I4)
    DISP_PROPERTY_NOTIFY(COCXEXMPLCtrl, "StdButtonType", m_stdButtonType,
OnStdButtonTypeChanged, VT_I4)
    DISP_STOCKPROP_CAPTION()
    DISP_STOCKPROP_ENABLED()
    DISP_STOCKPROP_FONT()
    //}}AFX_DISPATCH_MAP
    DISP_FUNCTION_ID(COCXEXMPLCtrl, "AboutBox", DISPID_ABOUTBOX, AboutBox,
VT_EMPTY, VTS_NONE)
END_DISPATCH_MAP()


/////////////////////////////////////////////////////////////////////////
// Event map

BEGIN_EVENT_MAP(COCXEXMPLCtrl, COleControl)
    //{{AFX_EVENT_MAP(COCXEXMPLCtrl)
    EVENT_STOCK_CLICK()
    EVENT_STOCK_KEYDOWN()
    EVENT_STOCK_KEYPRESS()
    EVENT_STOCK_KEYUP()
    EVENT_STOCK_MOUSEDOWN()
    EVENT_STOCK_MOUSEMOVE()
    EVENT_STOCK_MOUSEUP()
    //}}AFX_EVENT_MAP
END_EVENT_MAP()


/////////////////////////////////////////////////////////////////////////
// Property pages

// TODO: Add more property pages as needed.  Remember to increase the count!
BEGIN_PROPPAGEIDS(COCXEXMPLCtrl, 1)
    PROPPAGEID(COCXEXMPLPropPage::guid)
END_PROPPAGEIDS(COCXEXMPLCtrl)


/////////////////////////////////////////////////////////////////////////
// Initialize class factory and guid
```

```
IMPLEMENT_OLECREATE_EX(COCXEXMPLCtrl, "OCXEXMPL.OCXEXMPLCtrl.1",
    0xd8d77e03, 0x712a, 0x11cf, 0x8c, 0x70, 0, 0, 0x6e, 0x31, 0x27, 0xb7)

/////////////////////////////////////////////////////////////////////////
// Type library ID and version

IMPLEMENT_OLETYPELIB(COCXEXMPLCtrl, _tlid, _wVerMajor, _wVerMinor)

/////////////////////////////////////////////////////////////////////////
// Interface IDs

const IID BASED_CODE IID_DOCXEXMPL =
    { 0xd8d77e01, 0x712a, 0x11cf, { 0x8c, 0x70, 0, 0, 0x6e, 0x31, 0x27, 0xb7 }
  };
const IID BASED_CODE IID_DOCXEXMPLEvents =
    { 0xd8d77e02, 0x712a, 0x11cf, { 0x8c, 0x70, 0, 0, 0x6e, 0x31, 0x27, 0xb7 }
  };

/////////////////////////////////////////////////////////////////////////
// Control type information

static const DWORD BASED_CODE _dwOCXEXMPLOleMisc =
    OLEMISC_ACTIVATEWHENVISIBLE |
    OLEMISC_SETCLIENTSITEFIRST |
    OLEMISC_INSIDEOUT |
    OLEMISC_CANTLINKINSIDE |
    OLEMISC_RECOMPOSEONRESIZE;

IMPLEMENT_OLECTLTYPE(COCXEXMPLCtrl, IDS_OCXEXMPL, _dwOCXEXMPLOleMisc)

/////////////////////////////////////////////////////////////////////////
// COCXEXMPLCtrl::COCXEXMPLCtrlFactory::UpdateRegistry -
// Adds or removes system registry entries for COCXEXMPLCtrl

BOOL COCXEXMPLCtrl::COCXEXMPLCtrlFactory::UpdateRegistry(BOOL bRegister)
{
    if (bRegister)
        return AfxOleRegisterControlClass(
            AfxGetInstanceHandle(),
            m_clsid,
            m_lpszProgID,
            IDS_OCXEXMPL,
            IDB_OCXEXMPL,
            FALSE,                          //  Not insertable
            _dwOCXEXMPLOleMisc,
            _tlid,
```

```
            _wVerMajor,
            _wVerMinor);
    else
        return AfxOleUnregisterClass(m_clsid, m_lpszProgID);
}


/////////////////////////////////////////////////////////////////////////
// COCXEXMPLCtrl::COCXEXMPLCtrl - Constructor

COCXEXMPLCtrl::COCXEXMPLCtrl()
{
  InitializeIIDs(&IID_DOCXEXMPL, &IID_DOCXEXMPLEvents);

  // TODO: Initialize your control's instance data here.
}


/////////////////////////////////////////////////////////////////////////
// COCXEXMPLCtrl::~COCXEXMPLCtrl - Destructor

COCXEXMPLCtrl::~COCXEXMPLCtrl()
{
  // TODO: Cleanup your control's instance data here.
}


/////////////////////////////////////////////////////////////////////////
// COCXEXMPLCtrl::OnDraw - Drawing function

void COCXEXMPLCtrl::OnDraw(
      CDC* pdc, const CRect& rcBounds, const CRect& rcInvalid)
{
  DoSuperclassPaint(pdc, rcBounds);
}


/////////////////////////////////////////////////////////////////////////
// COCXEXMPLCtrl::DoPropExchange - Persistence support

void COCXEXMPLCtrl::DoPropExchange(CPropExchange* pPX)
{

  // Default actions on the part of the Class Wizard.
  ExchangeVersion(pPX, MAKELONG(_wVerMinor, _wVerMajor));
  COleControl::DoPropExchange(pPX);

  // Make all of our properties persistent.
  PX_Bool(pPX, "OnOff", m_onOff, FALSE);
  PX_Long(pPX, "ModalResult", m_modalResult, mrNone);
```

```
    PX_Long(pPX, "StdButtonType", m_stdButtonType, 0);

}

////////////////////////////////////////////////////////////////////////
// COCXEXMPLCtrl::OnResetState - Reset control to default state

void COCXEXMPLCtrl::OnResetState()
{
  COleControl::OnResetState();  // Resets defaults found in DoPropExchange

  //Modify the Microsoft control to match Delphi property settings.
  COleControl::SetText("Button");
  COleControl::SetControlSize(75, 25);
}

////////////////////////////////////////////////////////////////////////
// COCXEXMPLCtrl::AboutBox - Display an "About" box to the user

void COCXEXMPLCtrl::AboutBox()
{
  CDialog dlgAbout(IDD_ABOUTBOX_OCXEXMPL);
  dlgAbout.DoModal();
}

////////////////////////////////////////////////////////////////////////
// COCXEXMPLCtrl::PreCreateWindow - Modify parameters for CreateWindowEx

BOOL COCXEXMPLCtrl::PreCreateWindow(CREATESTRUCT& cs)
{
  cs.lpszClass = _T("BUTTON");
  return COleControl::PreCreateWindow(cs);
}

////////////////////////////////////////////////////////////////////////
// COCXEXMPLCtrl::IsSubclassedControl - This is a subclassed control

BOOL COCXEXMPLCtrl::IsSubclassedControl()
{
  return TRUE;
}

////////////////////////////////////////////////////////////////////////
// COCXEXMPLCtrl::OnOcmCommand - Handle command messages

LRESULT COCXEXMPLCtrl::OnOcmCommand(WPARAM wParam, LPARAM lParam)
{
```

2

```
#ifdef _WIN32
  WORD wNotifyCode = HIWORD(wParam);
#else
  WORD wNotifyCode = HIWORD(lParam);
#endif

  // TODO: Switch on wNotifyCode here.

  return 0;
}

////////////////////////////////////////////////////////////////////////
// COCXEXMPLCtrl message handlers

void COCXEXMPLCtrl::OnOnOffChanged()
{
  //If the programmer set the OnOff property true, take appropriate action.
  if (m_onOff)
  {
    COleControl::SetText("On");    //Change the caption.
    m_SetOn = TRUE;                //Set an internal caption flag.
    m_modalResult = mrOn;          //Set the modal result value.
  }
  else
  {
    COleControl::SetText("Button");   //Restore default caption.
    m_SetOn = FALSE;                  //Turn our caption flag off.
    m_modalResult = mrNone;           //Use the default modal result.
  }

  SetModifiedFlag();                //Perform the default action.
}

void COCXEXMPLCtrl::OnClick(USHORT iButton)
{
  // See if the OnOff flag is set.  If so, change the caption and internal
  // caption flag.  The effect you should see from this code is a toggling
  // of the caption text.
  if (m_onOff)
  {
    if (m_SetOn)
    {
      COleControl::SetText("Off");
      m_SetOn = FALSE;
      m_modalResult = mrOff;
    }
    else
```

```
    {
      COleControl::SetText("On");
      m_SetOn = TRUE;
      m_modalResult = mrOn;
    }
  }

  // Call the default OnClick processing.
  COleControl::OnClick(iButton);
}


void COCXEXMPLCtrl::OnModalResultChanged()
{
  // We don't need to do anything here except set the modified flag.
  SetModifiedFlag();
}


void COCXEXMPLCtrl::OnStdButtonTypeChanged()
{
  // Change the modal result and button caption to match the user selection.
  switch (m_stdButtonType)
  {
  case 0:
    m_modalResult = mrNone;
    COleControl::SetText("Button");
    break;
  case 1:
    m_modalResult = mrOK;
    COleControl::SetText("OK");
    break;
  case 2:
    m_modalResult = mrCancel;
    COleControl::SetText("Cancel");
    break;
  case 3:
    m_modalResult = mrAbort;
    COleControl::SetText("Abort");
    break;
  case 4:
    m_modalResult = mrRetry;
    COleControl::SetText("Retry");
    break;
  case 5:
    m_modalResult = mrIgnore;
    COleControl::SetText("Ignore");
    break;
```

```
case 6:
  m_modalResult = mrYes;
  COleControl::SetText("Yes");
  break;
case 7:
  m_modalResult = mrNo;
  COleControl::SetText("No");
  break;
case 8:
  m_modalResult = mrOn;
  COleControl::SetText("On");
  break;
case 9:
  m_modalResult = mrOff;
  COleControl::SetText("Off");
}

//Set the OnOff property to false since the user selected another type.
m_onOff = FALSE;

//Set the modified flag.
SetModifiedFlag();
}
```

Listing 2-2

```
// OCXEXMPLCtl.h : Declaration of the COCXEXMPLCtrl OLE control class.

/////////////////////////////////////////////////////////////////////////////
// COCXEXMPLCtrl : See OCXEXMPLCtl.cpp for implementation.

class COCXEXMPLCtrl : public COleControl
{
  DECLARE_DYNCREATE(COCXEXMPLCtrl)

// Constructor
public:
  COCXEXMPLCtrl();

// Overrides

  // Drawing function
  virtual void OnDraw(
      CDC* pdc, const CRect& rcBounds, const CRect& rcInvalid);
```

```
    // Persistence
    virtual void DoPropExchange(CPropExchange* pPX);

    // Reset control state
    virtual void OnResetState();

    // A new OnClick routine.
    virtual void OnClick(USHORT iButton);

// Implementation
protected:
  ~COCXEXMPLCtrl();

  DECLARE_OLECREATE_EX(COCXEXMPLCtrl)      // Class factory and guid
  DECLARE_OLETYPELIB(COCXEXMPLCtrl)        // GetTypeInfo
  DECLARE_PROPPAGEIDS(COCXEXMPLCtrl)       // Property page IDs
  DECLARE_OLECTLTYPE(COCXEXMPLCtrl)        // Type name and misc status

    // Subclassed control support
    BOOL PreCreateWindow(CREATESTRUCT& cs);
    BOOL IsSubclassedControl();
    LRESULT OnOcmCommand(WPARAM wParam, LPARAM lParam);

// Message maps
  //{{AFX_MSG(COCXEXMPLCtrl)
    // NOTE - ClassWizard will add and remove member functions here.
    //      DO NOT EDIT what you see in these blocks of generated code !
  //}}AFX_MSG
  DECLARE_MESSAGE_MAP()

// Create a new enumerated type for the modal result.
  typedef enum
  {
    mrNone = -1L,
    mrOK = 1L,
    mrCancel = 2L,
    mrAbort = 3L,
        mrRetry = 4L,
        mrIgnore = 5L,
        mrYes = 6L,
        mrNo = 7L,
        mrOn = 8L,
        mrOff = 9L,
  }MODALTYPE;
```

```
// Dispatch maps
  //{{AFX_DISPATCH(COCXEXMPLCtrl)
  BOOL m_onOff;
  afx_msg void OnOnOffChanged();
  long m_modalResult;
  afx_msg void OnModalResultChanged();
  long m_stdButtonType;
  afx_msg void OnStdButtonTypeChanged();
  //}}AFX_DISPATCH
  DECLARE_DISPATCH_MAP()

  afx_msg void AboutBox();

// Event maps
  //{{AFX_EVENT(COCXEXMPLCtrl)
  //}}AFX_EVENT
  DECLARE_EVENT_MAP()

// Special On/Off state variable.
  BOOL m_SetOn;

// Dispatch and event IDs
public:
  enum {
  //{{AFX_DISP_ID(COCXEXMPLCtrl)
  dispidOnOff = 1L,
  dispidModalResult = 2L,
  dispidStdButtonType = 3L,
  //}}AFX_DISP_ID
  };
};
```

Breaking the Code into Pieces

Your initial reaction to all this code might be one of sheer terror, but it's actually pretty easy to figure it out if you take it one function at a time. In fact, about 20 percent of this code is generated automatically for you as part of the procedure we followed to get to this point. The application framework will save you quite a bit of time.

Let's start taking this code apart. The first function that you'll need to modify is DoPropExchange. This function only performs one service in this example—it allows you to make your custom properties persistent. Essentially, the PX_ series of function calls allow you to store the value of a particular property from one session to the next. There is one function call for each variable type that you define. Each one of them accepts four variables like this:

    PX_Bool(pPX, "OnOff", m_onOff, FALSE);

The first variable is a pointer to a property exchange structure. Visual C++ defines this structure for you automatically—all you need to do is use it. The second parameter contains the external name of the property, the one that the user will see in the Property Inspector. (There are a variety of names for the Property Inspector—Delphi uses the term Object Inspector, for example.) The third parameter is the internal name for the property. That's the one you'll use throughout the program to define the property. Finally, we have to define a default value for the property (unless you want the user to see a blank field in the Property Inspector).

The next function you have to modify is OnResetState. This function provides some of the aesthetic details that users will see when they add the component to a form. In this case, we'll give the component a default caption and resize it to match those provided with most programming languages, such as Delphi and Visual Basic. You'll need to change this setting to meet the needs of the programming language you use most often.

TIP: The default component size used by Microsoft is about twice the size of the one provided by Borland products such as Delphi.

At least two of the three modified functions in the message handlers section of the code require some kind of change. (The ModalResultChanged function doesn't require any modification, so I won't talk about it here.) The OnOnOffChanged function is the first one we'll look at. What we need to do is set an internal caption flag and the initial caption. If the programmer set the OnOff property to True, we'll set the control up as an OnOff switch button by setting its caption to On. We also provide a different modal result value when the pushbutton is used as an OnOff switch. Notice that the m_onOff internal property variable tracks the status of the flag. The m_SetOn internal property tracks the current condition of the OnOff switch (on or off). Since the button is initially On, we set the m_SetOn flag to True.

The OnClick() message handling function is active during run time. There are two levels of action here. First we need to determine whether the programmer defined this button as an OnOff switch. If this is an OnOff switch, we change the internal state variable (m_SetOn) and the button caption. The function switches the button state between on and off as needed. Once we finish with the internal processing needed to make the button work, we call the default OnClick processing routine. Failure to call this default routine will cause the OCX to skip any code specific to the programming environment that you attach to button events. For example, if you were to use this control in a Delphi application, any code attached to the exposed events in Delphi would be ignored.

Now it's time to look at the processing required for the Property Page feature of this OCX. The OnStdButtonTypeChanged function is nothing more than a simple case statement. It changes the button's Caption and ModalResult properties as needed to create various default button types. Notice that we also have to turn off the OnOff pushbutton processing if the user selects a default button type.

The header file requires only a few changes, but they're pretty important. The first is the addition of a virtual void OnClick(USHORT iButton); declaration to the public section of the component definition. Visual C++ doesn't add this declaration automatically. Since we need it to modify the handling of OnClick events, you'll have to add it manually. This is an important point to remember when writing your own components as well. Assume that nothing is declared public until you actually see it in the code.

The only other addition to the header is an enumerated type definition—MODALTYPE—which allows me to use the same ModalResult settings in the source code that Delphi uses. You'll need to modify this area to match the settings used by your favorite programming language. (In most cases you'll find that the ModalResult settings are pretty standard from language to language.) I found that this was a small but very important change. Otherwise, the code I wrote could easily get out of sync with that provided by Delphi. It's going to be less of a consideration for you if you plan to write generic OCXs that could work in any environment. In that case you'll need to publish the various modal results that users of your control can expect to receive, and it will be up to them to adapt. You'll want to keep this idea handy, though, if the OCXs you create are for use with specific language applications. For example, customizing a control to match the settings used by Visual Basic is one way to reduce a programmer's learning curve, especially for in-house projects.

Before you can use this component, you'll have to build it within Visual C++. Part of the build process automatically registers the OCX for you with Windows. I really liked this feature because it saved me some time when testing the OCX later. The only downside is that preregistration contaminates your working environment. You'll have to go to another machine to test this component from an Internet point of view as an ActiveX control.

Testing the Control

Once you create a new ActiveX control of any kind (whether your compiler calls it an OCX or not), you have to perform some type of testing to make sure it works as anticipated. The best way to do this for an ActiveX control you want to use on the Internet is to follow a four-phase approach: three levels of internal testing and a fourth level of external testing. The following list illustrates the importance of each phase.

♦ **Internal testing phase 1: Use the control in a standard environment** You'll want to see if the control is going to work at all before you move it off your standard programming platform. The reason is simple: testing an ActiveX control from within a browser leaves you without a debugger. Testing the basic functionality of an ActiveX control before you move it out of the C++ (or other OCX/ActiveX) programming environment means that you'll have a debugger handy for finding the really critical problems.

♦ **Internal testing phase 2: Test locally within a browser** Setting up a very short test on your local machine to see if the ActiveX control will even load into an HTML page could save some time later. You'll want to verify that enough properties are available to actually use the control and that it works when you view your test page.

♦ **Internal testing phase 3: Use a network connection to test a full Web page** Once you've tested the basic functionality of the ActiveX control and verified that it works with your browser, you have to determine whether it works with a full page of HTML tags. After all, what good is a control that won't work with other controls on the same page? Interaction between controls can cause some really odd problems. You could test for interaction problems using a standard form in an application, but that really won't help much. The problem is that a browser won't look at the ActiveX control the same way that your favorite compiler will.

♦ **External testing: Check control functionality on an uncontaminated machine** One of the biggest problems you're going to run into is contamination. Remember that most compilers automatically register an OCX or ActiveX control that you create. Someone checking into your Internet site won't have the same advantage. It's crucial to have an uncontaminated client and server handy to test your new control within the context of a Web page. In other words, this final stage of testing will look at the control the same way that anyone accessing your Internet site will see it.

Now that you have a good idea of where we're headed, let's look at some testing for the control we just created. This example purposely uses a pre-Internet version of Visual C++ for a good reason. We'll also take a look at some of the non-bug errors you'll see when using a straight OCX on the Internet.

Internal Testing Phase 1— Use the Control in a Standard Environment

Performing the first phase of internal testing doesn't have to be a long drawn-out affair. All you really need to do is create a project using your standard programming environment, and then add the ActiveX control (OCX) you've created. You'll want to make sure all of the properties work as expected. Take time to check out the property page thoroughly as well.

Start by creating a new project in your favorite programming environment (it has to support OCXs to work). For the purposes of this example, you could easily test the control by creating a dialog-based application in Visual C++. The MFC AppWizard takes care of most of the work for you.

Once you have a new project in place, create a form (if needed) and add the ActiveX control to it. Visual C++ automatically registers ActiveX controls for you, so the control we created in the previous section should appear in the list of controls available to you. (Other programming environments may force you to register your ActiveX control separately.) Figure 2-10 shows the dialog for the test program I created to debug this example. It also shows the Properties dialog with the Control page selected. Figure 2-11 shows the All page. Notice that the OnOff property is set to True.

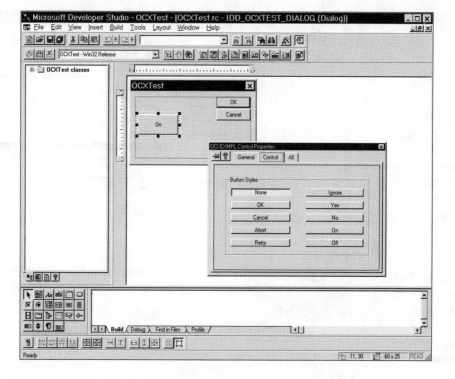

The Control page of the Properties dialog shows the special features for this pushbutton.
Figure 2-10.

2

You'll probably want to add some test code to the program as well. That way you can check the effects of various control events. For example, the OnOff switch button in our example provides a variety of modal result return values depending on how you set the button properties. Setting the OnOff property to True creates a special switch button. The ModalResult property switches between two values. However, you could just as easily select one of the standard button values from the Control page of the Properties dialog. Listing 2-3 shows the C++ test code for this example. Notice the use of the GetModalResult() wrapper class function that Visual C++ automatically creates for the control. You'll find all of the declarations that Visual C++ makes for you in the OCXEXMPLE.H file. It's educational to look at this header file since it shows how Visual C++ is interacting with your control. Looking at this file could help you find interface problems that you might not otherwise see (especially if you don't test every property of the control completely).

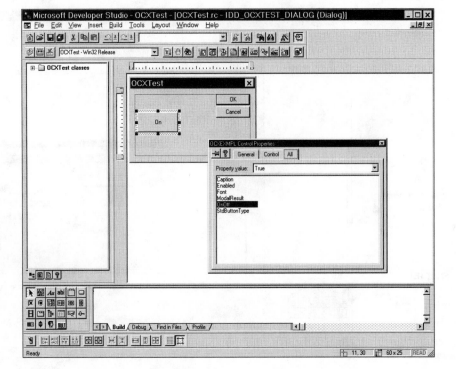

The All page of the Properties dialog allows you to change the properties that you made visible for a particular control.

Figure 2-11.

NOTE: You can create the OnClickOcxexmplctrl1() function in several ways. The easiest way to do it is using the MFC ClassWizard (which you can display using the View I ClassWizard command). Highlight the IDC_OCXEXMPLCTRL1 entry in the Object IDs list box, then the Click entry in the Messages list. Clicking the Add Function button at this point will add the function to your program.

Listing 2-3

```
void COCXTestDlg::OnClickOcxexmplctrl1()
{
    //Get the current ModalResult value.
    long liModalResult;
    liModalResult = m_OnOffButton.GetModalResult();

    //Determine which modal result was returned and display a message.
```

```
switch (liModalResult)
{
case -1:
    MessageBox("None button pressed", "State of Control", MB_OK);
    break;
case 1:
    MessageBox("OK button pressed", "State of Control", MB_OK);
    break;
case 2:
    MessageBox("Cancel button pressed", "State of Control", MB_OK);
    break;
case 3:
    MessageBox("Abort button pressed", "State of Control", MB_OK);
    break;
case 4:
    MessageBox("Retry button pressed", "State of Control", MB_OK);
    break;
case 5:
    MessageBox("Ignore button pressed", "State of Control", MB_OK);
    break;
case 6:
    MessageBox("Yes button pressed", "State of Control", MB_OK);
    break;
case 7:
    MessageBox("No button pressed", "State of Control", MB_OK);
    break;
case 8:
    MessageBox("Button is On", "State of Control", MB_OK);
    break;
case 9:
    MessageBox("Button is Off", "State of Control", MB_OK);
    break;
}
}
```

Now that you have a simple form with your control attached to it, try testing it. The example program will display a simple dialog box with the ActiveX control on it. Click the control and you'll see another dialog telling you the state of the button, as shown in Figure 2-12. A click on either the OK or Cancel button (provided free of charge by Visual C++) will end the program. As previously stated, this is a simple test of basic control functionality. What we've done so far is check the property page, the properties, and the results of using the control.

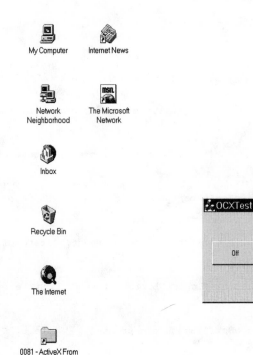

The on/off
button works
as predicted
by returning
alternate
modal result
values.

Figure 2-12.

Internal Testing Phase 2—
Test Locally Within a Browser

So far we haven't done anything even remotely close to working with a Web
page, much less adding an ActiveX control to one. That's about ready to
change. The next step in the testing process is to insert the control into an
HTML document. We'll use a very simple setup again.

Microsoft provides the ActiveX Control Pad utility as one of the ways you
can quickly build HTML pages for testing your controls. Figure 2-13 shows
what this utility looks like the first time you open it. You can also use it to
create full-fledged Web pages, but we'll look at that process in Chapter 4.

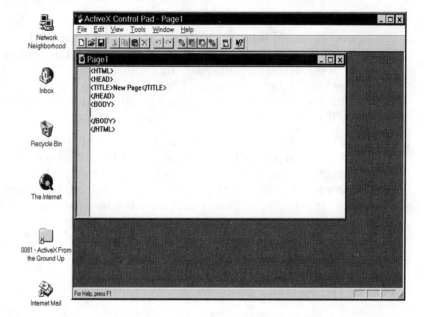

The ActiveX
Control Pad
utility allows
you to design
an HTML
page for
testing your
ActiveX
control
quickly.
Figure 2-13.

2

TIP: At the time of this writing it was uncertain whether Microsoft
would include ActiveX Control Pad with any of their programming
products. It isn't included as part of the ActiveX SDK. You can download a
copy of this very useful utility at http://www.microsoft.com/workshop
/author/cpad/. Make sure you look at the rest of the tools in the
SiteBuilder Workshop arsenal as well. You'll find all the details at
http://www.microsoft.com/workshop/.

To create a test HTML page for your ActiveX control, use the Edit | Insert
ActiveX Control command to display the Insert ActiveX Control dialog.

Select your control from the list provided. Click on OK and you'll see the ActiveX Control loaded, as shown in Figure 2-14. Normally you'd place the control within a form somewhere, but our only purpose is to test it alone for right now.

Every time you load a new control, ActiveX Control Pad will automatically display the Properties dialog shown in Figure 2-14. It contains the standard list of published properties for the control. Notice that Figure 2-14 also shows the General properties page. You display it by right-clicking on the control and selecting the desired context menu entry. For our example, you'll want to select the second Properties entry.

The only property we need to change is the OnOff property in the Properties dialog. Change it to True, and then close the dialog containing the Control. ActiveX Control Pad is going to add a tag to the HTML page script. (Don't worry if all of this HTML page lingo seems foreign right now; we'll cover it in detail in Chapter 4.) Notice that the entry includes the control's CLASSID along with all of the properties needed to set it up.

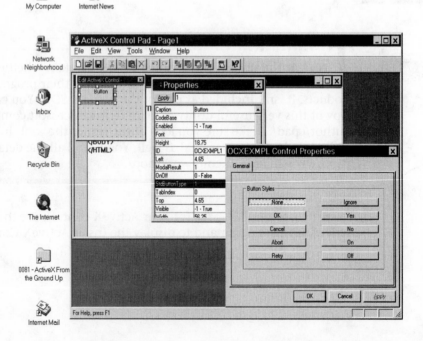

The ActiveX
Control Pad
utility displays
your control
after loading it.
Figure 2-14.

TIP: You'll see a little button next to the <OBJECT> tag in the HTML script. Clicking this button displays the control again so that you can edit its properties. Whenever you place an ActiveX control or an HTML page layout in a script, ActiveX Control Pad will display this button, making it easy for you to edit the control or page layout as needed.

2

Save the sample HTML page using the Save button on the toolbar. (Make sure you save it using the HTM extension.) Close ActiveX Control Pad, and then open the sample HTML page using your favorite Web browser. You'll see something like Figure 2-15. It doesn't look very awe-inspiring right now, but that control can do something that a standard HTML page button can't do. Click on the button, and you'll see that it switches between on and off. You could monitor the modal result value of that button as well and determine what state it was in—all without writing a single line of CGI script code. (We'll look at getting information from an ActiveX control in Chapter 3.)

The ActiveX control on this page does something you couldn't normally do—it changes between two states as you click it.

Figure 2-15.

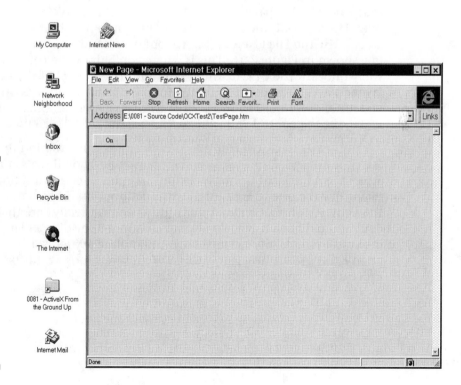

NOTE: You'll probably see a Safety Violation dialog telling you that the ActiveX control in this page contains unsafe code. That's because we haven't marked it as safe. You'll learn all about security in Chapter 6, and that includes marking your controls as safe once they're fully tested. Just ignore the message for now. Version 4.2 of Microsoft Visual C++ provides tools that take care of this detail for you (or at least provide a menu item so you don't have to resort to using the DOS prompt). This is one of the areas that I talked about at the beginning of the chapter in which you could write an ActiveX control using an older compiler, but a newer compiler would make doing so more convenient.

At this point, we've tested the control's basic functionality within C++ and a local ActiveX document. Before you move to the network, you may want to try various permutations of the control. For example, the OnOff switch pushbutton can also work in several standard configurations. Try them out to see if they actually work.

Now it's time to use the OnOff switch pushbutton with other controls. Let's start a new HTML page in the ActiveX Control Pad. We're going to create a new HTML layout, then place the OnOff switch pushbutton within the layout. Use the File | New HTML Layout command to create a form like the one shown in Figure 2-16. This is where you'll draw the components that will work with the OnOff switch pushbutton. Notice that the example layout places a few controls on the form for testing purposes. At this point you really don't need to add a lot of complexity, just enough information to make sure the control will work within a standard HTML environment.

Adding our ActiveX control is a bit different in this situation than it was the last time around. Right-click on the Toolbox and you'll see a context menu. Select the Additional Controls option, and you'll see an Additional Controls dialog like the one in Figure 2-17. This dialog contains a complete list of all the ActiveX controls on your machine (it doesn't really care that these controls could be OCXs). You can also choose to display a complete list of insertable objects. For example, you could place a Microsoft Word document or an Excel spreadsheet into a form. We'll take a look at this particular process in Chapter 5.

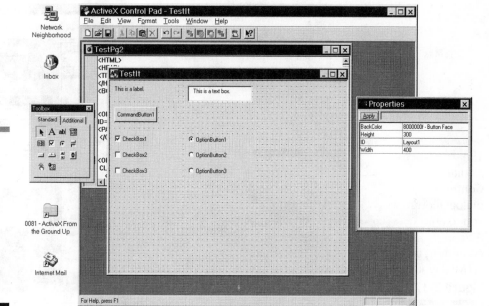

The second step in testing the ActiveX control is to see if it works with other HTML controls present.

Figure 2-16.

It's interesting to see that all of the controls in the Toolbox are actually ActiveX controls and not the standard HTML equivalent.

Select the OCXExmpl option (or whatever you named your control) from the list. Make sure you actually check the box next to the control, or ActiveX Control Pad won't install it. Click on OK to complete the process. You'll see a new control added to your Toolbox. Just grab it and place it next to the Command button shown in Figure 2-16. As before, make sure you set the OnOff property to True if you're using the example control in this chapter.

Once you complete all your edits, save your layout and then close the page. ActiveX Control Pad will add an <OBJECT> tag to the HTML script, just like it did for the ActiveX Control page we tested earlier. Of course, the difference in this case is that we're looking at a whole page of controls, not just a single control sitting on the page by itself. You'll want to save the new test page, then open it with your browser to see if the control works. After you've tested the ActiveX control in this environment, you can move on to network testing using the two pages we've just constructed.

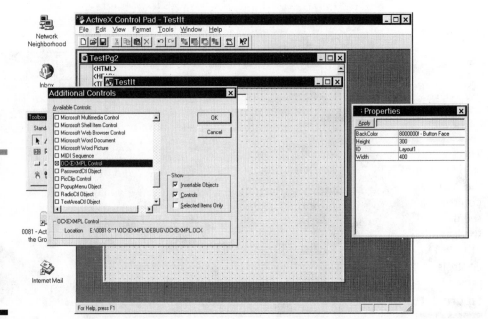

The Additional Controls dialog allows you to add ActiveX controls to an HTML layout.

Figure 2-17.

Internal Testing Phase 3—Use a Network Connection to Test a Full Web Page

There are quite a few ways to go about testing your control on a network. The only criteria is to have two machines: a server and a client that are connected using the TCP/IP protocol. You'll also want to run an HTTP server on the server. Fortunately, both versions of Windows NT 4.0 are going to ship with a small HTTP server that you can use for testing purposes. In fact, this new version of Windows NT will include FTP and Gopher servers as well.

You'll want to make sure that you can communicate with the server using a standard browser and the domain name that you've assigned. Don't make the mistake of accessing the server drive through something like Explorer, then double-clicking on the test pages. Sure, this will open the browser and you'll see your test pages, but you'll defeat the whole purpose of this test phase. Opening the page through Explorer or File Manager will place the browser in file mode. It won't allow you to test the HTTP server capabilities. The reason for this phase of the test is to simulate as closely as possible the environment typical users will have when they access your Web site.

Once you've established a link to the server and can see the default Web page that it provides, add a link to your test page. Use this link to test both the single control and the full HTML pages that we created in the previous section. In most cases, you'll find that simply testing the link is going to be sufficient for this phase of the test. In other words, if your control works in one mode, it should work in all of the other modes that you've provided for it as well. For example, in the case of our example control, I simply tested it as an OnOff switch. The standard button modes worked just fine because I had already tested them thoroughly during the first two phases of testing. That's why local testing is so important—it saves you time at this phase. (Imagine having to re-create several versions of that same Web page and testing them over a server connection—that's a pretty counterproductive way to program.)

External Testing—Check Control Functionality on an Uncontaminated Machine

We've completely tested the control in our private environment. Every type of control access was looked at, and we made sure that the control worked with standard HTML controls. Now it's time for the external testing phase.

Actually this is just an extension of the third internal phase. However, instead of accessing the Web site from the network, you'll want to access through a phone connection, just like your users will. In addition, you've been testing the control using a contaminated machine—one that has the control installed on it and all the appropriate registry entries.

The purpose of this testing phase is twofold. First, you want to make sure that the control still works when accessing from an uncontaminated machine. Otherwise, you may find that your control relies on some registry entries or other criteria that the client machines accessing your Web site won't meet. Second, you want to check the download time of your page. To this point we've been accessing the test pages using high-speed connections. People using your site won't have that privilege. The majority of them will access your site through a dial-up connection.

T IP: You'll want to install your test pages in a private section of your Web site to prevent other people from accessing them. Unlike the network testing phase, don't place an actual link to the test pages on your main Web page. Use direct addresses to access the test pages since you've already tested connectivity in the previous testing phase.

To complete this portion of the testing process, move the test pages to the private section of your Web server. Dial into your Web server from an uncontaminated machine using an ActiveX-enabled browser. You'll need to use the URL for the private section of your network instead of the URL for the main page. Try accessing the single-control test page first to see if the ActiveX control works at all. You'll also want to see how long it takes to download the control outside the influences of a full-page implementation. Once you've checked out the single-control test page, move on to the second page that uses a full HTML layout. If this connection works, you've got a working ActiveX control that you can use to enhance your regular HTML pages.

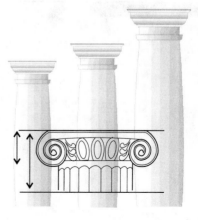

Chapter

3

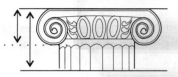

OLE and ActiveX

OLE has been with us for quite some time. You'll find it in Windows 3.*x* in a variety of forms. In fact, OLE is probably the most logical outcome of a sequence of events that Microsoft set in motion when they introduced the idea of a clipboard for cutting and pasting bits of text. (We looked at the history of ActiveX in Chapter 1, so I won't repeat it here.)

Most people still associate OLE with the cut and paste functions of yesteryear; but as a programmer you know better. OLE today has more to do with the component object model (COM) of programming than it does with data transfer. OCXs (OLE Control eXtensions), a form of OLE for programmers, have been making life easier for quite a while now. In their most basic form, OCXs are simply mini-applications that talk to your application; they're also viewed as libraries of precompiled routines. You design your application to take advantage of an OCX's capabilities using a standard interface.

Nothing's changed now that Microsoft has renamed OCXs as ActiveX controls. Sure, you'll start to find those controls in interesting places, but as we saw in Chapter 2, the basic functionality is the same. ActiveX controls still use COM as the basis for their existence. You can place an ActiveX control within an application with the same ease that you could OCX. Only the name has changed, not the technology.

Placing a control that does something really interesting on a Web page is one of the newer ways to use an ActiveX control. We looked at that scenario in Chapter 2 by creating a control and watching what it would do on an HTML page. However, as the Web grows larger and more complex, users are expecting a higher level of interaction and the ability to do more with the Web sites they visit. Such tasks currently require a lot of script programming (when you can do them at all). ActiveX provides a way for you to interact with a Web page—in order to get feedback from the reader as well as provide information.

It's this combination of old and new that we're going to explore in this chapter. We'll begin by looking at COM. What can COM do for me?—that's the question you should be asking yourself as you read this section. We aren't going to take an exhaustive look at COM, but it's important to at least understand the ideas that COM presents to you as a programmer. COM is not a form of library, although some programmers think so. Nor is COM a form of OLE, although some programmers confuse OCXs with OLE. Instead, COM represents a new way of looking at reusable code.

Sticking a control on a page like we did in Chapter 2 is nice, but you really won't get much out of it that way. The test application in Chapter 2 interacted with our sample control and provided you with some feedback on its current state. That's what the second section of this chapter is all about. How can you convince an ActiveX control sitting on a Web page to interact with anything? We'll look at a couple of approaches you can use for now. Microsoft is probably working on other methods even as you read this.

You can't avoid the registry when it comes to working with ActiveX controls or OLE. The third section of this chapter gives you a good overview of the OLE portion of the registry. You'll find yourself referring to this information more often than you'd like as you try to troubleshoot problem installations or controls that don't quite work as expected. Registering your ActiveX control properly is essential to making it work right.

The fourth and fifth sections of this chapter look at two tools that Microsoft thoughtfully provided for working with ActiveX controls. The first utility is *OLEViewer*. After you spend some time with RegEdit, you'll really come to appreciate the ease of use that this utility provides. OLEViewer allows you to look at your OLE controls without moving from place to place in the registry. It also provides a few handy tools that you can use with ActiveX Control Pad to make some types of script writing faster.

The second utility program is *ODS_Tool*, which stands for object data stream. This tool helps you manage OLE control streams, an important part of managing Internet data. You'll find this utility invaluable when it comes to creating data stream from the Internet server to the client.

A Quick Look at the Component Object Model (COM) and OLE

The component object model (COM) is the basis for the ActiveX controls sitting on your machine right now. As a result, COM garners more than its share of discussion in a variety of places, and gurus who know all its gory details abound. This isn't the place to look if you're in the mood for some heavy philosophical discussion of COM. What we're going to look at are some COM nuts and bolts that you'll need to know as a programmer. In other words, we'll cover the programming basics, but we probably won't cover every minuscule detail that some tomes take hundreds of pages to accomplish. With this in mind, here are a few things you'll need to know when we talk about COM.

In the days of DOS there was the *library*. A library allowed you to store routines—object modules—in precompiled format. The advantage to using a library was pretty obvious. Once you wrote a piece of code and debugged it, you could rely on it to work (that is, at least in theory; things like interaction problems made libraries a less-than-perfect solution). The problem with libraries is that they are linked statically. This means that every application using the code within the library carries a copy of that code with it. Obviously, since DOS was only designed to run one application at a time, static libraries weren't much of a problem.

Windows came along and introduced the *DLL (dynamic link library)*. Notice that we're still talking about a library of routines—object modules that you compile and test. In this case, however, the modules don't get linked with the application until you run the application on your machine. This means that the functions within a DLL, unlike those found in a DOS library, are executable code. The advantage here is that you can run multiple applications that require the code in the DLL without using multiple copies of the DLL itself. Using DLLs saves memory and, in some cases, processor cycles as well. The problem with DLLs is that you have to know all about them before you can use them. Every function within the DLL has a different interface, making it very difficult to reuse the code. In addition, DLLs are implementation-specific—meaning that a DLL function written to use C strings has to be called with C string arguments. This isn't such a big deal if you're already using C to write your application, but some people prefer to use Pascal.

VBXs (Visual Basic eXtensions) arrived on the scene and took some of the pain out of using DLLs. A VBX uses a standard interface (one that is implementation-independent) and provides a representation of the component that the programmer sees during the design phase. In addition, a VBX provides a method for determining what the control needs to operate by exposing properties. It also exposes functions contained within the VBX. Now a programmer can reuse code created by someone else with ease. No longer do you need to spend a lot of time looking at the documentation to figure out how to use the code because the property values and function calls provide clues. Finally, unlike static library code or DLLs, a VBX is designed to fully integrate with the application and provide a response to events. Unfortunately, VBXs are part of the 16-bit world that we left behind in Windows 3.x—Windows NT and Windows 95 are both 32-bit operating systems.

COM came along in the form of OCXs (now called ActiveX controls). The starting point for an ActiveX control is the VBX. An ActiveX control is simply an enhanced 32-bit version of a VBX. From a program design point of view, you may not even notice the difference from within your compiler's IDE. Like a VBX, an OCX provides a programmer interface by exposing properties. We saw how this works in Chapter 2 while designing our example control. However, an ActiveX control only uses the ideas presented by VBX technology as a starting point. They also add an OLE component to the picture. We'll see how this works in the next section.

TIP: You can download a special ActiveX Template Library for Visual C++ 4.x from http://www.microsoft.com/visualc. This template library allows you to create the smaller, more efficient form of OCX required for Internet use more easily. It also adds some of the special interface elements to your ActiveX control that you'll need for a full server implementation.

OK, so now that we've opened the COM can of worms, let's look at what COM is all about from a simple programming point of view. The first thing you need to understand is that COM is a specification. That's where the model part of the acronym comes into play. COM doesn't tell anyone how to implement a control; instead, it concentrates on the way that two programs communicate with each other. An application interacts with an ActiveX control as an object, not as a bit of code that it's borrowing. What this implies is that there's a binary level of standardization. An application always interacts with every ActiveX control in the same way because every control supports specific interfaces. Another term that Microsoft originally applied to ActiveX controls was Windows object. In reality, that's what an ActiveX control is still about—although the platform has changed from only Windows to other operating systems.

3

ActiveX controls are object-oriented. An application doesn't need to know anything about the control's implementation to use it. In addition, this makes ActiveX controls programming language-independent as well. No longer does a Pascal user have to perform strange string manipulations to access a much-needed function. Likewise, a C++ programmer doesn't need to know that an ActiveX control was written in Pascal before using it. The use of Windows objects makes the language of choice something for the programmer to decide, not the writer of a library.

OLE Control Hosting

In the previous section we looked at a progression of programming libraries, from DOS to present-day ActiveX controls. The level of communication provided by an ActiveX control doesn't happen by accident. Windows provides a special DLL, COMPOBJ.DLL, that contains a small number of basic API functions. One of these API calls allows you to *instantiate* a component object—essentially a special form of Windows object. Every component object is identified by a 128-digit class identifier. We'll talk about this identifier in the "An Overview of the OLE Portion of the Windows Registry" section of this chapter. Instantiation is one of those thousand- dollar words that means nothing more than creating a copy of the object you need. In return for creating the object, you get a list of the functions that the object supports. We'll see later in the chapter that a lot of those functions are precisely the same—that you have to support specific functions to create a specific kind of ActiveX control. (Chapter 5 tells you about the four special interface functions required to create an ActiveX Document control.)

Instantiation performs another service for you as well. Since you request an object of a specific class from COMPOBJ.DLL, your application doesn't need to know where the component resides. Sure, the location of the component normally appears in your machine's registry, but we'll see in Chapter 4 that even though the location always appeared in the registry in the past, browsers such as Internet Explorer 3.0 have circumvented this requirement through the use of a CODEBASE attribute in the HTML <OBJECT> tag. (The component object still gets downloaded to the local machine and registered before you use it, so the requirement still remains intact.) As far as your application is concerned, it doesn't need to know anything about the location of a component object. This means that the object could appear in an EXE or DLL or OCX—it doesn't matter. A component object could also appear on the local machine or in a remote location (although OLE 2 doesn't really support this capability right now). Eventually you'll find that COM will allow you to create distributed applications that help a network distribute the burden of processing to several machines.

There is, however, one problem with the current implementation of ActiveX controls. Every time you download a control from the Internet, the person designing the Web page can specify one of three places for the control to go: the OCCACHE, main Windows, or SYSTEM folder. If the control ends up in either the main Windows or SYSTEM folder, it'll stay there until you figure out some way of getting rid of it. We'll see in Chapter 7 that there are ways of extricating the control's entries from the registry. Once you perform this step, you can erase it from disk. However, that still leaves one very sticky problem: how do you know which controls are safe to remove? There isn't any good answer to that question. Fortunately, the majority of the ActiveX controls you download should end up in your OCCACHE folder. Internet Explorer will hold on to them for a while, then remove unneeded controls for you automatically. Any control you see in the OCCACHE folder is safe to get rid of if Internet Explorer isn't running at the time.

TIP: You don't have to use Internet Explorer 3.0 to access a Web site using ActiveX controls. NCompass Labs Inc. produces a plug-in called NCompass ActiveX Pro that allows you to view HTML pages containing ActiveX controls using Netscape Navigator 3.0. At the time of this writing, the NCompass plug-in and Internet Explorer 3.0 ActiveX control capabilities are exactly the same. You'll probably want to spend a little time researching the plug-in before you use it. You can view an assortment of ActiveX plug-ins and controls at http://www.caboose.com/cwsapps/95activx.html. Go to: ftp://ftp.ncompasslabs.com/public/ and download NCPRO3.EXE if you only want this particular plug-in.

Another problem you need to tackle when looking at ActiveX controls is the environment in which they'll work. Even though you can only use an ActiveX control with a 32-bit application like Internet Explorer 3.0, there are still times when it may need to send data to a 16-bit application. COMPOBJ.DLL steps in here as well. It performs a process called marshaling to allow a 32-bit application to talk to a 16-bit application. In fact, the same feature takes care of all function call and parameter passing across process boundaries—even when both applications are 32-bit. The reason is simple: 32-bit applications always reside in their own address space, so any parameters (as a minimum) would have to get moved from one address space to the other as the two applications talked with each other.

TIP: As you use Internet Explorer 3.0, you'll find that there is a lot more to the OLE-to-Internet Explorer connection than you first thought. For example, it's not easy to figure out how to turn off all of those features that get added by ActiveX controls on some sites. You can learn a lot of different techniques for using Internet Explorer efficiently at http://www.cnet.com/ Content/Features/Howto/Explorer/ss03.html.

3

Creating an Interface

By now you've gotten the idea that ActiveX control communication consists of a client, a server, and an interpreter named COMPOBJ.DLL between them. That's not all there is to know about the communication, though—an ActiveX control needs to provide a standard interface to make it useful. When an application instantiates a copy of an ActiveX control (the component object), it receives a pointer to a list of functions. That list of functions is housed in what's termed an interface. To make it easier for you to understand what an interface is (at least in the context of an ActiveX control), think of it as a set of semantically-related functions implemented as part of a component object. You'll normally see an interface as an array of functions defined in the OLE 2 headers for your programming language.

An interface can perform a variety of tasks. For example, you might add a data operation interface like GetData or SetData. You'll see in the registry section of this chapter that you'll actually see registry entries for these interface elements. The more complex an ActiveX control, the more interfaces it requires to perform its task.

There is one interface called *IUnknown* that every ActiveX control must provide. It's the basis of all other interfaces—every other interface inherits from this basic interface. This is the interface that gets passed back to your application when you instantiate a copy of the control as a component object. Within this interface (and every other interface supported by an ActiveX control) are the three function calls listed here.

♦ **Query Interface**   This function allows the application to determine what interfaces the object supports. If the application queries an interface and the ActiveX control supports it, the application receives an array of pointers to the functions supported by the interface. Otherwise, the application receives a null pointer.

♦ **AddRef**   This function creates a new relationship to a component object interface. Using this function creates another pointer to the array of function pointers supported by the interface. A component object maintains a reference count of the number of relationships that it has established. The component object only gets unloaded from memory when the reference count is 0.

♦ **Release**   This function allows you to destroy the relationship between an application and an ActiveX control. It decreases the reference count by 1. If the component object's reference count is 0, then this function call also requests the destruction of the component object.

The presence of IUnknown means that your application can communicate with any component object it encounters. If your application recognizes the interfaces that the component object supports, it can communicate with that object at a fairly high level. For example, an ActiveX control provides very specific interfaces that your programming environment will know about if it supports them. If your application only recognizes a few of the interfaces, it still might be able to communicate with the component object, but at a much lower level.

There are a lot of interfaces that the OLE 2 specification already supports for specific kinds of component objects. The Microsoft OLE 2 SDK provides a full synopsis of all of these component object types and the interfaces that they're required to support. We'll also cover a few of the ActiveX-specific requirements throughout this book. However, just because Microsoft hasn't defined a particular interface doesn't mean that you can't define it yourself. The specifications we'll talk about throughout this book and those that you'll learn from other sources are the minimum interfaces that you can implement. Nothing says that you can't implement more interfaces, then publish an API that tells how to use them. That's the beauty of using COM—you can extend it as needed to meet specific requirements.

Storing the Data

The whole purpose of creating an ActiveX component (at least in most cases) is to exchange some kind of information with the client. Why else would you take the time to build a control when there are other methods of performing other kinds of tasks that take a lot less time and effort? Data exchange occasionally implies data storage as well. For example, even if you create an ActiveX control that simply tells the user that she or he is the 402nd person to visit your Web site, you still have to store that number somewhere. Obviously, this is a simple case—forms tied to a database somewhere are probably becoming the rule rather than the exception on the Internet. (They'll certainly be the rule on the intranets that will make the heaviest use of ActiveX controls until they become fully accepted by the majority of browser vendors.)

The OLE 2 specification (and, as a result, ActiveX itself) provides the means to store data in a number of ways. It also provides a number of data storage interfaces commonly known as structured storage when referenced as a whole. Structured storage is a technique for accessing data that doesn't rely on the old system used by DOS—a single file handle with a single data pointer keeping track of the current read position within the file. Instead, structured storage looks at data in two ways—storages and streams—which look more like the folders and files that Explorer uses to display the directory structure of your hard drive.

A stream object contains data. That data could consist of anything and in any format you like. For example, a stream can just as easily hold a graphic image as it could an entry for your database. In fact, a stream could conceivably hold an ActiveX control that you're sending from an Internet site to the client machine. Streams always provide one data pointer and you can assign rights to it. You identify them with a text string up to 31 characters in length. (We'll talk more about streams in the "Creating OLE Control Streams Using ODS_TOOL.EXE" section of this chapter.)

A storage object is just like the folders (directories) used by the disk on your machine. It can contain any number of stream or storage objects. Unlike a stream, a storage object cannot contain any user data and you don't get to determine its structure. However, you can assign rights to a storage object and perform operations such as enumerate, copy, move, rename, or delete on the elements within it. You can also do things like change the date and time stamps of elements within the storage object.

As with compound objects, Windows provides a special library of functions for working with OLE data storage in STORAGE.DLL. This DLL works

3

through COMPOBJ.DLL to get its work done. Whenever an application creates a compound document, it relies on the API calls contained in STORAGE.DLL to do so.

We could probably get into a lot of theory at this point, but it's probably easier to show you how this compound document storage system works. The OLE 2 SDK comes with a handy utility named DFVIEW.EXE. It's probably one of the better utilities you can keep around to enhance your knowledge of how OLE storage works. Figure 3-1 shows a typical Word for Windows document. It contains several kinds of OLE objects along with some native text. You could create a similar test document by opening a new Word document, then using the Insert Object command to insert some OLE objects. Creating the objects from a file will save some time. This particular example contains two different graphics documents (I picked two at random from the Windows 95 main folder). You could use sound or other OLE objects to see how the information differs from that shown here.

The first thing you should notice is that there's an overall storage object that uses the filename. This is also called the root storage object—just like the first directory on a drive is called a root directory. Below this is a stream

This Word for Windows compound document contains several examples of stream and storage objects.

Figure 3-1.

```
OLE 2.0 DocFile Viewer
File  List  Help
Storage file H:\WINWORD\0081-W~1\TESTDOC.DOC
  'CompObj', Type: Stream, Size: 106
  'ObjectPool', Type: Storage, Size: 0
    '_901011332', Type: Storage, Size: 0
      'Ole', Type: Stream, Size: 20
      'PIC', Type: Stream, Size: 76
      'META', Type: Stream, Size: 2176
      'PRINT', Type: Stream, Size: 2176
      'CompObj', Type: Stream, Size: 76
      'ObjInfo', Type: Stream, Size: 4
      'Ole10Native', Type: Stream, Size: 25896
    '_901011374', Type: Storage, Size: 0
      'Ole', Type: Stream, Size: 430
      'PIC', Type: Stream, Size: 76
      'META', Type: Stream, Size: 2176
      'ObjInfo', Type: Stream, Size: 4
      'LinkInfo', Type: Stream, Size: 20
    '_901011445', Type: Storage, Size: 0
      'Ole', Type: Stream, Size: 20
      'PIC', Type: Stream, Size: 76
      'META', Type: Stream, Size: 50424
      'PRINT', Type: Stream, Size: 50424
      'CompObj', Type: Stream, Size: 77
      'ObjInfo', Type: Stream, Size: 4
      'Ole10Native', Type: Stream, Size: 49220
  'WordDocument', Type: Stream, Size: 4096
  'SummaryInformation', Type: Stream, Size: 56112
  'DocumentSummaryInformation', Type: Stream, Size: 236
```

object named CompObj. You'll find this particular object in just about every compound document (but not necessarily by this name) since it contains the description information for the application that created the document. Some programs call this object Contents, others Book, and still others by other names. The main idea here is to define the application that created the compound document using an object name that will be fairly easy to figure out. There are several other stream objects at this level too—they're Word for Windows-specific and tell you what the document is about (SummaryInformation) and what it contains (WordDocument). Notice the ObjectPool storage object. Below it are three numbered storage objects that correspond to the three OLE objects contained in this document. Two of the objects are embedded, one is linked. You can tell which one of the documents is linked because it contains a LinkInfo stream object. The objects appear in the same order as they appear in the document.

An Overview of the OLE Portion of the Windows Registry

The first thing we need to define is the term *registry*. It's meant a lot of different things over the years and some people still aren't quite sure what it really represents. The Windows 3.x registry was so simple that most people never gave it a second thought. About the only thing it contained were some file associations and a few OLE settings. You might have found a few bits and pieces of other information in there as well, but for the most part, even Windows ignored the registry. The lack of support for the Windows 3.x registry showed in the tools that Microsoft provided to manage it; about the only thing you could do with the tools for this version of the registry was edit the file associations. There wasn't much a developer could do to see how well an application was registered short of breaking out a hex editor and going through the registry one line at a time.

Along came Windows NT. This product contains a registry that is so complex you need a four-year degree just to figure out the basics. (All you need to do is look at the Windows Resource kit for a few moments to realize just how complex the registry is.) The Windows NT registry contains every piece of information about everything that the operating system needs to know, including equipment settings, software configuration, network setup, and all the DLLs it needs to run applications. The tools for this version of the registry are also much improved from its predecessor. You can view all the various registry components using the editor that Microsoft provides. In addition, you can use the editor to modify more than simple file associations. The new version of RegEdit allows you to add and remove keys.

You can also save specific keys out to disk for future reference. It's important to know that developers now have a tool that will actually help them find problems in the way their application is registered with Windows. This added functionality should help reduce the problems that some users encounter trying to making OLE work.

Windows 95 uses a Windows NT-style registry. However, because Windows 95 is designed for workstation use and not as a file server, its registry is a bit less complex, but you'll still see all the file associations that you did with Windows 3.x. The Windows 95 registry also contains all your equipment settings, software configuration information, and a list of DLLs to load. In essence, the registry has become the central repository of information for the Windows 95 operating system.

The registry's also the heart of OLE in many ways. Unless you register your application (or have your programming environment do it for you) it won't recognize data files or perform even the most basic OLE functions. Because of the intimate relationship between OLE and the registry, it's important to at least know the basics of how the OLE section of the registry works. This section doesn't give you a blow-by-blow description of every part of the registry, but it does provide a detailed description of the sections you'll need to work with to implement OLE.

NOTE: This section concentrates on the Windows 95 form of the registry since both Windows 95 and Windows NT provide similar capabilities when it comes to OLE. The additional Windows NT registry entries are server- and security-specific.

A Look at the Registry

You use the RegEdit utility to view and change the contents of the registry. It displays the registry in the format shown in Figure 3-2. Windows 95 uses two hidden files, USER.DAT and SYSTEM.DAT, to store the registry information, but RegEdit displays them as one contiguous file. The same idea holds true with Windows NT even though it uses a different set of files to hold the registry information (security concerns are the main reason for the differences in file structure). Even though the RegEdit display might seem a bit difficult to understand at first, it's really not. The big difference between the registry and the Windows 3.1 alternative of SYSTEM.INI and WIN.INI is that the registry uses a hierarchical organization and plain English descriptions that you'll find easy to edit and maintain. Every application you

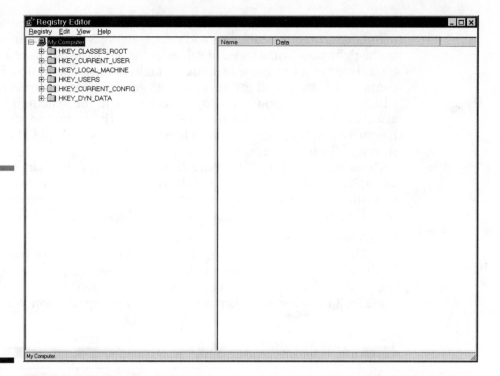

A typical
RegEdit
opening
screen. Each
HKEY key
controls a
different part
of the
Windows
setup.
Figure 3-2.

add will add entries to this file, but the file's organization makes it easy for an application to remove the entries when you uninstall it. Even if you install an older application that doesn't understand the registry, you can still remove its entries with ease.

CAUTION: Always make a backup copy of your registry before editing using the Registry | Export Registry File command of RegEdit. Simply accept the default options shown in the Export Registry File dialog and type the name of a file in the File Name field. Windows 95 provides a DOS command line method for restoring the registry using RegEdit. You will need to restore the registry from within the Administrator account under Windows NT. Never modify the registry for the Windows NT Administrator account. Windows NT always maintains separate user-specific registry files for each user. All users share the same hardware configuration registry file. Whether you'll have a separate registry file for each user under Windows 95 depends on the configuration—in most cases it's safe to assume that all users share the same registry files.

The Windows 95 and Windows NT registry uses two types of entries to maintain its organization: keys and values. Figure 3-3 shows a series of keys in the right pane and a series of values in the left pane. Keys are a registry topic; think of a key as the heading that tells you what a particular section contains. Looking at all the keys provides an outline for a particular topic, which could range from the setup of each drive in the system to the file associations needed to configure the machine. The key at the top of the hierarchy usually contains generic information. For example, the six keys shown in Figure 3-2 break the registry up into six categories of information. Each subkey provides a little more detail about that particular topic. For example, in Figure 3-3 we see that the HKEY_USERS key is broken down by user (there's only one in this case named Default) and the settings for that user. Keys always appear in the left pane of the RegEdit window.

Values are the definition of a RegEdit topic; they describe the key in some way. Think of a value as the text that fills out the heading provided by a key. Values are like the text in this book, while keys are the headings that organize the text. A value can contain just about anything—for example, the value for a file association key can tell you which application Windows will

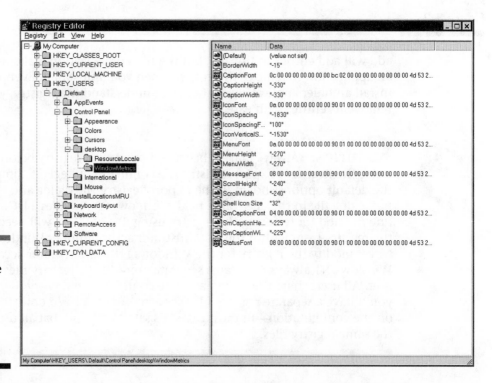

Keys and values are the two types of information you'll find in the registry.

Figure 3-3.

start when you double-click on a file that has that extension in Explorer. A value could tell you which interrupt and I/O port settings a piece of hardware uses as well. Keys and values work together to completely define a registry entry; you'll find the value you need by using the keys, but you'll find the actual information you need by reading the values.

There are three types of values: binary, string, and DWORD. Usually, only applications use the binary and DWORD value types. (Figure 3-3 shows what a binary type looks like—CaptionFont is an example.) Binary and DWORD values usually store configuration data in a format that can't be understood by humans unless you sit there with a hex editor to figure things out manually. Some applications use DWORD or binary values to store data in a general sense. For example, you might find the score from your last game of FreeCell here. Binary values can be any length and RegEdit displays them in byte-sized increments. DWORD values always appear in the 0x00000000 format and can store a DWORD-sized value. (The decimal value appears in parentheses next to the DWORD entry.) String values provide a lot of information about the application and how it's configured. Figure 3-3 shows several typical examples like BorderWidth. Notice that strings use a different icon than either binary or DWORD values do. Strings are always used to store configuration or other forms of data in human-readable format. Values always appear in the right pane of the RegEdit window.

As you can see from Figure 3-2, there are six main keys that Windows 95 uses to organize everything else. The current version of Windows NT uses only five main keys—it lacks HKEY_DYN_DATA since that information is stored elsewhere. The category that we're interested in for this chapter is HKEY_CLASSES_ROOT. It contains both file associations and OLE entries.

Figure 3-4 shows the typical HKEY_CLASSES_ROOT organization. There are two main types of entries under the HKEY_CLASSES_ROOT key. The first key type is a file extension. Think of all the three-letter extensions you've used, such as DOC and TXT. Windows 95 and Windows NT still use them to differentiate one file type from another, and also to associate that file type with a specific action. For example, even though you can't do anything with a file that uses the DLL extension, it appears in this list because Windows needs to associate DLLs with an executable file type. The second entry type is the association itself. (Look at Figure 3-4 and you'll notice that the ZIP entry is highlighted—this is where the file extension entries end.) The file association entries normally associate a data file with an application or an executable file with a specific Windows function. Below the association key are entries for the menus you see when you right-click on an entry in the

3

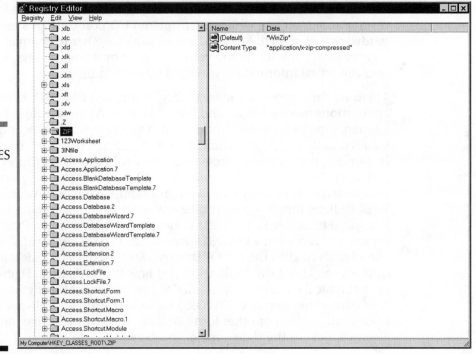

A typical HKEY_CLASSES _ROOT display. Notice the distinct difference between file extension and file association keys.

Figure 3-4.

Explorer. It also contains keys that determine what type of icon to display and other parameters associated with a particular file type.

NOTE: There is actually a third key type under the HKEY_CLASSES _ROOT key consisting of a single key, CLSID, that we'll discuss later in this chapter (in theory) and in Chapter 9 (in practice). This key is the entry point for all OLE 2 entries. For the most part it's better to simply think of the HKEY_CLASSES_ROOT key as consisting of two main sections.

Understanding Special Extension Subkeys

Some file extensions such as TXT provide a ShellX subkey (see Figure 3-5). In the case of TXT and WAV, the standard subkey is ShellNew (the most common key). There are some cases where you won't see the ShellX subkey immediately, as in the case of the SHW key. In this case there are entries for

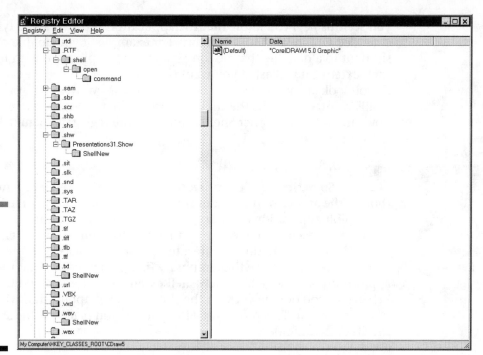

3

The shell extension is a powerful OLE 2 feature that few applications implement.

Figure 3-5.

specific applications: SHW provides only one, but there could be more. Notice that the RTF entry also contains a Shell key, but in this case it defines a special action for the file extension, Open, and an associated Command key that tells how to open files of this type. This isn't a Shell*X* key—it's a holdover from the OLE 1 days. A Shell*X* key will always have something following the word *shell*.

The term Shell*X* means *shell extension*. Think of a shell extension as an automated method of extending the functionality of Windows as a whole. When you right-click on the Desktop and look at the New option on the context menu, all the types of files you can create are the result of shell extensions. Even though ShellNew is the most common type of shell extension, a variety of other shell extensions are available. The actual number is limited only by the imagination of the programmer writing the associated application. For example, Microsoft Excel provides no less than three different shell extension entries for the XLS file extension.

A shell extension is an OLE hook into Windows 95 or Windows NT (Windows 3.x doesn't support this feature). Only an application that supports OLE 2 extensions can place a Shell*X* key into the registry. When you see this key, you know that the application provides some type of extended OLE-related functionality. For example, if you double-click on a shortcut to a data file that no longer exists, an application with the ShellNew shell extension will ask if you want to create a new file of the same type. (If you look at the values associated with ShellNew, there's always a NullFile entry that tells the shell extension what type of file to create.) You can look at the other Shell*X* entries in the registry as a guideline for creating your own.

TIP: Sometimes a file type won't appear on the context menu even though the application provides support for it. Most of the time it happens with 16-bit applications that don't install correctly. You can use the shell extension procedure to create new files as if the context menu entry did exist. All you need to do is create a temporary file, place a shortcut to it on your Desktop, and erase the temporary file. (Make certain that the application provides a ShellNew shell extension before you do this.) Whenever you double-click on the shortcut, your application will create a new file for you. This procedure also works if you place the file shortcut in the Start menu folder.

There are other, more generic, shell extensions as well. For example, the * extension has a generic Shell*X* subkey. Below this you'll see a PropertySheetHandler key and a 128-digit key that looks like some kind of secret code. Actually, the 128-digit value is a class identifier—you'll see them a lot in this book. It's a reference identifier for the DLL or other executable that takes care of the * extension. You'll find this key under the CLSID key. (CLSID stands for *class identifier*.) In this case the class identifier points to the OLE Docfile Property Page. Looking at the value of the next key will tell you if it exists in DOCPROP.DLL. This DLL provides the dialog that asks which application you want to use to open a file when no registry entry is associated with that extension.

Understanding the OLE 1 Registry Entries

Windows 95 and Windows NT both provide OLE 1 and OLE 2 support; so do many of the applications you'll use with them. It's easy to tell the OLE 1 and OLE 2 entries apart because they appear in different areas of the registry. You can always tell what kind of OLE support an application provides by checking its registry entries. If you see registry entries in one area of the registry, then you'll know that the application provides OLE 1 support. Registry entries in a second area of the registry show that the application provides OLE 2 support.

Let's begin by looking at the OLE 1 support. In previous sections we discussed the idea that the HKEY_CLASSES_ROOT key is divided into two areas: file extension and file association. That distinction is important. When you look at the file extension section you'll see a reference for that extension in the file association section. Figure 3-6 shows a typical file association section in the registry—in this case we're looking at the entry for Corel DRAW! 5.0.

What you'll find in the file association section are some OLE 1 keys (which we'll talk about in a few moments) and a Shell key (in some cases). Under the Shell key are actions associated with the application and instructions for executing them. Explorer uses the contents of the Shell section to define

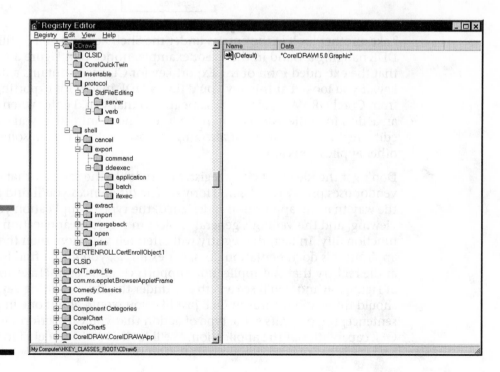

Windows places OLE 1 support in the file association area of the registry.

Figure 3-6.

what entries it'll display for a particular file type on the context menu as shown here.

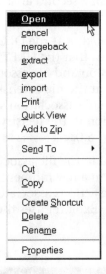

Take another look at the entries under the Shell key and you'll still see some DDE hanging around in there. For example, notice that Figure 3-6 shows that the extended form of the Export key for CDraw5 contains a ddeexec key. If you looked at this key you'd find a DDE macro for exporting a file from Corel DRAW!. This is the same macro that you'd enter when defining an action for a file association in Explorer. The point is that you can't simply edit a registry entry without affecting at least Explorer and in some cases other applications as well.

Don't get the idea that every registry entry looks the same or that every vendor uses precisely the same format. The differences you'll find are due to the way that the application is designed, the type of application you're viewing, and the vendor's general choices in regard to application functionality. In fact, the registry will often tell you more than the application's documentation does. For example, you might find by looking at the registry that the application supports certain verbs. (Take another look at Figure 3-6 and you'll see a verb key under the StdFileEditing key.) You should think about verbs in OLE just like you would about one in a sentence; it represents some type of action that you can perform using the OLE capabilities of the application. We'll look at verbs in detail in Table 3-1.

There are a few things you can always count on. For one thing, Windows always places OLE 1 support information in the file association area. (We'll look at the way OLE 2 support appears in the registry after we look at OLE 1.) Table 3-1 describes the various OLE 1 entries that you might find in this area. Some of these entries aren't supported by Corel DRAW! 5.0, but you'll probably find another application that does. Remember that the OLE support provided by each application on your machine will probably differ from the one shown in Figure 3-6—this is only a sample for you to look at right now.

3

Entry	Description
CLSID	This is actually part of the OLE 2 entry even though it appears in the OLE 1 section. It's a pointer to an entry in the CLSID section of the HKEY_CLASSES_ROOT key. C programmers use a special application to generate this 128-digit class identifier. (Newer programming environments always generate the class identifier automatically—reducing the workload on the programmer.) If you look for this number under the My Computer I HKEY_CLASSES_ROOT I CLSID key (as we'll do in just a bit), you'll find the OLE 2 entries for this file association.
Insertable	Normally you won't see any value associated with this key. A blank value means that Windows can place this file association in the Insert Object (or equivalent) dialog provided by many applications, such as Word for Windows. Some OLE 1 objects aren't insertable for a variety of reasons.
Protocol	This is a header key (think of it as a heading in a book, a means to group like information together in one place). Underneath it you'll find all the standard OLE-related actions that this OLE 1 application can perform. The only supported function in most cases is a standard file edit. (An application can support a lot of shell-related actions without supporting a lot of OLE 1-related actions.)
StdFileEditing	This key is another header. In this case it's the heading for all the keys that will define a particular action: standard file editing.

OLE 1 Entries in the Windows Registry
Table 3-1.

Entry	Description
Server	You'll find the name of the application Windows will call to service any OLE 1 calls for this file association. The string always includes the application's name, extension, and path. If you ever run into a situation in which your OLE links worked yesterday but won't work today, check this value to make certain the path matches the actual application location.
Verb	Several verbs are associated with an OLE 1 object. Each verb defines a specific action that the server will perform. This key doesn't have a value associated with it; its sole purpose is to organize actual verb entries. A client application can use only the verbs that are defined for a specific server. The following entries show both the keys and their associated values (<key>=<value>). The word values like Hide are the actual verb names. The numbers are false (0) or true (1), with the default being true (if you don't see a number in the value part of the verb key).

Key	Value
3 = Hide, 0, 1	This verb allows the client application to hide the server window. The first number following the verb is a menu flag. The second number is the verb flag. Normally you don't need to worry about either value as long as you supply the values shown here (or use the settings provided by the vendor).
2 = Open, 0, 1	This verb allows the client to open the server in a separate window rather than allow it to take over the client window.
1 = Show, 0, 1	A client would use this verb to display the server window in its preferred state. The whole idea of a state can get to be quite complex. Think of it as the way the window looks, and you'll have a pretty good idea of what to expect.
0 = &Edit, 0, 2	Every server provides this verb. It allows the client to call the server to edit the object.

OLE 1 Entries
in the
Windows
Registry
(*continued*)
Table 3-1.

Key	Value
1 = &Play, 0, 3	The only time you'll see this verb is when you're looking at some form of multimedia object.

OLE 1 Entries in the Windows Registry (*continued*)
Table 3-1.

Entry	Description
RequestDataFormats	This entry allows the server to define what data formats it supports for retrieval purposes.
SetDataFormats	This entry allows the server to define what data formats it supports for storage purposes.

3

Understanding the OLE 2 Registry Entries

Now it's time to look at the OLE 2 part of the registry. You'll find these entries under the HKEY_CLASSES_ROOT | CLSID key. Each of the 128-digit numbers here represent a specific class of information. Not all of the entries under the HKEY_CLASSES_ROOT | CLSID key are OLE 2 entries, but most of them are. You'll also find that not every application supports OLE 2. Your first clue that Corel DRAW! supports it is the CLSID entry in the OLE 1 section shown in Figure 3-6. The HKEY_CLASSES_ROOT | CDraw5 | CLSID entry is a pointer to the OLE 2 entry under the HKEY_CLASSES_ROOT | CLSID key. Figure 3-7 shows this key for CDraw5—the same application we looked at as an OLE 1 registry entry. Table 3-2 describes these entries in detail. An application doesn't necessarily need to provide every OLE 2 entry described in Table 3-2 in the registry. It depends on what OLE 2 features the application vendor decided to support. You can use these registry entries to determine the capabilities of your application, just like you can with OLE 1.

Using the OLEViewer Utility

If you found the prospect of digging your way through the registry to find the information you needed a little less than appealing, don't fear. The ActiveX SDK provides an alternative to RegEdit for viewing the various types of OLE information on your system. The OLEViewer utility appears in Figure 3-8. This is the default view that you'll see. We'll look at some alternatives later in this section.

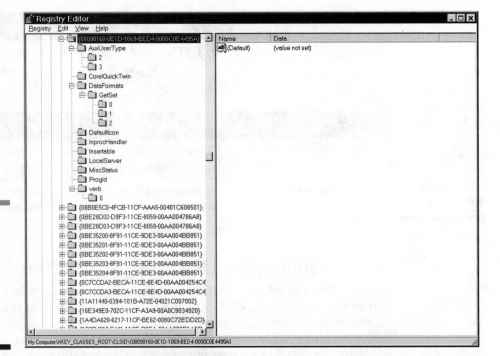

Figure 3-7.

Entry	Description
AuxUserType	This key is a heading for all the user type keys that follow.

Key	Description
2	The 2 AuxUserType always contains the short name for the application. A client can use this name in a list box to identify the object's owner.
3	This key contains the full name of the application that created the object. Like the 2 key, a client could use the 3 key value to provide an English application name for the object.

Table 3-2.

3

Entry	Description
DataFormats	This key is a heading for all the data format keys that follow. There are two standard data format keys: GetSet and DefaultFile. A vendor can implement any number of additional keys depending on the kinds of service that the application provides.
GetSet	This key is a subheading for all the data formats the server can store and retrieve. For example, an OLE server like Word for Windows would support a DOC, RTF, and standard text format. Its OLE 2 entries would reflect this fact. Each entry below this one defines a specific format type. Every GetSet subkey uses this format: n = format, aspect, medium, flag, as described in the next table entry.
n = format, aspect, medium, flag	Each of the sequentially numbered keys contains a different format. Format contains the type of format as a string. You might find some as easy to read as "Rich Text Format" or as cryptic as "Embed_Source". In every case, this string tells you the name of the format that the application supports. The client displays this string (for get formats) in the dialog box where you select the format you want to use when performing a Paste Special command. Aspect tells the client what display orientation the object supports. This usually means portrait and/or landscape. You'll usually find a value of 1 here for portrait. Medium contains the supported format as a computer-readable number. The Flag argument tells the client whether this is a get, set, or both format—a value of 1 is get, a value of 2 is set, and a value of 3 is both.
DefaultFile	This entry works much like GetSet, except it identifies the default file format for this particular object. Normally this entry is in plain English like the MSWordDoc value for the DefaultFile key included with Word for Windows.
DefaultIcon	The value of this key tells the client which application icon to use when displaying the object as an icon.

OLE 2 Entries
in the
Windows
Registry
(*continued*)
Table 3-2.

Entry	Description
InProcHandler	This key contains the name of the in-process handler. In most cases, this is OLE2.DLL unless the application provides its own OLE 2 handler. (A handler is a special program that helps two programs communicate.)
Insertable	Normally you won't see any value associated with this key. A blank value means that Windows can place this file association in the Insert Object (or equivalent) dialog provided by many applications such as Word for Windows. Some OLE 2 objects aren't insertable for a variety of reasons.
LocalServer	Every OLE 2 object must have a server. This key contains the name of the server on the local machine. Since OLE 2 doesn't support RPCs (remote procedure calls), you'll always need a local server for a standard OLE 2 application. Some Internet-enabled applications may be able to use a remote server—it depends on how the application is set up and whether the user can download it as an ActiveX control.
MiscStatus	This key contains the default value for all data format aspects.
ProgID	The program identifier is a pointer back to the file association that this class identifier belongs to. The file association is always a character string of some sort. It's the same string that you look for when you try to find the file association that goes with a file extension in the HKEY_CLASSES_ROOT category. For example, if you looked at the ProgID value for Corel DRAW! 5.0, you would see CDraw5. That's the same value we see in Figure 3-6 as the first key for the file association.
Verb	Several verbs are associated with an OLE 2 object. Each verb defines a specific action that the server will perform. This key doesn't have a value associated with it; its sole purpose is to organize actual verb entries. A client application can use only the verbs that are defined for a specific server. See Table 3-1 for a list of verbs and their meanings.

OLE 2 Entries in the Windows Registry (*continued*)
Table 3-2.

Entry	Description
InProcServer	This is a special form of OLE server. Instead of calling the application that created the object, the client calls a DLL to handle any necessary display or editing functions. This has the advantage of speed; a DLL is faster than calling the executable. However, the programmer has to do a lot more coding to make this kind of interface work.
TreatAs	When this key is present, it contains the CLSID for another file format. The client can treat the current file format like the specified file format. For example, if you looked at the Paintbrush Picture OLE 2 entry, you would find a TreatAs value with the same 128-digit value as a Bitmap Image. This tells you that Windows 95 uses the same application to service Paintbrush Picture files as it does for Bitmap Image files. A little more research would tell you that the OLE 2 server for Paintbrush Pictures is Microsoft Paint.
AutoTreatAs	This key forces the client to treat the current file format the same way it would treat the file format specified by the CLSID. From a user perspective it works just like the TreatAs entry that we looked at previously.
AutoConvert	Some objects' context menus contain a Convert option. This key allows you to automatically convert the current file format to the one identified by CLSID. For example, Word for Windows allows you to convert many types of data to a format that it specifically supports. This conversion process changes the embedded or linked object into a Word for Windows object. In other words, it changes the data into something that Word might have created itself.

3

OLE 2 Entries in the Windows Registry (*continued*)
Table 3-2.

Entry	Description
Convertible	There are two levels of subkeys below this one. The first level contains two keys, Readable and Writeable. Below them are keys that contain a list of readable or writeable file formats that you can convert this file format to. For example, you'll find that Word for Windows supports several formats including Word Document. The number of entries in this area usually varies by the number of file filters you install for the application. For example, if you install WordPerfect file support for Word for Windows, then you'll likely find an entry for it here. Remember that these are OLE 2 entries; even if an application supports another application's file format as part of a Save As option, it still might not support it for OLE purposes.
Interfaces	This key contains a list of interfaces supported by the server. The value for this key will eventually contain the names of other ways of accessing the OLE server (other than from the local machine), but there aren't any applications that support it right now. For example, this entry could contain the types of network protocols that the application supports.

OLE 2 Entries
in the
Windows
Registry
(*continued*)
Table 3-2.

Notice that there are two panes. The pane on the left contains various objects. The pane on the right tells you about the object that you've currently selected based on the contents of the registry. You won't need to wander around looking at the various sources of information provided by the registry because OLEViewer gathers them all in this one place.

Figure 3-8 shows all of the categories of objects that you can see with OLEViewer—at least using the current configuration. Let's take a look at one of those categories. Figure 3-9 shows all of the Controls that are in the Safely Scriptable category. This is the list of controls that contain the proper interfaces to work with scripts on an HTML page. Notice that all of the controls you get with the ActiveX Control Pad are listed, but the control we created in Chapter 2 isn't.

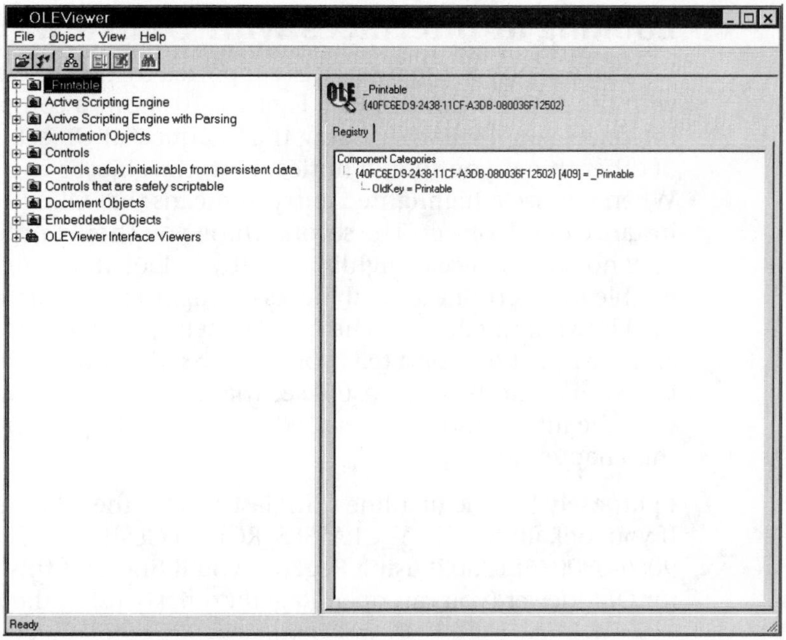

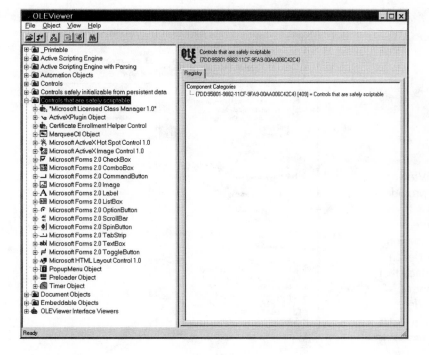

The OLEViewer utility starts with this categorized view of the objects loaded on your machine.

Figure 3-8.

Below each category is a list of objects that fit in that category— including controls of various types.

Figure 3-9.

Looking at Interfaces with OLEViewer

Let's take a look at the interfaces supported by the ActiveX controls provided with the ActiveX Control Pad. Figure 3-10 shows a complete list of the interfaces you'll see when using the MarqueeCtl Object. There are a couple of other things you should notice. First, the object's entry is highlighted. When you see a highlighted entry, it means that OLEViewer has created an instance of the object. The second thing you should notice is that the IUnknown interface is highlighted. If you look in the right pane, you'll be able to determine several pieces of important information about IUnknown immediately. The first line tells you that this is an interface entry, while the second tells you the class identifier for it. If you look at the NumMethods entry, you'll see that there are three, which is consistent with the information you learned in the "Creating an Interface" section of this chapter.

I purposely left the first line until last. It's for the OLEViewer | ViewerCLSID. If you look under HKEY_CLASSES_ROOT | CLSID | {7CE551EA-F85C-11CE-9059-080036F12502} using RegEdit, you'll find that this particular entry is for OLEViewer (you can open RegEdit quickly using the File | Run the

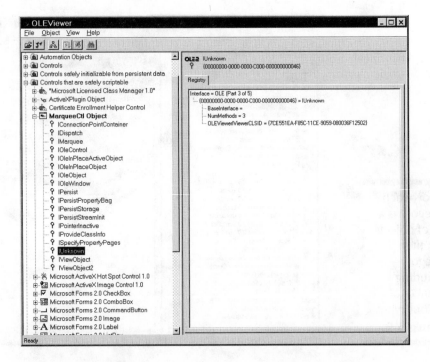

OLEViewer can provide you with detailed information about each interface that a control provides.

Figure 3-10.

Registry Editor command provided with OLEViewer). Now look at the InProcServer32 subkey and you see that the VIEWERS.DLL file is the one that allows users to see the IUnknown interface shown here. It's not always essential to know what every entry you see in OLEViewer is about, but a little digging can usually provide you with some interesting insights. What if you were having a problem getting a particular control to work? Digging around and finding out which applications on your machine affected a particular control might give you places to look once you'd exhausted the usual list of suspects.

IUnknown is somewhat unusual when it comes to interface. Take a look at the IOleObject interface shown in Figure 3-11 and you'll see a more common entry. Notice that the first section of this entry tells you about the interface itself. For example, you'll find that there are both a 16-bit and a 32-bit proxy stub. In the second section you'll find out what those proxy stubs are—both in-process servers in this case. The 32-bit server is OLE32.DLL, while the 16-bit server is OLE2PROX.DLL. So, how would this information help you? One way this information might come in handy is to check the files that your application relies on to work properly. A user might be having a problem getting one of your controls to work properly, then find out that one of these files was corrupted (or even missing).

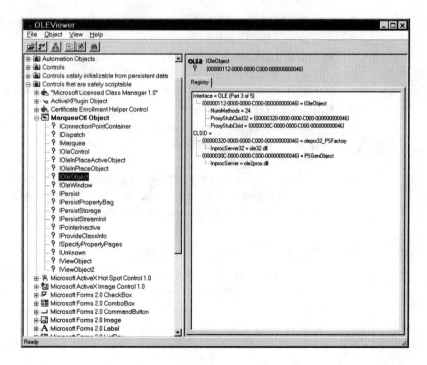

Most interface entries shown in OLEViewer tell you about the files needed to make a control work as well as the control itself.

Figure 3-11.

3

Freeing Memory Used by Object Instances

By now it should be obvious that every instance of a control that you create eats up system memory. Open enough controls with OLEViewer and you'll find your system without enough memory to do anything else. How do you get around this problem? Right-click on the MarqueeCtl Object entry and you'll see a context menu like this one.

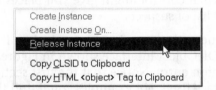

Notice that this context menu contains five entries. The following list describes each one in detail.

♦ **Create Instance** Tells OLEViewer to create an instance of this particular object so that you can view its interface elements. Every instance of an object consumes memory, so you'll want to keep them to a minimum.

♦ **Create Instance On** This option creates an instance of the object, but does so by using another application in place of OLEViewer.

♦ **Release Instance** Use this option to release the memory used by an instance of an object. Obviously this will also close any displays of the object hierarchy associated with the released instance as well.

♦ **Copy CLSID to Clipboard** This option comes in handy when you need to reference the CLSID for an object somewhere. For example, you may need to do this within one of your application programs or on an HTML page.

♦ **Copy HTML <OBJECT> Tag to Clipboard** Use this option to create the <OBJECT> tag that we'll talk about in Chapter 4. Essentially, the <OBJECT> tag is the one used to access ActiveX objects.

Seeing the Bigger Picture

Up until this point we've been looking at the default picture provided by OLEViewer. It does provide two enhanced views that you can use to find various registry entries. You activate both of these views using the View menu shown here.

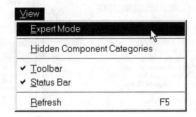

The first entry we'll want to talk about on this menu is the View | Hidden Component Categories command. There are situations where you might not see all of the information about a particular control or an actual component category (like Active Scripting Engine) won't appear in the initial OLEViewer display because the application hid them. Checking the Hidden Component option will reveal all of these hidden items. Of course, the question that most of you are probably asking at this point is why you wouldn't keep them visible all of the time. If a vendor goes through the trouble of hiding a component or component category, you can be sure it was for a good reason. In general, you can't use the components to build your own application.

Take a look at the Expert Mode entry of the View menu. If there was ever a case of information overload, checking this option will give it to you. Figure 3-12 shows a typical OLEViewer display after you enable this option.

As you can see, not only will the OLE 2 objects appear, but everything else the registry has to offer as well. It's still organized after a fashion, but you'll find yourself doing a lot more digging in this mode. There are some occasions when this information does come in handy. One of the better ways to use the information offered by this particular view is checking for OLE 1 entries in the registry. You may need to access one of these entries from time to time if the application is old and the vendor has no desire to update it.

Check out the Type Libraries section and you'll find a wealth of information. For example, how else would you get the version number of the type library used with a specific application? You'd probably find yourself doing a lot of digging around before you got it. At the rates that some vendors charge now for helping to troubleshoot inter-application problems, you'll want to be able to find this information quickly.

3

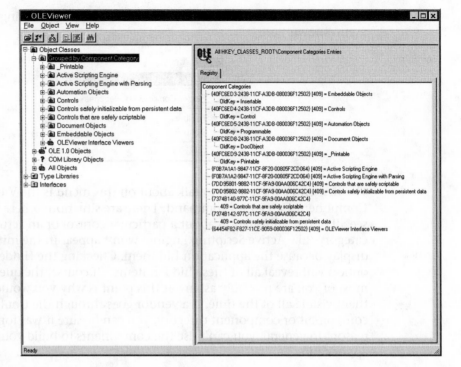

Placing
OLEViewer in
Expert Mode
is one sure
way to find
everything out
about your
system, but at
the expense of
information
overload.
Figure 3-12.

Creating OLE Control Streams Using ODS_TOOL.EXE

We talked about the need for data storage when working with ActiveX controls in the "Storing the Data" section of this chapter. Compound documents aren't the only way to store information—you can use memory as well. Think of streams of data flowing from the client to the server (and vice-versa). The Object Data Stream Tool (ODS_TOOL.EXE) allows you to manage stream objects, but in an Internet environment. It helps you create the flow of data between the client and server using a data stream built of memory.

You'll see a blank page when you initially open the Object Data Stream Tool. The first thing you'll want to use is the Edit I Insert New Control command to add an ActiveX control to the page. The control you choose depends on the kind of data stream you want to create between client and server. You'll see the Insert Object dialog shown here.

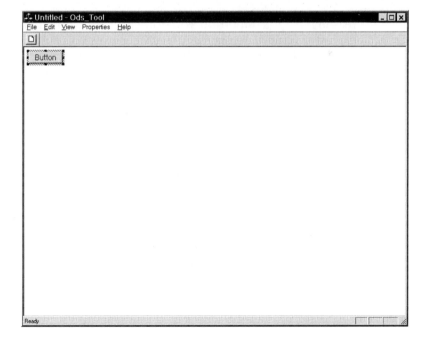

Select one of the ActiveX controls from the list and click OK. What you'll see is a copy of the control using the default configuration. For the purpose of this example, we'll use the OCXEXMPL control we created in Chapter 2. Figure 3-13 shows what our screen looks like now. Notice that the control appears much as it has in every other place we've used it. The noticeable exception is the in-place activation box (denoted by the hatched lines) surrounding the control. Unlike a programming environment, you must activate the control before you can do anything with it.

Normally you'd expect to see an Object Inspector as well, but this utility doesn't work that way. Use the Properties | Properties command to display the Properties page of the control, as shown in Figure 3-14. This is one of the

Removing the control is just as easy as creating it. Simply highlight the control you want to remove, then use the Edit | Delete Control command to remove it.

3

The
OCXEXMPL
control looks
much the
same here as
it has in other
places we've
used it.

Figure 3-13.

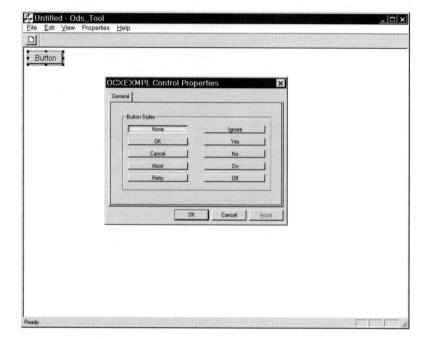

The OCXEXMPL Control Properties dialog box is the only direct form of access we have to the control in this case.

Figure 3-14.

reasons that it's important you don't rely on exposed properties as the exclusive form of access for ActiveX controls you build. You never know when the Properties page (displayed here as the OCXEXMPL Control Properties dialog) will be the only form of access you'll have.

Choose the On button, then click on OK to make the change permanent. What you'll see is a change in the control's caption. It'll still look like the original control in Figure 3-13. The only time you can change a control's appearance is if it provides this capability as part of the Properties page. You can resize and move the control around. (Moving the control around doesn't appear to do anything with the current version of the utility—future versions may allow you to change the control's position on an HTML page based on the changes you make here.)

The <OBJECT> tag provides a DATA attribute that's supported by some ActiveX controls. (Don't worry if some of this <OBJECT> tag information doesn't make sense right now; we'll cover it in Chapter 4 in theory and in other areas of the book in practice.) The DATA attribute acts much like a command line parameter when you use it. The control has to parse the command line, then act on the input it receives. The Object Data Stream Tool provides the capability to send the equivalent of a DATA attribute to the currently selected control. All you need to do is use the Properties I Load Text command to display the Create from DATA Attribute dialog shown here.

Create from DATA attribute   ☒

                [OK]

Paste the DATA attribute into the edit control below.
For example: [Cancel]

DATA="AJABwNQBAA1NUyBTYW5zlFNIcmlmAQAAAP8AAA=="

A new control will be created based on this
information

    Data: [_____]

3

Type in the command line text that you would normally supply for the DATA attribute of the <OBJECT> tag in the Data field of the dialog. Click on OK and the Object Data Stream Tool will create the object with the additional text attached. (The OCXEXMPL control that we created in Chapter 2 doesn't provide support for the DATA attribute. We'll cover the requirements for this support in some of the examples in Part 3 of the book.)

T **IP:** If you make a mistake while configuring a control, simply use the Properties I Reset command to return the control to its native state. The only downside is that you'll have to start configuring it from scratch again. This command only affects the control you have selected—other controls are unaffected.

Now that you've created the object and configured it, you'll want to save the changes you've made. There are two stages to this process. The first step involves creating an entry in an HTML file. Use the Properties I Save Content command to display the Save Content dialog shown here.

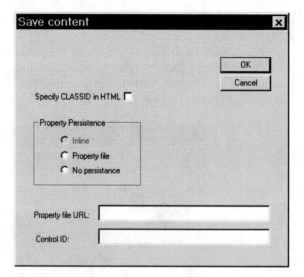

You'll almost always want to check the Specify CLASSID in HTML check box. This tells the Object Data Stream Tool to add the class identifier information to the <OBJECT> tag—a prerequisite to actually using the addition. The Property Persistence group defines how your control's configuration information gets stored. The standard method is to store it inline as a group of <PARAM> tags between the <OBJECT> and </OBJECT> tags. You can also choose to store the properties in a separate file (Property File) or not at all (No Persistence). If you choose to store the settings in a property file, you'll need to include an URL for it. Finally, you'll need to define a Control ID for the control. This is the name you'll use to access it within scripts.

The second step is saving the control configuration information as an ODS file. If you choose to create a property file, then you'll see a File Save dialog immediately after the Save Content dialog. Just type in a filename as usual and you'll be able to reload the control and its current settings the next time you use the Object Data Stream Tool with the File | Open command.

If you decide not to store the control as a persistent file, you can save it as a compound document instead. The Object Data Stream Tool will ask you if you want to create the file before you exit the program. Figure 3-15 shows what this compound document looks like for a simple control using OCXEXMPL.

OK, so you might be thinking to yourself, what's the big deal? I've created an ODS file, but what does that buy me? Microsoft hasn't provided documentation for this utility at the time of this writing, but there are quite

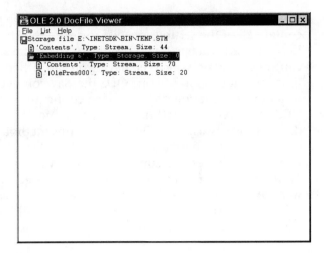

You can also create compound documents using the Object Data Stream Tool.

Figure 3-15.

3

a few practical ways you can use it. For one thing, you can use this utility to examine the control if it doesn't want to work with ActiveX Control Pad for whatever reason. Because of the way that this utility creates the control, there are some situations where it works when ActiveX Control Pad won't. You'll also find the tool handy for its intended purpose—storing data streams. However, it's the third use that you'll find most intriguing. There is a way to use this ODS file to create what might be termed prefabricated controls. We'll see in Chapter 4 precisely how the <OBJECT> tag works, but here's an example of how you would use the ODS file with it.

```
<OBJECT ID="OCXEXMPL1" WIDTH=75 HEIGHT=25
 CLASSID="CLSID:D8D77E03-712A-11CF-8C70-00006E3127B7"
 CODEBASE="http://www.mycompany.com/OCXEXMPL.OCX"
 DATA="PBSetting.ODS">
</OBJECT>
```

Normally the <OBJECT> tag relies on one or more <PARAM> tags to configure the ActiveX control. The ODS file lets you get around this particular requirement. Instead of using one or more <PARAM> tags to set your control up, you can specify a single ODS file to do it. This ODS file will contain all of the settings needed to create the kind of control you want. Here's the advantage: if you decide for stylistic reasons to change some control setting on your Web page, you can either modify each file one at a time, or you can modify one ODS file. Say you need a whole bunch of on/off pushbuttons, but you don't want to configure them one at a time. Using an ODS file provides a method for creating one control and using it in a lot of different places. The disadvantages to this method are pretty significant. For one thing, you have to deal with another file and there isn't any guarantee that every browser that supports ActiveX will know what to do with that file. Another problem is that the control is no longer self-documenting. If you want to find out what that control does, you'll have to do so using the ODS_TOOL utility. Problem areas aside, ODS files are one way to give the <OBJECT> tag more flexibility in an environment where flexibility is key.

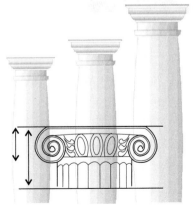

Chapter 4

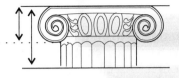

HTML and ActiveX

No matter how hard you try to avoid it, any kind of Internet experience will require some level of HTML (hypertext markup language) knowledge. It seems like a pretty broad statement until you figure out that any kind of normal access to the Internet is going to involve a visit to a Web page. Any time you type **http:**, you'll find yourself accessing a Web page that uses HTML through HTTP (hypertext transfer protocol). And there's little you can do in the way of information exchange without typing those letters.

As an ActiveX programmer, you may or may not spend a lot of time creating Web pages. You will, however, need to know how they work so that you can help other people use your controls. Learning HTML might seem a bit daunting at first. There is a wealth of tags (like programming statements) that you can use to create a page. Viewing these tags isn't a problem. Just about any browser on the market provides a View | Source command that you can use to look at the underlying HTML for any page on a Web site. Figure 4-1 shows a typical example.

T IP: You can use the View | Source command to your advantage if you design a lot of Web pages. Simply find a Web site that contains a feature you want to use; then look at the underlying source to see how the programmer accomplished the task. Unlike many programming situations in which the code is hidden, encrypted, or otherwise inaccessible, HTML retains its English-like syntax even when used at an Internet site.

There's a simple way at least to begin the learning process, and that's part of what we'll cover here. You could essentially put together a Web site using a mere 12 HTML tags, then embellish them using additional tags later. That's what the first section of this chapter will look at. We'll examine the 12 tags that you'll find on any Internet site that provides just about any level of functionality at all.

You can view the source for most Web pages—a handy feature when you want to learn to do something new.

Figure 4-1.

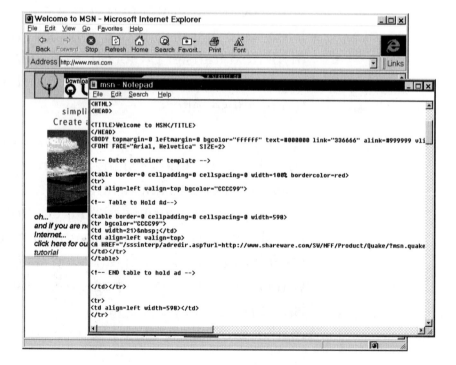

Once you have these 12 tags in mind, we'll look at one additional tag that you'll need to make ActiveX work. We'll combine everything you know with the example that we created in Chapter 3 to produce a very simple Web page. You'll be able to do something with this page and could even use it as a template for new pages later. The idea is to provide you with a baseline knowledge of HTML, not make you an HTML programming guru.

NOTE: This chapter won't teach you everything you need to know about HTML. Whole books are devoted to this topic, and some people complain that even that isn't enough to do the job. What we're going to do is look at HTML at a very basic level—a level that most of these other books miss. By the time you finish this chapter, you'll have just enough information to make learning additional HTML tags easy.

It may seem strange that an ASCII text file could contain enough information to make ActiveX work. Once you learn about the ActiveX-specific tag, we'll take a look at how the browser interprets this tag and makes ActiveX work. It's not a difficult task once you know the little secrets that Microsoft included with Internet Explorer 3.0.

4

The final section of this chapter looks at one of the utilities provided with the ActiveX SDK—DIANTZ.EXE. It allows you to compress one or more ActiveX controls and reduce the download time. This same utility will produce the CAB files that Microsoft uses to distribute Windows 95. You'll find that the DIANTZ utility comes in handy for more than just ActiveX development.

Quick Overview of HTML

You could write a whole book about HTML and not cover all of the variations of all the various tags. Let's take a look at that term first. Every HTML statement is composed of one or more tags. A *tag* is like a programming statement. There are tags for beginning and ending the various sections of an HTML document and others that allow various kinds of processing. As companies become more involved with the Internet, the complexion of tags is changing. We'll take a look at a couple of these changes within the confines of this chapter, but there are other changes we won't cover due to space considerations. (The chapter will provide some leads as to where you can find some of this additional information.)

The HTML tag list tells you whether or not a tag is mandatory.

The most basic HTML document will likely contain 12 different kinds of tags. Some of these tags are mandatory; others are only used to provide specific types of functionality. We'll look at the tags in their simplest form—you can add modifiers to most tags to affect the way they work. For example, you could add a font specification or tell the tag to center any text it contains on the page. The following list provides a quick overview of the 12 basic tags that we'll look at.

♦ **<HTML> and </HTML> (mandatory)**   Every HTML document begins with <HTML> and ends with </HTML>. This is how the browser knows where to start and stop reading.

♦ **<HEAD> and </HEAD> (normally used)**   When you look at any HTML document, you'll see a heading and a body. The heading normally identifies the Web site and defines the page setup.

♦ **<BODY> and </BODY> (normally used)**   You'll place the main section of the content of your Web page within these two tags. The body normally contains the information that the user visited your site to find.

♦ **<H***x***> and </H***x***> (optional)**   Books and other forms of text normally divide the information they contain into sections using headings. This tag allows you to add headings to your Web site.

♦ **<P> (optional)**   HTML always assumes that all the text you type, whether it appears on the same line or not, is part of the same paragraph. You use this tag to add a carriage return and two line feeds (marking the end of a paragraph).

♦ **
 (optional)**   There are times when you'll want to go to the left margin without adding a new line to the page. That's what this tag is for. It adds a carriage return with a single line feed.

♦ **<HR> (optional)**   The horizontal rule tag allows you to place a line across the page. It also adds white space between paragraphs.

♦ **<A HREF="Destination Document"> and </A> (optional)**   Hyperlinks to other documents are the most common component of a Web page.

♦ **<A NAME="Anchor Name"> and </A> (optional)**   Anchors allow you to move from one point on the page to another. The hyperlink to access this tag looks like this: <A HREF="Current Document#Anchor Name">.

♦ **<EM> and </EM> (optional)**   Different browsers react differently to the emphasis tag. However, the majority simply display text in italic type.

♦ **<STRONG> and </STRONG> (optional)** As with the emphasis tag, it's up to the browser to determine how it will react to the <STRONG> tag. Most browsers display text in bold type when they see this tag.

♦ **<PRE> and </PRE> (optional)** There are times when you don't want a browser to reformat your text. The preformatted tag tells the browser to leave the text formatting alone.

Never make your Web page larger than 60 KB including graphics— it takes too long to download otherwise.

Now that you have the basic idea of what these tags are about, let's look at a few of them in detail. The following sections talk about some of the tags that you'll use on a more or less consistent basis and require more than a modicum of work to use in most cases. Don't worry if you can't quite grasp everything during this discussion; we'll look at actual usage details in the section on creating simple HTML documents. Seeing how the tags work will help you understand how they interact with the browser.

Understanding the <HEAD> Tag

A heading tells the browser what you want to do with the page before it gets displayed—it doesn't provide any form of actual content. For example, look at the source for http://www.microsoft.com in Figure 4-2. Notice that the heading contains a title, some style commands, and a few meta commands. In fact, these three entries represent the only three kinds of tags that you'll find in an HTML page heading.

Don't get the idea that the <META> tag is the only form of scripting you'll find in the heading area. For example, if you visit http://www.netscape.com, you'll find JavaScript commands in the heading area. It doesn't matter which scripting language the page designer uses; the point is that the script is there to add instructions for certain elements of the page. One way to look at the heading is as a definition area for the rest of the page. It affects the appearance of the page as a whole but doesn't provide any form of content. In fact, you'll normally want to hide the contents of this area from a visitor to your Web site.

Adding Headings Using the <H*x*> Tag

Just as a heading separates various sections of text in a book, headings (the <H*x*> tag) in an HTML document separate various areas of content. The HTML specification provides six levels of headings. For the most part, the only difference you'll see between heading levels is the size of the font used to display them. The aesthetic appeal of headings is about all you get. There isn't any magic involved when using headings—they won't create a physical

4

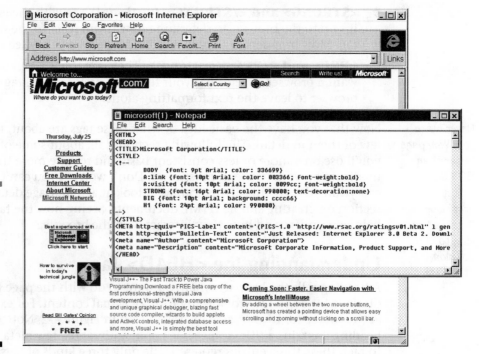

The <HEAD> tag won't help much in the content area, but it does define the appearance of the page.
Figure 4-2.

separation between sections of text; it's more the way a visitor to your site will perceive the material you have to provide.

TIP: A lower-number heading level uses larger type than a higher number. Users would see a larger font for an <H1> tag than they would for an <H2> tag.

So how do you create a heading? Simply replace the *x* in the <H*x*> tag with a number from 1 to 6, type your heading text, then end the line with a </H*x*> tag as follows:

```
<H1>This is a Heading</H1>
```

Another point to remember with headings is that you don't need to add any of the end-of-line tags, such as <P>, <BR>, or <HR>, to the end of the heading. The end tag, </H*x*>, automatically adds the required amount of space for you. Of course, this doesn't prevent you from adding extra space if you so desire.

Links and Anchors

Links and anchors provide the special feeling of visiting a Web site. Every time you visit a Web site and see some text underlined, you're probably looking at a link. A link connects your current location with some other location. In fact, two common forms of links are used on most Web pages. The first type creates a link to another page (a URL in Internet terminology), and it's the one you'll see most often. The second type creates a link to another section of the current page or a specific area of another page. You'll use it to find an anchor (which we'll look at in a few seconds). Here's an example of the two common types of links. Notice that they both use the HREF keyword along with the <A> tag.

```
This is a <A HREF="http://www.microsoft.com">Document</A> link.


This is an <A HREF="http://www.microsoft.com#MyAnchor">Anchor</A> link.
```

4

In both cases the text that appears between the <A> and </A> tags is the part of the sentence that appears underlined on the Web site. You should always place some text here or else your link will appear invisible to the user. Notice that the links look exactly alike except for one difference—the anchor link uses a # sign to separate the URL from the anchor name. In this case we've used MyAnchor as the anchor name. The second link would look for the URL first, then for a specific anchor location on that page before displaying any content to the user.

TIP: If you want to create an anchor link to an anchor on the current page, you don't need to provide the URL part of the <A> tag. You could abbreviate it as <A HREF="#Anchor Name">.

An anchor link also requires you to create an anchor somewhere on the page you specify as part of the <A> tag (unless you want to find a specific location on the current page, in which case you don't need to provide a URL). For example, we looked at an anchor link to MyAnchor on http://www.microsoft.com. How would an anchor look for this location?

```
This is the <A NAME="MyAnchor">Anchor</A> for this page.
```

As you can see, the big difference between an anchor and a link is the NAME keyword. An anchor always uses NAME in place of HREF. In addition, most browsers won't highlight or underline the text between the <A> and </A> tags since you really can't use them for anything.

Creating a Simple HTML Document

In the previous section we looked at 12 basic tags for creating HTML pages. These are the tags that just about everyone will use somewhere along the way. Now it's time to look at how you'd actually use those tags to create a page on your Web site. Listing 4-1 shows the source for a sample Web page. Obviously, you would never create a page like this for actual use. The whole purpose of this page is to see how the 12 tags work.

Listing 4-1

```
<HTML>
<HEAD>
<TITLE>Sample HTML Page</TITLE>
</HEAD>
<BODY>
<H1>This is a <EM>Level 1</EM> heading.</H1>
Notice that the "Level 1" portion of the heading is emphasized using the
EM tag.<P>
We ended the previous paragraph with a <STRONG>P</STRONG> tag.
This paragraph will end with a <STRONG>BR</STRONG> tag.<BR>
Notice how we used the <STRONG>STRONG</STRONG> tag to add bold
text to the previous paragraph.<HR>
Horizontal rules also have a place on Web sites.  You'll use them most
often to provide separations between major areas of text.  Of course, most
Web sites are starting to use frames because they're more flexible.<HR>
Here are the other five levels of headings.<P>
<H2>Level 2</H2>
<H3>Level 3</H3>
<H4>Level 4</H4>
<H5>Level 5</H5>
<H6>Level 6</H6><HR>
Let's look at some other HTML tags.<P>
Click <A HREF="LISTS.HTM">Here</A> to display the list page.<BR>
Click <A HREF="GRAPH.HTM">Here</A> to display the graphics page.<BR>
Click <A HREF="TABLE.HTM">Here</A> to display a page with tables.<BR>
Click <A HREF="FORM.HTM">Here</A> to display a page with forms.<BR>
Click <A HREF="#MyAnchor">Here</A> to see another
```

```
area of this page.<P><P><P><P><P>
This is an <A NAME="MyAnchor">Anchor</A> link area.
</BODY>
</HTML>
```

This source might look a bit daunting at first, but there isn't anything here that we haven't already looked at in the previous section. The first tag, <HTML>, defines the start of the page. You see its counterpart, </HTML>, at the end of the source listing. Next, we divide the document into two sections using the <HEAD> and <BODY> tags (along with their counterparts). The only tag that might mystify you is the <TITLE> tag. It defines the title that you'll see in the browser's title bar. This tag isn't absolutely necessary, but it's nice to give your Web page a title so that other people will know what they're looking at. In addition, the title will help you navigate your own pages as you troubleshoot any problem areas.

The body of the page begins with a level 1 heading, some text with special attributes added, and then a horizontal rule. You'll also find some text that shows the difference between the <P> and <BR> tags here. We'll see what they look like in a few seconds.

4

The next section of the listing shows you the differences between the five remaining headings. Most browsers will simply use a different type size as you change headings. Unfortunately, most browsers run out of readable font sizes before they run out of heading levels. You'll want to avoid using level 6 headings because some people won't be able to read them. Level 5 headings are pretty marginal as well.

The last section of this example page contains some links. We won't look at the linking pages just now; that's an exercise for upcoming sections. However, look at the fifth link, and you'll notice that it's to an anchor on the current page. The last working line of the body area contains this anchor. Make sure you take the time to see how this works with your browsers.

So, what does our sample HTML page look like? Figure 4-3 shows how it would look when using Internet Explorer 3.0. You might want to take time to compare the screen shot in the book to the one on your screen if you use another kind of browser. You'll find that not all browsers are the same—there are subtle differences in the way they display things. Differences between machines will only intensify the display differences. Considering that these are common tags, imagine what will happen when you start using some of the more exotic tags that some browsers support, but others don't.

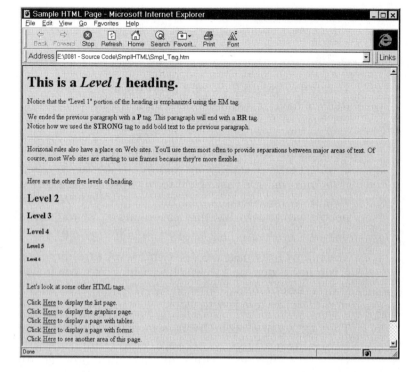

The sample HTML page shows how the basic 12 tags would appear within Internet Explorer 3.0.
Figure 4-3.

It's time to expand our HTML horizons just a bit. The next few sections show you how some of the other standard tags work. We won't look at all the details in these sections, but they will provide enough of an overview so that you'll know what you're looking at when you visit other Web sites and view their source codes.

Working with Lists

How many technical books have you seen that don't include any form of bulleted lists or procedures? Putting complex ideas into easily grasped pieces is one of the most basic tasks that any writer can perform. Lists—short bits of text that enumerate ideas—are the answer in most cases. Considering the size limits of most Web pages, lists become even more important. HTML supports three different kinds of lists:

♦ **Unordered list** This kind of list uses bullets. You start it with the <UL> tag and end it with the </UL> tag. Items within the list use the <LI> tag.

♦ **Ordered list** Procedures and other numbered forms of text are considered ordered lists. This list format depends on the <OL> and </OL> tags. As with unordered lists, each item begins with the <LI> tag.

♦ **Glossary** This particular list uses two kinds of item entries surrounded by a <DL> and </DL> tag pair. The term that you want to define is preceded by a <DT> tag. The definition gets a <DD> tag.

Even though there are only three list types, you can still get a variety of effects by nesting them just like you would in any other programming scenario. You'll see an example of how to do this later in Listing 4-2 when we discuss the sample page code.

Of the three list types we've talked about, the glossary list type is the most flexible in some ways. The use of two list element types can provide a little more in the way of aesthetics when you try to display text. The big difference between the <DT> (term) and <DD> (definition) tags is that one of them is indented. You can use this feature to create special effects not related to the display of glossary-type entries. As with some of the other special text tags that we've talked about in this chapter, list tags (<LI>, <DT>, and <DD>) automatically insert a <BR> tag for you at the end of the line. Using a <BR> tag advances the text to the next line but keeps the list together.

It's time to take a look at some examples of list coding. Listing 4-2 shows the first link page from the first page we looked at in Listing 4-1. It contains the three basic list types along with one example showing how to nest them. Notice especially that this is the first page to use comments (the <!-*Text*-> tag).

4

> Always add plenty of comments to your HTML pages since you may have nonprogrammers editing them from time to time. Even though there may be other ways of creating comments, use the <!-*Text*-> tag for consistency.

Listing 4-2

```
<!-The purpose of this page is to show how to use the list tags.->
<HTML>
<HEAD>
<TITLE>Creating Lists</TITLE>
</HEAD>
<BODY>
<H2>There are three different kinds of Lists:</H2>

<!-Display an unordered list.->
<H3>Unordered</H3>
<UL>
<LI>Item 1
<LI>Item 2
</UL><HR>

<!-Display an ordered list.->
```

```
<H3>Ordered</H3>
<OL>
<LI>Item 1
<LI>Item 2
</OL><HR>

<!-Display a glossary list showing the two list entry types.->
<H3>Glossary</H3>
<DL>
<DT>A Term
<DD>This is the definition for it.
<DT>Another Term
<DD>Yet another definition.
</DL><HR>

<!-Show one method of nesting lists.->
<H3>Nested List</H3>
<OL>
<LI>Item 1
     <UL>
     <LI>Subitem 1
     <LI>Subitem 2
     </UL>
<LI>Item 2
</OL>
</BODY>
</HTML>
```

Now that you have a better idea of how to code the various kinds of list tags, let's see what this page looks like. Figure 4-4 shows a typical example of how you could use lists. Notice that the three list types aren't all that decorative, but they do work.

Adding Graphics

Graphics can really dress up a page of text. Most of us would agree that technical manuals are a lot easier to understand when the author adds enough of the right kind of graphic image. You can add graphics to a Web page as well. However, there are a few limitations in the way that you can add them.

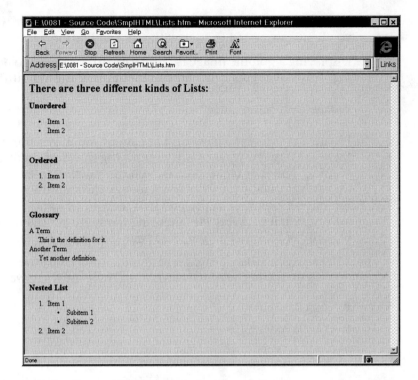

List tags make it easy to enumerate specific points on a Web page or provide glossary-type entries.
Figure 4-4.

4

TIP: Some people are overzealous when adding graphics to their Web site. The result is that most people don't even get to see most of those graphics. Just about any user will press the Stop button on the browser after a minute or so of waiting for graphics to download. In fact, a good rule of thumb is to make the total size of any Web page 60 KB or less including graphics and ActiveX controls.

One of the bigger limitations that you'll face is the kinds of graphics you can display. Many browsers only handle two formats—the ones supported directly by HTML—including GIF (also known as CompuServe format) and JPEG images. Any other kind of image you see displayed in your browser is the result of using a plug-in. Both Netscape and Internet Explorer support various kinds of plug-ins. For example, one of the more popular plug-ins will allow you to view AVI (movie) files using your browser. The problem for a Web page designer is that you can't depend on other people owning these plug-ins. As a result, if you plan to create an Internet site with wide appeal, you'll probably need to stick with GIF and JPEG images.

Displaying a graphic image is fairly easy. All you need to do is use the <IMG> tag. This tag accepts a filename as input using the SRC attribute, like this:

```
<IMG SRC="Figure1.Gif">
```

Placing graphics on a page isn't as easy as you might think. As with text, there are very few ways of predetermining the location of a graphic outside of using frames or tables because you can't define an exact position for them. Text usually provides some leeway through the use of tricks like the list tags we looked at in the previous section. Graphics provide no such leeway. You'll probably end up using frames to get the right effect on the majority of browsers if your Web page is very complex in design.

You can define the way text and graphics mix using the <IMG> tag. All you need to do is add the ALIGN attribute. There are three ways to align text:

♦ ALIGN=TOP

♦ ALIGN=MIDDLE

♦ ALIGN=BOTTOM

Let's take a look at some simple code for adding graphics to a Web site. We'll take a deeper look at graphics placement in the "Using Forms" section. All the code in Listing 4-3 does is display a graphic image and show you how to use the ALIGN attribute. This method is suitable for those times when you want to display a company logo or some other simple graphics on a page. Figure 4-5 shows how this code looks in the viewer.

Listing 4-3

```
<HTML>
<HEAD>
<TITLE>Using Graphics</TITLE>
</HEAD>
<BODY>
<H2>You can align text and graphics in one of three ways.</H2>
<H3>Top</H3>
<IMG SRC="ColorBlk.Gif" ALIGN=TOP>This is at the TOP.<HR>
<H3>Middle</H3>
<IMG SRC="ColorBlk.Gif" ALIGN=MIDDLE>This is in the MIDDLE.<HR>
<H3>Bottom</H3>
<IMG SRC="ColorBlk.Gif" ALIGN=BOTTOM>This is at the BOTTOM.<HR>
</BODY>
</HTML>
```

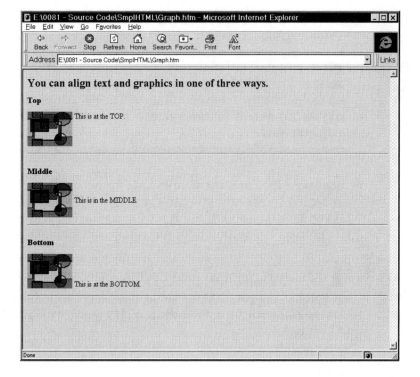

Adding simple
graphics is
fairly easy—
complex
graphic
layouts
require
advanced
techniques
like frames.
Figure 4-5.

4

Creating Tables

Tabular data is part of just about any kind of business display. Spreadsheets
are just one example of the accountant's ledger sheet brought alive in the
computer. It makes sense then that you can create tables on an HTML page
as well. However, you'll need an entire set of tags to make tables work, as
shown in the following list.

♦ **<TABLE> and </TABLE>**   This set of tags define the beginning and
end of the table as a whole.

♦ **<TR> and </TR>**   Each row is defined with these tags. Normal
procedure is to define rows, then columns.

♦ **<TD> and </TD>**   Every data element, or column, is enclosed within
this tag pair.

♦ **<CAPTION> and </CAPTION>**   These tags define the table's title.

♦ **<TH> and </TH>** With this pair of tags, you create headings for each table row or column.

TIP: The <TABLE> tag includes a special BORDER attribute that allows you to enclose the table within lines. The default border size is a width of 1, but you can usually set this value to any width between 1 and 6 depending on the browser.

Let's take a look at some sample code for two different kinds of tables. Listing 4-4 shows how you can create two different effects using the simple tags we've talked about in this section so far. The first table contains simple text entries. The second table mixes text and graphics in complex ways.

TIP: You can center the text in a table using the <CENTER> and </CENTER> tag pair. This same tag pair works with any text you may want to place within a document. It also works with graphics, as shown in Listing 4-4.

Listing 4-4

```
<HTML>
<HEAD>
<TITLE>Creating Tables</TITLE>
</HEAD>
<BODY>

<!-Create a simple text table.->
<H3>Tables are an important part of Web pages.</H3>
<CAPTION>A Simple Text Table</CAPTION>
<TABLE BORDER>
    <TR>
        <TH></TH>
        <TH>Column A</TH>
        <TH>Column B</TH>
        <TH>Column C</TH>
    </TR>
    <TR>
        <TH>Row 1</TH>
        <TD>Entry A1</TD>
        <TD>Entry B1</TD>
        <TD>Entry C1</TD>
    </TR>
```

```
        <TR>
                <TH>Row 2</TH>
                <TD>Entry A2</TD>
                <TD>Entry B2</TD>
                <TD>Entry C2</TD>
        </TR>
        <TR>
                <TH>Row 3</TH>
                <TD>Entry A3</TD>
                <TD>Entry B3</TD>
                <TD>Entry C3</TD>
        </TR>
</TABLE><HR>

<!-Create a complex table with mixed text and graphics->
<H3>You aren't limited to text in a table.</H3>
<TABLE BORDER=3>
        <TR>
                <TD><IMG SRC="ColorBlk.Gif"></TD>
                <TD><IMG SRC="ColorBlk.Gif" ALIGN=MIDDLE> Text and
Graphics. </TD>
                <TD>Text Alone</TD>
        </TR>
        <TR>
                <TD>Some more text.</TD>
                <TD><CENTER><IMG SRC="ColorBlk.Gif"></CENTER></TD>
                <TD>Some more text.</TD>
        </TR>
        <TR>
                <TD><IMG SRC="ColorBlk.Gif"></TD>
                <TD><CENTER>Some more text.</CENTER></TD>
                <TD><IMG SRC="ColorBlk.Gif"></TD>
        </TR>
</TABLE>
</BODY>
</HTML>
```

4

This looks like a lot of code, and it was a bit tedious to write by hand. (Code like this demonstrates yet another reason why you should invest in some kind of GUI front end for writing your HTML page code if you plan to write a lot of it.) Figure 4-6 shows what it looks like in the browser. The code also illustrates the one basic rule to follow—always work on the rows first, the columns second. If you follow that one simple rule, you won't experience any problems putting tables together. Notice that the second table mixes text and graphics. Even though the table looks a lot more complex, the same

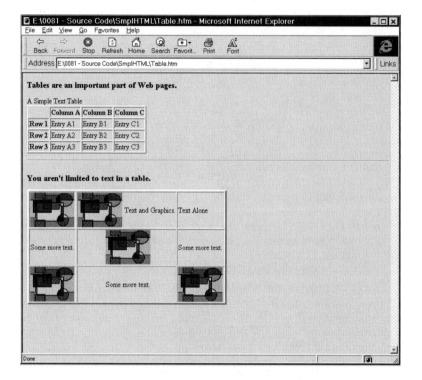

Tables are easy once you figure out that rows come first, columns second.

Figure 4-6.

Indenting your code can help you keep rows and columns in a table separate and easy to see.

pattern of rows, then columns holds true. Notice the difference between the standard 1-width border used for the first table and the 3-width border used for the second table. The 3-width border takes up a lot more space, but it's also more dramatic.

The first table also includes the <TH> tag for both rows and columns. There are two main differences between the standard text and header text. Standard text is normally left-justified, while heading text is centered. You can change this behavior using the <CENTER> tag, as shown in Listing 4-4. In addition, the heading text uses a bold font.

Using Forms

The last fundamental piece of HTML coding we'll look at is forms. You can use forms in a variety of ways—most of which have to deal with data entry rather than data dissemination. Of all the techniques we've looked at so far, forms provide the only method for adding things like radio buttons and check boxes to your Web site using standard HTML. We won't go into all of the vagaries of using forms here since ActiveX largely replaces the need to use them at all. It's important to know that there are alternatives to using ActiveX though.

Every form begins with a <FORM> tag. You must include two attributes in addition to the tag itself. The METHOD attribute defines how you intend to work with the data gathered in the form. There are two standard methods: POST and GET. The POST method is used most often for data entry forms. It allows you to send data from the client machine to the host. The GET method is used for data query forms. For example, when you go to your favorite Web search page, you're really filling out a form using the GET method. The other attribute is ACTION. It tells the Web server where to find a CGI script for handling the input from the form. A typical <FORM> tag looks like this:

```
<FORM METHOD=GET ACTION="/cgi-bin/query">
```

The main tag that you'll use in creating a form is the <INPUT> tag. There are a variety of ways to use this particular tag—more than we'll cover here. In addition to the basic information you'll find here, the <INPUT> tag is usually enhanced by the browser's vendor to provide additional functionality. For example, you may find that one browser supports more kinds of buttons than another one will. With that in mind, let's take a quick look at the various attributes used with this tag:

4

♦ **TYPE** The kind of control—button, text box, and so on—is defined with this attribute.

♦ **VALUE** The impact of this attribute depends on the kind of control. It defines the caption for a button, but the contents of a text box, for example.

♦ **NAME** This attribute references the variable used to hold the output from this particular control.

♦ **SIZE** The size of the control—usually the width in characters—is defined with this attribute.

♦ **CHECKED** Use this with radio buttons and other controls that have a checked or unchecked state.

♦ **ROWS** The number of rows to allocate for a particular control—usually the height of the control—is defined with this attribute.

Besides the <INPUT> tag, you can use the <SELECT> tag to create pop-up lists or menus. It works about the same way as the lists we created previously in the "Working with Lists" section of this chapter. You end the list with a

</SELECT> tag. In between the <SELECT> and </SELECT> tags you use either <OPTION> or <OPTION SELECTED> tags to create a list of entries for your pop-up list. The <OPTION SELECTED> tag indicates which option you want selected when the user initially views the page.

The final form-specific tags allow you to create a text area. This allows you to display a lot of text in a small area or provide a large area for user notes or comments. A text area uses the <TEXTAREA> and </TEXTAREA> tag pair. You can also add an optional attribute, NAME, to the <TEXTAREA> tag so that you can retrieve its contents later.

Now that you have a basic idea of how these tags work, let's take a look at some actual code. Listing 4-5 shows the example code for a form. It includes one example of each type of basic control you can use, plus one extended control that we'll look at in more detail near the end of this section. Figure 4-7 shows what this page would look like when viewed from Internet Explorer—your view may vary slightly if you're using a different browser. Notice that the three button types are centered at the bottom of the page using the <CENTER> tag.

Listing 4-5

```
<!-This is a very simple nonfunctional form.  It won't->
<!-show you how to write the CGI scripts normally required->
<!-to make the form functional.  To see a full form->
<!-implementation, look at a Web site like http://www-msn.lycos.com/.->

<HTML>
<HEAD>
<TITLE>New Page</TITLE>
</HEAD>
<BODY>
<H2>This is our sample form.</H2>

<!-Create a simple form using standard controls.->
<FORM METHOD=GET ACTION="/cgi-bin/query">

<!-Create a text field.->
<STRONG>This is a text field: </STRONG>
<INPUT TYPE="text" VALUE="Some Text" NAME="Text1" SIZE=20><P>

<!-Add some radio buttons.->
<STRONG>These are some radio buttons.</STRONG><P>
<INPUT TYPE="radio" NAME="Radio1" VALUE="Button 1" CHECKED>Button 1<BR>
<INPUT TYPE="radio" NAME="Radio1" VALUE="Button 2">Button 2<BR>
<INPUT TYPE="radio" NAME="Radio1" VALUE="Button 3">Button 3<P>
```

4

```
<!-Add some check boxes.->
<STRONG>These are some check boxes.</STRONG><P>
<INPUT TYPE="checkbox" NAME="Checkbox 1" VALUE="Checkbox 1">Checkbox 1<BR>
<INPUT TYPE="checkbox" NAME="Checkbox 2" VALUE="Checkbox 2">Checkbox 2<BR>
<INPUT TYPE="checkbox" NAME="Checkbox 3" VALUE="Checkbox 3">Checkbox 3<P>

<!-Popup lists and menus require a different format.->
<STRONG>Here's a popup list: </STRONG>
<SELECT NAME="Popup 1">
    <OPTION>
Item One
    <OPTION SELECTED>
Item Two
    <OPTION>
Item Three
</SELECT>
<P>

<!-You can also create areas of text onscreen.->
<STRONG>Adding text areas is easy using the TEXTAREA tag.</STRONG><P>
<TEXTAREA ROWS=3 NAME="Text Area 1">
This is some text that got added to the display to show the effect of the
TEXTAREA tag.  You'll find it quite handy as you create Web pages with
a lot of information to convey.  It's very important to provide the users of
your site with complete information, and this tag helps you do it.
</TEXTAREA><P><P>

<!-Every form requires a Submit button to send data to the server.->
<CENTER>
<INPUT TYPE=submit VALUE="Submit">

<!-This optional Reset button will save the user time.->
<INPUT TYPE=reset VALUE="Reset">

<!-This is a standard button type.  We'll use it to cancel the form.->
<INPUT TYPE=button VALUE="Cancel">

</CENTER>
</FORM>
</BODY>
</HTML>
```

As you can see, the majority of the controls shown use the <INPUT> tag. The main difference between control types is defined by the TYPE attribute. You can select any of the controls if you want to see how they work. The only

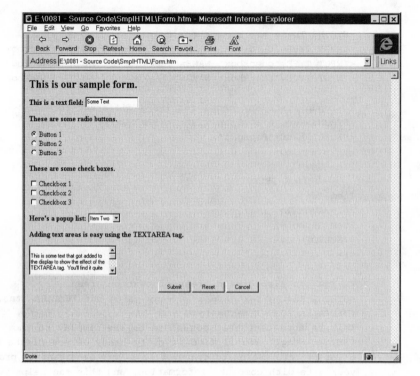

Forms allow
you to get
feedback from
the viewer.
Figure 4-7.

button that doesn't work correctly is the Submit button because we haven't written a CGI script to do something with the information on the form. The Cancel button is nonfunctional, but we'll fix that in a moment.

Something else you should notice about the source code are the two specific button types: Reset and Submit. A Reset button always resets the contents of any controls on a form to their initial state. This allows the user to restart the form from scratch without leaving the site first and reentering. The Submit button always takes the action listed in the ACTION attribute of the <FORM> tag. You must provide a Submit button if you intend to process the information in the form using standard methods.

The Cancel button in this example is still nonfunctional. You could click it, but nothing would happen. The Cancel button represents the standard button type for HTML documents. To make it work you have to add an ONCLICK argument that calls a script or performs some other action. ActiveX Control Pad provides an easy method for you to create this script once you create the button itself. The following procedure shows a quick

The Script Wizard displays a list of your controls and the actions associated with them.
Figure 4-8.

method for assigning just about any default action to a button (or other control for that matter).

1. Use the Tools | Script Wizard command to display the Script Wizard dialog shown in Figure 4-8. What you'll see is three list boxes and some buttons. The first list box contains a list of the controls you've defined. The second list box contains a list of actions you can associate with events of those controls. The third list box contains a list of actions currently assigned to a particular event.

2. Click on the plus sign next to the Cancel entry in the first list box, and then click on the onClick event. This tells Script Wizard that you want to assign some action to the onClick event of the Cancel button.

3. Click on the Go To Page action in the second list box. When you click on the Cancel button, you'll go to another page. In this case we'll go to the previous page of our example Web site.

4. Click on the Insert Action button. You'll see the Go To Page dialog shown in Figure 4-9. This is where you tell Script Wizard where you want to go.

5. Type the name of a page on your Web site in the Enter a Text String field. In the case of this example, you would type **SMPL_TAG.HTM**. Notice that you don't need to include double or single quotes—the Wizard takes care of that for you automatically.

6. Click on OK. You should see an action associated with the onClick event of the Cancel button now, as shown in Figure 4-10. If you saved this document back to disk, then looked at the page with a browser, pressing the Cancel button would take you back to the previous page.

The Script Wizard automatically makes any needed changes to your code. In this case it added an ONCLICK attribute to the Cancel button we defined in Listing 4-5. The code now appears as follows:

```
<!-This is a standard button type.  We'll use it to cancel the form.->

<INPUT LANGUAGE="VBScript" TYPE=button VALUE="Cancel"
ONCLICK="Window.location.href = 'SMPL_TAG.HTM'">
```

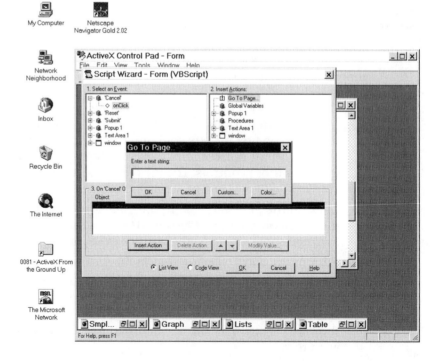

Once you decide on a control and an action, the Insert Action button allows you to define what you want to do.

Figure 4-9.

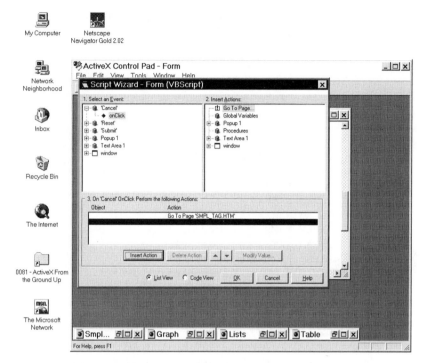

The Script
Wizard
completes
the script you
created by
showing you
the event and
associated
action in the
third list box.
Figure 4-10.

4

Where Does ActiveX Fit In?

We've spent just about the entire chapter talking about coding techniques
that you could use with any browser. These techniques are important to the
ActiveX developer as well since it's unlikely that you'll want to write controls
for every aspect of your Web site. Even if you did write all of the required
controls, it's unlikely that anyone would wait for all of them to download.
The coding techniques we've looked at so far are generic. Not only will they
work with just about every browser available, but they're platform independent.
ActiveX doesn't provide the same level of support; for the time being it's
very much tied to Internet Explorer.

You will be able to build on the knowledge you've gained so far as you work
with ActiveX controls. Adding an ActiveX control to your HTML document
requires a tag as well, just like all of the other controls we looked at in
previous sections. In this case you'll use the <OBJECT> tag. In Chapter 2 we
quickly added an example of an ActiveX control to a Web page for testing
purposes, but didn't really look at the HTML code. Let's take a look at what

ActiveX Control Pad created automatically now. That sample module code appears in Listing 4-6.

Listing 4-6

```
<HTML>
<HEAD>
<TITLE>This Page Contains an ActiveX Control</TITLE>
</HEAD>
<BODY>

<OBJECT ID="OCXEXMPL1" WIDTH=75 HEIGHT=25
 CLASSID="CLSID:D8D77E03-712A-11CF-8C70-00006E3127B7">
    <PARAM NAME="_Version" VALUE="65536">
    <PARAM NAME="_ExtentX" VALUE="1984">
    <PARAM NAME="_ExtentY" VALUE="661">
    <PARAM NAME="_StockProps" VALUE="70">
    <PARAM NAME="Caption" VALUE="On">
    <PARAM NAME="OnOff" VALUE="1">
    <PARAM NAME="ModalResult" VALUE="8">
</OBJECT>

</BODY>
</HTML>
```

As with most complex tags, the <OBJECT> tag begins the definition and the </OBJECT> tag ends it.

Let's begin with the first line of the <OBJECT> tag. The ID attribute tells what kind of control we're dealing with. Notice that no extension is listed—Internet Explorer defaults to an extension of OCX. Internet Explorer currently supports three extensions: OCX, CAB, and INF. We'll discuss the merits of the various types later in this section. You could also specify an URL as part of the ID attribute string. Notice that this first line also includes a WIDTH and HEIGHT attribute to define the size of the control.

Just like every other ActiveX control on your machine, one downloaded from the Internet has a CLASSID attribute. This is the unique number that identifies a particular control to Windows. The number is stored in the Windows registry. We'll see later that this particular feature can help reduce the download time for your controls if you use controls that users are likely to have installed on their machine.

Not shown here is an optional attribute, CODEBASE. Adding the CODEBASE attribute tells the browser where to find the control on your Internet site if it isn't already installed on the host machine. Think of it as a remote PATH statement like the ones you've placed in AUTOEXEC.BAT. If you don't add a CODEBASE attribute to your <OBJECT> tag, you've effectively disabled download of the control from your Internet site. We'll see how this feature works in the next section.

NOTE: We didn't set the CODEBASE property for the first three testing phases in Chapter 2 since the control was already loaded on the test machine. Normally you would set this property in the control's Properties dialog once the page you were working on was ready for testing and implementation on the Internet. (See Figure 2-14 for an example of the Properties dialog. The figure also shows the CodeBase property entry.)

Now that we've defined an object, a whole string of <PARAM> tags follows. These tags define how you want the control configured when you display it for the user. The <PARAM> tag always includes two attributes: NAME and VALUE. The NAME attribute defines the name of the parameter you want to set. The VALUE attribute assigns a value to the parameter. All values are enclosed in double quotes—even if they're numeric.

The last three parameters in the list should look familiar to you from Chapter 2. They're the parameters that we added to the OCX we created. As you can see, you haven't lost the ability to set up the control as needed. The _Version parameter comes into play during the download process. It helps the browser determine when the version of a control on the client machine is out of date with the one on the server. The _ExtentX and _ExtentY properties position the control on the Web page. Finally, the _StockProps property defines the stock properties of a control—you won't normally need to set them.

Previously we talked about the three kinds of files you can download from the Internet. The OCX file format—also known as the portable executable (PE) format—allows you to send the control to a client in its final format. No additional processing is required at the other side, meaning less support problems for you in the long run. The CAB file format is the same one used by Microsoft for shipping products such as Windows. It has the distinct advantage of letting you ship more than one control in a single package. This format also offers file compression, which will reduce download time for the user. The disadvantage is one of complexity. You have to create several installation files, including an INF file. In addition, users will need to wait for the CAB file to be decompressed and installed once they download it—making this method more likely to frustrate users and cause a lot of problems when they try to cancel the process. The final format, INF, allows you to selectively install one or more controls. It uses an INF file similar in

4

format to the ones that come with Windows. Users will see some type of an installation screen when they visit your site. The downside to this route is that you'll still need to create the INF file. Using an INF file means there is less chance of users getting totally annoyed while they wait for the page to download, and they'll feel that they're at least part of the process. We'll talk about the INF file format in the "Building Component Download (CAB) Files Using DIANTZ.EXE" section later in the chapter.

Downloading from the Internet

The inner workings of most of the tags in this chapter are pretty obvious. The browser looks at the tag, then displays what you requested. The whole process is straightforward and easy to understand. The ActiveX <OBJECT> tag isn't quite as easy to understand. What happens when the browser sees an <OBJECT> tag? We know it doesn't simply render the control onscreen—ActiveX controls provide a lot more functionality than that.

Microsoft has included a new Windows API call for browsers to use—CoGetClassObjectFromURL. When a browser sees an <OBJECT> tag, it parses out the CLASSID, CODEBASE, and _Version parameters. It passes these parameters to CoGetClassObjectFromURL, which downloads, verifies, and installs the control if necessary. The first thing this API call does though is to check whether the registry currently contains a reference to the CLASSID. You'll find this reference under the HKEY_CLASSES_ROOT | CLSID key of the registry, as shown in Figure 4-11.

T IP: The specification for the <OBJECT> tag and associated API calls is in a constant state of flux. If you want to find out the latest information about the <OBJECT> tag, look at http://www.w3.org/pub/WWW/TR/WD-object.htm.

If CoGetClassObjectFromURL finds an instance of the ActiveX control installed on the client machine, it checks the version number. When the version number of the control installed on the client machine matches the one on the HTML page, CoGetClassObjectFromURL loads the local control instead of downloading the control from the Internet. Once the control is loaded, CoGetClassObjectFromURL creates a class factory for it and passes the class factory back to the browser. (A *class factory* works just like any other factory would—it produces some item. In this case it allows the browser to

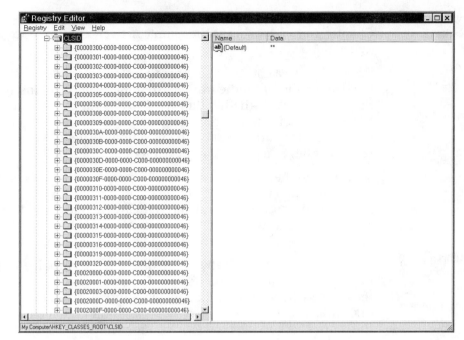

Windows
stores ActiveX
control class
identifiers
under the
HKEY_CLASSES
_ROOT |
CLSID key.
Figure 4-11.

produce an instance of the object.) Otherwise, the API call asks the browser to download the code from the Internet site.

Downloading is an asynchronous process—Windows can perform other ActiveX-related tasks while it waits for a download to complete. Once the browser completes the download and decompresses the file if needed, the Windows Trust Provider Service function WinVerifyTrust is called. This service looks inside the ActiveX control and determines whether there is a signature block. The signature block contains the author's name, a public key, and the encrypted digest of the control's contents. Think of an ActiveX control signature block just as you would the signature field on a check, a driver's license, or a contract—it not only tells who you are, but verifies that you are who you say you are. If the WinVerifyTrust call finds a signature block (also called a certificate), it validates the certificate. Each certificate can contain the name of a parent certificate. WinVerifyTrust travels the hierarchical tree of certificates until it comes to the root certificate. It then verifies that this root certificate appears in the list of trusted root certificates. If the certificate does appear, CoGetClassObjectFromURL automatically loads the control and creates a class factory for it. Otherwise, the user gets a

A public key works like the security gate key for a condominium or apartment—it lets you into the main building. A private key is like the door key for the condominium or apartment—it lets you into your living quarters.

message saying that the control isn't trusted. This is the message we got in Chapter 2 when looking at the sample ActiveX control, since we hadn't signed it.

Users still have a choice of whether to install an ActiveX control or not, even if it doesn't appear on the trusted list. If users choose to install the control, they also are asked whether they want to add the control's author to their trusted list. Adding the author's name to the list means that any new controls from that same author will be accepted immediately. We'll look at the security issues in more detail in Chapter 6.

So, where do these controls get installed? ActiveX controls downloaded from the Internet don't automatically appear in the user's System folder. They are added to a special folder named OCCACHE that could literally appear anywhere on the user's machine. Normally you'll find this folder located in the main Windows folder, the /SYSTEM folder, or the user's Internet folder.

Loading the control isn't all that involved. The control has to register itself during the installation process. In most cases this means calling the DllRegisterServer API function. Once installed and registered, the CoGetClassObjectFromURL function passes the class factory associated with the control back to the browser. The browser uses the class factory to create an instance of the object. It initializes any parameters passed with the <OBJECT> tag and displays the control onscreen (if necessary).

Building Component Download (CAB) Files Using DIANTZ.EXE

You learned earlier that you could save the user some time by placing your ActiveX controls in a CAB file. This file format offers the ability to transfer more than one file in a single download and file compression as well. Creating a CAB file doesn't have to be difficult, but you will want to test it thoroughly before using it in a production environment.

The first step is to figure out which files to send to users. For example, users will probably have a copy of all the MFC (Microsoft Foundation Class) files from using other programs. You don't want them to waste time downloading these files over and over again if they don't need to. In most cases you'll want to limit yourself to the files that are unique to your Web site.

The second step is to create an INF file. There are several reasons for including this file. For one thing, it can include installation instructions that will make the user's life a lot easier and reduce your support calls. Another good reason for including an INF file is that it contains those common files that your ActiveX control needs, but didn't get downloaded as part of the CAB file. You can include instructions for downloading those files from your Internet site if the user really does need them. The Internet Component Download service portion of your browser doesn't understand the full-fledged INF file specification—it can only use a subset of the standard entries. Table 4-1 shows the entries you can use and the order you should use for including them.

4

Entry	Description
[Add.Code]	
<Filename1>=<Section-Name1> <Filename2>=<Section-Name2> <Filename n>=<Section-Name n>	The [Add.Code] section provides a complete list of all the files that you want to install. This won't include all of the files in the INF file since you won't want to install the INF file as a minimum. The <Section-Name> part of the entry tells Internet Component Download service where to find the installation instructions for a particular file. (See the next section.)
[Section-Name1]	
Key1=Value1 Key2=Value2 Key n=Value n	Each file-specific section contains one or more keys, just like the keys you've used before with INI files. The following entries explain the key values that Internet Component Download will understand.
File=[<URL> | ThisCAB]	This key tells whether you can download the file from a specific location on the Internet or from this cabinet. Using this key allows you to define locations for files needed by the ActiveX control but not included in the CAB file. Normally these additional support files are located on the Internet server.
File Version=<a>,<b>,<c>,<d>	This key specifies the minimum acceptable version number for a file. If you don't specify a value, Internet Component Download assumes any version is fine. Each letter designates a level of revision. So if your control's version is 1.0, you'd use Version=1,0,0,0.

INF File Format for Internet Component Download Service
Table 4-1.

Entry	Description
File-[Mac | Win32]-[x86 | PPC | Mips | Alpha]=[<URL> | IGNORE]	This key allows you to differentiate required support for various platforms. First you define an operating system, then the CPU type. The <URL> parameter allows you to specify a location for the file. The IGNORE argument tells Internet Component Download that the file isn't needed on the specified platform.
CLSID=[<Class ID>]	This key allows you to define a class identification for the file. You won't actually create the CLSID—Visual C++ does this step for you automatically, based on a complex equation developed by Microsoft. There are two places to get this value: your C++ source code and the Windows registry. To find it in the Windows registry, just open the registry editor and use the Edit | Find command to find the name of your OCX under the HKEY_CLASSES_ROOT | CLSID key. The registry form of the CLSID for the example in Chapter 2 is {D8D77E03-712A-11CF-8C70-00006E3127B7}. The C++ source location is in the control file. For example, the Chapter 2 source code file to look in is OCXEXMPLCTL.CPP. You'll find the identifier in this call: // // Initialize class factory and guid IMPLEMENT_OLECREATE_EX(COCXEXMPLCtrl, "OCXEXMPL.OCXEXMPLCtrl.1", 0xd8d77e03, 0x712a, 0x11cf, 0x8c, 0x70, 0, 0, 0x6e, 0x31, 0x27, 0xb7) // The CLSID value for an ActiveX control never changes (unless you change something very basic like the name—code changes have no effect), so you only need to find this value once.

INF File
Format for
Internet
Component
Download
Service
(*continued*)

Table 4-1.

Entry	Description
DestDir=[10 | 11]	This key defines where you want to place the file. A value of 10 places it in the main Windows folder. A value of 11 places it in the SYSTEM folder. If you don't specify a value, Internet Component Download will place it in the browser cache directory. Placing a component in the browser cache directory usually won't cause any problems unless the user clears the contents of the cache. If this happens, the control will be downloaded again the next time the user needs it since Windows won't be able to find it in the location specified in the registry. (For this same reason you won't want the user to move the control once it's installed.)

INF File
Format for
Internet
Component
Download
Service
(*continued*)
Table 4-1.

4

Creating an INF file is fairly easy. All you really need to do is think about what you need to include and where it's located. Listing 4-7 shows a typical INF file for a two-file installation. The first file, OCXEXMPL.OCX, is actually located in the CAB. The user will also need MFC40.DLL, but there's a good chance it's already installed on the client machine. The example includes a site to find the file on the Internet server, just in case the client machine doesn't have the required file. Once you have a list of files and an INF file, you can create the Diamond Directive File (DDF) needed by DIANTZ.EXE to create the CAB file. The format of this file is not difficult to understand. Listing 4-8 shows a typical example that you can use to create your own DDF.

Listing 4-7

```
;INF File for OCXEXMPL.OCX
[Add.Code]
OCXEXMPL.OCX=OCXEXMPL.OCX
MFC40.DLL=MFC40.DLL

[OCXEXMPLE.OCX]
File=thiscab
Clsid=[D8D77E03-712A-11CF-8C70-00006E3127B7]
FileVersion=1,0,0,0

[MFC40.DLL]
File=http://aux/files/MFC40.DLL
FileVersion=4,0,0,5
```

Listing 4-8

```
;Diamond Directive File
;Generate a complete error listing for any variable typos.
.OPTION EXPLICIT
;Define the name of the CAB file.
.SET CABINETNAMETEMPLATE=ActiveX.CAB
;Create a cabinet.
.SET CABINET=ON
;Compress the files.
.SET COMPRESS=ON
;List the files.
Install.INF
File1.OCX
File2.OCX
...
```

Once you get to this point, creating the CAB file isn't hard. Just use the command line shown here:

```
DIANTZ /F MY.DDF
```

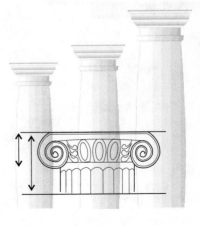

Chapter

5

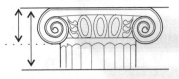

ActiveX Documents

So far, we've talked about all kinds of new technology, especially ActiveX, which promises to make the Internet into a business tool for everyone. There are a lot of different ways in which ActiveX is getting used. For example, Microsoft has recently released a new ActiveX API called ActiveX Accessibility. This API is designed to add to the Internet what the Accessibility applet added to Windows 95. Things like *Sticky Keys* (a method for creating control key combinations by pressing one key at a time instead of all the keys simultaneously) won't only appear on your Windows 95 and Windows NT 4.0 desktop, they'll also appear within your ActiveX-compatible Internet browser.

There are other ActiveX-based technologies in the works as well (by Microsoft and other companies)—too many to talk about here. Some of the more important ones include ActiveX Movie and ActiveX VRML (virtual reality modeling language), both of which are already available.

143

In fact, the MSNBC Internet site is already using ActiveX Movie to show you clips from the NBC news network. Essentially, ActiveX Movie allows you to view film clips on the Internet, and play AVI and other kinds of movie files. Gamers will find that ActiveX VRML allows them to play games against other humans on the Internet instead of against the computer. VRML by itself allows the browser to create realistic 3-D animation sequences that depend on virtual reality modeling techniques. The ActiveX portion of the picture adds a live connection and other elements that only OLE can provide up to this point. The main difference between VRML and other technologies that you may have seen is that you are able to react in all three dimensions, just as you would in the real world. (At a recent seminar, some of the other ideas for using this technology included architectural modeling and long-distance engineering sessions.)

The most important ActiveX technology, though, isn't a new and exciting one—it's that old and mundane problem, sharing documents on the Internet. This has always been a problem because the interface is static—just consider the number of tags you'd need and the complexity of the program required to create any kind of a dynamic interface after reading Chapter 4. Sure, you can export a word-processed document into HTML and come up with a realistic representation of the data, but that data won't change and it will be difficult for the user to edit it. The same holds true for spreadsheet data. Showing the data isn't too hard as long as you're willing to sacrifice up-to-the-minute information. ActiveX provides an answer in this case. It allows you to create a dynamic document—one that you can edit and see change in real time.

So, where did this technology mysteriously appear from? It's not new at all: Microsoft has simply modified the technology found in Microsoft Office. The original name for ActiveX Document is *OLE Document Objects*. It's part of the Microsoft Office Binder technology and was never meant to become a public specification. Originally you had to sign up for the Office-compatible program before you could even get a specification for OLE Document Objects. It was only after the appearance of Windows 95 that this specification became something that anyone could get. However, it only makes sense that Microsoft would make this specification public since it's the next logical step in the evolution of OLE.

ActiveX Document is what this chapter is all about. We're going to examine what will be the most important use of ActiveX besides database applications. You'll learn just how easy it is to create ActiveX Documents for browser use. We'll also examine what you need to do to create custom document setups of your own.

What Are ActiveX Documents (A.K.A. OLE Document Objects)?

Up to this point in the book we haven't looked very much at the kinds of documents a user would be familiar with. Instead, what we've looked at is a scripting language used to display specific page elements in a way that only a programmer would love. Of course, this begs a question that nearly everyone will ask—what's in the Internet for the user besides a bit of information and a few forms? ActiveX Documents provide part of that answer. They are a means for just about anyone to create content and display it on a Web page.

However, ActiveX Documents are more than merely a way to share information—you can actually use them to get real work done. Think about this scenario: your company has its own intranet that employees can contact as needed from anywhere in the world. They use it to get their email and perform a variety of other tasks. Now your boss tells you that the marketing department has to create a report and that most of the sales representatives are on the road. How do you get the job done?

NOTE: Netscape Navigator and earlier versions of Internet Explorer provided the ability to view non standard documents through the use of helpers. The browser would start a full copy of the application and then pass it the contents of the file on the Web site. The problem with this approach is that you use more memory to start another application and you don't have a live connection to the Internet server. Changes made to the file wouldn't get reflected in the server copy. Even though Microsoft still uses the term "helpers" with regard to Internet Explorer 3.0 and above, the view from the user's standpoint is completely different.

5

ActiveX Documents are the answer in this case. Simply place a link to the document in an HTML document using the tags we discussed in Chapter 4. When users click on the document reference, they'll see an editable copy of the document in their browser with the appropriate changes to their menu and toolbar. Figure 5-1 shows a Word for Windows document displayed in an Internet Explorer browser window. Notice that all of the browser features are still intact: the only thing that's changed is the way the document gets displayed. This particular technique isn't new—it's called *in-place editing*. Most OLE 2 servers can now provide this capability to an OLE 2 client. Try it out in Word for Windows or CorelDRAW! some time. The menu and toolbar will change to match that of the client anytime you click on an OLE object. The big difference is that this is happening in a browser through an Internet connection.

NOTE: You may get a dialog asking whether you want to open or save the file if you test this sample on a LAN-based Internet server. In most cases you'll definitely get it when testing the connection over a live Internet connection (depending on how you set security up for your browser). Simply open the file to see it as shown in Figure 5-1.

You'll notice another difference as well. If you were to make a change to this document, then click the Back button on the Internet Explorer browser toolbar, you'd see the following dialog asking if you want to change the file. If you click on Yes, you'll see a typical File Save dialog. The unfortunate part of this setup is that saving the file using this technique will place it on your local hard drive—something that won't work in our scenario, but possibly

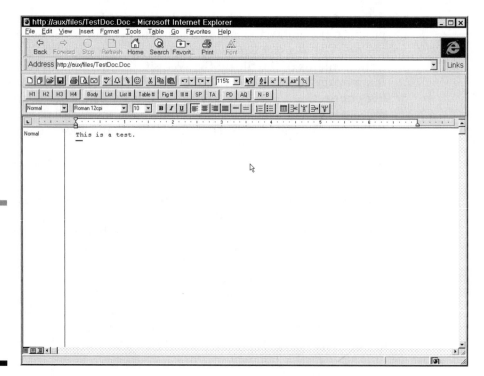

Internet Explorer 3.0 shows the effects of in-place editing—an OLE 2 feature of COM.
Figure 5-1.

could in other circumstances. There are other ways of saving the file. You could use the File | Save As File command. You could also use the File | Send To | Web Publishing Wizard command to actually send it back to the Web server—that would be our choice in this situation. We'll look at the steps needed for using the Web Publishing Wizard in the "Using the Web Publishing Wizard" section of this chapter.

TIP: There are some situations where none of the techniques for posting changes in this section will help very much. For example, you may want to post the document on the Web server, but you may want each post to arrive individually. In that case you could always tell the user to use the File | Send To | Mail Recipient command. Obviously this would mean coordinating all of the documents you receive, but this method will work when others won't.

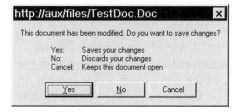

5

TIP: The current HTTP 1.0 specification doesn't allow the user to publish a document to the WWW server. The newer 1.1 specification will remedy this oversight. If you want to allow users to publish documents back to the server from a Web page, then providing a server that uses the 1.1 specification is the way to go. Not only will you save time and effort writing mundane scripts or jumping through other hoops, you'll reduce support calls by making things easier for the user as well. (All current versions of both Netscape and Microsoft products support this 1.1 specification—check your documentation if you own an older version of either vendor's product.)

ActiveX Document also presents some changes in the way that a programmer has to think about OLE. There are three levels of object participation within a client. An object can simply appear in the viewing area, or it can take over the window, or it can take over the entire application frame. Let's look at how these three levels differ.

Originally you could create an object and place it in a container. The container would simply display an icon showing the presence of the object and nothing more when OLE 1 came out. To edit an object, you double-clicked on its icon within the container. Windows would bring up a full-fledged copy of the document in a separate window. This is what someone means when they say an object simply appears in the viewing area.

OLE 2 changed the way that clients and servers interact. Now you could actually see the contents of the object. For example, if you placed a spreadsheet object within a word processing document, you could see its contents without double-clicking on the object. This is the window level of participation. The client and server share a window; and the client displays its data, then relies on the server to display any information within an object. OLE 2 also provides in-place activation. Double-clicking on the object in most cases starts an out-process server that actually takes over the entire client frame. The server takes over the menus and toolbars normally reserved for client use. From a user perspective the application was the same; the tools just changed to meet their needs for editing an object.

ActiveX Document moves this technology from desktop to the Internet through the use of a browser. Now your browser tools will automatically change to meet the needs of the user, and they no longer need to open a separate program to edit a document. An out-process server will take care of changing the browser menus and toolbars to match the ones normally used by the application. In fact, future versions of Windows will go still farther.

Windows 95 and Windows NT 4.0 both use the Explorer interface. If you right-click on just about any document that's associated with a registered application, you'll see a menu with a variety of choices. The most common choices are to open or print the document. In some cases you'll also see an option to use the Quick View utility to see what the document contains.

The interface will probably change in the near future. Double-clicking on a document will perform an in-place activation. The server will actually take over the Explorer menus and toolbars. No longer will the user leave Explorer to open another application window. In addition, Internet sites will appear within Explorer as hard drives, combining the functionality of a browser with what we have today.

Are all of these changes welcomed by the programmer community? Not by a long shot. A few people are already claiming that this technology is only increasing Microsoft's grip on the computing world. Of course, that would only happen if you couldn't install another server in the place of Internet Explorer—which is something that definitely won't happen. ActiveX

Document is going to be an extremely important technology as computing matures. That's why this chapter is so important—its purpose is to get you up-to-speed on this emerging technology so that you can use it to meet your current computing needs.

Creating the Connection

Now that we've seen the result of using an ActiveX Document and discussed why this technology is important, let's take a look at the HTML code required to implement it. Listing 5-1 shows the code used to create this example (it's short and to-the-point). I didn't add any bells or whistles so that you could see the absolute minimum required to create an ActiveX Document link. As you can see, the code uses a simple link and nothing more. All of the "magic" behind this application is located in Internet Explorer. We've used this kind of link to display other pages on a Web site in Chapter 4.

Listing 5-1

```
<HTML>
<HEAD>
<TITLE>ActiveX Document</TITLE>
</HEAD>
<BODY>
<Center>
<H2>ActiveX Document Test Page</H2>
<EM>Requires Microsoft Word or WordPad</EM><P>
</Center>
<A HREF="http://aux/files/TestDoc.Doc">Test Document</A>
</BODY>
</HTML>
```

5

OK, so you've got a document displayed in your browser that you can edit. That really isn't such a big deal, is it? Sure it is. Since the document remains in the browser, you save memory. There is only one application running, and although you do have to pay the cost of some additional processing overhead and memory to view and process the document, it's a lot less than running two applications. For example, the in-place activation features are the result of using an *out-process server*. An out-process server is essentially a fancy form of DLL that provides the right kinds of interfaces to communicate with the client application. The point is that the DLL will take less memory than a full-fledged application if for no other reason than it doesn't have to worry about displaying anything (that's the job of the client). We'll take a look at some of the requirements for this DLL in the "An Overview of the ActiveX Document Architecture" section of this chapter.

There are two other ways to create an ActiveX document connection that we won't spend much time looking at here. The Microsoft Web Browser Control allows you to browse the Internet looking for any kind of document—including those that you don't normally associate with the Internet like Word for Windows documents. There are several advanced <OBJECT> tag attributes that will help you in this regard as well. You'll want to take the time to look at the <OBJECT> tag information in Chapter 4, then go to the Web site listed there to download the associated specification. The advanced attributes for the <OBJECT> tag are currently in a state of flux: that's why we won't look at them here.

Using the Web Publishing Wizard

You don't have to settle for the old methods of keeping documents up-to-date. It only takes a little bit of effort to use the Web Publishing Wizard to keep a document current on the Web server. These changes won't solely appear on your local machine as they would with older browser technology. They'll actually appear on the Internet server. By providing a written procedure for using the Web Publishing Wizard (and possibly setting up the connection information in advance), you've allowed an employee to make a change to what's essentially an HTML page from a remote location.

So, how do you start the process? The following procedure will get you going the first time around. You can make this an easy four-step process after this first attempt—we'll look at that part of the procedure once we go through this first phase. We'll start with a document like the one shown in Figure 5-1 and assume that you've already edited it. Now you want to save the change to your Internet site.

1. Use the File | Save As File command to display a File Save dialog. You'll need to save the file locally before you can send it to the Web server. Perhaps Microsoft will change this part of the procedure later, but for now you'll have to take the time to make a local copy. Give the file the same name as the Web site page. In the case of our sample Internet site, the name of the file is TESTDOC.DOC (as shown in the Internet Explorer title bar in Figure 5-1).

2. Use the File | Send To | Web Publishing Wizard command to display the Web Publishing Wizard dialog shown here.

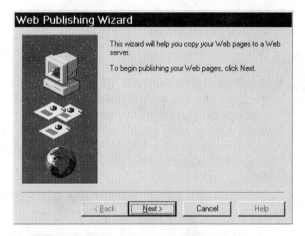

3. Click Next. You'll see the next page as follows. Notice that Web Publishing Wizard automatically places a filename in the File or Folder Name field. You won't want to use this filename right now.

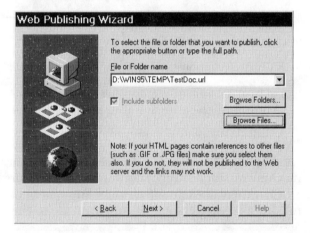

5

4. Click the Browse Files button to display a Browse dialog (it looks like a standard File Open dialog). Locate the local copy of the document you just saved, then click on Open. Now you'll see the name of the Web document in the Field or Folder Name field.

5. Click Next. If you've defined a Web server connection in the past, you'll see a single drop-down list box that contains names of the connections. You can select one of those connections or define a new one by clicking the New button. We'll assume that you need a new connection for the purposes of this example. (If you really don't need a new connection, select an existing connection and skip to step 13.) Whether you click the New button or you've never defined a server connection in the past, you'll see the next page as illustrated here. This page is where you begin to define the connection between the client machine and the Internet server. Fortunately, you only have to do it once.

T IP: A network administrator could perform this task once on each machine to reduce support calls from users. Unfortunately (at least as of this writing) there doesn't appear to be any way of doing this automatically like making a registry change or copying a file to the target machine.

6. Type the name you want to use for your Internet connection. In most cases leaving My Web Site is just fine if you only need one entry. Select an Internet Service Provider from the second list box. If you're creating a connection for a LAN Internet site, then select Other Internet Provider as shown.

7. Click Next. You'll see the next page, as follows. Notice that you'll need to define a connection to the Internet server. Simply type in the URL for your site.

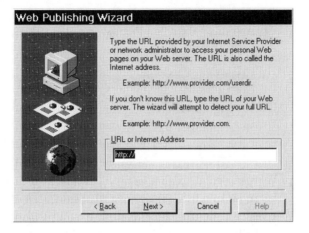

8. Click Next. You'll see the next page, as shown here. This page allows you to select a connection type: LAN or dial-up. Don't be fooled by the description provided by the dialog. You can create a dial-up connection for an intranet just as easily as you can for an Internet.

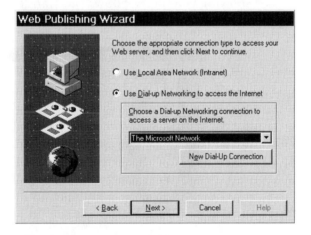

5

9. Choose between a LAN connection (no modem connection) or a dial-up connection. If you select a dial-up connection, you'll also need to select one of the dial-up connections in the list box. Clicking the New Dial-Up Connection button allows you to create a new connection definition.

10. Click Next. The Web Publishing Wizard displays the next page which simply states that it needs to verify the information you provided. Click Next to begin the verification process. If you're trying to create a LAN connection, you'll almost certainly get the error message shown next.

Don't worry about it—the next few steps will show you how to fix the problem. If the Web Publishing Wizard successfully found your site, you can proceed to step 14.

11. Click OK to clear the error message dialog. You'll see the first page of an extended connection configuration, as follows. This is where you'll select a file transfer method. If you're working with an Internet site through a dial-up connection, you can choose between an FTP or HTTP file transfer. The HTTP method is only available to Web sites using HTTP version 1.1 or above. If you're working with a LAN, the FTP and Windows File Transfer options are available. At this point the various connections require a bit more definition. The procedure will continue by showing you the Windows File Transfer option since it's the one you'll need most often.

TIP: When configuring a LAN connection, use the Windows File Transfer method whenever possible since it's faster. The FTP connection requires an added file transfer layer that really isn't needed in the LAN environment. However, on a WAN, the FTP method could provide an added layer of security.

12. Click Next. You'll see the next page as shown in Figure 5-2. This is where the connection problem will become obvious. Web Publishing Wizard almost never gets the *UNC* (uniform naming convention) destination for your file right. The reason is pretty simple: the name is obscured by the server in most cases. You'll need to provide a fully qualified UNC to your storage directory like the one shown in Figure 5-2. Make absolutely certain that you provide a UNC name, not a standard DOS drive and directory location. The reason for using a UNC is that it allows you to use the same entry technique no matter what file system the server is using.

13. Click Next. The Web Publishing Wizard displays the next page, which simply states that it needs to verify the information you provided. Click Next to begin the verification process. This time you should see a success message.

14. Click Finish. This will allow you to complete the file transfer process. You'll see a file transfer dialog while Web Publishing Wizard copies the file for you. Once it's finished, you'll see the success dialog shown here. You've just modified this document—anyone visiting the Web site will see the changes automatically.

5

Once you complete these setup steps the first time, the user can complete the process in four easy steps. All you need to do is save the document to a local drive, use the File | Send To | Web Publishing Wizard command to start the Wizard, select the file, select a connection, and then click Finish to complete the process, which are steps 1 through 4, and 14 if you want to look at it from a procedural view.

An Overview of the ActiveX Document Architecture

It's important to understand how the controls that you use work—at least to a certain extent—so that you can easily troubleshoot them when the time

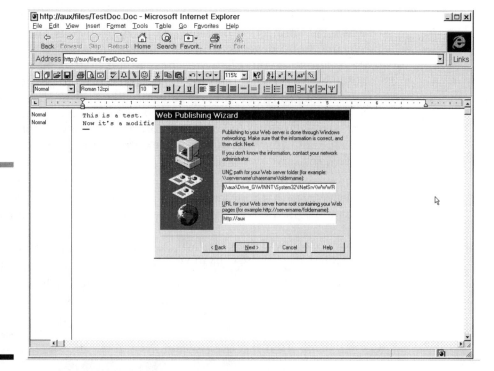

Figure 5-2.

comes. There isn't room in this book to go over the theory behind OLE in detail; some books on the market are devoted to that task and have a hard time doing it in even 1,000 pages. However, an ActiveX Document control requires some special features and those are the ones we'll look at in this section.

The first thing you need to understand is that an OLE control works because it uses a common interface. Every OLE control that you'll ever use must support specific classes (actually interface elements) to allow applications to access it. For example, if a client needs to ask the server for in-place activation support, it makes a call to one of the methods associated with IOleInPlaceActivateObject. Every server that supports in-place activation has to provide a class of this name and expose it for the client to use. The equivalent client class in this case is IOleDocumentSite. There are literally hundreds of classes (and associated methods) that you could support to provide various kinds of OLE functionality (it's inconceivable that you would need to support them all, though, since some forms of functionality simply aren't needed by specific controls). Figure 5-3 shows the classes (interface elements) for Excel Worksheet using OLEViewer (the utility we discussed in Chapter 3). Notice that each one of them begins with an *I* instead of the more familiar *C*. This represents the exposed interface classes—the ones that a client would access to gain some type of functionality from the server.

NOTE: Figure 5-3 shows three IMso functions. This represents the pre-specification names for the ActiveX Document functions. The ActiveX specification now states that these are standard IOle classes. Fortunately, it appears that Internet Explorer 3.0 will support document objects using either interface. However, this support may not last long and you should use the IOle versions of the calls we'll talk about in this chapter.

Obviously, you could drive yourself crazy trying to remember if you implemented all of those calls in your control. Fortunately, an IDE like Visual C++ that provides direct support for building ActiveX controls (or OCXs) normally takes care of creating the myriad of classes for you. (There

OLEViewer provides a convenient method for seeing what kind of interface elements you need to support when creating a control.

Figure 5-3.

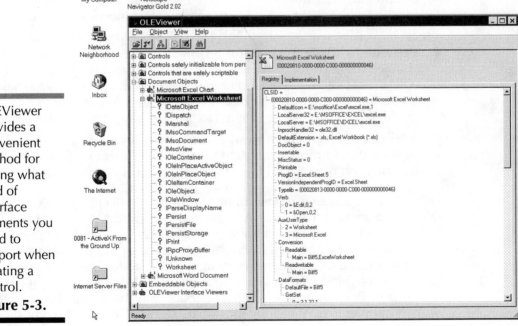

are more than a few compiler vendors creating ActiveX add-ons for their products as you read this. Products like Borland's Delphi already include an Internet control pack add-on to help you build Internet-aware applications.) They implement a default behavior for each of the required classes as well. The only time that you really need to change a behavior is if you want to add some special kind of functionality not supported by the compiler. We saw in Chapter 2 that building a simple control doesn't have to involve a lot of work if you build an appropriate application framework. That's why the example spends so much time getting everything set up before adding even a single line of code.

There's actually an easy way of looking at the OLE interface functions required to create ActiveX Documents. In fact, we can summarize the functionality of an ActiveX document using what you've learned so far in the book as a basis for understanding. If you want your application to support this specification, it has to perform the four steps listed below.

♦ **Implement IPersistentStorage** Your application must support this class and associated methods so that it can use OLE compound files as a storage medium.

♦ **Support OLE Document Embedding Features** This particular feature is implemented in many different ways. The current trend is toward providing the user with two embedding methods through menu functions: Insert Object and Paste Special. The functions used to do this are IPersistFile, IOleObject, and IDataObject.

♦ **Provide In-Place Activation Support** There are two classes that you need to implement in order to support in-place activation: IOleInPlaceObject and IOleInPlaceActivateObject. To implement these classes you'll have to gather information about the container using methods provided by the IOleInPlaceSite and IOleInPlaceFrame classes.

♦ **Add the ActiveX Document Extensions** Most OLE 2 servers perform the first three steps right now. To make them work on the Internet, you have to add the four functions we'll discuss in this section.

Let's talk about the fourth item on this list in greater detail. ActiveX Documents are fairly new in some ways. Since Microsoft kept the specification for them a secret for so long, few compilers out there provide direct support for an ActiveX Document server. What this means to you as a programmer is that you'll either have to build the added interfaces yourself (not really too difficult) or upgrade your compiler. What we'll look at in the next four sections are the four added interface calls that you'll have to support in order to create a fully functional ActiveX Document server.

(Fortunately, they aren't all required—Figure 5-3 shows that Excel only implements three of them.) The good news is that the ActiveX SDK provides the header and other support files needed to create these interface elements. We'll take a look at those in this section as well.

TIP: The soon-to-be-released 4.2 version of Microsoft Visual C++ includes direct support for creating most ActiveX object types including ActiveX Document. This means that the new version will literally build all of the elements we'll talk about in this section for you—reducing the time it will take for you to create your new control or application.

IOleDocument

Whenever an Internet client sees a server that implements the IOleDocument class, it knows that the server can act as an ActiveX Document server. This is the first thing that Internet Explorer and other Internet client applications will look for when they see a document that's associated with your application. Don't confuse standard in-place activation with the kind used by an ActiveX Document server. You can build an application that supports in-place activation alone and it will work fine on a local machine, but it won't support in-place activation over the Internet.

NOTE: In many cases it doesn't matter if you implement this interface—you can still support OLE 2 without it. A server that's missing this interface will simply be opened in a separate window, even if it normally supports in-place activation with local clients like Word for Windows.

So, what does this class do besides telling Internet Explorer that your application supports ActiveX Documents? The methods it supports get called every time the client needs to create new server views (CreateView method), enumerate those views (EnumViews method), or retrieve the MiscStatus bits associated with the ActiveX Document (GetDocMiscStatus method). In essence, this class helps you manage the server as a whole. It provides the low-level functionality required for the client and server to communicate.

A server view is not the same thing as the view that the user sees when they click on a link to one of your documents—that's managed by the IOleDocumentView function we'll talk about in the next section. What a server view provides is a single instance of the server itself. A client application uses this view for communication purposes. For example, if the client needs to find out what features the server supports, it would use a server view to do so. We'll see how this works when we get into the actual application code.

There are four standard miscellaneous status bits. The first bit, DOCMISC_CANCREATEMULTIPLEVIEWS, tells the client whether the server can create multiple views. In other words, this bit defines whether you can run multiple copies of the application at one time. In most cases a modern server can do this. About the only exceptions are for CAD or drawing programs where the memory requirements might be too prohibitive. Another class of application that may not support this is a communications program, since most people only have one modem. The second bit, DOCMISC_SUPPORTCOMPLEXRECTANGLES, tells whether the server can support complex view area commands. An example is whether or not the server will allow the client to determine the position of things like scroll bars and sizing boxes. The third bit, DOCMISC_CANOPENEDIT, is used to tell the client whether the server can open a document for editing. Setting this bit prevents the user from editing a document online (something you may want to consider for security reasons or if you want to create a server for viewing purposes only). The final bit, DOCMISC_NOFILESUPPORT, tells whether the server supports any kind of file manipulation. Setting this bit usually forces the client to display an error message since the user won't even be able to read the selected file.

IOleDocumentView

Like the IOleDocument class, you must implement IOleDocumentView to make ActiveX Document work. This particular interface element is reliant on the IOleDocument class. You need to have a server running before you can open a document. In addition, the client relies on information it gets from the GetDocMiscStatus method of IOleDocument to know how to interact with this class. Each copy of the IOleDocumentView class controls a single instance of an ActiveX Document view. In most cases this means that the single instance of the IOleDocumentView class controls a single document. However, you could just as easily create one instance of the class for each view of the single document you have opened.

The IOleDocumentView class supports a variety of methods. Table 5-1 lists the most common methods that you'll find. As you can see, the methods allow you to resize the screen or create another copy of the view that you're looking at. Some of the other methods allow you to reset the view's bounding area or determine which document is currently displaying within the view.

Method	Description
SetInPlaceSite	Associates a view site object with this view. The client supplies the view site object. In essence, this is the method that will associate a document with the current view.
GetInPlaceSite	Returns a pointer to the view site object associated with the view.
GetDocument	Returns a pointer to the document associated with the view.
SetRect	Defines the bounding area for the view. In other words, this method sets the size of the window that the user will see.
GetRect	Returns the coordinates for the view's bounding area.
SetRectComplex	Defines a complex bounding area for the view. Not only does this method determine the size of the window the user will see, but things like the placement of scroll bars and other view elements. A view doesn't have to support this feature. You do need to set a miscellaneous status bit if your application doesn't provide the support. (See the IOleDocument class description for more details.)
Show	The client can use this method to either show or hide the view.
UIActivate	Determines whether the user interface is active or not. Normally the user interface is only active when the view has the focus. It is normally deactivated at all other times to prevent conflicts with the view that does have focus.

5

Methods Associated with the IOleDocument View Class
Table 5-1.

Method	Description
Open	Requests that the server open the view in a separate window. You can turn off this feature using a miscellaneous status bit. (See the IOleDocument class description for more details.)
CloseView	Shuts the view down.
SaveViewState	Writes the current view status information to an IStream.
ApplyViewState	Requests that a view return its state to the settings defined in a previously saved IStream.
Clone	Creates a copy of the current view. The cloned view will have the same context, but use a different view port (instance of the IOleDocumentView class).

Methods
Associated
with the
IOleDocument
View Class
(*continued*)
Table 5-1.

IOleCommandTarget

This is one of the classes you don't have to implement to make ActiveX Document work. However, it's a lot more than a simple convenience item. IOleCommandTarget allows the client and server to talk with each other without resorting to tricks like assigning fixed-menu IDs. Of course, there are limitations to this communication. For one thing, the communication is still limited to a fixed number of commands (which we'll talk about a little further down). There is a two-step procedure required to make this part of the interface work.

The first part of the client-to-server communication is to find out what commands the server supports. The client does this using the Query method. Table 5-2 provides a complete list of the commands that the server can support along with their associated identifiers. The first thing you should notice is that most of the commands are standard menu entries.

The second phase of the client/server communication uses the Exec method. The client passes the server one or more OLECMD structures. Each structure contains a single command, any required input arguments, and a place to put informational flags on return from the call. You won't need to provide any input arguments, so that part of the structure will contain a NULL. The standard options appear in Table 5-3. Table 5-4 describes the flags that you'll see on return from an Exec call.

Command	Identifier
Edit Clear	OLECMDID_CLEARSELECTION
Edit Copy	OLECMDID_COPY
Edit Cut	OLECMDID_CUT
Edit Paste	OLECMDID_PASTE
Edit Paste Special	OLECMDID_PASTESPECIAL
Edit Redo	OLECMDID_REDO
Edit Select All	OLECMDID_SELECTALL
Edit Undo	OLECMDID_UNDO
File New	OLECMDID_NEW
File Open	OLECMDID_OPEN
File Page Setup	OLECMDID_PAGESETUP
File Print	OLECMDID_PRINT
File Print Preview	OLECMDID_PRINTPREVIEW
File Properties	OLECMDID_PROPERTIES
File Save	OLECMDID_SAVE
File Save As	OLECMDID_SAVEAS
File Save Copy As	OLECMDID_SAVECOPYAS
Not a standard command. This identifier asks the server if it can perform the following three tasks: return a zoom value, display a zoom dialog, and set a zoom value. This identifier is normally associated with View menu commands (or their equivalent) if the server supports them.	OLECMDID_ZOOM
Not a standard command. This identifier retrieves the zoom range supported by the server. It's normally associated with the View Zoom command if the server supports it (or an equivalent).	OLECMDID_GETZOOMRANGE
Tools Spelling	OLECMDID_SPELL

5

Common Commands Supported by IOleCommand Target
Table 5-2.

Flag	Description
OLECMDEXECOPT_PROMPTUSER	Prompts the user for some kind of input prior to executing the command. For example, you'd want to use this option with a File Open command.
OLECMDEXECOPT_DONTPROMPTUSER	Don't ask the user for any kind of input. For example, you might want to use this option when the user asks you to print a document.
OLECMDEXECOPT_DODEFAULT	You're not sure whether to prompt the user or not. In this case you want the application to perform the default action. In most cases this means it will prompt the user for input.
OLECMDEXECOPT_SHOWHELP	Don't execute the command at all, display its help screen instead. You might want to use this command if your ActiveX document provides an alternative help button.

Standard Exec
Method Input
Arguments
Table 5-3.

IPrint

IPrint is another optional class that you can implement. In fact, it's the one missing from Figure 5-3. This class allows an object to support programmatic printing. There are three methods supported by IPrint: print (Print), retrieve print-related information (GetPageInfo), and set the initial page number for a print job (SetInitialPageNum). Of the three methods, only the Print method accepts any flags as input. Table 5-5 provides a list of these flags and tells how to use them.

Flag	Description
OLECMDF_SUPPORTED	The view object supports the requested command.
OLECMDF_ENABLED	The command is available and the view object has enabled it.
OLECMDF_LATCHED	This command uses an on-off toggle and it is currently set to on.
OLECMDF_NINCHED	The view object can't determine the state of a command that uses a toggle state. In most cases this means that the command uses a tri-state configuration and that it's in the indeterminate state. For example, a three-state check box will return this value if the user has selected some suboptions for an install program, but not others. (The check box appears grayed onscreen.)

Standard Exec
Method
Return Values
Table 5-4.

Flag	Description
PRINTFLAG_MAYBOTHERUSER	Tells the server that user interaction is allowed by the client. If this flag isn't set, then any print requests have to run by themselves. In most cases the client will allow user interaction—the only exception will probably involve batch printing jobs or situations where the print operation proceeds in the background.

Flags
Supported
by the Print
Method
of IPrint
Table 5-5.

5

Flag	Description
PRINTFLAG_PROMPTUSER	Prompts the user for input regarding the print job using the standard print dialog (like the one supported by Windows). For example, the user can select the number of copies when this option is specified. You must also specify the PRINTFLAG _MAYBOTHERUSERflag to use this option.
PRINTFLAG_USERMAYCHANGEPRINTER	Allows the user to change the printer. There are some situations where you won't want to enable this option—like network setups where the user can't easily access the printer. You must also specify the PRINTFLAG _PROMPTUSER flag to use this option.
PRINTFLAG_RECOMPOSETODEVICE	Tells the print job to recompose itself for the target printer. For example, if the target printer supports a higher resolution than currently specified as part of the print job, then the print job should make use of that higher resolution.
PRINTFLAG_DONTACTUALLYPRINT	Test the print job out, but don't actually create any output. This option allows you to test a user interface feature like prompting without wasting paper in the process.
PRINTFLAG_PRINTTOFILE	Send the printed output to a file instead of a printer.

Flags
Supported
by the Print
Method
of IPrint
(*continued*)
Table 5-5.

PART 2

ActiveX and the Environment

Chapter

6

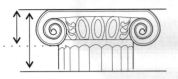

Addressing Security Concerns

Security is one of the major issues facing anyone building an Internet site today. It's hard to know who's harder pressed, the company building a public access Internet or the one trying to hide their presence with an intranet. No matter which environment you work in, a host of companies are preparing tools of various kinds and capabilities to address the needs of those who want to protect their data from harm. Unfortunately, all the nifty tools in the world won't prevent you from shooting yourself in the foot when building your own controls. (They also don't work very well when you use them in the wrong way.)

It would be ridiculous to attempt to cover in one chapter all of the various technologies available today, or even every security issue you'll ever run into. What we'll concentrate on instead is the programmer's perspective on security matters.

In fact, the focus will be even tighter than that—we'll spend most of our time looking at ActiveX controls in particular. This chapter will answer the question of what a programmer can do to protect not only data, but application code from harm. From a programmer's perspective, an ActiveX control isn't only a source of new browser capabilities, it's a potential source of viruses. Even the most careful attempts at protecting a control could prove inadequate unless the browser, programmer, and Internet site all work together to make security a reality.

We'll spend some time at the beginning of this chapter looking at the kinds of things that a programmer needs to think about in regard to security. Just who is involved with an Internet site and how? It's also important to know about the weak links in your organization and what harm they could cause by downloading controls from the Internet without too much thought. Unless you know who you're protecting and from what, the effort is a lost cause from the start.

The chapter will also spend some time on Internet security standards. Some programmers view standards of this type as a nuisance because they don't directly relate to programming. We won't waste a lot of time covering the content of those standards, but it's important to know that they exist and where you can find them. Most of you will agree that there isn't a good reason to reinvent the wheel when it comes to security. If someone else has already figured out a way to prevent harmful access in a standardized way that everyone can use, why not make use of that information? That's what the standards section is all about, letting you know what's available and how you can use the information that the standards contain.

Once we get past some of the more mundane concerns of security, we'll start looking at what you can do to implement it. Here's the problem. When Sun started creating Java applets, they took what's termed the "sandbox" approach to security. A Java applet can only play in its own sandbox—it can't access the operating system or even the hardware hosting the applet outside the strict areas that Sun thought the applet should access (which is pretty close to no access at all). The run-time engine you need in order to use a Java applet ensures that access is strictly controlled. The advantage of this approach is immediately clear—lack of access also means lack of security concerns. Unfortunately, this lack of access also severely limits what you can do with a Java applet, especially when it comes to data exchange of various sorts.

sn't bulletproof. Hackers have already found holes in
it make Java a less-than-perfect solution. For example,
ew Dean (ddean@ICS.Princeton.EDU) and Ed Felton
EDU), of the Princeton Department of Computer
a Java that allowed them to create an applet that
er's local disk. They did this by downloading a file
hrough the Netscape caching mechanism and then
ng the applet. Fortunately, this bug was fixed in the
e. You can find out about other potential security
http://www.cs.princeton.edu/sip/pub/secure96.html.

r tack with ActiveX controls, called the "shrink-wrap"
iveX control, you have full access to the system, just
shrink-wrapped piece of software. What this means
ome extremely flexible controls that make full use of
offer. There are no limitations from a data access
vever, from a security perspective, ActiveX could turn
it would prevent a control that you downloaded from
our system as you watched in horror? There's another
piece to this approach—vendor identification. When you buy a piece of
software at the store, you know who produced it. If the software contains a
virus or even a nasty bug, you know who to contact. We'll look at a certification
method that Microsoft is proposing for ActiveX controls that does the same
thing as the packaging for a piece of software you buy in the store—identifies
with certainty the vendor who created the software you're using.

Lest you think that scripts are easily monitored, we'll look at some of the
security concerns about running them in the "Making Windows NT Security
Work for You" section of the chapter. The short version is that neither VBScript
nor JavaScript are even close to safe (though more work has been done finding
the security holes in JavaScript). You can find out about the currently known
security problems with JavaScript at http://www.osf.org/~loverso/javascript/.
The following list presents three of the most common problems.

♦ **Tricking the user into uploading a file** Even though JavaScript
  has to ask the user's permission to upload a file, a hacker could hide this
  request in a variety of ways. All a hacker really needs is a button with an
  interesting caption. Uploaded password files like those used for Windows
  95 are easily broken—making the hacker's job of breaking into your
  system easy.

6

♦ **Obtaining file directories** A JavaScript doesn't have to ask anyone's permission to upload a directory of your machine. In fact, it can upload the directories of any network machines you have access to as well. Knowing the organization of your hard drive can go a long way toward allowing a hacker to break into your system.

♦ **Tracking sites visited** Hackers can learn a lot about you by keeping track of the Web sites you visit. A JavaScript makes this easy to do. It can track every URL you visit and send the addresses to the hacker's machine. As with the file upload problem, the user has to give permission to do this, but the hacker can disguise this permission as just about anything.

Finally, we'll spend some time looking at the various APIs and other tools that Microsoft has provided to make writing ActiveX controls at least a little safer. Especially important is a look at the native security provided by products such as Windows NT. Since you have full access to the operating system, why not use the security features that it provides to your advantage? The flexibility provided by ActiveX controls is both a benefit and a burden. The benefit is obvious to everyone. Some added security measures on your part will keep the burden pretty much out of view.

The Internet—Wild and Untamed

Some people view the Internet as today's Wild West of computers. There are few standards in place and even fewer security measures. Growth is exponential, as more people move onto the Internet to sell their wares. Even the growth of technology reflects the kind of environment that we often associate with the Wild West. It's the combination of home grown, new, and old technology, however, that threatens the Internet the most. For example, the current version of IP (Internet protocol) doesn't provide any method for encrypting data (at least not at the protocol level). The problem with this is that people need to send data over the Internet in such a way that no one else can easily read it, and you just don't have the tools to ensure that security 100 percent right now. Future versions of IP are supposed to fix this, but they aren't available today. The theme of future fixes prevails on the Internet—just as it did in the Old West, when people looked toward the promise of a brighter tomorrow. A lot of upgrades have been promised, but few are in place today. Surfing the Internet is fun for some people in part because it's so wild and untamed.

T IP: You can find out what kinds of security risks you're facing, especially when running a Web server, by reading The World Wide Web Security FAQ at http://www.genome.wi.mit.edu/WWW/faqs/www-security-faq.html. This white paper is a work in progress and includes specifics about the security risks of using certain browsers and servers. It includes Windows NT, UNIX, and Macintosh servers at the moment, with a definite bias toward the UNIX end of the spectrum. The paper also addresses many general questions, such as trying to find a balance between user privacy and your need to know who's accessing your site. You'll even find a What's New section to tell you how the document is growing as the Internet matures.

Just as the Wild West eventually became a much tamer environment, we'll eventually see changes in the Internet as well. Technologies such as ActiveX will help shape that future and make the Internet a place where people can transact business without fear of loss. These technologies will also make the Internet a friendlier place—just as cars and highways have made the West a lot easier to travel, these new technologies will help speed people on their way from one point to another.

One thing that will never change in the West—or on the Internet for that matter—is the need for security. Working in a secure environment is one of the ways in which society fosters innovation and all of the good things we associate with modern times. After all, if you're not spending all your time fighting the enemy (whoever that might be), you actually have time to work on artistic goals. The following sections discuss some of the concerns behind Internet security. It's important to define the security problem before you try to tackle it within an application. If you've already defined your security problems and want to get on with the task of implementing security, take a look at the section, "Internet Security Standards." Otherwise, let's take some time to consider a few of the problems you'll face as you try to make the Internet a viable tool for your company.

6

The Business Perspective of the Internet

As previously mentioned, part of the thrill of the Internet for many users is the fact that it's untamed—you can literally find anything on the Internet because no one's regulating it. (Even though the U.S. government recently tried to regulate online services, they weren't very successful.) If you're a programmer, the untamed environment of the Internet may have a certain appeal, but you won't be building applications for yourself. You must consider the needs of the businesspeople that you'll work with. Businesspeople tend not to be in the crowd searching for cheap thrills. The idea of an untamed environment is more of a nightmare than a fantasy for your typical business user, who wants everything defined, well ordered, and most of all, secure.

The extreme growth rate of the Internet isn't doing anything to instill confidence in business users either. New and untested technology is simply an accident waiting to happen in some business users' minds. Consider the potential gains and losses of ActiveX controls. Sure, they'll allow business users to get things done more quickly, but there's still that security element to take into consideration. Anyone with a modicum of programming skills could create a potentially devastating control that would destroy everything that a company holds dear.

Recent trade paper surveys show that big companies are taking things slow when it comes to the Internet. One of the biggest factors they cite for this slow approach is the lack of security. Businesses want to be sure that the technology is stable and that their data will be safe before making any kind of commitment. One way to build the perceived trust level of the Internet is to write good applications in-house. Stated another way, building ActiveX controls that really work is even more critical than for many other application classes.

NOTE: Business users will need to deal with a host of issues that don't affect the programmer in a general sense, such as whether to allow employees to access the Internet and what level of access to allow. Certainly the debate over these issues will remain heated for quite some time, but we won't cover them in this chapter. Only the programmer-specific issues appear here.

So, how do you tackle this problem of security? Talking with management at the company you're working for is one way to pursue things. If you can find out what concerns they have in regard to the applications you write, you can likely address those needs specifically as part of the application. For example, we'll look at the methods you can use to access the built-in security provided with a Windows NT server later in this chapter. The downside to this approach is that addressing security concerns with a lot of added code will definitely slow the application down and could make it harder for users as well. Make sure you also tell management the trade-offs they're making during the design phase of the application (and ultimately the Web site).

Defining the Object of Protection—Data

So what are you trying to protect? You'll get a surprising number of answers, but they all point to one thing. When all is said and done, keeping data safe is the most important reason for security on the network. Hardware and application concerns take a back seat to data concerns. Lose a hard drive and you can replace it—kill a software configuration and you can reinstall it—lose last week's report on the company's finances and you're the only person who can reproduce it. Data is the most precious part of the computing environment simply because you will have to fight hard to replace it once it's lost.

Securing data has always been a major concern for anyone responsible for its use (and potential misuse). Some network administrators spend more time looking after security concerns than just about anything else. In most cases, the security concerns deal with who has access to what data and why. Look in any trade press, and you'll find article after article on data security— it doesn't matter whether you're looking at a magazine or weekly paper, the effect is the same. The data we produce with computers fills every second of every day; there isn't any doubting its value to you and your company. When you build an ActiveX control and attach it to an HTML page, your major security concern is the data that you'll provide access to.

Data security revolves around access. Whether it's access to a local machine or access to your network, the goal of preventing unauthorized access is the same. Trying to create a secure environment on a local machine is fairly easy. Besides all of the software mechanisms available, many computers also come with BIOS-level password protection. If this isn't enough, you can always resort to physical security to make sure that no one can access your system. Keeping things secure on a LAN gets a little harder, but you can still do it without too much effort. Network operating system products such as Novell's NetWare and Windows NT are rife with various kinds of security measures designed to make local data access difficult at best (unless someone physically cuts through the cabling and starts to ferret things out with a network sniffer). Implementing security on a WAN can be a nightmare— especially if you have a lot of dial-in connections. No longer are all your connections in one place—software and hardware entry points abound, making it a lot easier for someone to break in without your knowing it (at least for a while). Some people have gone so far as to say that implementing security on the Internet might be impossible. Not only do you have the significant problems posed by a WAN environment, but you have the public access provided by the Internet itself. Anyone reading recent trade presses

6

knows how hard vendors are trying to plug security holes in their products, only to find that someone has found yet another way through the system.

Creating Some Form of Protection

Even if you try to ignore Internet-specific security problems for the moment, there are other issues to consider when it comes to data protection. For example, what kind of protection do you want to provide? Let's take a non-Internet view for a second. In this environment, you can view protection from a hardware or software perspective as a physical means for preventing access to your computer or network by unauthorized persons. Providing a secure workstation as a separate entity from everything else is one way that some companies deal with data requiring special care. This physical separation from the network means that anyone requesting access to the data on the workstation actually has to use that workstation. You can prevent access using locks if necessary in this case. Other companies deal with this issue through the use of data encryption or by performing security audits—both of which are software-specific security schemes.

Unfortunately, you can't set a computer in the corner of a room and lock it up to protect data you have on the Internet. This means that the hardware alternatives that a company used in the past are probably out of the picture as far as the Internet goes—at least when looking at the workstation view of things. The loss of hardware-level protection places an additional burden on the programmer. As a programmer, you'll be responsible for adding some measure of security to the ActiveX controls you create. Fortunately, you can look at the way things are done now for dealing with the new security issues posed by the Internet. For example, document encryption is still a valuable data protection technique. An encrypted document is just as secure on an Internet site as it is on the WAN—the only difference is the number of people that your company allows to access that document.

Now that we've looked at workstations (which you'll find difficult at best to protect) and data (which you could protect using encryption), let's look at the server. From an Internet perspective, some companies are implementing their site using a server that's physically separate from the rest of their network (which definitely reduces the number of ways in which you can use that server for company-specific needs). Using a separate server is the hardware approach to keeping your network secure. No one can see the data on your network if there isn't any connection from your Web server to the rest of the network. The software solution comes in the form of firewalls—essentially another form of the same login procedure we've used for years on LANs.

There are practical limitations to what you can take from the setup you currently use and the one you'll need to implement. One of the main concerns as far as Internet access goes is flexibility. Sure, you can lock down your site to the point that no one can access it, but what's the point? Resorting to inflexible and harsh tactics to enforce security probably won't buy you much because it runs counter to the free access that the Internet is supposed to espouse. Learning new ways to make security strong without impinging on the level of access enjoyed by people using your Web site is the challenge you'll face. From a programmer's perspective, this means that you'll have to learn about the capabilities of the hardware and software installed on the network before you'll even begin to make a dent in the security concerns that the Internet introduces.

Implementing a Solution

It doesn't take long to figure out that creating a secure environment is a big issue. It takes time and effort to create even a basic security plan. Implementing the plan takes even longer, especially if you're trying to reduce the impact on the working environment by taking a phased approach. Even if you write a great security plan and do your best to cover every contingency, you can never be quite sure that you've covered all the bases. When someone finally breaks through your security and damages some data—it could mean the end of your job. Situations like this are enough to make any network administrator paranoid.

Once you consider all of these potential problems, it's not too hard to figure out why network administrators are constantly clamping down on user freedom when it comes to even the most innocuous things. For example, some network administrators are firmly against any form of Internet access for their company, while others take a Big Brother approach to monitoring user activity once Internet access is approved.

Network administration and data protection aren't the only security issues you'll face when setting up a Web site of any kind. It's also important to consider the user end of the question. How would you like it if someone told you that a connection was secure and you found out it wasn't? A lot of credit card users really don't want to take that risk. A non-secure connection from their computer to a Web site could mean thousands of dollars in credit card charges before they get the chance to even stop payment.

When it comes time to implement a security solution, make sure you have all of the facts. The ActiveX controls you create can go a long way toward ensuring that the data exchanged by a client and server is secure. Taking time to consider the full impact of all the needs of everyone using the

6

Internet is essential if you want to make your Internet site as bulletproof as possible. Then, when the unthinkable happens and someone does break through your security, a security plan can help you react quickly, to plug any holes in your security net.

Internet Security Standards

The previous section concentrated on telling you all of the problems you'll face when writing code for the Internet. All of those problems are real, but you don't have to face them alone. Standards groups are working even as you read this to come up with methods for protecting data. All you need to do is learn the methods that these groups come up with for managing security on your Web site. The advantages to going this route are twofold. First, you won't have to reinvent the wheel and come up with everything from scratch. Second, your security methods will mesh with those used by other sites, reducing the user learning curve and making it possible for you to use tools developed for other programmers.

T IP: If you want to find out the latest information on where the Internet is going with security standards, take a look at http://www.w3.org/pub/WWW/Security/. This page of general information won't provide everything you need, but it will give you places to look and links to other sites that do provide additional material. Another good place to look for information is the WWW Security References page of Rutgers University Network Services at http://www-ns.rutgers.edu/www-security/reference.html. For the most part this site tells you who to contact and provides abstracts of various security meetings rather than actual specifications. Developers will want to get the commercial view of security at http://www.rsa.com/. The RSA site covers a pretty broad range of topics, including the current status of efforts by MasterCard and VISA to create secure credit card transactions. You can also find out the current status of IETF efforts by viewing the document at ftp://ftp.isi.edu/internet-drafts/1id-abstracts.txt.

Let's take a quick look at the various types of standards that have either become fact or should be emerging soon. Table 6-1 shows the standards or standards drafts that were available at the time of this writing. You may find even more available by the time you read this. It's a surprising fact that vendor standards are probably the fastest growing area of the Internet right now besides browser technology (which seems to be growing at such a fast rate that even the beta testers have a hard time keeping up). You'll also notice that the majority of standards listed here aren't from Microsoft or some other company—they come from one of two groups: the IETF (Internet Engineering Task Force) or a group known as W^{3}C (World Wide Web Consortium). IETF has been around for a long time—we discussed this organization in Chapter 1 as part of the Internet history section. They're one of the very first groups to work with the Internet. Be prepared to read a lot about the W^{3}C group as you delve into Internet security issues (and to a lesser extent other standards areas such as HTML tags as well). They're the ones responsible for newer standards of every kind when it comes to the Internet. For example, Microsoft is currently trying to get them to accept the <OBJECT> tag and other ActiveX-related HTML extensions.

Most of the IETF RFC documents can be found at http://ds.internic.net/rfc/.

The security standards in Table 6-1 represent the Internet end of the security picture. It's important to keep this fact in mind. All that these standards really cover is the connection between the client and server. You can still add other security measures at the client, the server, or both. Most of these standards don't cover Internet add-on products such as firewalls either. Your company can add these additional security features and at least make it more difficult for someone to break into their system.

TIP: Just in case you don't have enough security information yet, you can always spend time looking at the IETF informational sites. Two of the current sites are gopher://ds1.internic.net/00/fyi/fyi8.txt (Site Security Handbook) and gopher://ds1.internic.net/00/fyi/fyi25.txt (A Status Report on Networked Information Retrieval).

6

Who Is W^{3}C?

Before we go much further, let's take a quick look at the W^{3}C organization. They first appeared on the scene in December 1994 when they endorsed SSL (Secure Sockets Layer). In February 1995 they also endorsed application-level security for the Internet. Their current project is the Digital Signature Initiative—W^{3}C presented it in May 1996 in Paris. As you can see, W^{3}C started as a standards organization devoted to security needs. Some of their other functions have evolved from that starting point.

TIP: There's a lot of concern over the safety of using SSL right now because some computer hackers could conceivably break the encryption in specific cases. The U.S. government restricts exported encryption technology to a 40-bit key. A computer could break such a key by trying all 2^{40} key combinations. Encryption programs made for U.S. use only can use a 128-bit key, which means that someone would have to have the patience to wait until the computer tries all 2^{128} key combinations (not in your lifetime). So, how do you determine the safety level of a transaction? Netscape makes it easy. Just look at the key in the lower-left corner of the screen. A broken key means no encryption, a single-toothed key means 40-bit encryption, and a double-toothed key means 128-bit encryption. Both Netscape and Internet Explorer also offer a Document Properties dialog as part of the File menu. Simply check this dialog to see what kind of protection a particular site offers.

So, why do we need yet another standards organization? The main idea is to get the major industry players to work together toward the goal of creating a secure Internet environment. In addition, some standards groups—the IETF for one—are staffed by volunteers and move too slowly to make the changes currently required by the industry. W^3C is an effort to add some semblance of order by allowing change to happen faster, yet in an organized way.

Standard	Description
Distributed Authentication Security Service (DASS) IETF RFC1507	DASS is an IETF work in progress. It defines an experimental method for providing authentication services on the Internet. The goal of authentication in this case is to verify who sent a message or request. Current password schemes have a number of problems that DASS tries to solve. For example, there is no way to verify that the sender of a password isn't impersonating someone else. DASS provides authentication services in a distributed environment. Distributed environments present special challenges because users don't log onto just one machine—they could conceivably log onto every machine onto the network.

Current Security Standards for the Internet
Table 6-1.

Standard	Description
DSI (Digital Signatures Initiative)	This is a standard originated by W^3C to overcome some limitations of channel-level security. For example, channel-level security can't deal with documents and application semantics. A channel also doesn't use the Internet's bandwidth very efficiently because all the processing takes place on the Internet rather than the client or server. DSI defines a mathematical method for transferring signatures—essentially a unique representation of a specific individual or company. DSI also provides a new method for labeling security properties (PICS2) and a new format for assertions (PEP). This standard is also built on the PKCS7 and X509.v3 standards.
Extended Internet Tag SHTTP (EIT SHTTP)	This extension to SHTTP (described later in this table) would add security-related tags to the current HTTP list. There is no standards organization support for this technology now, but there could be in the future. (The Web Transaction Security—WTS—group of the IETF was recently formed for looking at potential specifications like this one. You can contact them at http://www-ns.rutgers.edu/www-security/wts-wg.html.)
Generic Security Service Application Program Interface (GSS-API) IETF RFC1508	This is an approved IETF specification that defines methods for supporting security service calls in a generic manner. Using a generic interface allows greater source code portability on a wider range of platforms. IETF doesn't see this specification as the end of the process, but rather the starting point for other, more specific, standards in the future. However, knowing that this standard exists can help you find the thread of commonality between various security implementation methods.

Current Security Standards for the Internet (*continued*)

Table 6-1.

Standard	Description
Generic Security Service Application Program Interface (GSS-API) C-bindings IETF RFC1508	This is an approved IETF specification that defines methods for supporting service calls using C. It's one of the first specific implementation standards based on RFC1508.
Internet Protocol Security Protocol (IPSec)	IETF recently created the IP Security Protocol working group to look at the problems of IP security, such as the inability to encrypt data at the protocol level. They're currently working on a wide range of specifications that will ultimately result in more secure IP transactions. You can find out more about this group at http://www.ietf.cnri.reston. va.us/html.charters/ipsec-charter.html.
JEPI (Joint Electronic Payment Initiative)	A standard originated by W^3C, JEPI provides a method for creating electronic commerce. Transactions will use some form of electronic cash or credit cards. Data transfers from the client to the server will use encryption, digital signatures, and authentication (key exchange) to ensure a secure exchange. This is an emerging standard—some items, such as transport-level security (also called privacy), are currently making their way through the IETF.
PCT (Private Communication Technology)	The IETF is working with Microsoft on this particular protocol. Like SSL, PCT is designed to provide a secure method of communication between a client and server at the low protocol level. It can work with any high-level protocol such as HTTP, FTP, or TELNET. We'll discuss this protocol in detail in the "Private Communication Technology (PCT)" section of the chapter. You can find updates at http://www.lne. com/ericm/pct.html.

Current Security Standards for the Internet (*continued*)

Table 6-1.

Standard	Description
Privacy Enhanced Mail Part I (PEM1) Message Encryption and Authentication Procedures IETF RFC1421	This is an approved IETF specification for ensuring that your private mail remains private. Essentially, it outlines a procedure for encrypting mail in such a way that the user's mail is protected, but the process of decrypting it is invisible. This includes the use of keys and other forms of certificate management. Some of the specification is based on the CCITT X.400 specification— especially in the areas of Mail Handling Service (MHS) and Mail Transfer System (MTS). You can contact the PEM working group at http://www.ietf.cnri.reston.va.us/html.charters/pem-charter.html.
Privacy Enhanced Mail Part II (PEM2) Certificate-Based Key Management IETF RFC1422	This is an approved IETF specification for managing security keys. It provides both an infrastructure and management architecture based on a public key certification technique. IETF RFC1422 is an enhancement of the CCITT X.509 specification. It goes beyond the CCITT specification by providing procedures and conventions for a key management infrastructure for use with PEM.
Privacy Enhanced Mail Part III (PEM3) Algorithms, Modes, and Identifiers IETF RFC1423	This is an approved IETF specification that defines cryptographic algorithms, usage modes, and identifiers specifically for PEM use. The specification covers four main areas of encryption-related information: message encryption algorithms, message integrity check algorithms, symmetric key management algorithms, and asymmetric key management algorithms (including both symmetric encryption and asymmetric signature algorithms).

Current
Security
Standards for
the Internet
(*continued*)
Table 6-1.

6

Standard	Description
Privacy Enhanced Mail Part IV (PEM4) Key Certification and Related Services IETF RFC1424	This is an approved IETF specification that defines the method for certifying keys. It also provides a listing of cryptographic-related services that an Internet site would need to provide to the end user.
Secure/Multipurpose Internet Mail Extensions (S/MIME)	This is a specification being promoted by a consortium of vendors, including Microsoft, Banyan, VeriSign, ConnectSoft, QUALCOMM, Frontier Technologies, Network Computing Devices, FTP Software, Wollongong, SecureWare, and Lotus. It was originally developed by RSA Data Security, Inc. as a method for different developers to create message transfer agents (MTAs) that used compatible encryption technology. Essentially, this means that if someone sends you a message using a Lotus product, you can read it with your Banyan product. S/MIME is based on the popular Internet MIME standard (RFC1521).
Secure/Wide Area Network (S/WAN)	S/WAN is only a glimmer in some people's eyes at the moment. It's an initiative supported by RSA Data Security, Inc. The IETF has a committee working on it as well. RSA intends to incorporate the IETF's IPSec standard into S/WAN. The main goal of S/WAN is to allow companies to mix-and-match the best firewall and TCP/IP stack products to build Internet-based Virtual Private Networks (VPNs). Current solutions usually lock the user into a single source for both products.

Current Security Standards for the Internet (*continued*)

Table 6-1.

Standard	Description
SHTTP (Secure Hypertext Transfer Protocol)	This is the current encrypted data transfer technology used by Open Marketplace Server, which is similar in functionality to SSL. The big difference is that this method only works with HTTP. There is no standards organization support for this technology now, but there could be in the future. (The Web Transaction Security—WTS—group of the IETF was recently formed for looking at potential specifications like this one.)
SSL (Secure Sockets Layer)	This is a W^3C standard originally proposed by Netscape for transferring encrypted information from the client to the server at the protocol layer. Sockets allow low-level encryption of transactions in higher-level protocols such as HTTP, NNTP, and FTP. The standard also specifies methods for server and client authentication (though client site authentication is optional). You can find details about SSL at http://home.netscape.com/info/SSL.html.
The Kerberos Network Authentication Service (V5) IETF RFC1510	This is an approved IETF specification that defines a third-party authentication protocol. The Kerberos model is based in part on Needham and Schroeder's trusted third-party authentication protocol and on modifications suggested by Denning and Sacco. As with many Internet authentication protocols, Kerberos works as a trusted third-party authentication service. It uses conventional cryptography that relies on a combination of shared public key and private key. Kerberos emphasizes client authentication with optional server authentication.

Current
Security
Standards for
the Internet
(*continued*)

Table 6-1.

6

Standard	Description
Universal Resource Identifiers (URI) in WWW IETF RFC1630	URI is an IETF work in progress. Currently, resource names and addresses are provided in clear text. An URL (uniform resource locator) is actually a form of URI containing an address that maps to a specific location on the Internet. URI would provide a means of encoding the names and addresses of Internet objects. In essence, to visit a private site, you would need to know the encoded name instead of the clear text name. You can contact the URI workgroup at http://www. ietf.cnri.reston.va.us/html.charters/uri-charter.html.

Current Security Standards for the Internet (*continued*)
Table 6-1.

Finally, the W^{3}C is there to provide the actual specifications (a place where you can find out what a specification is all about), demonstrations of applications that comply with the standards, and prototype code as needed so others can create applications that comply with the standards.

Another project that W^{3}C is working on is the Joint Electronic Payment Initiative (JEPI), one of the standards that will affect future commerce on the Internet. It's amazing to think that someone from England, France, Germany, or America could visit the same Web site and buy the exact same items for the same price. Before this can be done, there are some problems that need to be worked out. For example, do you ask "customers" to provide a method of payment before they enter your electronic store, or do you wait until they've "filled their shopping cart," then ask for some method of payment? What kind of payment do you need to accept? You have to think beyond paper currency, since there isn't any way to exchange it electronically. Credit cards offer one solution, but W^{3}C is also exploring other avenues such as electronic checks, debit cards, and electronic cash. This is one of the smaller issues. A major issue is coming up with some kind of noncurrency-related method for pricing. How do you tell people in Germany that the price of a coat is $80? Would they really understand what a dollar is if they haven't been exposed to it? As for Americans, they could visit an English store and find that they needed to deal with the pound.

So what does JEPI have to do with security? Think about transactions as a whole. Your company may not have to deal with a customer wanting to buy a coat, but you may have to deal with other transaction-related issues. A large company may want to provide a faster, more efficient means to move money from one area of the world to another. Electronic commerce over the Internet could eventually provide an answer. OK, so that's not in your immediate future. What about travel? Just about every company has to deal with traveling employees. What do you do when they run out of cash? Right now you issue a credit card and hope for the best. Wouldn't it be nice, though, if you could get a daily report on expenditures over the Internet? Right now, it's not really a good idea to do so because there are too many security holes. These commerce standards will help companies create new methods of transferring sensitive information from one place to another.

Standard Methods of Handling Money

You may run into a situation in which you have to find a way to accept money at your Web site. The most obvious situation is if your company sells a product of any kind—whether it's something you would buy at the mall or not is probably immaterial. You could sell widgets just as easily over the Internet as you could any other way. In fact, you might even be able to sell them better. Other situations could include services. For example, you might provide a method for customers to pay their bills electronically rather than send you a check in the mail. There are rumors that at least one telephone company is looking into this possibility. A small business might find Internet transactions more trouble than they're worth, but certainly medium and large companies will embrace this method somewhere along the way. Banks and credit card companies will eventually get into the picture as well. In fact, you can already get a Web Conductor VISA card by filling out a form online (check out http://www.conductor.com/ for more details). This particular card allows you to view statements and request services online. In the near future it will also allow you to make payments online, reducing the amount of time spent filling checks out by hand.

6

There are currently three different common schemes for implementing a cash-handling capability on your Web server: First Virtual Accounts, DigiCash, and Cybercash. Each one has different strengths and weaknesses that we'll talk about in the next few paragraphs. The important thing to realize now is that none of these schemes is perfect, and you'll probably have to compromise in some areas to make a solution work for right now. If that statement makes you feel uneasy, it should. A lot of major financial companies are currently working toward some method of making financial transactions totally secure, but it wouldn't be safe to say they're available today.

From an implementation point of view, the First Virtual Accounts scheme is the easiest to use. Users sign up for a First Virtual Account over the phone and receive a special account number that has nothing to do with the credit card they supplied. Vendors who support this scheme accept the account number using a secure certificate. Every transaction uses this special number instead of a real credit card number—reducing the risk of someone stealing your credit card and using it without your knowledge. The vendor turns any transactions over to First Virtual Accounts, and they verify the transaction with the user. When the user approves the transaction, the vendor receives payment and ships whatever product the user requested. You can find out more about First Virtual Accounts at http://www.fv.com/.

DigiCash has the advantage of using real money for transactions instead of credit. This means vendors don't have to pay credit card surcharges. In addition, DigiCash has the advantage of working just like an ATM debit card—vendors get real money today instead of waiting for the credit card company to honor a transaction. This particular scheme requires the user to make a deposit at a special bank. The bank sets up an account, just like a checking account, except that it works online. When the user makes a purchase, he or she uses "E-cash" instead of credit. The vendor simply turns in the E-cash and gets real money in return. Obviously, the user must replenish the account from time to time, just as you would any other bank account. You can contact DigiCash at http://www.digicash.nl/.

Cybercash is a combination of the previous two transaction schemes. It provides both debit and credit capabilities—sort of like a bank account with overdraft protection. Unlike the other two schemes, Cybercash uses real account information. This represents a risk to users since their account information could end up anywhere in unencrypted form if the vendor is of the less scrupulous sort. When users make a purchase, Cybercash pops up a window that requests their account information. In credit mode users supply the name and number of their credit card. In debit mode they provide the name of a local bank and their account number at that bank. You can find out more about Cybercash at http://www.cybercash.com.

NOTE: The banks and credit card companies aren't the only ones talking about online transactions. At least one browser company, Netscape, is talking about them as well. Netscape Communications Corporation has made deals with both First Data, a large credit card processor, and MasterCard to incorporate credit card processing into the Netscape/Netsite combination. You can find out more at http://www.mcom.com/. Open Market, Inc., the Web server company, is also working on an online transaction scheme based on SHTTP. They'll act as the bank and credit card company if you sign up for this scheme. You can find out more about this endeavor at http://www.openmarket.com.

Making Windows NT Security Work for You

Windows NT provides a level of security that almost verges on paranoia for an operating system. It allows you to set security in a variety of ways, including both the familiar user and file levels. You can also create groups and assign security by using groups instead of individuals. In addition, you can monitor every aspect of the security system using various alarms and log files. Windows NT excels in the way that it actually monitors system activity. Not one event goes without some kind of scrutiny. It's this level of security that makes Windows NT an excellent platform for a Web site. In addition, you can actually improve on most of the standard features provided by a Web site if you go through the added trouble of actually writing code to use the features that Windows NT provides.

So, why would you want to go to all the effort of building additional Windows NT-specific security into your application? For one thing, there are holes in the current API specifications for Internet security. For example, we've already talked about Internet Component Download service— we looked at the process itself in Chapter 4 as part of the discussion on downloading from the Internet. There are methods that an unscrupulous person could use to bypass all of the security features we discussed in that chapter as a result of holes in the current defenses provided by the various browsers on the market. (We'll concentrate on Internet Explorer, but you can be sure Netscape and other browsers have the same, slightly different, or even worse problems.) These security holes aren't in the API itself, but in some of the creative solutions people used in the past to make the Internet work. In essence, problem-solving in the past created security back doors in the present. The following list tells you about three of the holes in Internet Component Download service (though it's almost certain that more holes exist).

6

♦ **HTML <A HREF> tag** There are ways to download and run an EXE file using the <A HREF> tag. The current method used by Internet Explorer 3.0 to keep this problem in check is to have the HTML parser use the URL moniker directly to download the code, then the parser calls WinVerifyTrust to check code validity (this is the same technique described in Chapter 4). Is this method 100 percent safe? No, because you're using something other than the standard procedure to verify the contents of a file. In this case you're relying on the HTML parser.

♦ **Scripts** Right now scripts are totally free of any kind of security check. There is no way to verify who created the script or what it might do to your machine. Microsoft is working right now to create some kind of script certificate. Once script certificates become a reality, the browser can call WinVerifyTrust to check a script before running it.

♦ **Full applications or other complex download situations**
Internet Explorer does a good job of checking specific kinds of downloads
right now. For example, downloading an OCX initiates a WinVerifyTrust
sequence. What happens if the download parameters fall outside the
limited scope of things checked by Internet Explorer? For example, a
user might want to download and install *Doom* or some other game
program. The installation sequence might include unpredictable actions
such as making registry entries and rebooting the machine. Internet
Explorer can't handle that situation at the moment. Microsoft plans
to make future versions of component download more robust so that it
can handle such events.

TIP: Part of your protection strategy is going to include testing multiple
browsers to see how they react—especially if you're creating a public access
Web site. As a programmer working with multiple products, you still have to
keep track of all the Web sites you visit on a regular basis for ideas. A product
called NavEx allows you to create copies of your Internet Explorer Favorite
Places folder as Netscape bookmarks and vice versa. You can download it at
http://mach5.noc.drexel.edu/navex/download.html.

We've also looked at holes in other types of Internet technology in this
chapter. For example, Table 6-1 is full of new specifications designed to
plug the holes in the technology we use today. SHTTP, S/WAN, and other
technologies like them wouldn't be needed if security didn't present a problem.
There's even a new version of MIME called S/MIME to make sure that no
one reads your mail.

One of the first steps in understanding how Windows NT can help you
enhance the security of your Internet site is to look at the basic security
features offered by the operating system itself. You can access those features
using an OCX. Of course, some features, such as mapping a drive, don't
make much sense in the realm of Internet security. However, other features
do make sense. For example, you could use the password protection features
of Windows NT to display a logon dialog every time someone requests secure
access to your site. This actually accomplishes two things. First, the password
security provided by Windows NT is a lot better than that provided by
Windows 95. A hacker will have a pretty tough time getting past the logon
dialog without the right password. Second, you can tell the server to log every
secure access—remember that Windows NT gives you the capability of
monitoring everything. If someone does manage to break into your system,

you'll at least know which account they used. Having an account name will allow you to assess the level of damage the hacker could inflict based on the security level of the person whose account was broken into.

The next few sections of the chapter take a look at several new technologies that you'll either find embedded in Windows NT, one of the Internet servers that it supports such as Microsoft Internet Information Server or Peer Web Services (provided free with Windows NT 4.0), or one of the new browsers. It's interesting to see that Internet Explorer 3.0 provides built-in SSL support, as does the new version of Netscape Navigator. You'll also find PCT support in at least Internet Explorer (the new version of Netscape Navigator is still in beta as of this writing). We'll also take a look at the Authenticode (digital signature) technology used by several vendors now to allow programmers to digitally sign their work. Any tampering with the code after that will show up when the user tries to download the program. The result is that it's less likely that you or one of your users will download a virus-infected program.

Encryption is another potential way of keeping your data safe, so we'll visit the CryptoAPI that Microsoft has developed. This particular bit of technology is included in at least a rough form in Internet Explorer. However, even though you can do some work with it now, the CryptoAPI is really a work in progress. In addition, the development kit required to expand on the CryptoAPI is only available in the United States and Canada—making this feature one of limited appeal for the moment.

Built-in Security Features

Windows NT is about the most overengineered operating system on the market today when it comes to security. If you have any doubt as to the importance of security with Microsoft, just look at some of the qualifications that Windows NT presents. You can use that capability to your advantage. For example, you could make use of those advanced capabilities within an OCX or grant access to specific features over the Internet. You'll have to use a lot of restraint in doing this because you don't want to damage your security net. In addition, it's impractical to use some features from the Internet because they just aren't important.

6

Fortunately, ActiveX controls aren't necessarily restricted to the Internet either. There isn't any rule saying that you couldn't create a control designed specifically for use within applications. An ActiveX control in a database or other application normally used by a network administrator (or other qualified person) could make that task a lot easier and more secure. In fact, an ActiveX control can take on multiple personalities if you want it to. You could even add the capability to detect the control's current location or perhaps add a special location field as part of a property page setup. Someone could choose a subset of features for Internet use, another set of features for LAN use, and still another set of features for local use.

About now, many of you are asking what kind of administrator would need to access security, but wouldn't use the tools provided by the NOS to do so. Windows NT actually provides a lot of very easy-to-use tools, so adding a lot of functionality isn't worthwhile in the minds of some programmers. There are actually a few good answers to this, but there's one situation that almost always comes to mind when most people think about security under Windows NT. What if the person administering the application isn't a network administrator—someone with the training to work with the NOS itself? Say that person is a workgroup manager or other individual who doesn't need the whole network picture—just enough information to maintain the application he or she is responsible for managing. You'll find yourself in that situation a lot more often than you might think. Large companies with a lot of small workgroups frequently fall into this category. The network administrator doesn't have the knowledge needed to administer the application correctly, but he or she doesn't want the workgroup manager crawling around the network either.

Whether you're creating a control for Internet, local, WAN, or LAN use, you'll find that a good understanding of the underlying network security architecture is essential. Windows 95 doesn't provide the same level of security that Windows NT does, so you'll find yourself doing without added security under Windows 95 at times. However, when Windows 95 does provide a security feature, it uses the same setup as Windows NT, so one security module will work with both of them. (In other cases you'll definitely want to use a separate module for Windows NT to make better use of its enhanced security capabilities—see the following note for details.)

NOTE: Windows NT does support a lot more Windows security API calls than Windows 95 does, because its security is a lot more robust. In fact, you'll find that your ability to manage security when using Windows 95 is severely hampered by its lack of support for Windows NT security features. For example, you can't use the GetUserObjectSecurity call under Windows 95. Most of the access token calls that we'll look at in the next section won't work either. The best way to figure out whether a call is supported or not is to test it. If you get ERROR_CALL_NOT_IMPLEMENTED (value 120) returned from the call, you know that you can only use it under Windows NT.

Windows NT and Windows 95 both use the term *object* rather loosely. It's true that a lot of objects are lurking beneath the surface, but you may not find that they fit precisely within the C++ usage of the term. In general, in the next few sections, we'll look at an object as the encapsulation of code and data required to perform a specific security task. In other words, each security object is a self-contained unit designed to fulfill a specific role. (In many places in both Windows 95 and Windows NT, Microsoft chose to use the full C++ version of an object mainly because they implemented the required functionality as part of MFC. However, you shouldn't depend on the definition of an object when reading either the Microsoft documentation or this chapter to mean a strict C++ object—think of objects more in the COM sense of the word.)

Knowing that everything is an object makes security a bit easier to understand—at least it's a starting point. However, objects are just a starting point. Users are the other part of the security equation. An object is accessed by a user—so security in Windows is a matter of comparing the object's protection to the user's rights. If the user has sufficient rights (rights that meet or exceed those of the object), then he or she can use the object. The Windows documentation refers to an object's level of protection as a *security descriptor*. This is the structure that tells the security system what rights a user needs to access the object. Likewise, the user has an *access token*, which is another structure that tells the security system what rights a user has in a given situation. *Token* is a good word here because the user will give Windows NT the token in exchange for access to the object. (Think of the object as a bus with Windows NT as the driver and the user presenting the required token to board.) Figure 6-1 shows both of these structures.

This is the shortest look you can take at security under either Windows 95 or Windows NT. Simply knowing that there are security objects and user tokens will go a long way toward helping you make sense out of the Windows security API calls. In the following sections we'll take a more detailed look at precisely what a token is and how it works. We'll also look at the security descriptor. You don't absolutely have to know this information to implement security using ActiveX if your only interest is the Internet, but knowing it can help you design ActiveX controls of a more general nature and wider appeal.

6

Understanding Access Tokens

You'll find that there are two of ways of looking at a user's rights under Windows—both of them related to objects in one form or another. The user's access token has a security identifier (SID) to identify the user throughout the network—it's like having an account number. The user

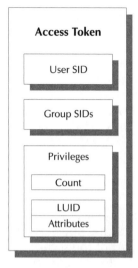

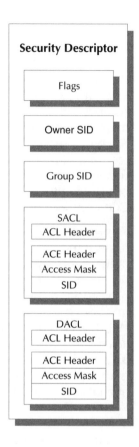

Access tokens
define the
user's rights,
while security
descriptors
define the
protection
level for a
process.

Figure 6-1.

token that the SID identifies tells what groups the user belongs to and what privileges the user has. Each group also has a SID, so the user's SID contains references to the various group SIDs that the user belongs to, not to a complete set of group access rights. You would normally use the User Manager utility under Windows NT to change the contents of this access token.

So, what's the privileges section of the access token all about? It begins with a count of the number of privileges that the user has—not the groups that the user belongs to, but the number of special privilege entries in the access token. This section also contains an array of privilege entries. Each privilege entry contains a locally unique identifier (LUID)—essentially a pointer to an object—and an attribute mask. The attribute mask tells what rights the user has to the object. Group SID entries are essentially the same. They contain a privilege count and an array of privilege entries.

T **IP:**   Now would probably be a good time to look at the Windows API help file provided with your copy of C, Visual Basic, or Delphi and see what kind of SID- and token-related API calls you can find. Examples of SID-related calls include CopySID and AllocateAndInitializeSID. You'll also find that the OpenProcessToken and GetTokenInformation calls are essential to making security work correctly with any language you use.

Using Access Tokens

Let's talk briefly about the Token calls that the Windows API provides, since they are the first stepping-stone that you'll need to know about when it comes to security. To do anything with a user's account—even if you want to find out who has access to a particular workstation—you need to know about tokens. As previously stated, tokens are the central part of the user side of the security equation. You'll almost always begin a user account access with a call to the OpenProcessToken call. Notice the name of this call—it deals with any kind of a process—user or otherwise. The whole purpose of this call is to get a token handle with specific rights attached to it. For example, if you want to query the user account, you need the TOKEN_QUERY privilege. (Your access token must contain the rights that you request from the system, which is why an administrator can access a token, but other users can't.) Any changes to the user's account require the TOKEN_ADJUST_PRIVILEGES privilege. There are quite a few of these access rights, so we won't go through them all here.

Once you have an access token handle, you need to decide what to do with it. If you decide you want to change a user's privilege to do something, you need the LUID for the privilege you want to change. All of these appear in the WINDOWS.PAS file with an SE_ attached to them. For example, the SE_SYSTEM_PROFILE_NAME privilege allows the user to gather profiling information for the entire system. Some SE values aren't related to users (for example, the SE_LOCK_MEMORY_NAME privilege that allows a process to lock system memory). You get the LUID for a privilege using the LookupPrivilegeValue call. Now you can combine the information you've gotten so far to change the privilege. Most generally, you'll use the AdjustTokenPrivileges call to make the required change.

Querying the user's account (or other access token information) is fairly straightforward. You use the GetTokenInformation call to retrieve any information you might need. This call requires a token class parameter, which tells Windows what kind of information you need. For example, you would use the TokenUser class if you wanted to know about a specific user.

6

You'll also need to supply an appropriate structure that Windows can use for storing the information you request—which differs based on the token class you request.

Understanding Security Descriptors

Now let's look at the security descriptor. Figure 6-1 shows that each security descriptor contains five main sections. The first section is a list of flags. These flags tell you the descriptor revision number, format, and ACL (access control list) status.

The next two sections contain SIDs. The owner SID tells who owns the object. This doesn't have to be an individual user; Windows allows you to use a group SID here as well. The one limiting factor is that the group SID must appear in the access token of the person changing the entry. The group SID allows a group of people to own the object. Of the two SIDs, only the owner SID is important under Windows. The group SID is used as part of the Macintosh and POSIX security environment.

The final two sections contain ACLs. The security access control list (SACL) controls Windows' auditing feature. Every time a user or group accesses an object and the auditing feature for that object is turned on, Windows makes an entry in the audit log. The discretionary access control list (DACL) controls who can actually use the object. You can assign both groups and individual users to a specific object.

NOTE: There are actually two types of security descriptors: absolute and self-relative. The absolute security descriptor contains an actual copy of each ACL within its structure. This is the type of security descriptor to use for an object that requires special handling. The self-relative security descriptor only contains a pointer to the SACL and DACL. This type of descriptor saves memory and reduces the time required to change the rights for a group of objects. You would use it when all the objects in a particular group require the same level of security. For example, you could use this method to secure all the threads within a single application. Windows requires that you convert a self-relative security descriptor to absolute format before you can save it or transfer it to another process. Every descriptor you retrieve using an API call is of the self-relative type—you must convert it before you can save it. You can convert a security descriptor from one type to another using the MakeAbsoluteSD and MakeSelfRelativeSD API calls.

An ACL consists of two types of entries. The first entry is a header that lists the number of access control entries (ACEs) that the ACL contains. Windows uses this number as a method for determining when it has reached the end of the ACE list. (There isn't any kind of end of structure record or any way of determining a precise size for each ACE in the structure.) The second entry is an array of ACEs.

WARNING: Never directly manipulate the contents of an ACL or SID, since Microsoft may change their structure in future versions of Windows. The Windows API provides a wealth of functions to change the contents of these structures. Always use an API call to perform any task with either structure type to reduce the impact of changes in structure on your application.

So, what is an ACE? An ACE defines the object rights for a single user or group. Every ACE has a header that defines the type, size, and flags for the ACE. Next comes an access mask that defines the rights that a user or group has to the object. Finally, there's an entry for the user's or group's SID.

There are four different types of ACE headers (three of which are used in the current version of Windows). The *access allowed* type appears in the DACL and grants rights to a user. You can use it to add to the rights that a user already has to an object on an instance-by-instance basis. For example, say you wanted to keep the user from changing the system time so that you could keep all the machines on the network synchronized. However, there might be one situation—such as daylight savings time—when the user would need this right. You could use an access allowed ACE to give the user the right to change the time in this one instance. An *access denied* ACE revokes rights that the user has to an object. You can use it to deny access to an object during special system events. For example, you could deny access rights to a remote terminal while you perform some type of update on it. The *system audit* ACE type works with the SACL. It defines which events to audit for a particular user or group. The currently unused ACE type is a *system alarm* ACE. It allows either the SACL or DACL to set an alarm when specific events happen.

6

TIP: Now would be a good time to look through the Windows API help file to see what types of access rights Windows provides. You should also look at the various structures used to obtain the information. Especially important are the ACL and ACE structures. Look for the ACE flags that determine how objects in a container react. For example, check out the CONTAINER_INHERIT_ACE constant that allows subdirectories to inherit the protection of the parent directory.

Using Security Descriptors

Understanding what a security descriptor is and how the various structures it contains interact is only one part of the picture. You also need to know how to begin the process of actually accessing and using security descriptors to write a program. The first thing you need to understand is that unlike tokens, security descriptors aren't generalized. You can't use a standard set of calls to access them. In fact, there are five classes of security descriptors, each of which uses a different set of descriptor calls to access the object initially. (You must have the SE_SECURITY_NAME privilege to use any of these functions.)

♦ **Files, directories, pipes, and mailslots** Use the GetFileSecurity and SetFileSecurity calls to access this object type.

NOTE: Only the NTFS file system under Windows NT provides security. The VFAT file system provides it to a lesser degree under Windows 95. You cannot assign or obtain security descriptors for either the HPFS or FAT file systems under either operating system. The FAT file system doesn't provide any extended attribute space, one requirement for adding security. The HPFS file system provides extended attributes, but they don't include any security features.

♦ **Processes, threads, access tokens, and synchronization objects** You need the GetKernelObjectSecurity and SetKernelObjectSecurity calls to access these objects. All of these objects, even the access tokens, are actually kernel objects. As such, they also have their own security descriptor for protection purposes.

♦ **Window stations, desktops, windows, and menus** The GetUserObjectSecurity and SetUserObjectSecurity calls allow you to access these objects. A window station is a combination of keyboard, mouse, and screen—the hardware you use to access the system. Desktops contain windows and menus—the display elements you can see onscreen. These four objects inherit rights from each other in the order shown. In other words, a desktop will inherit the rights of the window station.

♦ **System registry keys** This object type requires use of the RegGetKeySecurity and RegSetKeySecurity calls. Notice that these two calls start with Reg, just like all the other registry-specific calls that Windows supports.

♦ **Executable service objects** The QueryServiceObjectSecurity and SetServiceObjectSecurity calls work with this object. For some strange reason, neither call appears with the other security calls in the Windows API help file. You'll need to know that these calls exist before you can find them. An executable service is a background task that Windows provides—such as the UPS monitoring function. You'll find the services that your system supports by double-clicking the Services applet in the Control Panel.

Once you do gain access to the object, you'll find that you can perform a variety of tasks using a generic set of API calls. For example, the GetSecurityDescriptorDACL retrieves a copy of the DACL from any descriptor type. In other words, the descriptors for all of these objects follow roughly the same format—even though the lengths of most of the components will differ. One reason for the differences in size is that each object will contain a different number of ACEs. The SIDs are different sizes as well.

The next step in the process of either querying or modifying the contents of a security descriptor is to disassemble the components. For example, you could view the individual ACEs within a DACL or a SACL by using the GetACE API call. You could also use the owner and group SIDs for a variety of SID-related calls (we discussed these calls in the access token section of the chapter). Suffice it to say that you could use a generic set of functions to manipulate the security descriptor once you obtain a specific procedure.

6

In essence, any security descriptor access will always consist of the same three steps: getting the descriptor itself, removing a specific component, then modifying the contents of that component. To change the security descriptor, you follow the reverse process. In other words, you use a call like AddACE to add a new ACE to an ACL, then SetSecurityDescriptorSACL to change SACL within a descriptor, and finally, save the descriptor itself using a call like SetFileSecurity (assuming that you want to modify a file object).

ACEing Security in Windows

Once you start thinking about the way Windows evaluates the ACEs in the DACL, you'll probably discover a few potential problem areas—problems that the Windows utilities take care of automatically, but which you'll need to program around in your application to derive the same result. (The SACL has the same potential problem, but it only affects auditing, so the effect is less severe from the standpoint of system security.)

Windows evaluates the ACEs in an ACL in the order in which they appear. At first this might not seem like a very big deal. However, it could become a problem in some situations. For example, what if you want to revoke all of a user's rights in one area, but his or her list of ACEs includes membership in a group that allows access to that area? If you place the access allowed ACE first in the list, the user would get access to the area—Windows stops searching the list as soon as it finds the first ACE that grants all the user's requested rights (or an ACE that denies one of the requested rights). Granted rights are cumulative. If one ACE grants the right to read a file and another the right to write to it, and the user is asking for both read and write rights, Windows will view the two ACEs as granting the requested rights. The bottom line is that you should place all your deny ACEs in the list first, to prevent any potential breach in security.

You also need to exercise care in the ordering of group SIDs. Rights that a user acquires from different groups that he or she belongs to are cumulative. This means if a user is part of two groups, one that has access to a file and another that doesn't, the user will have access to the file if the group granting the right appears first on the list.

Obviously, you could spend all your time trying to figure out the best arrangement of groups. As the number of groups and individual rights that a user possesses increases, the potential for an unintended security breach does as well. That's why it's important to create groups carefully and limit a user's individual rights.

Other Security Concerns

There are two other concerns when you look at security under Windows 95 or Windows NT. The first deals with a client's ability to access data he or she isn't supposed to when accessing data through a server. (I'm not talking about a file server here, but some type of DDE or other application server.) Think about it this way: what if a client didn't have rights to a specific type of data, but he or she accessed the data through a DDE call to a server that did have the required rights? How could the server protect itself from being an unwilling accomplice to a security breach?

Windows provides several API calls that allow a server to impersonate a client. In essence, the calls allow a server to assume the security restrictions of the client in order to determine whether the client has sufficient rights to access a piece of data or a process. For example, a Word for Windows user might require access to an Excel data file. The user could gain access to that file using DDE. In this case, the server would need to verify that the Word for Windows user has sufficient rights to access the file before it sends the requested data. A server might even find that the client has superior rights when he or she uses this technique. The bottom line is that the server's only concern is for the protection of the data, resources, and environment that it manages.

This set of API calls supports three different types of communication: DDE, named pipes, and RPCs. You need to use a different API call for each communication type. For example, to impersonate a DDE client, you would use the DDEImpersonateClient call. There are some limitations to the level of impersonation support that Windows currently provides. For example, it doesn't currently support TCP/IP connections, so you'd have to resort to using other methods to verify that a user has the proper level of access rights in this case.

The other security concern is protecting the server itself. When a user calls Excel from Word for Windows, what prevents the user from doing something with Excel that damages the server itself? Ensuring that security concerns are taken care of isn't difficult to do with files and other types of named structures since the file server automatically attaches a security descriptor to these objects. (A DDE server like Excel wouldn't need to do anything in this case because the file is under the control of the file server.) However, many of the DDE or application server's private objects aren't named and require special protection. Windows also provides API calls to help a server protect itself. For example, the CreatePrivateObjectSecurity call allows the server to attach a security descriptor to any of its private objects—say, a thread or other process. The security descriptor would prevent anyone other than the server from accessing the private object.

6

Private Communication Technology (PCT)

Microsoft and the IETF are working together to create a new low-level protocol named PCT. Like SSL, PCT is designed to prevent hackers from eavesdropping on communications between a client and server through the use of encryption, authentication, and digital signatures. As with SSL, client authentication is optional.

TIP: If you want to find out about the current status of PCT, look at ftp://ftp.isi.edu/internet-drafts/draft-benaloh-pct-01.txt. This document contains the current draft of the second version of PCT.

PCT assumes that you have a reliable transport protocol in place such as TCP. Some people look at TCP/IP as a single protocol, but it isn't. TCP is the transport part of the protocol, while IP is the data transfer portion of the protocol. IP doesn't provide any form of data encryption. So, when you use TCP/IP, your data is open to anyone who wants to see it. Using a protocol such as TCP/PCT or TCP/SSL makes your communications secure. The first version of PCT corrects several problems with SSL, as described in the following list.

♦ **Simplified message and record structures** Reconnected sessions require a single message in each direction if you don't enable client authentication. Even with client authentication, a reconnection requires only two messages in each direction.

♦ **Extended cryptographic negotiation** PCT supports a wider variety of algorithms than SSL. This means it can support a broader range of protocol characteristics and that those characteristics get negotiated individually. For example, the common characteristics include cipher type, server certificate type, a hash function type, and a key exchange type.

♦ **Improved message authentication keys** The message authentication keys are separate from the encryption keys under PCT. This means that messages can use a very long key, ensuring secure transmission even if the encryption key is short or nonexistent. The main reason for this feature is to circumvent the 40-bit key limitation imposed by the U.S. government for secure transmissions.

♦ **Patched security hole** PCT uses a client authentication based on the cipher negotiated during a session. This prevents someone from capturing the client authentication key, disconnecting the original client, then reconnecting to the server using the stolen key. The client must know both the cipher and the key to gain access to the server.

♦ **Addition of Verify Prelude field** During the original handshaking process, communication between the client and server is carried out in the clear. The addition of this field makes it possible for the client and server to detect any tampering with these "in the clear" communications.

NOTE: Even though SSL version 3 also provides a Verify Prelude field type capability, a hacker can get around it by changing the protocol version number to 2, which didn't include this feature. Since SSL version 3 is fully version 2 compliant, neither client nor server will notice the change.

Microsoft is currently working on the second version of PCT. It's fully compatible with the first version, but offers several important features that the first version didn't. The following list provides an overview of these features.

♦ **New datagram record type** Individual records are sent independently as "datagrams." In essence, this means that the protocol doesn't guarantee an order of delivery or that the record will even get to its destination. It's up to the client to put the records it receives in order, then verify that they're all present. The main advantage of this approach is speed.

♦ **Recognizable record types** The record header contains information that tells the receiver what kind of record to expect.

♦ **Continuation records** PCT version 1 allowed data to span more than one record even though the record header didn't indicate any form of continuation. Version 2 adds a continuation field to the record header, which allows protocol messages to span more than one record as well.

♦ **Intermediate processing of data records** Data records are encapsulated now, which allows the sender to perform some form of intermediate processing, such as compression.

♦ **Independent decryption of datagram records** Since datagram records could be sent across an unreliable transport, this particular feature is essential to secure communication. Each record is encrypted individually, making it possible for the receiver to decrypt them one at a time even if they're received out of order.

♦ **New key management record type** This record type allows the sender to temporarily change either the encryption or message authentication keys during a session. In essence, this allows PCT to transmit pre-encrypted data.

♦ **New closing connection key management message** This is a special message that tells the other party to close a connection. Since this is an encrypted message, it's harder for a hacker to send a simulated message and close the connection prematurely.

6

♦ **Enhanced message authentication**   Message authentication now includes record headers.

♦ **Improved handshaking**   Both the client and server authentication phase include a wider variety of options, including key exchange, signature public key, and certificate.

♦ **New private authentication feature**   This feature allows a client and server to authenticate each other using a previously shared identity-associated private key, rather than a certified public key.

Now that we have a few of the basics down, let's look at how PCT works. PCT uses variable length records as a means of communication. Every record contains a header that defines the kind of message it contains. There are two kinds of messages: application and protocol. Application messages always contain data and can use either the standard PCT or datagram formats. A protocol message can key management, error, or handshake information. PCT uses two additional layers. Records are always transmitted using a connection. Normally there is one connection between a client and server, but there isn't any reason why there can't be more. Every connection is part of a session. Again, normally you'll only see one session between a client and server, but you could have more. (Multiple sessions would require more than one physical connection between the client and server.)

A PCT protocol connection begins with a handshake phase. This is where the handshake management message type comes into play. The client and server exchange several pieces of information, beginning with the negotiation of a session key for the connection. In other words, the client and server decide on a secret password to use for talking to each other. The client and server authenticate each other during this time as well. It doesn't pay for them to talk if the client or server doesn't know who the other party is and that they can be trusted. Once the client and server determine that they can trust each other, they decide on a master key that is used for encrypting all other messages.

Using Digital Signatures

Figuring out the precise technology behind digital signatures right now is a little like nailing JELL-O to the wall—you might be able to do it, but who would want to try. The first thing you need to understand is that the digital signature is also referred to as a certificate. Think of it as you would a driver's license, since it has the same function. A digital signature identifies some Internet object, who created it and when, and could potentially provide a

The code-signing process described in the "Mechanics of Downloading Internet Components" section of this chapter will eventually incorporate a digital certificate even though it doesn't now.

wealth of other information. If the object happens to be a client or server, a digital signature shows the current owner of that object. The digital signature certificate, like a driver's license, also expires—forcing vendors to keep proving they are who they say they are. The expiration date also gives hackers a lot less time to figure out how to steal the certificate. (Since each certificate is a separate item, learning to steal one won't necessarily buy the hacker anything.) Using a digital signature helps to keep everyone honest because it forces everyone to go through a central verification point. A digital signature avoids the one big problem with the honor system used by the Internet to date—it doesn't rely on one person to maintain the security of your machine. Now you have direct input into who gets access and when. (This implies some level of user training to ensure that people actually know how to use this feature.)

Implementing a digital signature—especially from the client end—is pretty straightforward. In most cases you'll find that vendors provide a standard certificate recognized by any browser or server designed to do so, but that there are some differences in the way the certificates actually accomplish the task. For example, the Authenticode Web page shown in Figure 6-2 shows one of the potential problem areas. If you're getting a client certificate, how do you determine what level to get? (Most people will go for the Class 1 Digital ID certificate since it's free for the asking.)

From an implementation standpoint, it doesn't matter whether you get a Class 1 or 2 certificate in this case—even the vendor doesn't really matter, though you'll probably want to stick with VeriSign (the place you end up when you follow the prompts) for compatibility purposes. The methods for using digital signatures are pretty much the same from vendor to vendor since the interface is defined by the Web server or browser vendor. What you'll do is submit an application, and once the vendor verifies who you are, you'll get a PIN or other means of identification in your email. Installing the certificate is a matter of following the instructions provided with your browser or Web server. In the case of VeriSign, you go to their Web site, plug in your PIN, and the browser will take care of the download and installation details.

Browser compatibility isn't the only reason that you can get a certificate and expect it to work with a variety of software. There's also a plethora of digital signature-oriented specifications in the works (see Table 6-1), and you'll find that most digital signature certificate vendors are adhering to those standards now. However, there is still a problem with Figure 6-2. There is no way for the user to figure out that a Class 2 certificate will provide a lot higher level

6

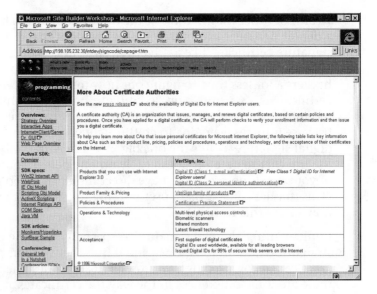

Client-side authentication is an important part of future Internet security, but figuring out what to get can be confusing. **Figure 6-2.**

The free Class 1 Digital ID being offered to Internet Explorer 3.0 users normally costs $6 per year.

of protection than a Class 1 certificate. Digging through about eight or nine pages finally yielded some answers, as listed here:

♦ **Class 1** Provides the user with a unique name and address within a repository. VeriSign (or whatever certificate vendor you choose) will be able to verify that the person and the address go together. The mail-back process is the only verification that VeriSign uses in this case. You have to own an email address to receive the certificate, making it hard for a hacker to obtain a fake certificate. This class of certificate costs $6 per year to maintain.

♦ **Class 2** To obtain a Class 2 certificate, you must provide third-party evidence of your identity. (This limits access to a Class 2 certificate to people in the United States and Canada at the moment.) The big difference between a Class 2 certificate and a Class 1 certificate is that VeriSign actually checks information you provide against a consumer database maintained by EquiFax. You'll also go through a hardware signing process, which requires multiple keys instead of one. This class of certificate costs $12 per year to maintain.

♦ **Class 3** This level isn't even listed in Figure 6-2. It provides the same level of security that a Class 2 certificate does. However, the initial checking procedure is much more intense. You must provide VeriSign with a notarized application. This means that someone will physically check your identification to make sure you are who you say you are. This class of certificate costs $24 per year to maintain.

OK, so now you have a digital certificate assigned to your ActiveX control, a Web server, or your browser (or all of the above). How do you identify someone who has a certificate versus someone who doesn't? You'll always see some kind of warning dialog when accessing a non-secure site. Likewise, accessing a site with a digital certificate always looks the same. You'll see a digital certificate dialog like the one shown here:

Notice that the dialog gives you a few options for optimizing your system. First, you'll want to check the certificate to make sure it's valid. For example, check to see that the vendor listed is the one that you expected. Also check the date to make sure that the certificate hasn't expired. Second, you'll have the ability to bypass the verification stage for this vendor if you want to. The first check box below the certificate always allows you to add a particular company to the list checked by WinVerifyTrust (we covered the download process in Chapter 4). If you check this box, you won't get asked each time you request a download from that particular vendor. This is a good risk with some vendors, but may not be such a smart thing to do with others. What you have to determine is how far you trust the vendor. The second check box always allows you to accept all access from any vendor certified by a specific certificate authority, such as VeriSign (the vendor shown in this case). Unless you're very comfortable with the certification process, you'll probably want to leave this box unchecked.

6

You're probably wondering what all this has to do with ActiveX controls. Like users and Webmasters alike, you'll find yourself requesting certificates somewhere along the way if you decide to make your site public. People won't want to download the controls you create unless they're digitally signed and they see the certificate associated with your company. The process for getting a certificate shouldn't be too much different than the one we just looked at for browser users. Right now you don't actually need a certificate to sign your controls, but you will in the near future. We'll cover the process for actually signing your ActiveX control in the "Mechanics of Downloading Internet Components" section of this chapter.

Understanding the CryptoAPI

Preventing someone from reading your data has been the topic of just about every area of this chapter so far. We've studied protocols and a variety of security techniques that are going to help you make the job of a hacker nearly impossible. However, there isn't a lock that can't be picked given enough time. In fact, that's the whole purpose behind using a 128-bit key instead of a 40-bit key. Picking the 128-bit lock is too time intensive (at least at the moment) to make the data contained in a record attractive to a hacker. It's not that the hacker can't pick the lock, it simply isn't efficient to do so.

Layers of Protection

Adding layers of protection is another way to guard against hackers. Encrypting the data at several different levels adds "doors" that the hacker must pass through to get to the data. Put enough doors between your data and the hacker, and the hacker will find something easier to break.

Microsoft's CryptoAPI (Cryptography Application Programming Interface) falls into the layer category of protection. It's a means of adding yet another layer of protection to your sensitive data. Are the encryption techniques you'll find supplied here unbreakable? No, but they do extend the time required for someone to unlock your data and read it. Using the routines in the CryptoAPI will help you better protect the data transferred between a client and server on the Web.

NOTE: As with just about everything else dealing with the Internet, the CryptoAPI is brand new and evolving. At the time of this writing, the CryptoAPI is only mentioned as part of the ActiveX SDK—you'll need to download a copy of the specification from the Internet. Even though this section provides the best overview possible at the time of writing, you'll want to visit the CryptoAPI site at http://www.microsoft.com/intdev/security/cryptapi-f.htm for the latest information.

The CryptoAPI has another purpose though. It's a general-purpose tool designed to allow encryption of data in any environment, not just the Web. For example, you could build an application that stores data using the same encrypted format whether the information was stored locally, transferred through a modem, uploaded to a Web site, or sent through the mail on a disk. That's a big advantage to your company. Using encryption all the time for sensitive data means that a hacker breaking into your system will find that the job has suddenly gotten a lot harder, yet a common encryption technique means that your users won't be inconvenienced by the added security. You can bet that a user is more likely to use encryption when it's convenient (and for the most part automatic). Making things difficult, hard to understand, or simply too time consuming is the best way to convince the user that it's too much trouble to protect the data on your system.

Microsoft has also moved to a modular approach to their operating design in the past few years, so it's no surprise that the CryptoAPI is modular as well. The CryptoAPI could be compared to the GDI (Graphics Device Interface) API under Windows. Any vendor can add a new device driver that tells the GDI how to work with a particular display adapter. The same holds true for the CryptoAPI. It uses the idea of a Cryptographic Service Provider (CSP) just as you would a display adapter device driver. Windows will come with one CSP—the one provided by Microsoft. However, if Microsoft's encryption feature set doesn't meet your needs, you could either design a new CSP yourself or buy one from a third party. The installation procedure would work much like the one you currently use to add a device driver. In fact, this device driver approach makes it easy for you to mix encryption hardware and software on your machine—a real plus in a world where you normally install hardware and software as separate entities.

6

NOTE: Microsoft is currently developing a DDK (Device driver Development Kit) for the CryptoAPI called the Cryptographic Service Provider Developer's Kit (CSPDK). You can get more information about this DDK and sign up for the beta program at http://pct.microsoft.com/capi/cspref1.html. Since the CSPDK uses 128-bit encryption technology, Microsoft is only accepting requests from the United States and Canada.

Encrypting a File

One of the easiest ways to show you the functionality provided by the CryptoAPI is to give an example. Encrypting a file is fairly simple. Microsoft follows a straightforward procedure using an eight-step process (six of the steps involve cryptographic-specific calls). You begin by opening a source and destination file, just as you would in any program. (The example code in this section is written in C, but you could easily port the required header files to other languages.) Once you have valid file handles, you need to get the handle for a CSP, like this:

```
// Get handle to the default provider.
if(!CryptAcquireContext(&hProv, NULL, NULL, PROV_RSA_FULL, 0))
    {
    MessageBox("Error during CryptAcquireContext", NULL, MB_OK | MB_ICONEXCLAMATION);
    PostQuitMessage(1);
    }
```

CryptAquireContext() can accept up to five parameters, but only two of them are essential in this case. The first parameter stores a handle for the CSP. The second parameter specifies the type of CSP that you're looking for. Every CSP has both a name and a type. For example, the name of the CSP currently shipped with Windows is "Microsoft Base Cryptographic Provider v1.0," and its type is PROV_RSA_FULL. The name of each provider is unique; the provider type isn't. The second parameter contains the key container name. If you specify a value here, Windows will look for a specific key container. A vendor can store the key container in hardware, within the registry, or on the hard drive, so you normally won't know the name of the key container. Using NULL (as shown) tells Windows to return the default key container. The third parameter contains the name of a CSP. You can retrieve the values of any installed CSPs using the CryptGetProvParam() function. Supplying a NULL value returns the default CSP. The final parameter contains one or more flags. Normally you'll set this value to 0 unless the CSP provides specific flag values for you to use. (Microsoft does provide some default flag values, but they're for administrative purposes only.)

The next step is either to encrypt the file using a random key or to generate a key using a password. The random key method is the one you'll probably use most often within an ActiveX control, so that's the one described here. The password method is similar and actually requires fewer steps than the random key method.

```
// Create a random session key.
if(!CryptGenKey(hProv, ENCRYPT_ALGORITHM, CRYPT_EXPORTABLE, &hKey))
{
    MessageBox("Error during CryptGenKey", NULL, MB_OK | MB_ICONEXCLAMATION);
    PostQuitMessage(1);
}
```

The CryptGenKey() function provides you with a unique key. Notice that the very first parameter is the CSP handle that we obtained in the previous step. The second parameter contains the name of an encryption algorithm. Microsoft supports two: CALG_RC2 (block cipher) and CALG_RC4 (stream cipher). You'll probably find that the algorithm names vary by vendors— so it's important to know which vendor the user intends to use as a CSP. The third parameter contains flags. There are three default flag values. CRYPT_EXPORTABLE tells Windows that it can export the random key value into a blob (we'll look at blobs in a few moments). CRYPT_CREATE_SALT tells Windows to use something other than 0 for the random key seed value. Finally, CRYPT_USER_PROTECTED tells Windows to notify the user when certain actions take place while using this key. Each CSP will probably define a unique set of actions. The last parameter is a container for the returned random key.

Sometime during the process of getting a certificate, the user received a public key. This is the key that the CSP keeps stored in a central place—it identifies the user. To make data transfers absolutely safe then, it's important to get a copy of the user's public key to use in the encryption process. That's what we do in the next step.

```
// Get handle to key exchange public key.
if(!CryptGetUserKey(hProv, AT_KEYEXCHANGE, &hXchgKey))
{
    MessageBox("Error during CryptGetUserKey", NULL, MB_OK | MB_ICONEXCLAMATION);
    PostQuitMessage(1);
}
```

The very first parameter we supply to CryptGetUserKey() is the handle to the CSP. The next parameter tells what kind of key to retrieve from that provider. Every CSP will support two keys: AT_KEYEXCHANGE (exchange the public key provided for a personal certificate used in an application like a browser) or AT_SIGNATURE (get a signature key like the one we'll generate later for an ActiveX control). The third parameter provides a place to store the key returned by the function.

6

Now comes the fun part. We take the random key and the user's public key and mix them together. Mixing the two keys together means that even if the user's key has been compromised in some way, the data will still get encrypted in a way that forces the hacker to start from scratch every time. It's the random element that makes this encryption technology at least a little more secure than other methods.

```
// Determine size of the key blob and allocate memory.
if(!CryptExportKey(hKey, hXchgKey, SIMPLEBLOB, 0, NULL, &dwKeyBlobLen))
{
    MessageBox("Error computing blob size.", NULL, MB_OK | MB_ICONEXCLAMATION);
    PostQuitMessage(1);
}

if((pbKeyBlob = malloc(dwKeyBlobLen)) == NULL)
{
    MessageBox("Error allocating memory for blob.", NULL, MB_OK | MB_ICONEXCLAMATION);
    PostQuitMessage(1);
}

// Export session key into a simple key blob.
if(!CryptExportKey(hKey, hXchgKey, SIMPLEBLOB, 0, pbKeyBlob, &dwKeyBlobLen))
{
    MessageBox("Error during CryptExportKey", NULL, MB_OK | MB_ICONEXCLAMATION);
    PostQuitMessage(1);
}
```

Notice that the process of exporting the *blob* key (the combination of the user's public key and the random key) is actually a three-step process. We call the CryptExportKey() function twice. The first two values are the keys we created: random and user. The third parameter tells Windows what kind of blob to create. Most CSPs support two values: SIMPLEBLOB or PUBLICKEYBLOB. The fourth parameter is for flags. Always set this value to 0 unless a CSP uses it for some purpose. The fifth parameter points to a buffer used to store the blob. If you call CryptExportKey() with this parameter set to NULL, it simply returns the size of the buffer you need in the sixth parameter. That's what we've done in the first call to the function. The sixth parameter normally contains the size of the buffer when you actually call CryptExportKey() to create the blob. (The source code displayed here also contains a memory allocation function call.)

Now that we have a blob to work with, it's time to do a little maintenance. One of the things you'll want to do without waiting around too much is destroy the user's public key. Just think about a hacker looking around in memory for some way of breaking down your code. Leaving the key in memory is one of the fastest ways to do this. Killing the key, then, isn't only a good idea from the standpoint of memory and good coding practice, it's a necessary part of maintaining a secure environment. The following source code calls the CryptDestroyKey() function to get rid of the public key.

```
// Release key exchange key handle.
CryptDestroyKey(hXchgKey);
hXchgKey = 0;
```

At this point you would send the blob data to the destination file on disk. The blob actually forms a header that the receiving computer will use later to decrypt the file. However, a header isn't much good without some data, so that's what we'll take care of next. The first thing you'll want to do is define a block size for the data. If you're using a block cipher, the CSP will provide a block size for you to use. A block cipher normally requires you to add one additional blank block at the end of the file as well. When using a stream cipher, you can define any convenient block encryption size (though Microsoft recommends a block size of 1,000 bytes). Now you'll read the data into a buffer one block at a time, use the following code to encrypt it, then write the block to the destination file.

```
// Encrypt data
if(!CryptEncrypt(hKey, 0, eof, 0, pbBuffer, &dwCount, dwBufferLen))
{
    MessageBox("Error during CryptEncrypt", NULL, MB_OK | MB_ICONEXCLAMATION);
    PostQuitMessage(1);
}
```

You can process the data in a loop until you run out of blocks. Make sure you pad the end of any incomplete blocks. The CryptoAPI depends on an even block size as part of the decryption process.

Ensuring the Safe Download of Internet Code

6

It seems like every time you look in the trade press another vendor is promising to upload their application to the Internet as a series of ActiveX controls. For example, Lotus plans to migrate a series of Notes-specific viewers to the Internet in the form of ActiveX controls. Quarterdeck also plans to convert its entire line of utility programs into ActiveX controls and upload them to the Internet. Soon, you'll be able to at least view just about any kind of data you want to directly from a browser. In some cases you'll be able to edit it directly as well. (We'll probably have to wait awhile for those full-fledged editors.)

Trying to keep all of that code virus-free could cause vendors major problems if they didn't have a plan in mind for ensuring it doesn't get damaged. We've already discussed some of the mechanics behind the Windows Verify Trust API in Chapter 4. In this section we'll look at the API itself. You'll get an overview of how this technology works and ideas of places to go for detailed information.

We'll also look at the Windows Software Publishing Trust Provider in this section. It's actually an add-on to the Windows Verify Trust API that verifies the trustworthiness of downloaded software components. It does this through several different methods that include checking local rules (like the security-related check boxes in your browser) and cryptographic information in the file itself (like digital signatures).

Finally, we'll take a look at the process for signing your ActiveX controls. Signing your control allows you to place it on the Web without forcing users to see those "not trusted" messages each time they download a page containing it. This section also takes a quick look at a procedure you can use to clean up your machine for testing—at least in a small way. You'll learn how to uninstall an ActiveX control so that you can test ActiveX control signing and other downloading features of your Web site without having to run to a clean machine every time.

Using the Windows Trust Verification API

This particular API is stable in some ways right now—Microsoft has already implemented parts of it in Internet Explorer 3.0 and within Windows itself. Other sections are in a state of flux as you read this because the various software vendors are trying to hash out the best methods for checking downloaded software (along with other trust verification items). You can always get the most current version of the Windows Trust Verification API at http://www.microsoft.com/intdev/signcode/wintrust.htm.

So what precisely is the Windows Trust Verification API? It's a general method for determining whether you can trust any Windows object. It doesn't matter whether that object is a client requesting services, a server requesting information, a downloaded document, or even an ActiveX control. The final form of this API will allow you to check the trustworthiness of any object.

Like most of the APIs supported by Windows, the Windows Trust Verification API is extensible—you can add new features to allow it to perform extended checks. One of the extensions that comes as part of Internet Explorer 3.0 is the Windows Software Publishing Trust Provider. We'll take a look at it in the next section. For right now, all you really need to know is that the Windows Trust Verification API is a general-purpose API and will probably require various extensions as more people use it.

The Windows Trust Verification API uses a variety of methods to check the trustworthiness of a file. Some of those methods are up for debate right now, but the two most common methods are checking system rules and verifying any certificates or digital signatures accompanying the object. You'll also find that the Windows Trust Verification API relies on external certificates. For example, many popular Internet encryption standards currently use the idea of a public and private key. The public key gets passed around in the header of a file (to see one example of how this works look at the "Encrypting a File" section of this chapter). The private key resides on the user's machine. To decrypt a file, you need both the public and the private key. Since only the user has that key, no one else can view the file. Obviously, there is more involved than just two keys. Some of the simpler schemes also add a random key, which when combined with the public key, makes it nearly impossible for a hacker to break into more than one file without individually decrypting each one.

System rules could reside in a number of places. For example, browsers store their "trust" information as part of a configuration file or within the registry. The system administrator also sets policy. Those settings could appear in an individual user's registry file or within the general registry files used by everyone. The exact placement of a policy depends on which version of Windows you're using, whether you have multiple users enabled (under Windows 95), and the type of policy that the system administrator wants to implement (system or individual). You also have the trust provider (CPS) rules to work with. (The exact term used by the specification is a *trust provider* since the source of rules could be any trusted authority, not just a CPS.) For example, telling your browser that anyone certified by a certain trust provider is trustworthy places the burden for verification on the trust provider. A trust provider will always define a specific object type and level of trust provided along with a specific list of owner names as part of the trust verification rules. User actions can also affect the rules that the Windows Trust Verification API will use. For example, when a user tells the system that a certain vendor is trustworthy, that information gets placed in the registry. Every time the Windows Trust Verification Service sees that vendor's name on a certification from that point on, it passes the object without checking further.

Now that you have an overview of what this API will do for you, let's take a quick look at the API itself. The call that you'll be most interested in is this:

```
WinVerifyTrust(HWND hwnd, DWORD dwTrustProvider, DWORD dwActionID,
LPVOID ActionData);
```

As you can see, the call requires four parameters. Most of you should know the first parameter by heart—it's a handle for the current window. The purpose of this parameter is to let WinVerifyTrust() know that there's a user available to make decisions. For example, the call may want to ask whether

6

to download a file even though it hasn't been signed. If you want to check the trustworthiness of an object without bothering the user, simply substitute INVALID_HANDLE_VALUE for the window handle. You can also use a value of 0 if you want the user's desktop to take care of any interaction instead of the current application. The second parameter defines who to ask regarding the matters of trust. Windows recognizes two values as a default (though a vendor could certainly define any special values needed to make the actual trust provider clear): WIN_TRUST_PROVIDER_UNKNOWN (find a trust provider based on the action you want performed) or WIN_TRUST_SOFTWARE_PUBLISHER (an actual software publisher). If you choose the WIN_TRUST_PROVIDER option, Windows will try to find a registry entry containing the action you want performed. If it can't find such an entry, the WinVerifyTrust() function will return TRUST_E_PROVIDER_ UNKNOWN. The third parameter specifies an action. For the most part it tells the trust provider what you want to do. Since each trust provider is different, you'll have to check trust provider documentation for a list of valid actions. The precise contents of the final parameter are also dependent on the trust provider you use. In most cases you'll at least need to tell the trust provider what data you want checked. Some trust providers may also request information about the level of trust required or context for the trust decision.

Once you make a call, WinVerifyTrust will usually return some kind of value specific to the trust provider. In some cases it could also return one of four standard values. You'll notice that all four of them are error values—the Windows Trust Verification API doesn't define any default success messages. The following list shows the four values and provides an explanation for each one.

♦ **TRUST_E_SUBJECT_NOT_TRUSTED** Normally the trust provider will give you a more specific error message than this one. This return value simply states that the object wasn't trusted for the action you specified. It doesn't necessarily mean that the object isn't trusted at all, just that it wasn't trusted for the current action. Unfortunately, you'll need to call WinVerifyTrust() once for each action unless the trust provider supplies some type of generic action or you only need to perform a single action with this particular object.

♦ **TRUST_E_PROVIDER_UNKNOWN** As previously stated, Windows returns this error message when it can't find a specific trust provider based on the action you requested.

- **TRUST_E_ACTION_UNKNOWN** Windows returns this error value if the action you requested isn't supported by the trust provider. At the time of this writing, WinVerifyTrust uses registry entries instead of actually talking with the trust provider to verify valid actions. This means that even if a trust provider does support a specific action, you might not be able to use it if the registry has been damaged somehow.

- **TRUST_E_SUBJECT_FORM_UNKNOWN** There are a variety of reasons for getting this error message. For the most part you'll get it if the data parameter isn't formatted right or contains incomplete information. A trust provider may not be able to find the object you want verified and return this message as well. If you're lucky, the trust provider will supply a more precise set of data-related error messages, but you may still see this value if the trust provider can't determine what the source of the problem is.

Understanding the Windows Software Publishing Trust Provider

The Windows Software Publishing Trust Provider is an add-on to the Windows Trust Verification API discussed in the previous section. The main purpose for this add-on is to allow an application to check whether a software component contains digital signatures or certificates. Either of these items will identify the document as being authentic software released by a publisher trusted on the local user's system. As with the Windows Trust Verification API, this API uses a variety of techniques and sources of information to determine whether a particular document is trustworthy or not.

You'll also find that the Windows Software Publishing Trust Provider uses the WinVerifyTrust() function that we talked about in the previous section. There are, however, a few differences. For one thing, you should always use the WIN_TRUST_SOFTWARE_PUBLISHER trust provider unless the trust provider supplies a different value. If you do use the WIN_TRUST_PROVIDER_UNKNOWN trust provider, Windows will simply select the default trust provider. Windows also defines two actions you can perform (the trust provider you choose may offer others): WIN_SPUB_ACTION_TRUSTED_PUBLISHER (checks to see that the publisher of the document is in the trusted list) and WIN_SPUB_ACTION_PUBLISHED_SOFTWARE (checks the document itself for the proper verification certificate). The WIN_SPUB_ACTION_TRUSTED_PUBLISHER action isn't supported by the current version

6

of the Windows Software Trust Provider. If you select the WIN_SPUB_ACTION_ PUBLISHED_SOFTWARE action, then WinVerifyTrust() will also expect the WIN_TRUST_ACTDATA_SUBJECT_ONLY data structure shown here:

```
typedef LPVOID WIN_TRUST_SUBJECT

typedef struct _WIN_TRUST_ACTDATA_SUBJECT_ONLY
{
   DWORD                dwSubjectType;
   WIN_TRUST_SUBJECT    Subject;
} WIN_TRUST_ACTDATA_SUBJECT_ONLY , *LPWIN_TRUST_ACTDATA_SUBJECT_ONLY
```

Notice that the structure contains two variables. dwSubjectType defines the type of object you want to verify. You can choose either WIN_TRUST_ SUBJTYPE_RAW_FILE for most data file types or WIN_TRUST_SUBJTYPE_ PE_IMAGE executable files (including DLLs and OCXs). The Subject structure points to the object that you want to verify. It has the following format.

```
typedef struct _WIN_TRUST_SUBJECT_FILE
{
   HANDLE               hFile;
   LPSTR                lpPath;
} WIN_TRUST_SUBJECT_FILE, *LPWIN_TRUST_SUBJECT_FILE;
```

As you can see, the two variables in this structure point to the file and the path where it can be found. In most cases you'll find the file in one of the cache folders for the particular browser (or other application) you're using. For example, Internet Explorer 3.0 stores its cache in the Temporary Internet Files (data files) or OCCACHE (executable files) folders under the main Windows directory. Just to be different, you'll find most ActiveX controls for Netscape Navigator stored in the ActiveX Control Cache folder (also located under the main Windows directory).

Now that you have all of the information together and have made the call to WinVerifyTrust(), how does Windows actually verify the document? The first thing it looks for is a PKCS #7 signed data structure. This is the data structure that we'll create in the upcoming section on signing your control. The next thing it does is look for a series of X.509 certificates. In the current implementation of Windows Software Publishing Trust Provider, you must provide a root private key along with the software publisher's public key. (We'll also look at what that means in an upcoming section.) In the future, Windows Software Publishing Trust Provider will also look for appropriate X509.3 extensions defining key-usage restrictions and other attributes of the certified parties. If the PKCS #7 data structure and X.509 certificates are correct, then WinVerifyTrust returns a success message to your application.

Mechanics of Downloading Internet Components

You could also entitle this section, Signing Your Code. There are actually four parts to this process, and you may have to repeat them several times to get the right results. The first action you need to take is to create a document using your ActiveX control on a local Web server. You need to access the server as an Internet site, or any testing you do won't mean a thing. We already looked at this process in Chapter 2, so we won't look at it again here. The second action is to unregister your ActiveX control. Most programming languages automatically register the control for you when you create it. Even if they didn't, you'd have to register it as part of the testing process we discussed in Chapter 2. Unregistering the control removes all of the registry entries that WinVerifyTrust() would use to look for a local copy of the control. Since it won't find any, you'll see the same trust screens that the user will. The third action is to sign your ActiveX control. The fourth, and final, action is to visit your test Web site and take a look at the page. This action will download the control and allow you to test the signing process. You may need to perform these last three actions several times before you get the signing process right.

Unregistering Your Control

In your SYSTEM (or SYSTEM32) folder you'll find a little program called RegSvr32. It's the program responsible for adding entries for your ActiveX control to the registry. The same program can unregister your control using a little-known command line switch, -U. So, if you wanted to unregister the control we created in Chapter 2, you'd type **REGSVR32 OCXEXMPL.OCX -U** at the command line. If you're successful, you'll see a dialog like this one:

Signing Your Control

Signing your control is a four-step process. The first step is to create an X.509 certificate (we talked about this certificate from a security standpoint in the

6

Make sure the CryptoAPI is running on your machine by typing two commands: INIT *, then API *. You may need to stop API by pressing CTRL-C.

previous section on the Windows Software Publishing Trust Provider). You'll use the MAKECERT utility as follows to create a basic certificate. The documentation for this utility (and all of the others needed in this section) is in SIGNCODE.TXT, which appears in the BIN folder of your ActiveX SDK installation.

```
MAKECERT -u:AKey -k:AKey.PVK -n:CN=MyCompany -d:A-Company TESTCERT.CER
```

All this command line does is create a random public/private key pair and associate the key pair with a friendly name. We also created a private key file (PVK) that holds a copy of the private key. Once you create a certificate, you have to combine it with a root X.509 certificate from a CSP such as VeriSign (this is step 2). Since there aren't any CSPs that deal with this kind of certificate right now, Microsoft provides a test certificate for you to use called ROOT.CER. It's in the BIN directory along with everything else.

We'll use the CERT2SPC (certificate to Software Publishing Certificate) utility to place both certificates into a PKCS #7 signature block object (we discussed this object from a security standpoint in the earlier section). Essentially, this object acts as a holder for any certificates you want to include within a signed object. Normally there are only the two certificates that we've described so far. You use the CERT2SPC as follows:

```
CERT2SPC ROOT.CER TESTCERT.CER TESTCERT.SPC
```

The three parameters in this case are the root certificate supplied by Microsoft, the certificate we created in the first step, and the name of a new file used to store the PKCS #7 signature block object. Now that you have a completed certificate, you have to place it within the ActiveX control (step 3). You do that using the following command line.

```
SIGNCODE -prog OCXEXMPL.OCX -spc TESTCERT.SPC -pvk MYKEY.PVK
```

This command line actually performs quite a few tasks, even though you don't end up with any more files than you had before. The first thing it does is to create a cryptographic digest of the image file (OCXEXMPL.OCX in this case), then sign it with the private key found in MYKEY.PVK. This cryptographic digest allows the client to compare the current state of the image file with the state it receives the file in. The client will use this comparison to detect any form of tampering along the way. Next, SIGNCODE removes any X.509 certificates it finds from the SPC file. It creates a new PKCS #7 digital signature object using the serial number of the X.509 certificate and the signed cryptographic digest. Finally, it embeds the new PKCS #7 digital signature object along with the X.509 certificates into the image file.

You'll want to check the work of the SIGNCODE utility, considering the amount of work it's done. That's the fourth step of the process. The first thing to check is whether the digital signature was implanted successfully. Use the PESIGMGR utility to do this. All you need to supply is the name of the file you want to check. If you get a success message, check to make sure the executable code is properly represented by the digital signature object by using the CHKTRUST utility. This utility does the same thing that a user's browser will do. It examines the digital signature object, then the X.509 certificates. If they both check out, CHKTRUST will also perform a check on the image file's code to see if it compares with the signed cryptographic digest. CHKTRUST performs one final act not usually performed by your browser. It checks the linkage between the various certificates and makes sure that dependency chain eventually ends up at the root.

Performing a Live Test

The last step in checking your signed control is to actually use it. You have to do this over an Internet connection; nothing else will do. Simply move the control over to your Internet server, make certain that it's no longer registered at your local machine, then try to view the test page using your browser. If everything works right, you should see a certificate displayed instead of the usual warning message when your browser goes to download the control.

There are a few ways that your test can fail even if the control was signed properly. The first error to look for is an improperly formatted <OBJECT> tag. We discussed this tag in Chapter 4. However, one reminder here is in order. Make sure your CODEBASE attribute points to the location of the control. In addition, use an URL instead of a directory location on your machine. For example, if your control is located in the CONTROLS subdirectory of the Web site root, then use an URL like http://www.mycompany.com/CONTROLS/OCXEXMPL.OCX with the CODEBASE attribute.

You may want to double-check your control after signing locally as well. Even though it's unlikely that the control will get damaged during the signing process, it could happen. Make sure that the control works on your local test page if it doesn't work properly the first time you test it at the remote location.

6

Chapter 7

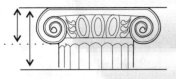

Scripting and ActiveX

If you thought you'd get rid of scripting by using ActiveX controls on your Web site, forget it. ActiveX controls are actually more reliant on scripting than other kinds of Web interface elements. Theoretically, you could place an ActiveX control on a page and allow it to just sit there looking pretty without any scripting, but that's about it. One of the reasons you didn't see any feedback from the on/off button control in Chapter 4 is that we were missing the script required to do so.

Fortunately, there are some positive features to using scripting languages other than the fact that you need them to use ActiveX controls. Have you ever sat waiting for a CGI script to complete on the host (Internet server) only to find out that the data you entered was incomplete or wrong in some way? A lot of people have had that experience. Since VBScript and JavaScript both execute on the host (in this case the user's machine), you'll find that you can validate information as soon as the user enters it. This saves network bandwidth and makes user feedback instantaneous. Anything that keeps the user happy is bound to save you some time as well.

Obviously, if you're going to spend some time working with a scripting language, it pays to know the players. Some scripting languages are more popular than others, and right now, VBScript and JavaScript seem to be the two getting the most media attention, so those are the two languages we'll focus on in this chapter. ActiveX Control Pad currently supports both VBScript and JavaScript. You'll find that most of the other tools you see on the market right now support them as well.

We'll also take a look at ActiveX Scripting, which is an OLE communication technology rather than a scripting language. This particular technology is still at the workbench as this book is being written, so we won't look at any working example. You'll get an overview of what the technology involves though, so you can be prepared to use ActiveX Scripting once it does become available. For the most part you'll find that ActiveX Scripting relies on current OLE technology with some new interface elements added and a couple of new bells and whistles borrowed from other places. The actual technology is a little more complicated, but we'll visit as much of the specification as possible at this time. (We'll definitely look at those new interface elements.)

This chapter spends most of its time looking at how scripting and ActiveX controls work together. We'll begin with a simple example using some of the controls provided with ActiveX Control Pad. For example, you may have noticed that you can't define any of the entries for a drop-down list box by sticking it on the page and accessing the Properties dialog. The reason is simple: you need a script to add those entries at run time. All sections of this chapter will look at both VBScript and JavaScript (we'll use different examples though, so you can get the maximum benefit from the information you get). Using both scripting languages will help you make a personal decision about which language you want to use.

Once we get past the basics, we'll spend a little time looking at some intermediate scripting examples. For example, we'll take a look at how you can use scripting to interact with controls you've created. There is a real lack of complex controls available to demonstrate, but we'll view enough of them to give you the general idea of how to use scripts in complex situations.

Overview of ActiveX Scripting

At the present, ActiveX Scripting isn't a language (macro or otherwise) like the VBScript or JavaScript languages we'll look at in the next two sections. It's better defined as a communication method between a client and server. In essence, it's Microsoft's new name for OLE automation. Saying that OLE automation and ActiveX Scripting are precisely the same wouldn't be correct since Microsoft hasn't left the capabilities of ActiveX Scripting at the application level. (Most Microsoft products and a few other products such as CorelDRAW! support OLE automation at the application level.) ActiveX Scripting also takes the Internet into account.

Since ActiveX Scripting isn't a language, but a communication specification, the scripting language, including syntax, is left to the scripting vendor. The purpose of this standard is to define a method for a scripting host to call on various scripting engines and allow communication between objects within an OLE container. In essence, the script is more a blob of executable code than anything else. It could consist of text, pcode, or even executable code in native binary format. The essence of ActiveX Scripting is that it's an OLE-based communication medium designed for both application and Internet use.

NOTE: The ActiveX Scripting specification is a moving target as of this writing. You'll want to spend time looking at the latest news if you intend to use ActiveX Scripting in place of or as an addition to other technologies. In addition, this section doesn't provide complete coverage of the calling syntax for all the interface methods required by the OLE host and scripting engine. Look at http://www.microsoft.com/intdev/sdk/docs/olescrpt/ for additional information about the current ActiveX Scripting specification.

Let's take a few moments to define some terms here. First, what precisely is a *scripting host*? It's an application that supports a scripting engine. When you define a script, it's the host that accepts it and then sends the commands to the engine. The most common example of an ActiveX scripting host right now is Internet Explorer 3.0. You can also add this capability to Netscape Navigator using a plug-in. We discussed one of these plug-ins, NCompass ActiveX Pro, in Chapter 3. A scripting engine isn't limited to either of these

7

products, of course. You could build it into a custom browser application or find it in any number of applications. For example, it's likely that Microsoft will bring all of its application products (such as Microsoft Word) up to this standard in the near future.

An ActiveX *scripting engine* is the object that actually interprets the script. There are no limitations on the precise language syntax or even the form of the script. You could theoretically write an ActiveX scripting engine for any language, including VBScript, Java, and JavaScript. An ActiveX scripting engine will provide special interfaces, just like any other OLE object that we'll discuss later in this section. In addition, you can write to an ActiveX scripting engine using an OLE automation wrapper (Microsoft plans to provide a special form of OLE automation wrapper for ActiveX Scripting). The advantage to using the wrapper format is that it keeps the code small and lightweight—ideal for browsers and online scripting engines. The disadvantage is that you lose control over the run-time namespace, persistence model, and other authoring elements that you would have if you wrote to the ActiveX Scripting interface directly.

There are four new interface elements required for ActiveX Scripting. The IActiveScriptSite and optional IActiveScriptSiteWindow interfaces are host specific. The IActiveScript and optional IActiveScriptParse interfaces are scripting-engine specific. Each interface element performs a specific function, as described in the following list.

- ◆ **IActiveScriptSite** The main purpose of this interface is to create a site for the ActiveX scripting engine. This corresponds to the idea of a container in other OLE implementations—it's where everything else, such as ActiveX controls, are placed. Since this is a container interface, it monitors events such as the starting and stopping of scripts and when a script error occurs.

- ◆ **IActiveScriptSiteWindow** Any ActiveX scripting host that provides a user interface also needs to provide this interface (servers need not apply). It provides two essential methods: GetWindow( ), which creates a window, and EnableModeless( ), which allows you to set the modal condition of the window. GetWindow( ) is similar in functionality to IOleWindow::GetWindow( ), and EnableModeless( ) is similar in functionality to IOleInPlaceFrame::EnableModeless( ).

- ◆ **IActiveScript** This interface allows you to work with the script itself. You can use it to get the scripting site, start or stop the script, work with script items, close the script, or establish thread state and parameters.

♦ **IActiveScriptParse**   This interface accepts scripts from the scripting host. It allows you to create a new script, add *scriptlets* (pieces of raw script text) to an existing script, or parse an existing script.

Three different elements are actually involved in an ActiveX Scripting session: the host, an engine, and the window (page) containing the code and controls. Establishing communication between the three elements is an eight-step process, as described here:

1. The host loads a document or project as needed. This isn't an ActiveX Scripting-specific task since any environment needs to perform this step.

2. The host creates a scripting engine. Normally it uses the PROGID attribute of the <OBJECT> tag to do this. A call to CoCreateInstance( ) completes the task.

3. Loading the script comes next, and the host can follow several routes to accomplish it. If the script is stored as persisted data, then the host uses the engine's IPersist::Load( ) to reload it into memory. If the host needs to load a new script, it calls IActiveScriptParse::InitNew( ) or IPersist::InitNew( ) to create an empty script. Hosts that maintain scripts as text can then call IActiveScriptParse::ParseScriptText( ) to load the script into the engine. (Hosts that use other formats to maintain the script will have to devise their own loading method.)

4. Once the host has loaded the script in some way, it has to populate the engine's namespace with entities. An entity is a form, page, or other document. The host uses the IActiveScript::AddNamedItem( ) method to accomplish this task. Obviously, it doesn't need to load any entities stored as part of the script's persistent storage. Lower-level items such as ActiveX controls require a different loading technique. The host uses the ITypeInfo and IDispatch interfaces to get the job done.

5. Now that the ActiveX scripting engine has everything it needs to run the script, the host issues an IActiveScript::SetScriptState(SCRIPTSTATE _CONNECTED) call. This tells the scripting engine to start the script—it's equivalent to calling the Main( ) function in a standard C program.

6. Before the scripting engine actually starts running the script, it needs to take care of a few housekeeping tasks. For example, it needs to associate a symbol with every top-level item. The scripting engine does this using the IActiveScriptSite::GetItemInfo( ) method.

7

7. One of the final steps before the scripting engine actually runs the script is to make the proper connections between script elements and events associated with objects. For example, if there's a script item that deals with the onClick event for a pushbutton, the scripting engine needs to make the connection before it runs the script. The scripting engine uses the IConnectionPoint interface to perform this work.

8. The scripting engine can finally run the script. As it runs the script, the scripting engine will need to access the methods and properties associated with the objects on your HTML page or other document. It does this using the IDispatch::Invoke( ) or other standard OLE binding methods.

Now that you have a pretty good idea of how a script works, let's take a very quick look at some of the ways in which a scripting engine reacts when running. The scripting engine doesn't simply have two operating states: on and off. It provides several states that you can use to determine what needs to be done to get it running. (You obtain the current state using the IActiveScript::GetScriptState( ) method.) The following list tells you about the various scripting engine states.

♦ **Uninitialized** This means that the scripting engine isn't ready to do anything. Normally the host will have to load a script and any entities required for the script to run before the scripting engine will leave this state.

♦ **Initialized** The script is loaded (usually with IPersist) and the site for running it is set (using IActiveScriptSite), but the scripting engine isn't actually associated with a host yet. You can't run any code while the scripting engine is in this state. Any code executed with IActiveScriptParse::ParseScriptText( ) will run once the scripting engine enters the started state.

♦ **Started** This is a transition state from which you can run code using IDispatch. All the code is loaded along with the objects. However, the scripting engine hasn't created connections between script elements and the object events yet. If the script runs into a situation where it needs to perform event processing, it will become blocked (stopped) until the scripting engine completes the required initialization.

♦ **Connected** You'll only get this state when the scripting engine is ready to perform every task required of it.

♦ **Disconnected** The script essentially pauses when the scripting engine enters this state. The script is still loaded and all the connections made, but the scripting engine isn't prepared to answer requests from the host. The scripting engine can go from this state back to the connected state without losing the current script running position.

♦ **Closed** The scripting engine will no longer answer calls when in this state. It enters this state after you send an IActiveScript::Close( ) call.

Overview of Visual Basic Scripting (VBScript)

VBScript is actually a special version of Visual Basic for Applications (VBA), which in turn is a subset of the full Visual Basic product. In fact, Microsoft's full name for this particular product is Visual Basic Scripting Edition. What does that mean for most developers? If you already know how to use Visual Basic, then VBScript is simply a few steps away.

Developers will realize several benefits from using VBScript. If you're a browser developer, Microsoft is licensing the source implementation for VBScript free of charge (at least at this writing). It's also one of two languages designed to work with Java applets and ActiveX objects. You can use this language to interface with ActiveX controls you create. In addition, since VBScript is a true subset of the other languages in the Visual Basic family, any applications you write with it will also run in those environments. Theoretically this means you could write code for an HTML page and move it to your application programming environment as well. VBScript could be used in environments other than the Internet, but there aren't any implementations of this sort right now.

 NOTE: Microsoft currently provides VBScript implementations for the Windows and Macintosh platforms. Future UNIX versions will allow you to run it on the IBM, Hewlett-Packard, Sun, and Digital platforms. Even though none of the current versions of VBScript offers a development environment or debugging capabilities, Microsoft plans to provide these features at some future date.

7

You'll find that VBScript places some pretty significant restrictions on what you can and can't do. Since VBScript is a true subset of VBA, it's easier to show what VBScript doesn't allow you to do. Table 7-1 shows the VBA features you can't use with VBScript. As you can see, the limitations are somewhat severe. Microsoft recommends that if you need a feature that VBScript doesn't provide, you use VBA instead. (In fact, VBA is missing quite a few features as well, so you may have to resort to using the full-fledged product if VBA won't work.) The idea is to make VBScript very small and fast. Using a very discrete subset also makes it possible for VBScript to potentially run in some environments that won't support the other two products.

Feature Category	Missing Features
Arrays	Option Base, declaring arrays with a starting point other than 0
Calling DLLs	Declare
Classes	Dim x As New <TypeName>, Set x = New <TypeName>, If TypeOf x Is <TypeName>, With...End With
Collection access using !	MyCollection!Foo
Conditional compilation	#Const, #If...Then...#Else...#End If
Constants (data types)	Currency type, CCur
Constants (module level)	Const, Private, Dim, Public, Global
Constants (procedure level)	Const
Control flow	DoEvents, GoSub...Return, GoTo, line numbers and labels, On Error...GoTo, Select Case
Data types	Boolean, Byte, Currency, Date, Double, Integer, Long, Object, Single, String, type suffixes (%, $, !, etc.), user-defined classes (no Me)
Debugging	Debug, Print, End, Stop
Error trapping	Erl, Error, Error$, On Error...Resume, Resume, Resume Next
File I/O	There are actually too many missing features to mention here. For the most part, if you need to perform all but the most basic file I/O, you need VBA.

VBA Features
Not Found in
VBScript
Table 7-1.

Feature Category	Missing Features
Graphics	Cls, Circle, Line, Point, PSet, Scale, Print, Spc, Tab
Literals	There are three classes of missing user-defined literals: 1. Based real numbers, such as 1.2345E+100 2. Dates, such as #4/7/69# 3. Trailing type characters, such as the highlighted ampersand &hFF**&**
Named arguments	Named arguments in calling members. For example, you can't use Call MyFunction (Variable1:= 4).
Operators	Like
Options	Def <Type>, Option Base, Option Compare, Option Private Module
Procedures (declaring)	Property Get/Let/Set, specifying Public/Private
Procedures (exiting)	Exit property
Procedures (parameters)	ParamArray, Option
Strings	Fixed-length strings, Mid, LSet, RSet
Structs	Type...End Type, LSet, RSet
Variables (data types)	Currency type, CCur
Variables (module level)	Const, Private, Dim, Public, Global
Variables (procedure level)	Const

VBA Features
Not Found in
VBScript
(*continued*)

Table 7-1.

TIP: You can find full documentation for VBScript at http://
www.microsoft.com/vbscript/. This includes the full language feature
set as well as calling syntax. The ActiveX Control Pad utility we've talked
about in several chapters also provides assistance in using VBScript. We'll
see how later in the chapter. It's also important to join a newsgroup so that
you can exchange information with other people. Microsoft provides such
a newsgroup at Microsoft.Public.VB (there are actually 19 groups from
which to choose—each group covers a different programming topic).

7

The news isn't all bad. VBScript does provide substantial run-time features. In fact, the new version adds better string handling and objects for performing file I/O. Even though these features don't give you any new functions to work with, you'll definitely notice the performance boost they provide. (VBA doesn't include these two features yet—one of the few areas where VBScript is actually superior.) Of course, you'll also find that VBScript is missing quite a few of the VBA run-time features, as shown in Table 7-2. For the most part these features were removed to improve security or to make VBScript more portable.

Feature Category	Missing Features
Classes	TypeName
Clipboard	Clipboard object
Collection	Add, Count, Item, Remove
Constants	For the most part you can't use the full capabilities of constants in the run-time environment. As of this writing, Microsoft hasn't listed all of the shortcomings of VBScript in this regard. Personal experience has shown that there are a lot of missing constant features in the run-time environment.
Conversion	Chr$, Hex$, Oct$, CVar, CVDate, CCur, Format, Format$, Str$, Str, Val
Date	Date statement, Date$, Timer
DDE (dynamic data exchange)	LinkExecute, LinkPoke, LinkRequest, LinkSend
Financial	Most of the financial functions don't work at all or provide very limited functionality. Since Microsoft hasn't provided a complete list of nonimplemented financial functions, you'll need to test a function before using it in a production environment.

VBA
Run-Time
Features Not
Found in
VBScript
Table 7-2.

Feature Category	Missing Features
Graphics	TextHeight, TextWidth, LoadPicture, SavePicture, QBColor, RGB
Miscellaneous	Environ, Environ$, SendKeys, Command, Command$, DoEvents, AppActivate, Shell, Beep
Objects (general)	GetObject
Objects (manipulation)	Arrange, ZOrder, SetFocus, InputBox$, Drag, Hide, Show, Load, Unload, Move, PrintForm, Refresh, AddItem, RemoveItem
Printing	TextHeight, TextWidth, EndDoc, NewPage, PrintForm
Strings	LCase$, UCase$, LSet, RSet, Space$, String$, Format, Format$, Left$, Mid$, Right$, Trim$, LTrim$, RTrim$, StrConv
Time	Time statement, Time$, Timer
Types	TypeOf
Variant support	IsMissing

VBA Run-Time Features Not Found in VBScript (*continued*)

Table 7-2.

One of the more interesting uses that Microsoft sees in VBScript's future is as a hardware-independent batch processing language. A hardware vendor could potentially use it as part of an installation program. This may work out eventually, but so far no hardware vendors are using VBScript in place of more standard languages. As with hardware vendors, software vendors could potentially use VBScript to write an installation program that would run on just about any machine. Again, there doesn't appear to be much interest in doing this today, but it could happen in the future.

How does VBScript compare to other forms of Visual Basic? Microsoft is quick to point out that most of the omissions in the language are either to make it fast or safe. It's pretty obvious that some of the features you find in the full-fledged packages, such as the Clipboard object, just aren't good bets on other platforms either. Some sacrifices were made in the name of compatibility. Of course, the fact that VBScript is free is one of the things that Microsoft tends to hit hard any time they talk about it.

7

Overview of Java Scripting (JavaScript)

Before we go any further, let's get one thing out of the way. Java and JavaScript are two entirely different entities. If you're looking for a full-fledged programming environment, then Java, not JavaScript, is the language you're looking for. On the other hand, if you're looking for a macro language of the same caliber (although not the same functionality) as VBScript, but with a C orientation, you're looking for JavaScript. Also, Java is a Sun innovation, while JavaScript comes to you from Netscape. Some marketing person at Netscape must have come up with this rather confusing idea of giving both products essentially the same name—the original name for JavaScript was LiveScript.

Now that we've gotten the distinction between Java and JavaScript out of the way, let's look at the language itself. For the most part you'll find JavaScript used for the same purposes as VBScript—as a means for working with ActiveX controls and Java applets on an HTML page. In fact, you can work with any kind of an object with JavaScript—sometimes the only limiting factor is figuring out how to do so. JavaScript also comes in handy for a variety of other purposes, most of which we'll see in the next few sections of the chapter. For right now it's only important to know that JavaScript provides a distinctly different feature set from VBScript that allows you to enhance your Web site.

Unlike VBScript, there aren't any directly compatible versions of anything to compare JavaScript to. Comparing it to C (or even Java) wouldn't provide you with much information because JavaScript was designed as a separate product with a feature set oriented toward Internet use. What we'll do is take a quick overview of what JavaScript does provide, then look at it in action during the rest of the chapter.

JavaScript takes an object map approach to working with HTML documents. It builds a hierarchy of objects starting with the window, the documents within the window, forms within the document, and finally, any objects within the form. Using JavaScript allows you to communicate with each object by defining a path to it. For example, if you wanted to do something to a form, you'd separate the form name from the window name like this: Window1.Form1. Notice that the window name is separated from the form name by a period—many programmers refer to this as a *dot syntax reference*.

There are a few very non-C-like things to know about JavaScript. First, JavaScript is a loosely typed language. That means you don't have to declare your variables. Second, there are objects in JavaScript, but there aren't any classes or inheritance. This means that you can't create new object types.

You can, however, extend existing object types to a certain extent. The objects you get to use are the ones contained within an HTML document or form. The method of extension depends on what properties and methods the control author exposed for you to use. In essence, for an ActiveX control, the properties would appear on the Properties page and the methods would be events that you exposed. (Look at the example in Chapter 2 if you need to know more about building a basic control.) It's important to remember that JavaScript is object based, not object oriented. Finally, JavaScript is dynamically bound. This means it checks for objects at run time. C and Java are both statically bound; they check for objects during compile time.

TIP: There are a lot of places to learn about JavaScript. The best place to view the language guide is http://home.netscape.com/eng/mozilla /Gold/handbook/javascript/index.html. You'll not only find a language guide there, but good discussions on various language elements. (Netscape used to provide a ZIPped copy of their documentation, but the site isn't active anymore.) Fortunately, you can get a tutorial-sized version of the JavaScript documentation in Windows help format from http:// www.jchelp.com/javahelp/javahelp.htm or an Adobe Acrobat version from http://www.ipst.com/docs.htm. (You can also get a free Acrobat reader or plug-in from ftp://ftp.adobe.com/pub/adobe/Applications/Acrobat/.) Another good resource page is http://www.c2.org/~andreww/javascript/. It contains source listings for example programs and a wealth of other information. It's also important to find a place where you can share information about JavaScript with other people. You'll find a great newsgroup at Comp.Lang.JavaScript.

The most important thing to remember about JavaScript is that like Java, you're extremely restricted as to what you can do with the system hardware. The reason behind this limitation is to prevent (as much as possible) security breaches. Unfortunately, the amount of protection you'll actually get from JavaScript is limited (see Chapter 6 for details). One of the hardware access restrictions you'll run into is that you can't write to files. The only exception to this rule is that you can write to cookies. A *cookie* is a bit of data that you can store to the browser's cache directory. The purpose of a cookie is to store configuration information from one session to the next. Some programmers use the cookie for other small storage purposes as well. For example, you could use it to store the URL of the last site explored by the user so that you can return the user to that site during the next session.

7

JavaScript supports four different variable types: numbers, strings, Boolean, and a special null value. You can use function calls to convert one variable type to another. However, you can just as easily mix variable types. For example, you could create a variable named nANumber and assign it a numeric value. In the very next line of code you could assign the same variable a string value, and JavaScript won't complain. You can also mix variable types in one line of code. For example, nANumber = "Some Answer Equals " + 42 is perfectly legal in JavaScript. This is one of the reasons you'll want to enforce some kind of variable typing yourself through the use of a notation like Hungarian Notation (explained in the Introduction).

Functions are the only form of modular coding you can use within JavaScript. In fact, this is one of the first places where JavaScript actually takes on a C-like look. As with most programming languages, you can accept parameters as part of the function call and provide a return value. The following example shows a typical JavaScript function. Notice that it uses the Document.Write( ) method—one of the methods you'll use most often in beginning scripts. Not only can you use it to display text, but as we see here, you can use it to write HTML code as well.

```
function MyFunction(nSomeValue)
{
    Document.Write("The value received was: ",nSomeValue,".","<BR>")
    Return nSomeValue + 1
}
```

Most languages support some kind of conditional statement, and JavaScript is no exception. The easiest conditional to use is in this form: (<Condition>) ? <Value1> : <Value2>. You'd use it to assign one of two values to a variable. For example, lIsGreater = (Value1 > Value2) ? true : false. If Value1 is greater than Value2, the lIsGreater will equal TRUE. You can use the If...Else conditional statement like this. JavaScript doesn't currently support any form of case (or switch) statement—making it a lot more difficult to write code that checks a lot of different values.

```
if (Value1 > Value2)
{
    Document.Write("Value 1 is greater than Value 2.")
    Return true
}
else
{
    Document.Write("Value 2 is greater than Value 1.")
    Return false
}
```

Looping is another operation that all programming languages support. You'll find that JavaScript supports two different looping constructs: for and while. Here's an example of each type. You'll notice that they look almost exactly like the equivalent structure in C.

```
for (nCounter = 0, nCounter < 10, nCounter++)
{
    Document.Write(nCounter)
}

while (nCounter < 10)
{
    Document.Write(nCounter)
    nCounter++
}
```

This gives you a very basic overview of JavaScript. You'll get to see a lot of JavaScript code throughout this chapter, so don't worry right now about what you don't know. The biggest thing that you need to remember is that JavaScript is C-like—it's not C by any stretch of the imagination (you should have noticed quite a few differences by now).

The Basics of Working with Scripts

Writing a script, especially if you use a scripting language similar to the programming language you normally use, doesn't have to be a long or difficult task. In fact, most of the scripts you'll write will actually be short and to the point. One of the tricks you might employ when learning script writing is to check out the source code used by sites you really like. Unlike other forms of programming, the source code you need is usually available to you in some form on the Internet—the trick is finding it. (Simply use the View | Source command in your browser to see the source code used by other programmers to accomplish a task.)

Fortunately, learning from an online manual, local help file, or other documentation, coupled with real-world examples, isn't the only route you can travel to learn script programming techniques. Since JavaScript is better established than VBScript for right this second, the Internet contains a wealth of information you can use and even a few tutorials. Just check out the sites in the tip in the previous section. There may be a lack of VBScript-specific tutorials right now (it won't take long for programmers to catch up here either), but you can always use tutorials and training materials meant for VBA and full-fledged Visual Basic. Remember that VBScript is a

7

true subset of these languages. That's one of the reasons we looked at how VBScript differs from VBA in Tables 7-1 and 7-2.

You'll get some help learning a new scripting language from this book as well. This section of the chapter is going to look at some very easy scripts. They aren't meant to dazzle anyone—their only intent is to help you understand the basics of scripting a little bit better. We look at two different programming examples in the next two sections. Each one is meant to show you a different concept of script language programming. We'll also examine the scripts in two different languages. That will help you decide which scripting language you prefer to use on a regular basis.

Using VBScript

Always place scripts within an HTML (<! ->) comment so that older browsers will bypass your code.

We looked at how VBScript differs from its siblings in an earlier section. Now it's time to look at some coding examples for it. The first thing we'll do is take a look at a simple text processing example with HTML code. Listing 7-1 shows some sample HTML code with scripts added to support the buttons and other features. The initial page appears in Figure 7-1. All we're going to do with this example is process the color settings and a text entry. Color changes take place immediately—you can change both the foreground and background colors. The results of any text changes will appear in a text block each time you click the Try It! button.

Listing 7-1

```
<HTML>
<HEAD>
<TITLE>First VBScript Processing Example</TITLE>

<!Placing your scripts here tends to produce less problems than->
<!they could elsewhere.  There two scripts used to process user selections.->
<!The first displays the results in a text block.  The second changes the->
<!foreground and background colors.->
<SCRIPT LANGUAGE="VBScript">
<!--
Sub ChangeText()
    'Create a form reference.
    Dim Form1
    Set Form1 = Document.SampleForm1

    'Send the text to our Results variable.
    Form1.Results.Value = Form1.Results.Value + " " + Form1.TextInput.Value
End Sub
```

```
Sub ChangeColor(sColor)
    'Determine what color text to use.
    Select Case sColor
        Case "Black"
            Window.Document.FgColor="Black"
        Case "Blue"
            Window.Document.FgColor="Blue"
        Case "Green"
            Window.Document.FgColor="Green"
        Case "Purple"
            Window.Document.FgColor="Purple"
        Case "Red"
            Window.Document.FgColor="Red"
        Case "Silver"
            Window.Document.BgColor="Silver"
        Case "White"
            Window.Document.BgColor="White"
        Case "Fuchsia"
            Window.Document.BgColor="Fuchsia"
        Case "Teal"
            Window.Document.BgColor="Teal"
        Case "Aqua"
            Window.Document.BgColor="Aqua"
    End Select
End Sub
-->
</SCRIPT>
</HEAD>
<BODY>
<!Add a heading->
<CENTER><H1>Our First Script Example</H1></CENTER>

<!Use a form to test out the VBScript.->
<FORM NAME="SampleForm1">

<!Create a text entry control.->
Enter a short text string:
<INPUT TYPE="text" VALUE="Some Text" NAME="TextInput" SIZE=20><P><P>

<!Add some color selection radio buttons.->
Select a foreground and background color: <P>
<TABLE WIDTH=300>
<TR>
    <TH><CENTER>Foreground</CENTER></TH>
```

7

```
   <TH><CENTER>Background</CENTER></TH>
<TR>
   <TD><INPUT TYPE="radio" NAME="Radio1" VALUE="Black" CHECKED
      ONCLICK=ChangeColor("Black")>Black</TD>
   <TD><INPUT TYPE="radio" NAME="Radio2" VALUE="Silver" CHECKED
      ONCLICK=ChangeColor("Silver")>Silver</TD>
<TR>
   <TD><INPUT TYPE="radio" NAME="Radio1" VALUE="Blue"
      ONCLICK=ChangeColor("Blue")>Blue</TD>
   <TD><INPUT TYPE="radio" NAME="Radio2" VALUE="White"
      ONCLICK=ChangeColor("White")>White</TD>
<TR>
   <TD><INPUT TYPE="radio" NAME="Radio1" VALUE="Red"
      ONCLICK=ChangeColor("Red")>Red</TD>
   <TD><INPUT TYPE="radio" NAME="Radio2" VALUE="Fuchsia"
      ONCLICK=ChangeColor("Fuchsia")>Fuchsia</TD>
<TR>
   <TD><INPUT TYPE="radio" NAME="Radio1" VALUE="Green"
      ONCLICK=ChangeColor("Green")>Green</TD>
   <TD><INPUT TYPE="radio" NAME="Radio2" VALUE="Teal"
      ONCLICK=ChangeColor("Teal")>Teal</TD>
<TR>
   <TD><INPUT TYPE="radio" NAME="Radio1" VALUE="Purple"
      ONCLICK=ChangeColor("Purple")>Purple</TD>
   <TD><INPUT TYPE="radio" NAME="Radio2" VALUE="Aqua"
      ONCLICK=ChangeColor("Aqua")>Aqua</TD>
</TABLE><P><P>

<!Define a place to put the results.->
<TEXTAREA ROWS=5 NAME="Results">
</TEXTAREA><P><P>

<!-This is a standard button type.  We'll use it to display the text using the script.->
<INPUT TYPE=button VALUE="Try It!" ONCLICK=ChangeText()>

</FORM>
</BODY>
</HTML>
```

Now that you've had a look at the code, let's break it apart. Look at the HTML part of the page first. All we do is display a heading, a text input box (with associated prompt), some radio buttons (also with associated prompt), and a text area. Most of this code shouldn't be any surprise; we covered it as part of Chapter 4. There are, however, some tricks that you should notice. First, take a look at the way we use a table to line up the various radio

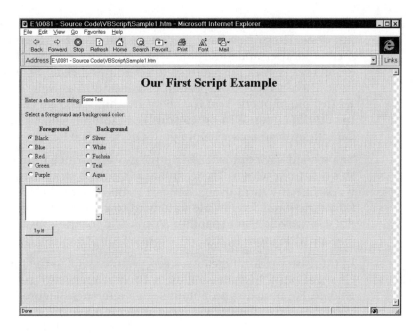

The first
VBScript
sample uses
a variety of
HTML and
VBScript
techniques to
display the
information
in a pleasing
way.

Figure 7-1.

Always select
a procedure
(Sub) when
you don't
require any
output from
the VBScript.
Otherwise,
use a function
in its place.

buttons. This is one of the techniques that you'll see used almost constantly on production sites. Notice also that there are actually two sets of radio buttons. You need two sets so that the user sees a highlighted entry for both foreground and background selections.

We're using a new attribute—ONCLICK—for the radio buttons. All of them point to the same VBScript procedure, ChangeColor. We also pass the color that we want to use to the procedure. The Try It! button is of the same type we saw in Chapter 4. Notice, however, that it too uses an ONCLICK attribute in this example. We need to point to the ChangeText procedure to update the Results text box. Notice that this particular procedure doesn't require any input from the button.

Now it's time to look at the VBScript procedures. ChangeText( ) is the first one on the list. Notice that we begin by creating a form reference (actually a constant) that points to the form. This will make your code shorter in most cases and also help you avoid ambiguities when you reference a particular object on the form, such as a control. You can use this technique at virtually any form level, though you'll see it most commonly used as shown here. The second task is to take the text out of TextInput and place it in Results. We do this with a simple equality in this case.

7

This may seem like an overly simple example until you consider what you've just done. How often have you seen a standard HTML form provide any method of user update? That's what we've just done with this VBScript. Results won't wait for a refresh to get some work done, it will update right now. There's another important consideration as well. All of the processing we just did happened on the client machine. You'll find that this allows you to perform all kinds of processing. For example, you could validate all of the data input from a user before you send it to the server.

The second VBScript is fairly simple as well. Notice that we accept input for this one from sColor. There isn't anything too strange in that—VBScript works like any form of Visual Basic in this regard. Notice that we use the fully functional Select Case statement to change the color value. JavaScript doesn't provide this capability. You'll find for the most part that VBScript does provide more in the way of statements than its counterpart.

We used Script Wizard for the first time in Chapter 4 — look there for additional usage details.

In this case we don't create a reference constant to the form as we did in ChangeText( ). Instead we'll use a direct reference to the object we want to change. So, how do you obtain such a reference? Figure 7-2 shows Script Wizard. Notice that the Window object is open and shows the same hierarchy to BgColor and FgColor defined in our VBScript. (The FgColor entry is two below the BgColor entry highlighted in the Insert Actions field.) Even if you can't use Script Wizard to create a particular script, you'll find that it's a very good tool in other respects—one of which is figuring out how to access the methods and properties you need.

There are two other things you should know about. First, notice that the color settings are changed using standard HTML colors. This is a lot more readable than the hex values that Script Wizard will supply. You'll still have to rely on hex values for custom colors, but it's normally better if you can make do with a standard HTML color. Sometimes the added readability is worth a loss of a little pizzazz on your Web page. If nothing else, use graphics when a particular situation demands more than the usual amount of color.

The second thing you need to know about is that you can't change the font color using VBScript. Normally you'd use the Window.Document.Write( ) method shown in Figure 7-2 (four entries above the highlighted BgColor entry) to accomplish this, but VBScript doesn't support it. Here's another difference between JavaScript and VBScript. You'll find that JavaScript currently provides better object support in some cases than VBScript will.

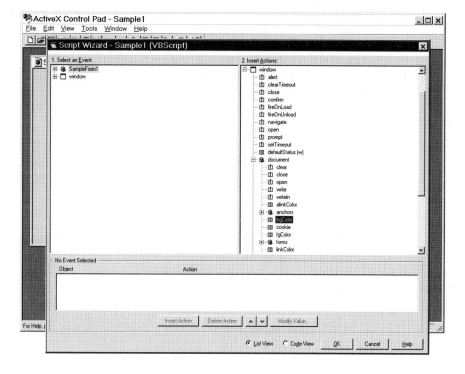

Script Wizard is a valuable tool for determining the hierarchy of objects on your page.

Figure 7-2.

For example, if you wanted to change the font color to blue using JavaScript, you'd simply write a line of code like this:

```
Window.Document.Write("<FONT COLOR=Blue>")
```

Using JavaScript

JavaScript is pretty straightforward to learn if you know C. Since we've already taken a preliminary look at JavaScript's syntax in the previous sections of this chapter, let's take a look at an example script. Listing 7-2 shows a fairly simple JavaScript (and associated HTML) that allows us to display an order form and automatically calculate the amount that the user owes. This particular program is a bit more complicated than the VBScript example in the previous section—especially in the HTML area. Take a close look at the listing and you'll see a tag or two that you haven't seen before,

7

along with some unique uses for ones you've already seen. Figure 7-3 shows what this form looks like when you first open it up. Notice that the table is in full view this time. This particular form doesn't include a Submit button yet. We'll cover data processing needs in Chapters 12 and 13. The important piece of information to get from this example is how to process data contained in a form locally.

Listing 7-2

```
<HTML>
<HEAD>
<TITLE>Typical Entry Form</TITLE>

<SCRIPT LANGUAGE="JavaScript">
<!--
function CalculateItem1(nAmount)
{
   Window.DataEntry.Item1Ex.Value = nAmount * Window.DataEntry.Item1.Value
   CalculateTotals()
}

function CalculateItem2(nAmount)
{
   Window.DataEntry.Item2Ex.Value = nAmount * Window.DataEntry.Item2.Value
   CalculateTotals()
}

function CalculateItem3(nAmount)
{
   Window.DataEntry.Item3Ex.Value = nAmount * Window.DataEntry.Item3.Value
   CalculateTotals()
}

function CalculateTotals()
{
   with (Window.DataEntry)
   {
   // Calculate the item subtotals.
   nTotalItems = parseInt(Item1.Value) + parseInt(Item2.Value) +
parseInt(Item3.Value)
   nTotalAmount = parseFloat(Item1Ex.Value) + parseFloat(Item2Ex.Value) +
parseFloat(Item3Ex.Value)

   // Calculate the total amounts.
   nHandling = nTotalItems * 5
   nTax = nTotalAmount * .05
   nTotal = parseFloat (nTotalAmount) + parseFloat (nHandling) + parse Float (nTax)
```

```
        // Store the data.
        Handling.Value = nHandling
        Tax.Value = nTax
        Total.Value = nTotal
        }
}
-->
</SCRIPT>

</HEAD>
<BODY>
<!Add a heading.->
<CENTER><H1>Sam's Special Order Form</H1><CENTER>
<H3><MARQUEE WIDTH=50% LOOP=INFINITE>
    Get It While It's Hot!  Sam's is known the world over for really HOT items!
    Sams will not be held responsible for stolen items,
    but then you're not really worried about that if you're shopping here.
</MARQUEE></H3>

<!Create a form.->
<FORM NAME="DataEntry">

<!Place a table of order items within the form.  The table will->
<!include four columns: quantity, description, unit price, and->
<!extended price.  The user will only have to type something->
<!in the quantity column.->
<TABLE WIDTH=100% BORDER=1>
<TR>
    <TH WIDTH=30> Quantity </TH>
    <TH> Description </TH>
    <TH WIDTH=75> Unit Price </TH>
    <TH WIDTH=75> Extended Price </TH>
<TR>
    <TD><INPUT TYPE="text" NAME="Item1" VALUE=" " SIZE=3
        ONCHANGE=CalculateItem1(24.99)></TD>
    <TD>Remove It Shaving Mug</TD>
    <TD>$24.99</TD>
    <TD>$<INPUT TYPE="text" NAME="Item1Ex" VALUE="0" SIZE=7></TD>
<TR>
    <TD><INPUT TYPE="text" NAME="Item2" VALUE=" " SIZE=3
        ONCHANGE=CalculateItem2(39.99)></TD>
    <TD>Rampaging Willy Doll</TD>
    <TD>$39.99</TD>
    <TD>$<INPUT TYPE="text" NAME="Item2Ex" VALUE="0" SIZE=7></TD>
<TR>
    <TD><INPUT TYPE="text" NAME="Item3" VALUE=" " SIZE=3
```

7

```
            ONCHANGE=CalculateItem3(19.95)></TD>
    <TD>You Said It! Game</TD>
    <TD>$19.95</TD>
    <TD>$<INPUT TYPE="text" NAME="Item3Ex" VALUE="0" SIZE=7></TD>
<TR>
    <TD><INPUT TYPE="hidden"></TD>
    <TD ALIGN=Right><H3>Shipping and Handling (@ $5.00 / Item)</H3></TD>
    <TD><INPUT TYPE="hidden"></TD>
    <TD>$<INPUT TYPE="text" NAME="Handling" VALUE="0" SIZE=7></TD>
<TR>
    <TD><INPUT TYPE="hidden"></TD>
    <TD ALIGN=Right><H3>Tax (@ 5%)</H3></TD>
    <TD><INPUT TYPE="hidden"></TD>
    <TD>$<INPUT TYPE="text" NAME="Tax" VALUE="0" SIZE=7></TD>
<TR>
    <TD><INPUT TYPE="hidden"></TD>
    <TD ALIGN=RIGHT><STRONG><H3>Total</H3></STRONG></TD>
    <TD><INPUT TYPE="hidden"></TD>
    <TD>$<INPUT TYPE="text" NAME="Total" VALUE="0" SIZE=7></TD>
</TABLE>
</FORM>
</BODY>
</HTML>
```

Let's begin by looking at the HTML code in this example. First, it contains a new tag, <MARQUEE>, that allows you to display scrolling text. You can also use this tag to scroll an image—which is what the vast majority of programmers do. The text capabilities you get with this tag are a little limited. Any "fancy" text that you add within the <MARQUEE> tag won't appear onscreen. The text that you start with is the text you keep throughout. This means doing any formatting you want before you actually display the marquee (it also explains why so many programmers prefer to use an image).

CAUTION: The <MARQUEE> tag won't work with Netscape Navigator browsers older than version 2.0. You'll also want to provide a LOOP attribute whenever you use this tag because some browsers that do support it react strangely if you don't. It's important to get user feedback when you first implement this particular tag since it is so prone to causing problems with older browsers. A little tweak here or there could make the tag work for everyone's browser that does support it at your site.

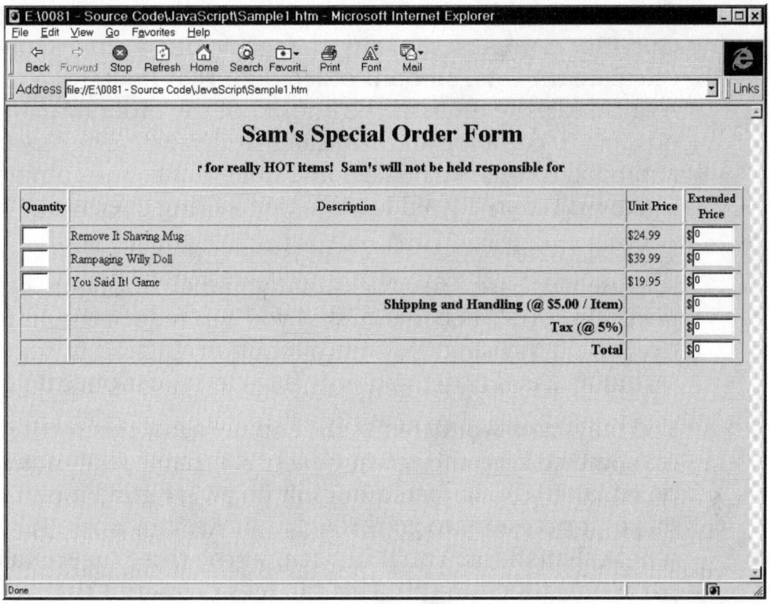

The order
entry form
for Sam's
automatically
calculates the
totals for all
the items
ordered by
the user.
Figure 7-3.

The next piece of HTML code you'll see bears a striking resemblance to the previous example. We're using a table again to create the order form. Notice the use of the WIDTH attribute in several areas. There are two ways to use it: as a percentage of the total screen or as a specific amount of screen real estate. If you use the percentage method, the amount of space used will remain proportional as the user resizes the display. Also notice that three of the four table headings use a WIDTH attribute. The Description heading gets whatever is left after the other three take what they need. You'll find that this is a very convenient way to present users with an appealing form no matter what their screen resolution or how they resize the browser window.

There are a few changes in the <INPUT> tag as well. Notice that the code uses the SIZE attribute to keep the text input to a specific size. You'll also find a new type of <INPUT> tag. The "hidden" control can get rid of those raised areas in a table. If you look at Figure 7-3 again, you'll notice that the hidden control keeps the Quantity field from retaining a raised appearance when we calculate the totals.

Now let's look at the JavaScript. Notice that we keep all of the functions within a comment, as we did with VBScript. The reason is the same—to prevent older browsers from having problems reading the form.

7

The first three functions are pretty simple. All we do is monitor the three Quantity row entries for any change. When a change does occur, we calculate the total amount ordered for that item, then call a function that recalculates the totals at the bottom of the order form. It may have been possible to combine all three calculations into one function, but this approach is somewhat faster and does reduce the complexity of the code. There isn't even any added function calling overhead.

The CalculateTotals( ) function is the one that you'll want to look at closely because there are a few tricks that you may not figure out at first when using JavaScript on forms. Notice that you can reduce the amount of typing you need to do by using the with( ) function. Instead of constantly typing "Window.DataEntry," you only have to type it once if you use this approach.

About the only time you really have to use parseInt( ) and parseFloat( ) is when you are adding numbers together—JavaScript does a good job of keeping variable types straight during other math operations.

You may have wondered at the beginning of this section how JavaScript managed to keep the actual type of a variable straight since it's a loosely typed language. In fact, it doesn't do a very good job in some places—which makes it necessary to go through a little extra work. Take a look at the first set of calculations. You'll notice that the three object values are within a parseInt( ) function call. This call tells JavaScript that you want to convert the string to a number. If you don't use this function, you'll end up concatenating the three strings into one large string instead of adding them as intended. The same note holds true for the next line. In this case, we need to use the parseFloat( ) function though, since these are dollar values. It's not the most elegant solution, but it works.

The last thing you should notice is that the CalculateTotals( ) function uses a lot of intermediate variables. In this case, the intermediate variables help JavaScript keep the types of the variables straight and make the code a little easier to read. There isn't any reason you couldn't get rid of one or two of the intermediate variables if the memory they took was cause for concern.

TIP: Make sure you use the Tools | Options | Script command to change your language type if you intend to use JavaScript instead of VBScript with the ActiveX Control Pad. The current version tends to lose this setting after each session, and reversing any changes made by Script Wizard can become time consuming.

Working with ActiveX Controls

Believe it or not, you have just about everything you need to create some really astounding Web pages using a combination of scripts, HTML, and

ActiveX controls. The only thing you need to do now is put everything you've learned so far together and add just a tad more information to it.

As with the previous section, we're going to look at two different examples using the two scripting languages: VBScript and JavaScript. The difference is that this time we'll put everything together along with objects. The examples are purposely simple because we'll explore more complex avenues throughout the rest of the book. It's very important to get the basics down for now.

Using VBScript

Working with an ActiveX control under VBScript is much the same as working with the document as a whole. You really don't need to work all that hard at it if you take a few precautions before you start coding. Of course, it helps to have the full vendor documentation for a control before you try to use it. (This isn't a problem when you write your own controls.)

Make sure you always check which language ActiveX Control Pad is set up to use before going into Script Wizard.

The first thing you'll want to do is place your controls on a page or within an HTML layout. We'll work with a standard HTML page in this section. The next section will show you what to do with an HTML layout generated by the ActiveX Control Pad utility. Once you have the controls in place, open Script Wizard and have a look around. Figure 7-4 shows a typical view of what you'll see for the OCXEXMPL control we created in Chapter 2.

Notice that there are several events located on the left side of the display. The idea that we'll look at next is going to be a little tough for you to remember at first, but it's essential that you do. If you want to attach a script to a particular event listed for an ActiveX control, combine the name you gave the control (OCXEXMPL1 in this case) with an underscore "_" and the name of the event to create a procedure name. Case is important—unlike many other things in VBScript, you have to work with the browser to make a connection. If we wanted to attach a script to the Click event of OCXEXMPL1, we would create a procedure with the name OCXEXMPL1_Click. Don't make the mistake of using onClick because it doesn't exist in your browser's world.

7

Another surprise is in store for you. You can change the characteristics of your control while the user is viewing it. That sounds pretty strange, but the example program we'll look at in this section does just that. We'll make our special button change state while it's running on the HTML page. Listing 7-3 contains the source code for this example. Figure 7-5 shows the initial display you'll see once you have the source code completed.

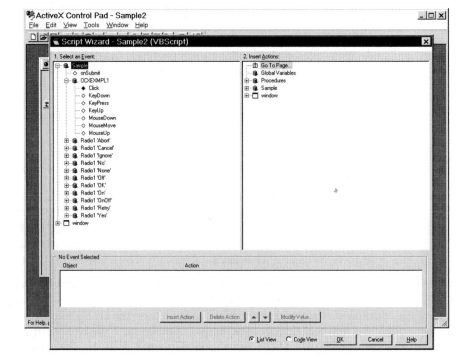

Script Wizard can deliver some essential information about your control before you use it on an HTML page.
Figure 7-4.

NOTE: Listing 7-3 shows the setup for the ActiveX control we created in Chapter 2. Make sure to substitute any control you create and want to test for the <OBJECT> tag currently shown. You'll at least want to change the CODEBASE attribute for the current object tag to match your system's setup. Use an URL to point to the control's location on your Internet server.

Listing 7-3

```
<HTML>
<HEAD>
<TITLE>Sample VBScript with ActiveX Object</TITLE>

<SCRIPT LANGUAGE="VBScript">
<!--
'This function displays the current caption on the ActiveX control
'when the user clicks it.
Sub OCXEXMPL1_Click()
    'Create a form reference.
    Dim Form1
```

```
        Set Form1 = Document.Sample

        'Check the ModalResult value.  Display its value along with the Caption.
        Select Case Form1.OCXEXMPL1.ModalResult
            Case -1
                MsgBox "ModalResult Value is: -1 or " + Form1.OCXEXMPL1.Caption
            Case 1
                MsgBox "ModalResult Value is: 1 or " + Form1.OCXEXMPL1.Caption
            Case 2
                MsgBox "ModalResult Value is: 2 or " + Form1.OCXEXMPL1.Caption
            Case 3
                MsgBox "ModalResult Value is: 3 or " + Form1.OCXEXMPL1.Caption
            Case 4
                MsgBox "ModalResult Value is: 4 or " + Form1.OCXEXMPL1.Caption
            Case 5
                MsgBox "ModalResult Value is: 5 or " + Form1.OCXEXMPL1.Caption
            Case 6
                MsgBox "ModalResult Value is: 6 or " + Form1.OCXEXMPL1.Caption
            Case 7
                MsgBox "ModalResult Value is: 7 or " + Form1.OCXEXMPL1.Caption
            Case 8
                MsgBox "ModalResult Value is: 8 or " + Form1.OCXEXMPL1.Caption
            Case 9
                MsgBox "ModalResult Value is: 9 or " + Form1.OCXEXMPL1.Caption
        End Select
End Sub


Sub SetControlState(sState)
        'Create a form reference.
        Dim Form1
        Set Form1 = Document.Sample

        'Determine which radio button has changed.
        Select Case sState
            Case "None"
                Form1.OCXEXMPL1.StdButtonType=0
            Case "OK"
                Form1.OCXEXMPL1.StdButtonType=1
            Case "Cancel"
                Form1.OCXEXMPL1.StdButtonType=2
            Case "Abort"
                Form1.OCXEXMPL1.StdButtonType=3
            Case "Retry"
                Form1.OCXEXMPL1.StdButtonType=4
            Case "Ignore"
                Form1.OCXEXMPL1.StdButtonType=5
```

7

```
        Case "Yes"
            Form1.OCXEXMPL1.StdButtonType=6
        Case "No"
            Form1.OCXEXMPL1.StdButtonType=7
        Case "On"
            Form1.OCXEXMPL1.StdButtonType=8
        Case "Off"
            Form1.OCXEXMPL1.StdButtonType=9
        Case "OnOff"
            Form1.OCXEXMPL1.OnOff=-1
    End Select
End Sub
-->
</SCRIPT>


</HEAD>
<BODY>

<!-Display a heading.->
<CENTER><H1>Using an ActiveX Control with VBScript</H1></CENTER>

<!-Create a form.->
<FORM NAME="Sample">

<!-Give the user the ability to change the control parameters.->
<H3>Select a Button Type:</H3>
<INPUT TYPE="radio" NAME="Radio1" VALUE="None"
   ONCLICK=SetControlState("None") CHECKED>None<BR>
<INPUT TYPE="radio" NAME="Radio1" VALUE="OK"
   ONCLICK=SetControlState("OK")>OK<BR>
<INPUT TYPE="radio" NAME="Radio1" VALUE="Cancel"
   ONCLICK=SetControlState("Cancel")>Cancel<BR>
<INPUT TYPE="radio" NAME="Radio1" VALUE="Abort"
   ONCLICK=SetControlState("Abort")>Abort<BR>
<INPUT TYPE="radio" NAME="Radio1" VALUE="Retry"
   ONCLICK=SetControlState("Retry")>Retry<BR>
<INPUT TYPE="radio" NAME="Radio1" VALUE="Ignore"
   ONCLICK=SetControlState("Ignore")>Ignore<BR>
<INPUT TYPE="radio" NAME="Radio1" VALUE="Yes"
   ONCLICK=SetControlState("Yes")>Yes<BR>
<INPUT TYPE="radio" NAME="Radio1" VALUE="No"
   ONCLICK=SetControlState("No")>No<BR>
<INPUT TYPE="radio" NAME="Radio1" VALUE="On"
   ONCLICK=SetControlState("On")>On<BR>
<INPUT TYPE="radio" NAME="Radio1" VALUE="Off"
   ONCLICK=SetControlState("Off")>Off<BR>
```

```
<INPUT TYPE="radio" NAME="Radio1" VALUE="OnOff"
   ONCLICK=SetControlState("OnOff")>On/Off<P><P>

<!-Add our example ActiveX control.->
<H3>See How the Control Changes -- Click It to See the Result</H3><P>
<OBJECT ID="OCXEXMPL1" WIDTH=75 HEIGHT=25
   CLASSID="CLSID:D8D77E03-712A-11CF-8C70-00006E3127B7"
   CODEBASE="http://aux/controls">
   <PARAM NAME="_Version" VALUE="65536">
   <PARAM NAME="_ExtentX" VALUE="1984">
   <PARAM NAME="_ExtentY" VALUE="661">
   <PARAM NAME="_StockProps" VALUE="70">
   <PARAM NAME="Caption" VALUE="Button">
</OBJECT>

</FORM>
</BODY>
</HTML>
```

There isn't anything new in the HTML code in this example. All we really needed was a set of radio buttons, some explanatory text, and the ActiveX control itself. Since we've visited the techniques used here before, we'll go on to the VBScript procedures.

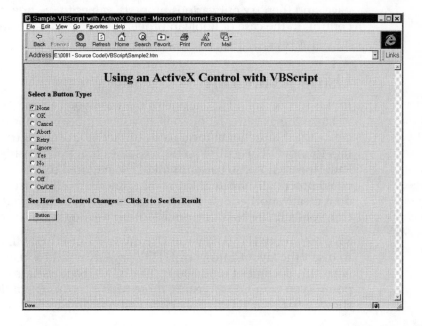

VBScript allows you to modify the functionality of a control in real time.

Figure 7-5.

7

This example uses two procedures. The first procedure, OCXEXMPL1_Click( ), allows us to check the state of the ActiveX control. We could have looked at just about any of the control parameters, but ModalResult and Caption provide the most useful information in this case. Notice that we use a Case Select structure to detect the current ModalResult setting, just like we did in the sample test code in Chapter 2. (You may want to revisit Chapter 2 at this point to make comparisons between the test C code and the VBScript code shown here.) Using the caption is simply a matter of concatenating its value to the end of the MsgBox message.

The second procedure doesn't look all that formidable until you figure out what we're really doing here. The radio buttons send this procedure a specific value each time the user clicks on them. That, in turn, does one of two things within the Select Case statement. Most of the button states are changed using the StdButtonType property. Changing that one property causes the ActiveX control to change both the Caption and ModalResult properties—all while the control is active on a form. Notice that there's one case where we don't use the StdButtonType. To create the special On/Off button that this control was designed to provide, you have to set the OnOff property to -1.

The question now is where the value of -1 for the OnOff property comes in. You can usually determine what value to give a control by working with it for a while within ActiveX Control Pad. Simply add the control to a blank page, and then try out various property values to see how they affect the control. In the case of Boolean properties, the values are always -1 for True and 0 for False.

Using JavaScript

Remember that the HTML page will have an HTM extension, and the HTML Layout will use an ALX extension.

In this section we'll look at one of the ways you can use ActiveX Control Pad to make things easier (though it may seem more complicated at first). We'll create a semifunctional form using all ActiveX controls (no more <INPUT> tags for now). This entire section assumes that you're using ActiveX Control Pad. However, it also contains all of the required source code so that you could potentially create it using other methods. The first thing you'll need to do is create another new HTML page and an HTML Layout using ActiveX Control Pad. The New button will allow you to create either document.

Save the empty HTML Layout. Use the Edit | Insert HTML Layout command to insert the layout into your HTML page. Now add a heading that explains what this document is all about. The HTML page itself is finished at this point—you won't do anything more with it in this example. Listing 7-4 shows what your HTML page code will probably look like.

Listing 7-4

```
<HTML>
<HEAD>
<TITLE>Using ActiveX Control with JavaScript and HTML Layout</TITLE>
</HEAD>
<BODY>

<!-Add a heading->
<CENTER><H1>Using JavaScript with ActiveX Controls on an HTML Layout</H1>

<!-Insert our layout->
<OBJECT CLASSID="CLSID:812AE312-8B8E-11CF-93C8-00AA00C08FDF"
    ID="Layout1_alx" STYLE="LEFT:0;TOP:0">
    <PARAM NAME="ALXPATH" REF VALUE="Layout1.alx">
</OBJECT>

</BODY>
</HTML>
```

Now that we've gotten the easy part out of the way, let's start looking at the HTML Layout. Figure 7-6 shows the set of ActiveX controls used for this example. All you need to do is click on a control in the Toolbox, and then drop it onto the canvas. (ActiveX Control Pad also allows you to use drag and drop to add controls to the canvas if you prefer that method.) Once the control is placed on the canvas, you can drag it to wherever it's needed, and then resize it to match other controls in the same area. A functional layout would differ from the one shown in Figure 7-6, but this one is designed to show you specific features for using ActiveX controls and JavaScript together. Notice that all the controls are ActiveX controls taken from the Toolbox.

You can also use Script Wizard as shown in this section to get VBScript procedure names.

It's time to make this example functional. Like VBScript, JavaScript requires that you perform some special function name formatting before you attach a function to a button or other control. There's also an easy way to come up with the name. In this case though, we'll use Script Wizard to get it for us.

Open Script Wizard using the Tools | Script Wizard command. Select the Click event for one of the pushbuttons. At the bottom of the dialog you'll see List View and Code View radio buttons. Click on the Code View radio button and you'll see the bottom of the dialog change, as shown in Figure 7-7. Look at the gray bar in the lower third of the dialog—notice that it now shows you precisely how to format your function call for JavaScript. If you had selected VBScript in place of JavaScript as your language of choice, the dialog would show the VBScript version of the procedure call (similar to the examples shown in Listings 7-1 and 7-3 of this chapter).

7

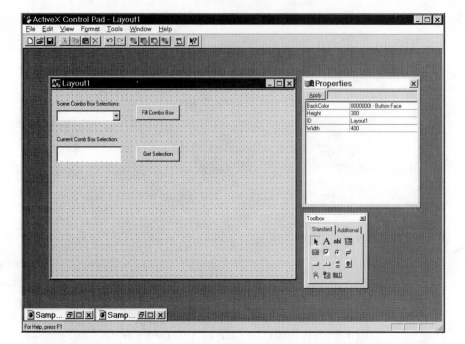

Layout of
ActiveX
controls.
Figure 7-6.

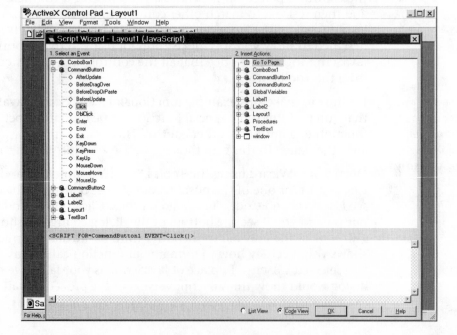

Script Wizard
will help you
figure out the
required
procedure or
function
names for
accessing
an object.
Figure 7-7.

Now it's time to add some JavaScript to make our controls functional. Close Script Wizard (if you haven't already). Right-click on the layout and you'll see a context menu. Select View Source from the context menu. ActiveX Control Pad may ask you to save the layout first; do so if it does. What you'll see next is a Notepad or Wordpad (depending on how large your layout is) text file. Don't disturb the <OBJECT> tags already in place. Add the script code shown in Listing 7-5. (The listing also shows the <OBJECT> tags, should you wish to create this file by hand.) Figure 7-8 shows how the combination of HTML, scripts, and layout page look in a browser.

Listing 7-5

```
<!-This script fills the combo box with data.->
<SCRIPT FOR="CommandButton1" EVENT="Click()">
    for (nCount = 1; nCount < ComboBox1.ListRows; nCount++)
        {
        ComboBox1.AddItem("Item " + nCount)
        }
    ComboBox1.ListIndex = 0
</SCRIPT>

<!-This script retrieves the current combo box value.->
<SCRIPT FOR="CommandButton2" EVENT="Click()">
    TextBox1.Text = ComboBox1.Text
</SCRIPT>

<!-All of these objects are machine created, don't touch.->
<DIV ID="Layout1" STYLE="LAYOUT:FIXED;WIDTH:400pt;HEIGHT:300pt;">
    <OBJECT ID="Label1"
     CLASSID="CLSID:978C9E23-D4B0-11CE-BF2D-00AA003F40D0"
     CODEBASE="http://aux/controls"
STYLE="TOP:17pt;LEFT:8pt;WIDTH:124pt;HEIGHT:17pt;ZINDEX:0;">
        <PARAM NAME="Caption" VALUE="Some Combo Box Selections:">
        <PARAM NAME="Size" VALUE="4374;600">
        <PARAM NAME="FontCharSet" VALUE="0">
        <PARAM NAME="FontPitchAndFamily" VALUE="2">
        <PARAM NAME="FontWeight" VALUE="0">
    </OBJECT>
    <OBJECT ID="ComboBox1"
     CLASSID="CLSID:8BD21D30-EC42-11CE-9E0D-00AA006002F3"
     CODEBASE="http://aux/controls"
STYLE="TOP:33pt;LEFT:8pt;WIDTH:107pt;HEIGHT:18pt;TABINDEX:1;ZINDEX:1;">
        <PARAM NAME="VariousPropertyBits" VALUE="746604571">
        <PARAM NAME="DisplayStyle" VALUE="3">
        <PARAM NAME="Size" VALUE="3775;635">
        <PARAM NAME="MatchEntry" VALUE="1">
```

7

```
            <PARAM NAME="ShowDropButtonWhen" VALUE="2">
            <PARAM NAME="FontCharSet" VALUE="0">
            <PARAM NAME="FontPitchAndFamily" VALUE="2">
            <PARAM NAME="FontWeight" VALUE="0">
        </OBJECT>
        <OBJECT ID="CommandButton1"
          CLASSID="CLSID:D7053240-CE69-11CD-A777-00DD01143C57"
          CODEBASE="http://aux/controls"
STYLE="TOP:25pt;LEFT:140pt;WIDTH:72pt;HEIGHT:24pt;TABINDEX:2;ZINDEX:2;">
            <PARAM NAME="Caption" VALUE="Fill Combo Box">
            <PARAM NAME="Size" VALUE="2540;847">
            <PARAM NAME="FontCharSet" VALUE="0">
            <PARAM NAME="FontPitchAndFamily" VALUE="2">
            <PARAM NAME="ParagraphAlign" VALUE="3">
            <PARAM NAME="FontWeight" VALUE="0">
        </OBJECT>
        <OBJECT ID="Label2"
          CLASSID="CLSID:978C9E23-D4B0-11CE-BF2D-00AA003F40D0"
STYLE="TOP:74pt;LEFT:8pt;WIDTH:107pt;HEIGHT:17pt;ZINDEX:3;">
            <PARAM NAME="Caption" VALUE="Current Combo Box Selection:">
            <PARAM NAME="Size" VALUE="3775;600">
            <PARAM NAME="FontCharSet" VALUE="0">
            <PARAM NAME="FontPitchAndFamily" VALUE="2">
            <PARAM NAME="FontWeight" VALUE="0">
        </OBJECT>
        <OBJECT ID="TextBox1"
          CLASSID="CLSID:8BD21D10-EC42-11CE-9E0D-00AA006002F3"
STYLE="TOP:91pt;LEFT:8pt;WIDTH:107pt;HEIGHT:25pt;TABINDEX:4;ZINDEX:4;">
            <PARAM NAME="VariousPropertyBits" VALUE="746604571">
            <PARAM NAME="Size" VALUE="3775;882">
            <PARAM NAME="FontCharSet" VALUE="0">
            <PARAM NAME="FontPitchAndFamily" VALUE="2">
            <PARAM NAME="FontWeight" VALUE="0">
        </OBJECT>
        <OBJECT ID="CommandButton2"
          CLASSID="CLSID:D7053240-CE69-11CD-A777-00DD01143C57"
STYLE="TOP:91pt;LEFT:140pt;WIDTH:72pt;HEIGHT:24pt;TABINDEX:5;ZINDEX:5;">
            <PARAM NAME="Caption" VALUE="Get Selection">
            <PARAM NAME="Size" VALUE="2540;847">
            <PARAM NAME="FontCharSet" VALUE="0">
            <PARAM NAME="FontPitchAndFamily" VALUE="2">
            <PARAM NAME="ParagraphAlign" VALUE="3">
            <PARAM NAME="FontWeight" VALUE="0">
        </OBJECT>
    </DIV>
```

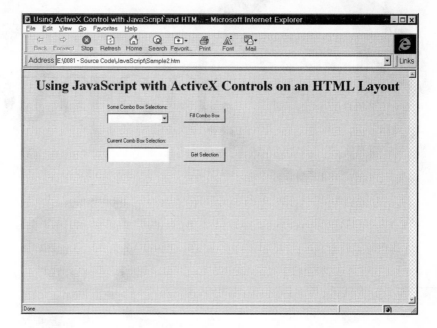

The HTML
layout isn't
visible in the
browser, but
the effects of
using it are.

Figure 7-8.

The two scripts shown in Listing 7-5 are fairly simple. The first script shows how you would fill a combo box. All you really need to do is use the AddItem method to tell the combo box what you want to add. Once you do fill the combo box, use the ListIndex property to set the default selection. If you don't do this, the user will continue to see a blank combo box, even after you fill it. The list index starts at 0.

One of the problems with using ActiveX objects is that you can't do certain setups until run time. For example, you can't fill a combo box with values until run time (just try doing it with the Properties dialog sometime). The whole idea behind using a scripting language with ActiveX is to give you a margin of flexibility you've never seen before.

There are quite a few ways to figure out what selection the user made. If you need a numeric selection number, you can get it from the ListIndex property. We needed a string value, so the Text property was the best place to go. That's what the second script does. It merely copies the value of the ComboBox1.Text property into the TextBox1.Text property.

7

Chapter

8

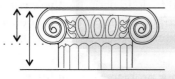

The Internet Is Not Your Computer

One of the biggest problems that some developers have when moving from the LAN or local machine to the Internet is recognizing that they are no longer working on their own computer—they're actually working on someone else's computer. Added to this problem is that they don't even know the people using the computer and will probably never get to meet them. Programming for the Internet means that you're leaving home. The ideas that may have worked on your local machine or within your company may not work so well in the Internet environment. For example, how many users would condescend to wait half an hour for your favorite control library to download just so they could see the image of a madman jumping up and down? It won't happen—so you may as well get used to the idea that large files just won't make it on a Web page.

This chapter is all about starting to think of the Internet as someone else's computer. We'll look at what precisely that means in the following sections. The first thing we'll look at is what you need to do to design ActiveX controls, Web pages, graphics, content, and even scripts. It's important to look at the total package when you think about the Internet, because that's what users will download from your site.

Next, we'll look at one of the most infamous problems on the Internet—too many pixels (or sometimes not enough of them). Some people will immediately think that this section is graphics specific. However, we'll look at pixels from a variety of perspectives. For example, what's the best way to grab users' attention without overwhelming them with input overload? We'll look at that issue and more.

Remember that speed is one of the biggest issues on the Internet right now. In fact, Microsoft and Netscape are duking it out in the browser wars. Microsoft is trying to win by providing a phenomenal feature set. Netscape, on the other hand, is trying to provide a very functional feature set combined with great download speeds and a small memory footprint. It's also interesting that Microsoft is giving their browser away, while Netscape charges a modest price. The next few months will show which strategy is right. However, it's probably safe to bet that some people will want speed, and others features. As a programmer, you have to cater to both crowds. That's what the third section in this chapter is about. We'll explore some alternatives that will make both kinds of users drool over your Web site without costing them in either the memory or speed arenas.

NOTE: The average user visiting your Web site will probably have a 14.4 Kbps modem, which can download information from the Internet at 1 Kbps on a good day. That means if you have a 10 KB GIF on your site, it will take ten seconds for the user to download it. It doesn't take too many of these small files to convince the user to click the Stop button and go to the next site. A good rule of thumb to follow is that a user will wait no longer than 60 seconds to download a Web page.

We'll look at one specialty graphics item in this chapter as well—animated GIFs. You'll find more of these little graphics on the Internet than you can shake a stick at. The reason is simple: animated GIFs are exceptionally memory efficient, yet they can really dazzle the average user. Some of the animated GIFs on the Internet right now are quite complex, but even a modest graphic image can add pizzazz to a site. For example, one site on the Internet uses a ball that changes color, in place of bullets, for major points of interest. This is a tiny animated GIF, but it really enhances the appeal of the site.

So far the chapter has provided a lot of "fun" information that you can use to keep your site looking great without making any mortal enemies over downloading time. We still haven't covered the issue of getting from one point to the other. So, how do you do it? The last section of this chapter looks at what you need to include in an ActiveX control to make it easy to get from point A to point B. The idea here is that the Internet is an interrelated set of sites, and you need to provide access to sites that complement your own. Doing so will make a lot of friends for you among users looking for detailed information about specific topics. In the past you could do this with links—which is still a good approach in many cases. However, links are static. Wouldn't it be nice if you could tailor a set of links based on a user's needs? That's one of the advantages to using the ActiveX approach to creating links from your site to others on the Internet.

Designing with the Internet in Mind

We'll take a look at some physical Web characteristics in this section of the chapter. How does your Web site appear to other users? You may think that the answer is easy, but it's not easy at all. For example, how accessible is your Web site to someone who's physically challenged? If you force someone to zoom all over the page trying to accomplish even the smallest task, it's not very accessible to this group. Creating a Web site that's user friendly means taking all of the users into account. Some programmers forget about blind users who are using some kind of reader to access the site. Did you include text prompts as alternates in your tags? A simple text prompt like

Even though you can't do anything about it right now, Microsoft is planning on adding the features found in the Accessibility applet in the Control Panel of Windows 95 and Windows NT 4.0 to their browser.

```
<IMG SRC="MyHouse.GIF" ALT="A picture of a house">
```

could help several categories of users—not just those who lack graphics capabilities with their browser. If you fail to include little features such as text prompts, you'll find that a blind person who really needed your product probably got left out in the cold.

There are some categories of users that you might need to pay special attention to depending on whom you're trying to attract. For example, what would your Web site look like to someone who only spoke Spanish? If your goal was to attract more than one nationality, you might want to provide links to pages that use alternate languages, not just English.

8

It's even reasonable to try and take some cultural differences into account (although this is a really tough nut to crack because you'll inevitably offend someone along the way). For example, even a name could cause problems, which is something most of us might not think about. In England, the name Wally is a derogatory term for someone who's stupid. Some book publishers, realizing that this is a problem, have gone so far as to change the author's name on a book to Wallace. If you're planning on attracting an international crowd, you'll want to spend some time learning about local taboos before you prepare your Internet site.

Let's talk about some of the problems you'll encounter with ActiveX controls and graphics. Some things that you'll want to avoid are obvious. Depicting someone in the nude is probably the fastest way to alienate potential visitors to your site—at least if you're in the United States. Some countries overseas don't have such taboos. However, no matter whom your audience is, you should practice at least a modicum of restraint—especially if your site is designed to attract users under 18.

Downloading controls can cause quite a problem. You'd think that it would be safe to place a control in the user's main Windows or SYSTEM folders. Nothing could be further from the truth. Who cleans those files up when the user no longer needs access to your control? Some users are already voicing concerns that they'll eventually end up with a hard disk full of old ActiveX controls that they won't be able to get rid of. If you're creating a public Internet site, you'll want to download your control to the OCCACHE directory (we covered downloading in Chapter 4). Downloading a control to OCCACHE allows the browser to get rid of it for you after a certain period of time. Of course, if you're providing access to a private intranet, placing the ActiveX control in the user's main Windows or SYSTEM folder is the appropriate thing to do, since you want the control to hang around for a while.

Sound bites—short sounds normally stored in WAV file format—are OK in many situations. In fact, a good sound bite can really dress up your Web site. For example, a sound bite telling users they completed a task successfully is a good way to provide positive feedback and improve their responses in other areas. However, there are situations in which you'll probably want to sharply curtail or avoid the use of sound bites. For example, most businesses frown on users receiving too many sound bites in a crowded office environment, especially when users aren't separated from each other by partitions. If using your Web site creates disturbances, users probably won't visit it even if they want to because the network administrator (or other management) will ask them not to. So, how do you determine what kind of sound bites to include?

If you're running a site designed for business use, you'll probably want to use them sparingly or not at all. If you're running a site that's for entertainment purposes, use as many as you think the user will want to hear. In other words, continuous sounds aren't good; sounds that stress some particular event are.

NOTE: The WAV file format is the most common media for sound files. However, your browser may support other sound file formats. Check your vendor documentation to be sure, if you plan to implement an intranet and need the added support of a special browser capability. You can also add other sound file formats using Java applets or ActiveX controls. If you plan to present sound bites on an Internet though, using the WAV file format is always the safest bet.

Music can be another problem area on some sites. Playing the *1812 Overture* when someone enters your financial Web site isn't the way to win friends or influence people. About the only thing you'll do is discourage anyone from visiting. Don't use music at all in business situations (unless there is a very special reason to do so, such as a promotional offer). Entertainment sites are another matter. You can use music as needed to make the user feel comfortable. However, you'll want to avoid playing the same tune over and over again. The "noise" will begin to grate on the user's nerves. Even if users don't consciously make a decision not to return, they'll still do it subconsciously. If you do want to play music continually, provide a variety of tunes and play them in random order. Of course, this technique eats up transmission bandwidth, so you may have to choose between music and getting other data downloaded quickly. The one advantage ActiveX technology gives you here is that you can provide an on/off switch for the music if you want to. That way users can simply turn the music off if things start moving too slowly.

There's also a problem on the Internet with what some people term jittery script. The same script program runs over and over again to produce some effect (usually visual) of dubious value. Drawing a graph or chart with a script is fine—trying to produce animation with one probably isn't the best use of resources. Scripts are about the handiest tool that the Webmaster has right now to dress up a Web site in a way that most browsers can use. People have the option of turning this capability off, so misusing scripts not only hurts you, but other Web sites as well. We'll look at animated GIFs later in

8

the chapter. Using an animated GIF is a lot more efficient than using a script in the wrong place.

Avoiding the Pixel Trap

In the previous section we looked at some Web site configuration traps of a general nature. In this section we'll look at one specific trap that every Webmaster falls into at one time or another—overuse of pixels on a Web page. *Pixels* are what make up the individual pictorial elements of any display. As a programmer, you know that each dot on the screen is individually drawn and that adding more colors necessarily slows the process down because there are more bits per pixel. In addition, higher-resolution displays take longer to redraw than lower-resolution screens. Add to that any activity that you've created using animated GIFs and ActiveX controls. By now you should be starting to see a potential problem. Pixels represent a major area of data movement between your Web site and the client machine.

To get a better idea of how severe this problem could get, just think about how much time it takes to move pixels over the PC bus. Look at any of the trade presses—even major newspapers—and you'll see an advertisement of some sort or another for the latest display adapter. What do all of these advertisements have in common? They all tell you how much faster they can move pixels around onscreen—that the improved speed can best be used to display higher-resolution images with more colors. Sound familiar? You've probably read hundreds of such advertisements along the way. (A quick poll of four weekly newspapers sitting on my desk showed that the average trade press newspaper contains a whopping six advertisements for display adapters.)

Now extend the information you've just learned to the Internet. If it takes a lot of bandwidth to move pixels around on a PC, just how much bandwidth do you think you're eating up by moving that 200 KB image across a 28.8 Kbps connection? The pixel trap is easy to fall into. It's easy to forget that the Web page you're designing locally and testing over a LAN intranet setup will have to travel to a client machine somewhere out there. Even if you try to test all of your pages using a live connection, you're going through at most two routers to reach your Web site. Some of the people accessing your Web site will go through ten or more routers. Each router slows those pixels down as well. What might look acceptable to you in a lab environment will most certainly drive users of your site crazy.

So, how do you test for the pixel trap? The previous section contained a valuable note that bears repeating here. A 14.4 Kbps modem will download at most 1 KB of data per second. That means a 200 KB image will take 200 seconds to download, given less than optimal conditions. Would you sit around for a little over 3 minutes waiting for an image to download? Even if the user had a 28.8 Kbps modem, the image would take 1.5 minutes to download. (Fortunately, a newer high-speed modem is arriving on the market in a 33.3 Kbps form, but few ISPs will be able to support this higher speed any time soon.)

WARNING: If you're saying to yourself right now that the average user has a 28.8 modem, don't believe everything you read. Conduct a survey, if nothing else, and you'll probably find about the same results that most Webmasters have. About 20 percent of the users visiting your Web site will use a 28.8 modem, 55 percent will use a 14.4 modem, 15 percent will still have a 9600 modem sitting around, and the remaining 10 percent will use something else (some of which will be direct high-speed connections). In fact, conducting a survey is probably the best thing you can do to learn just how many pixels your users will be able to tolerate.

Here's a rule of thumb you should write down. The entire size of any Web page should never exceed 60 KB if your average user owns a 14.4 modem. If your average user owns a 28.8 modem, you can safely bump that limit up to 100 KB or even 110 KB, but no more than that. Always strive to hit well below this mark if at all possible, and try to make your pages about the same size so that the user will see consistent page transitions. (A user who expects to wait a certain length of time between pages will notice any large deviations—reducing the effectiveness of those well-designed Web pages you created.)

It should be obvious at this point that you'll have to perform some kind of programmer magic to provide great-looking content without extended download times. So how can you achieve this goal of 60/100 KB? The following list describes several ways.

♦ **Reduce image size** A number of products on the market will help you shrink the size of an image. In many cases you can shrink the image by half in each direction without making it hard to see or too grainy. A reduction of that amount will reduce the size of an image by a factor of 4. So, if your image is currently 100 KB, it will only take 25 KB when you finish shrinking it.

8

◆ **Reduce the number of colors**   Some people think that every image has to use 24-bit color, but how many computers can actually display that many? A good rule of thumb is to use 256 colors for art and 16 colors for icons. Pictures—actual images that are captured with a camera—will probably need more colors, depending on the quality of the image that you want to present. A color reduction will usually reduce your image size by a factor of 2.

◆ **Avoid realistic art**   You may want to see that picture of your best friend displayed on your Web site, but it's pretty safe to say that no one else will be too thrilled about it. Unless you absolutely must have a pictorial image of some idea or concept, use art instead. Try to present your ideas in the simplest ways possible. Using realistic art will almost always increase image size by a factor of 10.

◆ **Use compression if possible**   This may seem a bit weird when you first think about it, but what is stopping you from downloading compressed graphics to a user's machine and then blowing them back up using an ActiveX control? Even if you don't want to go this route, there are some Netscape plug-ins that will help you accomplish the same thing. But you will have to give up something to get the incredible space savings that compression can provide—compatibility. Compression can reduce an image by a factor of 5 or more.

◆ **Use animation sparingly**   Animated GIFs are actually created using a series of images. Even if you use the image-cropping techniques we will look at later in this chapter, you'll find that an animated GIF can quickly become more bother than it's worth. Make sure that you keep animated images small and pertinent.

◆ **Use HTML tags**   Don't forget that you can create some nice effects using the <MARQUEE> tag, and it costs you a lot less download time than just about any other form of onscreen action.

WARNING: Some browsers provide support for specialty tags such as <MARQUEE>, and others don't. You always use these tags at your own risk. The worst that will happen in most cases is that the browser will simply ignore a tag it doesn't understand. Many Web sites now contain a message stating, "Best when viewed with <Browser X>." This tells your audience which browser you used in creating the site and at least gives them some idea of where to look for problems when your site doesn't work as anticipated.

♦ **Display data using efficient methods** Some people think they need a really huge ActiveX control that displays almost live data to make an impression. But users won't care if the graph you display is a few minutes old—the only major concern is that the data is at least fresh and not out of date. There are times when you'll simply want the server to update a static graph at specific intervals instead of relying on ActiveX to transfer the image.

♦ **Give users a method of escape** There are many ways to do this, but most Web sites simply provide a link that turns off the graphic display. Users still get the use of the site, but they'll see text instead of graphics. You could even provide an intermediate level of user interface by including a tag that allows users to turn off animation without affecting the rest of the graphics they'll see.

This section has covered a lot of ground from a theoretical point of view. We looked at the optimal situation, in which a site provides a perfect balance between beauty and the needs of the user. Life is seldom so kind. You're going to find that marketing wants to load some huge graphic on the main page and a ton of little graphs on other pages. Someone in management will get the bright idea that it would be nice to have live data after all. You'll even have trouble from users who want you to provide more functionality, but at no cost to them.

When you run into one of these situations, see if one of the bullets we just looked at will help you get your Web page to that magic 60 KB level. If you can't achieve that level despite your best efforts, you may want to take another more drastic step. Simply tell people that they're going to need a 28.8 modem or better to visit your Web site. You'll still get some people who complain, but at least you'll be able to say that they were warned.

Using Tricks of the Trade to Reduce Processing Needs

Trying to find a balance between really intriguing Web pages and those that take so long to download that no one sees them is more than just an interesting problem. Some Webmasters never do seem to find the right combination for their Web site. You'll see some truly boring Web sites out there simply because the Webmasters who designed them didn't have the artistic talent required to provide substantial art or simply didn't want to increase download time after user complaints.

8

There is no shortage of ways to make your Web site user friendly and still allow the user to download each page in a reasonable amount of time. The first thing you'll want to do is use the divide and conquer technique. You'll find that looking at a Web site as if it were a book is a good way to go. In fact, you should create a Web site outline just like an author would create an outline for a book. Define where each page begins and ends—try to make each page equal in regard to download time. If you find that one page takes too long to download, you may want to divide its content into two or even three pages. Don't try to place every bit of information you have to offer on one page. Use links effectively to present the user with an overview and a method to get more detail if needed.

Sound bites (in the form of WAV files) go a long way toward dressing up a Web site as well. However, some users will find them distracting if you continuously play sound bites every time users perform the smallest task. Make your sound bites short and to the point. Add them like a cook would add a spice. A little spice goes a long way toward making a tasty dish. Using too much spice will ruin whatever it is that you're trying to create.

Using a marquee is one way to add a form of animation to your Web page. All a marquee does is display a scrolling message or graphic image. We looked at an HTML tag for doing this in Listing 7-2 in Chapter 7. Microsoft also provides an ActiveX version of the marquee as part of the ActiveX Control Pad utility.

Animation can really enhance a site without adding too much overhead (although it does add some). The problem, of course, is spending the time to create some kind of animation routine. Some of you may be tempted to write a script or create an ActiveX control to get the job done, but there's a better way. You don't have to create fancy animation schemes if you don't want to, just use an animated GIF. If you're like me, you're probably asking what an animated GIF is by now, since most programmers have never seen such a thing. In reality, if you've spent much time on the Internet, you probably have seen one or two of these files. All an animated GIF consists of is a series of images that are displayed one at a time on your Web site.

TIP: You can see animated GIFs in action on many Internet sites. One of the more interesting places to look is http://www.wanderers.com/rose /animate.html. This site offers an index of sites you can visit to see various kinds of animated GIFs. Looking at a variety of sites will help you understand what works and what doesn't. You can also download an animated GIF Wizard, make your own animated GIF online, and learn all about how to make animated GIFs.

Small is better when it comes to Web sites. A recent visit to some Web sites showed that some of them were remarkably colorful and interesting, yet proved remarkably fast to download. Looking at the code showed one common element. All of these authors used tables and frames to divide the page into smaller areas. Each area used small icons and graphics to make the page look nice. In addition, the author usually used some kind of coordinating color scheme to allow each frame an individual appearance without making the page look gaudy.

Let's take a look at an example page that demonstrates the concepts we've talked about so far in the chapter. Listings 8-1 through 8-5 show how this page is put together. Notice that it includes some small graphics and frames to organize the information. You also see many of the other tricks that you've seen in the book so far (and a few new ones as well). Figure 8-1 shows how this page would look—at least in shades of gray. You'll need to construct the page to appreciate the use of color in this case.

NOTE: This example doesn't cover everything you can do. In the next section we'll look at animated GIFs. We'll also look at other kinds of graphic displays in Chapter 11. Make sure you spend some time looking at what you can do with text displays in Chapters 10 and 12. Finally, if multimedia is your way of expressing yourself, take a look at the techniques in Chapter 14. The chapter covers a few things you can do to make multimedia at least palatable for the user in today's computing environment.

Listing 8-1

```
<!-FRAME.HTM->
<HTML>
<HEAD>
<TITLE>Sample Web Page</TITLE>
</HEAD>
<!-Play a sound for those entering the Web site.->
<BGSOUND SRC=TwilZone.WAV>

<!-Set the frame parameters.->
<FRAMESET COLS="15%, *" ROWS="20%, 80%">

<!-Add an icon->
<FRAME SCROLLING=NO SRC=Icon.HTM>

<!-Create a heading.->
<FRAME SCROLLING=NO SRC=Heading.HTM>

<!-List some other sites that may be of interest.->
```

8

```
<FRAME SRC=OthrSite.HTM>

<!-Display the main content for our page.->
<FRAME SRC=Main.HTM>

</BODY>
```

Listing 8-2

```
<!-HEADING.HTM->
<HTML>
<HEAD>
<TITLE>New Page</TITLE>
</HEAD>
<BODY BGCOLOR=WHITE>

<!-Define a heading and marquee for our site.->
<CENTER><H1> Welcome to The TIME Site</H1>
<H3><FONT COLOR=WHITE>
<MARQUEE BGCOLOR=BLUE BEHAVIOR=ALTERNATE WIDTH="75%" LOOP=INFINITE>
    One of the best places on earth to learn that time is money!
</MARQUEE>
</H3><FONT COLOR=BLACK>
</CENTER>

</BODY>
</HTML>
```

Listing 8-3

```
<!-ICON.HTM->
<HTML>
<HEAD>
<TITLE>New Page</TITLE>
</HEAD>
<BODY BGCOLOR=YELLOW>

<!-Display our icon.->
<IMG SRC=TimeIt.GIF ALT="From 9 to 5">

</BODY>
</HTML>
```

Listing 8-4

```
<!-OTHRSITE.HTM->
<HTML>
<HEAD>
<TITLE>New Page</TITLE>
</HEAD>
```

```
<BODY BGCOLOR=YELLOW>

<!-Display a heading.->
<CENTER><FONT COLOR=BLUE>
<H2>Other Interesting Sites</H2>
</CENTER><FONT COLOR=BLACK>

<!-Display the time management links.->
<P><P><CENTER><H3>Time Management</H3></CENTER>
<A HREF="http://www.time101.com">Time Management 101</A><P>
<A HREF="http://www.businesstime.com">Time Management for Business</A><P>
<A HREF="http://www.killerhelp.com">Killer Time Management Techniques</A><P>

<!-Display the added help links.->
<P><P><CENTER><H3>Getting Help</H3></CENTER>
<A HREF="http://www.superserve.com">Super Services</A><P>
<A HREF="http://www.irons.com">Too Many Irons in Fire</A><P>
<A HREF="http://www.business.com">Business Help to Go</A><P>

</BODY>
</HTML>
```

Listing 8-5

```
<!-MAIN.HTM->
<HTML>
<HEAD>
<TITLE>New Page</TITLE>
</HEAD>
<BODY BGCOLOR=BLUE LINK=YELLOW VLINK=SILVER>

<!-Display a heading.->
<CENTER><FONT  COLOR=YELLOW>
<H2>What's Happening This Week?</H2>
</CENTER><FONT COLOR=WHITE>

<!-Display a list of current events.->
<UL>
<LI>Learn how to create time in a bottle--get your own genie.  Demonstrations of how
    to work with a genie every Tuesday and Friday.  Call (555)555-1212 or send email
    care of this site for more details.
<LI>Tired of working too hard for too little time off?  Learn the secrets of cloning
    yourself.  There should be more of you.  Click <A HREF="Clone">HERE</A> for more
    details.
<LI>Be the envy of every salesperson out there.  Hire an inflatable dummy to sit in
    for you at the office while you go out and make a killing in new sales.  We'll
    show you how at <A HREF="http://www.dummy.com">Dummies Unlimited</A>.
```

8

```
</UL>

<!-Present an ad for potential future sales.->
<CENTER><HR WIDTH=75%></CENTER>
<STRONG><H3><CENTER><PRE>
Get your ad on this site.  We'll run just about any ad at any time
since we really need the money.  If you want to line our pockets
with your extra cash, give us a call at (555)555-1212.  You can
also send us email which we'll gladly answer Tuesday for some
money today.
</PRE></CENTER></H3></STRONG>

<!-Send us email.->
<CENTER><HR WIDTH=75%></CENTER>
<FONT COLOR=YELLOW SIZE=-1>
&#169;1996 MyCompany and Associates, All Rights Reserved.    Send us some
email: <A HREF="mailto:admin@mycompany.com">&lt;Admin@MyCompany.com&gt;</A>

</BODY>
</HTML>
```

As you can see, this site presentation isn't overly fancy, but it's more interesting than some of the places you've probably visited in the past. Let's take some time to break down the more interesting sections of the code. The

Our example Web page is well under 60 KB, yet shows the diversity of things you can do to make a page interesting.
Figure 8-1.

first thing you'll notice is that the site is broken into five files. You'll find it easier to maintain sites with frames if you use separate files. In addition, you could use the same heading and icon file for all of the pages on your site—saving download time for the user. All that the code in Listing 8-1 does is divide the browser area into frames, then define what belongs in each cell. Notice that you can specifically define the area for each frame as a percentage or use an asterisk (*). The browser will give defined areas their percentage of the viewable screen first, then divide the remaining area among the other cells equally. You could use this feature to force a certain aspect ratio on your Web pages. This page also uses a new tag, <BGSOUND>. It allows you to play a sound bite when the user enters your Web site. A special attribute allows you to define how many times the sound bite gets played. Using the <BGSOUND> tag by itself plays the sound one time.

Make sure the browser you intend to use for an intranet actually supports the <BGSOUND> tag before you use it.

Listing 8-2 contains the heading for our Web site. About the only interesting bit of coding here is the use of color to set off the marquee area. Using coordinating colors throughout your Web site will dress things up, yet won't cost the user much in download time. Also notice that this marquee bounces back and forth instead of going around in circles. The BEHAVIOR attribute is responsible for this change. Using a variety of attributes to provide special effects can make your site more appealing. You'll also notice that this is the only use of animation right now on the site—anything more might prove distracting.

All you'll find in Listing 8-3 is an <IMG> tag for our icon. Notice that the <BODY> tag does contain a BGCOLOR attribute so that the background of the page will match that of the icon. That way if users resize the display area, they won't see the page color peeking out from underneath the icon.

A lot of Web sites include links to other sites, but in a way that doesn't interfere with the Web site as a whole. That's the purpose of the code in Listing 8-4. It organizes the links from the current site to other sites on the Internet, without taking up space on the Web page itself. Not only does this tend to make the information easier to find, but you could use it as an index of sorts for your own site.

You'll find some interesting coding techniques in Listing 8-5 (at least ones that we haven't used in the book so far). The first thing you'll want to look at is how tag attributes are used throughout this page to obtain special effects. For example, notice how the <PRE> tag is used to present special formatting for the note in the middle of the page. You'll also notice that this page uses reverse colors (light text on a dark background instead of the normal arrangement). This special effect sets off the main section of your page from the ancillary areas surrounding it. Several sites on the Internet use this same

8

effect. For example, look at http://www.pacbell.com. Down at the bottom of Listing 8-5, you'll see two new ways of doing things as well. The first new technique is the use of &#*<number>* for special characters. For example, you can produce a copyright symbol using &#169. If you want one of these special characters to appear right beside a normal character, separate the two with a semicolon, like this: ©1996. The second new technique shows one way to allow someone to send you mail about your Web site. All you need to do is provide an HREF like this:

```
<A HREF="mailto:admin@mycompany.com">&lt;Admin@MyCompany.com&gt;</A>
```

The secret here is the "mailto" part of the link. Notice that the link text also uses another form of special character. In this case &lt and &gt provide less-than and greater-than symbols around the link text.

TIP: The HTML reference provided with the ActiveX Control Pad may be a little incomplete in some areas, but it does provide a full listing of these special characters. Just look at the Character Set category found in the main index.

Creating an Animated GIF

If the previous section didn't show you enough techniques to make your Web site sparkle, then there are a host of other ideas you can use. A favorite idea of Webmasters the world over is the use of animated GIFs. All that an animated GIF does is pack several pictures into one file. The browser plays these pictures back one at a time—allowing you to create the illusion of continuous animation. You can also use special effects to create a slide show using a GIF. The only problem with this approach is the download time—a slide show tends to put quite a strain on the user's download capability.

NOTE: This section will show you how to create a GIF using the GIF Construction Set from Alchemy Mind Works. You can download it from several places. The best place is straight from the vendor at http://www.mindworkshop.com/alchemy/gifcon.html. You can also download it from the animated GIF viewing site mentioned earlier in the chapter: http://www.wanderers.com/rose/animate.html.

We'll use the GIF Construction Set for this section for two reasons. First, since it's shareware, all of you can download it from the Internet and follow along with the examples. Second, it's a really great program, and most people find that it works just fine for creating animated GIFs. At most, you'll notice the lack of an actual drawing program with this program, but Windows already supplies that in the form of Paintbrush or MS Paint. You'll also need a graphics conversion utility if your drawing program doesn't support the GIF file format directly (neither Paintbrush nor MS Paint do). Both Graphics Workshop from Alchemy Mind Works and Paint Shop Pro by JASC, Inc. are excellent graphics conversion programs. Both vendors provide shareware versions of their product. You can find Alchemy Mind Works at the Internet site provided in the previous note. The JASC product appears on various BBS and CompuServe forums (they may also have an Internet site by the time you read this). The first thing you'll see when you open GIF Construction Set is a File | Open dialog like the one shown here:

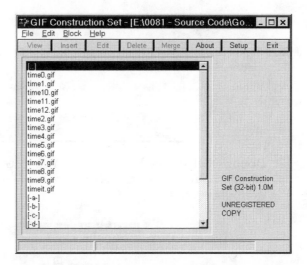

Notice that the directory shown has several GIF files in it already. TimeIt.GIF is the static file you saw in Figure 8-1. Time0.GIF is a base file—a blank used to create the animation effect. You can save a substantial amount of time by creating such a blank whenever you create an animation. In fact, cartoonists use this very technique. They draw the common elements of an animation once on separate sheets, then combine them to create the animation. Only unique items are drawn one at a time. Time1.GIF through Time12.GIF are the actual animation files—think of each one as an animation cel.

8

Let's create an animated GIF using these "cel" files. The following procedure isn't meant to lock you into a particular regimen, but it does show one way to use the GIF Construction Set to create one.

1. Use the File | New command to create a new GIF. You'll see a blank GIF dialog like the one shown in the following illustration. GIF Construction Set always assumes a standard display size of 640 × 480 pixels. We'll need to change that value.

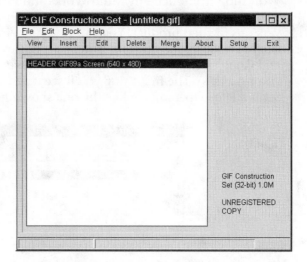

2. Double-click on the Header entry. You'll see the dialog shown next. It allows you to change characteristics associated with the GIF—for example, its size.

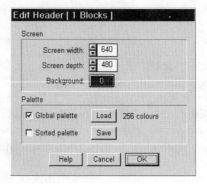

3. Type a new size in both the width and height fields to match the size of your image. For this example, you'd use 90. Click OK to make the change permanent.

4. Click on the Merge button. This allows you to add an image to the GIF. You'll see a standard File | Open dialog.

5. Double-click on the first file you want to use in the animation. In this case you'd double-click Time1.GIF. You'll see the dialog change as shown next. The palette for this graphic doesn't match the standard palette used by GIF Construction Set.

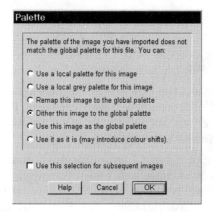

6. Since all of the images in this animation use the same palette, you'll want to select the Use This Image as the Global Palette setting. Click OK to complete the process. GIF Construction Set will insert a new graphic into the GIF, as shown in the following illustration. If you click on the Image entry, you'll see an actual copy of the image. Don't worry about this capability right now, but it does come in handy if you want to make sure you have your animated files in the right sequence.

8

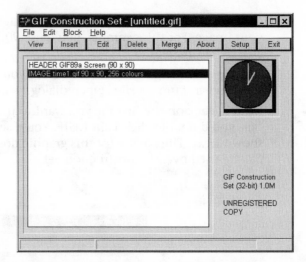

7. Click the Merge button. You'll see the same File | Open dialog as before.

8. Select the next image in the series and click OK. Click OK again if GIF Construction Set asks you about the palette setting. GIF Construction Set will automatically insert the image in the next position of the animation sequence.

9. Repeat steps 7 and 8 for the remaining GIFs in this animation. Once you complete this step, your dialog should look like the one shown here. Notice that all 12 images are in order. Now we have to insert some controls to make this image work properly.

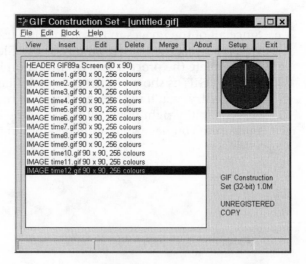

10. Click the Insert button. You'll see the menu shown here:

This menu contains every kind of object you can insert into an animated GIF. The two you'll use most often are Loop and Control. A Loop allows you to define how long the animation continues to go through a sequence of pictures. Wise use of Loop objects can create some pretty interesting effects. Unfortunately, many browsers ignore this particular entry, so you may want to use it sparingly. (If a browser ignores the Loop object, it simply keeps the animated GIF looping forever.) Controls allow you to modify the behavior of the animated GIF. For example, you can use a control to set the time between pictures. The Image entry is pretty obvious; every picture you want to add to the animated GIF is an Image. You'll use comments to document the behavior of your animated GIF, which is especially important if you plan to allow other people to use it. Plain Text is simply that—text that gets displayed as part of the animation.

11. Select the Loop entry in the menu. GIF Construction Set will automatically place it under the Header entry. Now we need to place Control objects between each picture to time the animation sequence.

12. Click the first Image entry. GIF Construction Set normally places the next entry right below the one you click.

13. Click the Insert button and select Control from the menu. You'll see a Control entry added to the list, as shown here:

8

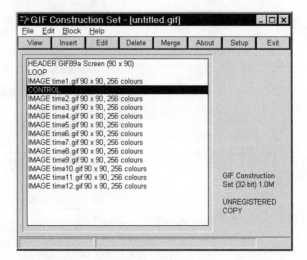

14. Click the next Image entry.

15. Repeat steps 13 and 14 for each of the images. You'll end up with a series of Image and Control objects, as shown in the next illustration. (Make sure you add a Control object after the last image, since the animated GIF will automatically loop back to the first image.)

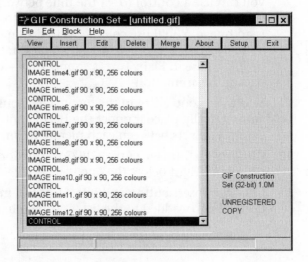

16. Normally you'll find that the default time period between pictures works pretty well. However, let's take a look at what you'd need to do to change the setting. Double-click on the last Control object entry. You'll see the dialog shown here:

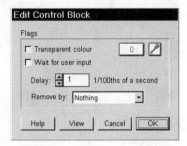

The most commonly used entry is the Delay field. You can use it to control the speed of the animation. The Transparent Color check box will allow whatever appears below the GIF to show through in the areas that are displayed with a certain color. Clicking the pushbutton allows you to select the transparent color. The Wait for User Input check box tells the animation to pause at this point in the animation and wait for the user to provide some kind of input. Normally the user will press a key. Finally, the Remove By field allows you to determine what to do with this animation cel once the browser displays it. Make sure you leave this entry alone because you'll get very unpredictable results from some browsers otherwise.

17. Click Cancel to close the dialog.

18. Let's view the completed animation. Click the View button, and you'll see a screen similar to the one shown in Figure 8-2. Press ESC to exit the viewing area.

19. The only thing left to do is save your animated GIF file. Use the File | Save As command to do that. You could use any filename, but for the purposes of this example, save the file as TimeIt.GIF. That's how we'll access the file later within an HTML page.

If you look at the size of even the modest animation created for this example, you'll find that it consumes about 16.7 KB of memory. That's almost one third of your memory budget for this page. What you've got to consider at this point is whether the animation is worth the added memory burden.

8

Fortunately, there's another way to deal with the problem. Double-click on any of the Image objects, and you'll see a dialog like this one:

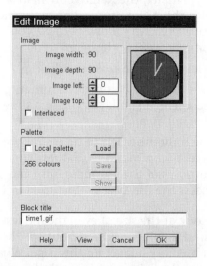

Notice the Image Left and Image Top fields. These fields allow you to choose a starting point for each image in the animation. You really don't need to redisplay the entire clock every time the animation cel changes. All you need to do is overwrite the previous hour hand position and replace it with the next one in the series. Cropping each image so that the previous hour hand gets covered and the new one displayed could reduce the size of your animated GIF by 75 percent. In other words, that 16.7 KB file would be reduced to about 4.7 KB. The only thing you need to do is crop the image with your paint program, reinsert it into the animated GIF file using the procedure we just covered, and then use the Image Top and Image Left fields to place the cropped image correctly on the display. This dialog also allows you to choose a new palette for the picture and assign it a different name.

TIP: Unless your animated GIF is very large or your download budget very small, you won't want to take the time to crop every image individually. For example, our sample GIF would probably work fine if it were the only image on the page.

The Interlaced check box is pretty interesting too. If this GIF were designed as a static image, you'd want to check this box. Interlaced images are displayed one line at a time. It's the effect you see on most Web sites when downloading a large graphic. Using an interlaced graphic gives users some visual feedback during the download process—it lets them know that the machine hasn't frozen. You'll want to leave this box unchecked for animated GIFs though, because it takes more time to display an interlaced image. Checking the Interlaced check box could actually make the animation look pretty jumpy in this case.

Getting Where You Want to Go

People in the northeastern part of the United States are famous for a saying: "You can't get there from here, you have to go somewhere else first." Some people feel the same way about the Internet. It always seems as if you have to cross a minimum of four or five Web pages before you find the one site you were looking for to begin with.

It's this very principle that has caused some Webmasters to place a number of links on their Web sites. Each link points to information related to the current topic—information that augments the Web site in some way. There isn't a single user who will complain about the presence of these added links. In fact, you'll find that they would complain if the links were missing.

There's a problem with the current system of links though. Just like everything else on the Internet, they're static. You get the same set of links

8

on a particular site no matter how you entered it or what set of conditions you're operating under. Wouldn't it be nice if the Web site had at least a little intelligence to help you find what you needed? In addition, wouldn't it be nice if you could enter some criteria to make the process of moving from one site to the other a bit easier? For example, you could type in some kind of criteria to locate a specific kind of site based on current needs. ActiveX provides a way to take care of this dynamic need through the use of *URLs* (a string that defines where to find something) and *monikers* (the actual resource object provided by the system).

Overview of URL Monikers

Let's begin this section by looking at what those two terms—URLs and monikers—mean. An URL (uniform resource locator) is the method we've all become accustomed to using for getting from one site to another. It's the http://www.mycompany.com that you type when using a browser. URLs have three parts: the protocol (http in this case), the host (www), and the domain (mycompany.com). What makes this scheme so useful is that you can extend it almost infinitely. For example, if you want to use another protocol, just specify it at the beginning of the URL. The Internet has quite a few such protocols, including FTP, Gopher, and News.

Monikers originated with the OLE 2 specification. Essentially, a moniker is a system-generated object. You can use this object to find another object or to retrieve data from it. Some types of custom monikers may support other operations as well, but these are the two basic operations that are provided by any moniker. The OLE 2 specification provided synchronous monikers, which means that the application would wait until the system had retrieved whatever data it was looking for from the specified object.

If you combine the idea of an URL with a moniker, you get the URL moniker provided by the ActiveX API. So what's the difference between the URL moniker used by ActiveX and the synchronous monikers that the OLE 2 specification talks about? For one thing, URL monikers provide both synchronous and asynchronous binding. This is important for looking on the Internet because you don't know how long it will take to find something. If you use synchronous binding for an Internet search, the application could get blocked and cause all kinds of problems on the client machine. An URL moniker also provides a framework for building and using URLs—something the OLE 2 specification didn't have to take into account. If you want to access remote data using a standard OLE 2 application, it has to support UNC (uniform naming context) drive locations across a network.

This implies mapped drives of some sort, which you obviously can't get with an Internet location.

You'll need three pieces to create an URL moniker: client, system, and transport. The client part of the equation is built into your application. The system component is part of the operating system (you don't have to worry about this part because Microsoft takes care of it). The transport part of the equation is variable—it depends on what transport you want to implement. When it comes to the Internet, you'll probably use TCP.

Just like every other special OLE capability discussed in this book so far, implementing URL monikers requires you to create or use some special interfaces. There are two each in the client, system, and transport components of the URL moniker. The following list describes each interface.

♦ **IEnumFormatETC (client)**   This optional interface allows you to provide protocol-specific information that affects the bind operation. For example, if you want to provide MIME capabilities, you'd need to provide this interface to enumerate the formats your application supports.

♦ **IBindStatusCallback (client)**   The transport uses this interface to notify the client about specific events such as the progress of a download. More importantly, once the binding from the client, through the system, to the transport is complete, the transport uses the IBindSystemCallback::OnStartBinding method to pass back an IBinding interface.

♦ **IBindCtx (system)**   You'll begin the process of finding an Internet resource by passing a pointer to your IBindStatusCallback interface (and optionally, the IEnumFormatETC interface) using the CreateAsyncBindCtx ActiveX API call. This returns a pointer to the IBindCtx interface, which performs the actual binding between client and transport.

♦ **IMoniker (system)**   You use this interface element for a lot of purposes. The main functions it performs include retrieving moniker names in human-readable form using the GetDisplayName method and transport instantiation using the BindToStorage or BindToObject method.

♦ **IParseDisplayName (transport)**   The current version of the MkParseDisplayNameEx() function supported by ActiveX will allow you to create monikers from either files or URLs. You may find that you need to create monikers from other kinds of objects. This interface allows your application to work with the transport to create new

8

moniker types. You'll also need to register these new moniker types with the registry.

♦ **IBinding (transport)**   The system creates a transport defined by the type of protocol that the application wants to access. IBinding is the resulting protocol-specific transport interface. It parses the protocol string, drives any download of data, and provides status information to your application through its IBindStatusCallback interface. The application can use the IBinding interface to start, stop, pause, or resume the binding operation.

Creating an URL Moniker

As with every other kind of OLE communication, creating an URL moniker follows a pretty standard routine. There are several levels of communication, and you can choose whether or not to implement some interfaces fully or at all (IEnumFormatETC). The following steps outline a typical communication session using the minimum number of interface elements. In other words, this procedure tells you what you'll always see—anything else either increases flexibility or provides additional information exchange.

1. Create a binding context. You can do this using the CreateAsyncBindCtx( ) function call provided with the ActiveX API. This call requires that you provide a pointer to your application's IBindStatusCallback function. Without this interface, there isn't any way for the system and transport to communicate with your application. You can also pass a pointer to the optional IEnumFormatETC interface if your application implements special features such as MIME. The format enumerator allows the server and transport to determine what data formats your application can handle (they always assume you can handle text data).

2. The system will pass back a pointer to its IBindCtx interface. This interface also registers your IBindStatusCallback with the bind context.

3. Once your application has an IBindCtx to work with, it can use either the CreateURLMoniker( ) or MkParseDisplayNameEx( ) function calls to create an URL moniker. The choice of which function to use is simple. If you have a moniker, use the CreateURLMoniker( ) function. Otherwise, use the MkParseDisplayNameEx( ) function that parses the text string, creates a moniker from it, then passes this information to the CreateURLMoniker( ) function.

4. The next step is to create a transport capable of working with the URL moniker by using the system's IMoniker interface. There are two

Only the new Win32 API provided with your MSDN subscription contains the extended version of the MkParse-DisplayName-Ex() function that supports URLs.

methods for doing this: BindToObject( ) and BindToStorage( ). The BindToObject( ) call allows you to instantiate an object that points to the moniker. This object allows you to interact with the moniker. Normally you'd use it with a Web site or other live connection. The BindToStorage( ) call retrieves the data pointed to by the moniker and stores it. This process is referred to as "binding" the moniker. Essentially, you grab the information and stick it on disk. You'd use this call with something like an FTP site. In either case, you have to pass the pointer to the IBindCtx that you received in step 2 as part of the call.

5. The system's IMoniker interface will launch a transport-specific server for whatever protocol you requested. It determines which protocol to use based on the moniker you passed. As soon as the transport-specific server becomes active, it sends the application a pointer to its IBinding interface using the application's IBindStatusCallback::OnStart-Binding( ) method.

6. Now that you've established communication between all three elements—application, system, and transport—and provided the application with two interfaces for working with the other elements (IBindCtx and IBinding), your application can begin the process of downloading a file, Web page, or other resource. There's one other piece to the communication puzzle though. Whenever the application requests data, the transport will tell it the progress of the download using the IBindStatusCallback::OnDataAvailable( ) method. The application uses the status information passed through this method to determine whether or not the download is complete. (You can also use this status information to update a progress bar or other status indicator for the user.)

Hyperlinking Basics

URL monikers are the low-level part of an OLE implementation for getting from one place to the other on the Internet. There's a higher level interface as well—the one seen by the user. Whenever you see a bit of underlined text in your browser, you're probably looking at a hyperlink to another site. We've already covered the HTML part of this process in several chapters of the book (see Chapter 4 for an overview of HTML).

Microsoft provides an ActiveX hyperlink interface you can use to emulate specific browser's actions within an ActiveX control. Like other forms of OLE, this means that you can extend browser technology to an application or simply use it within an HTML page to provide an added level of functionality for an ActiveX control. Wherever you use ActiveX

8

hyperlinks, you can perform a few basic services that include the items in the following list.

♦ **Application to application** You can create a hyperlink between two applications in the absence of a browser. This is an especially handy feature if you implement some type of intranet site on your LAN.

♦ **Application to ActiveX/HTML document** We saw how ActiveX documents work in Chapter 5. The document is actually displayed in the browser window. You make the connection from the Internet to the document using a standard HTML <A HREF> tag. What if you could place a control in an application that automatically connects you to a document on the Internet? In other words, this link would act just like an HTML <A HREF> tag in reverse. ActiveX hyperlink controls can help you accomplish this task. For example, you can use this capability to provide links from a company policy document to sources of additional information on the Internet.

♦ **ActiveX document to ActiveX document** You're in a browser looking at a document. Wouldn't it be nice to be able to move from one place to another in that document using anchors, just like you can on an HTML page? ActiveX hyperlinks allow you to do just that. You can also use this capability to move from one document to the next, just like you would move from one HTML page to the next on the Internet.

♦ **Browser ActiveX document to Microsoft Office Binder ActiveX document** A company could potentially use this capability on a local intranet. It would allow users to move from a document displayed in a browser to one located on the local machine through the Microsoft Office Binder. For example, you could use this capability to provide links to a local glossary. Whenever users didn't know the meaning of a word, they could follow a link located on the Internet to the local copy of the glossary for clarification.

A navigation stack is a list of URLs visited during the current session and is maintained by the browser.

Before you can perform any of these neat tricks, you need to create an URL moniker. We looked at this process in the previous two sections. You'll also need to work with the hyperlink interface provided with the ActiveX API. Fortunately, you don't have to resort to using a low-level interface like that provided for URL monikers. If all you want to do is get from point A to point B, you can use a set of four functions that Microsoft thoughtfully provided. The following table describes each function.

Function	Description
HlinkSimpleNavigateToString( )	This function allows you to go to a new location based on a string—one that's formatted just like the strings you would type in at the browser. You'll normally use this function to go to a new HTML document or another location within the same HTML document, but could use it with objects as well.
HlinkSimpleNavigateToMoniker( )	This function moves you from one place to another using a moniker as a source of information. Normally you'd use it with objects.
HlinkGoBack( )	This function emulates the Go Back button on a browser's toolbar. It moves you to the previous position in the navigation stack.
HlinkGoForward( )	This function emulates the Go Forward button on a browser's toolbar. It moves you to the next position in the navigation stack.

TIP: The simple hyperlink functions are located in the URLHLINK.H header file provided with the ActiveX SDK. You'll find the actual functions in the URLMON DLL by the time the ActiveX SDK is released.

Using these functions is fairly simple. Let's begin with the easier functions: HlinkGoBack( ) and HlinkGoForward( ). Both of these functions require a single argument, a pointer to the IUnknown interface for the current document. To retrieve it, simply use the ExternalQueryInterface( ) function with IID_IUnknown as the first argument and a pointer variable as the second argument.

8

The HlinkSimpleNavigateToString() and HlinkSimpleNavigateToMoniker() functions are a bit more complicated. The following command lines show what arguments the functions will accept.

```
HlinkSimpleNavigateToString(szTarget, szLocation, szTargetFrame,
    pIUnknown, pIBindCtx, pIBindStatusCallback,
    grfHLNF, dwReserved)
HlinkSimpleNavigateToMoniker(pmkTarget, szLocation, szTargetFrame,
    pIUnknown, pIBindCtx, pIBindStatusCallback,
    grfHLNF, dwReserved)
```

Except for the first argument, both functions allow you to use the same list of arguments. The first argument for HlinkSimpleNavigateToString() is a string containing the URL (or other identifying information) of the site you want to visit. The first argument for HlinkSimpleNavigateToMoniker() is a pointer to a moniker.

Let's look at the common arguments. szLocation contains the name of a location on the same page. We looked at how this works in Chapter 4. The szTargetFrame argument contains the name of a frame within the document. This is HTML specific and only works with pages that use frames. Neither of these arguments are required; you only need to provide them if you want to provide extended navigation information. Use a value of NULL for both arguments when you don't want to include them.

There are three interface-specific arguments: pIUnknown, pIBindCtx, and IBindStatusCallback. Of these three, only the pIUnknown argument is required. You can retrieve it using the ExternalQueryInterface() function. You'd only need to specify a pIBindCtx value if you wanted to provide additional processing information. For example, if your application provides MIME capability, you could use this parameter to pass the location of the IEnumFormatETC interface (it's passed as part of the IBindCtx parameter—don't pass a pointer to the IEnumFormatETC interface itself). You'll want to pass a pointer to the IBindStatusCallback interface for your application if you want status information during the transfer.

The grfHLNF argument is the only one remaining. It allows you to specify certain behaviors on the part of the browser. For example, if you provide HLNF_OPEN_INNEWWINDOW for this argument, the browser will display the specified site in a new window. You can see a complete list of HLNF values in the HLINK.H header file provided with the ActiveX SDK.

Understanding the Hyperlink Interface

In some situations, the simple hyperlink function calls discussed in the previous section won't do the job. For example, you may want to implement a full-fledged browser as part of your application. Another situation in which the simple calls won't work is if you want to provide some type of extended functionality not supported by the calls, for example, working with a history list. The calls in the previous section are best used in situations where navigation is the only concern.

As with any ActiveX control, you'll need to provide a few additional interfaces to implement hyperlinking within an application. In fact, there are five new interfaces, as follows:

♦ **IHLink (mandatory)** This is the center point of the ActiveX hyperlinking interface. It's the interface that provides everything another application would need to hyperlink. This includes the target moniker (actual object identification), URL-style string, and a friendly name. You'll find that it also provides other kinds of information, but they're not normally needed to create a simple hyperlink. All simple hyperlinking is done through the Navigate method, which is what the simple functions described in the previous section use.

♦ **IHLinkTarget (optional)** You'll use this to find your way around the document or to download additional information. For example, this interface would allow you to point to a specific cell within a spreadsheet. IHLinkTarget also provides the means for passing a pointer to the document's IBrowseContext interface to the calling application. An application can still hyperlink to a document that doesn't provide this interface, but that's about it.

♦ **IHLinkFrame (optional)** Remember that in OLE, a frame is an application's container for an OLE container. It contains the menu and the outside box. This interface allows the frame to maintain contact with the OLE container (usually a document of some sort).

♦ **IHLinkSite (optional)** This is the interface that manages the hyperlink site. It performs two essential services and many miscellaneous ones. The first major task is gaining access to a document's HLink object. Gaining access to this object provides a wealth of information, such as the current site name. The second major purpose for this interface is to provide feedback to the client application. For example, the OnNavigationComplete method will tell the client that a download or other task is complete.

8

♦ **IBrowseContext (optional)**   An application gains access to the browse context object through this interface. All that the browse context object does is keep track of the navigation stack—the sites visited during the current session. The HlinkGoForward() and HlinkGoBack() functions described in the previous section rely on this interface to do their work.

There are actually two levels of implementation within this group of interfaces. We'll assume that the first level is an application—a browser in this case. The second level is an OLE container—a document in this case. The browser implements the IHLinkFrame and IBrowseContext interfaces. There is only one occurrence of both of these interfaces—the browser either implements them or it doesn't. The document implements the IHLinkTarget, IHLink, and IHLinkSite interfaces.

The document is a little more difficult to define in terms of interfaces. The container portion of the document implements the IHLinkTarget interface, so you'll only see one of them even when working with a document containing more than one object. Likewise, there is only one IHLinkSite interface per document no matter how many objects it contains. You can, however, have more than one hyperlink within a document.

Let's take a quick look at hyperlinks. Each hyperlink requires a separate IHLink interface, and there are four functions you can use to create one: HlinkCreateFromMoniker(), HLinkCreateFromString(), HlinkCreateFromData( ), and HlinkQueryCreateFromData(). HLink objects can use persisted data, meaning that the control must implement an IPersistStream interface. Since you can create an HLink from data, you can also cut, copy, and paste it using the Clipboard. In addition, since an HLink uses monikers, you can point to any kind of OLE document, including things you don't normally see displayed in a browser, such as a Word for Windows file.

PART

3

Real World ActiveX

Chapter 9

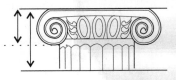

Utilities and ActiveX

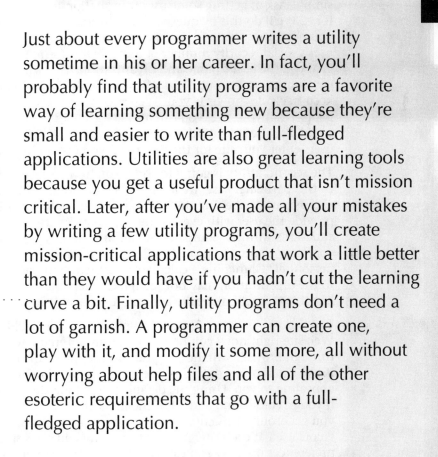

Just about every programmer writes a utility sometime in his or her career. In fact, you'll probably find that utility programs are a favorite way of learning something new because they're small and easier to write than full-fledged applications. Utilities are also great learning tools because you get a useful product that isn't mission critical. Later, after you've made all your mistakes by writing a few utility programs, you'll create mission-critical applications that work a little better than they would have if you hadn't cut the learning curve a bit. Finally, utility programs don't need a lot of garnish. A programmer can create one, play with it, and modify it some more, all without worrying about help files and all of the other esoteric requirements that go with a full-fledged application.

If you haven't guessed yet, we're going to spend some time looking at utility ActiveX controls in this chapter. These are little bits of code you can stick on a page and do something useful with that don't require a lot of additional work later. The difference between a utility and a control used for developing a full-fledged application (like the control we created in Chapter 2) is that the utility is stand-alone. Of course, you still interact with the utility, you just don't need to do as much hand-holding as a standard control such as a pushbutton would require.

Three different utilities are presented in this chapter. The first performs the simple task of getting some user information for you without asking the user for it. We'll do this by querying the Windows registry. All of the information you need appears there in a special place. Now, this utility won't get you the user's social security number or any secret information, but it will at least give you the user's name and organization. That's a lot more than you could get from using a script. How will you use this information? One way is to keep track of who visits your Web site. Besides keeping track of how many people visit your site, you can also keep track of who visits and when. You could also use this utility to personalize your Web page. Just think, when users enter your site for the first time, you can address them by name.

The second utility is going to show you how to automate tasks for the user. In this particular case, we'll launch a common Windows application for the user as part of opening the Web page. You could use this capability to provide the user with everything needed to get the job done—especially in situations within a company (on an intranet). For example, what if a company wanted to provide a financial page for their traveling sales personnel? Launching a calculator for them to use while they send data back to the organization may not seem like a very big deal, but it's little touches like this that will make life a lot more enjoyable for everyone.

The third application is something that everyone will like. When you go to a Web site right now, you have the option of forcing it to use one set of colors through browser switches, or you can use the colors provided by the site itself. The browser option is fine if seeing every site in one set of colors is appealing to you. Using the default colors for a site might be nice, but what if you're color-blind and all of the links are in red? The color utility will help you get around this entire problem by making it possible to customize the colors used at each site. All that the utility will do is store the user's color preferences on disk. You can check for the file when users enter the site and change the colors to the user's preferred settings before displaying the page.

NOTE: We looked at the basic procedure for creating an ActiveX control in Chapter 2. You may want to review that procedure now if you're a bit rusty at creating controls. This chapter will only detail differences between that standard procedure and setups required to create the example controls shown here.

Grabbing User Information

The ability to work with the registry is one of the fortes of working with ActiveX controls versus many of the other technologies we've looked at in this book. This example will show you some registry access basics. In this case you'll see how to create a control that accesses the user information and allows you to place that information on a Web page. This way you can greet users by name when they access your site. The same programming techniques will work with other kinds of registry access as well.

WARNING: You can access any part of the Windows 95 registry at any time, but Windows NT is not nearly as helpful. In Windows NT the network administrator can cordon off certain areas of the registry as inaccessible, unless the local administrator does so first. There are also structural differences in some areas of the registry between the two operating systems. It's always best to test your application in both the Windows NT and Windows 95 environments unless you can guarantee the user will use one or the other.

You'll use the same basic setup that you did for creating a control in Chapter 2 when starting this control, with a few small differences. The name of the workspace for the example control is UserInfo, but you could use any other name. When you get to the second page of the OLE Control Wizard, you'll need to check the Invisible at Runtime check box. This prevents the user from seeing your control on the Web page. You also won't need to subclass an existing control—we want a blank ActiveX control in this case.

This control won't require you to expose any special events—it does everything it needs to do during initialization. It does require you to create two custom properties using the MFC ClassWizard: UserName and

UserCompany. (We looked at the process for doing this in Chapter 2.) They're both of type CString and use a Member variable implementation. Your OLE Automation page should look like this once you complete this step:

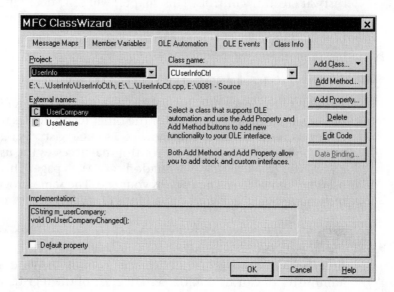

 NOTE: We won't go through the About Box dialog in this chapter. In addition, this particular control doesn't require a property page since you can't really set anything. It retrieves the needed information for you automatically. All you need to do is grab it from the exposed properties.

Amazingly, this is all the setup you need to do. Before you start adding some code though, let's take a look at a few things you'll need to know to make this example work. First, Figure 9-1 shows a view of the registry from RegEdit. Notice that we're looking at some user information located under the HKEY_CURRENT_USER | Software | Microsoft | MS Setup (ACME) | User Info key. Every registry—no matter what version of Windows you're using—should contain this information if the user provided it during installation. (If you're using Windows NT 4.0, you may have to look in a different place for the required information. HKEY_LOCAL_MACHINE | Software | Microsoft | Windows NT | CurrentVersion contains a

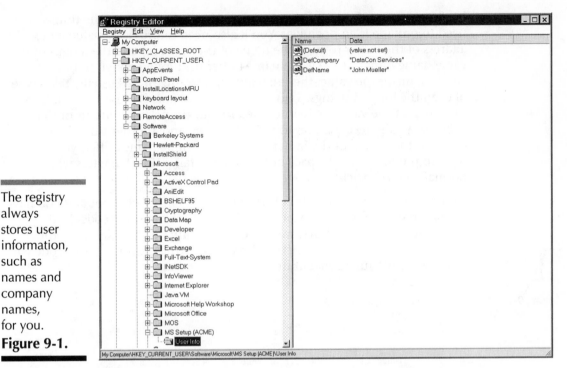

The registry always stores user information, such as names and company names, for you.

Figure 9-1.

RegisteredOwner and a RegisteredOrganization value that you can use in place of the normal values.) Since most users do provide this information, you can use it to your advantage.

You'll need to perform a two-step process to gain access to the key that we need. First, you need to open the key. This step gives you a handle to it just like opening a file gives you a handle. Windows provides two functions to perform this part of the task: RegOpenKey() for Windows 3.1, and RegOpenKeyEx() for Windows 95 and Windows NT. You'll need to provide several values, including a null terminated string pointing to the key that you want to open, the access rights you want, and a pointer to a variable used to store the key. (You'll see how this works when we look at the source code.)

The second step in the process is to query the key. Each value uses an index. In this respect the registry values within a key work much like an array would (though it's not even close to the same thing). You use the

RegEnumValue() function to access the information. One of the things you need to provide is an open key. You'll also need to provide a value index, the address of the buffer to store the name of the value in, and the length of the value name buffer. If the value name buffer isn't long enough to hold the entire name of the value, the call will fail. A setting of 128 usually takes care of even the longest strings. Two optional parameters are also needed. It's not the name of the value we're interested in, but the actual contents of that value, so you'll need a buffer to hold the value and another variable that contains the length of the buffer. As with the value name buffer, you'll need to provide enough space or the call will fail—128 characters will normally do the trick.

Now that you have some idea of what this program is all about and you have the program skeleton put together, let's take a look at some code. Listing 9-1 shows the only method that we'll need to modify for this example—the CUserInfoCtrl::CUserInfoCtrl() method or constructor. Adding this code will give you a fully functional utility.

Listing 9-1

```
CUserInfoCtrl::CUserInfoCtrl()
{
    InitializeIIDs(&IID_DUserInfo, &IID_DUserInfoEvents);

    LONG    ulResult;       //Result of function calls.
    LPCTSTR lpSubKey;       //Key value that we're looking for.
    HKEY    hkUser;         //Handle of key.
    CHAR    sNVName[128];   //Name of the user name value.
    DWORD   dwNVNameLen;    //Length of the user name value.
    UCHAR   sNValue[128];   //User name.
    DWORD   dwNValueLen;    //Length of the user name.
    CHAR    sCVName[128];   //Name of the company name value.
    DWORD   dwCVNameLen;    //Length of the company name value.
    UCHAR   sCValue[128];   //Company name.
    DWORD   dwCValueLen;    //Length of the company name.

    // Begin by opening the registry key.
    lpSubKey = "Software\\Microsoft\\MS Setup (ACME)\\User Info";
    ulResult = RegOpenKeyEx(HKEY_CURRENT_USER, lpSubKey, NULL, KEY_READ, &hkUser);
    if (ulResult != ERROR_SUCCESS)
    {
        MessageBox("Failed to Open Registry Key", "Initialization Error", MB_ICONERROR | MB_OK);
    }

    //Get the user name from the information in the registry
    //and place it in our UserName control property.
```

```
dwNVNameLen = sizeof(sNVName);
dwNValueLen = sizeof(sNValue);
ulResult = RegEnumValue(hkUser, 0, sNVName, &dwNVNameLen, NULL, NULL, sNValue, &dwNValueLen);
if (ulResult != ERROR_SUCCESS)
{
    MessageBox("Failed to Get Name", "Value Read Error", MB_ICONERROR | MB_OK);
}
m_userName = sNValue;

//Get the user company from the information in the registry
//and place it in our UserName control property.
dwCVNameLen = sizeof(sCVName);
dwCValueLen = sizeof(sCValue);
ulResult = RegEnumValue(hkUser, 1, sCVName, &dwCVNameLen, NULL, NULL, sCValue, &dwCValueLen);
if (ulResult != ERROR_SUCCESS)
{
    MessageBox("Failed to Get Company", "Value Read Error", MB_ICONERROR | MB_OK);
}
m_userCompany = sCValue;

// Close the opened registry key.
RegCloseKey(hkUser);
}
```

As you can see, there are three main events: getting the key, getting the user's name, and getting the user's company name. Let's look at getting the key first. About the only thing we haven't covered here yet is the method of describing a key location. Notice that it's much like defining a directory on a hard drive. Obviously, we need to use the double backslash (\\) so that the compiler won't look at the path information as escape sequences. The next two sections are equally easy. All you need to do is call RegEnumValue with the proper index values. In this case the user's name is stored at index 1, and the company name is stored at index 2. In both cases we simply store the result in the property memory variables.

Once you add this code, you can build the OCX and test it. Make sure you follow the test steps that we went through in Chapter 2. What you should get at the end is a control you can insert into an HTML page using ActiveX Control Pad. Create a blank HTML page and insert the control. Figure 9-2 shows what the control looks like when you insert it. Notice that the UserName and UserCompany properties will already contain values. That's because the control gets those values during initialization. There's a valuable lesson to learn here. If we had made the registry calls after an event, you wouldn't see the values immediately after adding the control to a page.

9

You'd have to write some test code in an HTML page first, and that would have wasted time. This method gives you instant results.

NOTE: Figure 9-2 shows a shape for the control when displayed on the canvas. This is only so the programmer can see the control. You won't be able to see it when the control is displayed as part of the HTML page.

Adding the control to the page is only the first step of the process though. Right now you won't see anything at all if you save the page and display it. That's because we made this control invisible. Now you have to add the usual tags and text for your site along with a bit of JavaScript or VBScript. Listing 9-2 shows the very small amount of text added to this page for test purposes. It also shows you how to access the UserInfo control using JavaScript. Notice that unlike the examples we looked at in Chapter 7, this script is in-line with the rest of the page. You'll see how this works in a few moments.

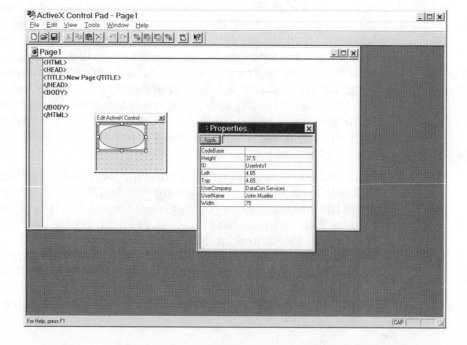

You can see the results of the registry query immediately after adding the control to an HTML page.
Figure 9-2.

Listing 9-2

```
<HTML>
<HEAD>
<TITLE>User Information Control</TITLE>
</HEAD>
<BODY>

<!-Insert the control anywhere at the beginning of the page.->
<OBJECT ID="UserInfo1" WIDTH=100 HEIGHT=51
 CLASSID="CLSID:A019B364-FD9F-11CF-8C70-00006E3127B7"
 CODEBASE="http://www.mycompany.com/controls/UserInfo.OCX">
    <PARAM NAME="_Version" VALUE="65536">
    <PARAM NAME="_ExtentX" VALUE="2646">
    <PARAM NAME="_ExtentY" VALUE="1341">
    <PARAM NAME="_StockProps" VALUE="0">
</OBJECT>

<!-Display a heading.->
<CENTER><H1>Welcome to our site!</H1></CENTER>

<!-Give the user a personal greeting.->
<CENTER><H2>

<!-A JavaScript method of displaying the user information.->
<SCRIPT LANGUAGE="JavaScript">
<!--
    Window.Document.Write("Hello to " + UserInfo1.UserName + " of ")
    Window.Document.Write(UserInfo1.UserCompany + "!")
-->
</SCRIPT>

</H2></CENTER>

</BODY>
</HTML>
```

The two Window.Document.Write() calls in the JavaScript allow us to send a combination of text and parameter values to the display area. Using the Write() method always places the text in the current window position, meaning that you can't choose a spot as an afterthought—you have to place this code in-line as shown. Notice how this example embellishes the output text using an <H2> and <CENTER> tag. The JavaScript appears between the beginning and end of the tags without any problem. There is one caution when using this approach—limit the amount of work you do to writing to the document.

9

Let's take a look at the results of using the utility program. Figure 9-3 shows the resulting page. Of course, you could dress up the display with a little added processing, but this example shows the potential of this particular control.

TIP: If you see a sunken square with a red "X" through it in the upper-left corner of the browser display area and the browser display doesn't match the one shown in Figure 9-3, it means that the control didn't download properly from the Web server. Make sure you set the CODEBASE attribute of the <OBJECT> tag properly. In addition, make sure you set the Active Content Security Level on the Safety Level dialog to Medium. You can access the Safety Level dialog from the Security page of the Internet Explorer Options dialog. What you should see when downloading a new, unsigned control are three dialogs: one that asks if you want to download the control, a second that warns you that the page contains ActiveX controls, and a third that warns about using an unsigned control. Even if you test the control on a machine that already contains the control, you'll see the second and third dialogs.

Our UserInfo
ActiveX utility
works just as
planned—it
displays a
somewhat
personal
message to
the user.
Figure 9-3.

Launching a Program

There are more than a few limitations in trying to provide customized support for users on an intranet. The fact that users are far from home and you don't have any direct way to support them by automating applications doesn't really help matters. In fact, you'll find that many users really miss that touch of home when they're away. This particular utility helps you overcome part of that problem. It's a simple ActiveX control designed to run an application.

You'll find that Windows provides a number of ways to run an application (or process for that matter). However, in this section, we'll cover the easiest method of getting an application to run by using the WinExec() function. It takes two parameters. The second parameter is the easiest to figure out—you simply select how you want to open the window. For example, you can choose between the minimized and maximized settings. You'll see how to add some flexibility to any ActiveX controls you create later in this section. Now let's look at a more difficult problem, the first parameter. It contains the program name. You can provide a path if you want to, but since the user is bound to be far from home, it's probably a better idea not to do so. You never know what configurations users have for their machines, and it's unlikely that you'll have more than a few machines using the same configuration anyway. However, WinExec() is pretty flexible in this regard. If you provide an application name, it will look in the following places to see if it can find the program for you.

♦ **Application directory** In most cases this is going to be the browser's starting directory, so it's unlikely that WinExec() will find the program here. However, it's handy to know that you could place special utility programs here just in case you need to launch one of them.

♦ **Current directory** It's pretty difficult to tell what the current directory will be. You could find yourself starting just about anywhere on the hard drive. Even if you set the directory to a specific location, there isn't any way to tell that the application you need is actually there.

♦ **System folder** You'll find this option handy for most of the system applications you'll need to launch, but that won't happen very often.

♦ **Main Windows folder** Windows 95 and Windows NT extend this to mean all of the applications provided with Windows—even if they're in the Program Files folder. This means you can always run any Windows-specific application without worrying too much about location.

♦ **PATH environment variable** If you make sure all the applications you plan to execute are referred to by the PATH statement in AUTOEXEC.BAT, you can count on them running. So, if you're setting up a laptop for use on the road, you'd better add all of the important applications to the PATH statement. It will cost you a little bit in load time, but it's worth it to use this feature of ActiveX.

Let's take a look at what you'll need to do to create the sample application. The name of the workspace for the example control is LaunchIt—you'll use the same steps as you did in Chapter 2 to start the creation process. When you get to the second page of the OLE Control Wizard, you'll need to check the Invisible at Runtime check box. As with the previous example, setting this option prevents the user from seeing your control on the Web page. You also won't need to subclass an existing control—we want a blank ActiveX control in this case.

The LaunchIt control needs something we haven't used before, a custom method. You want to make sure you have positive control over the actual launching of an application. Adding a method to the ActiveX control is the best way to accomplish this. You'll add the method using the same OLE Automation page of the MFC ClassWizard dialog that you used to add properties. The only difference is that you'll click the Add Method pushbutton instead of the Add Property pushbutton. This illustration shows what the Add Method dialog looks like:

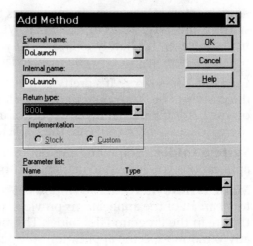

This dialog is filled out so that you can see where the various settings go. All you need to do is type **DoLaunch** in the External Name field and select a Return Type field value from the drop-down list box. The MFC ClassWizard will take care of the internal name for you automatically. Notice the list box at the bottom of the dialog. This is where you would normally place a list of parameters for the method. There are two columns: one for the parameter name and another for its type. In this case we don't need any, so you can leave the list blank.

We'll also need two properties for this ActiveX control. The first is ProgramName, and it's of type CString. This is the parameter that will eventually hold the name of the program we want to execute. The second parameter is Size. It's of type SHORT. It will hold a number that tells what size to make the window. We'll provide three numbers: 1 is default, 2 is minimized, and 3 is maximized. You could extend this parameter to hold any of the values that Windows API allows. Your MFC ClassWizard should look like this when you get finished—it will contain two parameters and one method.

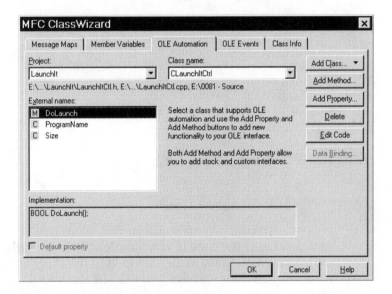

At this point you could add some information to the About box, but we won't take the space here to do it. You might want to add a property page to this example as well, but again, it's not really necessary to do so since you'll usually want to access the control using code. Now that we have a structure in place, let's see how you would make this control come alive. Listing 9-3

9

shows the code for the DoLaunch method—the only coding we need to do to make this control work.

Listing 9-3

```
BOOL CLaunchItCtrl::DoLaunch()
{
    SHORT    WinSize;

    // See if there is a program to run.
    if (m_programName == "")
    {
        MessageBox("You must provide a program name!", NULL, MB_OK | MB_ICONERROR);
        return FALSE;
    }

    // Define the window's size.
    switch (m_size)
    {
    case 1:
        WinSize = SW_SHOWDEFAULT;
        break;
    case 2:
        WinSize = SW_SHOWMINIMIZED;
        break;
    case 3:
        WinSize = SW_SHOWMAXIMIZED;
        break;
    }

    // Execute the program.
    WinExec(m_programName, WinSize);

    // Exit.
    return TRUE;
}
```

As you can see, the code is very simple. All we do is make sure that there's some kind of program name provided in the ProgramName property. If not, we display an error message and exit the method. There's one note of caution you should observe at this point. Normally it's better to handle errors outside of the ActiveX control. The reason is simple: you don't want users to see strange error messages that they can't understand. Most of the time, when users can't understand what the computer wants, they will use brute force to make it do something that you probably didn't want it to do. Save yourself some time and use error messages sparingly or not at all within the ActiveX control unless you plan to take the time to put them in plain English. In fact, that's one of the principles that this control demonstrates. A user can understand a missing value and report it to you. This message isn't perfect, but it's a lot better than most of the ones that you've probably seen that contain obscure wording.

The next thing we do is look at the Size property to see what size the user wants to make the window. As previously stated, there are three sizes to choose from, though you could certainly provide more. The switch statement merely places a constant value into the WinSize variable. At this point we can use WinExec to actually start the application. All you need to do at this point is build and test your new control.

NOTE: At this point you should be thinking to yourself that this control doesn't provide any form of feedback. How do you know that the application actually gets launched? The actual process of sending information back to the Web server can get quite convoluted, and even if we did send it back in this case, what would you do with it? Could you trigger an alert of some kind to tell you that a user accessing the Web site is having trouble getting an application to run? That's a problem we'll tackle in the database-specific chapters later in the book (see Chapters 12 and 13 for details).

Let's look at the way we'd use this control at a Web site. The first thing you should look at is how ActiveX Control Pad reacts to this control. We already saw how the control will appear, in Figure 9-2. Since ActiveX Control Pad doesn't have an actual control to display, it displays a rectangle with an oval inside it. What you may want to look at is how Script Wizard sees the control. Add the control to a blank HTML page within ActiveX Control Pad, and then view it with Script Wizard. What you'll see is something similar to Figure 9-4. Notice that there aren't any events associated with the control and that the DoLaunch method appears on the right side of the page. There's an important reason for going through this exercise. If you wanted the control to react in a certain way to outside stimulus, you would have to define an event. Events appear in the left pane, methods appear on the right.

Now it's time to see this control in action. Listing 9-4 shows a quick program for testing the LaunchIt ActiveX control. You've seen most of these items previously, but this page does provide a few new tricks for getting the job done. Building this page requires the same process as we've used before. Add the control to the page, then the HTML input controls required to interact

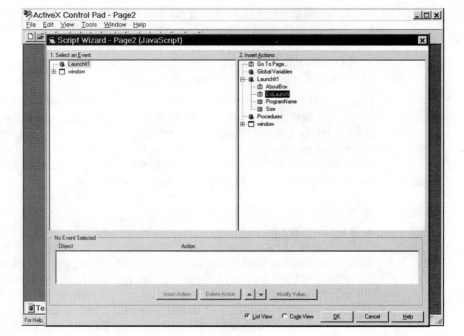

Always think
ahead when
you design an
ActiveX
control. How
do you want it
to interact
with your
HTML page?
Figure 9-4.

with it, and finally, the JavaScript (or VBScript) required to perform that
actual communication with the object.

Listing 9-4

```
<HTML>
<HEAD>

<!-This script will assist in launching an application.->
<SCRIPT>
<!--
function StartProgram()
{
    //Detect if there is a program name.
    if (ProgramName.Value != " ")
        {
        //Get the name of the program.
        LaunchIt1.ProgramName=ProgramName.Value;
        }

    //Run the program.
    LaunchIt1.DoLaunch();
}
```

```
-->
</SCRIPT>

<TITLE>Program Launching Test</TITLE>
</HEAD>
<BODY>

<OBJECT ID="LaunchIt1" WIDTH=100 HEIGHT=51
CLASSID="CLSID:D4082A43-FDD5-11CF-8C70-00006E3127B7"
CODEBASE="http://www.mycomputer.com/controls/LaunchIt.OCX">
    <PARAM NAME="_Version" VALUE="65536">
    <PARAM NAME="_ExtentX" VALUE="2646">
    <PARAM NAME="_ExtentY" VALUE="1323">
    <PARAM NAME="_StockProps" VALUE="0">
</OBJECT>

<!-Display a heading.->
<CENTER><H1>Program Launching Example</H1></CENTER><P>

<!-Add some controls to the page.->
Program Name:
<INPUT TYPE="text" NAME="ProgramName" VALUE=" "><P>

Display Size:<P>
<INPUT LANGUAGE="JavaScript" TYPE="radio" NAME="Radio1" VALUE="Default"
   ONCLICK="LaunchIt1.Size=1" CHECKED>Default<BR>
<INPUT LANGUAGE="JavaScript" TYPE="radio" NAME="Radio1" VALUE="Minimized"
   ONCLICK="LaunchIt1.Size=2">Minimized<BR>
<INPUT LANGUAGE="JavaScript" TYPE="radio" NAME="Radio1" VALUE="Maximized"
   ONCLICK="LaunchIt1.Size=3">Maximized<P>

<INPUT TYPE="button" NAME="Launch" VALUE="Run Program" ONCLICK=StartProgram()>

</BODY>
</HTML>
```

Let's talk about the new tricks in this particular piece of code. Check the
<INPUT> tags for the radio buttons. Remember that JavaScript doesn't
provide the case statement that you'll find in VBScript. The easiest way to
get around this limitation is to take care of whatever you want the control to
do as part of the <INPUT> tag. That's what we've done with the radio
buttons in this case. The two important things to notice are the addition of a
LANGUAGE attribute and an ONCLICK attribute. Unlike ONCLICK
attributes we've used in the past, this one's in quotes. That's because we're

actually performing a task instead of calling a function. Contrast this with the ONCLICK attribute for the Launch button.

The JavaScript for this example is pretty straightforward. When the user presses the Run Program button, the StartProgram() function is called. The first thing that happens is that the script checks to make sure that the user has actually entered a value; if not, the ProgramName property doesn't receive the ProgramName text box value. There's a reason for this. If you don't check for the empty string first, JavaScript will fill the ProgramName property with spaces. We could make extra checks within the ActiveX control for this condition, but it's easier to do it here.

Figure 9-5 shows what this program looks like in action. All the user needs to do is fill in a program name, select a window size, then click the Run Program button to start an application on the client machine. Obviously, you'd normally take care of these tasks in code in response to a user-initiated event. (If the program doesn't start, make sure it's in one of the five search paths that we discussed earlier—you can always add it to the PATH statement if required.)

NOTE: Even though this example will normally work with a path, there are times when it won't. If you experience problems getting the example to work with a full path, such as D:\Windows\MyApp.EXE, try just the application name, MyApp. In addition, some applications don't run with the Default button clicked on the first attempt. If this happens, try running the application with the Maximized button clicked on the first attempt. Subsequent attempts will allow you to use the Default setting. Most of these problems are due to the way that Internet Explorer and the Windows shell interact. They should be fixed with the next release of Internet Explorer.

Working a Color Change

Users want things their way, and when it comes to certain aspects of a Web site, there isn't any good reason not to accommodate them—or is there? It's pretty obvious that Webmasters want their sites to look as attractive as possible. This is especially true when it comes to environmental settings. Just look at the wide variety of setups on the Internet. Not only do sites vary by style, but they vary in font usage, color, and other features. Graphics and a whole host of other innovations also play an important part in the look and feel of a Web site.

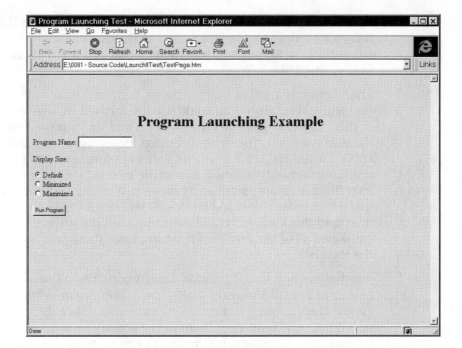

The LaunchIt ActiveX control allows you to run applications on the client machine.
Figure 9-5.

You may feel that a mauve background with country blue lettering is the height of fashion when it comes to Web site design, but there are going to be some users who feel a tad intimidated by such a color scheme. Add a really soft font that's barely readable on a laptop display and you have just given someone a good reason not to visit a site that he really wanted to explore.

So, how do you give users the opportunity to change their site settings? There is always the browser alternative. The user can force your site to use specific colors based on the browser settings. Unfortunately, that individuality problem comes into play. Colors that work just fine for one site may obscure graphics on another. Besides, how can you really get into the mood when looking at a sci-fi page using a white background? The browser alternative is good, but limited.

You could write CGI script and have users fill out their preferences as part of a sign-in process. Unfortunately, that solution is going to cost you a lot in time and effort to implement, the user will feel just a bit put out by the added time and trouble to fill out the form, and you'll find that the page takes a lot longer to download. Sign-in sheets allow users to customize each site as they see fit, but let's face the fact that this method just won't work as well as you'd like.

The solution is another utility ActiveX control. You could attack this problem several ways. You could use the method we used in the first section of this chapter to gain user information and set your site colors to those on the user's desktop. The current settings are always stored under the HKEY_CURRENT_USER | Control Panel | Colors key. Using the current color settings is certainly the most automatic method for ensuring the user will at least like the colors you're using on your Web site, but it doesn't necessarily mean that those colors will work well with your site content. (If you wanted to extend this idea, you could even provide a drop-down list box that contained all of the user's color setups, since those setups are stored in the registry.)

Another method would provide a button onscreen. The user could click this button to display a page (or dialog) containing color settings. You could even include a font selection if you wanted to. Once the user made the selections, you could store them in the registry or a text file. The settings would always be handy, you wouldn't end up writing a lot of scripts, and the user wouldn't be faced with extended download problems.

There's only one more problem to solve. Where do you store the color data? Two solutions come to mind immediately: the registry or a file. Let's take a look at these two solutions. Users will complain if you use the registry and they only visit your site once. After all, who wants an already crowded registry filled with still more information? This solution also assumes that the user has a registry to fill. Not everyone has a Windows 95 or Windows NT machine. The file solution is more appealing in this regard because users can simply erase the file if they don't want to preserve their settings. However, this leads to a situation in which you'd get user complaints because they lost their settings file. You'd also have to figure out somewhere to store the file on a hard drive whose configuration you don't understand. You could use the main Windows directory for storage—the solution that probably makes the most sense if the vast majority of your callers use Windows.

We won't tackle all of these issues with the example in this section, but we'll look at a simple implementation that you could expand to meet specific needs. This example shows how to create an ActiveX control, associated HTML, and JavaScript script to make individual color settings a reality. We'll store the file on disk since this chapter already shows one registry implementation. Besides, writing to a foreign registry isn't necessarily the best idea unless you have more than a little experience under your belt. Let's look at what you need to do to build the ActiveX control first. (We'll use an abbreviated procedure here—look at Chapter 2 for details on creating a basic control.)

Start by creating a new workspace. You'll want to use the OLE Control Wizard, as we have for the other examples in this chapter. In addition, make sure you check the Invisible at Runtime check box. Setting this option prevents the user from seeing your control on the Web page. You also won't need to subclass an existing control—we want a blank ActiveX control in this case.

This project is a little more complex than the other two in this chapter. We need a way to store individual color settings and retrieve them later. This example will use four properties to store the color settings: BackgroundColor, ForegroundColor, LinkColor, and VisitedColor. All four of these properties are of type CString. You'll need to use the MFC ClassWizard to create them, just as we have in the other examples in this book. In addition, we'll need two methods: GetColor and SetColor. The first will retrieve the color settings stored on disk. The second will send the colors to disk. They won't require any input, but they will return a BOOL value to let you know whether color setting or getting was successful. We saw how to add methods to a control in the previous section, so we won't revisit that issue here. What you have now is a control framework that can get and set the four basic colors used to display an HTML page. We also need another property. In this case it's the ColorAvailable property, which is of type BOOL. It doesn't help much if users visit your Web site and you request their custom color settings if none are available. This property will tell you if they are. When you finish adding all of these methods and properties, your OLE Automation page in the MFC ClassWizard should look like the one shown here:

Remember that BackColor and ForeColor are stock properties of type OLE_COLOR, so you can't use those property names for this control.

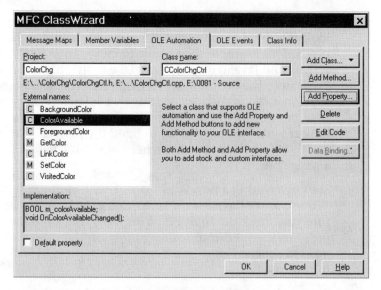

There is one other consideration you may not have thought about—it's better to decide on color settings before you display the HTML page. This is the first control in which we'll have to add an event. We'll call it OnColorLoad, and it will signify the completion of a color loading procedure. It will allow you to synchronize the loading of custom colors with the display of your HTML page. You add events using the OLE Events page of the MFC ClassWizard shown here:

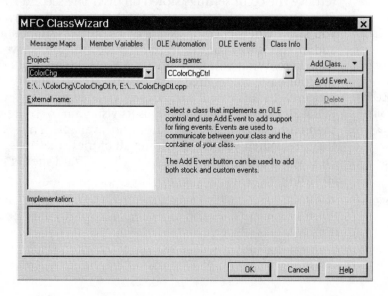

As you can see, this page looks much like the OLE Automation page. The list box (now empty) contains a list of the events that you've defined. This page also shows you the current project name and class. Clicking the Add Event button will display the following dialog. This is where we'll add the OnColorLoad event. All you need to do is type the name of the event, and then click OK.

As with methods, you can define a set of input parameters, though we don't need them in this case. You'll also notice that this event gets called within the ActiveX control using FireOnColorLoad. Calling the fire function actually sends the signal outside the control that the loading process is complete. (From the users' point of view, they've made some color selection choices, then clicked a Save Colors button.) We'll see how everything works in the code that follows in Listing 9-5.

NOTE: The CColorChgCtrl::OnColorAvailableChanged() method at the end of Listing 9-5 is provided in the following listing for the sake of completeness. The ClassWizard will add it for you automatically if you create the application correctly. There's no need to add any code to this method unless you want to enhance the example to perform some type of special processing. However, you will want to make certain that the method does appear somewhere in your code listing. (If it doesn't appear, you probably missed defining the ColorAvailable property needed by the control.)

Listing 9-5

```
//////////////////////////////////////////////////////////////////////////
// CColorChgCtrl::CColorChgCtrl - Constructor

CColorChgCtrl::CColorChgCtrl()
{
    char*           szFileName;     // Name of the file to open.
    CFileStatus     oStatus;        // Status of file object.

    InitializeIIDs(&IID_DColorChg, &IID_DColorChgEvents);

    // Initialize our color properties to some default value.
    m_backgroundColor = "WHITE";
    m_foregroundColor = "BLACK";
    m_linkColor = "GREEN";
    m_visitedColor = "RED";

    // See if there's a color file on disk.
    szFileName = "C:\\COLORSET.TXT";
    m_colorAvailable = CFile::GetStatus(szFileName, oStatus);

}

BOOL CColorChgCtrl::GetColor()
{
    char*           szFileName;     // Name of the file to open.
    CFileStatus     oStatus;        // Status of file object.
    CFile           oFile;          // File object for sending data to the drive.
    CFileException  oException;      // File opening exception.
    char            szData[99];      // Data storage variable.

    // See if there's a color file on disk.
    szFileName = "C:\\COLORSET.TXT";
    if (! CFile::GetStatus(szFileName, oStatus))
    {
        // Make sure the color detection variable is set right.
        m_colorAvailable = FALSE;

        // Exit the routine.
        return FALSE;
    }

    // Open the file for reading.
    if (oFile.Open(szFileName, CFile::modeRead, &oException))
    {
        // Read the file.
        oFile.Read(szData, sizeof(szData));
```

```
        // Store the color settings in our properties.
        m_backgroundColor = strtok(szData, ",");
        m_foregroundColor = strtok(NULL, ",");
        m_linkColor = strtok(NULL, ",");
        m_visitedColor = strtok(NULL, ",");

        // Close the file.
        oFile.Close();
    }
    else
    {
        // We couldn't read the settings.
        MessageBox("File Exception: " + oException.m_cause, "Error", MB_OK | MB_ICONERROR);
        return FALSE;
    }

    return TRUE;
}

BOOL CColorChgCtrl::SetColor()
{
    CFile           oFile;          // File object for sending data to the drive.
    CFileException  oException;     // File opening exception.
    char*           szFileName;     // Name of the file.
    CString         oData;          // Data storage variable.

    // Open the file for writing, don't save the old settings.
    szFileName = "C:\\COLORSET.TXT";
    if (oFile.Open(szFileName, CFile::modeCreate | CFile::modeWrite,
&oException))
    {
        // Store the color settings in an easily parsed form.
        oData = m_backgroundColor + ",";
        oData = oData + m_foregroundColor + ",";
        oData = oData + m_linkColor + ",";
        oData = oData + m_visitedColor + ",";

        // Write the data to the file.
        oFile.Write(oData, oData.GetLength());

        // Close the file.
        oFile.Close;

        // Update the ColorAvailable status.
        m_colorAvailable = TRUE;
```

```
      // Tell the world that we've changed the colors.
      FireOnColorLoad();
   }
   else
   {
      // We couldn't save the settings.
      MessageBox("File Exception: " + oException.m_cause, "Error", MB_OK | MB_ICONERROR);
      return FALSE;
   }


   return TRUE;
}

void CColorChgCtrl::OnColorAvailableChanged()
{
   // TODO: Add notification handler code

   SetModifiedFlag();
}
```

As you can see, you'll actually need to change three methods to implement this control. The first method is the control's constructor. You need to initialize the properties to specific values just in case the user hasn't visited your site before. These default color values will allow you to use very generic code when creating your Web site. Even more important than the color settings is the detection of the color settings file. You'll see how this works when we look at the HTML part of the project. For right now, all you need to know is that setting this property is essential to setting up the HTML page correctly.

The next method, GetColor(), allows us to retrieve the color values that the user previously saved. There aren't any real surprises here. The first item of business is to make sure the file exists. Once we establish that it's actually there, all we do is use standard file functions to open the data file and store its contents in szData. Notice that the strtok() function makes parsing the data values and placing them in the various properties easy.

SetColor() is the third method you'll need to implement. Notice that it grabs the data it needs from the properties, forms them into a string of values separated by a comma delimiter, then writes them to disk. The last thing we do is fire the OnColorLoad() event. This allows the control's user to perform some action based on the new color selections we just stored to disk.

Now that we have a control to look at, it's time to look at the code required to set up the sample Web page. As with the other controls we've looked at so far, you'll start with a clean HTML page, add the control, then add the code required to make it work. Notice that we placed the control outside of the body area, just like before. You'll find the code for this part of the example in Listing 9-6.

Listing 9-6

```
<HTML>
<HEAD>
<TITLE>Saving Color Settings</TITLE>

<!-Use our OnColorLoad event to automatically update the display.->
<SCRIPT FOR=ColorChg1 EVENT=OnColorLoad()>
<!--{
    Document.fgColor = ColorChg1.ForegroundColor;
    Document.bgColor = ColorChg1.BackgroundColor;
    Document.linkColor = ColorChg1.LinkColor;
    Document.vlinkColor = ColorChg1.VisitedColor;
-->
</SCRIPT>

<!-Insert our color saving object.->
<OBJECT ID="ColorChg1" WIDTH=1 HEIGHT=1
 CLASSID="CLSID:7510C6E3-FE7B-11CF-8C70-00006E3127B7"
 CODEBASE="http://www.mycompany.com/controls/ColorChg.OCX">
    <PARAM NAME="_Version" VALUE="65536">
    <PARAM NAME="_ExtentX" VALUE="35">
    <PARAM NAME="_ExtentY" VALUE="35">
    <PARAM NAME="_StockProps" VALUE="0">
</OBJECT>

</HEAD>

<!-This script will create a custom body tag.->
<SCRIPT LANGUAGE="JavaScript">
<!--
    // If the user previously saved the color settings, restore them.
    if (ColorChg1.ColorAvailable)
    {
        ColorChg1.GetColor();
    }
```

```
    // Build a <BODY> tag.
    Window.Document.Write("<BODY BGCOLOR=" + ColorChg1.BackgroundColor);
    Window.Document.Write(" TEXT=" + ColorChg1.ForegroundColor);
    Window.Document.Write(" LINK=" + ColorChg1.LinkColor);
    Window.Document.Write(" VLINK=" + ColorChg1.VisitedColor + ">");
-->
</SCRIPT>

<!-Display a heading->
<CENTER><H1>Custom Settings Example</H1>
<H2>You can save a user's settings to disk!</H2></CENTER>

<!-Display a fake link.->
This is a <A HREF="SAMPLE.HTM">fake link</A>.<P>

<!-Display a table of radio buttons for making color selections.->
<CENTER>
<H2>Select Your Color Choices</H2>
<TABLE WIDTH=75% BORDER=2>
<TR>
    <TH>Background</TH>
    <TH>Foreground</TH>
    <TH>Link</TH>
    <TH>Visited Link</TH>
<TR>
    <TD><INPUT TYPE="radio" NAME="Radio1" VALUE="Black"
        ONCLICK=ColorChg1.BackgroundColor="BLACK">Black</TD>
    <TD><INPUT TYPE="radio" NAME="Radio2" VALUE="Black" CHECKED
        ONCLICK=ColorChg1.ForegroundColor="BLACK">Black</TD>
    <TD><INPUT TYPE="radio" NAME="Radio3" VALUE="Black"
        ONCLICK=ColorChg1.LinkColor="BLACK">Black</TD>
    <TD><INPUT TYPE="radio" NAME="Radio4" VALUE="Black"
        ONCLICK=ColorChg1.VisitedColor="BLACK">Black</TD>
<TR>
    <TD><INPUT TYPE="radio" NAME="Radio1" VALUE="Red"
        ONCLICK=ColorChg1.BackgroundColor="RED">Red</TD>
    <TD><INPUT TYPE="radio" NAME="Radio2" VALUE="Red"
        ONCLICK=ColorChg1.ForegroundColor="RED">Red</TD>
    <TD><INPUT TYPE="radio" NAME="Radio3" VALUE="Red"
        ONCLICK=ColorChg1.LinkColor="RED">Red</TD>
    <TD><INPUT TYPE="radio" NAME="Radio4" VALUE="Red" CHECKED
        ONCLICK=ColorChg1.VisitedColor="RED">Red</TD>
<TR>
    <TD><INPUT TYPE="radio" NAME="Radio1" VALUE="White" CHECKED
        ONCLICK=ColorChg1.BackgroundColor="WHITE">White</TD>
    <TD><INPUT TYPE="radio" NAME="Radio2" VALUE="White"
```

```
                ONCLICK=ColorChg1.ForegroundColor="WHITE">White</TD>
      <TD><INPUT TYPE="radio" NAME="Radio3" VALUE="White"
          ONCLICK=ColorChg1.LinkColor="WHITE">White</TD>
      <TD><INPUT TYPE="radio" NAME="Radio4" VALUE="White"
          ONCLICK=ColorChg1.VisitedColor="WHITE">White</TD>
  <TR>
      <TD><INPUT TYPE="radio" NAME="Radio1" VALUE="Green"
          ONCLICK=ColorChg1.BackgroundColor="GREEN">Green</TD>
      <TD><INPUT TYPE="radio" NAME="Radio2" VALUE="Green"
          ONCLICK=ColorChg1.ForegroundColor="GREEN">Green</TD>
      <TD><INPUT TYPE="radio" NAME="Radio3" VALUE="Green" CHECKED
          ONCLICK=ColorChg1.LinkColor="GREEN">Green</TD>
      <TD><INPUT TYPE="radio" NAME="Radio4" VALUE="Green"
          ONCLICK=ColorChg1.VisitedColor="GREEN">Green</TD>
  <TR>
      <TD><INPUT TYPE="radio" NAME="Radio1" VALUE="Blue"
          ONCLICK=ColorChg1.BackgroundColor="BLUE">Blue</TD>
      <TD><INPUT TYPE="radio" NAME="Radio2" VALUE="Blue"
          ONCLICK=ColorChg1.ForegroundColor="BLUE">Blue</TD>
      <TD><INPUT TYPE="radio" NAME="Radio3" VALUE="Blue"
          ONCLICK=ColorChg1.LinkColor="BLUE">Blue</TD>
      <TD><INPUT TYPE="radio" NAME="Radio4" VALUE="Blue"
          ONCLICK=ColorChg1.VisitedColor="BLUE">Blue</TD>
  <TR>
      <TD><INPUT TYPE="radio" NAME="Radio1" VALUE="Silver"
          ONCLICK=ColorChg1.BackgroundColor="SILVER">Silver</TD>
      <TD><INPUT TYPE="radio" NAME="Radio2" VALUE="Silver"
          ONCLICK=ColorChg1.ForegroundColor="SILVER">Silver</TD>
      <TD><INPUT TYPE="radio" NAME="Radio3" VALUE="Silver"
          ONCLICK=ColorChg1.LinkColor="SILVER">Silver</TD>
      <TD><INPUT TYPE="radio" NAME="Radio4" VALUE="Silver"
          ONCLICK=ColorChg1.VisitedColor="SILVER">Silver</TD>
  </TABLE>
  </CENTER>

  <!-Allow the user to save their color selections.->
  <P><INPUT LANGUAGE="JavaScript" TYPE="button" VALUE="Save Colors"
     ONCLICK=ColorChg1.SetColor()>

  </BODY>
  </HTML>
```

Take a look at this example code for a few minutes—try to find the <BODY>
tag. You won't find it all in one place. This example shows you yet another
way to extend your page using JavaScript. In this case we're using JavaScript

to determine the color of the various page elements before we display them onscreen. There isn't a function name, but you'll find the code right below the </HEAD> tag. What we're actually doing is building a <BODY> tag out of the properties of our ActiveX control. Look at how the Document.Write( ) calls are put together. You can easily extend this methodology to other areas of the document.

We've seen a few tables so far in the book, so I won't go into detail here. The only thing of note is the method used to change the property values using the ONCLICK method of the various radio buttons in the table. Notice how the WIDTH attribute in the <TABLE> tag helps to make this table a little more readable in Figure 9-6.

The last thing to look at in the body of the document is the final <INPUT> tag, which contains our button code. Notice that all we need to do is call the ActiveX control's SetColor( ) method here. You won't need a lot of added code to get the job done because the control does it all for you.

One last detached-looking piece of code in this example appears at the very top of the document in the heading area. That's right, it contains a function designed to work with the OnColorLoad( ) event. Every time the user presses

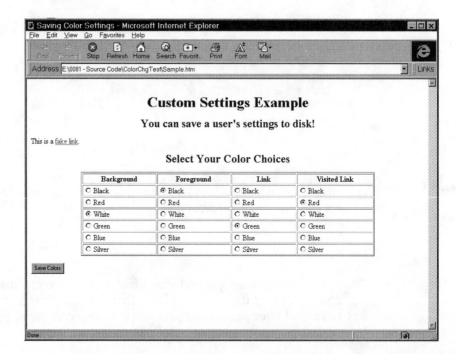

This page may look ordinary, but it provides all kinds of surprises.

Figure 9-6.

the pushbutton to save the new color settings, the control fires this event. Even though you never specifically update the colors in the HTML code, they are updated anyway as a result of using this event code.

TIP: We'll see more uses for events as the book progresses. However, one of the most important events you could add to error-prone controls is an OnError event. You could use this event to alert the client machine of problem situations. A property could hold a custom message that explains the precise cause of the problem. All that you'd need to do is use one of the JavaScript dialog commands to display the message onscreen.

Chapter 10

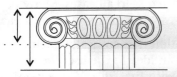

New Technologies and ActiveX

So far in this book we've looked at a lot of ways of making old technology work in new ways with the Internet. The first section of this chapter will take a close look at the new capabilities provided by Microsoft Visual C++ version 4.2. In many cases the new technology we'll look at is simply an extension of the old. For example, ActiveX Document is an extension of the Microsoft Binder technology. (Chapter 5 provides full details on the history of ActiveX Document.) There are a few places where the new technology is specially designed for the Internet. For example, when we look at URLs and monikers (see Chapter 8 for a discussion of the theory behind this technology), we'll look at methods of connecting to other data sources that's Internet-specific.

There are all kinds of ways to work with text in Internet applications. In fact, Web pages originally used text alone to communicate their messages. Today's use of graphics, sound, and full motion

329

video is a recent addition to the Internet repertoire of communication methods. The obvious reason for the addition of these other communication forms is that text wasn't quite enough to get the message across in all cases. Many people also consider text to be a somewhat bland way to talk about some ideas.

Almost every form of Internet communication that comes in document form is one-way—the Webmaster presents an idea to the user, but the user doesn't really have any way of interacting with that idea. We saw one way of remedying this situation in the "Using the Web Publishing Wizard" section of Chapter 5. Using Word for Windows or other applications that can act as ActiveX Document containers can make the presentation of information a two-way street. It can even allow people in distant places to collaborate on a document through an Internet connection. Another section of Chapter 5, "What Are ActiveX Documents," described the theory behind creating an ActiveX Document. The second section of this chapter will show you one way to actually create an ActiveX Document using Microsoft Visual C++.

URLs and monikers provide specific methods for finding a resource on the Internet or on your local intranet. Anyone who has spent time on the Internet has used URLs extensively. Monikers are probably an alien concept to users, but programmers will probably become quite familiar with them, in some cases because they require one less step of processing. We've already looked at the theory behind both URLs and monikers in Chapter 8. This chapter will look at the technique for implementing them within an application. We'll look at some of the more common questions that programmers have regarding the use of both URLs and monikers. For example, how would you allow a user to access a link to data on the Internet when that link appears within a standard document? Creating and maintaining connections is one of the more important issues that you'll have to deal with when working with the Internet today.

NOTE: All of the examples in this chapter use Microsoft Visual C++ 4.2. You must have this version of the product to follow the examples from start to finish. (Borland has recently released a version of its C++ compiler that will allow you to do many of the things demonstrated in this chapter, but not quite in the way shown. The new version of the Borland compiler does make using ActiveX a lot easier than even Microsoft's 4.1 version of their product.) There are ways of at least using the examples with Visual C++ 4.1, but you may need to work with them a little first. For example, you'll need to add references to the various new classes supported as a default by Visual C++ 4.2. In addition, creating the examples won't be as automatic as when using the newer product. Theoretically, it's possible to create these examples with Visual C++ 4.0 as well, but the amount of work required will certainly make getting an updated version of the compiler seem like a good idea.

New Features of Visual C++ 4.2

The latest version of Microsoft Visual C++ is Internet-enabled in more ways than one. It not only extends current technology, but it adds a few new application types as well. For example, the new Internet Information Server (IIS) has spawned the need for additional application types that can work at the server end of the picture. We'll look at this area in the next section.

It's the extensions to existing technologies that you'll appreciate the most. If you take a look at some of the programming examples provided with the ActiveX SDK, you'll appreciate just how easy it is to become mired in detail when it comes to Internet applications. A programmer has to learn a lot of new technology just to create the most basic of applications, since the Internet requires a lot of new interfaces to work. (We've seen all of these interfaces in the theory section of this book—look at Chapter 5 for ActiveX Documents or Chapter 8 for URL and moniker support.)

History is repeating itself with the Internet just as it has for all kinds of other environment changes. Just as many programmers had a hard time at first writing applications for Windows, early adopters will have some problems working with Internet applications. (There is an expression that some programmers live by because it's so true—you can always tell the pioneers by the arrows in their back.) Even though writing an Internet application is difficult today, it won't always be that way. You need to consider what makes Windows applications almost effortless to write today—it's RAD environments and other tools that make life easy when it comes to plain vanilla Windows applications. Likewise, new tools will eventually make Internet applications a breeze to write. Microsoft Visual C++ 4.2 represents a leap in tool support that will make it easier to write Internet-enabled applications—though you'll still need to do some serious work to make the application fully functional.

CAUTION: Before you even begin to read this section, make sure you update your copy of Microsoft Visual C++ to the 4.2a version. You can find the required patch at http://www.microsoft.com/visualc/v42/v42tech/v42a /vc42a.htm. This patch fixes some problems between the ActiveX SDK and the Visual C++ compiler. Not applying this patch means that you'll run into some unexpected bugs while writing controls for ActiveX Document servers. (In fact, you'll find that you'll run into problems when trying to write just about any kind of ActiveX-specific code.) Even though the patch was in beta at the time of this writing, it should be in released form by the time you read this.

A Look at the ISAPI Wizard

Let's take a look at a basic example of the new functionality provided by the Microsoft C++ 4.2 compiler. Start the Microsoft Developer Studio and use the File | New command to open the New dialog. Double-click on the Project Workspace selection, and you'll see the familiar New Project Workspace dialog. All of the entries should look at least vaguely familiar—though Microsoft renamed some entries, such as the OCX Wizard to OLE Control Wizard. At the very end of this list you'll find a new Internet-specific entry like the one shown here:

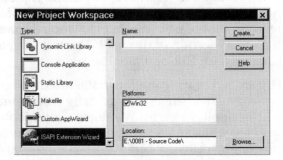

The ISAPI (Internet Server Application Programming Interface) Wizard is a new workspace type that allows you to add functionality to your Web server. Essentially, these applications will sit on the server and allow the user to perform some types of tasks that might have been impossible in the past. Other application types will perform user monitoring or allow you to detect certain types of intrusions into your network. You might even use this workspace to make some types of data access easier. Even though you can create many kinds of applications, they all fall within two levels of functionality, as shown here (the first page of the ISAPI Wizard):

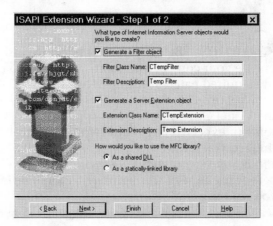

The default setting is Generate a Server Extension Object. Selecting this option means that you want to create some sort of server-specific application. For example, if you want to perform some type of special forms handling that allows you to enter information into a database without resorting to scripts, you select this option. Server extensions aren't a one-way street. You can use them to provide additional information to the user as well. For example, every time the user requests data from a standard server, a CGI (or other) script executes. It begins by opening the database, then requests the information, and finally, closes the database again. All of this opening and closing activity can chew up a big chunk of your Web server's performance. It can also result in some pretty strange errors, such as overrunning the lock limit on some types of database managers. Server extensions will allow the user to get the information faster, reduce the cost of server hardware by extending the number of users that you can attach to one server, and reduce the number of administrator headaches caused by scripts.

TIP: The ISAPI Wizard offers you the option of loading the MFC library routines dynamically or statically. If you choose the first option, you'll need to distribute a copy of the MFC libraries with your application. However, this option makes for a smaller application, reduces disk space requirements if you have two or more MFC applications running on the host machine, and reduces the memory footprint of the application in memory since it shares one copy of the code with other applications. The advantages to using the static method are fairly obvious as well. You can always be sure that the application has everything it needs to execute even if the MFC libraries get wiped off the host machine. In addition, since the libraries load with the application, you'll normally find that an application that uses the static MFC library option takes longer to load but runs slightly faster afterward. Since the performance benefits are slight, you'll normally want to keep the dynamic (default) selection highlighted. Most Web servers will have a copy of the MFC libraries, and the amount of memory you'll save using the dynamic option is significant (not to mention the disk space savings).

There is a second kind of object that you can add to your server extension. A filter object allows you to detect certain Internet events. That event could be as simple as someone requesting access to your server. You can even monitor things like mapping requests from a user moving from one place to another on your Web site. Filters can also work with both secured and non-secured connections. (In Internet parlance, a non-secured connection usually means that someone has logged in using an Anonymous connection. This is an extremely common connection for all types of Internet access and is one of the reasons for security problems on the Internet today.) Whenever you select the Generate a Filter Object option, the ISAPI Wizard presents a second page of configuration options, as shown in Figure 10-1.

So how does a filter object work with the server extension object (which will be some type of application in this case)? Every time the filter detects something that your application has requested to know about, it sends an event message that tells your application what it found. Your application can then decide whether or not to react to the event. In addition to reacting with a server extension, you can use filter objects by themselves. A filter object could manipulate an incoming URL or request a password from the user. Most filters will provide some type of utility function, but nothing says that you have to restrict them to this mode of operation. However, the distinction between a server extension object and a filter object is pretty clear. A filter object always interacts with the data stream; the server extension object always interacts with the Web server itself. What this means is that you can't use a filter object to query a database or other server-specific information—likewise, a server extension object can't monitor Internet events.

Notice that the dialog shown in Figure 10-1 also allows you to choose a priority for your filter. A high-priority filter will get to look at Internet events

The second page of the ISAPI Wizard allows you to define the kind of monitoring your filter object will perform.

Figure 10-1.

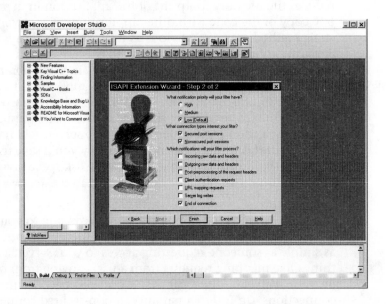

first. If it doesn't need to react to the event, the filter will pass the event to the next filter in line. If you load two or more filters with the same priority level on your Web server at the same time, the one loaded first will get to see the Internet events first. What this means is that you could achieve a specific level of monitoring by changing the filter load order rather than unnecessarily increasing the filter priority level.

TIP: Using the Low priority setting whenever possible assures that your application will have the least possible effect on the server, freeing it to do the work that you set it up to do in the first place. High-priority applications will always adversely affect the performance of your server and may not garner any more events than a low-priority application would. When creating an application, you always need to ask yourself whether the event you want to monitor is common or not. If it is a common event and you must absolutely see the event messages first, your only choice is to use either the Medium or High settings; but this should be the option of last resort. Use the default Low setting whenever possible.

When creating a filter, you also have to decide on what to monitor. You can monitor all Internet events, or simply a subset. Every event you choose to monitor does reduce server performance, so you'll want to choose the events you monitor carefully. There are seven different kinds of filters you can create. The following list provides an overview of each type.

- ♦ **Incoming Raw Data and Headers** Selecting this filter notification type adds an OnReadRawData() method to your application. This filter method will get called every time a client makes any request of the server. You can return any of several success messages, the most common of which tells the server to disconnect the session. Unlike a script, though, you can return a special message— SF_STATUS_REQ_FINISHED_KEEP_CONN—which maintains the session and allows the client to make additional requests.

- ♦ **Outgoing Raw Data and Headers** This filter notification type selection will add an OnSendRawData() method to your application. It allows you to modify the information going from the server to the application. For example, you could use this method to compress the data before it leaves the server. You're only allowed to call the next filter in the chain or indicate failure when using this method.

♦ **Post-Processing of the Request Headers**   Whenever a server processes client requests, it sends notification to the client that it is doing so. For example, when you enter a newsgroup on the Internet and see a progress indicator showing the current download status for the messages on that newsgroup, that's an effect of server notification. Selecting this option adds an OnPreprocHeaders() method to your application—allowing you to monitor the notification messages sent from the server to a client.

♦ **Client Authentication Requests**   We talked about client authentication from a variety of perspectives in Chapter 6. This option tells the server that you want to be notified each time it requests client authentication. Selecting this option adds an OnAuthentication() method to your application.

♦ **URL Mapping Requests**   The server always notifies the client when it maps a logical URL to a physical location on the server. Normally the server uses a directory structure similar to the link structure of the Web site, but it doesn't necessarily have to do so (which is the reason for URL mapping). You can add a filter to handle URL mapping in other than the default manner. For example, you might want to intercept specific URLs and map them to a secure location. Selecting this option adds an OnUrlMap() method to your application.

♦ **Server Log Writes**   Most servers log specific events. The kind of events logged depends on the server configuration. You can select this option to intercept the event log and perform some processing with it before sending it to disk. This comes in especially handy for handling statistical surveys of server usage. Selecting this option adds an OnLog() method to your application.

♦ **End of Connection**   A session on the Internet doesn't just end—a little communication goes on first so that both the client and server can take care of any housekeeping chores. The End of Connection option adds an OnEndOfNetSession() method to your application. You can use this method to perform any housekeeping chores required by a server extension or simply for statistical purposes.

 WARNING: You must select at least one item in the connection type area and one item from the notification type area of the dialog shown in Figure 10-1 to make the filter work. Failure to do this will result in a nonfunctional filter as a minimum and a nonfunctional server as a maximum.

Application Enhancements

Visual C++ 4.2 has quite a few application-specific enhancements, but we're only interested in one of them. Unlike previous versions of Visual C++, in which the ActiveX Document features were hidden in the MFC classes (used with the Microsoft Office Binder), you can now access these features with a mere check box selection. We're going to look at this particular feature in detail in the "Creating an ActiveX Document" section of this chapter.

NOTE: Microsoft Visual C++ 4.2 does support ActiveX Document servers. It doesn't support the container part of the equation. (Internet Explorer is an example of a container.) For a more detailed discussion about the requirements for servers and containers, read the theoretical information in Chapter 5.

ActiveX Control Improvements

You've already seen quite a few ActiveX control examples in the book (both Chapters 2 and 9). All of those controls were built using Microsoft Visual C++ 4.0 so that they would work with a broader range of compilers. There isn't a single thing wrong with any of those controls—they'll work just as expected. However, you should consider these controls to be more of the Volkswagen persuasion than a full-fledged Cadillac. Microsoft Visual C++ 4.2 adds some options that will make your controls look just a bit better than the garden variety control. The following illustration shows the Advanced ActiveX Features dialog that this product includes.

As you can see, the improvements aren't in any specific area of program development. Some of the enhancements, such as Optimized Drawing Code, will improve overall control performance (depending on whether your control provides any drawing features or uses images, of course). Some are more in the area of appearance. For example, Flicker-Free Activation will help your control look better in a browser window. The following list provides an overview of the various new ActiveX-related features you'll be able to use with controls.

◆ **Windowless Activation**   Every control we've created so far has a window. Even the transparent controls we created in Chapter 9 displayed a window with an oval in them. This option allows you to create controls that don't require a window—they depend on the server container for that function. Using this feature reduces control code size and allows it to load more quickly.

◆ **Unclipped Device Context**   When you do draw within the confines of a control, the control normally performs checks to make sure it doesn't draw outside its window. Selecting this option will eliminate that check. The positive side is that you'll see a small, but noticeable, gain in drawing speed. The negative side is that you'll have to perform additional checks to make sure the control always remains within its drawing area. You can't use this option with windowless controls.

◆ **Flicker-Free Activation**   One of the most basic messages that a control will receive is to repaint itself. Normally this isn't any cause for alarm because the redraw operation goes quickly on a local machine. However, when working with an ActiveX control, the redraw can become noticeable and cause the screen to flicker. This option turns off redrawing between the active and inactive states—reducing flicker by quite a margin.

◆ **Mouse Pointer Notifications When Inactive**   This is a general-purpose option that could come in handy with any control— not just those used on the Internet. It allows your control to monitor two mouse messages, WM_SETCURSOR and WM_MOUSEMOVE, even when inactive. You can use this feature to display bubble help or provide other added functionality.

◆ **Optimized Drawing Code**   You'll find that this feature can provide a substantial speed increase, but only if the container supports it. Instead of redrawing the entire control every time some type of touch-up is needed, the control only repaints the affected area. The container will also perform other optimizations, such as looking for a copy of the control in local memory rather than performing a redraw over the dial-up connection.

◆ **Loads Properties Asynchronously**   All of the controls we've created in the book load synchronously. This means that Windows waits until the control is completely loaded before it does anything else. Normally this isn't a big deal on a local drive—the control loads fairly fast.

Checking this option allows you to compensate for the loading speed difference over an Internet connection by loading the control asynchronously. The only provision you need to make is calling the COleControl::InternalSetReadyState() method when you've accomplished the task of loading all the control properties.

Besides all of these new features, you'll find that there are a few additional controls you can subclass from when using Visual C++ 4.2. All of these new controls reflect the Windows 95 interface that both Windows 95 and Windows NT now use. In addition, all of the new controls are fully 32-bit (as reflected by the new "32" added to the control names). You'll also find all the old standards here, such as the BUTTON class that we've used so often in the book.

Creating an ActiveX Document

In Chapter 5 we looked at what you can do with an ActiveX Document application such as Word for Windows or Excel. That's fine if you're a power user who needs to get a little added performance or a Webmaster who wants to optimize a Web site; but you're a programmer who needs to create an application with these capabilities.

Trying to add all four of the required interfaces that we looked at in Chapter 5 manually might prove troublesome even to the most accomplished programmer. In addition, there really isn't any need to go through the trouble now that Microsoft has released their new version of C++. What we'll look at in this section is the quick method for creating an ActiveX Document-enabled application. We'll skip some of the details that you'd find in just about any application and concentrate on the ActiveX-specific portions of the project instead.

The first thing you need to do is create a new project workspace. We saw how to do that in the previous section. You'll want to select the MFC Application Wizard and give your application a name—the sample application uses ActivDoc. Click on Create to start the process, and you'll see the first page of the MFC Application Wizard. To make life a little simpler, check the Single Document option on the page of the Wizard. Click Next twice to get past the first and second pages of the Wizard. What you'll see next is the third page.

The third page is where you'll do most of the ActiveX Document configuration for the application. You can provide five different levels of OLE support with your application. The last three levels also allow you to add ActiveX Document support. The Mini-Server option won't allow you to run the application alone—you'd have to run it from Word for Windows, or Internet Explorer 3.0, or some other container. This level of support is fine if you want to create some kind of file browser. The next option is Full-Server, which allows the application to execute by itself. You can use this kind of application to support objects, but not to display them. Paint programs are usually good examples of an application that acts as a server, but not necessarily as a container. The final level, Both Container and Server, is the one that we'll select for this application. It allows you to provide full OLE 2 capabilities in your application, including embedding objects. You'll also want to check the ActiveX Document Server option, as shown in the following illustration. (You could also add OLE Automation and OLE Control support at this point, but we won't do so for the sample application.)

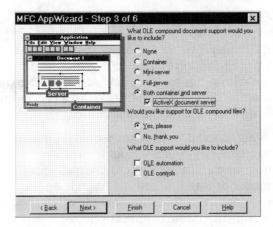

Click Next to see the fourth page of the MFC Application Wizard. Most of the settings on this page are just fine. You may want to set the Recent File List setting higher since most people really like this feature (it sure beats hunting around on the hard drive). A setting of 9 or 10 works fine in most cases; the example program uses a setting of 10.

This page also contains an Advanced button—which most programmers might whiz right by if they didn't look hard enough. Unfortunately, this really shouldn't be labeled Advanced (or perhaps Microsoft should consider reworking the Application Wizard a bit to make one of the required settings more obvious). Click on the Advanced button, and you'll see a dialog similar to the one in Figure 10-2.

The Document Template Strings page of the Advanced Options dialog allows you to set the file extension for your application. It also performs some important behind-the-scenes work for you automatically. The example program uses a file extension of AXD. All you need to do is type the extension in the first field (which starts out blank). You may want to change some additional strings, for example, the Main Frame Caption field. The example uses "ActiveX Document Editor". You may want to make the entry in the Filter Name field a little more descriptive as well. It starts out as "ActivD Files (*.axd)", but changing it to "ActiveX Document Files (*.axd)" is a lot more readable. Some people really don't care too much about the File Type Name field (which defaults to ActivD Document), but changing it to "ActiveX Document" will certainly help later as you search through the registry. In addition, this is the string used to display your new document within the Windows context menu (more on this in a few paragraphs). Once you make all of these changes, your Advanced Options dialog should look like the one in Figure 10-2.

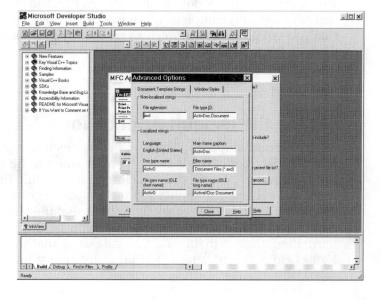

The Advanced Options dialog contains at least one entry that you really need to change before creating an application.

Figure 10-2.

At this point we've made all the selections required to create a simple ActiveX Document server. Click on Close to close the Advanced Options dialog. Then, click on Finish to complete the project shell. You'll see a New Project Information dialog like the one shown here:

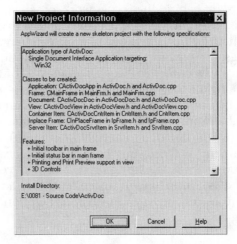

Take a few seconds to look through the list of features to ensure that the ActiveX support is complete. (After working with a few projects, you'll find that you can detect any problems very quickly by looking at this dialog.) Click on OK to generate the project shell.

Testing the Default Application—Step 1

Right now our sample application can't do much, but there are a few things it can do right out of the Wizard. Compile and run the application once the MFC Application Wizard finishes creating it. Running the application is important because the application makes some registry entries the first time you do so. The first change you'll notice is that the Windows context menu now contains an entry for your application file type, as shown in the following illustration. (Notice that this is the same name that we typed in the File Type Name field of the Advanced Options dialog shown in Figure 10-2.)

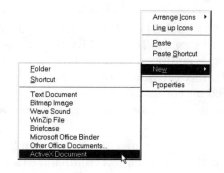

You'll see another change as well. Figure 10-3 shows the ActiveX Document application within the OLEView utility (we worked with this utility in Chapters 3 and 5 as well). As you can see, it's listed with the other Document Objects, such as Word for Windows. You should immediately notice that none of the four interfaces we talked about in Chapter 5 are listed here, as they would be for Word for Windows or other Binder programs. We'll see later in this section that checking your interfaces before saying that a program is ready for testing can save you a lot of time and effort later.

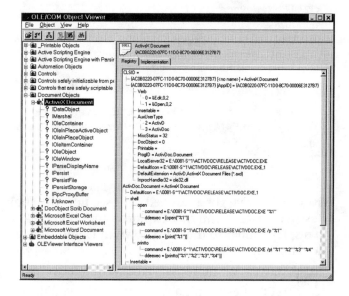

The ActivDoc application appears within OLEView as a Document Object.

Figure 10-3.

TIP: Visual C++ 4.2 provides a utility similar to OLEView. You can access it using the Tools | OLE Object View command. The ActiveX SDK still comes equipped with the OLEView utility shown throughout this book. Either utility provides essentially the same information about the controls installed on your machine.

The ActivDoc program can also create a basic container file. All you need to do is use the Insert | Object command to add an existing object to the current document. You can save the file to disk. Try creating one now so that you can test the application frame with Internet Explorer. Make sure you insert an object, then save the file, or you won't see anything when opening the document. This example uses the ColorBlk.BMP file shown in other parts of the book (Chapter 4, for example) as the object—the file itself is saved as TESTDOC.AXD. Once you create the test document, you'll need to create an HTML page to test it. Listing 10-1 shows the code we'll use in this case.

Listing 10-1

```
<HTML>
<HEAD>
<TITLE>New Page</TITLE>
</HEAD>
<BODY>

<!-Display a heading.->
<CENTER><H2>ActiveX Document Test</H2></CENTER>

<!-Create a link to the test document.->
Click <A HREF="TestDoc.AXD">Here</A> to test the AXD file.

</BODY>
</HTML>
```

Now that we've got a test bed, let's see how the application works. Open the test Web page in Internet Explorer, and then click on the test link. You'll see a display similar to the one shown in Figure 10-4, which isn't what we were looking for.

NOTE: If everything works properly, you'll see a dialog asking if you want to either save or open the file (assuming, of course, that you haven't turned the dialog off during a previous session). Make sure you tell the browser to open the file so that you can actually view it.

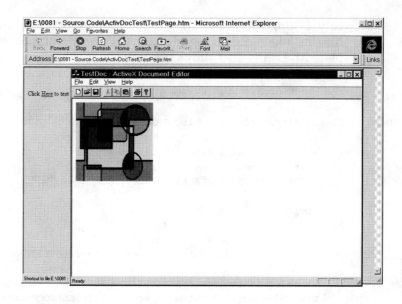

The first attempt at creating an ActiveX Document server is close, but not close enough.
Figure 10-4.

There is an important lesson regarding Wizards to learn here. Even though the application shell created with the MFC Application Wizard contains everything you need, you'll find that not everything is actually implemented. It's like building a house and leaving room for future expansion—your application contains all the basic structures needed to complete ActiveX Document support, but you'll need to do some additional work before those structures can do what you originally intended them to do. The next section will show how to fix this problem.

Fixing the ActiveX Document Server

You'll have to read the theoretical discussion in Chapter 5 before any of this section will make much sense. The short version is that even though the application we created in previous section has the capability of being an ActiveX Document server, it lacks the proper interface elements. If you remember from our discussion in Chapter 5, you must always implement a special interface to tell Windows that your application is capable of providing ActiveX Document support—it's the IOleDocument interface. In addition, you should implement three other interfaces: IOleDocumentView, IOleCommandTarget, and IPrint. You'll quickly find that none of these interfaces are provided with the sample application, and for good reason— you may not always want to provide ActiveX Document support in your application even if it can act as an in-place server. Adding the support is very easy. Listing 10-2 shows the code you'll need to add to the ActivDocDoc.H file (the added code is highlighted; the surrounding code shows where to place it). Listing 10-3 shows the addition for the ActivDocDoc.CPP file. In this case, you can place the entire method at the end of the ActivDocDoc.CPP source file.

Listing 10-2

```
class CActivDocDoc : public COleServerDoc
{
protected: // create from serialization only
    CActivDocDoc();
    DECLARE_DYNCREATE(CActivDocDoc)

// Attributes
public:
    CActivDocSrvrItem* GetEmbeddedItem()
        { return (CActivDocSrvrItem*)COleServerDoc::GetEmbeddedItem(); }

    // Added to implement ActiveX Document Interface.
    CDocObjectServer* GetDocObjectServer(LPOLEDOCUMENTSITE pSite);

// Operations
public:

// Overrides
    // ClassWizard generated virtual function overrides
    //{{AFX_VIRTUAL(CActivDocDoc)
    protected:
    virtual COleServerItem* OnGetEmbeddedItem();
    public:
    virtual BOOL OnNewDocument();
    virtual void Serialize(CArchive& ar);
    //}}AFX_VIRTUAL
```

Listing 10-3

```
// Added for ActiveX Document interface.
CDocObjectServer* CActivDocDoc::GetDocObjectServer(LPOLEDOCUMENTSITE pSite)
{
    return new CDocObjectServer(this, pSite);
}
```

As you can see, all four of the required interfaces are implemented using the CDocObjectServer class. It's important to understand that each interface doesn't have to be a separate class when creating an OLE application. One of the benefits of using OLE is that you can bundle interfaces together. The interfaces, in turn, bundle groups of functions together, which makes them easier to use (or at least find). You'll find all of the declarations for this class in the AFXDOCOB.H header file provided with Visual C++. Listing 10-4 shows an excerpt from this file that we'll use for discussion purposes. Notice that the CDocObjectServer class is subclassed from the CCmdTarget base class.

Listing 10-4

```
/////////////////////////////////////////////////////////////////////////////
// CDocObjectServer class

class CDocObjectServer : public CCmdTarget
{
    DECLARE_DYNAMIC(CDocObjectServer)

// Constructors
public:
    CDocObjectServer(COleServerDoc* pOwner,
        LPOLEDOCUMENTSITE pDocSite = NULL);

// Attributes
public:

// Operations
public:
    void ActivateDocObject();

// Overridables
protected:
    // Document Overridables

    // View Overridables
    virtual void OnApplyViewState(CArchive& ar);
    virtual void OnSaveViewState(CArchive& ar);
    virtual HRESULT OnActivateView();

// Implementation
public:
    virtual ~CDocObjectServer();
    void ReleaseDocSite();
    void SetDocSite(LPOLEDOCUMENTSITE pNewSite);
    COleDocIPFrameWnd* GetControllingFrame() const;
protected:
    STDMETHODIMP OnExecOleCmd(const GUID* pguidCmdGroup,
        DWORD nCmdID, DWORD nCmdExecOpt, VARIANTARG* pvarargIn,
        VARIANTARG* pvarargOut);
    BOOL DoPreparePrinting(CView* pView, CPrintInfo* printInfo);
```

```
    void DoPrepareDC(CView* pView, CDC* pdcPrint, CPrintInfo* pprintInfo);
    void DoPrint(CView* pView, CDC* pdcPrint, CPrintInfo* pprintInfo);
    void DoBeginPrinting(CView* pView, CDC* pDC, CPrintInfo* pprintInfo);
    void DoEndPrinting(CView* pView, CDC* pDC, CPrintInfo* pprintInfo);

#ifdef _DEBUG
    virtual void AssertValid() const;
    virtual void Dump(CDumpContext& dc) const;
#endif

    // Overrides
protected:
    // ClassWizard generated virtual function overrides
    //{{AFX_VIRTUAL(CDocObjectServer)
    public:
    virtual void OnCloseDocument();
    //}}AFX_VIRTUAL

    // Implementation Data
protected:
    // Document Data
    LPOLEDOCUMENTSITE m_pDocSite;
    COleServerDoc* m_pOwner;

    // Print Data
    LONG m_nFirstPage;
    LPCONTINUECALLBACK m_pContinueCallback;

    // View Data
    LPOLEINPLACESITE   m_pViewSite;

    // Implementation Helpers
protected:
    void OnSetItemRects(LPRECT lprcPosRect, LPRECT lprcClipRect);
//   LPUNKNOWN GetInterfaceHook(const void* iid);

    // Generated message map functions
protected:
    //{{AFX_MSG(CDocObjectServer)
        // NOTE - the ClassWizard will add and remove member functions here.
    //}}AFX_MSG
    DECLARE_MESSAGE_MAP()

// Interface Maps
public:
    BEGIN_INTERFACE_PART(OleObject, IOleObject)
```

```
        INIT_INTERFACE_PART(CDocObjServerDoc, DocOleObject)
        STDMETHOD(SetClientSite)(LPOLECLIENTSITE);
        STDMETHOD(GetClientSite)(LPOLECLIENTSITE*);
        STDMETHOD(SetHostNames)(LPCOLESTR, LPCOLESTR);
        STDMETHOD(Close)(DWORD);
        STDMETHOD(SetMoniker)(DWORD, LPMONIKER);
        STDMETHOD(GetMoniker)(DWORD, DWORD, LPMONIKER*);
        STDMETHOD(InitFromData)(LPDATAOBJECT, BOOL, DWORD);
        STDMETHOD(GetClipboardData)(DWORD, LPDATAOBJECT*);
        STDMETHOD(DoVerb)(LONG, LPMSG, LPOLECLIENTSITE, LONG, HWND, LPCRECT);
        STDMETHOD(EnumVerbs)(IEnumOLEVERB**);
        STDMETHOD(Update)();
        STDMETHOD(IsUpToDate)();
        STDMETHOD(GetUserClassID)(CLSID*);
        STDMETHOD(GetUserType)(DWORD, LPOLESTR*);
        STDMETHOD(SetExtent)(DWORD, LPSIZEL);
        STDMETHOD(GetExtent)(DWORD, LPSIZEL);
        STDMETHOD(Advise)(LPADVISESINK, LPDWORD);
        STDMETHOD(Unadvise)(DWORD);
        STDMETHOD(EnumAdvise)(LPENUMSTATDATA*);
        STDMETHOD(GetMiscStatus)(DWORD, LPDWORD);
        STDMETHOD(SetColorScheme)(LPLOGPALETTE);
    END_INTERFACE_PART(OleObject)

    BEGIN_INTERFACE_PART(OleDocument, IOleDocument)
        INIT_INTERFACE_PART(CDocObjectServer, OleDocument)
        STDMETHOD(CreateView)(LPOLEINPLACESITE, LPSTREAM, DWORD,
LPOLEDOCUMENTVIEW*);
        STDMETHOD(GetDocMiscStatus)(LPDWORD);
        STDMETHOD(EnumViews)(LPENUMOLEDOCUMENTVIEWS*, LPOLEDOCUMENTVIEW*);
    END_INTERFACE_PART(OleDocument)

    BEGIN_INTERFACE_PART(OleDocumentView, IOleDocumentView)
        INIT_INTERFACE_PART(CDocObjectServer, OleDocumentView)
        STDMETHOD(SetInPlaceSite)(LPOLEINPLACESITE);
        STDMETHOD(GetInPlaceSite)(LPOLEINPLACESITE*);
        STDMETHOD(GetDocument)(LPUNKNOWN*);
        STDMETHOD(SetRect)(LPRECT);
        STDMETHOD(GetRect)(LPRECT);
        STDMETHOD(SetRectComplex)(LPRECT, LPRECT, LPRECT, LPRECT);
        STDMETHOD(Show)(BOOL);
        STDMETHOD(UIActivate)(BOOL);
        STDMETHOD(Open)();
        STDMETHOD(CloseView)(DWORD);
        STDMETHOD(SaveViewState)(LPSTREAM);
        STDMETHOD(ApplyViewState)(LPSTREAM);
```

```
        STDMETHOD(Clone)(LPOLEINPLACESITE, LPOLEDOCUMENTVIEW*);
    END_INTERFACE_PART(OleDocumentView)

    BEGIN_INTERFACE_PART(OleCommandTarget, IOleCommandTarget)
        INIT_INTERFACE_PART(CDocObjectServer, OleCommandTarget)
        STDMETHOD(QueryStatus)(const GUID*, ULONG, OLECMD[], OLECMDTEXT*);
        STDMETHOD(Exec)(const GUID*, DWORD, DWORD, VARIANTARG*, VARIANTARG*);
    END_INTERFACE_PART(OleCommandTarget)

    BEGIN_INTERFACE_PART(Print, IPrint)
        INIT_INTERFACE_PART(CDocObjectServer, Print)
        STDMETHOD(SetInitialPageNum)(LONG);
        STDMETHOD(GetPageInfo)(LPLONG, LPLONG);
        STDMETHOD(Print)(DWORD, DVTARGETDEVICE**, PAGESET**, LPSTGMEDIUM,
                LPCONTINUECALLBACK, LONG, LPLONG, LPLONG);
    END_INTERFACE_PART(Print)

    DECLARE_INTERFACE_MAP()
};
```

It's time for a quick overview of what's happening in Listing 10-4. CCmdTarget is the base class that is used for all MFC classes of objects that can send and receive messages. It provides the message map architecture used by all the applications you create with Visual C++. (Another reason to subclass from the CCmdTarget class is that it provides a full implementation of the IUnknown interface.) Dispatch and interface maps are similar to message maps, so you can use the CCmdTarget class as a basis for creating a class that works with these other types of mapping. The CDocObjectServer class uses a set of interface maps to expose the interface elements required by a browser to recognize your application as an ActiveX Document server.

Take a look at the section of Listing 10-4 that begins with the "Interface Maps" comment. There are five interface maps shown in this section of code. The first interface declared is OleObject—which doesn't affect our ActiveX Document server-specific interfaces at all. (This is extremely important for other reasons that we won't discuss here.) However, the next four interfaces are part of the ActiveX Document interface. You'll see four interface maps here that correspond to the IOleDocument, IOleDocumentView, ICommandTarget, and IPrint interfaces we discussed in Chapter 5.

An interface declaration always begins with a BEGIN_INTERFACE_PART() macro and ends with an END_INTERFACE_PART() macro. The BEGIN_INTERFACE_PART() macro always takes two arguments: the name of the object you want to use and the name that you want to give to

An interface is not an implementation —it most commonly contains a list of pointers to the actual functions within an application or control.

the interface. The second parameter is what you see within utilities such as OLEView when you create an instance of the object. This macro also automatically declares the AddRef, Release, and QueryInterface functions for you; all you need to do is declare functions that are specific to your interface. The END_INTERFACE_PART() macro takes a single argument—the name of the object you want to use. You initialize the instance using an INIT_INTERFACE_PART() call that accepts the class name and the name of the interface object as input. The purpose of this macro is to define a link between the class and the interface elements it supports. In this case, it also allows the CDocObjectServer class to override the default interfaces provided by CCmdTarget.

Declaring the functions specific to your interface is the whole reason for creating an interface declaration in the first place. The STDMETHOD() macro allows you to declare one function at a time. It's the only macro requiring two sets of arguments in parentheses. Using this macro is easy. All you need to do is provide the name of the function within the first set of parentheses and the argument types for that function within the second set of parentheses. For example, if you look at the IOleDocument interface map, you'll see an entry that looks like this:

```
STDMETHOD(GetDocMiscStatus)(LPDWORD);
```

This entry defines a function named GetDocMiscStatus(), which requires a single argument—a pointer to a DWORD variable. The function will use the variable to store the status information.

There is one last step in declaring an interface. The DECLARE_INTERFACE_ MAP() function at the very end of Listing 10-4 is the secret to publishing your interface. This function tells the compiler to declare all of the interface elements you've defined with macros and make them public. It also tells the framework that your class will use a custom interface map. The next time you view the control or application using the new class, you should see the new interface elements. (Even if you can't see them using OLEView or another utility, other applications can still see and use the interfaces.)

Don't get the idea that you have to accede to some rigid interface implementation when using Visual C++. If you wanted to add something more than the default interface elements or modify the view, you could always inherit from the CDocObjectServer class and override its default methods. Look at Listing 10-4 again, and you'll notice that there is a special section of overridable functions at the beginning of the class declaration. Some of the view setup methods include OnActivateView() (displays the document object view), OnApplyViewState() (restores the state of the document object view), and OnSaveViewState() (saves the document object view state). In addition to these view methods, the ActivateDocObject() tells the document object to activate itself through the ActivateMe() method of the IOleDocumentSite interface.

Testing the Default Application—Step 2

Now that you've added all the required code, let's take a look at the results. Compile the application again. After Visual C++ finishes compiling the new version of the application, make sure that you run it again by itself. This ensures that any new required registry entries are made. In fact, it's a good idea when working with ActiveX-enabled applications to get into this habit. However, even if you run the application again, the four interfaces we added in the previous section won't show up using the OLEView utility—for some reason they remain invisible even after adding the CDocObjectServer class. You can see them using the OLE 2 Object View utility provided with Visual C++ 4.2 for our sample application. (Make sure you select the Show All Interfaces button on the toolbar.) However, despite the lack of visible evidence, you'll find that the application acts a lot different this time around.

Run the application using the same test document and same test page as before (Listing 10-1). This time you'll see a different result, as shown in Figure 10-5. Notice that the sample application has taken over the menus and toolbar of the browser, just as a Word for Windows document would. In addition, you can insert new objects and perform other tasks using the menu, just as if the application were working on a local document. You can also use the Web Publishing Wizard to save changes (see Chapter 5 for details on this utility).

Is this application complete? Not by a long shot—you can't even type any text into it or use it for any other document-related purpose. The only purpose for this application example is to show you the very minimum you have to do to make an application work as an ActiveX Document server. Anything else is up to you and your imagination.

Converting an Existing Application

Don't worry if you have a perfectly good application lying around that just doesn't happen to support ActiveX Document. You can convert it to provide this level of support with a minimum of effort—well, at least a lot less effort than writing the program from scratch. In this section we're going to look at

10

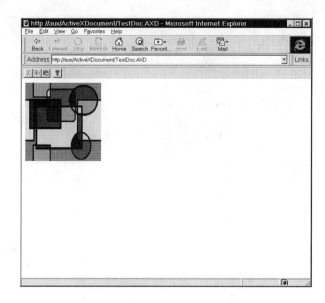

Our sample document appears within the browser window, just as any ActiveX document would.

Figure 10-5.

a five-step process that you can use to convert just about any existing OLE server to a rudimentary ActiveX Document server. However, it's important to remember that you'll only provide rudimentary support. Some applications will work just fine with this rudimentary level of support, others won't. Spend some time reading Chapter 5 again to get the theory down before you start adding support items. Once you do get the additional support items worked out, make sure you test them using an actual Internet setup rather than a local drive. This ensures that you test the complete interface and that the application won't try to do an end around by using standard OLE interfaces rather than the ActiveX Document interfaces that you really want to test.

The first and most obvious step is to implement the classes required to create an ActiveX Document server. If you look at the example we just created in the previous section and any other pre-C++ 4.2 application, you'll notice some very basic differences in the way the classes are declared. That's because Microsoft has subclassed the original MFC classes and added some functionality to them. The following table shows which classes have changed and how. The first column shows the class declarations used in a pre-C++ 4.2 application. The second column shows the new declarations. The third column tells you which file is affected. The fourth column shows an alternate class declaration that you may find implemented in older MFC class files—they're based on the Microsoft Office Binder declarations.

Original Class Declaration	New C++ 4.2 Declaration	ActivDoc Example Program File	Alternate MFC Class Declaration
class CInPlaceFrame : public COleIPFrameWnd	class CInPlaceFrame : public COleDocIPFrameWnd	IPFrame.H	class CInPlaceFrame : public CDocObjectIPFrameWnd
class CActivDocDoc : public COleServerDoc	class CActivDocDoc : public COleServerDoc	ActivDocDoc.H	class CActivDocDoc : public CDocObjectServerDoc
class CActivDocSrvrItem : public COleServerItem	class CActivDocSrvrItem : public CDocObjectServerItem	SrvrItem.H	class CActivDocSrvrItem : public CDocObjectServerItem

Once you replace these declarations in your header files, you'll also need to replace them in the associated CPP files. Using the search and replace capability of Microsoft Developer will make this easier. You won't have to worry too much about missing any of the places where the new class names are used—the compiler will point out any discrepancies automatically once you make the header file changes. Therefore, it's important to make the header file changes first and double-check them before you move on. (Notice that if you're trying to implement an ActiveX Document server using the ActiveX SDK and an older set of MFC files, you'll need to change three header files, whereas moving to Visual C++ 4.2 requires a change of only two header files.)

The second step is to add a simple declaration to the STDAFX.H file for your application:

```
#include <afxdocob.h>
```

This header file contains all of the declarations needed by your application to get document object support. In fact, a quick look at this file can be quite educational, as it shows exactly how the four ActiveX Document interface elements get implemented. (We looked at this header file in the "Fixing the ActiveX Document Server" section of this chapter.)

The third step is to change the way you make one of the registry entries. The application you're creating is no longer just an in-place server, so you'll need to change the registry entry in your CWinApp.CPP file (in the case of the example program, it's the ActivDoc.CPP file) from OAT_INPLACE_SERVER to OAT_DOC_OBJECT_SERVER. The actual line of code looks like this:

```
m_server.UpdateRegistry(OAT_DOC_OBJECT_SERVER);
```

The fourth step is to change some of the parse maps, since you'll need to tell your application where to send the print commands and other OLE-related information. You'll need to change two files. The first is the application document header file—ActivDocDoc.H in the case of our sample program. You'll need to add the following highlighted line:

```
// Generated message map functions
protected:
    //{{AFX_MSG(CActivDocDoc)
        // NOTE - the ClassWizard will add and remove member functions here.
        //    DO NOT EDIT what you see in these blocks of generated code !
    //}}AFX_MSG
    DECLARE_MESSAGE_MAP()
    DECLARE_OLECMD_MAP()
};
```

If the message map includes a DECLARE_MESSAGE_MAP() message map function, make sure the DECLARE_OLECMD_MAP() line appears after it. The second file is the application document CPP file. At the very beginning of the file, you'll find at least one mapping area for messages. You'll need to add another mapping area, as shown here:

```
BEGIN_OLECMD_MAP(CActivDocDoc, COleServerDoc)
    ON_OLECMD_PAGESETUP()
    ON_OLECMD_PRINT()
END_OLECMD_MAP()
```

As you can see, these additions allow the application to print by routing the print functions through their handler functions using the ID_FILE_PAGE_SETUP and ID_FILE_PRINT standard identifiers. All you need to do to complete the picture is add command maps for the actual handler functions, like this:

```
ON_COMMAND (ID_FILE_PRINT, OnFilePrint)
```

The fifth (and last) step is to add a new function to your application document header and CPP files. We covered this part of the process in the "Fixing the ActiveX Document Server" section of this chapter. The code for the example program appears in Listings 10-2 and 10-3.

Once you've completed these modifications, you'll need to compile and test the updated application. In most cases, you'll want to test it locally first to make sure you haven't broken anything with the changes. After you're satisfied that the changes haven't affected local performance, try to open a document from the browser. You should see the document open within the browser instead of within a separate window (just like the example program does in Figure 10-5). Make sure the application provides the same level of functionality (sans File | Save command) as it would when used locally.

Working with URL Monikers

With the special focus that some companies are placing on the Internet today, it's not going to be very long before the information on the Internet becomes as easy to access as the information on a local hard drive. In fact, Microsoft plans to blur this distinction as part of the next release of Internet Explorer. You'll find that your hard drive and favorite places on the Internet share a common Explorer view.

Of course, this blurring of data sites will open up some new opportunities for the user and programmer alike. For example, as a user you'll find it less cumbersome to get the data you need into the application you need in order to edit it. As a programmer, you'll find that there are now additional ways in which to tweak a program and make it special.

NOTE: You must install the ActiveX SDK to create the example in this section. The SDK provides the URLMON.H, HLINK.LIB, and URLMON.LIB files required to make the code work.

One of the most common ways that you'll probably find to make your application special is to add hyperlink capability to it. The easiest way to do this is to stick a button on the application's toolbar that takes the user to the

We discussed
the theory
behind URL
monikers in
"Overview
of URL
Monikers" in
Chapter 8.

company's intranet. You could extend this idea with another button that
would allow the user to select a specific site or choose from a list of company
authorized Internet sites. That's what we'll look at in this section. The sample
program will show you how to add two buttons to a typical application that
will give the user a fast and easy way to make a link to the Internet.

The first step, of course, is to create a new application. As with the previous
example, you could create this code using older versions of Microsoft's
Visual C++ compiler. The text in this section assumes that you're using the
4.2 version of that product. Since we looked at the process of creating an
application with MFC Application Wizard in the previous section, we'll use
an abbreviated procedure here. There are a few options you'll need to select
during the creation process in order for the example to work. First, the name
of the example is ViewURL (though you could choose any name you want).
Second, you'll want to select Single Document on the first page of the Wizard.
Finally, you'll want to select Windows Sockets support on the fourth page
of the Wizard. You could add ActiveX Document support as well, but the
example program doesn't include this feature, to keep things simple.

Adding Library Support

Once the Wizard finishes creating the application, you'll need to start making a
few changes. The first thing you'll want to do is add hyperlink support to the
application. To do this, add the following include in the STDAFX.H file.

```
//Added for URL support.
#include "URLMon.h"
```

This header file contains all the defines that you'll need in order to use
the various URL moniker-related commands. We discussed a few of these
commands in Chapter 8—you'll get to see them in action here.

The next thing you'll need to do is add some static library support. The two
libraries, HLINK.LIB and URLMON.LIB, are in the LIB folder of the ActiveX
SDK. Use the Insert | Files Into Project command of Visual C++ to add the
required library support to your application. Double-check that the support
was actually added by checking the list of included files in the File View
of the program (just click the File View tab on the left side of your display
work area).

TIP: Microsoft intends to fold the static library support found in HLINK.LIB and URLMON.LIB into URLMON.DLL at some future date. Make sure you check for this dynamic library support before writing an URL moniker-enabled application.

Creating the Required Resources

Now that you've added the required library support, let's add the buttons to the toolbar. Click on the Resource View, open the Toolbar folder, and then double-click on the IDR_MAINFRAME entry. You'll see the standard toolbar, shown in Figure 10-6. Adding a new button is easy—just click on the blank button at the end of the toolbar and start drawing on the blank button displayed in the drawing area. Moving the button a little to the right will separate it from the other button groups already displayed on the toolbar. The following figure shows the two buttons added for this example program.

Adding the buttons will provide the user with a visual display. You also need to add some button identification information for the application.

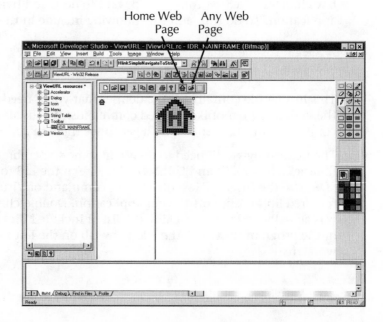

Home Web Page   Any Web Page

The standard toolbar with the Home Web Page and Any Web Page buttons

Figure 10-6.

Simply double-click on the toolbar representation of the button you wish to configure (don't click on the button icon you just created). What you'll see is a dialog like the one shown here. Use the settings shown in the following table for the two buttons.

Identifier	Caption	Height	Width
ID_GO_HOME	Click here to go to the home Web page. \ nHome Web Page	15	16
ID_GO_SITE	Click here to go to any Web page.\nAny Web Page	15	16

T **IP:** Notice that the Caption column has a long description, a \n, and then a short description. The long description will appear on the application's status bar. The short description appears as bubble help when you rest your mouse over the control. Make sure you include the \n to separate the two entry types. You can use this particular entry method just about anywhere you normally see bubble help in a Visual C++ application.

Clicking the first button will take the user to the company's home page—so you don't really need anything more in the way of resources to make this button work. All you need to add is a little code to perform the actual work. The second button, however, will allow users to type in their own site and, if they so desire, a location within that site. This button will also support frames for those sites that use them. This means adding a special dialog box. Open the Dialog folder in the Resource View. Right-click on the Dialog folder, and you'll see a context menu. Select the Insert Dialog entry, and you'll see a new dialog named IDD_DIALOG1 added to the list in the folder (the only other dialog currently provided with the application is the About Box dialog).

Let's rename the dialog. Right-click on the IDD_DIALOG1 entry and select Properties from the context menu. Type **IDD_SITE_SELECT** in the ID field, and then click on the X in the upper-right corner of the properties dialog. You'll see the new name appear in the list of dialogs within the Dialog folder.

Adding the required controls to the dialog is fairly easy. The first thing you'll want to do is resize the dialog to 250 × 120 pixels (the current dialog size appears on the right-hand side of the status bar). This will buy you a little room for those long URLs the user may want to type. Once you resize the dialog, add three labels and three edit controls, as shown here:

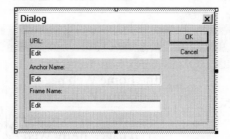

Double-click on each of the edit controls to display their property dialogs. We'll want to give them IDs that are easy to remember. The first control ID is IDC_URL, the second is IDC_ANCHOR_NAME, and the third is IDC_FRAME_NAME. You'll see how these names come into play later.

Defining New Classes and Writing Code

All of the resources we'll need are defined. It's time to create some code to go with the two buttons we've added to the toolbar. Make certain you have the IDD_SITE_SELECT dialog selected. Use the View | Class Wizard command to display the ClassWizard dialog. In this case, you'll see a dialog like the one shown here, telling you that the IDD_SITE_SELECT dialog is new and you need to create a class for it.

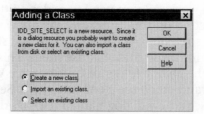

Click on OK, and you'll see the Create New Class dialog. All you need to provide is a class name. The example program uses SiteSelect—which makes the class name and its associated resource very easy to identify. Use the default CDialog base class in this case. Click Create to complete the action.

Select the Message Maps tab of the ClassWizard. Select the CMainFrame class name from the Class Name field. Scroll down the list of Object IDs on the left side of the dialog until you find ID_GO_HOME. Click on this entry, then on the Command entry in the Messages field on the right side of the dialog. Click Add Function to add the required function to your application. You'll see an Add Member Function dialog box. Click OK to accept the default function name. Follow this same procedure for the ID_GO_SITE object identifier. Your MFC ClassWizard dialog should look like this when you get through:

Make sure to set the first parameter in the Hlink SimpleNavigate ToString() function call to match your Web server's default page address.

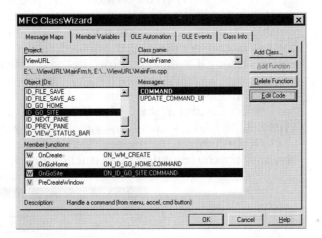

Select the OnGoHome entry and click Edit Code. The MFC ClassWizard will take you right to the shell for the new function. Listing 10-5 shows the code for this button. You'll see the OnGoSite() function right below the OnGoHome() function. Add the code shown in Listing 10-6 to it. Make certain that you include SiteSelect.H at the beginning of the MainFrm.CPP file (you could also include it in the STDAFX.H file if desired).

Listing 10-5

```
void CMainFrame::OnGoHome()
{
    // Go right to the company's home page.
    HlinkSimpleNavigateToString(L"http://aux/default.htm",
        NULL, NULL, NULL, 0, NULL, NULL, 0);

}
```

Listing 10-6

```
void CMainFrame::OnGoSite()
{
    // Create a copy of the dialog.
    SiteSelect    NewSiteSelect;

    // Display it.
    NewSiteSelect.DoModal();

}
```

So far we have enough code to send the user to the home page (Listing 10-5) or display a dialog (Listing 10-6). You'll also need to add some code to the SiteSelect dialog. When users click on OK, you'll want to take them to the site they selected. The first thing we'll need to do is add some memory variables to record what the user types. Look at the IDD_SITE_SELECT dialog box again. CTRL-double-click the first edit box. You'll see an Add Member Variable dialog like the one shown in the following illustration. It will allow you to assign a variable to the IDC_URL edit box. For the purposes of this example, name it URL (the name will actually appear as m_URL in the dialog box). Select Control in the Category field—this will change the Variable Type field to CEdit, which is the variable type we need for this example. Click OK to complete the process. Do the same thing for the other two edit boxes. Name the second variable Anchor and the third variable Frame.

Now that we have variables to work with, it's time to add another function. Open the MFC ClassWizard using the View | Class Wizard command. The dialog should still show the Message Maps tag; if not, select it. Select the SiteSelect entry in the Class Name field. You'll see the list of Object IDs on the left side of the dialog change to match those provided by the SiteSelect dialog. Highlight the IDOK object identifier, then the BN_CLICKED entry in the Messages field. Click Add Function, then OK on the Add Member Function dialog. Your MFC ClassWizard dialog should look like the one shown here:

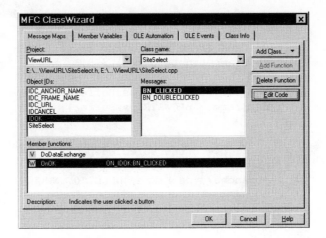

10

Now display our function skeleton by clicking Edit Code. This function has to accept the information users type in the dialog, then send them to the specified location on the Internet. Listing 10-7 shows the code to accomplish this task.

Listing 10-7

```
void SiteSelect::OnOK()
{
    LPCWSTR    pszURL = NULL;        //Local copy of URL string.
    LPCWSTR    pszAnchor = NULL;     //Local copy of Anchor string.
    LPCWSTR    pszFrame = NULL;      //Local copy of Frame string.
    LPTSTR     pszBuffer = "";       //Conversion buffer.

    // Get the URL string and convert it.
    if (m_URL.LineLength(0) > 0)
    {
        m_URL.GetLine(0, pszBuffer, m_URL.LineLength(0));
        pszURL = LPCWSTR(pszBuffer);
    }
    else
    {
        MessageBox("You must enter an URL", "Error", MB_OK);
        return;
    }

    // Get the Anchor string and convert it.
    if (m_Anchor.LineLength(0) > 0)
    {
        m_Anchor.GetLine(0, pszBuffer, m_Anchor.LineLength(0));
        pszAnchor = LPCWSTR(pszBuffer);
```

```
    }

    // Get the Frame string and convert it.
    if (m_Frame.LineLength(0) > 0)
    {
        m_Frame.GetLine(0, pszBuffer, m_Frame.LineLength(0));
        pszFrame = LPCWSTR(pszBuffer);
    }

    // Go right to the selected page.
    HlinkSimpleNavigateToString(pszURL,
        pszAnchor, pszFrame, NULL, 0, NULL, NULL, 0);


    CDialog::OnOK();
}
```

There are a few little tricks in this code, but nothing that most C programmers wouldn't already do. First, you need to set all three of the variables used to hold location information to NULL. That way they'll be ready to go if there isn't any information for them to hold. In this case the code also forces users to provide an URL. There is only one situation in which they wouldn't need to do this. If you wanted to let users jump to an anchor on the same page that they're currently on, you could leave the URL parameter NULL and simply have them specify the anchor name instead. The method used to store the information on the dialog requires the use of a buffer variable. However, the conversion from LPTSTR (long pointer to either a Windows or Unicode null terminated string) to LPCWSTR (long pointer to a null terminated Unicode string constant) is fairly straightforward. The meat of this particular routine is the call to HlinkSimpleNavigateToString, which converts the location information into an actual URL.

Let's take a look at how this application looks. Compile and run your application as usual. If you click on the Home Web Page button, you'll see a copy of Internet Explorer (or other default browser) start, then take you to whatever Internet site you set as a home page. Figure 10-7 shows the results of pressing this button for the example program. (The home page shown in the figure reflects the author's Internet server setup—your screen should reflect your setup.) Make sure you set the address in the HlinkSimpleNavigateToString() call in Listing 10-5 to your home Web site, or you may get some unusual results.

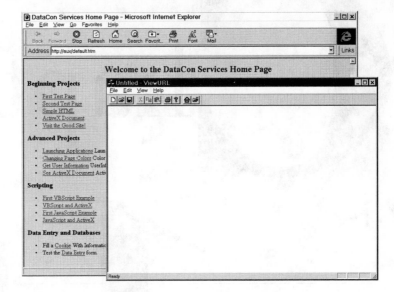

You can add
buttons like
this to any
application
and allow
users to access
the Internet
with ease.
Figure 10-7.

Clicking the Any Web Page button will display a dialog like the one shown here:

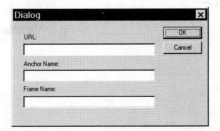

It allows you to enter an URL, along with an optional anchor name or frame name. Your target Web page must support the anchor or frame name you specify, or the function call will fail. The application also requires a live Internet connection if you enter any URL values outside the addresses supported by your local test machine.

Chapter

11

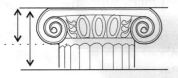

Graphics and ActiveX

From a programmer's perspective, there are probably more graphics in a typical application than you'd like to think about. There are the obvious sort of graphics that you'll deal with as the main document in some applications. You'll also find more than a few charts and pieces of art displayed by graphics. However, these aren't the only graphics you need to worry about. Think about some of the graphics that may be fun for you to create (depending on your desire to take a side trip from your programming). The most common example is the icon that you'll display for users when they see your application. In a lot of cases, you'll also need to create the icons used on buttons and in other areas of the application. Think for a second about dialog boxes. Even though most of us use the default icons provided with Windows, there isn't any reason why we couldn't create special dialog boxes using our own icons. The list goes on, but you get the idea. Graphics are everywhere in Windows.

The Internet has surprised more than a few programmers who are used to working with desktop applications all day. For example, these applications restrict you to two graphics formats: GIF and JPEG. While these are perfectly good formats, using them does create problems in some cases. For example, how do you use all those neat icons you've been creating for the past few years? It would seem impossible to do so. About the best you can hope to achieve is to convert them into a format that the Internet will accept. In some cases the conversion isn't all that great, and you lose the flavor of the graphics you so painstakingly created.

Displaying graphics on the Internet isn't the only problem you'll run into. Drawing a simple image can present some problems as well. Consider this—there is no way to define a specific spot on a page when you're working with the Internet. How have we been defining the placement of objects on a page in our examples throughout the book? Through the use of <P> or <BR> tags and the use of tables. Trying to draw an image on your Web page will prove problematic without some kind of enabling technology such as ActiveX.

If simple drawings prove less than accessible, trying to display a graph or chart will prove downright impossible. Some people actually resort to outputting the graphs or charts from their spreadsheet, converting them to a GIF, then placing them on their Web site to update the data used by coworkers each day. Not only is this a lot of manual labor, but the information is a day old by the end of the day. Considering how forgetful some people can be when their schedules get too hectic, the process is also error prone. Let's just say that you wouldn't want to use that information for major business decisions, once you consider how susceptible to damage and misuse it really is.

Now that you have an idea of where graphics are hiding in your applications and what the problems are with using them on the Internet, let's look at the examples for this chapter. The first example is simple. Have you ever tried to display both text and graphics on a button? This example will show how to do it. Now your Internet site can get dressed up with buttons that communicate in more than one way—making it more accessible for a variety of people (or more appealing at the very least).

As previously stated, the Internet appears to have more than its share of problems with graphic formats. We'll look at one technique for making those graphics more accessible in the next example. You'll learn how to create an ActiveX control that displays the graphics that an HTML tag won't. Of course, your ability to actually display graphics will become more limited as the graphics format becomes more esoteric, but at least you'll be able to

Make sure you take a look at Appendix A for a list of vendors who professionally create ActiveX controls for a variety of graphic display purposes.

display four or even five times the number of graphics formats you could using the Internet's native capabilities.

Do you want up-to-the-minute graphs and charts immediately available at your Web site any time day or night? Well, that might be out of the range of probability even for this book. However, we'll look at an example of how you can use OLE automation along with some basic graphing techniques to create a control that will update the appearance of a graph or chart within a few minutes. Unlike many of the other examples in this book, we'll also make this a static control that the user will have to initiate manually. The reason is simple: you can offer the user the choice of looking at new data or at material that may be a few minutes old using this technique.

Implementing an Icon and Text Button

Drawing icons has become one of those artistic elements that some programmers take quite seriously when they actually get to draw them. More than a few products on the market today use icons drawn by professional artists. Trying to get a realistic picture in the small area of an icon is a difficult task—especially if the idea you're trying to present is abstract or complex. For example, imagine designing an icon for George the Dragon Slayer software—brings more than a few difficulties to mind, doesn't it?

There's also a large investment in icons on your computer—much larger than most people even begin to understand. Just look at your word processor sometime. The main screen alone can contain upwards of 50 icons. Someone had to draw all of those icons, and it's almost certain that they didn't take just a few seconds to do it. If you're a small software company, you can ill afford to get rid of all those icons no matter what their quality level is. The sheer number of icons you own should make it apparent that you'll want to keep as many of them active as possible and in as many environments as you can.

OK, so if icons are so great, why do we need text too? Some users may not understand your icon, or they may need a text version of it due to a handicap. Another problem arises on international sites, where an icon may make perfect sense to someone from Australia, but not to someone in China because of cultural differences. You could easily write a macro that changes the text of the button to match the language of the person visiting your site (along with all of the other text on the page—see Chapter 8 for more details on the need to maintain site friendliness).

Once you decide to use an icon button at your site, you'll have to choose from one of the buttons available on the market or create one of your own. Making the decision won't be as easy as simply picking one from a catalog. There are quite a few picture button considerations for a Web page that you won't have to think about with a desktop application.

A few button selection issues involve appearance. For example, where do you place the graphic in relation to the text? Most buttons allow you to choose from one of several fixed locations. You'll also need to consider what kind of graphics to allow. Some buttons will allow you to use a wide selection of graphics and don't put too many limitations on size either. We'll stick to standard Windows icons for this example, but the techniques you'll learn work equally with other graphic types.

Graphic storage is another consideration. The buttons provided with ActiveX Control Pad store their data right within the HTML file. This is a good way of doing things if you want to limit the number of files you need to track on your Web server. It also tends to reduce confusion as to what picture to use and where. (Just remember that you may have to use the same graphic in several locations and that their Internet addresses will vary from your hard drive setup—making testing of a large page an interesting experience.) However, storing the graphic locally does make it rather difficult to read HTML files, since you'll have a lot of hexadecimal code to wade through each time you want to make a change. In many cases you'll want to store your icons in their standard format on disk. This has the advantage of not cluttering up the HTML file and allowing you to perform some tricks with your buttons that aren't allowed in the Microsoft version. Disk storage does require one additional consideration. You need to decide whether you want to store the file locally or on the Web server. If you're only going to download one copy of the image, storing it on the Web server saves disk space on the user's machine. Storing the file locally is a better idea if you plan to use the image more than once.

NOTE: Even though we won't add elements of the on/off button shown in Chapter 2 to this example, you could easily do so. The on/off button features weren't included in this example for the sake of clarity.

Now that you've got the basics down, let's look at the project itself. We'll begin with the same basic control we used in Chapter 2. Simply create a blank control using the same procedure as before. Make sure you subclass the BUTTON class by selecting it on the second page of the OCX Control Wizard. The big difference between this setup and the one you used for OCXExmpl is that you'll need to check the Acts as a Simple Frame Control check box on the second page of the OCX Control Wizard. This selection will make it possible to add a picture to the standard button control later.

Adding Properties and Events

11

We have to add some properties and methods to the control first. The ModalResult and StdButtonType properties (type long) from Chapter 2 are important here. (We saw how to use these properties in Listing 3 of Chapter 7.) You'll also want to add three stock properties: Caption, Enabled, and Font.

That takes care of the properties we've seen in the past; now let's look at a new property named IconType. It's of type long and works much the same way as StdButtonType does. The only difference is that you're storing the number of a standard Windows icon in place of the button type. The second new property is IconPosition. It's of type long and determines whether the icon appears on the right or left side of the button. We could have used type BOOL for this property, but using an integer allows for future expansion (you may want to add a top or bottom value) and makes it easier to use the property in some cases.

Theoretically, you can define as many events for this example as you like. However, the only two that we really need are Click and DblClick. You can select both stock events on the OLE Events page of the MFC ClassWizard dialog.

Defining the Property Pages

Every time you create a control, the OLE Control Wizard automatically creates a default property page for you. However, you may find that one page isn't enough—you may need two or more property pages to provide the user of your control with full access to all its features. We're going to look at the methods for adding two different kinds of property pages to your controls in this section. The first property page will be a custom page, just like the original created by the OLE Control Wizard. The second will be a stock property sheet.

NOTE: You should already have the first property page defined if you started this example by copying from the OCXExmpl control in Chapter 2. Otherwise, please use the procedure in that chapter to define a new first property page. You may want to take this opportunity to create a standard property page size by using the IDD_OLE_PROPPAGE_LARGE property page type for both pages, as discussed in the next paragraph. Make sure you name the first property page IDD_OLE_PROPPAGE_PBUTTON, give it a class name of CPButtonPropPage, and a base class property of COlePropertyPage.

Let's begin by creating the custom property page. This will actually be the second property page when viewed from ActiveX Control Pad (Visual C++ adds its own General property page, making this the third property page). Go to the Resources section of the example program. Open the Dialog folder. Right-click on the Dialog folder, and you'll see a context menu. Select the Insert... option, and you'll see an Insert Resource dialog. Open the Dialog section and select the IDD_OLE_PROPPAGE_LARGE entry. Click OK. You'll see a new dialog added to the list of dialogs shown (there should be three once you add the new dialog). Right-click on the new dialog entry and select Properties from the context menu. Change the ID field to read IDD_OLE_PROPPAGE_PBUTTON2, and then close the Dialog Properties dialog.

Before we go much further, we need to do some work in the ClassWizard. Double-click on the new dialog, and you'll see a blank dialog screen. Right-click on the blank dialog and select ClassWizard. The ClassWizard will detect that this is a new dialog and display the Adding a Class dialog shown here:

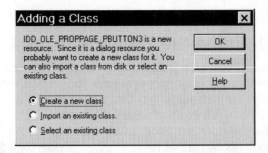

Click OK in the Adding a Class dialog to accept the default choice of creating a new class. You'll see a Create New Class dialog. In the Name field, type

CPButtonPropPage2. Select COlePropertyPage in the Base Class field. Click Create to complete the new class definition, then OK to close the MFC ClassWizard dialog.

Now that we have a dialog skeleton, let's add some controls to it. Add two groups of radio buttons to the dialog, as shown in Figure 11-1. The first group has ten radio buttons, and the second has two. Placing the second group within a group box will make it easier to tell where each group starts and ends. Make sure you change the Caption property of each radio button to match that shown in Figure 11-1. For the purpose of this example, we also changed the ID property of each radio button to match its caption. For example, the None radio button has an ID of IDC_ICON_NONE.

If you remember from Chapter 2, we also need to do a little work to make the radio buttons fully functional. Begin by double-clicking on each button in turn and selecting the Tabstop check box. We also need to check the Group option for the None and Left buttons—this signifies the start of each radio button group. Once you have the radio buttons configured, you need to perform some OLE-specific configuration. CTRL-double-click on the None button, and you'll see the Add Member Variable dialog shown here:

Remember that capitalization and spelling are very important when making class entries for Visual C++.

Type **m_iconType** in the Member Variable Name field and **IconType** in the Optional OLE Property Name field. Do the same thing for the Left button. In this case, however, you'll want to type **m_iconPosition** in the Member Variable Name field and **IconPosition** in the Optional OLE Property Name field.

Let's look at the stock property sheet now. Microsoft provides three of them: one for fonts (CLSID_CFontPropPage), another for pictures

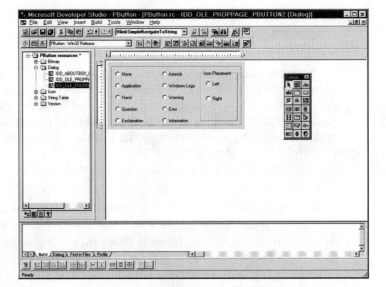

The custom property page includes two groups of radio buttons.
Figure 11-1.

(CLSID_CPicturePropPage), and another for colors (CLSID_CColorPropPage). These stock property sheets are designed to work with the stock properties for a control. So, if your control provides a stock font property, like the example control does, you can support it using the stock Fonts property page. All of the connections are automatic—you don't have to perform one iota of additional programming. You do need to add the stock property (we did that in the previous section), and then add a single line of code to the control file of your ActiveX control (PButtonCtl.CPP in the case of our example control). Listing 11-1 shows the code we added for a default font page in boldface—all you need to do to use the other stock property page types is use one of the parameters given at the beginning of this paragraph. (Notice that the code shows the entry for the first and second custom property pages as well.) We'll see later how this set of three property pages looks when used within an application. If you don't see this automatic linkage, you know that there's a problem with the way the stock property is defined, that you used the wrong stock property page name, or that you're using the control in an environment that doesn't support fonts (within an HTML page, for example). Also notice that the macro entry for a stock property page in Listing 11-1 follows a different format than the custom property pages—you don't need to provide a custom guid in this case.

Listing 11-1

```
BEGIN_PROPPAGEIDS(CPButtonCtrl, 3)
    PROPPAGEID(CPButtonPropPage::guid)
```

```
    PROPPAGEID(CPButtonPropPage2::guid)
    PROPPAGEID(CLSID_CFontPropPage)
END_PROPPAGEIDS(CPButtonCtrl)
```

Make sure you update the number of pages shown in the second parameter of the BEGIN_ PROPPAGEIDS() macro to match the actual number of property pages.

You may be wondering how to give each property page tab its own name. The method for doing this is less than straightforward, but it isn't hard. Open the String Table folder in ResourceView. Double-click on the String Table entry. You'll see a list of strings there. This is where Microsoft Visual C++ creates strings that you'll eventually associate with controls or other program features. All you need to do is make certain that the following entries appear in the String Table to give names to the two property page tabs. (The IDS_PBUTTON_PPG_CAPTION entry should already be there, but you'll need to change the caption as shown.)

ID	Value	Caption
IDS_PBUTTON_PPG_CAPTION	101	Button Type
IDS_PBUTTON_PPG_CAPTION2	102	Picture Settings

Now we have to associate the string for the second property page (IDS_PBUTTON_PPG_CAPTION2) with the actual property page. Look at the CPButtonPropPage2::CPButtonPropPage2() method in the PButtonPropPage2.CPP file. In that method you'll see an entry for the COlePropertyPage() function. Change it as shown here to add the property page string we've just created to the tab of the second property page (the first property page tab is taken care of for you automatically since it was already entered into the String Table as part of the program shell creation process).

```
COlePropertyPage(IDD, IDS_PBUTTON_PPG_CAPTION2)
```

Defining a Message Map

This is the first time we'll have to work with message maps. All that a message map does for the most part is allow you to intercept the messages that Windows normally sends to the application and do something special with them before passing them to the default message handler.

Graphics require special handling in a number of ways. For example, since a button doesn't handle graphics by default, you have to provide special code to perform any work with them. Redrawing the graphic when it changes or gets overwritten by another application is one of these events. You can't simply draw the graphic once, then assume it will remain in place (unless the control you draw on provides some level of graphics support as a default).

There are a number of ways to monitor the need to redraw a control, but one of the easiest ways to do it is simply to monitor mouse movement. That's what we'll do in this example. Every time the mouse moves, the picture on the control will be redrawn. This may seem like a lot of redrawing, but you'll find out that the control actually works very fast, and you won't even notice the redraws.

You'll need to open the MFC ClassWizard to add the message map support required to intercept the mouse movement messages. Select the Message Maps page. We'll work with the CPButtonCtrl class, so you'll need to select it in the Class Name field. Find the CPButtonCtrl entry in the Object IDs field (it should be the first entry in the list and selected as the default option). Select the WM_MOUSEMOVE message in the Messages field. Click Add Function to add a function for monitoring this message to your application. The MFC ClassWizard will add the function to the PButtonCtrl.CPP file for you. Your MFC ClassWizard dialog should look like the one in the following illustration. Notice that it displays the name of the new function you just created in the Member Functions list. If you want, you can click Edit Code to go right to the new function entry.

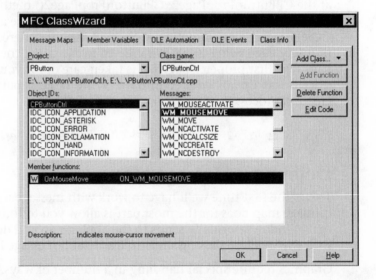

Adding Some Code

The skeleton of the program is complete, so now it's time to add some code. Most of the code you'll need to add appears in the PButtonCtl.CPP file. Listing 11-2 shows all of the code in that file. We'll discuss the changes you need to make right after you get a chance to look at the code.

Listing 11-2

```cpp
// PButtonCtl.cpp : Implementation of the CPButtonCtrl OLE control class.

#include "stdafx.h"
#include "PButton.h"
#include "PButtonCtl.h"
#include "PButtonPpg.h"
#include "PButtonPropPage2.h"


#ifdef _DEBUG
#define new DEBUG_NEW
#undef THIS_FILE
static char THIS_FILE[] = __FILE__;
#endif


IMPLEMENT_DYNCREATE(CPButtonCtrl, COleControl)


/////////////////////////////////////////////////////////////////////////////
// Message map

BEGIN_MESSAGE_MAP(CPButtonCtrl, COleControl)
    //{{AFX_MSG_MAP(CPButtonCtrl)
    ON_WM_MOUSEMOVE()
    //}}AFX_MSG_MAP
    ON_MESSAGE(OCM_COMMAND, OnOcmCommand)
    ON_OLEVERB(AFX_IDS_VERB_PROPERTIES, OnProperties)
END_MESSAGE_MAP()


/////////////////////////////////////////////////////////////////////////////
// Dispatch map

BEGIN_DISPATCH_MAP(CPButtonCtrl, COleControl)
    //{{AFX_DISPATCH_MAP(CPButtonCtrl)
    DISP_PROPERTY_NOTIFY(CPButtonCtrl, "StdButtonType", m_stdButtonType,
OnStdButtonTypeChanged, VT_I4)
```

11

```
        DISP_PROPERTY_NOTIFY(CPButtonCtrl, "ModalResult", m_modalResult,
OnModalResultChanged, VT_I4)
        DISP_PROPERTY_NOTIFY(CPButtonCtrl, "IconType", m_iconType,
OnIconTypeChanged, VT_I4)
        DISP_PROPERTY_NOTIFY(CPButtonCtrl, "IconPosition", m_iconPosition,
OnIconPositionChanged, VT_I4)
        DISP_STOCKPROP_CAPTION()
        DISP_STOCKPROP_ENABLED()
        DISP_STOCKPROP_FONT()
        //}}AFX_DISPATCH_MAP
        DISP_FUNCTION_ID(CPButtonCtrl, "AboutBox", DISPID_ABOUTBOX, AboutBox,
VT_EMPTY, VTS_NONE)
END_DISPATCH_MAP()


/////////////////////////////////////////////////////////////////////////////
// Event map

BEGIN_EVENT_MAP(CPButtonCtrl, COleControl)
    //{{AFX_EVENT_MAP(CPButtonCtrl)
    EVENT_STOCK_CLICK()
    EVENT_STOCK_DBLCLICK()
    //}}AFX_EVENT_MAP
END_EVENT_MAP()


/////////////////////////////////////////////////////////////////////////////
// Property pages

// TODO: Add more property pages as needed.  Remember to increase the count!
BEGIN_PROPPAGEIDS(CPButtonCtrl, 3)
    PROPPAGEID(CPButtonPropPage::guid)
    PROPPAGEID(CPButtonPropPage2::guid)
    PROPPAGEID(CLSID_CFontPropPage)
END_PROPPAGEIDS(CPButtonCtrl)


/////////////////////////////////////////////////////////////////////////////
// Initialize class factory and guid

IMPLEMENT_OLECREATE_EX(CPButtonCtrl, "PBUTTON.PButtonCtrl.1",
    0x43d22016, 0xb1, 0x11d0, 0x8c, 0x70, 0, 0, 0x6e, 0x31, 0x27, 0xb7)


/////////////////////////////////////////////////////////////////////////////
// Type library ID and version
```

```
IMPLEMENT_OLETYPELIB(CPButtonCtrl, _tlid, _wVerMajor, _wVerMinor)


/////////////////////////////////////////////////////////////////////////
// Interface IDs

const IID BASED_CODE IID_DPButton =
        { 0x1bb92a1, 0xf2, 0x11d0, { 0x8c, 0x70, 0, 0, 0x6e, 0x31, 0x27, 0xb7
} };
const IID BASED_CODE IID_DPButtonEvents =
        { 0x1bb92a2, 0xf2, 0x11d0, { 0x8c, 0x70, 0, 0, 0x6e, 0x31, 0x27, 0xb7
} };


/////////////////////////////////////////////////////////////////////////
// Control type information

static const DWORD BASED_CODE _dwPButtonOleMisc =
    OLEMISC_SIMPLEFRAME |
    OLEMISC_ACTIVATEWHENVISIBLE |
    OLEMISC_SETCLIENTSITEFIRST |
    OLEMISC_INSIDEOUT |
    OLEMISC_CANTLINKINSIDE |
    OLEMISC_RECOMPOSEONRESIZE;

IMPLEMENT_OLECTLTYPE(CPButtonCtrl, IDS_PBUTTON, _dwPButtonOleMisc)


/////////////////////////////////////////////////////////////////////////
// CPButtonCtrl::CPButtonCtrlFactory::UpdateRegistry -
// Adds or removes system registry entries for CPButtonCtrl

BOOL CPButtonCtrl::CPButtonCtrlFactory::UpdateRegistry(BOOL bRegister)
{
    if (bRegister)
        return AfxOleRegisterControlClass(
            AfxGetInstanceHandle(),
            m_clsid,
            m_lpszProgID,
            IDS_PBUTTON,
            IDB_PBUTTON,
            FALSE,                      //  Not insertable
            _dwPButtonOleMisc,
            _tlid,
            _wVerMajor,
            _wVerMinor);
```

```
       else
           return AfxOleUnregisterClass(m_clsid, m_lpszProgID);
   }


   /////////////////////////////////////////////////////////////////////////
   // CPButtonCtrl::CPButtonCtrl - Constructor

   CPButtonCtrl::CPButtonCtrl()
   {
       InitializeIIDs(&IID_DPButton, &IID_DPButtonEvents);

       EnableSimpleFrame();

       // TODO: Initialize your control's instance data here.
   }



   /////////////////////////////////////////////////////////////////////////
   // CPButtonCtrl::~CPButtonCtrl - Destructor

   CPButtonCtrl::~CPButtonCtrl()
   {
       // TODO: Cleanup your control's instance data here.
   }



   /////////////////////////////////////////////////////////////////////////
   // CPButtonCtrl::OnDraw - Drawing function

   void CPButtonCtrl::OnDraw(
           CDC* pdc, const CRect& rcBounds, const CRect& rcInvalid)
   {
       HICON   hIcon;   // Handle of the icon we'll display.

       int     iWidth;  // Control Width
       int     iHeight; // Control Height


       // Get the control width and height.
       COleControl::GetControlSize(&iWidth, &iHeight);

       // Calculate the right position of the icon.
       iWidth -= 36;

       // Perform default paint behavior.
       DoSuperclassPaint(pdc, rcBounds);

       // Load the requested bitmap.
```

```
        switch (m_iconType)
        {
        case 1:
            hIcon = LoadIcon(NULL, IDI_APPLICATION);
            break;
        case 2:
            hIcon = LoadIcon(NULL, IDI_HAND);
            break;
        case 3:
            hIcon = LoadIcon(NULL, IDI_QUESTION);
            break;
        case 4:
            hIcon = LoadIcon(NULL, IDI_EXCLAMATION);
            break;
        case 5:
            hIcon = LoadIcon(NULL, IDI_ASTERISK);
            break;
        case 6:
            hIcon = LoadIcon(NULL, IDI_WINLOGO);
            break;
        case 7:
            hIcon = LoadIcon(NULL, IDI_WARNING);
            break;
        case 8:
            hIcon = LoadIcon(NULL, IDI_ERROR);
            break;
        case 9:
            hIcon = LoadIcon(NULL, IDI_INFORMATION);
        }

        // Display the icon on screen.
        if (m_iconPosition == 0)
        {
            DrawIcon(pdc->m_hDC, 4, 4, hIcon);
        }
        else
        {
            DrawIcon(pdc->m_hDC, iWidth, 4, hIcon);
        }
    }


    /////////////////////////////////////////////////////////////////////////
    // CPButtonCtrl::DoPropExchange - Persistence support

    void CPButtonCtrl::DoPropExchange(CPropExchange* pPX)
```

```
{
    //Default Wizard Code
    ExchangeVersion(pPX, MAKELONG(_wVerMinor, _wVerMajor));
    COleControl::DoPropExchange(pPX);

    // Make all of our properties persistent..
    PX_Long(pPX, "ModalResult", m_modalResult, mrNone);
    PX_Long(pPX, "StdButtonType", m_stdButtonType, 0);
    PX_Long(pPX, "IconType", m_iconType, 1);
    PX_Long(pPX, "IconPosition", m_iconPosition, 0);

}


/////////////////////////////////////////////////////////////////////////////
// CPButtonCtrl::OnResetState - Reset control to default state

void CPButtonCtrl::OnResetState()
{
    COleControl::OnResetState();  // Resets defaults found in DoPropExchange
}


/////////////////////////////////////////////////////////////////////////////
// CPButtonCtrl::AboutBox - Display an "About" box to the user

void CPButtonCtrl::AboutBox()
{
    CDialog dlgAbout(IDD_ABOUTBOX_PBUTTON);
    dlgAbout.DoModal();
}


/////////////////////////////////////////////////////////////////////////////
// CPButtonCtrl::PreCreateWindow - Modify parameters for CreateWindowEx

BOOL CPButtonCtrl::PreCreateWindow(CREATESTRUCT& cs)
{
    cs.lpszClass = _T("BUTTON");
    return COleControl::PreCreateWindow(cs);
}


/////////////////////////////////////////////////////////////////////////////
// CPButtonCtrl::IsSubclassedControl - This is a subclassed control

BOOL CPButtonCtrl::IsSubclassedControl()
```

```
{
    return TRUE;
}


/////////////////////////////////////////////////////////////////////////
// CPButtonCtrl::OnOcmCommand - Handle command messages

LRESULT CPButtonCtrl::OnOcmCommand(WPARAM wParam, LPARAM lParam)
{
#ifdef _WIN32
    WORD wNotifyCode = HIWORD(wParam);
#else
    WORD wNotifyCode = HIWORD(lParam);
#endif

    // TODO: Switch on wNotifyCode here.

    return 0;
}


/////////////////////////////////////////////////////////////////////////
// CPButtonCtrl message handlers

void CPButtonCtrl::OnStdButtonTypeChanged()
{
    // Change the modal result and button caption to match the user selection.
    switch (m_stdButtonType)
    {
    case 0:
        m_modalResult = mrNone;
        COleControl::SetText("Button");
        break;
    case 1:
        m_modalResult = mrOK;
        COleControl::SetText("OK");
        break;
    case 2:
        m_modalResult = mrCancel;
        COleControl::SetText("Cancel");
        break;
    case 3:
        m_modalResult = mrAbort;
        COleControl::SetText("Abort");
        break;
    case 4:
```

```
        m_modalResult = mrRetry;
        COleControl::SetText("Retry");
        break;
    case 5:
        m_modalResult = mrIgnore;
        COleControl::SetText("Ignore");
        break;
    case 6:
        m_modalResult = mrYes;
        COleControl::SetText("Yes");
        break;
    case 7:
        m_modalResult = mrNo;
        COleControl::SetText("No");
        break;
    case 8:
        m_modalResult = mrOn;
        COleControl::SetText("On");
        break;
    case 9:
        m_modalResult = mrOff;
        COleControl::SetText("Off");
    }


    //Set the modified flag.
    SetModifiedFlag();
}


void CPButtonCtrl::OnModalResultChanged()
{
    // We don't need to do anything special here.

    SetModifiedFlag();
}


void CPButtonCtrl::OnMouseMove(UINT nFlags, CPoint point)
{
    HICON   hIcon;    // Handle of the icon we'll display.
    CDC*    pdc;       //device context
    int     iWidth;   // Control Width
    int     iHeight;  // Control Height

    // Get the control width and height.
    COleControl::GetControlSize(&iWidth, &iHeight);
```

```
// Calculate the right position of the icon.
iWidth -= 36;

// Get the current device context.
pdc = COleControl::GetDC(NULL, 0);

// Load the requested bitmap.
switch (m_iconType)
{
case 1:
    hIcon = LoadIcon(NULL, IDI_APPLICATION);
    break;
case 2:
    hIcon = LoadIcon(NULL, IDI_HAND);
    break;
case 3:
    hIcon = LoadIcon(NULL, IDI_QUESTION);
    break;
case 4:
    hIcon = LoadIcon(NULL, IDI_EXCLAMATION);
    break;
case 5:
    hIcon = LoadIcon(NULL, IDI_ASTERISK);
    break;
case 6:
    hIcon = LoadIcon(NULL, IDI_WINLOGO);
    break;
case 7:
    hIcon = LoadIcon(NULL, IDI_WARNING);
    break;
case 8:
    hIcon = LoadIcon(NULL, IDI_ERROR);
    break;
case 9:
    hIcon = LoadIcon(NULL, IDI_INFORMATION);
}

// Display the icon on screen.
if (m_iconPosition == 0)
{
    DrawIcon(pdc->m_hDC, 4, 4, hIcon);
}
else
{
    DrawIcon(pdc->m_hDC, iWidth, 4, hIcon);
```

```
    }

    // Release the device context.
    COleControl::ReleaseDC(pdc);

    // Perform the default action.
    COleControl::OnMouseMove(nFlags, point);
}

void CPButtonCtrl::OnIconTypeChanged()
{
    // Paint the control.
    COleControl::Refresh();

    // Perform default action.
    SetModifiedFlag();
}

void CPButtonCtrl::OnIconPositionChanged()
{
    // Paint the control.
    COleControl::Refresh();

    // Perform default action.
    SetModifiedFlag();
}
```

The first change you'll notice in the source code is the addition of a stock property page. We already discussed this change in the "Defining the Property Pages" section of this chapter, so we won't discuss it again here. However, it's essential that you add this entry, and you may want to check it again now.

The next function that requires change is CPButtonCtrl::OnDraw(). This is the function that draws your control when you place it in a container. It's also the function responsible for displaying the control when you first start an application. The first thing we do (after declaring some variables) is to get the current control size using the COleControl::GetControlSize() function. You'll find that the COleControl class of functions is invaluable when writing controls that provide more than the default level of functionality (members of this class appear over and over again in the code presented in this section). Once we know the current size, we can calculate the position of an icon if we place it on the right side of the control. The value of 36 represents the pixel size of 32 in addition to the 4 pixels used by the control to provide a 3-D effect. Next you'll see a call to DoSuperclassPaint(). This is the only call that originally appeared within the function. It displays a basic pushbutton with a caption.

Now that we have a basic control painted, we need to add an image to it. First we need to load the correct icon. To do this, we use the m_iconType variable to determine which icon to load (m_iconType is the internal name for the IconType property). The LoadIcon() function does the actual work of loading the icon. The first parameter for this function is an instance handle for the current application. Normally you would retrieve this value using the AfxGetInstanceHandle() function. Since we're using internal Windows icons, we need to provide a NULL value. The second property is a string containing the name of the icon we want to use. The icons listed here are all standard Windows icons found in WinUser.H. If you wanted to use an internal icon, you'd have to use the string name for it instead. Now we are ready to draw the icon using the DrawIcon() function. This function accepts four parameters—the first of which is a device context handle. You can use the CDC structure (pdc) sent to the OnDraw() function as a source for this information. The function also requires positioning information—which is normally on the left side of the button. The 4 pixel offsets allow us to display the icon without destroying the button's 3-D effect. If the user decides to display the icon on the right side of the button, we'll use the value of iWidth that we calculated earlier. The final parameter is the icon handle that we obtained using the LoadIcon() function.

The next major function modification on the agenda is CPButtonCtrl::DoPropExchange(). This function affects the control's persistence. There are four entries to make—all of them much the same. The PX_Long() function accepts four parameters. The first is a CPropExchange structure (pPX). The second parameter is a string containing the external property name of the structure. Next comes the internal member value that actually contains the value we want to exchange. Finally, you can provide an optional initial value—which is usually a good idea.

If you created this control from scratch, you'll need to look at the CPButtonCtrl::OnStdButtonTypeChanged() function next. We've already discussed this function in Chapter 2, so we won't go into it again here. The overall purpose for this function is to make any changes required as the result of selecting a standard button type in either the Object Inspector or the Property Page dialog.

The CPButtonCtrl::OnMouseMove() function works much the same as the CPButtonCtrl::OnDraw() function. The biggest change you'll notice is that since this function isn't passed a device context, we have to obtain it from Windows. That's what the COleControl::GetDC() function does. It retrieves a CDC structure like the one we used in the OnDraw() function. You'll notice a corresponding COleControl::ReleaseDC() function call near the end of the OnMouseMove() function. Always release a device context before a function goes out of scope. The alternative is a slow memory leak at best, or unexplained system crashes when people use your control at worst. Notice that the last thing we do in this function is call the original function with the parameters passed to OnMouseMove(). This is an essential part of intercepting Windows messages if you intend to support a default level of functionality.

The CPButtonCtrl::OnIconTypeChanged() and CPButtonCtrl::OnIcon-PositionChanged() functions both work the same way. Since we've already defined the required drawing actions in other parts of the program, we don't need to define them again here. The COleControl::Refresh() function allows us to make use of those previously defined drawing actions—saving coding time now. (Amazingly, the SetModifiedFlag() function doesn't force an automatic redraw of the control—you have to perform this step manually.)

Creating a Simple Test Program

The PButton control is now finished. You can compile it to get it ready for use. Visual C++ will automatically register it for you. This particular control provides a special feature that you won't be able to see when it's used on a Web page—the stock Fonts property page. That's one of the purposes of this section—to demonstrate the capabilities of that page.

Begin by creating a standard application—the example program uses PBTest as a name, but you can use anything you like. Select Dialog Based on the first page of the MFC Application Wizard. You'll also want to check the OLE Controls option and type a dialog title, such as Picture Button Test, on the second page. At this point you can click on Finish to complete the program shell.

You'll need to insert the PButton control using the Insert | Component command. The control appears on the OLE Controls tab of the Component Gallery dialog. To insert the control, just highlight it and click on Insert. You'll see a Customize dialog. Click on OK to close the Customize dialog, then on Close to close the Component Gallery dialog.

Now that we have a program shell and a control to use with it, let's format the dialog itself. Add a Static Text control (or use the existing one) to the dialog. This control will contain the instructions: "Click to change icon type. Double-click to change icon position." To add the instructions, just double-click on the control and type the words in the Caption property. Close the Properties dialog when you get done. We'll also need to add our PButton control. Since the previous sections didn't tell you to modify the control icon, it will probably look like a standard button with the letters "OCX" on it when viewed in the Controls dialog. Double-click on the control. Change the entry on the Button Type page to OK. Change the entries on the Picture Settings page to None (for the IconType property) and Left (for the IconPosition property). Select the Fonts page. You'll see something similar to the display shown in Figure 11-2. This figure shows you the placement of the various controls on the dialog and the special property page we created for the control. Notice that our control appears in the Controls dialog. If you change the font properties, they'll change on the PButton control caption as well. Close the Properties dialog when you get done.

Before you leave this view of the dialog, we'll need to add a member variable for the PButton control. This will allow us to modify it within the program later. To add the variable, CTRL-double-click the PButton control. You'll see an Add Member Variable dialog. Type **PButton1** in the Member Variable Name field (don't remove the m_), and then click OK to complete the action. We're ready to add some code.

We'll take the easy route for creating the function shells. Use the View | ClassWizard command to display the MFC ClassWizard dialog. Select the Message Maps page. In the Class Name field, select CPBTestDlg. Highlight the IDC_PBUTTONCTRL1 entry in the Object IDs list. There should be two entries in the Messages list: Click and DblClick. Select Click, then click Add Function. Do the same thing for DblClick. Your MFC ClassWizard dialog should look like this:

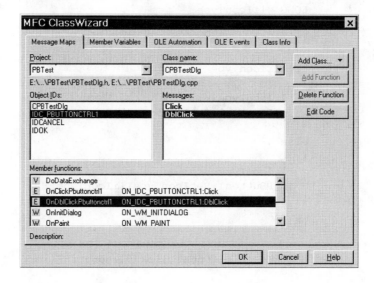

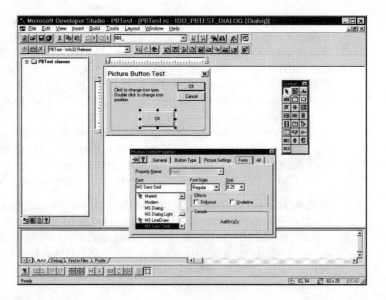

Adding a
stock Fonts
property page
allows you to
modify the
fonts used
with your
control and
requires
very little
programming.
Figure 11-2.

Click the Edit Code button, and MFC ClassWizard will take you directly to
the new functions. Listing 11-3 shows the code for the two new functions.
Don't worry about any other code; Visual C++ took care of it automatically
for you as part of the application shell creation process.

Listing 11-3

```
void CPBTestDlg::OnClickPbuttonctrl1()
{
    LONG   liIconType;

    liIconType = m_PButton1.GetIconType();

    if (liIconType < 9)
    {
        liIconType++;
        m_PButton1.SetIconType(liIconType);
    }
    else
    {
        liIconType = 0;
        m_PButton1.SetIconType(liIconType);
    }

}


void CPBTestDlg::OnDblClickPbuttonctrl1()
```

```
{
    LONG   liIconPosition;

    liIconPosition = m_PButton1.GetIconPosition();

    if (liIconPosition == 0)
    {
        liIconPosition = 1;
        m_PButton1.SetIconPosition(liIconPosition);
    }
    else
    {
        liIconPosition = 0;
        m_PButton1.SetIconPosition(liIconPosition);
    }

}
```

11

As you can see, this code is pretty simple. The first function, OnClickPbuttonctrl1(), works with the IconType property. Its only function is to let you cycle through the icons one at a time. The OnDblClick-Pbuttonctrl1() is even easier; it moves the icon from side to side, using the IconPosition property. Compile and run the sample application. A single click will display an icon similar to the one shown in Figure 11-3. This figure also shows the result of a double-click—the icon moves to the other side of the button.

NOTE: Your results when using this control will vary. For example, different versions of Windows support different default icons. In addition, the programming language and compiler you choose may affect the appearance of this control. Figure 11-3 represents a typical output when used under Windows 95. The compiler in this case is Visual C++ 4.0.

Using the New Control on a Web Page

You will encounter one surprise when using this control within ActiveX Control Pad. Create a new HTML page and use the Edit I Insert ActiveX Control command to add the PButton control to it. Right-click the control and select the bottom Properties option from the context menu. Configure

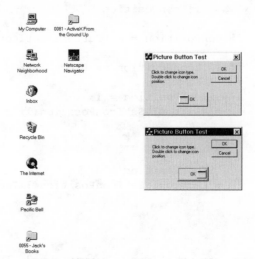

The sample
application
cycles through
the available
icons when
single-clicked
or changes
the icon
position when
double-clicked.
Figure 11-3.

the Button Type page for an OK button (StdButtonType property). On the
Picture Settings page, set the IconType property to None and the
IconPosition property to Left. Now take a look at the Fonts page. Here's the
same stock Fonts property page that you saw in the previous section (see the
following illustration). Notice that it's not enabled, and no amount of work
on your part will enable it either. A stock property will automatically enable
itself in environments that support it. When a control is used in
environments that don't support a particular property page, you'll see the
disabled version.

Close the properties page, then the control itself. ActiveX Control Pad will automatically add an <OBJECT> tag for you. Listing 11-4 shows the rest of the code we'll use with this example.

Listing 11-4

```
<HTML>
<HEAD>

<!-Define JavaScript code to change the icon type.->
<SCRIPT FOR="PButton1" EVENT="Click()">
   if (PButton1.IconType < 9)
      PButton1.IconType++
   else
      PButton1.IconType = 0;
</SCRIPT>

<!-Define JavaScript code to change the icon position.->
<SCRIPT FOR="PButton1" EVENT="DblClick()">
   if (PButton1.IconPosition == 0)
      PButton1.IconPosition = 1
   else
      PButton1.IconPosition = 0;
</SCRIPT>

<TITLE>Picture Button Test</TITLE>
</HEAD>
<BODY>

<!-Display  a heading.->
<CENTER><H2>Picture Button Example</H2></CENTER><P>

<!-Display a caption and the button.->
Click to change the icon.<BR>
Double click to change the icon position.<P><P>
<OBJECT ID="PButton1" WIDTH=100 HEIGHT=51
 CLASSID="CLSID:43D22016-00B1-11D0-8C70-00006E3127B7"
 CODEBASE="http://www.mycompany.com/controls">
    <PARAM NAME="_Version" VALUE="65536">
    <PARAM NAME="_ExtentX" VALUE="2646">
    <PARAM NAME="_ExtentY" VALUE="1341">
    <PARAM NAME="_StockProps" VALUE="70">
    <PARAM NAME="Caption" VALUE="OK">
    <PARAM NAME="ModalResult" VALUE="1">
    <PARAM NAME="StdButtonType" VALUE="1">
    <PARAM NAME="IconType" VALUE="0">
</OBJECT>

</BODY>
</HTML>
```

Most of the code shown here is typical of what we've done throughout the book. We begin by adding a heading to the page along with the regular text to explain how to use the control. The <OBJECT> tag was added automatically. There are also two scripts written in JavaScript. The first script activates when you click the button—it works with the IconType property. Clicking will allow you to cycle through the default icons provided by Windows, as in the previous section. A double-click activates the second script. As before, it works with the IconPosition property to move the icon to the right or left side of the button. Figure 11-4 shows how the control acts when used on an HTML page.

NOTE: You may notice slight variations in control presentation when using different versions of Windows. Different browsers may render the control differently as well. Figure 11-4 shows how the control looks when using it under Windows 95 and displaying it within Internet Explorer 3.0. The compiler in this case was Visual C++ 4.0.

Adding Custom Icons

After you cycle through the icons in our example program a few times, you'll notice that the standard Windows icons often have little to do with their names. For example, the hand icon looks more like a red circle with an X through it. The "Adding Some Code" section of this chapter mentioned that you could create your own icons and use them on a button. Let's look at the procedure for doing that.

The first thing you'll need to do is add an icon to the example control we've already created. All you need to do is select the Resources page of your application, right-click on the Icon folder, and select Insert Icon from the context menu. What you'll see is a blank icon. Right-click on the new icon and select Properties. Change the ID of the icon to IDI_HAND2. Now you'll need to double-click on the icon folder to display the blank icon drawing area. Figure 11-5 shows the icon used for this example. Of course, you can draw any icon you like.

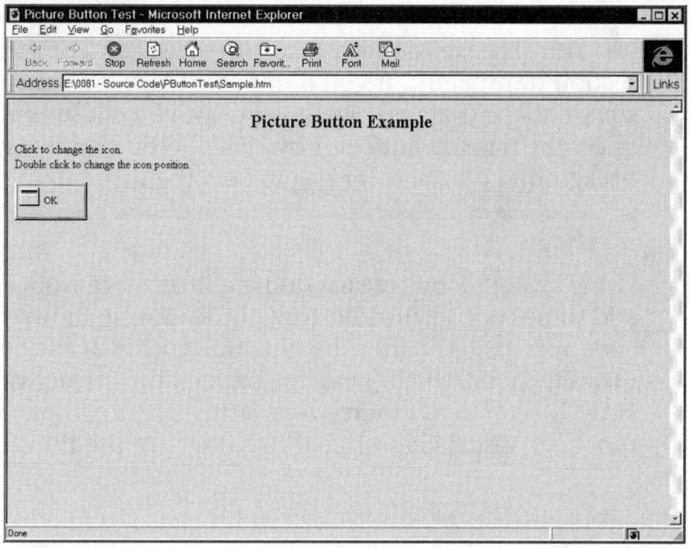

The PButton
control works
much the
same no
matter where
you use it.
Figure 11-4.

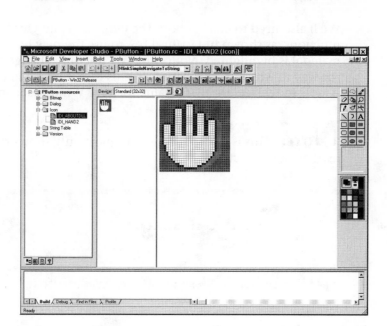

Our new icon
will actually
look like a
hand—notice
the shading
that will make
the icon look
like it's raised
from the
button surface.
Figure 11-5.

TIP: The weird green-looking background of the icon will make that section transparent. If you don't use this color, your icon will appear as a square shape that uses whatever color you chose as a background. You can select the transparent color by clicking the monitor with the green background on the color palette. It's the first entry you'll see.

Using custom icons means doing a little more work as well. You'll need to add some code to the PButtonCtl.CPP file, as shown in Listing 11-5. This code appears right after the #include entries at the beginning of the file. The MAKEINTRESOURCE() macro converts the integer value that represents the HAND2 icon to a resource type string that's compatible with the LoadIcon() function. Visual C++ will balk if you try to use the resource ID directly.

Listing 11-5

```
//Define our hand icon.
#define IDI_CUSTHAND MAKEINTRESOURCE(IDI_HAND2)
```

We'll also need to change both the OnDraw() and OnMouseMove() functions, as shown in Listing 11-6, to use the new hand icon. The new material is highlighted. Notice that we not only change the icon loaded, but the way in which it gets loaded. In this case we have to provide an instance handle to replace the NULL value used for Windows icons.

NOTE: This is a partial code listing—it only shows the case statement used by both functions.

Listing11-6

```
// Load the requested bitmap.
switch (m_iconType)
{
case 1:
   hIcon = LoadIcon(NULL, IDI_APPLICATION);
   break;
case 2:
   hIcon = LoadIcon(AfxGetInstanceHandle(), IDI_CUSTHAND);
   break;
case 3:
   hIcon = LoadIcon(NULL, IDI_QUESTION);
   break;
```

```
case 4:
   hIcon = LoadIcon(NULL, IDI_EXCLAMATION);
   break;
case 5:
   hIcon = LoadIcon(NULL, IDI_ASTERISK);
   break;
case 6:
   hIcon = LoadIcon(NULL, IDI_WINLOGO);
   break;
case 7:
   hIcon = LoadIcon(NULL, IDI_WARNING);
   break;
case 8:
   hIcon = LoadIcon(NULL, IDI_ERROR);
   break;
case 9:
   hIcon = LoadIcon(NULL, IDI_INFORMATION);
}
```

So what does the new hand icon look like? Compile the ActiveX control, and then run the PBTest application or example Web page again. You won't need to do anything with the two test programs—that's one of the beauties of using ActiveX controls. Figure 11-6 shows how the hand icon looks within a Web page.

Creating a Simple Drawing

Drawing on the screen is one of those things that you try to tackle when learning about any programming environment. After all, given a good set of graphics primitives and a little imagination, you can get almost any idea across to the user. Besides, there are simply some things you can't represent very well with bitmaps—especially if the presentation will change in any way. This section shows you how to use some graphics primitives in the ActiveX environment. We aren't going to create a full-fledged drawing program for the Internet, but you will learn how to make some graphics primitives work in that environment.

Building the DepictIt Control

We'll begin by creating an OLE control. The example project is named DepictIt, but you can name your version of the project anything you like. You won't need to set anything special during the shell creation process, so you can simply click Finish on the first page of the OLE Control Wizard.

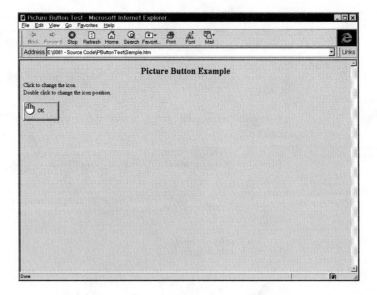

The new hand icon actually looks like a hand rather than a circle with an X through it.
Figure 11-6.

Like many graphics applications, this one will require a lot of properties to get the job done—especially in the light of its generic task. As usual, use the View | ClassWizard command so you can use the MFC ClassWizard to define them. There are three stock properties: ForeColor, BackColor, and Enabled. We'll use the ForeColor and BackColor properties in an interesting way in the example, so don't forget to add them. There is one boolean variable, CircleSquare. It lets you force the control to produce a perfect square or circle when necessary. We'll use several long variables to control the appearance of the display, including BrushType, DrawType, PenType, and PenWidth. There is a special pen color variable called PenColor—it's of type OLE_COLOR. This example will show you how handy this particular variable type can be when you need to keep track of more than two color settings. Finally, there are eight positioning variables of type long: X1, X2, X3, X4, Y1, Y2, Y3, and Y4. You'll also want to include two stock methods for experimentation purposes: DoClick and Refresh (we don't actually use them in the example, but you could use them to extend the example later).

NOTE: We'll skip defining the property pages this time around. You would, however, define the property pages for a production quality control.

This example also requires the use of a bitmap to demonstrate a special drawing feature—patterned brush drawing. Figure 11-7 shows how to create the bitmap used for the example, though you could certainly create anything you like. The only requirement is that the bitmap fit within an 8-X-8-pixel space.

The application is now ready for coding. Unlike other examples, you'll need to work with the control header file, DepictItCtl.H. Listing 11-7 shows the variable declarations you add to the header file right before the dispatch event IDs near the end of the file. All four of these variables will be used later to change specific graphic elements of the program. The first two affect the color of the brush used to paint some graphic elements. The other two are for the pen that is used to draw other graphic elements.

11

Listing 11-7

```
// Add some custom variables.
    CBrush    oBackBrush; //Background color brush.
    CBrush    oForeBrush; //Foreground color brush.
    CPen      oPen;       //Standard pen.
    COLORREF  liPenColor; //Default pen color.
```

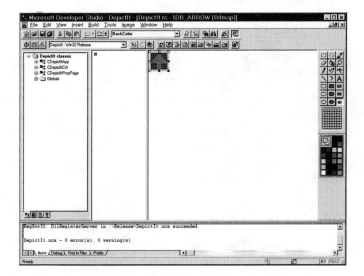

The sample bitmap will show how to use patterns in drawing.

Figure 11-7.

Once you have changed the heading, you'll need to modify the control code in DepictItCtl.CPP. You've already created all of the required function shells during the property definition process in the MFC ClassWizard, so the actual amount of coding is somewhat less than it first appears. Listing 11-8 contains the complete source for the DepictItCtl.CPP file, since there are so many changes to make.

Listing 11-8

```
// DepictItCtl.cpp : Implementation of the CDepictItCtrl OLE control class.

#include "stdafx.h"
#include "DepictIt.h"
#include "DepictItCtl.h"
#include "DepictItPpg.h"


#ifdef _DEBUG
#define new DEBUG_NEW
#undef THIS_FILE
static char THIS_FILE[] = __FILE__;
#endif

// Custom defines for drawing types.
#define DRAW_LINE            0
#define DRAW_SOLID_RECT      1
#define DRAW_HOLLOW_RECT     2
#define DRAW_ROUND_RECT      3
#define DRAW_ARC             4
#define DRAW_CHORD           5
#define DRAW_PIE             6
#define DRAW_ELLIPSE         7


// Custom defines for brush types.
#define BT_SOLID             0
#define BT_BDIAGONAL         1
#define BT_CROSS             2
#define BT_DIAGCROSS         3
#define BT_FDIAGONAL         4
#define BT_HORIZONTAL        5
#define BT_VERTICAL          6
#define BT_PATTERN           7

IMPLEMENT_DYNCREATE(CDepictItCtrl, COleControl)
```

```
//////////////////////////////////////////////////////////////////////
// Message map

BEGIN_MESSAGE_MAP(CDepictItCtrl, COleControl)
    //{{AFX_MSG_MAP(CDepictItCtrl)
    // NOTE - ClassWizard will add and remove message map entries
    //     DO NOT EDIT what you see in these blocks of generated code !
    //}}AFX_MSG_MAP
    ON_OLEVERB(AFX_IDS_VERB_PROPERTIES, OnProperties)
END_MESSAGE_MAP()


//////////////////////////////////////////////////////////////////////
// Dispatch map

BEGIN_DISPATCH_MAP(CDepictItCtrl, COleControl)
    //{{AFX_DISPATCH_MAP(CDepictItCtrl)
    DISP_PROPERTY_NOTIFY(CDepictItCtrl, "PenColor", m_penColor,
OnPenColorChanged, VT_COLOR)
    DISP_PROPERTY_NOTIFY(CDepictItCtrl, "PenWidth", m_penWidth,
OnPenWidthChanged, VT_I4)
    DISP_PROPERTY_NOTIFY(CDepictItCtrl, "PenType", m_penType,
OnPenTypeChanged, VT_I4)
    DISP_PROPERTY_NOTIFY(CDepictItCtrl, "DrawType", m_drawType,
OnDrawTypeChanged, VT_I4)
    DISP_PROPERTY_NOTIFY(CDepictItCtrl, "X1", m_x1, OnX1Changed, VT_I4)
    DISP_PROPERTY_NOTIFY(CDepictItCtrl, "X2", m_x2, OnX2Changed, VT_I4)
    DISP_PROPERTY_NOTIFY(CDepictItCtrl, "Y1", m_y1, OnY1Changed, VT_I4)
    DISP_PROPERTY_NOTIFY(CDepictItCtrl, "Y2", m_y2, OnY2Changed, VT_I4)
    DISP_PROPERTY_NOTIFY(CDepictItCtrl, "CircleSquare", m_circleSquare,
OnCircleSquareChanged, VT_BOOL)
    DISP_PROPERTY_NOTIFY(CDepictItCtrl, "BrushType", m_brushType,
OnBrushTypeChanged, VT_I4)
    DISP_PROPERTY_NOTIFY(CDepictItCtrl, "X3", m_x3, OnX3Changed, VT_I4)
    DISP_PROPERTY_NOTIFY(CDepictItCtrl, "X4", m_x4, OnX4Changed, VT_I4)
    DISP_PROPERTY_NOTIFY(CDepictItCtrl, "Y3", m_y3, OnY3Changed, VT_I4)
    DISP_PROPERTY_NOTIFY(CDepictItCtrl, "Y4", m_y4, OnY4Changed, VT_I4)
    DISP_STOCKFUNC_DOCLICK()
    DISP_STOCKFUNC_REFRESH()
    DISP_STOCKPROP_BACKCOLOR()
    DISP_STOCKPROP_FORECOLOR()
    DISP_STOCKPROP_ENABLED()
    //}}AFX_DISPATCH_MAP
```

```
      DISP_FUNCTION_ID(CDepictItCtrl, "AboutBox", DISPID_ABOUTBOX,
AboutBox, VT_EMPTY, VTS_NONE)
END_DISPATCH_MAP()


/////////////////////////////////////////////////////////////////////
// Event map

BEGIN_EVENT_MAP(CDepictItCtrl, COleControl)
    //{{AFX_EVENT_MAP(CDepictItCtrl)
    // NOTE - ClassWizard will add and remove event map entries
    //      DO NOT EDIT what you see in these blocks of generated code !
    //}}AFX_EVENT_MAP
END_EVENT_MAP()


/////////////////////////////////////////////////////////////////////
// Property pages

// TODO: Add more property pages as needed.  Remember to increase the
count!
BEGIN_PROPPAGEIDS(CDepictItCtrl, 1)
   PROPPAGEID(CDepictItPropPage::guid)
END_PROPPAGEIDS(CDepictItCtrl)


/////////////////////////////////////////////////////////////////////
// Initialize class factory and guid

IMPLEMENT_OLECREATE_EX(CDepictItCtrl, "DEPICTIT.DepictItCtrl.1",
    0x23db37e5, 0xe31, 0x11d0, 0x8c, 0x70, 0, 0, 0x6e, 0x31, 0x27, 0xb7)


/////////////////////////////////////////////////////////////////////
// Type library ID and version

IMPLEMENT_OLETYPELIB(CDepictItCtrl, _tlid, _wVerMajor, _wVerMinor)


/////////////////////////////////////////////////////////////////////
// Interface IDs

const IID BASED_CODE IID_DDepictIt =
     { 0x5db3d081, 0xed6, 0x11d0, { 0x8c, 0x70, 0, 0, 0x6e, 0x31, 0x27,
0xb7 } };
```

```
const IID BASED_CODE IID_DDepictItEvents =
        { 0x5db3d082, 0xed6, 0x11d0, { 0x8c, 0x70, 0, 0, 0x6e, 0x31,
0x27, 0xb7 }
};


////////////////////////////////////////////////////////////////////////
// Control type information

static const DWORD BASED_CODE _dwDepictItOleMisc =
    OLEMISC_ACTIVATEWHENVISIBLE |
    OLEMISC_SETCLIENTSITEFIRST |
    OLEMISC_INSIDEOUT |
    OLEMISC_CANTLINKINSIDE |
    OLEMISC_RECOMPOSEONRESIZE;


IMPLEMENT_OLECTLTYPE(CDepictItCtrl, IDS_DEPICTIT, _dwDepictItOleMisc)


////////////////////////////////////////////////////////////////////////
// CDepictItCtrl::CDepictItCtrlFactory::UpdateRegistry -
// Adds or removes system registry entries for CDepictItCtrl

BOOL CDepictItCtrl::CDepictItCtrlFactory::UpdateRegistry(BOOL bRegister)
{
    // TODO: Verify that your control follows apartment-model threading
rules.
    // Refer to MFC TechNote 64 for more information.
    // If your control does not conform to the apartment-model rules, then
    // you must modify the code below, changing the 6th parameter from
    // afxRegApartmentThreading to 0.

    if (bRegister)
        return AfxOleRegisterControlClass(
            AfxGetInstanceHandle(),
            m_clsid,
            m_lpszProgID,
            IDS_DEPICTIT,
            IDB_DEPICTIT,
            afxRegApartmentThreading,
            _dwDepictItOleMisc,
            _tlid,
            _wVerMajor,
            _wVerMinor);
    else
        return AfxOleUnregisterClass(m_clsid, m_lpszProgID);
}
```

```
/////////////////////////////////////////////////////////////////////
// CDepictItCtrl::CDepictItCtrl - Constructor

CDepictItCtrl::CDepictItCtrl()
{
   // Default action.
   InitializeIIDs(&IID_DDepictIt, &IID_DDepictItEvents);
}



/////////////////////////////////////////////////////////////////////
// CDepictItCtrl::~CDepictItCtrl - Destructor

CDepictItCtrl::~CDepictItCtrl()
{
   // TODO: Clean up your control's instance data here.
}



/////////////////////////////////////////////////////////////////////
// CDepictItCtrl::OnDraw - Drawing function

void CDepictItCtrl::OnDraw(
        CDC* pdc, const CRect& rcBounds, const CRect& rcInvalid)
{
   long     liDistance; // The distance between two points.
   CBitmap  oUpArrow;   // A bitmap object.

   // Create a standard foreground and background brush, and a pen.  Only
the
   // foreground brush type can be changed to something other than solid.
   oBackBrush.CreateSolidBrush(TranslateColor(COleControl::GetBackColor(),
NULL));

   switch (m_brushType)
   {
   case BT_SOLID:
      // Create a solid brush.
      oForeBrush.CreateSolidBrush(TranslateColor
(COleControl::GetForeColor(),
NULL));
      break;
   case BT_BDIAGONAL:
      // Create a backward diagonal brush.
      oForeBrush.CreateHatchBrush(HS_BDIAGONAL, TranslateColor
(COleControl::GetForeColor(), NULL));
```

```
                break;
            case BT_CROSS:
                // Create a vertical & horizontal cross brush.
                oForeBrush.CreateHatchBrush(HS_CROSS,
    TranslateColor
    (COleControl::GetForeColor(), NULL));
                break;
            case BT_DIAGCROSS:
                // Create a diagonal cross brush.
                oForeBrush.CreateHatchBrush(HS_DIAGCROSS,
    TranslateColor
    (COleControl::GetForeColor(), NULL));
                break;
            case BT_FDIAGONAL:
                // Create a forward diagonal brush.
                oForeBrush.CreateHatchBrush(HS_FDIAGONAL,
    TranslateColor
    (COleControl::GetForeColor(), NULL));
                break;
            case BT_HORIZONTAL:
                // Create a horizontal brush.
                oForeBrush.CreateHatchBrush(HS_HORIZONTAL,
    TranslateColor
    (COleControl::GetForeColor(), NULL));
                break;
            case BT_VERTICAL:
                // Create a vertical brush.
                oForeBrush.CreateHatchBrush(HS_VERTICAL,
    TranslateColor
    (COleControl::GetForeColor(), NULL));
                break;
            case BT_PATTERN:
                // Load the bitmap.
                oUpArrow.LoadBitmap(IDB_ARROW);

                // Create a pattern brush.
                oForeBrush.CreatePatternBrush(&oUpArrow);
                break;
        }

        oPen.CreatePen(m_penType, m_penWidth, TranslateColor(m_penColor));

        // Set some default colors.
        pdc->SelectObject(&oForeBrush);
        pdc->SelectObject(&oPen);
```

```
// Fill in the background.
pdc->FillRect(rcBounds, &oBackBrush);

// Determine which kind of graphics primitive to create.
switch (m_drawType)
{
case DRAW_LINE:
    // Move to the starting point, then draw a line.
    pdc->MoveTo(m_x1, m_y1);
    pdc->LineTo(m_x2, m_y2);
    break;
case DRAW_SOLID_RECT:
    // Check to see if we want a square.
    if (m_circleSquare)
    {
        liDistance = abs(m_x1 - m_x2);
        m_y2 = m_y1 + liDistance;
    }

    // Draw a solid rectangle.
    pdc->Rectangle(m_x1, m_y1, m_x2, m_y2);
    break;
case DRAW_HOLLOW_RECT:
    // Check to see if we want a square.
    if (m_circleSquare)
    {
        liDistance = abs(m_x1 - m_x2);
        m_y2 = m_y1 + liDistance;
    }

    // Draw a hollow rectangle. The only brush width is 1.
    pdc->FrameRect(CRect(m_x1, m_y1, m_x2, m_y2), &oForeBrush);
    break;
case DRAW_ROUND_RECT:
    // Check to see if we want a square.
    if (m_circleSquare)
    {
        liDistance = abs(m_x1 - m_x2);
        m_y2 = m_y1 + liDistance;
    }

    // Verify that the ellipse parameters used to round
    // the corners are within tolerance.
    if (!m_x3 > 0)
        m_x3 = 1;
    if (!m_y3 > 0)
```

11

```
                    m_y3 = 1;

            // Draw a rectangle with rounded corners.
            pdc->RoundRect(m_x1, m_y1, m_x2, m_y2, m_x3, m_y3);
            break;
        case DRAW_ARC:
            // Draw an arc.
            pdc->Arc(m_x1, m_y1, m_x2, m_y2, m_x3, m_y3, m_x4, m_y4);
            break;
        case DRAW_CHORD:
            // Draw a chord.
            pdc->Chord(m_x1, m_y1, m_x2, m_y2, m_x3, m_y3, m_x4, m_y4);
            break;
        case DRAW_PIE:
            // Draw a pie wedge.
            pdc->Pie(m_x1, m_y1, m_x2, m_y2, m_x3, m_y3, m_x4, m_y4);
            break;
        case DRAW_ELLIPSE:
            // Check to see if we want a circle.
            if (m_circleSquare)
            {
                liDistance = abs(m_x1 - m_x2);
                m_y2 = m_y1 + liDistance;
            }

            pdc->Ellipse(m_x1, m_y1, m_x2, m_y2);
            break;
    }
}


/////////////////////////////////////////////////////////////////////
// CDepictItCtrl::DoPropExchange - Persistence support

void CDepictItCtrl::DoPropExchange(CPropExchange* pPX)
{
    int    iWidth;  // Control Width
    int    iHeight; // Control Height

    // Perform some default actions.
    ExchangeVersion(pPX, MAKELONG(_wVerMinor, _wVerMajor));
    COleControl::DoPropExchange(pPX);

    // Get the control width and height.
    COleControl::GetControlSize(&iWidth, &iHeight);

    // Initialize the default pen color.
```

```
    liPenColor = 0x00000000;

    // Make our properties persistent
    PX_Long(pPX, "BrushType", m_brushType, 0);
    PX_Bool(pPX, "CircleSquare", m_circleSquare, FALSE);
    PX_Long(pPX, "DrawType", m_drawType, 0);
    PX_Color(pPX, "PenColor", m_penColor, OLE_COLOR(liPenColor));
    PX_Long(pPX, "PenType", m_penType, PS_SOLID);
    PX_Long(pPX, "PenWidth", m_penWidth, 1);
    PX_Long(pPX, "X1", m_x1, 0);
    PX_Long(pPX, "X2", m_x2, iWidth);
    PX_Long(pPX, "X3", m_x3, 0);
    PX_Long(pPX, "X4", m_x4, 0);
    PX_Long(pPX, "Y1", m_y1, 0);
    PX_Long(pPX, "Y2", m_y2, iHeight);
    PX_Long(pPX, "Y3", m_y3, 0);
    PX_Long(pPX, "Y4", m_y4, 0);
}


/////////////////////////////////////////////////////////////////////////////
// CDepictItCtrl::OnResetState - Reset control to default state

void CDepictItCtrl::OnResetState()
{
    COleControl::OnResetState();  // Resets defaults found in DoPropEx-
change

    // TODO: Reset any other control state here.
}



/////////////////////////////////////////////////////////////////////////////
// CDepictItCtrl::AboutBox - Display an "About" box to the user

void CDepictItCtrl::AboutBox()
{
    CDialog dlgAbout(IDD_ABOUTBOX_DEPICTIT);
    dlgAbout.DoModal();
}



/////////////////////////////////////////////////////////////////////////////
// CDepictItCtrl message handlers

void CDepictItCtrl::OnBrushTypeChanged()
```

```
{
    // Make sure our color changes take hold.
    COleControl::Refresh();

    // Perform default action.
    SetModifiedFlag();
}

void CDepictItCtrl::OnCircleSquareChanged()
{
    // Make sure our color changes take hold.
    COleControl::Refresh();

    // Perform default action.
    SetModifiedFlag();
}

void CDepictItCtrl::OnDrawTypeChanged()
{
    // Verify that the drawing type is valid.
    if ((m_drawType < DRAW_LINE) | (m_drawType > DRAW_ELLIPSE))
        m_drawType = DRAW_LINE;

    // Make sure our color changes take hold.
    COleControl::Refresh();

    // Perform default action.
    SetModifiedFlag();
}

void CDepictItCtrl::OnPenColorChanged()
{
    // Make sure our color changes take hold.
    COleControl::Refresh();

    // Perform default action.
    SetModifiedFlag();
}

void CDepictItCtrl::OnPenTypeChanged()
{
    // Make sure we have a valid pen type.
    if ((m_penType < PS_SOLID) | (m_penType > PS_INSIDEFRAME))
        m_penType = PS_SOLID;

    // Make sure our pen type changes take hold.
    COleControl::Refresh();
```

```
    // Perform default action.
    SetModifiedFlag();
}

void CDepictItCtrl::OnPenWidthChanged()
{
    // Make sure we have a valid pen width.
    if (m_penWidth < 1)
        m_penWidth = 1;

    // Make sure our pen width changes take hold.
    COleControl::Refresh();

    // Perform default action.
    SetModifiedFlag();
}

void CDepictItCtrl::OnX1Changed()
{
    // Make sure our color changes take hold.
    COleControl::Refresh();

    // Perform default action.
    SetModifiedFlag();
}

void CDepictItCtrl::OnX2Changed()
{
    // Make sure our color changes take hold.
    COleControl::Refresh();

    // Perform default action.
    SetModifiedFlag();
}

void CDepictItCtrl::OnX3Changed()
{
    // Make sure our color changes take hold.
    COleControl::Refresh();


    // Perform default action.
    SetModifiedFlag();
}
```

```
void CDepictItCtrl::OnX4Changed()
{
    // Make sure our color changes take hold.
    COleControl::Refresh();

    // Perform default action.
    SetModifiedFlag();
}

void CDepictItCtrl::OnY1Changed()
{

    // Make sure our color changes take hold.
    COleControl::Refresh();

    // Perform default action.
    SetModifiedFlag();
}

void CDepictItCtrl::OnY2Changed()
{
    // Make sure our color changes take hold.
    COleControl::Refresh();

    // Perform default action.
    SetModifiedFlag();
}

void CDepictItCtrl::OnY3Changed()
{
    // Make sure our color changes take hold.
    COleControl::Refresh();

    // Perform default action.
    SetModifiedFlag();
}

void CDepictItCtrl::OnY4Changed()
{
    // Make sure our color changes take hold.
    COleControl::Refresh();

    // Perform default action.
    SetModifiedFlag();
}
```

Even though this looks like a lot of code, it's fairly easy to break down if you take it one section at a time. At the very beginning of the file, you'll see two sets of the defines. The first set is program specific—they define the kinds of graphics primitives you'll see in this example. As you can see, we'll look at the kind of primitives you could use to build full-fledged applications or application-like controls. For example, there's a special Pie drawing primitive that you could use to create pie charts with ease. The second set of defines provides an easy way to manage the various brushes we'll use. Windows does provide a set of hatching-specific defines (as you'll see later), but there aren't any defines that allow you to look at all the brush capabilities as a whole.

The very first function you'll need to modify is OnDraw(). This is the main function for this particular example—which isn't too surprising. We start by defining two variables. liDistance will allow us to calculate the width of a graphics primitive, such as a square, and then use that value to adjust the height. In other words, we'll force the object to show a perfect square or circle. This variable doesn't affect some of the graphics primitives, for example, the line and the arc. The second variable contains the bitmap we defined earlier. We'll use it as one of the brush types defined in this example.

The next section of the OnDraw() function creates the brushes and pens we'll use to paint and draw the various graphics primitives. There are two brushes and one pen. The first brush contains the background color. Notice that we use the CBrush class CreateSolidBrush() member function. We'll get the color setting from the BackColor stock property. However, CreateSolidBrush() requires a standard Windows color, while the BackColor property will provide an OLE_COLOR—just like the one used for the PenColor property. Fortunately, the TranslateColor() function takes care of the transition for us. Take note of how we obtain the color as well—it's through the COleControl::GetBackColor() member function.

We create a solid color foreground color brush in much the same way as the background brush. However, we'll need to rely on a different CBrush member function to create other brush types. The first one we use, CreateHatchBrush(), provides one of several hatched brushes. A hatched brush comes in handy when you need to send output to a monochrome printer or simply want to achieve a different effect in displaying information without relying on patterns. In fact, there are more than the ones shown here, but this gives you a good idea of what they look like. The major difference between this call and the CreateSolidBrush() function is that you need to supply a hatch type in addition to a brush color. Surprisingly, the third type of brush we'll create relies on the PatternBrush() function. Notice that you have to use the CBitmap LoadBitmap() member function to load the bitmap into a variable before you can create a brush with it. The PatternBrush() function doesn't require any color input at all. It relies on the colors in an 8-X-8 bitmap pattern to provide both color and variety. This is the same kind of graphics effect provided by the Windows wallpaper patterns.

The process of creating a pen is entirely different from creating a brush. Notice that the CPen CreatePen() member function requires three kinds of input. The first is the pattern you want to display. Unfortunately, the pattern only comes into play when you use a pen width of 1. Any other width value negates the pattern effect—at least in Internet Explorer. The second variable is a pen width in pixels. You can choose any value from 1 up to the size of your screen. Finally, we define a color for the pen. Notice that we need to use the same technique here that we did for the hatched and solid color brushes.

Creating a pen or a brush doesn't mean that your control will use them. Think of the process of creating a brush or pen as you would if you were buying these items in the store—getting a pen or brush isn't the same as actually using it. Once you get the pen or brush, you need to take it out of your pencil holder to use it. That's what the process of pen or brush selection is all about. The next two statements in the example code, pdc->SelectObject(&oForeBrush) and pdc->SelectObject(&oPen), tell your control to select a specific pen or brush from the pencil holder and use them. Notice that you don't have to specify whether the object is a pen or brush since the SelectObject() function detects this automatically. You can only select one object at a time—similarly, so can your object. It can select one pen and one brush to use at a time. There's another way of selecting a pen or brush. Some functions allow you to specify this information directly. That's how the next function call, pdc->FillRect(rcBounds, &oBackBrush), works. It allows you to use a specific brush without using the SelectObject() function. Other drawing functions, such as pdc->LineTo(m_x2, m_y2), require that you select a pen or brush first—they always use the default settings.

Now that we've created something to draw with and those items are selected into the current context, it's time to decide what to draw. Normally you wouldn't draw one item at a time, but for the purposes of this example, we'll do just that. The switch statement determines what we'll draw. You'll want to take a look through this list to find the methods used to draw various types of objects, but let's talk about the more interesting types first. You can still use the familiar line drawing functions LineTo() and MoveTo() in an ActiveX control. Both of these functions accept two parameters—the X and Y positions of a specific point within the drawing area in pixel coordinates. These functions work just about everywhere. In fact, if you can't get some of the more complex functions to work in a specific situation, you can always draw what you want using complex line commands—it's not pretty, but it works. In addition to simple line commands, you can use the complex line command drawing functions such as Polyline(). However, since these complex drawing functions rely on building complex structures, you may find that they don't always work as expected.

A second type of drawing function is represented by the pdc->Rectangle(m_x1, m_y1, m_x2, m_y2) function call. You specify an upper-left and lower-right corner, and Windows takes care of the rest for you. Needless to say, this function requires you to provide four variables (representing two sets of X and Y coordinates) as input. You can also use a standard CRect object, but this isn't as convenient as you might think when working with an ActiveX control. The only time a CRect object does come in handy is if you want to fill the entire area taken by the control with a graphics primitive like this: pdc->FillRect(rcBounds, &oBackBrush). You should also notice that this is the first type of drawing that takes the CircleSquare property into account. If the control's user requests a square, the control performs a simple calculation to adjust the vertical axis length to match the horizontal axis.

The next two drawing types build on the second. In the first case we had to define an arc for the rounded edges of a rectangle like this: pdc->RoundRect(m_x1, m_y1, m_x2, m_y2, m_x3, m_y3). The third coordinate pair—m_x3 and m_y3—define how much rounding of the rectangle corners will occur. Notice that there's some additional code in this area to make sure that the values in m_x3 and m_y3 are always above 0. (A value of 0 means that no rounding occurs, and a negative value can have very unexpected results.) The next drawing type requires four coordinate pairs (eight variables). For example, pdc->Arc(m_x1, m_y1, m_x2, m_y2, m_x3, m_y3, m_x4, m_y4) falls into this category. The third and fourth coordinate pairs could be used for just about any purpose, but normally they form a bounding area of some kind. Unlike the rectangle and circle drawing functions, we don't check the CircleSquare property. Normally arcs, pies, and chords define irregular shapes.

It's finally time to move on to the next function after the OnDraw() function, CDepictItCtrl::DoPropExchange. As with all of the other examples in this book, we'll make all the properties persistent. Even though there are more properties to deal with, the function calls are pretty straightforward. The only difference from other examples that you'll want to note is the PX_Color(pPX, "PenColor", m_penColor, OLE_COLOR(liPenColor)) call. Notice that we have to convert the standard Windows color stored in liPenColor to an OLE_COLOR. The reason that this difference is so important is that we had to use the TranslateColor() function to translate an OLE_COLOR into a standard Windows color. You don't use the same function to perform the transition in reverse—a simple typecast takes care of the matter for you.

Most of the remaining function calls follow a simple pattern. Any time you make a change to a graphics setting, you must force a redraw of the drawing area. That's the purpose of the code shown here:

```
void CDepictItCtrl::OnBrushTypeChanged()
{
    // Make sure our color changes take hold.
    COleControl::Refresh();

    // Perform default action.
    SetModifiedFlag();
}
```

Simply setting the modified flag won't force the display to show any changes you've made to the graphics setup. This is important to remember when you start creating complex drawings. You can either make all the changes at once, and then display the drawing. Or, you can display the changes one at a time and create a sort of animation (especially if there is a discernible time delay between changes). That's why it's important to include the Refresh method with your control. It gives the user a choice of update methods.

Some of the remaining functions perform a variety of checks on the changed value. In some cases this is the best way to handle variables that are outside of the range you intended. Just set them back to a valid value if the user selects something out of range. You could even display a dialog telling the user what ranges are acceptable. However, in some situations you won't quite know what values are acceptable at the time a change takes place. For example, the X3 and X4 properties are used for a variety of purposes, so you can't check them at the time the user changes them. In this case you'll want to check the values right before you use the property, as we do with the rounded corners rectangle drawing. In a third case, it doesn't matter what value the user selects, so you really don't need to provide much in the way of range checking.

Testing the DepictIt Control

Once you have all of the functions implemented, it's time to compile and test your control. This one will work fine in a number of environments, so you should test it both locally and as part of a Web page. The code in Listing 11-9 will show you how to test it in the Internet environment using other ActiveX controls on an HTML layout. Begin by creating a new layout like the one shown in Figure 11-8.

The DepictIt control sits in the upper-left corner of the layout. Along the bottom are various options for the control that require radio button entries—the properties they affect are in parentheses: Background Color (BackColor), Foreground Color (ForeColor), Pen Color (PenColor), Pen Type (PenType), Brush Type (BrushType), and Drawing Type (DrawType). On the right side (near the top), you'll see a single check box. This changes the CircleSquare property. Below it is an edit box that controls the PenWidth property. Finally, you'll see eight sets of edit boxes for the drawing coordinate properties: X1, X2, X3, X4, Y1, Y2, Y3, and Y4.

As a minimum, you'll need to set the Caption and CodeBase properties for each control in Figure 11-8. You'll also find it very handy to give the controls a descriptive ID in this case, because there are so many of them. For example, the first radio button in the Background Color group might be called obBGBlack. This is an especially useful naming convention because it tells you what color to associate with this radio button. In other cases, you'll need

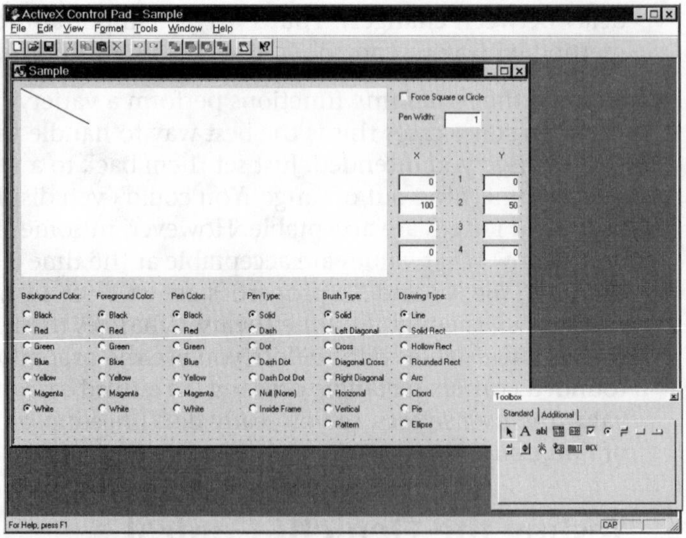

The sample HTML layout will allow you to test all of the capabilities of the DepictIt control.

Figure 11-8.

to assign a number to a particular control. For example, the first control in the Drawing Type group might be called obDType0. This lets you know what number to assign to the control later. The option (radio) buttons will also require an entry in the GroupName property. Using a subset of the ID value usually works well. For example, the GroupName property for all the controls in the Drawing Type group would be DType.

NOTE: The rest of this procedure assumes that you used some type of logical naming convention for the various controls. For example, it assumes that you gave the first control under the Background Color group a name like obBGBlack, which means option button, background, black.

11

At this point you're probably telling yourself that setting up all the scripts required to handle this control is an impossible task. Actually, you'll find that you can use Script Wizard to set up all the scripts, and you won't have to write a single line of code. There are several different ways to get this done. The easiest setup is for the color-associated radio buttons. Let's take a look at one example—all of the other radio buttons in this category work exactly the same way. Click on the + sign next to the obBGBlack entry in the Select an Event list. Highlight the Click entry under obBGBlack. Click on the + sign next to the DepictIt entry in the Insert Actions list. Highlight the BackColor property under the DepictIt entry. Click the Insert Action button, and you'll see a DepictIt BackColor dialog. Figure 11-9 shows what your screen should look like at this point. All you need to do is select a color (black in this case), and then click OK. Script Wizard will take care of all the details for you. Follow this same procedure for all of the color-related option buttons—changing the affected property under the DepictIt entry in the Insert Actions list and color to match the purpose of the control.

The Tools | Script Wizard command will always display the Script Wizard dialog box for you.

The Pen Type, Brush Type, and Drawing Type groups of radio buttons require a slightly different approach than the color settings. In this case you need to assign a number to the property. You'll still highlight the Click event for each option button in the Event list and select the associated property under the DepictIt entry in the Insert Actions list. However, the dialog box you'll see will look like the one shown in Figure 11-10. Notice that the rest of the setup looks similar to the one shown in Figure 11-9. (Now you can see why it's so important to add a number to the end of the control ID property.)

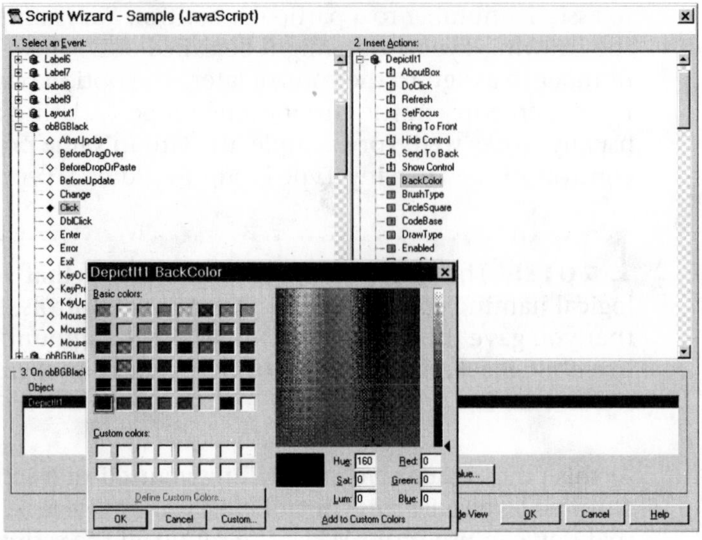

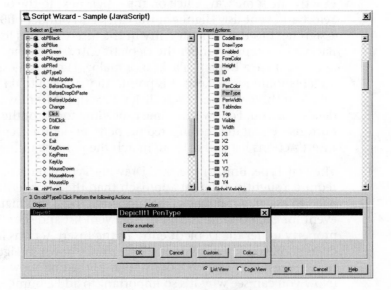

Setting up a script to change color is a matter of a few clicks in Script Wizard.
Figure 11-9.

Setting up the remaining option buttons requires numeric rather than color input.
Figure 11-10.

The remaining controls require a bit of added work. Let's look at the CircleSquare property control cbCircleSquare. In this case, you don't want to assign a specific number or color to the property. What you want to do is set the value of the CircleSquare property to true or false depending on whether cbCircleSquare is checked. You'll still select the Click entry under cbCircleSquare and the CircleSquare property under DepictIt—that part hasn't changed. However, when you click on Insert Action, you'll see a dialog asking whether you want to set CircleSquare to true or false. In this case you'll click Custom, then type **cbCircleSquare.Value**, as shown in Figure 11-11. Notice that all of the other selections are the same as before.

11

You still need to define nine text boxes: tbPenWidth, tbX1, tbX2, tbX3, tbX4, tbY1, tbY2, tbY3, and tbY4. Setting up the script for these controls works just like the cbCircleSquare control described in the previous paragraph. The only difference is that you need to select the Change event for each control rather than the Click event, as shown in Figure 11-12. Notice that this figure also shows how the custom entry for each of these controls would look.

You'll need to define a default action when using Script Wizard to create the CircleSquare property script.
Figure 11-11.

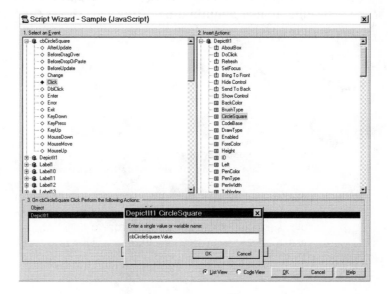

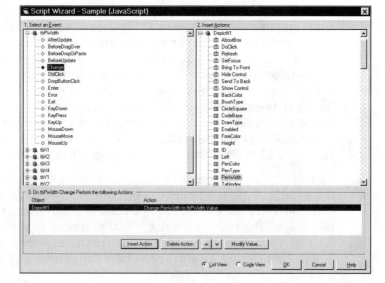

The remaining controls use the Change event rather than the Click event.
Figure 11-12.

That's all there is to setting up this layout. Get out of Script Wizard and save your layout. You'll need to insert the layout into an HTML page and add a heading to it as a minimum. Listing 11-9 shows the HTML code for the sample page.

Listing 11-9

```
<HTML>
<HEAD>
<TITLE>DepictIt Control Test</TITLE>
</HEAD>
<BODY>

<!-Display a heading.->
<CENTER><H2>A Sampling of Graphics Primitives</H2></CENTER>

<!-Display the layout.->
<OBJECT CLASSID="CLSID:812AE312-8B8E-11CF-93C8-00AA00C08FDF"
    ID="Sample_alx" STYLE="LEFT:0;TOP:0">
    <PARAM NAME="ALXPATH" REF VALUE="http://aux/DepictIt/Sample.alx">
</OBJECT>

</BODY>
</HTML>
```

We can finally see what this example looks like in action. Figure 11-13 shows the example control as it would look in an HTML layout. The appearance of this control will vary slightly depending on which version of Windows you're using. You'll also notice some differences when using the control in either a Visual C++ or Visual Basic program, since those environments offer additional capabilities that Internet Explorer doesn't offer. This is a good utility for you to use when you want to see the effects of using various drawing controls in various situations. You could even extend it to provide additional testing capabilities.

NOTE: Instead of the usual two- or three-message dialog sequence that you get when accessing an ActiveX control directly from an HTML page, using an HTML layout only displays one or two messages. The first message usually asks if you want to download the required controls—you won't see this message if all the controls are already loaded on your local hard drive. The second message will ask if you want to use the ActiveX controls on the layout. Just answer Yes to get past this dialog.

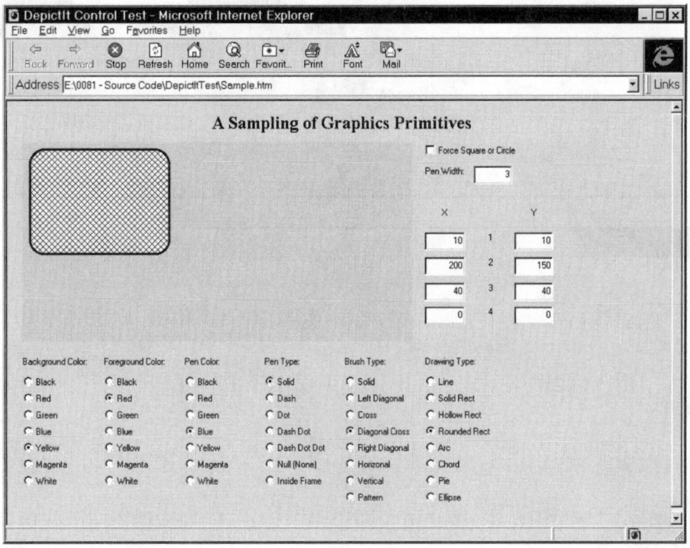

The DepictIt control comes in handy for making a utility program that determines the effects of various drawing control parameter choices.

Figure 11-13.

Chapter 12

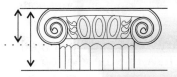

Data Entry and ActiveX

If you talk to many people about data entry, their first response will include something about database management. However, such a narrow view of data entry would limit you in ways that you really wouldn't think about at first. Data entry takes a variety of forms on a computer. For example, every time you visit one of the search sites on the Internet, what you're really looking at is a data entry form.

While most data entry forms either query a database or add to its contents, there are at least a few exceptions. There's at least one site out there that provides a financial calculator. You type in some figures; it provides output in the form of a chart showing your payments over the next few years. Such a calculator would neither have to query a database, nor add to its contents. Of course, this is just one example. Another example is some of the game programs you'll find on the

Internet. They accept input from the user and provide output in the form of game movement. While it could be argued that a state-of-the-art game would necessarily require some database interaction, you could potentially build one without it (consider card games as an example).

Whatever your reason for creating data entry forms, and whatever the source or destination of the information, they all have one thing in common: somewhere along the way the user will make some selections or type some information, then click a submit key to make the input permanent. To provide that kind of input, you have to add controls to a form that allow the user to enter information. Most user manuals call the inputs *fields*. Though some platforms might use another term, we'll use fields here as well.

Chapter 4 showed you the abundance of HTML-specific <INPUT> tags at your disposal for creating data input fields on a form. However, those tags have quite a few limitations that become obvious after a few minutes of using them to anyone experienced in using a RAD programming environment. For example, there aren't a lot of different kinds of pushbuttons—you get one type and that's it. ActiveX controls can provide you with a wealth of different pushbutton types. (We looked at an example of how to create these controls in both Chapter 2 and Chapter 11.) The same problem occurs with every other kind of input control you'll find provided with HTML. For example, working with combo boxes can become a real chore after a while. In addition, trying to add online help is going to become an exercise in frustration for the most part.

Make sure you take a look at Appendix A for additional ideas on where to find controls.

This is one of the few chapters in this third section of the book where we won't create any new controls. Instead, we'll look at the variety of controls provided with ActiveX Control Pad and see how to use them in different ways. The importance of this chapter is that it helps you understand when you don't need to reinvent the wheel to get what you want. (Up to this point, the idea may have been that ActiveX technology is so new that there isn't anything available for early adopters to use right off the shelf.) Our main focus will be the HTML Layout capability that ActiveX Control Pad provides and the controls that come with the program as a default.

This chapter has two main sections. The first looks at the requirements for creating a basic data entry form that relies exclusively on ActiveX. It's both harder and easier than the same task under HTML. It's harder because you may end up writing more code to get the job done. And it's easier because it will take less time to lay out the basic page, you'll find that you won't have as many problems getting the controls where you want them, and the user-friendly page you'll design will require fewer user support calls. In essence, you'll give up a little extra time in development to create a better prototype faster.

The second section shows you the benefit of enhancing your form using VBScript or JavaScript. The idea is to get as much of the processing done as possible before you send the information to your Web server. In fact, that's one of the biggest benefits of using ActiveX controls. You can process most of the information on the user's machine, then send only the finished product back to the Web server. Not only does this reduce Internet traffic, but it means that your server will have less of a burden as well. You'll be able to handle more users from the same site.

TIP: Any time you see a site that asks for your name and address, look at the underlying HTML code to see if it uses a mailbox as a destination. You might be surprised at the number of sites that do this. More importantly, you'll probably gain some invaluable methods to make the job of using this technique on your own site a lot easier.

12

The Basic Data Entry Form

Any form of data entry—whether you want to find a location on the Internet or answer a questionnaire—has to begin with a data entry form. Let's begin by looking at the controls that Microsoft provides with ActiveX Control Pad and the types of capabilities they give you. Table 12-1 provides a complete list of these controls and tells you something about what you can do with them.

The control names listed in Table 12-1 are the ones you'll see listed in the Insert ActiveX Control list box—the Microsoft name appears in parenthesis next to the actual name.

Form Aesthetics and Usability Considerations

Now that you have some idea of what controls are available—at least as part of ActiveX Control Pad—let's take a look at a basic form. Begin by opening ActiveX Control Pad and creating a new HTML layout. (We created a dummy HTML layout for testing the simple ActiveX control in Chapter 2 and for filling a combo box using JavaScript in Chapter 7, so we won't look at every detail of creating the page itself in this section.) What you should see is the layout page and the toolbar available for filling it with controls.

Control	Capability
ActiveMovie Control Object (ActiveMovie Control)	ActiveMovie allows you to play various types of multimedia files, including WAV, AVI, and Apple QuickTime file formats. The control uses a whole series of filters to provide playback capability. For example, six filters are used to play an MPEG file: source (reads data from disk), splitter (separates the video and audio), video transform (decompresses the video), video rendering (displays the video onscreen), audio transform (decompresses the audio), and audio rendering (sends the audio to the speaker). The control itself is active when you place it on an HTML page. All you really need to provide are a filename and a CODEBASE to make the control work properly on your Web site. Most of the controls you'll use are either on or off. For example, you can choose whether or not to display the position and selection controls. Hiding controls from the user doesn't mean they're inaccessible, you simply modify them with code instead of allowing the user to do so directly. You can also control specific playback environmental factors such as the size of the video screen. Unfortunately, only three methods are available: run, pause, and stop. Microsoft hadn't implemented the fast forward, seek, and rewind methods at the time of this writing (meaning you'll want to keep auto rewind enabled).
Microsoft ActiveX Hot Spot Control 1.0 (HotSpot Control)	A hot spot is a defined region on an HTML layout or page. In essence, hot spots are the ActiveX equivalent of image maps—you can use them to define actions for a specific area of an image—for example, going to another Web site. However, there's more to these controls than you may initially think. Like some of the other controls provided with ActiveX Control Pad, this one supports special mouse icon features, including the use of custom pictures. You can also visually place a hot spot control, which makes them fairly easy to use. Hot spots also sense mouse move, enter, and exit events, so you can use them to add bubble help to pushbuttons, text boxes, and other controls on the HTML layout. Naturally, they sense standard mouse events such as click and double-click.

ActiveX Controls Provided with ActiveX Control Pad

Table 12-1.

Control	Capability
Microsoft ActiveX Image Control 1.0 (Image Control)	This is a standard image display control. It contains all the usual features, including the ability to stretch, clip, or zoom the image. Unlike many of the other controls provided with ActiveX Control Pad, this one doesn't provide any special mouse features. However, the image control does sense mouse move, enter, and exit events, so you can use it to add bubble help to pushbuttons, text boxes, and other controls on the HTML layout. Naturally, it senses standard mouse events such as click and double-click.
Microsoft Forms 2.0	All Microsoft Forms controls provide some unique features that won't get covered in the individual descriptions. The first is the ability to choose a special mouse cursor. You can select from the standard cursors or use the custom category of 99. When using the custom category, make sure you include an icon in the MouseIcon property. All of these controls also support pictures. You can even use a picture with check boxes and other standard components. Simply add a picture to the Picture property and tell it where to appear with relation to the text, using the PicturePosition property. You can also choose a special effect. Just what values you'll get to choose from is determined by the type of control you want to access. Most of these controls also feature Locked and Enabled properties. A disabled control cannot receive the focus. Locking a control means the user can no longer edit its value. If a control is locked and enabled, it can still receive the focus and initiate events, but the user can't edit its value.
Microsoft Forms 2.0 CheckBox (CheckBox Control)	This is a standard check box control with a few added features. For example, you can choose between a normal true/false check box, or one that supports tri-state values (where a third null value is supported). The tri-state form of the control comes in handy when you need to show that a user selected only part of a particular option (you'll see this in installation programs that allow you to install some features, but not others).

ActiveX Controls Provided with ActiveX Control Pad (*continued*)

Table 12-1.

Control	Capability
Microsoft Forms 2.0 ComboBox (ComboBox Control)	You'll find that this combo box provides all the features that you're used to finding. However, unlike many of the controls you've probably used within a RAD programming environment, you'll have to fill the list of items in during run time. We looked at the procedure for filling a combo box in Chapter 7. Some of the special features of using this control include the ability to use multiple columns of text and column headings (you won't find full support for this second feature when using some browsers). When using multiple columns, you must also specify the column used to provide a value back to the calling application using the BoundColumn property. Make sure you ignore the IMEMode (input method editor mode) property provided with this control unless you're writing applications for the Far East.
Microsoft Forms 2.0 Command Button (Command Button Control)	There isn't anything too special about this command button. It doesn't even provide the ability to select standard button types. It does support the other special features of Microsoft Forms 2.0 controls.
Microsoft Forms 2.0 Frame (Undocumented)	The Frame control works just like it would in any programming environment; you can use it to group items together. The most common use, of course, is to group radio buttons together when a form contains more than one group. One of the special features of this control is the ability to use scrollbars. You could place a lot of controls into a confined area and know that the user can still access them all. Frames can also display pictures in the same way that the Microsoft Forms 2.0 Image control can. There's even a Zoom property for controlling the amount of zoom you get, something the Image control doesn't provide. Finally, this control provides five special effects consistent with its special uses: flat, raised, sunken, etched, and bump.

ActiveX
Controls
Provided
with ActiveX
Control Pad
(*continued*)
Table 12-1.

Control	Capability
Microsoft Forms 2.0 Image (Undocumented)	This ActiveX control provides a superset of the properties provided by the Microsoft ActiveX Image Control 1.0. The main difference between the two controls is that this one embeds the image within the HTML document using the Picture property. The other control uses a PicturePath property to describe the location of the picture you want to use. This control also provides the special features supported by all Microsoft Forms 2.0 controls.
Microsoft Forms 2.0 Label (Label Control)	This is a standard label without any frills other than the special features provided by all Microsoft Forms 2.0 controls.
Microsoft Forms 2.0 ListBox (ListBox Control)	You'll find that this list box provides all the features that you're used to finding. However, unlike many of the controls you've probably used within a RAD programming environment, you'll have to fill the list of items in during run time. We looked at the procedure for filling a combo box in Chapter 7—the procedure for a list box is the same. Some of the special features of using this control include the ability to use multiple columns of text and column headings (you won't find full support for this second feature when using some browsers). When using multiple columns, you must also specify the column used to provide a value back to the calling application using the BoundColumn property. Make sure you ignore the IMEMode (input method editor mode) property provided with this control unless you're writing applications for the Far East.
Microsoft Forms 2.0 MultiPage (Undocumented)	Most RAD programming languages provide a control similar to this one. It displays what equates to a configuration dialog with multiple pages of display area that you can use for various purposes. All you need to do is place the controls you want to display on each page, then write some script to interact with them. This control supports all of the special features that other Microsoft Forms 2.0 controls do. In addition, it supports a special property that's invaluable for Web page work. The Visible property allows you to hide this control until needed. This allows you to use the control as a dialog. You can provide a pushbutton or other triggering mechanism whose only purpose is to set the Visible property to TRUE.

12

ActiveX Controls Provided with ActiveX Control Pad (*continued*)
Table 12-1.

Control	Capability
Microsoft Forms 2.0 OptionButton (OptionButton Control)	This is a standard option button control with a few added features. For example, you can choose between a normal true/false option button, or one that supports tri-state values (where a third null value is supported). The tri-state form of the control comes in handy when you need to show that a user selected only part of a particular option (you'll see this in installation programs that allow you to install some features, but not others).
Microsoft Forms 2.0 ScrollBar (ScrollBar Control)	Some controls come without scrollbars attached. This control allows you to attach a scrollbar to any control displayed on an HTML page. This control requires some special handling because it's not actually attached to the control. For example, you need to provide glue code that reacts when specific events occur. You won't find any special features in this control except those associated with Microsoft Forms 2.0 controls as a whole.
Microsoft Forms 2.0 SpinButton (SpinButton Control)	This is a standard double-arrow spin button that you can use to update numeric values or automatically move between predefined choices in a list or text box. Monitoring the SpinUp and SpinDown events will tell you when to change the contents of the control associated with the spin button. You won't find any special features in this control except those associated with Microsoft Forms 2.0 controls as a whole.
Microsoft Forms 2.0 TabStrip (TabStrip Control)	This is for all intents and purposes a replica of the MultiPage control. See the text for that control for details. Some versions of ActiveX Control Pad come with the MultiPage control, others with this control.

ActiveX Controls Provided with ActiveX Control Pad (*continued*)

Table 12-1.

Control	Capability
Microsoft Forms 2.0 TextBox (TextBox Control)	You can use this control for standard text entry, just like any other text box control. However, it offers a few additional features beyond those provided by a standard Microsoft Forms 2.0 control. You can choose what you want to happen when the user enters the control using the EnterFieldBehavior property. For example, you can let the control act as if it were on a standard Windows application using the SelectAll option. The ENTER key normally submits the information in a field to the Web server. The EnterKeyBehavior property allows you to change this to the Windows behavior of moving to the next field on the form. (There's a TabKeyBehavior that changes the default behavior when the user presses the tab key, as well.) You can also make the control act as a password control by entering a character such as "*" in the Password property. Using the MultiLine and ScrollBars properties together allows you to use this control as a text area control. The control even provides the WordWrap property, which allows the user to automatically wrap long lines of text. Make sure you ignore the IMEMode (input method editor mode) property provided with this control unless you're writing applications for the Far East.
Microsoft Forms 2.0 ToggleButton (ToggleButton Control)	This control is more like a check box in button form than anything else. It allows the user to toggle a setting between the TRUE and FALSE states when set up in its standard configuration. You can also configure this button to support tri-state values (where a third null value is supported). The tri-state form of the control comes in handy when you need to show that a user selected only part of a particular option (you'll see this in installation programs that allow you to install some features, but not others).

12

ActiveX
Controls
Provided
with ActiveX
Control Pad
(*continued*)
Table 12-1.

Control	Capability
Microsoft WebBrowser Control (WebBrowser Object)	Unlike most of the controls in this table that perform standard data entry chores that you might find in any programming environment, the WebBrowser control performs an Internet-specific task. You can use this control to browse sites on the Internet, drives on a LAN, or drives on the local machine. Unfortunately, most of the capabilities of this control are only accessible at run time. For example, when you add the control to a page, you won't even see the LocationURL and LocationName properties that allow you to determine the current site (LAN and local drives use a special protocol of "file" in place of http or some other Internet-specific protocol). The Navigate method allows you to move from place to place on the Internet (or on a local drive). There are even special methods—for example, GoBack, GoForward, GoHome, and GoSearch—for navigating the Internet as you would from the browser. Monitoring the OnDownload Begin, OnProgress, and OnDownloadComplete events will allow you to provide the user with visual feedback concerning the current status of some Internet-related task. Needless to say, using this control could allow you to greatly reduce the complexity of getting a user from point A to point B on the Internet. It could also allow you to automate certain tasks for the traveler, such as downloading today's prices from the company's intranet or uploading sales information to a database.

ActiveX Controls Provided with ActiveX Control Pad (*continued*)
Table 12-1.

TIP: The size of the layout you create at the beginning of the process defines the size it will be on the user's display. Use a script to control the size of the user's window, and make it the same size as your layout. This way the user will see a clean layout without any additional material that may have found its way onto the page in other ways. (You can also use this technique to hide controls that you don't want the user to see.)

Filling a blank form with controls shouldn't be any problem if you've been programming for a while. What we'll do in this case is pretty simple. Our sample form will contain six fields corresponding to a user's name and address: FirstName, LastName, Address, City, State, and ZipCode. It will also contain some labels to identify the fields. Finally, we'll add two pushbuttons. The first will allow us to save a value to the cookie—the only file that you can normally save on disk. The second will allow us to read the cookie, essentially retrieving the data that we saved previously. (Don't worry if all this cookie stuff is a tad confusing. We'll look at it in detail in the next section.) Figure 12-1 shows what the sample form should look like when you are finished.

Simply sticking some controls on a page won't get the job done for you. We'll have to go a bit further and configure each of the controls. There are a number of reasons to configure the controls, but let's look at the mechanics first and the theory second. Table 12-2 shows how to configure each of the controls used in this example. (You'll also need to set the CODEBASE property for each control to point to the storage location on your Web server.)

12

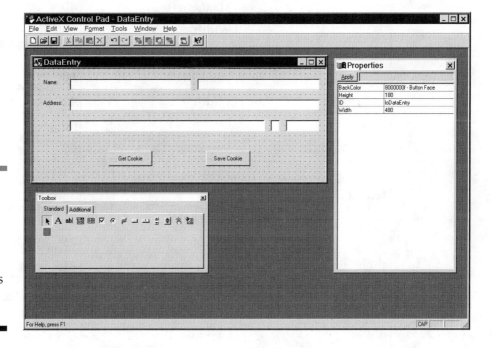

The sample data entry form contains the controls needed to create a simple address book.

Figure 12-1.

TIP: A ratio of 5 pixels to 1 character for text fields normally provides enough space for the user to visualize what the field should look like. For example, if you allow 40 characters for a field in a table, then using a 200-pixel width for the field onscreen should work just fine. Of course, you'll want to make some allowances for aesthetic reasons like lining up the fields. In addition, small fields (those less than 5 characters in length) usually work better using a 7 to 1 ratio.

Control ID	Property	Value
tbFirstName	Left	60
	MaxLength	40
	Width	200
tbLastName	Left	270
	MaxLength	40
	Width	200
tbAddress	Left	60
	MaxLength	80
	Width	410
tbCity	Left	60
	MaxLength	60
	Width	310
tbState	Left	380
	MaxLength	2
	Width	25
tbZIP	Left	415
	MaxLength	10
	Width	55
pbGet	Caption	Get Cookie
	Left	124

Changes for the Sample Data Entry Form

Table 12-2.

Changes for
the Sample
Data Entry
Form
(*continued*)
Table 12-2.

Control ID	Property	Value
pbSet	Caption	Save Cookie
	Left	284
loDataEntry	Height	180
	Width	480

NOTE: Table 12-2 contains an entry for a control ID of loDataEntry. This is the identifier for the data entry form itself. To access the data entry form properties, right-click on the data entry form and select Properties from the context menu. You'll see a Properties dialog containing entries for the control ID, background color, height, and width. Close the Properties dialog by clicking the X button in the upper-right corner.

At this point it's easy to say that most of these changes are mere appearance and really don't count for anything. However, there's more than meets the eye to these changes. Whenever you deal with a database, you're actually dealing with a collection of tables, just like the ones you might create using pencil and paper. Unlike your pencil and paper table though, a database table has some significant limitations. Each column on your table is a field. Database table fields are a specific length—you can add only so many characters to the field before it's full. They also handle only specific data types. If you say that a particular column contains numbers, it won't accept text. Your form has to signify these limits to the user visually and check for them within code. The length of a data entry field onscreen can tell users a lot about the size of the value they can provide. That's why the Address field is roughly twice the size of the FirstName and LastName fields.

Database table limitations aren't the only reason to present a well-formatted data entry form to the user. Aesthetics play an important part in the kind of input you'll receive. If a form looks sloppy, users will likely feel that you really don't care what kind of data input you get from them. In addition, a disorganized form will only serve to confuse users and make it more difficult for them to provide the kind of input you'd like. Finally, you want your electronic form to closely mimic the paper forms they'll replace. Someone used to a particular format (method of entering data) will be more efficient if you maintain that format as much as possible.

Working with Cookies

This chapter will show you one of the more common ways of storing information between sessions—the cookie. So what exactly is a cookie? The short answer is that it's a file that contains setting information. You can define a variable name and assign it a value. In addition, you can set an expiration date for the information, a path to its location, the domain it came from, and whether or not the data is secure. In most cases, the only thing you're really interested in is the variable itself and an expiration date. If you don't set an expiration date, none of the browsers (at least the ones tested for this book) will save the information to disk. The default expiration date and time is right now.

WARNING: Local testing of HTML pages on your machine is an error-prone process when working with cookies. Internet Explorer 3.0 won't save the cookie at all, even if you format the cookie information properly. Netscape will at least save the cookie, but not in the standard format, making it less useful than it could be. For the purposes of this chapter, you must have a functional Web server to act as a host for testing, and you must access that host using a standard URL. In other words, your test setup has to mimic a standard Internet setup, or none of the examples shown here will work properly.

Let's take a look at a very short example of how you can fill a cookie with the approximation of database information. Listing 12-1 shows some JavaScript code that will create the six initial data fields needed for the data entry form we just constructed in the previous section.

Listing 12-1

```
<HTML>
<HEAD>
<TITLE>Cookie Filler</TITLE>
</HEAD>
<BODY>

<!-Display a header.->
<CENTER><H2>Be a Cookie Monster with JavaScript!</H2></CENTER>

<!-This script fills the cookie, then displays its contents.->
<SCRIPT LANGUAGE="JavaScript">
<!--
```

```
// Fill the cookie.
document.cookie="FirstName=Ted;expires=Monday, 30-Sep-96 12:00:00;path=/"
document.cookie="LastName=Smith;expires=Monday, 30-Sep-96 12:00:00;path=/"
document.cookie="Address=2323 Auburn Lane;expires=Monday, 30-Sep-96
12:00:00;path=/"
document.cookie="City=Denver;expires=Monday, 30-Sep-96 12:00:00;path=/"
document.cookie="State=CO;expires=Monday, 30-Sep-96 12:00:00;path=/"
document.cookie="ZIP=77777;expires=Monday, 30-Sep-96 12:00:00;path=/"

// Get the cookie information and parse it.
// Parsing requires two substring method calls: one to get the variable, and
// another to get the value of the variable.
sCookie=document.cookie
sFirstName=sCookie.substring(sCookie.indexOf("FirstName"),
    sCookie.indexOf("LastName"))
sFirstName=sFirstName.substring(sFirstName.indexOf("=") + 1,
    sFirstName.indexOf(";"))

sLastName=sCookie.substring(sCookie.indexOf("LastName"),
    sCookie.indexOf("Address"))
sLastName=sLastName.substring(sLastName.indexOf("=") + 1,
sLastName.indexOf(";"))

sAddress=sCookie.substring(sCookie.indexOf("Address"),
sCookie.indexOf("City"))
sAddress=sAddress.substring(sAddress.indexOf("=") + 1, sAddress.indexOf(";"))

sCity=sCookie.substring(sCookie.indexOf("City"), sCookie.indexOf("State"))
sCity=sCity.substring(sCity.indexOf("=") + 1, sCity.indexOf(";"))

sState=sCookie.substring(sCookie.indexOf("State"), sCookie.indexOf("ZIP"))
sState=sState.substring(sState.indexOf("=") + 1, sState.indexOf(";"))

sZIP=sCookie.substring(sCookie.indexOf("ZIP"), sCookie.length)
sZIP=sZIP.substring(sZIP.indexOf("=") + 1, sZIP.length)

// Display the results of our parsing.
document.write("The cookie now contains these fields: " + sCookie + "<P>")
document.write("The first name is: " + sFirstName + "<P>")
document.write("The last name is: " + sLastName + "<P>")
document.write("The address is: " + sAddress + "<P>")
document.write("The city is: " + sCity + "<P>")
document.write("The state is: " + sState + "<P>")
document.write("The ZIP code is: " + sZIP + "<P>")
```

```
//-->
</SCRIPT>

</BODY>333
</HTML>
```

The coding may look a bit long and complicated, but it really isn't. You can break it into three main sections. The first section saves the cookie using six default variables and associated values. We'll see how these variables come into play in the next section of the book. Notice that each cookie has a very specific format and that the values are presented in a specific order. It's important to follow this order precisely if you want good results with all browsers. There are situations in which one browser will tolerate some variation that another won't. This code stores a cookie with one variable and a specific value for it, an expiration date, and the path information.

NOTE: Some browsers won't save the cookie to disk until it either needs memory or you exit the browser. If you want to inspect a cookie to see how the data gets stored, always create the cookie first, then exit the browser. This will force the browser to save the cookie to disk. If you have trouble getting the browser to actually save the cookie, check your expiration date—you must have one to get a stored disk file. Also look at the order of the various cookie elements. Avoid using the domain attribute supported within CGI scripts; most browsers won't support it within JavaScript.

The second section of the listing reads the cookie, parses the information it contains, and places the parsed value into a local variable. This may not be the most elegant way to get the job done, but it's easy to figure out and even easier to read. If you wanted to, you could probably combine everything into one statement rather than using several lines of code as shown in the example, but this would reduce the readability of your code and make it difficult for other people to work with you. Notice that JavaScript supports a standard substring() method. This method requires a starting and ending point within the string. There are several ways of deriving a starting and ending point. In this case we use the indexOf() method to find a specific keyword within the string. You could also provide a value of 0 for the beginning of the string. Notice that we use the length property of the string to provide an ending value. This is an important thing to remember because the last cookie won't have an ending semicolon (;).

The third section of our example simply displays the whole cookie, then the parsed cookie values. At this point you should note a few gotcha's about working with cookies. First, there is no way to specify an order of storage within a real cookie environment. This example shows what might be termed a rigged setup to simplify the code. In the real world you're going to need a slightly more complex parsing mechanism unless you can guarantee precise control over the cookie.

Another problem you'll experience when working with cookies is the way that browsers store them. You can't be guaranteed any particular storage method or location. The only thing that you're guaranteed is that you'll get the cookie back in a specific way, provided you use supported methods to access it. Let's look at the way two browsers store cookies. Figure 12-2 shows the Netscape method. Notice that all the cookies for every site you'll ever visit are stored in a single text file named COOKIES.TXT. This is the reason why Navigator can support local cookie storage—the name of the site gets left out of the cookie entry, but the information itself remains intact. The cookie is normally stored in the main Navigator folder, but there's no guarantee that Netscape will maintain this location.

WARNING: Never tamper with the contents of the cookie file using a text or other editor. The cookie file normally contains control codes that are difficult to see. In addition, some browsers index the cookie file, and any change in entry length will cause the browser to look in the wrong place for information. Accessing the cookie outside the normal environment will likely cause damage to the file. In most cases you can repair the damage by erasing the cookie and allowing the browser to create a new one.

Microsoft uses an entirely different technique than Netscape does for storing the cookie—even the storage method is different. Look in the Cookies folder that normally appears under your main Windows directory, and you'll find several files. Two of these files (the ones with the DAT extension) index the cookie files that you'll find in the directory. The cookie files use a special naming scheme to make them user- and site-specific. You'll see a user name, followed by an at (@) sign, followed by the name of the site. The advantage to this scheme is that each user maintains his own set of cookies. In addition, the individual file approach makes it less likely that the cookie will get damaged. There may be a performance gain as well, but it's slight in most cases. The disadvantage is that you could literally find yourself drowning in cookie files after a while. In addition, this method of cookie storage is very disk space intensive, since each cookie will consume far more hard disk space than it actually uses—at least on an uncompressed drive. You also can't view the cookie file using a standard text editor. Fortunately, you can

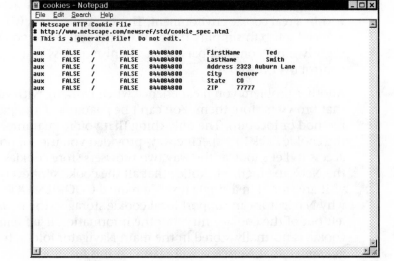

use the Quick View option on the file's context menu to see the contents of the cookie file, as shown here. (A Word for Windows-compatible editor will also work.)

Cookie storage locations and methods notwithstanding, you'll get similar results from the JavaScript code in Listing 12-1 no matter what browser you use. Figure 12-3 shows the results of using the script with Internet Explorer.

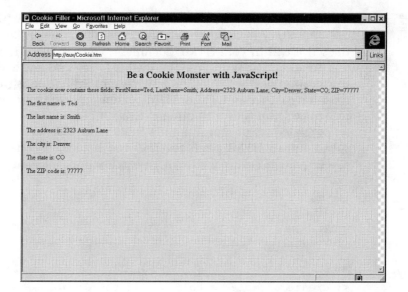

The cookie now contains these fields: FirstName=Ted; LastName=Smith; Address=2323 Auburn Lane; City=Denver; State=CO; ZIP=77777

The first name is: Ted

The last name is: Smith

The address is: 2323 Auburn Lane

The city is: Denver

The state is: CO

The ZIP code is: 77777

There's only one cookie for every document as far as JavaScript is concerned.
Figure 12-3.

12

Notice that even though both browsers store each cookie separately within the cookie file, you get one big lump of text when you retrieve it. That's the reason for all of the parsing code in our scripting example. You can store as many variables as you want, but you'll always get them back in one big string.

Data Entry Forms with Scripts

ActiveX controls will definitely allow you to dress up the appearance of your Web site forms. However, they can only do so much in regard to processing the information you receive unless you develop special utility controls like the ones we saw in Chapter 9. But before you break out the C compiler and start committing your ideas to code, you might want to consider a simpler alternative. Scripts, like the ones we looked at in Chapter 7, can do all of the processing work for you and even pass the data on to your Web site.

What we'll look at in this section is the script required to make the Get Cookie and Set Cookie buttons work. Actually, we've done a lot of the work already, but there are still a few tricks you'll need to use to make the example work with an HTML layout. The first thing you'll need to do, though, is to insert the layout we created in the previous section into an HTML document. You'll also want to add a title to the page, but nothing else of any significance. Listing 12-2 shows the code for the HTML page in this example.

TIP: You can build libraries of scripts if you want. Rather than including the script within your HTML document, you can place it within a separate file. To access the script, use the <SCRIPT> tag and add a SRC attribute with the location of the script. The only current limitation is that your script file must have either an HTM or HTML extension—most browsers won't recognize script files with other extensions. Maintaining one script or one set of related scripts per script file could reduce the amount of time you spend putting HTML pages together and encourage code reuse.

Listing 12-2

```
<HTML>
<HEAD>
<TITLE>Data Entry Design</TITLE>
</HEAD>
<BODY>

<!-Create a table to hold all of the display elements.->
<TABLE WIDTH=100%>

<!-Display a heading centered in the first row.->
<TR>
    <TD><CENTER><H2>An Example of Data Entry Design</H2></CENTER>

<!-Display the layout centered in the second row.->
<TR>
    <TD><CENTER><OBJECT
        CLASSID="CLSID:812AE312-8B8E-11CF-93C8-00AA00C08FDF"
        ID="DataEntry_alx" STYLE="LEFT:0;TOP:0">
        <PARAM NAME="ALXPATH" REF VALUE="http://aux/DataEntry.alx">
    </OBJECT></CENTER>
</TABLE>

</BODY>
</HTML>
```

This page is fairly ordinary. It does provide a few new tricks for you to try out. Notice that we create a single-column, two-row table to display the form and heading. Both rows center the information automatically as the user changes the window size. This is one of the better ways of keeping everything lined up as you display information from both tags and layouts onscreen.

Once you insert the layout and complete the necessary formatting, you can concentrate on adding some code to those two pushbuttons: Get Cookie and Set Cookie. Of course, this means adding some code to the ALX file used by the layout. Accessing the code for the layout is very easy. Just right-click on the layout and select View Source Code from the context menu. Listing 12-3 shows the complete source for the layout, including all of the controls, so that you can check your layout for problems if necessary. Normally, the source code generated by ActiveX Control Pad would start with the <DIV> tag shown immediately after the script code in Listing 12-3. The <DIV> tag differentiates an HTML layout from a standard HTML page. An older browser will simply ignore the entire page when it sees the <DIV> tag. Add only the script code to your layout.

Listing 12-3

The complete source code is provided for verification purposes and for anyone not using ActiveX Control Pad.

12

```
<!-This script is for the Get Cookie button.->
<SCRIPT FOR="pbGet" EVENT="Click()">
<!--
   // Get the cookie and parse the information it contains.
   sCookie=window.document.cookie
   sFirstName=sCookie.substring(sCookie.indexOf("FirstName"),
      sCookie.indexOf("LastName"))
   sFirstName=sFirstName.substring(sFirstName.indexOf("=") + 1,
      sFirstName.indexOf(";"))

   sLastName=sCookie.substring(sCookie.indexOf("LastName"),
      sCookie.indexOf("Address"))
   sLastName=sLastName.substring(sLastName.indexOf("=") + 1,
sLastName.indexOf(";"))

   sAddress=sCookie.substring(sCookie.indexOf("Address"),
sCookie.indexOf("City"))
   sAddress=sAddress.substring(sAddress.indexOf("=") + 1, sAddress.indexOf(";"))

   sCity=sCookie.substring(sCookie.indexOf("City"), sCookie.indexOf("State"))
   sCity=sCity.substring(sCity.indexOf("=") + 1, sCity.indexOf(";"))

   sState=sCookie.substring(sCookie.indexOf("State"), sCookie.indexOf("ZIP"))
   sState=sState.substring(sState.indexOf("=") + 1, sState.indexOf(";"))

   sZIP=sCookie.substring(sCookie.indexOf("ZIP"), sCookie.length)
   sZIP=sZIP.substring(sZIP.indexOf("=") + 1, sZIP.length)

   // Display the various cookie values.
   tbFirstName.Text = sFirstName
   tbLastName.Text = sLastName
   tbAddress.Text = sAddress
   tbCity.Text = sCity
   tbState.Text = sState
   tbZIP.Text = sZIP
```

```
//-->
</SCRIPT>
<!-This script is for the Get Cookie button.->
<SCRIPT FOR="pbSet" EVENT="Click()">
<!--
    // Fill the cookie.
    document.cookie="FirstName=" + tbFirstName.Text +
        ";expires=Monday, 30-Sep-96 12:00:00;path=/"
    document.cookie="LastName=" + tbLastName.Text +
        ";expires=Monday, 30-Sep-96 12:00:00;path=/"
    document.cookie="Address=" + tbAddress.Text +
        ";expires=Monday, 30-Sep-96 12:00:00;path=/"
    document.cookie="City=" + tbCity.Text +
        ";expires=Monday, 30-Sep-96 12:00:00;path=/"
    document.cookie="State=" + tbState.Text +
        ";expires=Monday, 30-Sep-96 12:00:00;path=/"
    document.cookie="ZIP=" + tbZIP.Text +
        ";expires=Monday, 30-Sep-96 12:00:00;path=/"
//-->
</SCRIPT>
<DIV ID="loDataEntry" STYLE="LAYOUT:FIXED;WIDTH:480pt;HEIGHT:180pt;">
    <OBJECT ID="Label1"
     CLASSID="CLSID:978C9E23-D4B0-11CE-BF2D-00AA003F40D0"
      STYLE="TOP:17pt;LEFT:17pt;WIDTH:33pt;HEIGHT:18pt;ZINDEX:0;">
        <PARAM NAME="Caption" VALUE="Name:">
        <PARAM NAME="Size" VALUE="1164;635">
        <PARAM NAME="FontCharSet" VALUE="0">
        <PARAM NAME="FontPitchAndFamily" VALUE="2">
        <PARAM NAME="FontWeight" VALUE="0">
    </OBJECT>
    <OBJECT ID="Label2"
     CLASSID="CLSID:978C9E23-D4B0-11CE-BF2D-00AA003F40D0"
      STYLE="TOP:50pt;LEFT:17pt;WIDTH:33pt;HEIGHT:18pt;ZINDEX:1;">
        <PARAM NAME="Caption" VALUE="Address:">
        <PARAM NAME="Size" VALUE="1164;635">
        <PARAM NAME="FontCharSet" VALUE="0">
        <PARAM NAME="FontPitchAndFamily" VALUE="2">
        <PARAM NAME="FontWeight" VALUE="0">
    </OBJECT>
    <OBJECT ID="tbFirstName"
     CLASSID="CLSID:8BD21D10-EC42-11CE-9E0D-00AA006002F3"
     CODEBASE="http://aux/controls"
      STYLE="TOP:17pt;LEFT:60pt;WIDTH:200pt;HEIGHT:18pt;TABINDEX:2;ZINDEX:2;">
        <PARAM NAME="VariousPropertyBits" VALUE="746604571">
        <PARAM NAME="MaxLength" VALUE="40">
```

```
        <PARAM NAME="Size" VALUE="7056;635">
        <PARAM NAME="FontCharSet" VALUE="0">
        <PARAM NAME="FontPitchAndFamily" VALUE="2">
        <PARAM NAME="FontWeight" VALUE="0">
   </OBJECT>
   <OBJECT ID="tbLastName"
    CLASSID="CLSID:8BD21D10-EC42-11CE-9E0D-00AA006002F3"
    CODEBASE="http://aux/controls"
      STYLE="TOP:17pt;LEFT:270pt;WIDTH:200pt;HEIGHT:18pt;TABINDEX:3;ZINDEX:3;">
        <PARAM NAME="VariousPropertyBits" VALUE="746604571">
        <PARAM NAME="MaxLength" VALUE="40">
        <PARAM NAME="Size" VALUE="7056;635">
        <PARAM NAME="FontCharSet" VALUE="0">
        <PARAM NAME="FontPitchAndFamily" VALUE="2">
        <PARAM NAME="FontWeight" VALUE="0">
   </OBJECT>
   <OBJECT ID="tbAddress"
    CLASSID="CLSID:8BD21D10-EC42-11CE-9E0D-00AA006002F3"
    CODEBASE="http://aux/controls"
      STYLE="TOP:50pt;LEFT:60pt;WIDTH:410pt;HEIGHT:18pt;TABINDEX:4;ZINDEX:4;">
        <PARAM NAME="VariousPropertyBits" VALUE="746604571">
        <PARAM NAME="MaxLength" VALUE="80">
        <PARAM NAME="Size" VALUE="14464;635">
        <PARAM NAME="FontCharSet" VALUE="0">
        <PARAM NAME="FontPitchAndFamily" VALUE="2">
        <PARAM NAME="FontWeight" VALUE="0">
   </OBJECT>
   <OBJECT ID="tbState"
    CLASSID="CLSID:8BD21D10-EC42-11CE-9E0D-00AA006002F3"
    CODEBASE="http://aux/controls"
      STYLE="TOP:83pt;LEFT:380pt;WIDTH:25pt;HEIGHT:18pt;TABINDEX:5;ZINDEX:5;">
        <PARAM NAME="VariousPropertyBits" VALUE="746604571">
        <PARAM NAME="MaxLength" VALUE="2">
        <PARAM NAME="Size" VALUE="882;635">
        <PARAM NAME="FontCharSet" VALUE="0">
        <PARAM NAME="FontPitchAndFamily" VALUE="2">
        <PARAM NAME="FontWeight" VALUE="0">
   </OBJECT>
   <OBJECT ID="tbZIP"
    CLASSID="CLSID:8BD21D10-EC42-11CE-9E0D-00AA006002F3"
    CODEBASE="http://aux/controls"
      STYLE="TOP:83pt;LEFT:415pt;WIDTH:55pt;HEIGHT:18pt;TABINDEX:6;ZINDEX:6;">
        <PARAM NAME="VariousPropertyBits" VALUE="746604571">
        <PARAM NAME="MaxLength" VALUE="10">
        <PARAM NAME="Size" VALUE="1940;635">
```

12

```
            <PARAM NAME="FontCharSet" VALUE="0">
            <PARAM NAME="FontPitchAndFamily" VALUE="2">
            <PARAM NAME="FontWeight" VALUE="0">
        </OBJECT>
        <OBJECT ID="tbCity"
         CLASSID="CLSID:8BD21D10-EC42-11CE-9E0D-00AA006002F3"
         CODEBASE="http://aux/controls"
           STYLE="TOP:83pt;LEFT:60pt;WIDTH:310pt;HEIGHT:18pt;TABINDEX:7;ZINDEX:7;">
            <PARAM NAME="VariousPropertyBits" VALUE="746604571">
            <PARAM NAME="MaxLength" VALUE="60">
            <PARAM NAME="Size" VALUE="10936;635">
            <PARAM NAME="FontCharSet" VALUE="0">
            <PARAM NAME="FontPitchAndFamily" VALUE="2">
            <PARAM NAME="FontWeight" VALUE="0">
        </OBJECT>
        <OBJECT ID="pbGet"
         CLASSID="CLSID:D7053240-CE69-11CD-A777-00DD01143C57"
         CODEBASE="http://aux/controls"
           STYLE="TOP:132pt;LEFT:124pt;WIDTH:72pt;HEIGHT:24pt;TABINDEX:8;ZINDEX:8;">
            <PARAM NAME="Caption" VALUE="Get Cookie">
            <PARAM NAME="Size" VALUE="2540;847">
            <PARAM NAME="FontCharSet" VALUE="0">
            <PARAM NAME="FontPitchAndFamily" VALUE="2">
            <PARAM NAME="ParagraphAlign" VALUE="3">
            <PARAM NAME="FontWeight" VALUE="0">
        </OBJECT>
        <OBJECT ID="pbSet"
         CLASSID="CLSID:D7053240-CE69-11CD-A777-00DD01143C57"
         CODEBASE="http://aux/controls"
           STYLE="TOP:132pt;LEFT:284pt;WIDTH:72pt;HEIGHT:24pt;TABINDEX:9;ZINDEX:9;">
            <PARAM NAME="Caption" VALUE="Save Cookie">
            <PARAM NAME="Size" VALUE="2540;847">
            <PARAM NAME="FontCharSet" VALUE="0">
            <PARAM NAME="FontPitchAndFamily" VALUE="2">
            <PARAM NAME="ParagraphAlign" VALUE="3">
            <PARAM NAME="FontWeight" VALUE="0">
        </OBJECT>
    </DIV>
```

There are two JavaScript code segments near the top of this listing. The first responds to the Click() event of the Get Cookie button. There are a few things you should notice about this function. First, it gets the cookie by looking at Window.Document.Cookie. You have to add the Window object, or the layout won't find what it needs. Add this same object to the HTML page and you'll get a JavaScript error. The reason for this difference is easy to understand: the layout resides outside of the HTML page in a separate document, so you need to add the additional reference level. It's an important distinction to remember. As far as parsing is concerned, this function uses the same technique as the example in the previous section. Notice that we place the results in the Text property of the various layout text box controls once we parse the cookie.

The second script doesn't contain many surprises. It acts much like the cookie filling example we saw earlier in the chapter. The difference is that instead of using static values, we get them from the Text property of the various text box controls. (By now you should see the reason for changing the control ID properties into something a little more readable.) The actual format for the cookie entries hasn't changed from the previous section, so we won't look at them again here.

It's time to see what this example looks like. Figure 12-4 shows what you should see when you put all the pieces together. If you click on the Get Cookie button, the various text box controls fill with appropriate values from the cookie. Clicking on the Set Cookie button saves those values to the cookie for later use. Since this example sets an expiration date, you should be able to view the contents of the cookies once you exit the browser.

This example not only shows you how to create a data entry form, but it shows how to work with the cookie as well.

Figure 12-4.

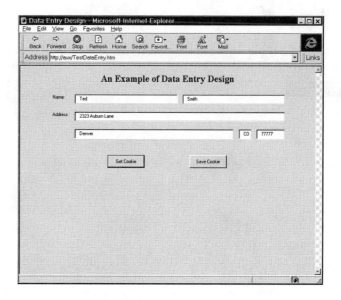

Chapter 13

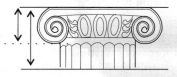

The Database Connection

For some people, the whole purpose of setting up a Web page is either the collection or dissemination of data. For example, you may have a Web site set up for the sales representatives in your company. One page may contain the latest prices on items that your company sells. A second page could have the latest company news, while a third may allow the salesperson to enter yesterday's invoices. Unlike any other programming example that we've discussed in the book so far, this kind of activity requires a database connection. If you haven't figured it out already, we're going to discuss database connectivity in this chapter.

There are several ways of providing access to a database when using a browser—most of which don't require the use of strange-looking scripting files. The following sections describe some of the more common techniques—most of which rely on some form of ActiveX to get the job done (though we'll discuss one non-ActiveX method for displaying data as well). If you plan to use these techniques, make sure you pay particular attention to the second section of the chapter, "Understanding the Objects in Data Access Objects (DAO)."

NOTE: All of the examples in this chapter were written using Access Version 7.0 as the database manager. The sample database contains a simple name and address listing, though you could use just about any type of database by extending the sample code.

You'll get to see an actual programming example in the section, "A Practical Example of Using DAO." This example focuses on using DAO within an HTML page. We won't access the data the way most people are used to doing it. This example will use a combination of standard HTML, some VBScript, and a few special objects to get the job done. Although this method is a tad limited when it comes to accessing mainframe databases or older databases that don't support ODBC (open database connectivity), it works fine for just about everything else.

This chapter features a second example that shows how to access data using a more complex, yet more aesthetically pleasing, method. It uses an HTML layout instead of placing data right on the HTML page. You might think that the two processes are essentially the same, based on the other examples so far in the book. In actuality, you have to go through several extra steps to get data access to work from an HTML layout. The results may be worth it for complex layouts though, because you have more control over the appearance of the page when using an HTML layout.

NOTE: The examples in this chapter assume you have a full-fledged copy of Microsoft Access at your disposal. The chapter also assumes that you've used Access to create at least one or two small projects.

We won't leave C++ out of the picture. The third example shows how you can use some of the new ActiveX controls provided with Visual C++ 4.2 to provide added functionality to your applications with very little work. The whole secret to this new functionality is the Microsoft RemoteData Control. Unfortunate as it may seem, this control won't currently work on an HTML page—let's hope Microsoft will figure out a way of fixing this problem with the next release of Visual C++.

NOTE: You must have Visual C++ 4.2 installed on your machine to use the third example in this book. In addition, you'll need Access 7.0 or another ODBC-compatible database manager (though the actual database manager doesn't matter in this case). Finally, you'll need to install the OLE controls provided with Visual C++ 4.2, since this particular example features two of the new controls provided with that product.

Using the HREF Anchor Technique

Ask the typical Webmaster about the requirements for setting up even the simplest database connection and you'll hear about endless scripts, hours of testing time, and even more complaints from users than usual. Fortunately, things are changing for the better for people who use a LAN instead of a mainframe to store their data (even some mainframe setups can benefit from the technique shown in this section). Creating a database connection doesn't have to be a heartbreaking task filled with endless scripts, especially when it comes to disseminating data. If you're setting up an intranet, where you can be certain of what kind of software each machine will have, you could simply create a link to the company's database using an HREF anchor tag. For example, the following code would allow you to open an Access database called MyData.MDB—the code assumes that users have Access installed on their machines.

13

```
<A HREF="http://aux/files/MyData.MDB">Test Access File</A><P>
```

Needless to say, you don't want to give access to the entire database using the HREF, so the database manager you choose has to provide programming capabilities. Some products, such as Access, support a form of auto-execution capability. This means that you could build a read-only query form into the database and have it auto-execute as part of the database loading process when the user clicks on the tag. Figure 13-1 shows a typical example of such a form for a name and address database.

NOTE: Refer to the manuals that come with your database manager to determine whether it offers an auto-execute capability. Make sure you provide any required macros or other required forms of code in addition to the read-only form.

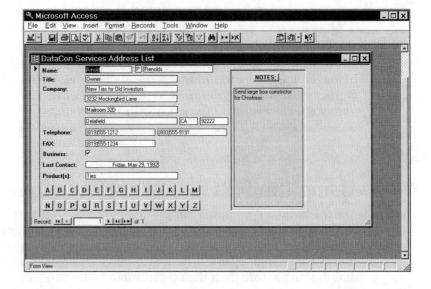

A query form can present a subset of data to the user in a way that prevents accidental changes.

Figure 13-1.

You don't have to lock everyone out of the database. A few more adjustments would add a password requirement for access to anything outside this form. Products such as Access support this capability through built-in utilities; other database managers require that you build this capability in through coding. Average users would only see the subset of data you wanted them to see, and the read-only nature of the form would prevent them from modifying anything; yet a manager could still access the data for editing. This kind of setup is perfect for a database of prices for salespeople on the road. A side benefit of this approach is that they could choose to download the database to their local machines on a regular basis (whatever the price change strategy of your company would require) —saving time and bandwidth. (Internet Explorer automatically asks if you want to open or save the file; Netscape Navigator allows you to right-click on the HREF link to perform the same task using a context menu option.)

Unfortunately, the HREF setup we've just looked at only works with smaller databases (usually within the 200 KB or lower range for dial-up connections). Imagine trying to download a 1 GB (or larger) database from the company's Web site if you're a salesperson on the road. Not only is it unlikely that the user would have enough free disk space to hold the database in the first place, but who would want to wait that long to find out that widgets have increased in price by two cents?

One way around this problem is to program the database manager to create a downloadable subset of the data in the database. Once you create the required code, a simple execute statement would take care of weekly maintenance for you (including the updating of the subset database). This works just fine for data that doesn't change a lot. For example, if your company updates prices monthly (or even weekly), you could probably get by with an HREF to display things like price lists that don't require data changes at the client machine. The best thing about creating a data subset is that it no longer matters where the original data resides. You could output an SDF (standard delimited file) from a mainframe database, load it into Access, and then use that data subset from an intranet without using any scripts.

Before you use this method, think ahead. It becomes pretty apparent after a few attempts at getting large quantities of data to the user that you'll have to come up with something better than a simple HREF if you have a lot of information to manage. That's what the rest of this chapter is all about. It answers the question, What do you do when a simple method like using an HREF link won't get the job done? However, it's equally important to keep this method in mind, since it works with every browser out there and requires very little effort on the part of the Webmaster to maintain.

13

TIP: If you can't find everything you need to get your database application up and running at one of the Microsoft Web sites, check out their directory of other sites at http://www.microsoft.com/activex/actx-gen/connect.htm. You'll find links there to some of the more common ActiveX vendors, many of which cater to the database programmer, since databases are such an important part of the business world. (A good grid control is one of the things lacking in the current Microsoft offerings, and some of these sites provide just what you'll need to get around the problem.)

Understanding the Objects in Data Access Objects (DAO)

There's a "magic" file hiding on your hard drive—at least it's magic when used to access a database remotely. Look in the Program Files\Common Files\Microsoft Shared\DAO folder on your machine and you'll see a file named DAO3032.DLL. This innocuous looking file does a lot more for you when it comes to data access than you might think. Let's look at why.

Open the OLEView utility. Click on the + sign next to the All Objects entry. Within this list you'll find a set of DAO objects like the ones shown in Figure 13-2. Notice that there are ten different DAO objects shown in the figure, though the actual number could vary on your machine. The most important of those objects—at least as far as this book is concerned—is DAO.DBEngine. This is the object that allows you to access a database remotely. If you look at the InprocServer32 entry, you'll see the DAO3032.DLL mentioned previously.

Defining DAO

So, what precisely is DAO? The short definition is that it's both a new and an old object-oriented database access technology. (Object oriented in this case probably won't meet with most programmers' definition of the term.) Microsoft has been using DAO for years—both Access and Visual Basic use DAO as the basis for data access at a low level. The new part of the equation is that, like the Microsoft Office Binder technology that has finally seen the light of day as ActiveX Documents, DAO has seen the light of day as an object-oriented means of accessing databases. Microsoft recently provided documentation for DAO in Visual C++ 4.2, along with the classes required to use it.

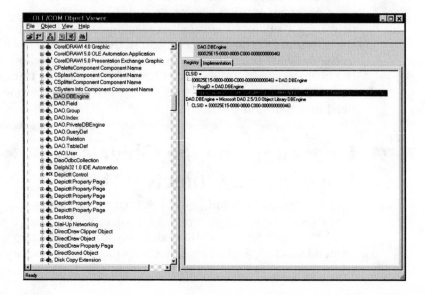

OLEView shows why the DAO3032.DLL file is so important to a Webmaster.
Figure 13-2.

The full definition for DAO is a little harder to pin down than the previous paragraph would lead you to believe. According to some of the documentation that Microsoft provides, it's a newer form of ODBC that you should try to use whenever possible. Other sources say that DAO is actually an adjunct to current ODBC technology. Just looking at these two definitions seems confusing. Once the media gets hold of DAO and tries to compare it to ODBC, we should have a real mess. The fact of the matter is that you can access any ODBC database using DAO as long as you have the driver loaded on your machine—the problem is that accessing the same database using ODBC classes is much faster in some cases.

TIP: Accessing a Microsoft-specific file format using DAO is just as fast as using ODBC. So, if you need to access an Excel spreadsheet or an Access database, using DAO doesn't impart any speed penalty. The speed penalty always occurs when you need to go through an ODBC driver to access the data—the driver adds several transition layers to the process.

13

To completely understand what DAO is offering, you need to understand a little about ODBC—the two products share a lot of common features. ODBC is a method for accessing databases. It features the use of a common language, SQL (structured query language), to find the data you need. This language also allows you to perform other standard database management tasks such as transaction tracking and adding new records or deleting old ones. ODBC relies on data source technology—you define a data source using either the ODBC or ODBC 32 icons in the Control Panel (we'll see how to do this in the section entitled "A Practical Example of Using DAO"). The main advantage of using ODBC technology is that you can gain access to information in a database even if the database file format isn't supported by your database manager. It's this connectivity angle that probably adds confusion to the DAO picture. When you look through the section, "A Practical Example of Using DAO," you'll see that you can reference ODBC sources within a DAO function call.

Let's quickly talk about some of the similarities between ODBC and DAO. The first similarity that you'll notice is that ODBC and DAO use nearly identical database and recordset object members. The procedures for performing specific database tasks such as querying datasets or adding records are nearly the same in both technologies as well. Both products also use a recordset object to hold the set of data returned by the database, and you use similar methods to access the data within the recordset. You'll also find that the ODBC and DAO classes use database objects to manage the underlying database management system (DBMS). In fact, the learning curve between ODBC and DAO is almost insignificant.

It may sound like ODBC is a really great technology, but there are a couple of problems with using it. For one thing, if you look through the list of objects shown in Figure 13-2, you won't find any entries for ODBC. The reason is simple: ODBC is more a methodology than an actual product. ODBC relies on SQL statements as a form of communication. It requires you to have a database manager installed to interpret those statements and act on them. For example, you can access a FoxPro database equally well using Access or Delphi (client/server edition) because both provide an ODBC-compatible database manager back end and provide the required FoxPro ODBC driver. Both products can also receive SQL statements and act on them in a predetermined way. DAO doesn't necessarily rely on this kind of technology—it provides the actual access technology. However, it does allow you to use ODBC to access a database file.

Another problem is that ODBC simply won't work with a Web site. The problem with using ODBC for you as a Webmaster is twofold. First, unless you install the database manager, you don't know what kind of capabilities users' machines will possess. They may have a database manager installed, but you don't know how it will work with ODBC. Second, there is no way to ensure the data source is properly configured. Remember that using ODBC requires that you have a properly configured source.

DAO Versus ODBC

So, what does DAO provide other than an object that we can place on a Web page? Let's take a little time to look at the details of how ODBC and DAO interrelate. DAO does provide a lot in the way of functionality, but as previously mentioned, some of that functionality is exactly the same as you would get from ODBC. For example, many DAO classes are the same as their ODBC counterparts, the only difference being the name that they use. Table 13-1 shows where ODBC and DAO provide equivalent functions or classes. This table doesn't show you places where either product provides extended functionality.

ODBC Class or Function	DAO Class or Function
CDatabase	CDaoDatabase
CDatabase::ExecuteSQL	CDaoDatabase::Execute
CFieldExchange	CDaoFieldExchange
CRecordset	CDaoRecordset
CRecordset::GetDefaultConnect	CDaoRecordset::GetDefaultDBName
RFX_Binary	DFX_Binary
RFX_Binary_Bulk	DFX_Binary
RFX_Bool	DFX_Bool
RFX_Bool_Bulk	DFX_Bool
RFX_Byte	DFX_Byte
RFX_Byte_Bulk	DFX_Byte
RFX_Date	DFX_DateTime
RFX_Date_Bulk	DFX_DateTime
RFX_Double	DFX_Double
RFX_Double_Bulk	DFX_Double
RFX_Int	DFX_Short
RFX_Int_Bulk	DFX_Short
RFX_Long	DFX_Long
RFX_Long_Bulk	DFX_Long
RFX_LongBinary	DFX_LongBinary
RFX_Single	DFX_Single
RFX_Single_Bulk	DFX_Single
RFX_Text	DFX_Text
RFX_Text_Bulk	DFX_Text

ODBC Data
Access
Functions and
Their DAO
Equivalents
Table 13-1.

13

There are a few things to note in Table 13-1. First, RFX stands for Record Field eXchange. You need to use these functions with CFieldExchange class objects. DFX stands for Data Field eXchange. You use these functions with CDaoFieldExchange class objects.

The second thing you need to realize is that the ODBC versions of these classes and functions don't handle data values precisely the same way as their DAO equivalents. For example, the RFX_Date_Bulk function uses an array of TIMESTAMP_STRUCT structures, while DFX_DateTime uses the COleDateTime object instead. A COleDateTime object is designed to work with the DATE OLE automation property type in the MFC ClassWizard. What does this mean to you as a Webmaster? If you take another look at the "Creating a Simple Drawing" example in Chapter 11, you'll notice that objects are easier to exchange on a Web page than structures are. If you need to exchange a structure, you have to provide separate properties (and associated code) for each structure member. An object requires a single property and associated code. Notice the special object code in the example program. In this case, we need to move a custom color object (PenColor) using the OLE_COLOR OLE automation property type from one place to another; but the theory is the same for other kinds of objects. There's even a VARIANT OLE automation property type designed especially for that purpose (if the MFC ClassWizard doesn't provide a specific OLE automation property type). Both the DFX_Byte (CByteArray) and DFX_LongBinary (CLongBinary) functions use objects to hold data values as well. Both of these functions are examples of places you'd need to use the VARIANT OLE automation property type.

A third thing you'll notice in Table 13-1 is that ODBC uses separate functions for single value and multiple value transfers (the functions that end in _Bulk are designed for multiple value transfers). DAO only requires one function for each type of transfer. Each of its associated functions can accept single or multiple values.

Finally, DAO provides an additional parameter that allows you to enable or disable MFC's double buffering mechanism for detecting changes in data fields. Normally this double buffering mechanism detects the change and saves you a lot of work in the interim. However, you can disable the double buffering and make the SetFieldDirty and SetFieldNull calls yourself. The advantage here is flexibility. You may want to provide some added level of functionality in your application that would normally require intervention before these functions get called.

Besides the common classes shown in Table 13-1, DAO provides a lot more in the way of classes and functions than ODBC does. For example, many databases provide a currency type field—ODBC doesn't have a function to handle this data type. DAO provides the DFX_Currency function for just this purpose. It uses a COleCurrency object to hold the field data. You'll use this object with the CURRENCY OLE automation property type in the MFC ClassWizard.

NOTE: There are a number of differences in the way DAO and ODBC handle recordsets and datasets. You'll want to spend some time becoming familiar with these differences when moving an application from one environment to the other. For example, even the method of handling the data queried from a database is different. DAO uses the dynaset recordset type as a default, while ODBC uses the snapshot recordset type. In addition, you can never edit the snapshots you get with DAO (they're read-only), while you may be able to edit those retrieved with ODBC, depending on the ODBC driver. This means you can depend on a specific level of functionality when using DAO, while the same can't be said of ODBC.

13

One of the more impressive additions that DAO provides is support for a DDL (data definition language). Unlike ODBC, you can use DAO to create databases and define tables through the use of a DDL. Using a DDL is also easier in some cases when it comes to complex operations. Most important of all, a DDL gives you better control over the database—it provides much needed flexibility when performing some types of operations, such as a join.

Understanding Double Buffering

The previous section mentioned the double buffering the DFX functions provide—it simply stated that using double buffering reduces the amount of work you have to do when creating controls for use on the Internet. We didn't talk very much about exactly what double buffering is or what it does for you. When your control or Web page uses double buffering, it actually retains an extra copy of the entire dataset locally as it sends the information to the Web server. A dataset is the sum of all the data retrieved from the server or added to the database as new records. Whenever the user makes a change to any data element, MFC compares the two copies of the dataset. It uses this comparison as the basis for knowing what data has changed and which changes to send to the Web server. Not using this methodology means that you'll need to make additional function calls to tell MFC which data has changed.

Obviously, you don't get something for nothing. Using double buffering does reduce the amount of code you need to write and ensures that all changes to the dataset actually get recorded at the Web site. The convenience factor is a big plus for using double buffering. However, you'll find that there are two negative points as well. The first thing you need to consider is the additional memory required to implement double buffering. This may not be a problem with small datasets, but it could cause significant problems when using large ones. In addition, you need to consider the housekeeping required to maintain two sets of data. These added calls reduce system efficiency by adding function call overhead and could make the Web site unnecessarily sluggish. You must also remember the added amount of bandwidth the calls will consume since the connection you'll want to make is over the Internet in most cases.

 TIP: Some types of data aren't double buffered by default. For example, variable length data usually isn't double buffered. Double buffering is always a good idea from the programmer's perspective, but Microsoft turned it off with some data classes for a good reason. Adding double buffering support can greatly reduce overall performance in some cases. In addition, you'll greatly increase the risk of suffering out-of-memory problems or other types of memory-induced errors as a result of using double buffering. The two copies of your data consume (obviously) twice as much memory, plus an additional amount for housekeeping. Large data elements will definitely use up system memory that could be used for other purposes. So, while you may want to turn double buffering on for an icon field, turning it on for a large bitmap probably isn't a good idea.

Because double buffering is such a potentially helpful option to the programmer, Microsoft gives you a lot of flexibility in turning it off or on. You can change the double buffering setting at both the field and the recordset levels. The m_bCheckCacheForDirtyFields variable allows you to set double buffering at the recordset level. A value of AFX_DAO_ENABLE_FIELD_CACHE sets double buffering on for every field type except the variable length field types of binary, long binary, and text—you still have to set double buffering for variable length fields at the field level. Setting double buffering off at the recordset level disables it for all fields in the recordset. As mentioned earlier, you set field-level double buffering using the special parameter provided by each of the DFX functions in Table 13-1. A value of AFX_DAO_ENABLE_FIELD_CACHE enables double buffering support.

Two function calls are specifically affected by double buffering: CDaoRecordset::Edit() and CDaoRecordset::AddNew(). Every time you edit the fields of the current record or add a new record to the recordset, DAO takes the current double buffering setting into account. You can reduce the impact of these calls by simply retrieving only the records you need. In addition, retrieving only the fields you use on a consistent basis, then using the CDaoRecordset::GetFieldValue() to get the values of fields that you only use on an occasional basis, will provide an additional savings in overhead.

A Practical Example of Using DAO

We could pursue a lot of different example programs at this point, but since this is an ActiveX book, let's look at what you would need to do to implement DAO on a Web page directly. (The next section, "Data Access in an HTML Layout," will show another technique that gives you more control over the appearance of the page, but you have to do more work to get it.) The first thing you'll want to do is open ActiveX Control Pad and create a new HTML page.

The question on your mind about now is how you'll even gain access to DAO. Even though it appears in OLEView under the All Objects category (see Figure 13-2), it won't show up in the Insert ActiveX Control dialog shown here. (You access this dialog by using the Edit | Insert ActiveX Control command.)

13

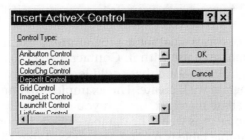

This is one of the cases that we talked about at the beginning of the book (Chapter 4) where you'll need to create an <OBJECT> tag by hand. In some situations you'll want to perform some type of complex operation, and ActiveX Control Pad just won't provide the capability you need. This is one of them—it only provides access to ActiveX controls, not all of the objects installed on your machine. The following source code shows how you would format the <OBJECT> tag.

```
<!-Insert the DAO object into our Web page.->
<!-This isn't an ActiveX control.->
<OBJECT ID="DAO"
   CLASSID="clsid:00025E15-0000-0000-C000-000000000046"
   CODEBASE="DAO3032.DLL">
</OBJECT>
```

Getting this <OBJECT> tag in place is easy. All you need to do is highlight the DAO.DBEngine entry in OLEView. Now use the Object | Copy HTML <OBJECT> Tag to Clipboard command in the OLEView utility to copy the DAO <OBJECT> tag to the Clipboard. You can then simply paste it into ActiveX Control Pad. The pasted tag doesn't quite contain everything you'll need. Make sure you add a CODEBASE attribute to the tag as well (though this isn't strictly necessary unless you want to allow the user to download the required files from your Web site).

TIP: Even though you could allow a user to download DAO3032.DLL and its associated files, the cost of doing so is fairly prohibitive. DAO3032.DLL weighs in at 473 KB, and the associated files bring the total up to 488 KB. Even though this is a lot smaller than most database managers out there today, it's still more than most users will be willing to download. Should you decide to use this technology on a Web site, you'll need to ascertain that users have a Windows platform and that they're actually willing to wait to download the needed files.

Since this is a database programming example, we'll also need an example database to use with it. Contact managers are a common database application—one that could lend itself to a Web site, so that's the kind of program we'll create. The example program will use Microsoft Access as a database manager, though you could easily use other kinds of database managers as well. The database needs to contain at least one table—the example table is named ADDRESS. Table 13-2 shows the field definitions for this table (any fields with asterisks are part of the primary key—highlight them, then use the Edit | Primary Key command to create the primary key). Make sure you format the names as shown if you plan to use the example as written.

Field Name	Data Type	Field Length	Description
LAST_NAME*	Text	30	Contact person's last name.
FIRST_NAME*	Text	20	Contact person's first name.
MIDDLE	Text	1	Contact person's middle initial.
TITLE	Text	40	Contact person's title.
COMPANY*	Text	40	Contact person's company.
ADDRESS1	Text	40	Contact person's address (normally company address).
ADDRESS2	Text	40	Contact person's address (normally company mail route).
CITY	Text	40	City
STATE	Text	20	State
ZIP	Text	10	ZIP code
TELEPHONE1	Text	30	Contact person's main phone number (use 800 number when possible).
TELEPHONE2	Text	30	Contact person's secondary phone number (direct office line or home phone number).
TELEPHONE3	Text	30	Contact person's fax number.
BUSINESS	Yes/No	N/A	Is this a business or personal contact?
NOTES	Memo	N/A	Temporary notes for next phone call or pertaining to current phone call.
CONTACTED	Date/Time	N/A	Last date contacted.
PRODUCT	Text	40	Product produced by the contact's company (use NOTES field if the product list won't fit here, and say "See Notes" in this field).

MyData.MDB
Database
Field Structure
Table 13-2.

13

NOTE: This programming example uses VBScript in place of JavaScript because JavaScript doesn't currently provide the capabilities required to use the DAO function calls properly (at least as of this writing). Perhaps future versions of this scripting language will provide the required support.

If you want to see the data in order, you'll also need to create a query. You can use the Simple Query Wizard to create the query. Just select the Query page, then click New on that page. You'll see the New Query dialog shown here:

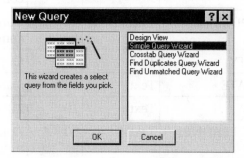

Select the Simple Query Wizard, then click OK. The next page allows you to select a data source and the fields you want to use from that source. Access allows you to select fields from more than one source. Select Table: ADDRESS in the Tables/Queries field. Click the double arrow (>>) to select all of the fields. The first page of the Simple Query Wizard should look like this:

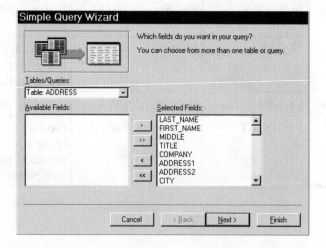

Click Next to go to the next page of the Simple Query Wizard. The next page will ask if you want to create a detail or summary query. Select Detail, then click Next to go to the next page. The last page will ask what you want to call your query and what mode you'd like to open it in. Type **LastName** in the "What title do you want for your query?" field. Click the Modify the Query Design option button. Click Finish to complete the process. Access will open the LastName query in design mode.

Even though our query will select the contents of the entire table for output, it won't sort those contents yet. To place the contents of the ADDRESS table in order, you'll need to change the contents of the Sort entry for the LAST_NAME, FIRST_NAME, and MIDDLE fields to Ascending. The final result should look like the dialog shown in Figure 13-3.

Now it's time to create the HTML page. Begin by inserting a text box or check box for each field in the database that we want to show. In addition, this example will require two buttons, Next and Previous. Table 13-3 provides a complete list of the ActiveX controls you'll need to insert along with the properties you'll need to change.

The LastName query selects all the fields in the ADDRESS table and sorts them by the LAST_NAME, FIRST_NAME, and MIDDLE fields.

Figure 13-3.

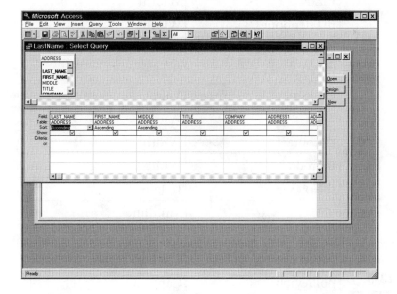

NOTE: Make certain that you set the CODEBASE property of all controls to point to the control storage location on your Internet site. The Control ID column of Table 13-3 contains the ID property value for each control. All tb controls are text boxes, all cb controls are check boxes, and all pb controls are command (push) buttons.

Control ID	Property	Value
tbFirstName	Width	115
tbMiddle	Width	20
tbLastName	Width	115
tbTitle	Width	250
tbCompany	Width	250
tbAddress1	Width	250
tbAddress2	Width	250
tbCity	Width	140
tbState	Width	40
tbZIP	Width	70
tbTelephone1	Width	83
tbTelephone2	Width	83
tbTelephone3	Width	84
cbBusiness	Value	False (0)
	Width	15
tbContacted	Width	70
tbProduct	Width	250
tbNotes	Height	54
	Multiline	True (-1)
	Width	250
pbNext	Caption	Next
pbPrevious	Caption	Previous

ActiveX
Control
Settings for the
DAO Example
Table 13-3.

After you insert the controls, you'll need to add some code to make them work. Listing 13-1 shows the code for this example. Make absolutely certain to add the hand-coded oWorkspace <OBJECT> tag. This is the DAO tag required to make the example work.

Listing 13-1

```
<HTML>
<HEAD>

<SCRIPT LANGUAGE="VBScript">
<!--
'Create any required global objects.
Dim oDB
Dim oRecord
Dim aCurrentRow
Dim iLastRow
Dim iCurrentRow

Sub Window_OnLoad()
    'Open the database.
    SET oDB = oWorkspace.OpenDatabase("http://aux/DAO/MyData.MDB")

    'Open the recordset.
    SET oRecord = oDB.OpenRecordset("LastName")

    'Go to the last record so that we can get the total number of records.
    oRecord.MoveLast
    iLastRow = oRecord.RecordCount

    'Close the recordset and reopen it so we can grab all the records.
    oRecord.Close
    SET oRecord = oDB.OpenRecordset("LastName")

    'Fill our data fields with the first record.
    aCurrentRow = oRecord.GetRows(iLastRow)
    tbLastName.Value = aCurrentRow(0, 0)
    tbFirstName.Value = aCurrentRow(1, 0)
    tbMiddle.Value = aCurrentRow(2, 0)
    tbTitle.Value = aCurrentRow(3, 0)
    tbCompany.Value = aCurrentRow(4, 0)
    tbAddress1.Value = aCurrentRow(5, 0)
    tbAddress2.Value = aCurrentRow(6, 0)
    tbCity.Value = aCurrentRow(7, 0)
    tbState.Value = aCurrentRow(8, 0)
    tbZIP.Value = aCurrentRow(9, 0)
    tbTelephone1.Value = aCurrentRow(10, 0)
```

13

```
        tbTelephone2.Value = aCurrentRow(11, 0)
        tbTelephone3.Value = aCurrentRow(12, 0)
        cbBusiness.Value = aCurrentRow(13, 0)
        tbNotes.Value = aCurrentRow(14, 0)
        tbContacted.Value = aCurrentRow(15, 0)
        tbProduct.Value = aCurrentRow(16, 0)

        'Set the current row.
        iCurrentRow = 0
    End Sub

Sub Window_OnUnload()
    'Close the database.
    oDB.Close
End Sub

Sub pbNext_Click()
    'See if we're at the last row.
    If iCurrentRow = iLastRow - 1 Then
        MsgBox("You're at the end of the file.")

    'If not
    Else
        'Go to the next record.
        iCurrentRow = iCurrentRow + 1

        'Fill our data fields with the first record.
        tbLastName.Value = aCurrentRow(0, iCurrentRow)
        tbFirstName.Value = aCurrentRow(1, iCurrentRow)
        tbMiddle.Value = aCurrentRow(2, iCurrentRow)
        tbTitle.Value = aCurrentRow(3, iCurrentRow)
        tbCompany.Value = aCurrentRow(4, iCurrentRow)
        tbAddress1.Value = aCurrentRow(5, iCurrentRow)
        tbAddress2.Value = aCurrentRow(6, iCurrentRow)
        tbCity.Value = aCurrentRow(7, iCurrentRow)
        tbState.Value = aCurrentRow(8, iCurrentRow)
        tbZIP.Value = aCurrentRow(9, iCurrentRow)
        tbTelephone1.Value = aCurrentRow(10, iCurrentRow)
        tbTelephone2.Value = aCurrentRow(11, iCurrentRow)
        tbTelephone3.Value = aCurrentRow(12, iCurrentRow)
        cbBusiness.Value = aCurrentRow(13, iCurrentRow)
        tbNotes.Value = aCurrentRow(14, iCurrentRow)
        tbContacted.Value = aCurrentRow(15, iCurrentRow)
        tbProduct.Value = aCurrentRow(16, iCurrentRow)
    End If
End Sub
```

```
Sub pbPrevious_Click()
    'See if we're at the first row.
    If iCurrentRow = 0 Then
        MsgBox("You're at the beginning of the file.")

    'If not
    Else
        'Go to the previous record.
        iCurrentRow = iCurrentRow - 1

        'Fill our data fields with the first record.
        tbLastName.Value = aCurrentRow(0, iCurrentRow)
        tbFirstName.Value = aCurrentRow(1, iCurrentRow)
        tbMiddle.Value = aCurrentRow(2, iCurrentRow)
        tbTitle.Value = aCurrentRow(3, iCurrentRow)
        tbCompany.Value = aCurrentRow(4, iCurrentRow)
        tbAddress1.Value = aCurrentRow(5, iCurrentRow)
        tbAddress2.Value = aCurrentRow(6, iCurrentRow)
        tbCity.Value = aCurrentRow(7, iCurrentRow)
        tbState.Value = aCurrentRow(8, iCurrentRow)
        tbZIP.Value = aCurrentRow(9, iCurrentRow)
        tbTelephone1.Value = aCurrentRow(10, iCurrentRow)
        tbTelephone2.Value = aCurrentRow(11, iCurrentRow)
        tbTelephone3.Value = aCurrentRow(12, iCurrentRow)
        cbBusiness.Value = aCurrentRow(13, iCurrentRow)
        tbNotes.Value = aCurrentRow(14, iCurrentRow)
        tbContacted.Value = aCurrentRow(15, iCurrentRow)
        tbProduct.Value = aCurrentRow(16, iCurrentRow)
    End If
End Sub
-->
</SCRIPT>

<TITLE>New Page</TITLE>
</HEAD>
<BODY>

<!-Display a heading.->

<CENTER><H2>Accessing a Database From a Web Page Using DAO</H2></CENTER>

<!-Insert the DAO object into our Web page.->
<!-This isn't an ActiveX control.->

<OBJECT ID="oWorkspace"
```

13

```
    CLASSID="CLSID:00025E15-0000-0000-C000-000000000046"
     CODEBASE="DAO3032.DLL">
</OBJECT>

<!-Add some record display objects.->

<CENTER>
<OBJECT ID="tbFirstName" WIDTH=153 HEIGHT=24
 CLASSID="CLSID:8BD21D10-EC42-11CE-9E0D-00AA006002F3"
 CODEBASE="http://aux/controls">
     <PARAM NAME="VariousPropertyBits" VALUE="746604571">
     <PARAM NAME="Size" VALUE="4057;635">
     <PARAM NAME="FontCharSet" VALUE="0">
     <PARAM NAME="FontPitchAndFamily" VALUE="2">
     <PARAM NAME="FontWeight" VALUE="0">
</OBJECT>

<OBJECT ID="tbMiddle" WIDTH=27 HEIGHT=24
 CLASSID="CLSID:8BD21D10-EC42-11CE-9E0D-00AA006002F3"
 CODEBASE="http://aux/controls">
     <PARAM NAME="VariousPropertyBits" VALUE="746604571">
     <PARAM NAME="Size" VALUE="706;635">
     <PARAM NAME="FontCharSet" VALUE="0">
     <PARAM NAME="FontPitchAndFamily" VALUE="2">
     <PARAM NAME="FontWeight" VALUE="0">
</OBJECT>

<OBJECT ID="tbLastName" WIDTH=153 HEIGHT=24
 CLASSID="CLSID:8BD21D10-EC42-11CE-9E0D-00AA006002F3"
 CODEBASE="http://aux/controls">
     <PARAM NAME="VariousPropertyBits" VALUE="746604571">
     <PARAM NAME="Size" VALUE="4057;635">
     <PARAM NAME="FontCharSet" VALUE="0">
     <PARAM NAME="FontPitchAndFamily" VALUE="2">
     <PARAM NAME="FontWeight" VALUE="0">
</OBJECT><P>

<OBJECT ID="tbTitle" WIDTH=333 HEIGHT=24
 CLASSID="CLSID:8BD21D10-EC42-11CE-9E0D-00AA006002F3"
 CODEBASE="http://aux/controls">
     <PARAM NAME="VariousPropertyBits" VALUE="746604571">
     <PARAM NAME="Size" VALUE="8819;635">
     <PARAM NAME="FontCharSet" VALUE="0">
     <PARAM NAME="FontPitchAndFamily" VALUE="2">
     <PARAM NAME="FontWeight" VALUE="0">
</OBJECT><P>
```

```
<OBJECT ID="tbCompany" WIDTH=333 HEIGHT=24
 CLASSID="CLSID:8BD21D10-EC42-11CE-9E0D-00AA006002F3"
 CODEBASE="http://aux/controls">
    <PARAM NAME="VariousPropertyBits" VALUE="746604571">
    <PARAM NAME="Size" VALUE="8819;635">
    <PARAM NAME="FontCharSet" VALUE="0">
    <PARAM NAME="FontPitchAndFamily" VALUE="2">
    <PARAM NAME="FontWeight" VALUE="0">
</OBJECT><P>

<OBJECT ID="tbAddress1" WIDTH=333 HEIGHT=24
 CLASSID="CLSID:8BD21D10-EC42-11CE-9E0D-00AA006002F3"
 CODEBASE="http://aux/controls">
    <PARAM NAME="VariousPropertyBits" VALUE="746604571">
    <PARAM NAME="Size" VALUE="8819;635">
    <PARAM NAME="FontCharSet" VALUE="0">
    <PARAM NAME="FontPitchAndFamily" VALUE="2">
    <PARAM NAME="FontWeight" VALUE="0">
</OBJECT><P>

<OBJECT ID="tbAddress2" WIDTH=333 HEIGHT=24
 CLASSID="CLSID:8BD21D10-EC42-11CE-9E0D-00AA006002F3"
 CODEBASE="http://aux/controls">
    <PARAM NAME="VariousPropertyBits" VALUE="746604571">
    <PARAM NAME="Size" VALUE="8819;635">
    <PARAM NAME="FontCharSet" VALUE="0">
    <PARAM NAME="FontPitchAndFamily" VALUE="2">
    <PARAM NAME="FontWeight" VALUE="0">
</OBJECT><P>

<OBJECT ID="tbCity" WIDTH=187 HEIGHT=24
 CLASSID="CLSID:8BD21D10-EC42-11CE-9E0D-00AA006002F3"
 CODEBASE="http://aux/controls">
    <PARAM NAME="VariousPropertyBits" VALUE="746604571">
    <PARAM NAME="Size" VALUE="4939;635">
    <PARAM NAME="FontCharSet" VALUE="0">
    <PARAM NAME="FontPitchAndFamily" VALUE="2">
    <PARAM NAME="FontWeight" VALUE="0">
</OBJECT>

<OBJECT ID="tbState" WIDTH=53 HEIGHT=24
 CLASSID="CLSID:8BD21D10-EC42-11CE-9E0D-00AA006002F3"
 CODEBASE="http://aux/controls">
    <PARAM NAME="VariousPropertyBits" VALUE="746604571">
    <PARAM NAME="Size" VALUE="1411;635">
```

13

```
    <PARAM NAME="FontCharSet" VALUE="0">
    <PARAM NAME="FontPitchAndFamily" VALUE="2">
    <PARAM NAME="FontWeight" VALUE="0">
</OBJECT>

<OBJECT ID="tbZIP" WIDTH=93 HEIGHT=24
 CLASSID="CLSID:8BD21D10-EC42-11CE-9E0D-00AA006002F3"
 CODEBASE="http://aux/controls">
    <PARAM NAME="VariousPropertyBits" VALUE="746604571">
    <PARAM NAME="Size" VALUE="2469;635">
    <PARAM NAME="FontCharSet" VALUE="0">
    <PARAM NAME="FontPitchAndFamily" VALUE="2">
    <PARAM NAME="FontWeight" VALUE="0">
</OBJECT><P>

<OBJECT ID="tbTelephone1" WIDTH=111 HEIGHT=24
 CLASSID="CLSID:8BD21D10-EC42-11CE-9E0D-00AA006002F3">
    <PARAM NAME="VariousPropertyBits" VALUE="746604571">
    <PARAM NAME="Size" VALUE="2928;635">
    <PARAM NAME="FontCharSet" VALUE="0">
    <PARAM NAME="FontPitchAndFamily" VALUE="2">
    <PARAM NAME="FontWeight" VALUE="0">
</OBJECT>

<OBJECT ID="tbTelephone2" WIDTH=111 HEIGHT=24
 CLASSID="CLSID:8BD21D10-EC42-11CE-9E0D-00AA006002F3"
 CODEBASE="http://aux/controls">
    <PARAM NAME="VariousPropertyBits" VALUE="746604571">
    <PARAM NAME="Size" VALUE="2928;635">
    <PARAM NAME="FontCharSet" VALUE="0">
    <PARAM NAME="FontPitchAndFamily" VALUE="2">
    <PARAM NAME="FontWeight" VALUE="0">
</OBJECT>

<OBJECT ID="tbTelephone3" WIDTH=112 HEIGHT=24
 CLASSID="CLSID:8BD21D10-EC42-11CE-9E0D-00AA006002F3"
 CODEBASE="http://aux/controls">
    <PARAM NAME="VariousPropertyBits" VALUE="746604571">
    <PARAM NAME="Size" VALUE="2963;635">
    <PARAM NAME="FontCharSet" VALUE="0">
    <PARAM NAME="FontPitchAndFamily" VALUE="2">
    <PARAM NAME="FontWeight" VALUE="0">
</OBJECT><P>

Business:
<OBJECT ID="cbBusiness" WIDTH=20 HEIGHT=24
```

```
      CLASSID="CLSID:8BD21D40-EC42-11CE-9E0D-00AA006002F3"
      CODEBASE="http://aux/controls">
          <PARAM NAME="BackColor" VALUE="2147483663">
          <PARAM NAME="ForeColor" VALUE="2147483666">
          <PARAM NAME="DisplayStyle" VALUE="4">
          <PARAM NAME="Size" VALUE="529;635">
          <PARAM NAME="Value" VALUE="False">
          <PARAM NAME="FontCharSet" VALUE="0">
          <PARAM NAME="FontPitchAndFamily" VALUE="3">
          <PARAM NAME="FontWeight" VALUE="0">
      </OBJECT>

Last Contacted:
<OBJECT ID="tbContacted" WIDTH=93 HEIGHT=24
 CLASSID="CLSID:8BD21D10-EC42-11CE-9E0D-00AA006002F3"
 CODEBASE="http://aux/controls">
          <PARAM NAME="VariousPropertyBits" VALUE="746604571">
          <PARAM NAME="Size" VALUE="2469;635">
          <PARAM NAME="FontCharSet" VALUE="0">
          <PARAM NAME="FontPitchAndFamily" VALUE="2">
          <PARAM NAME="FontWeight" VALUE="0">
      </OBJECT><P>

Product:<BR>
<OBJECT ID="tbProduct" WIDTH=333 HEIGHT=24
 CLASSID="CLSID:8BD21D10-EC42-11CE-9E0D-00AA006002F3"
 CODEBASE="http://aux/controls">
          <PARAM NAME="VariousPropertyBits" VALUE="746604571">
          <PARAM NAME="Size" VALUE="8819;635">
          <PARAM NAME="FontCharSet" VALUE="0">
          <PARAM NAME="FontPitchAndFamily" VALUE="2">
          <PARAM NAME="FontWeight" VALUE="0">
      </OBJECT><P>

Notes:<BR>
<OBJECT ID="tbNotes" WIDTH=333 HEIGHT=72
 CLASSID="CLSID:8BD21D10-EC42-11CE-9E0D-00AA006002F3"
 CODEBASE="http://aux/controls">
          <PARAM NAME="VariousPropertyBits" VALUE="2894088219">
          <PARAM NAME="Size" VALUE="8819;1905">
          <PARAM NAME="FontCharSet" VALUE="0">
          <PARAM NAME="FontPitchAndFamily" VALUE="2">
          <PARAM NAME="FontWeight" VALUE="0">
      </OBJECT><P>
</CENTER>
```

13

```
<!-Add a couple of buttons for moving around in the table.->

<CENTER>
<OBJECT ID="pbNext" WIDTH=96 HEIGHT=32
 CLASSID="CLSID:D7053240-CE69-11CD-A777-00DD01143C57"
 CODEBASE="http://aux/controls">
    <PARAM NAME="Caption" VALUE="Next">
    <PARAM NAME="Size" VALUE="2540;846">
    <PARAM NAME="FontCharSet" VALUE="0">
    <PARAM NAME="FontPitchAndFamily" VALUE="2">
    <PARAM NAME="ParagraphAlign" VALUE="3">
    <PARAM NAME="FontWeight" VALUE="0">
</OBJECT>

<OBJECT ID="pbPrevious" WIDTH=96 HEIGHT=32
 CLASSID="CLSID:D7053240-CE69-11CD-A777-00DD01143C57"
 CODEBASE="http://aux/controls">
    <PARAM NAME="Caption" VALUE="Previous">
    <PARAM NAME="Size" VALUE="2540;846">
    <PARAM NAME="FontCharSet" VALUE="0">
    <PARAM NAME="FontPitchAndFamily" VALUE="2">
    <PARAM NAME="ParagraphAlign" VALUE="3">
    <PARAM NAME="FontWeight" VALUE="0">
</OBJECT>
</CENTER>

</BODY>
</HTML>
```

This looks like a lot of code, but that's pretty familiar territory for anyone who creates many database applications. Moving data from place to place requires a lot of additional code that a little utility program or a simple control may not require. The main part of this application displays the controls that you created using the parameters in Table 13-3. It also contains a bit of text for explanatory purposes. This includes a main heading and headings for both the tbProduct and tbNotes controls. The cbBusiness and tbContacted controls also require a little explanatory text.

There are four functions in this example. All four of them require use of the global variables defined at the beginning of the script section. This is the first time we've used global variables in the book. Normally you'll want to avoid using them, but this is one case when we can't. The Window_OnLoad() function executes immediately after the form loads. It begins by opening the database. oDB contains a database object if the call is successful. (Don't worry. Internet Explorer will display an informative error message if the call isn't successful.) You could open the database in any of several ways. For example, you could define an ODBC connection. In this case, we use a direct connection.

The next thing the Window_OnLoad() function needs to do is open a recordset. This is a snapshot of the contents of one or more tables within the database. You could use any number of methods for defining the recordset. Either a table or query within the database is acceptable, as is an SQL statement defining what you want to retrieve. In most cases, you'll find that creating a query is the easiest way to go when using Access.

We do a pretty strange thing at this point, but it's for a good reason. Access provides an omnidirectional pointer into the table. This means that you can go forward, but not back. DAO does keep a count of the records you've visited in the table or query with the RecordCount property. So, the easiest way to see how many records we have is to move to the last record using the MoveLast method, and then see how many records DAO counted. In this case, we place the resulting value in iLastRow.

We're at the last row of the query now, so we can't do anything else. The next step is to close the recordset, then reopen it. This places the pointer at the beginning of the query again. Now that we know how many records the query contains, we can use a two-dimensional array with the query contents. We'll use the GetRows() method to accomplish this task. The first dimension of the aCurrentRow array contains the fields; the second contains the records. Now that we have an array containing the data we need, we'll display the first record, as shown in the listing. The very last thing we'll do in the Window_OnLoad() function is to set the value of the iCurrentRow variable to 0—the first record in our aCurrentRow array.

Any time you open a database, you want to close it when you're done using it. Most database vendors make this a requirement for using their product, not just a mere suggestion. The Window_OnUnload() function's only purpose in life is to close the database before we exit Internet Explorer or move on to another page.

The next two functions, pbNext_Click() and pbPrevious_Click(), are so similar that we'll only look at one of them. The first thing we do in both functions is check the current status of the iCurrentRow variable. If it equals the beginning or end of the query, we'll display a message. Otherwise, we display the data using iCurrentRow as a pointer into the aCurrentRow array.

It's time to look at our application in action—go ahead and save your HTML page (the example uses DAOAccess1.HTM for a filename). The second thing

13

you'll need to do is add some records to the ADDRESS table. Three or four records should be sufficient. Just open the table in Access as you normally would to add the records in a table view. Once you've finished adding the records, open the HTML page we've just created. Figure 13-4 shows what your Web page should look like at this point.

NOTE: Make absolutely certain that you test this example on a local drive first to be sure it works properly with your setup. Some older versions of the Access ODBC drivers and the DAO3032.DLL driver won't work properly in this configuration. This program was tested with the 3.000.2627 version of the DAO3032.DLL. Use a local path such as C:\Access\MyData.MDB when performing the local test.

Data Access in an HTML Layout

You don't have to settle for an inadequate layout and a bunch of <OBJECT> tags in your HTML code when accessing a database. There are other ways to use ActiveX technology to accomplish your goals. One of these methods involves creating some special file setups and using an HTML layout to display the data. The advantage of using an HTML layout is that you get precise control over the appearance of your display. In addition, getting a working prototype together using the layout technique is actually faster than

Using DAO access methods within an HTML page may not be very aesthetically pleasing, but you can put such a page together quickly.

Figure 13-4.

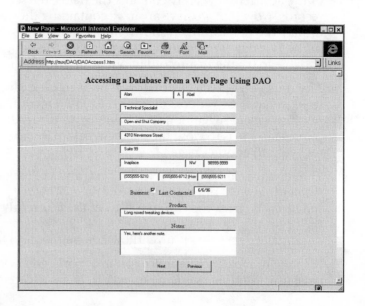

the method shown in the previous section. There are a few disadvantages as well. The most important of these disadvantages is that you will work harder in the long run to get a working Web page. Another problem is that this method uses more files—increasing the chances of potential corruption. Finally, this method does use a query approach to getting the data, which means that the connection is static.

TIP: Like everything else dealing with ActiveX, accessing databases using it is bound to change. You can keep up with current developments regarding this access technique by visiting http://microsoft.com/workshop/author/cpad/howto/container.htm#idc.

Gaining access to your data using this method doesn't have to be hard if you take a logical approach to doing it. You'll need to perform five main tasks to use this technique. The following steps are meant as an overview, not as a procedure. The example code provided here shows a minimal configuration. You could add a lot of other features, such as a password screen for accessing the data or a text box where the user could provide the search criteria for the form.

13

NOTE: This data access method should work with any type of data server. However, it currently appears to work only with Microsoft's SQL Server.

1. Create an ALX (HTML layout file) containing a single pushbutton and an associated script that sets the window location HREF to the location of your data. This location information must point to an HTML file. We'll call the ALX file Search.ALX for this example. The following code shows how you would implement this step.

```
<SCRIPT LANGUAGE="JavaScript" FOR="pbSearch" EVENT="Click()">
<!--
window.location.href = "http://aux/DAO/DataSelect.HTM"

-->
</SCRIPT>
<DIV ID="Layout1" STYLE="LAYOUT:FIXED;WIDTH:400pt;HEIGHT:300pt;">
    <OBJECT ID="pbSearch"
```

```
CLASSID="CLSID:D7053240-CE69-11CD-A777-00DD01143C57"
CODEBASE="http://aux/controls"
STYLE="TOP:74pt;LEFT:66pt;WIDTH:72pt;HEIGHT:24pt;TABINDEX:0;
    ZINDEX:0;">
  <PARAM NAME="Caption" VALUE="Search">
  <PARAM NAME="Size" VALUE="2540;847">
  <PARAM NAME="FontCharSet" VALUE="0">
  <PARAM NAME="FontPitchAndFamily" VALUE="2">
  <PARAM NAME="ParagraphAlign" VALUE="3">
  <PARAM NAME="FontWeight" VALUE="0">
</OBJECT>
</DIV>
```

2. Insert the ALX created in step 1 into an HTML file (which we'll call DAOAccess2.HTM). When users open this page, they'll see a Search pushbutton and a heading. You could add code that would accept input in the form of an employee's name.

```
<HTML>
<HEAD>
<TITLE>New Page</TITLE>
</HEAD>
<BODY>

<!-Display a heading.->
<CENTER><H2>Data Search in Layout Page Example</H2></CENTER>

<!-Insert the ALX file we created for changing the HREF.->
<OBJECT CLASSID="CLSID:812AE312-8B8E-11CF-93C8-00AA00C08FDF"
    ID="Search_alx" STYLE="LEFT:0;TOP:0">
    <PARAM NAME="ALXPATH" REF VALUE="http://aux/DAO/Search.alx">
</OBJECT>


</BODY>
</HTML>
```

3. Write an IDC file (we'll use Search.IDC for the example). This file will contain the name, location, user information, and data selection criteria for the data you want to view. It also contains the name of the layout HTX file—an ALX file in disguise. Here's some code that shows how to implement this step:

```
Datasource: MyData.MDB
Username: George
Password:
Template: Display.HTX
```

```
SQLStatement:
+SELECT *
+FROM ADDRESS
+ORDER BY ADDRESS.LAST_NAME, ADDRESS.FIRST_NAME, ADDRESS.MIDDLE;
```

4. Insert an ALX file object into an HTML file (we'll call our file DataSelect.HTM). Change the ALXPATH attribute to point to the IDC file created in step 3. The following code shows how to create the HTML file for this step. Notice that the reference change also includes a question mark.

```
<HTML>
<HEAD>
<TITLE>New Page</TITLE>
</HEAD>
<BODY>

<!-Display a layout showing the data search result.->
<OBJECT CLASSID="CLSID:812AE312-8B8E-11CF-93C8-00AA00C08FDF"
    ID="Display_alx" STYLE="LEFT:0;TOP:0">
    <PARAM NAME="ALXPATH" REF VALUE="Search.IDC?">
</OBJECT>


</BODY>
</HTML>
```

5. Create an ALX file that contains the layout and any required scripts for the data you want to display. Give this file an HTX extension (we'll use Display.HTX for the purposes of the example).

```
<SCRIPT LANGUAGE="VBScript">
<!--
    Sub window_onLoad()
    <%begindetail%>
    TextBox1.Value = "<%FIRST_NAME%>"
    <%enddetail%>
end sub
-->
</SCRIPT>

<DIV ID="Display" STYLE="LAYOUT:FIXED;WIDTH:466pt;HEIGHT:319pt;">
    <OBJECT ID="TextBox1"
      CLASSID="CLSID:8BD21D10-EC42-11CE-9E0D-00AA006002F3"
        STYLE="TOP:17pt;LEFT:33pt;WIDTH:72pt;HEIGHT:18pt;TABINDEX:0;ZINDEX:0;">
        <PARAM NAME="VariousPropertyBits" VALUE="746604571">
        <PARAM NAME="Size" VALUE="2540;635">
```

13

```
<PARAM NAME="FontCharSet" VALUE="0">
<PARAM NAME="FontPitchAndFamily" VALUE="2">
<PARAM NAME="FontWeight" VALUE="0">
</OBJECT>
</DIV>
```

So, how does this all work? Essentially, you build a query using the IDC file to get some data from the database. The IDC file inserts this information into the HTX file, which then gets built on the fly into an ALX file. The HTX file ends up being a template for constructing the ALX file that the user will actually see. Finally, the ALX file is displayed so that the user can interact with it. While this may seem like a long way to go about things at first, it's still a lot better than having to build and test a lot of script files.

There's one script added to the Display.HTX file shown in step 5. This script takes the data retrieved from the IDC file and places it in the various controls. The example only shows one control to make the code easier to see. Normally you'd have one control for each data field, as we did in the previous section's example.

Using the Microsoft RemoteData Control

We're going to switch gears now and look at one of the new features in Visual C++ 4.2 that you won't want to miss. The Microsoft RemoteData control is one of the handiest features that you'll find for building a database application quickly. In fact, you can build a functional database viewing utility using this control without writing a single line of code. That's what we'll do in this section—you'll only use the MFC Application Wizard and make property-level changes to create a functional viewer. This is one case where seeing is believing, so let's get a sample application started.

NOTE: You won't be able to actually connect to a Web site with this example unless you have an ODBC add-on product designed to allow you to publish databases on the Internet. This limitation will also prevent you from using a C++ application built using Visual C++ 4.2 on a general Internet site. However, this example will work fine for intranet site access, and you can always use it locally to see how the controls work before making an investment in additional software.

The first thing you'll need to do is create a data source using the ODBC or ODBC 32 Administration utilities provided in the Control Panel. Using the utilities is fairly easy. All you need to do is double-click on the applet in the Control Panel. Click Add when you see the Data Sources dialog. The next thing you'll see is an Add Data Source dialog, where you can select the driver you want to use. Once you select a driver, click OK. At this point you'll see one or more driver-specific configuration screens. Most ODBC drivers require you to enter a Data Source Name (DSN) and a database name as a minimum.

This example will use an Access 7.0 database as a data source, but you can use any ODBC data source that you'd like. The only criterion as far as this example is concerned is that you name the data source SampleData. (That's the DSN we'll use for all of the controls that require this entry—if you use a different data source name, make sure you change this setting in all the controls as well.) Nothing else about the ODBC connection is relevant (location, database name and type, and data logging are all hidden from the application).

TIP: You can use the rdoDataSource method to register a data source that the ODBC Administration utilities (the ODBC and ODBC 32 applets in the Control Panel) won't handle. Unfortunately, using this method requires an intimate knowledge of the driver you want to use, and the vendor information may be sketchy at best. The documentation provided with Visual C++ won't give you all of the information you need to use this method, so make certain you contact the ODBC driver vendor for driver-specific information before attempting to use this method.

13

Once you have a data source defined, you'll need to create a new application using the MFC Application Wizard. The example program is called RemData; but again, you could call your application anything. On the first page of the MFC Application Wizard, select Dialog Based. On the second page, you'll need to select the OLE Controls check box and give your dialog box a title. The example program uses Remote Data Access Example. Once you make these three changes, you can click Finish to complete the application shell. The MFC Application Wizard will copy some files to your application directory, then display the ClassView window as usual.

Most of the work you'll need to do involves changing dialog box-specific properties and adding controls. Open the ResourceView, click the + sign next to Dialog, then double-click the IDD_REMDATA_DIALOG entry. You'll see a blank dialog. The first thing you'll want to do is resize it to hold the controls we want to add. The example program uses a dialog size of 380 X 220, though the actual size you use isn't that important.

Now that we have a drawing area, let's add some controls. Use the Insert | Component command to display the Component Gallery dialog. Select the OLE Controls page. On this page you should see an Apex Data Bound Grid Control entry. If you don't, it could mean that you didn't install all of the controls with Visual C++ or that the control didn't get registered properly. Click Insert to add the control to your Controls palette. You should see a Confirm Classes dialog. Click OK to accept the defaults. Use the same procedure to add the RemoteData Control to your Controls palette. Click Close to close the Component Gallery dialog. You should see the two new controls added to your Controls palette.

Add an Apex Data Bound Grid control (IDC_DBGRID1) to your dialog box, then a RemoteData control (IDC_RDCCTRL1). The example program uses a size of 300 X 180 for the first control and 300 X 20 for the second. It's normal to place the grid above the positioning arrows, but you could just as easily reverse positions if you wanted to. If you go the standard route, your dialog should look similar to the one shown in Figure 13-5.

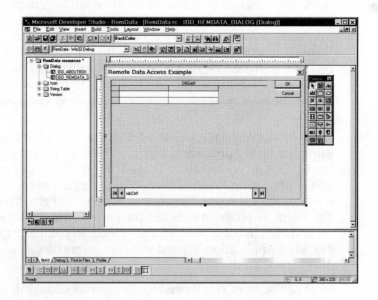

The sample program will display the contents of the MyData.MDB file in a data grid rather than a form.

Figure 13-5.

TIP: There are quite a few sites on the Internet that offer grid controls and other database-related resources. One site, http://www.gamelan.com/index.shtml (EarthWeb's Gamelan), is especially noteworthy for the number and variety of resources it provides. As of this writing, this site contains no less than 38 ActiveX resources and 365 JavaScript resources (among others—for example, the 451 multimedia and 337 utility resources). You'll even find a wealth of Java resources at this site. The one thing you won't find here are VBScript resources—right now you'll still have to rely on Microsoft in this regard.

There are some quick changes you'll want to make for aesthetic reasons. First, change the caption for the RemoteData control to a blank, and then change the caption for the Apex Data Bound Grid control to "MyData.MDB". You could always add code to change the RemoteData control caption to something like a record number or other status information later, but for now we'll leave it blank. Likewise, you could place the actual filename of the database the user is looking at in the Apex Data Bound Grid control caption, but we'll only be using this application to open one file so the static name is sufficient. Once you have changed the captions, open the Control page of the RemoteData Control Properties dialog. Select a data source, enter your user name, and a password. You'll also want to enter an SQL statement similar to the "Select * From ADDRESS" statement shown here:

13

RemoteData Control Properties	
General	Control	Colors	Fonts	All
DataSource	SampleData
UserName	Admin
Password	xxxxx
SQL	Select * From ADDRESS

TIP: Microsoft Access provides a handy feature if you're not proficient in SQL. Simply open any query you want to use in design mode. Use the View I SQL command to display the SQL required to get a specific result. You can simply copy the required code from the query window to the Clipboard, and then paste it into the RemoteData Control Properties dialog. Be sure the SQL statement actually fits though, since the dialog places a limit on the size of the query you can enter.

At this point you can make a connection to the database, provided you've set everything up correctly. You'll see in a few seconds whether you did or not. To check the connection, open the Apex Data Bound Grid Control Properties dialog. Select the All page. Click on the DataSource property and select IDC_RDCCTRL1 from the drop-down list box, as shown here. This action binds the grid control to the RemoteData control.

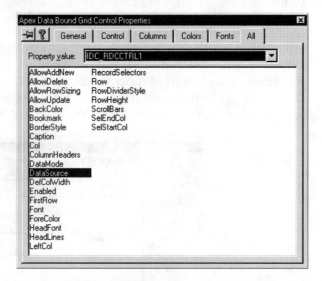

Now is the moment of truth. Close the properties dialog. Right-click the grid control and select the Apex Data Bound Grid Control Object I Retrieve Fields command. You may see a dialog asking if you want to replace the existing field definitions with new ones. After a few seconds, you should see a list of field entries similar to the ones shown in Figure 3-6.

Retrieving the fields may have entered the field names and provided new columns for you to use, but the fields aren't necessarily in the best order for

The Apex
Data Bound
Grid Control
automatically
loads all the
field names
for you from
MyData.MDB.
Figure 13-6.

The mouse
cursor will
change to a
down arrow
when you've
positioned it
correctly to
select a
column.

viewing. In addition, the column headings don't look as nice as they could. Let's fix the column ordering problem first. Right-click the grid control and select the Apex Data Bound Grid Control Object | Edit command. The grid control will change modes. You can now select a column; then right-click it to display a context menu, as shown here:

Moving fields around on the grid isn't as easy as it should be, but with a little thought you can get the job done. Use the Insert command on the context menu to add two columns. They'll appear to the left of the LAST_NAME field. Select both the FIRST_NAME and MIDDLE fields. Use the Cut command on the context menu to remove them. Now, select the two blank columns that you just inserted. Use the Paste command on the context menu to insert the FIRST_NAME and MIDDLE fields before the LAST_NAME field. (There are a lot of other ways to do this, but cutting and pasting is the least time consuming.) Click outside the Apex Data Bound Grid control to take it out of edit mode.

NOTE: There's a strange bug in the Apex Data Bound Grid control as of this writing. You may have to close, then reopen the workspace at this point to get more than two columns to appear in the properties dialog. If a dialog appears asking if you want to replace the grid definition with existing field definitions, click Cancel—you want to use the reordered grid. Make certain you save all your changes before closing the workspace. Microsoft Visual C++ will automatically take you back to the dialog when you reopen the workspace, so you shouldn't have to reset anything to continue with this section of the chapter.

Reopen the Apex Data Bound Grid Control Properties dialog. Select the Columns page. Type in a caption for each field. For example, change FIRST_NAME to First Name. (You can use the Column field of the dialog to change column headings that you're editing.) Your dialog should look similar to the one shown in Figure 13-7. Notice that the middle initial field has resized itself. This is an automatic function of the control. You can also place the control in edit mode and change the size of the fields manually.

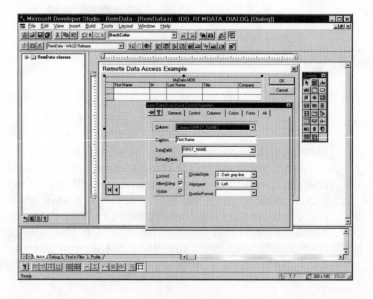

The Apex Data Bound Grid Control now provides aesthetically pleasing column headings.
Figure 13-7.

Close the properties dialog. It's time to compile the application and see what it looks like and how a non-coded application works. Figure 13-8 shows what the example program looks like. Notice that we didn't have to do one iota of programming to get this effect. Even adding or deleting records won't pose much of a problem. The Apex Data Bound Grid control includes the AllowAddNew property that allows you to add new records and the AllowDelete property that allows you to remove old ones. Of course, you can disallow any form of editing at all by setting the AllowUpdate property to false.

Try the arrows at the bottom of the dialog (the ones that were displayed as a result of adding the RemoteData control). Notice that they act much as you'd expect. Clicking the right arrow moves the record pointer down one position, and clicking the left arrow moves it up one position. You'll find that the beginning and end arrows are also functional. Even though you didn't program this functionality into the controls, MFC provides it automatically as part of the control behavior. This feature is called *data binding*.

Microsoft Visual C++ provides five controls that exhibit the data binding behavior: MSDataCombo control, MSDataList control, Apex Data Bound Grid control, Microsoft Masked Edit control, and Calendar control. All five of these controls are available through the Component Gallery.

13

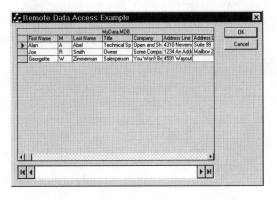

The completed application allows you to edit existing records. It doesn't allow you to append or delete records, but that's easily changed.

Figure 13-8.

You'll also find that they all provide a DataSource property. Setting this property to a RemoteData control will allow you to maintain the connection between them.

TIP: You won't find much information about any of these new controls in the standard C++ help files. Instead of searching help for information on how to use the controls, select the control in the Component Gallery and click on the ? (question mark) button. Visual C++ will display an appropriate help screen. You might be surprised to find that you're looking at a Visual Basic help screen though, instead of the standard C++ screens.

The big difference between the data binding behavior presented by Visual C++ 4.2 and other products such as Visual Basic at this point is that you can use the RemoteData control with both local and remote sources. Right now, the data binding provided by most products on the market only works with a local source. However, you must provide the proper source information to use it—in this case an ODBC source name.

Now that you've had a chance to create a non-programmed application in Visual C++, let's look at some of the problems with it. The bottom line is that even though this is a functional application, you'd still want to add a few features to it. For example, you'll probably want to add a password dialog of some sort to keep unwanted browsers out. If you decide to use this type of setup for creating a database editing tool, you'll need to add data safeguards as well. For example, you wouldn't want someone to enter a name in one of the telephone number fields or a nonexistent state. However, from a functional standpoint, the two controls used in this application are probably all you need.

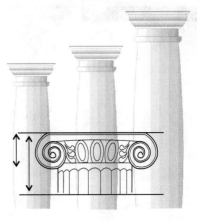

Chapter 14

Multimedia and ActiveX

Let's face it, multimedia is one of the "fun" areas to program because it's interactive. You get to make neat sounds and display pleasant pictures on the screen. Unlike a lot of types of programming that provide little or no feedback—at least of the dazzling variety—both user and programmer alike can derive pleasure from a well-designed multimedia presentation. Try to get that kind of an effect from a well-designed sort routine.

We visited some multimedia-like additions you could make to your Web site in Chapter 8. For example, a lot of people use animated GIFs to give their site a bit of glitz at a lower cost in download time than some of the techniques we'll visit in this chapter. Using <BGSOUND> is another addition you could make—again at a lower cost than the techniques we'll show here. However, let's face the fact that these alternatives aren't nearly as nice as seeing full-motion video or getting an ultrarealistic sound effect. If you really must have the best presentation possible at your Web site, using multimedia controls are the way to go. For example, it's hard to imagine how the various news media sites would look without some form of multimedia support. Some of them even provide a level of support for recorded broadcasts using movie files.

Before you grab a seat at the high-power workstation in your office and begin spewing out multimedia controls by the dozen, you'll want to spend a few seconds thinking about multimedia and the Internet. Unlike a lot of environments, users of the Internet have a definite bandwidth problem. We talked in Chapter 8 about the size limitations you should observe when building an Internet site to make it fun for everyone to use. Multimedia tosses those limitations out the window—you simply can't fit a multimedia presentation into a Web site size that the user will download in a reasonable amount of time. In addition, you'll want to think twice about writing your own multimedia controls. Using a multimedia control on a Web page is a whole different world than writing one from scratch.

Let's look at the file size problem first. You can't place a video of your latest product in action on an Internet site and expect the user to get any kind of performance from it. Multimedia files are huge, even when compressed, and it's going to cost the user some time to download your presentation. Some users will rightfully complain if you burden them with a long download without asking first. As a result, most Web sites that feature multimedia presentations place the multimedia portion on a second page. Users get a choice of whether they want to go to the second page or not. Another alternative is to place a pushbutton on the page. Users have to press the button to start the download process. This is obviously a lot more complicated than the second page method, but provides the advantage of making the multimedia presentation seamless. A third, and definitely unsatisfactory solution, is to start the download process anyway. The user can always abort the download, but now you've bought yourself a basket of ill will before the user has even seen your site. Some aficionados of this technique spruce up their sites in other ways—just in case the user did abort the download—but this isn't the best way to handle the situation.

No matter what technique you choose to present multimedia information, you've got another problem as well. Standards are a bit hard to come by when it comes to multimedia files, and even when they do exist, you're going to find that some companies don't abide by them. Trying to build your own multimedia control from scratch will provide you with more than a few challenges, most of which you could easily live without. Unless you're planning on building controls for a living, you'll probably be better off looking at what's available and using a standard control when building your Web site. That's part of what we'll look at in this chapter. We'll look at the ActiveMovie control provided with ActiveX Control Pad, along with a few other controls you can easily download from the Internet.

TIP: If you want to see what's available in the way of ActiveX multimedia controls, one of the better places to look is http://www.microsoft.com/activex/controls/. You may also want to look at http://www.caboose.com/cwsapps/95activx.html. Some of the control descriptions listed there will also take you to sites where the control is in use, so you can see it in action. In almost all cases, you'll need a license to actually use the control on your Web site.

Even if you do decide to use an off-the-shelf control, you're going to face some compatibility decisions. For example, the ActiveMovie control provided with ActiveX Control Pad is supposed to support the MOV file format used by products such as QuickTime. It does provide support, but only to a point (the exact limitations are a matter of much discussion on the Microsoft newsgroups on the Internet even now). If you need full support for the MOV file format, you might need to look at another kind of control. Some controls will support some, but not all, of the file formats you might need. You can be certain that visitors to your site will complain if they need to download more than one control, so getting one that supports everything you need from the outset is a real plus.

Finally, if you add multimedia to your Web site, you're going to get people who complain about it. This is true of intranets as well as the Internet. In fact, you'll probably get more complaints from users on an intranet site because they'll feel they have a vested interest in the appearance of the site and may not want to take the time required to look at multimedia when they have a meeting in five minutes. Then again, you'll see the opposite end of the spectrum as well. Even though people are far less likely to provide positive feedback than negative feedback, you'll still get some if your presentation is up to par.

14

Using Windows' Built-in Multimedia Capabilities

We're going to take another look at the multimedia capabilities that are built into Windows, but from a different perspective. In this case you need to provide the user with more information than will fit into a small file. This could include WAV, AVI, MID, or any number of other multimedia formats that Windows supports using standard utilities. For whatever reason, the file is just too large to make it an automatic download.

Of course, size isn't the only reason for providing a special multimedia download method. You may simply want to combine capabilities. For example, you could create a CAB file containing an animated GIF and a sound file. You could set everything up so the two files would play simultaneously—creating an animated movie of sorts. Don't count on any measure of synchronization if you use this method though; there just isn't any way to ensure you'll get it.

NOTE: You'll want to exercise care when using native Windows capabilities within your Web site for two reasons. First, not all visitors will use Windows as their operating system. Even if they do use Windows, there is no guarantee that they'll have the appropriate utility programs loaded for playing the files on your Web site. Second, some browsers react strangely to multimedia files. For example, Internet Explorer required some reconfiguration before it could play the AVI file in this example—Netscape Navigator handled the file with ease. On the other hand, Navigator required reconfiguration before it would play the MID file. Compatibility problems will almost certainly cause problems for you if you don't depend on a third-party product.

Let's get right into the example program since you're familiar with some of the specifics of working with Windows multimedia files already. Listing 14-1 shows the code for this particular example. Notice that it contains three different multimedia examples. Each one of them uses a different activation technique.

Listing 14-1

```
</HEAD>
<BODY>

<!-Netscape Navigator couldn't see the pushbutton without the FORM tag.->
<FORM>

<!-Add a heading.->
<CENTER><H2>Using Windows Multimedia Capabilities</H2>
<H3>Can Save Download Time</H3></CENTER>

<!-Display an anchor for a sound file.->
```

```
You can use a simple anchor for a
 <A HREF="http://aux/Multimedia/TwilZone.WAV">
Sound Byte</A>.<BR>

Netscape Navigator had problems playing this
 <A HREF="http://aux/Multimedia/Pinball.MID">
MIDI</A> file right out of the package.<P>

<!-Use a button for the AVI example.->
Buttons also work well (Microsoft's Internet Explorer had trouble with this file).<BR>
<INPUT LANGUAGE="JavaScript"
   TYPE=button
   VALUE=" See Movie "
   ONCLICK="location.href='http://aux/Multimedia/RobRoy.AVI'"><P>

</FORM>
</BODY>
</HTML>
```

This code should look pretty familiar by now. The two anchors provide access to our sound files. A button allows us access to the AVI file. Notice that we had to add a <FORM> tag to allow Netscape Navigator to see the <INPUT> tag. This is an important consideration if you're using Internet Explorer to test your Web pages. You could easily miss this requirement, effectively preventing Netscape users from visiting your site.

Let's take a look at a few other items with regard to the way Internet Explorer and Netscape Navigator handle multimedia files. The way they get the job done will present some interesting challenges in the way you handle standard files using what should be standard utility programs. Figure 14-1 shows Internet Explorer playing the WAV file. Figure 14-2 shows Netscape doing the same thing. Notice that Netscape uses a built-in utility—not the standard Windows utility. Does this make a difference in the way the file plays? You bet.

So, how can you ensure that the sound file you upload to the Internet sounds like it's supposed to? You can't. About the best thing you can do is try out your Web page with at least two browsers—more if you expect a heavy volume of traffic. That way you at least have an idea of the kinds of problems visitors to your site will have in experiencing the multimedia features you worked so hard to incorporate.

This same philosophy of support is what gets Netscape Navigator into trouble with the MID file. Since its built-in utility doesn't support this file type, you can't play it without performing some reconfiguration.

14

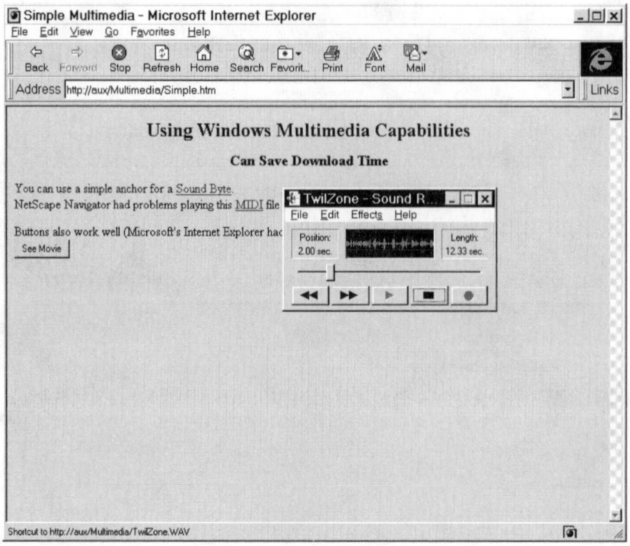

Microsoft's Internet Explorer uses the standard WAV utility to play the first sound file.

Figure 14-1.

Fortunately, Netscape Navigator handles the situation without too many problems. It displays a Save As dialog—offering to at least let you save the file and listen to it locally. Internet Explorer, on the other hand, appears to use a custom utility in this case that allows you to listen to the file, as shown in Figure 14-3.

Netscape Navigator uses a custom utility to accomplish the same task, though the user can force it to use the standard utility.

Figure 14-2.

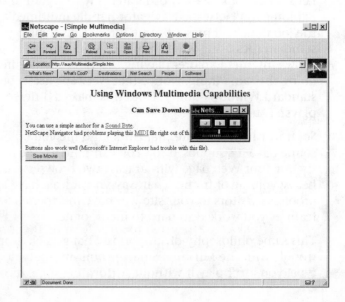

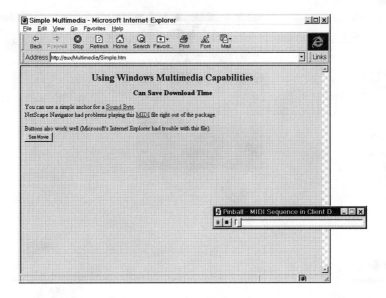

Microsoft's
Internet
Explorer
appears to
use a custom
utility, rather
than the
Media Player,
to play MIDI
files.

Figure 14-3.

The final file type for this example is AVI. In this case Internet Explorer
has a problem working with the file. However, instead of simply letting you
download the file, it defaults to displaying the error message shown here:

14

This particular example places the file reference in a button for a reason. If
you were the user visiting this site, you'd be out of luck if you were using
Internet Explorer. Using an <A HREF> tag in place of the button would allow
the user to bypass the problem by right-clicking on the link and selecting
Save Target As from the context menu. The button works fine for Netscape
Navigator users, and it really is a good idea for making your site look nicer,
but you'll want to make sure you test for problem areas like this before you
place a Web site in public view.

You might also be interested to know that neither browser uses the default
media viewing utility in this case. Figure 14-4 shows the custom way that
Netscape Navigator handles AVI files. The result is pretty nice, but lacks the
controls you usually associate with a media viewer. There aren't even any

Netscape
Navigator
provides a
seamless view
of AVI files,
but lacks
controls for
making the
viewing
experience
fun.
Figure 14-4.

instructions provided for turning the viewer on and off. (Clicking the viewer once will start the video; clicking a second time will stop it.)

Using the ActiveMovie Control

Using the utilities that come with Windows along with the native capabilities of any browser you happened to use does have the advantage of always being available. However, as we saw in the previous section, you can also rely on this method of displaying multimedia files to leave you with a Web site that provides an inconsistent appearance. The ActiveMovie control that comes with ActiveX solves at least part of the problems you'll experience. You can use it immediately with Internet Explorer and get consistent results. Add the NCompass plug-in to Netscape Navigator, and you can use it in that environment as well.

Figure 14-5 shows what the ActiveMovie control will look like when you insert it into an HTML page. As you can see, it looks just like any media player you've used in the past. The only property that you need to define is CODEBASE.

Unfortunately, using the NCompass ScriptActive plug-in (at least as of this writing) isn't a straight shot. You have to perform some special formatting of the <OBJECT> tag to get it to work. It's fortunate that the plug-in also includes the HTML Conversion utility for performing most of the work for

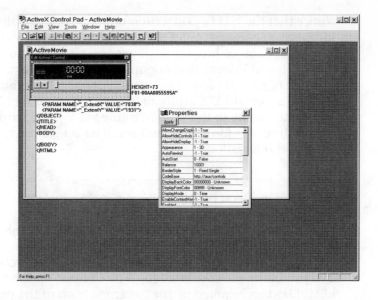

The ActiveMovie control looks like any standard media player.
Figure 14-5.

you. The results of using the utility on the standard ActiveMovie control appear in Listing 14-2.

14

Listing 14-2

```
<!-Insert an ActiveMovie control.->
<OBJECT ID="ActiveMovie1" WIDTH=267 HEIGHT=73
    CLASSID="CLSID:05589FA1-C356-11CE-BF01-00AA0055595A"
    CODEBASE="http://aux/controls">
  <PARAM NAME="_ExtentX" VALUE="7038">
  <PARAM NAME="_ExtentY" VALUE="1931">
<EMBED NAME="ActiveMovie1" WIDTH=267 HEIGHT=73
    CLASSID="CLSID:05589FA1-C356-11CE-BF01-00AA0055595A"
    CODEBASE="http://aux/controls"
    TYPE="application/oleobject"
  PARAM__ExtentX="7038"
  PARAM__ExtentY="1931"
></OBJECT>
```

WARNING: Don't edit the ActiveX control by clicking the <OBJECT> tag next to the entry on the HTML page once you make the transition from an <OBJECT> tag specific to an <OBJECT> tag, <EMBED> tag combination. In some situations the editor will change the <EMBED> tag in such a way that it won't work properly anymore. The best idea is to create your Web page, test it with Internet Explorer, then add the <EMBED> tags needed to make it work with the NCompass ScriptActive plug-in.

Notice that the HTML Conversion utility takes the <OBJECT> tag information and adds an <EMBED> tag with basically the same information. Since Internet Explorer doesn't understand the <EMBED> tag, the additional information doesn't cause any problems. The reason for this extra bit of code is pretty easy to understand. The ScriptActive plug-in requires a special TYPE attribute to specify the Internet MIME type for the object. According to the vendor, future versions of ScriptActive won't require this additional information, and you'll be able to use the <OBJECT> tag without modification.

T IP: Once you install the NCompass ScriptActive plug-in, you'll find a new NConvert context menu entry when you right-click on a file. The entry contains two options: Convert and Set Destination Folder. Use the Set Destination Folder option to tell the utility where you want converted files placed. Specify a special directory if you don't want your original file overwritten by the converted file. The Convert option inserts all of the <EMBED> tags required by the current version of the product.

Another problem with using ScriptActive is that it doesn't always allow you to access the properties associated with an object. In fact, the level of support even varies by machine—two machines with the same configuration and using the same hardware may show different results on a specific Web page. Different controls seem to provide varying levels of access as well—a more complex control usually presents more problems than a simple one will. All of these problems aren't too surprising considering the constant state of flux that the Internet is in and the relative newness of ActiveX technology. About the best you can hope to achieve is to display the control onscreen. Whether it will actually work or not is another matter.

Now that we have the preliminaries out of the way, let's look at an example that uses the ActiveMovie control. Listing 14-3 shows the code we'll use in this example. Notice that even though we include a filename for our control, we can change it on the fly. You'll definitely want to define the FileName property for the ActiveMovie control as part of the configuration process to avoid scripting errors. The advantage to using the on-the-fly filename changing technique is that you could provide a random movie or other display if you wanted to.

Listing 14-3

```html
<HTML>
<HEAD>

<SCRIPT LANGUAGE="JavaScript">
<!--

function PlayWAV()
{
    // Load the WAV file.
    window.ActiveMovie1.Filename = "TwilZone.WAV"
}

function PlayMIDI()
{
    // Load the MIDI file.
    window.ActiveMovie1.Filename = "Pinball.MID"
}

function PlayAVI()
{
    // Load the AVI file.
    window.ActiveMovie1.Filename="RobRoy.AVI"
}

function PlayerRun()
{
    // Start playing the loaded file.
    window.ActiveMovie1.Run()
}

function PlayerStop()
{
    // Stop the media player.
    window.ActiveMovie1.Stop()
}

function PlayerPause()
{
    // Pause the media player.
    window.ActiveMovie1.Pause()
}

function ModeDisplay()
```

14

```
{
    // Hide or display the media player.
    window.ActiveMovie1.ShowDisplay = !(window.ActiveMovie1.ShowDisplay)

    // Change the pbDisplay button caption as appropriate.
    if (window.ActiveMovie1.ShowDisplay)
    {
        Form1.pbDisplay.Value = "No Display"
    }
    else
    {
        Form1.pbDisplay.Value = "Display"
    }
}

function ModeControls()
{
    // Hide or display the media player.
    window.ActiveMovie1.ShowControls = !(window.ActiveMovie1.ShowControls)

    // Change the pbDisplay button caption as appropriate.
    if (window.ActiveMovie1.ShowControls)
    {
        Form1.pbControls.Value = "No Controls"
    }
    else
    {
        Form1.pbControls.Value = "Controls"
    }
}

    function ModeSelect()
{
    // Hide or display the media player.
    window.ActiveMovie1.ShowSelectionControls =
!(window.ActiveMovie1.ShowSelectionControls)

    // Change the pbDisplay button caption as appropriate.
    if (window.ActiveMovie1.ShowSelectionControls)
    {
        Form1.pbSelect.Value = "No Select"
    }
    else
    {
        Form1.pbSelect.Value = "Select"
    }
```

```
        }
        //-->
        </SCRIPT>

        <TITLE>ActiveMovie
        </TITLE>
        </HEAD>
        <BODY>

        <!-Insert an ActiveMovie control.->
        <OBJECT ID="ActiveMovie1" WIDTH=267 HEIGHT=73
          CLASSID="CLSID:05589FA1-C356-11CE-BF01-00AA0055595A"
          CODEBASE="http://aux/controls">
            <PARAM NAME="_ExtentX" VALUE="7038">
            <PARAM NAME="_ExtentY" VALUE="1931">
            <PARAM NAME="FileName" VALUE="TwilZone.WAV">
        <EMBED NAME="ActiveMovie1" WIDTH=267 HEIGHT=73
          CLASSID="CLSID:05589FA1-C356-11CE-BF01-00AA0055595A"
          CODEBASE="http://aux/controls"
            TYPE="application/oleobject"
            PARAM__ExtentX="7038"
            PARAM__ExtentY="1931"
            PARAM_FileName="TwilZone.WAV"
        ></OBJECT><P>

        <!-Create a form just for the buttons.->
        <FORM NAME=Form1>

        <!-Define some buttons for playing various file types.->
        <H4>File Types</H4>
        <INPUT TYPE=button NAME="pbWave"
          VALUE="WAV"
          ONCLICK=PlayWAV()>
        <INPUT TYPE=button NAME="pbMIDI"
          VALUE="MIDI"
          ONCLICK=PlayMIDI()>
        <INPUT TYPE=button NAME="pbAVI"
          VALUE="AVI"
          ONCLICK=PlayAVI()><P>

        <!-Define some control buttons.->
        <H4>Control Buttons</H4>
        <INPUT TYPE=button NAME="pbRun"
          VALUE="Run"
          ONCLICK=PlayerRun()>
        <INPUT TYPE=button NAME="pbStop"
```

```
  VALUE="Stop"
  ONCLICK=PlayerStop()>
<INPUT TYPE=button NAME="pbPause"
  VALUE="Pause"
  ONCLICK=PlayerPause()><P>

<!-Define some mode control buttons.->
<H4>Mode Controls</H4>
<INPUT TYPE=button NAME="pbDisplay"
  VALUE="No Display"
  ONCLICK=ModeDisplay()>
<INPUT TYPE=button NAME="pbControls"
  VALUE="No Controls"
  ONCLICK=ModeControls()>
<INPUT TYPE=button NAME="pbSelect"
  VALUE="Select"
  ONCLICK=ModeSelect()><P>
</FORM>

</BODY>
</HTML>
```

You'll probably take one look at this code and wonder about a few of the coding techniques used here—especially after looking at the rest of the examples in this book. You'll need to make a few changes to your standard coding techniques if you want both Netscape Navigator and Internet Explorer users to access the same page. The first consideration is the amount of code users will need to download. Notice that this page uses a lot of <INPUT> tags in place of the ActiveX command buttons we've used in other examples. If you used ActiveX controls everywhere, the source shown here would get significantly longer without providing much more in the way of functionality. When working with large examples that are going to take a long time to download, you owe it to the user to make them as space saving as possible in areas that don't really matter. In this case, an <INPUT> tag provides just as much functionality as a command button would.

Another coding technique that you'll have to get used to is non-direct function calls. We saw in other chapters that you could define a JavaScript <SCRIPT> tag like this: <SCRIPT FOR=pbCommand EVENT=Click()>. The problem with this approach is that Netscape Navigator will try to interpret the script before the page is in place and the ScriptActive plug-in has had time to do its work. Listing 14-3 shows the approach that you should use to get around this problem—at least one way of getting around it. In this case, the JavaScript calls won't become active until after the page is fully in place.

Always remember that Netscape Navigator doesn't understand VBScript, which means you have to use JavaScript in places where you want to use this browser.

You'll know if a function is causing problems because you'll get an unknown property, method, or control error from Netscape's JavaScript handler.

NOTE: There is a problem with the SelectionStart and SelectionEnd properties of the current version of the ActiveMovie control. The control properly detects the beginning and end of the first control it loads. After that, any new controls will automatically begin and end at the same time-counter settings as the first control did. You can get around this problem by setting the SelectionStart and SelectionEnd properties manually after loading a new file.

Of course, the bottom line is how the two displays look. Figure 14-6 shows the sample program as displayed in Netscape Navigator. Figure 14-7 shows the same display for Internet Explorer. Unlike our previous examples, these displays actually look close enough alike that you can count on a certain level of functionality.

Let's look at the functionality of this program for a few minutes. If you click on either the WAV or AVI buttons, Netscape Navigator and Internet Explorer will comply by loading one of the files we specified in Listing 14-3. Figure 14-8 shows how the ActiveMovie control changes when you load an AVI file.

14

ActiveMovie example using Netscape Navigator as the browser.
Figure 14-6.

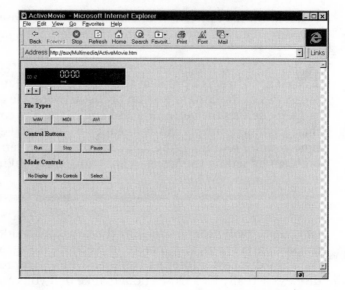

ActiveMovie
example using
Internet
Explorer as
the browser.
Figure 14-7.

You should see a download progress indicator like the one shown in the figure until the browser finishes the download process. Now click on the MIDI button. It will look for a second as if the file is going to load, then you'll see a quick glimpse of an error indicator in the display area of the ActiveMovie control, then the control will return to normal. Click Run, and you'll find out that the file you loaded last is still loaded. There are a number of ways that the control could have reacted when you tried to load a file type that it doesn't support, but this one is probably the best from a user's perspective (it's the worst from a programmer's perspective). Let's hope the next version of ActiveMovie supports MID files. Microsoft also plans to add several new features to the ActiveMovie control in the near future. One of these features is an Error event—which will allow the programmer to react to errors, such as the inability to load a media file. You'll also see more controls for controlling the actual media. For example, a future version of the control will probably include rewind, skip, fast forward, and fast reverse functions.

NOTE: The download indicator doesn't always work. For example, if users already have a copy of the file in their cache, they won't see the download indicator. Even with a copy of the file in the cache, the indicator should probably display the load status since it still takes about 30 seconds with a local copy. According to Microsoft, this control is a work in progress, and they'll probably add more features to take care of problems like this one.

The
ActiveMovie
control
normally
shows the
download
status of an
AVI file,
which is very
helpful from
a user's
perspective.
Figure 14-8.

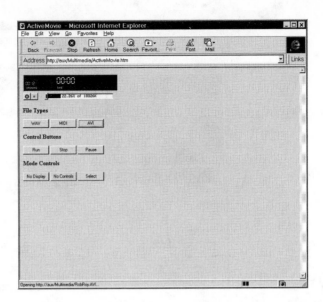

The function of the middle row of buttons is self-explanatory. The Run button allows you to play the media, the Stop button allows you to stop it, and the Pause button allows you to simply pause the media, then restart it with the Run button. As you can see from Listing 14-3, the code for adding this functionality is pretty easy to figure out.

ActiveMovie provides some configuration options that won't be obvious immediately, especially since you can't access the property pages from ActiveX Control Pad. The last three buttons show some of these configuration options (which you can change dynamically). The first is the No Display button. It allows you to remove the status display that contains the time indicator and selection options. The No Controls button removes all of the controls from view. However, you may not want to remove all of the controls from view, so the third button (Select) shows how you can enable or disable just one set of controls from the display.

Click the Select button, and you'll see two new buttons like those shown in Figure 14-9. As shown by the balloon help, the first button sets the SelectionStart property, while the second button sets the SelectionEnd property. All you need to do is set the slider to the starting or ending point, and then click the appropriate button when using this feature. Some displays, such as the one shown in Figure 14-9, show the Selection range all the time. Other displays—for example, the WAV file displays shown in Figures 14-6 and 14-7—only show the Selection range after you set it the first time.

14

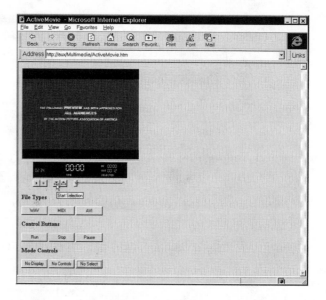

ActiveMovie doesn't show all the controls it supports as a default—you have to select some of them manually.
Figure 14-9.

Third-Party Multimedia Solutions

If you're serious about multimedia, you'll eventually get tired of trying to figure out some generic kludge for getting your site to work properly. Even with ActiveMovie, you'll still find the need to figure out a way of getting around some of the problems of displaying information until Microsoft provides a fully functional version of the control. (You'll probably want to check out their Internet site at http://www.microsoft.com/activex/controls/ from time to time to download new controls, such as the Gradient control that allows you to create a color transition in a certain area of the display.) Looking for better solutions usually means that you'll need to make an investment in a third-party product. That's what this section is all about. We're going to take a very quick look at a few third-party solutions that can really change the appearance of your Web site.

You're still going to run into problems when using a third-party product. For one thing, you'll need to incur the cost of a server for your Internet site in most cases. The majority of these third-party solutions rely on a method called *data streaming* to get the data from your Web site to the client site in an orderly manner. The file actually contains a pointer to a data stream on the Web server, which reduces the download to a few hundred bytes. Once the file loads, it tells a player to look in a specific place in the data stream. The media plays as users download the data stream from the Web site, greatly reducing any frustration they'll experience (at least in most cases) waiting for files to download. This solution also has the advantage of not leaving a file on the user's machine—a real advantage when using video clips or other media that could clog the viewer's system and cause copyright problems for the Webmaster. Unfortunately, while the plug-in or ActiveX control required to use the data is free, the server is far from cheap. You'll want to make sure that whatever product you choose fully supports all of the platforms that you think will visit your Web site.

Servers aren't the only problem you'll face. Several of these products provide a plug-in for Netscape Navigator users and an ActiveX control for Internet Explorer users. The difference in technology can (and probably will) affect the way the user sees your Web site. You'll still end up looking at your Web site using several products to make sure it looks the way you want it to, no matter what browser product the user selects.

Added to these other requirements is one item you may not have thought of. When you use the native capabilities that Windows provides—or simply ignore part of the market by using an ActiveX control such as ActiveMovie— you know for a fact that users will have the proper utility to view your site installed on their machine. You can't guarantee that when working with a third-party product. Unlike ActiveX controls, you can't help someone to download and install a plug-in for the most part. The bottom line is that you'll have to provide plenty of messages telling users what they need to view your site. In addition, you'll probably want to provide links to Internet sites where they can download the needed utilities or plug-ins.

14

RealAudio for Great Sounds

Playing music and other forms of audio enhancements is probably the most common way of making a Web site more attractive. RealAudio makes this process at least a little easier while enhancing the quality of sound that you'll get. RealAudio has several different forms, not just an ActiveX control. The current version of this multimedia player also comes as a plug-in for Netscape Navigator. You can contact the makers of RealAudio at http://www.realaudio.com/ for details on the player, SDK, and utility support. The SDK, RealAudio Encoder, RealAudio Timeline Editor, RealAudio Personal Server, and RealAudio Content Creation Guide are free for the price of a download. The RealAudio Personal Server supports two data streams— more than enough for demonstration or experimentation purposes.

Multiple levels of player support is only one of the things in favor of using this particular technology. It's also in use by quite a few Web sites. One of the more interesting sites that you can look at is http://www.cdnow.com/

(which connects to Magazine Warehouse). This is a CD/movie store that uses multimedia to good effect. For example, if you want to purchase a CD, you can hear selected tracks over your PC's speaker before you do so. They also sell T-shirts. You can view them before you buy if you'd like. About the only thing missing is the ability to view movie segments before you buy, but it's almost certain they'll add this capability eventually.

Getting started with RealAudio shouldn't be any problem. All you need to do is set up the server, encode your files, and then set up a Web page. The RealAudio Encoder utility dialog is shown in the following illustration. All you need to do is select the file you want to encode, enter any information needed in the Description area, and then click the Encode button to encode the file. (The RealAudio Encoder utility will automatically enter a destination filename for you.)

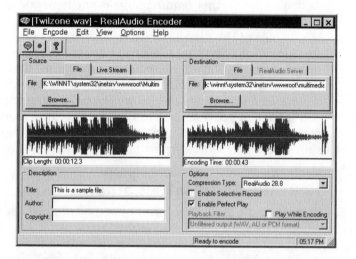

Adding the control to your Web page is pretty easy as well. All you need to do is select the RealAudio control from the list of controls in the Insert ActiveX Control dialog in ActiveX Control Pad—the same process that we've followed before. The only property you need to change other than CodeBase is shown here. Simply enter the URL where your sound file is located.

Listing 14-4 shows the code we'll use for this example. Notice that it contains the <EMBED> tag required by NCompass ScriptActive. This is one of the few controls that works absolutely flawlessly in both Netscape Navigator and Internet Explorer.

NOTE: You may need to change the HEIGHT and WIDTH attributes for the RealAudio1 <OBJECT> tag to work with your particular display configuration. The current values represent a default sizing that some people may find too small on high resolution displays.

14

Listing 14-4

```
<HTML>
<HEAD>
<TITLE>RealAudio Test</TITLE>
</HEAD>
<BODY>

<!-Display the heading.->
<CENTER><H2>Test of RealAudio ActiveX Control</H2></CENTER>

Click here to test the control:<BR>
<!-Display the control.->
<OBJECT ID="RealAudio1" WIDTH=49 HEIGHT=39
    CLASSID="CLSID:CFCDAA03-8BE4-11CF-B84B-0020AFBBCCFA"
```

```
            CODEBASE="http://aux/controls">
            <PARAM NAME="_ExtentX" VALUE="1296">
            <PARAM NAME="_ExtentY" VALUE="1032">
            <PARAM NAME="SRC" VALUE="http://aux/multimedia/TwilZone.RA">
            <PARAM NAME="AUTOSTART" VALUE="0">
            <PARAM NAME="NOLABELS" VALUE="0">
        <EMBED NAME="RealAudio1" WIDTH=49 HEIGHT=39
            CLASSID="CLSID:CFCDAA03-8BE4-11CF-B84B-0020AFBBCCFA"
            CODEBASE="http://aux/controls"
            TYPE="application/oleobject"
            PARAM__ExtentX="1296"
            PARAM__ExtentY="1032"
            PARAM_SRC="http://aux/multimedia/TwilZone.RA"
            PARAM_AUTOSTART="0"
            PARAM_NOLABELS="0" >
        </OBJECT>

        </BODY>
        </HTML>
```

Now that you have the code put together, let's look at the final result. Figure 14-10 shows how the example page will look. The user can simply click the RealAudio button to open the sound file. This particular control offers more than that, however. Right-click the control, and you'll see the context menu shown in Figure 14-10. Users can customize the control to meet their specific needs.

So, what does the control look like in action? Here's how our sample WAV file looks from the user's perspective:

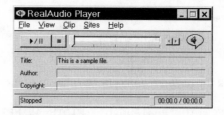

The
RealAudio
control
provides a
distinct
pushbutton
interface
along with
a context
menu for user
settings.

Figure 14-10.

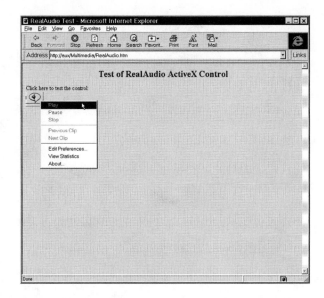

Notice that the dialog shows the description information added while in the RealAudio Encode utility. Unfortunately, the amount of information you can add is somewhat limited. It would have been nice to have one user-configurable field in addition to the default fields offered by the control.

14

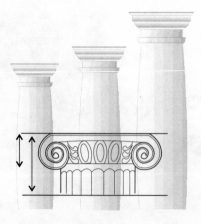

PART

4

Appendixes

Appendix A

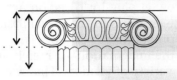

ActiveX Component Resources

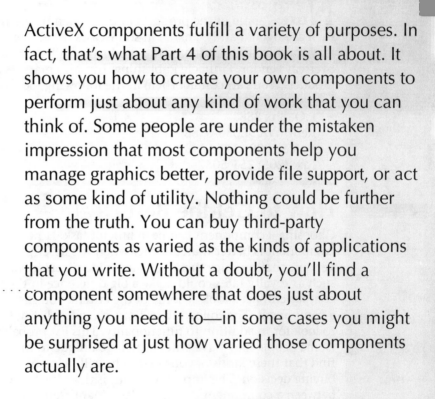

ActiveX components fulfill a variety of purposes. In fact, that's what Part 4 of this book is all about. It shows you how to create your own components to perform just about any kind of work that you can think of. Some people are under the mistaken impression that most components help you manage graphics better, provide file support, or act as some kind of utility. Nothing could be further from the truth. You can buy third-party components as varied as the kinds of applications that you write. Without a doubt, you'll find a component somewhere that does just about anything you need it to—in some cases you might be surprised at just how varied those components actually are.

This appendix looks at some of the third-party components available on the market. It's divided into three sections: OCXs waiting for conversion to true ActiveX controls, ActiveX controls, and browser plug-ins based on ActiveX controls. You'll probably find most of these products in the Visual Basic section of your favorite computer store or programmer's catalog. This appendix isn't complete by any stretch of the imagination—it merely shows a selection of ActiveX components from a variety of vendors. That way, if you don't see what you need, you can always contact one of the vendors listed here to see if they can provide the component you do need.

 NOTE: Some of the products in this appendix are from other countries, such as England and Canada. In some cases developers in the United States may want to try to purchase the products locally instead of relying on an overseas vendor. Pinnacle Publishing, Inc. also markets many of these products. You can contact them at the following locations:

P.O. Box 888
Kent, WA 98035-0888
Voice: (800) 231-1293
Fax: (206) 251-5057

How to Get the Best Deal

Choosing a component can be a difficult task. How do you know one component is better than another when the descriptions provided by the vendors that produce them are almost identical? In addition, other features such as royalty rates could make a big difference in the way you view a component. Let's look at some of the criteria you should use when selecting a component. The following sections provide a list of things you might want to look for in addition to functionality. This list probably isn't all-inclusive (some people may have criteria that are unique to their situation), but you'll find that these kinds of considerations will help you make an informed buying decision. The important point is that this list will help you choose between a component that provides a lot of really nice features and one that is best suited to your needs.

Royalties

Some companies charge a royalty when you use their product for commercial purposes. If you plan to use their product in your application and then sell your application to other people, you may have to pay the company royalties to maintain the licensing arrangement. Always look for products that don't charge a royalty first. That way you don't have to worry about licensing the product at all. If you don't find one in this category, start looking for an OEM licensing arrangement. Sometimes you can get by with an annual fee or other "one-shot" licensing scheme. Obviously, using a product that requires a royalty will also increase the price of your product, so looking around for a royalty-free product is always a good idea.

Source Code

There is that rare breed of components you can buy with some level of source code support. Some of them will require an additional purchase to get the source. If you're a professional consultant or someone who distributes applications commercially, the cost of buying that source is minimal compared to what you'll gain by having it. Not only will having the source allow you to learn new programming techniques, but you can use it to enhance the component you've purchased. Needless to say, source code is a rarity when buying an ActiveX component, but you do see it offered. Normally you'll need to know C to use the source code.

Recommendations from Other Programmers

Most of you have probably been bitten by a piece of software that was so buggy and ill-conceived it was unusable. Unfortunately, the companies that produce this kind of software are usually good at marketing and offer you just about everything you can imagine without delivering anything of the sort. It doesn't take most programmers very long to figure out that they should have gotten a few recommendations from other people before they bought the product. You should, too. Many times, someone has purchased a product that you're thinking about buying. See if you can get a few opinions before you buy.

Demo or Shareware Versions

There are times when you can't get a recommendation from another programmer. Perhaps no one has used the product in the same way that you intend to use it. In this case finding a demo or shareware version of the product that you want to use can save you a lot of grief later. Sure, they won't be full-featured, and some vendors actually make the shareware or demo version hide flaws in the full-featured product, but it's better than buying the product without even viewing it first. If you do try a shareware or demo version, see if other programmers have tried both the demo and final product. The feedback they provide will help you understand how the shareware or demo version of the product varies from what you'll actually buy.

TIP: Just about every product listed in this appendix includes the address of an online service. You'll find that most vendors place press releases and demonstration copies of their product on their Web site or forum. Make sure you spend the money to visit these sites before you buy a product. The visit may not only net a demo version of a product for you, but give you insights into the kind of support you can expect from the vendor.

Money-Back Guarantee

Vendors are getting smarter as the software industry matures. It's surprising to see how many vendors offer a 30- to 60-day money-back guarantee with their product these days. (At least one of the vendors in this appendix offers a whopping 90-day money-back guarantee.) What you'll need to find out first though are the terms of that money-back guarantee. Make sure you can try the product out on a small project or two, then return it if it doesn't work as advertised. You'll also need to check the return policy of the third-party vendor you buy a product through. In a few cases, vendors haven't honored their money-back guarantee when a programmer bought their product through a third party. Since the third-party seller didn't have a money-back guarantee either, the programmer ended up eating the cost of the purchase.

Company Stability and Support

Programmers rely on vendors to provide them with good updates on a fairly regular basis to remain competitive. If the one-man shop you buy your component from goes out of business tomorrow, how will you support the product you build with it? The problem doesn't only extend to practical matters like new technology; you'll need that support when a customer calls in with a bug that isn't in your code. You'll find that interactions between your program and a third-party product happen more often than you'd like. If the company you're working with goes out of business or charges by the minute for support, you may be out of luck when it comes time to fix that bug the user reported.

Cost per Component Versus Quality

Some vendors in this appendix offer a grab bag of all kinds of components at a very low cost. Be aware that those components may or may not be the best quality. Think about your own business. Could you afford to offer a lot of product for a low cost if it took a lot of time to put the application together? In most cases you'll agree that a vendor who offers a lot of product at a low cost must have cut corners somewhere. (Of course, some people just charge too much—the opposite side of the coin.) If someone's willing to offer you something for close to nothing, make sure you take a hard look at the product before you buy. You may find that you're simply getting an extra good buy, but more often than not, you'll find that you're buying a box of trouble. The component you get won't be worth the time and effort to install it, much less use in a project.

Flexibility

One of the products in this appendix—Graphics Server—offers no less than six levels of platform support: DLL, VBX, VCL (Delphi component), OCX, FLL, and C++ class (with ActiveX support coming soon). This is a real plus because you never know when you'll need to use a component you bought for Delphi or Visual C++, for example, on some other platform, such as Visual Basic. This is especially true for consultants because the job or the client often dictate which language you'll use for a particular project. Flexibility takes other forms as well. What about a communications package that lets you use nine or ten different protocols, or a network package that works with NetWare 3.*x* and 4.*x*? Products that allow you to do more than the minimum needed are always a better deal than those that don't.

Efficiency

There's a wealth of components you probably wouldn't use to build an application, much less add to a Web site, because they require too many resources to use. Some vendors try to stick every bit of functionality known to programmers into one component. Sure, it will allow you to write any kind of program in just ten minutes; but the fact that it requires 16 MB of memory to run should tell you something—no one is going to be able to run the application you build. In addition, even Microsoft is emphasizing the value of small modules when it comes to writing ActiveX components. Obviously there aren't any components, OCX or otherwise, that require

A

16 MB of memory to run, but there's an important reason to emphasize this point. You're going to run into situations when you think you just have to add one more bell or whistle to a Web page, only to find that users complain it's slow or won't run well on their machine. Look for the small and efficient component. Get the job done with the least number of resources possible, and you'll find that the people using your program are a lot happier.

Another form of efficiency when it comes to the Internet is the way a control is designed for downloading purposes. You might find that the control consumes very little space or resources by itself but requires help from a variety of support modules. A large component broken into a lot of small pieces isn't much better than a single large component. In fact, you'll find yourself spending time gathering all of the files together to ensure that a visitor to your Web site gets a complete copy of the control. An efficient ActiveX control will usually contain one, or maybe two, components. Look for vendors who have taken the time to create small controls that are actually the size they say they are. This is especially important when you know the vendor has converted an OCX to an ActiveX control. Make sure the conversion doesn't consist only of a name change.

NOTE: All prices in this chapter are current list prices as of the time of writing. The prices may change without notice.

OCXs—A Step Away from ActiveX

We looked at OCXs in Chapter 2. You can use them from a Web page if they aren't too resource intensive. The big thing you need to worry about is whether the OCX will actually work on the client machine and whether it stores a lot of persistent data (which increases download time and resource usage). Using an OCX instead of a bona fide ActiveX control also means that users will get the dreaded "not trusted" message when they try to download the control from your Web site. These problems aside, OCXs still represent a good value for the typical programmer—especially if you can't find what you need in an ActiveX control.

TIP: If you see a control in a catalog that only comes in VBX format, take time to call the vendor. You'll probably find that the catalog is out of date and that the vendor has already made the move from the 16-bit world to the 32-bit world. Even if the vendor hasn't made the change, your call may convince him to do so. Some vendors make business decisions based (at least in part) on input from people buying their products. A phone call at the right time could mean the difference between getting the control you need and programming it by hand.

Graphics Server SDK
$299.00
Bits Per Second, Ltd.
14 Regent Hill, Brighton BN1 3ED, UK
Telephone: 01273-727119
Fax: 01273-731925
CompuServe: >MHS:rflowers@bits
Internet: rflowers@bits.mhs.compuserve.com

This is the full-fledged version of the run-time product included with products such as Visual Basic and Delphi. It comes with DLL, VBX, VCL (Delphi component), OCX, FLL, and C++ class support; making it just about the most versatile tool in this appendix. Just like the run-time version, the server runs as an independent application outside of your Delphi or Visual Basic application. However, this product provides a lot more than the run-time version does.

TIP: Bits Per Second provides a special update offer for programmers who own Visual Basic or another product that comes with the run-time version of Graphics Server. Call them for the current price of this special deal.

A

Graphics Server is an OLE 2 graphics primitive engine. It supports commands that draw circles or squares. You can use it to perform a variety of complex drawing tasks with products other than Delphi or Visual Basic—even those that don't support OLE directly (CA-Visual Objects is one of them). This feature makes Graphics Server more than just an application programming tool; it's a tool that you could potentially use with a variety of products in a lot of different environments.

If you don't want to work with graphics primitives, and a graph or chart is your goal, you can use the included ChartBuilder product. This is the full-featured version of the Graph control included with Visual Basic. (The latest version of Graphics Server incorporates all of these capabilities into a single product.) All you need to do is tell ChartBuilder what data points you want to display and what type of graph or chart to display them on. It takes care of all the details.

There isn't room in this appendix to talk about all of the features of this product, but here are a few more:

♦ You can use Graphics Server SDK with Microsoft Excel and Word for Windows.

♦ Versions 4.5 and above fully support VBA.

♦ It includes support for spline graphs, floating bar graphs, and error bars on all log graphs.

About the only thing that you won't find here is source code. Bits Per Second wants to protect their investment, so you'll have to be satisfied with the compiled code. Graphics Server currently comes with a 30-day money-back guarantee.

ALLText HT/Pro and TList Enhanced Outline
$350.00
Bennet-Tec Information Systems
50 Jericho Turnpike
Jericho, NY 11753
Voice: (516) 997-5596
Fax: (516) 997-5597
CompuServe: GO BENNET-TEC
Internet: controls@bennet-tec.com

ALLText HT/Pro is essentially a word processor with a little extra oomph. It includes hypertext support, embedded OLE objects for graphics or other document embedding, RTF (rich text format) input and output, and data-aware support. The PEN edition provides support for pen-based computing—a nice feature if you have to provide this kind of support.

RTF is the word processing format used by the Windows help compiler. Many word processors use this format as a means for exchanging data with other word processors. The data-aware support means that ALLText includes the name of the application that created an object as part of the object. You could theoretically provide a small text processor in your application, then allow the user to export the file to a full-fledged word processor such as Microsoft Word without too many problems.

TList is an enhanced outlining control. It provides more features than your typical word processor will provide—making it more like the professional outlining tools that you see on the market. One of the special features of this product is the ability to customize items displayed in the outline. For example, you could give an item a special color or use a different icon to display it. This product also supports advanced features such as item hiding, bookmarks, category images, and drag and drop.

> **Communications Library 3**
> $149.00
> **Fax Plus**
> $249.00
> MicroHelp
> 4211 JVL Industrial Park Drive, NE
> Marietta, GA 30066
> Voice: (800) 922-3383 or (404) 516-0899
> Fax: (404) 516-1099
> Internet: http://www.microhelp.com

A

Communications Library 3 is a general communications library, which means that it provides a lot of generic capabilities that will allow you to build a specific type of communication program. It supports five terminal emulations: ANSI, TTY, VT52, VT100, and VT220. In addition, it provides support for eight file transfer protocols, including Kermit, CompuServe B+, X, Y, and Z modem. Unlike some packages, the Z modem support in this package also provides auto-recovery support. You can use Communications Library 3 up to speeds of 25.6 Kbps.

Trying to support the wide variety of modems is one of the big problems in writing a communications program. Communications Library 3 comes with over 150 initialization strings to support the most common modems. You'll also find a selection of Pascal subprograms and forms. The forms include those required for serial port and parameter selection, dialing the phone, and many other functions.

MicroHelp includes VBXs, DLLs, and 16/32-bit OCXs with Communications Library 3. It provides OLE 2 support for all of your file transfer needs. The library will support multiple communication ports (eight is the practical limit).

Fax Plus is another communications product from MicroHelp. You can use it with any class 1, 2, or 2.0 fax modem. Fortunately, the product also includes some components you can use to detect the type of modem—a requirement if you plan to distribute your application commercially.

One of the more interesting features of Fax Plus is that it supports faxes through printed output. In other words, you can build an application in such a way that it can take the printed output from another application and send it as a fax. You can also import BMP, PCX, DCX, or TIFF files to send as faxes. The standard fax format is ASCII text.

Unlike Communications Library 3, Fax Plus automatically handles the fax modem initialization for you. Of course, this is limited to the set of modems it supports, so you'll need to check whether the fax modem you want to use with Fax Plus is supported before you try to use it. The package also contains a variety of sample programs and other documentation to show you how to use the product. Both Fax Plus and Communications Library 3 are royalty free.

ActiveX Controls

ActiveX controls (at least for the purposes of this appendix) are different from OCXs only in the fact that they've been redesigned for Internet use. In most cases that means they have less persistent data, and any security concerns have been taken into account. Some of the ActiveX controls listed here are the same as the OCXs that you might find in a programmer's catalog somewhere, and that should give you some ideas. If you see a control you need that doesn't come in ActiveX format, it's probably time to call the vendor and see if they plan to produce an ActiveX version (they probably have and the catalog is simply out of date).

NOTE: Some of the controls listed in this section are so new that there wasn't any pricing information available. Be sure to contact the vendor for pricing information. You can also download sample copies of many of these controls from the ActiveX Component Gallery at http://www.microsoft.com/activex/gallery/.

MediaKnife
$399.00 (OCX version)
ImageKnife
$499.00 (OCX version)
Media Architects
1075 NW Murray Road, Suite 230
Portland, OR 97229-5501
Voice: (503) 297-5010
Fax: (503) 297-6744

MediaKnife is a fairly new offering from Media Architects. It allows you to
create all kinds of media presentations using a variety of file formats such as
AVI. You can use its WinG-based display technology to create transition
effects, background buffering of images and sound, irregular hot spots, and
custom cursors. This product also provides animated sprite capabilities.
The best part of all is that you can see all of these capabilities at design
time—meaning you won't spend as much time compiling an application or
setting up a Web site to test a particular design.

Some of the special MediaKnife capabilities include the ability to decompress
Iterated Systems' resolution-independent fractal files. The product includes
editors that allow you to perform a variety of tasks, including hot spot
definition, batch palette editing, and animated sprite assembly.

ImageKnife is a very complex graphics OCX that supports the Microsoft
Access Paintbrush Picture OLE Object format. It helps you acquire images
using the TWAIN scanner interface. That's the same interface used by
CorelDRAW and other similar products. Once you acquire an image, you
can change its appearance and store it in either a file or database. You could
use this library to provide an added level of support for graphics databases
using the Access database format. Of course, you aren't limited to Access
databases; you can also use this product with other DBMSs that support this
graphics format.

A

Don't get the idea that you can't use ImageKnife for some of the more
mundane graphics chores in your application. It also supports a variety of
other file formats, including BMP, DIB, JPEG, GIF, PCX, TIFF, and Targa. You
can display those files as true color (24-bit), Super VGA (8-bit), VGA (8-bit),
or monochrome images. This versatility makes ImageKnife a good graphics
library selection for most applications.

Both MediaKnife and ImageKnife come with a 90-day money-back guarantee. You can also include these products in your applications royalty free.

Command, Date Select, Masked Edit, and SysInfo

Aditi Inc.
10940 NE 33rd Place
Suite 204
Bellevue, WA 98004
Voice: (206) 828-9646
Internet: http://www.aditi.com

Command is a button that can adjust its shape in a number of ways, including ellipse, triangle, pentagon, and rhombus. If the control doesn't come with a shape to suit your needs, you can always draw your own. Like a lot of other controls of this type, Command allows you to use custom icons and captions for each button state.

Date Select provides a selection box for picking a date. Instead of entering a date by hand, the user simply presses a speed button. Highlighting a particular date element (month, day, or year) changes that element when the speed button is pressed. Clicking on another part of the control displays a calendar that the user can use to set the date as well.

You can never be certain of what a user will enter at a particular prompt. The results can be disastrous unless you include a lot of error trapping code. Masked Edit takes all of the work out of doing this for you. It restricts user entries to specific, predefined input. Database applications have had this capability for years—it's nice to see it available for the Internet as well. Aditi provides a number of predefined masks for you but allows you to add any custom masks that you need.

If you haven't noticed yet, trying to write an application for the Internet is a shot in the dark. At least if you write an application for general distribution in shrink-wrap, you can include some system requirements on the box. The same isn't true for an ActiveX control. It could encounter any kind of machine ever made. That's where SysInfo comes into play. This control allows you to scan the client machine and learn some basic parameters about it, such as what operating system it's using and the size of its hard drive. You can also detect the processor type and whether a math coprocessor is present. Detecting this kind of information frees you to provide users with a specific feedback message when they can't use your site due to equipment problems.

SmartHelp

Blue Sky Software
7777 Fay Avenue
Suite 201
La Jolla, CA 92037
Voice: (800) 677-4946
Internet: http://www.blue-sky.com

While Microsoft seems bent on moving you away from the Windows help format, Blue Sky seems equally determined to move you toward it. This control allows you to display a Windows help file from the user's browser. You might ask yourself why this particular control is even needed. HTML doesn't currently provide the same search capabilities that the Windows help file format does. In addition, using a help file format that the user is familiar with is one sure way to decrease support calls. Special features of this control include the ability to change the button bitmap (48 come with the product) and the type of help displayed (Windows 3.*x* or 95 style).

Light Lib

DFL Software, Inc.
55 Eglinton Avenue E.
Suite 208
Toronto, ON M4P 1G8
Voice: (416) 487-2660
Internet: http://www.dfl.com

There are four different versions of Light Lib that are ActiveX enabled (with more to come in all likelihood): Light Lib Business, Light Lib Images, Light Lib Multimedia Video, and Light Lib Multimedia Sound. Various versions of this product have appeared in programming languages. For example, you'll find it included with CA-Visual Objects.

A

Light Lib Business allows you to create charts and graphs. The actual number of charts and graphs wasn't available as of this writing, but you can be sure it will include the basic 2-D and 3-D chart types: bar, line, pie, gantt, complex ribbon, stacked, and percent. The context menu displayed when you right-click on the control is pretty special too. It allows the user either to save the current image as a file or place it on the desktop as wallpaper. The context menu contains the usual entries such as Copy and Properties as well.

DFL bills Light Lib Images as a complete document and image management library. It certainly provides a variety of controls for adjusting an image. For example, you can adjust the brightness and contrast of an image. The preliminary control also appeared to provide gamma correction capabilities. As with most libraries of this type you can perform a variety of image manipulations, such as rotating it. This control also includes the special context menu entries of the Light Lib Business control.

Both the Light Lib Multimedia Video and Light Lib Multimedia Sound controls are designed to make your animated presentations better. You'll find that they work well together even though DFL sells them as separate packages. The sound control provides a complete set of adjustments for a typical sound board that looks very much like the Volume Control dialog provided by Windows 95. In addition to the volume controls, you'll find a media player and set of file controls. The video control looks much like the AVI player provided by Windows 95. The difference is that the Light Lib player also provides volume controls. This control provides a speed setting as well that allows you to control the rate at which the video plays back.

Various Products
MicroHelp
4211 JVL Industrial Park Drive, NE
Marietta, GA 30066
Voice: (800) 922-3383 or (404) 516-0899
Fax: (404) 516-1099
Internet: http://www.microhelp.com

MicroHelp has a huge list of products to sell—more than I can tell you about in this appendix. A recent catalog containing the wares of many different vendors included 11 pages of MicroHelp products, while some vendors were having trouble filling one page.

You'll find that MicroHelp has fully embraced ActiveX technology. You can visit their Web site or the ActiveX Component Gallery to see what's available right now. What you'll see is a variety of 3-D control types, an alarm or two, some sliders and marquees, and even some game pieces such as cards and dice. Even Microsoft couldn't match this company's output of small but useful controls (widgets would be a better term) on the ActiveX Component Gallery at the time of this writing.

EarthTime
Starfish Software
1700 Green Hills Road
Scotts Valley, CA 95066
Voice: (800) 765-7839
Internet: http://www.starfishsoftware.com

The Internet is going to be a new experience for a lot of small and medium-sized companies because it will open up many more markets around the world. Take a simple thing like time. Everyone in a small company works at the same time (unless they're on the road in another city), and this didn't matter in the past. But now that they're doing business on the Internet, keeping everyone synchronized time-wise is going to be a nightmare. That's where EarthTime comes into play. It's a special control that shows you the local time in up to eight cities around the world. EarthTime includes over 375 world locations in its database, so you won't have a problem figuring out what time it is no matter where you are. You can use it to calculate time differences or to show seasonal changes in daylight and darkness. Some of EarthTime's special features include the ability to retrieve telephone codes, local language, and currency for many of the places employees will travel.

Browser Plug-Ins Based on ActiveX Controls

Plug-ins are part of the reason that your browser won't stay plain for very long. They allow you to add custom capabilities to your setup. In most cases you'll find that the plug-in is free, but the server for the plug-in is fairly expensive. What does this mean to you as a programmer? It means that if you decide to add a specific capability to your Web site, you'll need to pay server fees for it. In some cases there's a price for buying the server initially, then an annual maintenance fee after that. From a user's perspective it means that you can usually enhance your browser for free and gain the added features offered by a specific Internet site.

This section lists some of the more intriguing ActiveX plug-ins that you'll either see now or in the near future. If you don't see a price attached to a particular plug-in, it means that the browser part of the product is either free or that pricing information wasn't available at the time of this writing. Always assume that there's a cost associated with buying the server required to use the plug-in at an Internet site. Contact the vendor at the address shown to get pricing information.

A

VDOLive ActiveX for Windows 95
VDOnet Corp.
4009 Miranda Avenue
Suite 250
Palo Alto, CA 94304
Voice: (415) 846-7700
Fax: (415) 846-7900
Internet: http://www.vdo.net/enhanced.html

The basic purpose for VDOLive is to let you play real-time audio and video located on a Web site within your browser. It includes the capability for playing movies and other kinds of animated media presentations. The new 2.0 version promises better video quality (10 to 15 frames per second) and image size (352 X 288). It will also include an intriguing idea—storybook mode. In this mode, still images are synchronized with audio. In essence, you'll see the presentation unfold much like you would in a storybook.

NOTE: A product called VDOPhone is also in the works. It will allow you to send voice communications over the Internet. The product wasn't available at the time of this writing but probably will be by the time you read this.

VRML ActiveX for Windows 95
Microsoft Corp.
One Microsoft Way
Redmond, WA 98052-6399
Voice: (206) 882-8080
Fax: (206) 936-7329
Internet: http://www.microsoft.com/ie/ie3/vrml.htm

What if you were able to surf the net in 3-D? That's what VRML (virtual reality modeling language) is all about. It provides a method for displaying information in 3-D. Imagine the effect that VRML will eventually have on the engineering disciplines. For example, two architects could work on the same house over the Internet even though they lived miles apart. In addition, you could actually see what a product would look like before you bought it. VRML has already received a lot of attention from gamers, who will be able to play against each other across the Internet. This plug-in will help make that a reality because it allows the user to see the actions of other people as if they were in the same room. (They'll see the actions in the form of an avatar—a representation of the person—sent over the telephone line.)

Acrobat ActiveX for Windows 95
Adobe Systems Inc.
1585 Charleston Road
P.O. Box 7900
Mountain View, CA 94039-7900
Voice: (415) 961-4400
Fax: (415) 961-3769
Internet: http://www.adobe.com/

Adobe's Acrobat reader has already appeared in several places. If you're a programmer, you have probably used it to read help files in book form on your machine at one time or another. Acrobat uses PDF (Portable Document Format) to display information in a way that makes allowances for the display device. This new ActiveX version allows you to view PDF files using your browser instead of downloading the file and loading the entire Acrobat reader.

A

Appendix B

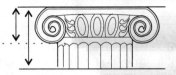

Glossary

This Glossary has several important features you need to be aware of. First, every acronym in the entire book is listed here—even if there's a better-than-even chance you already know what the acronym means. This way there isn't any doubt that you'll always find everything you need to use the book properly. The second thing you need to know is that these definitions are specific to the book. In other words, when you look through this Glossary, you're seeing the words defined in the context that they're used. This may or may not always coincide with current industry usage since the computer industry changes the meaning of words so often. Finally, the definitions here use a conversational tone in most cases. This means that they may sacrifice a bit of puritanical accuracy for the sake of better understanding.

128-bit/40-bit encryption key　(*See* Encryption level)

Access control entry　(*See* ACE)

Access control list　(*See* ACL)

ACE (access control entry)　A Windows NT-specific security component. Each object (which could include anything from a file to a piece of memory) contains two access control lists (ACLs). These lists determine what type of access a user, system element, or other type of object will have to the object. Within each ACL are one or more access control entries (ACEs). There is one entry for each user, group, or other object that has access to the object. This entry defines what type of access to grant. For example, a file object can grant read and write rights.

ACL (access control list)　A Windows NT-specific security component. There are two ACLs: the security access control list (SACL), which controls Windows' auditing feature, and the discretionary access control list (DACL), which controls who can actually use the object. The ACLs contain one or more access control entries (ACEs), which determine the actual rights for each user or object for which the ACL grants access.

ActiveX control　(*See* OCX)

ActiveX Document　One of several COM-based enabling technologies used on the Internet to display documents in formats that the Internet doesn't support natively, such as the Word for Windows DOC file format. Using ActiveX Document allows the OLE server to take over the browser's frame (menu and other features such as scroll bars) and present the document within the browser window.

ActiveX Movie　One of several COM-based enabling technologies used on the Internet to display real-time video and audio through the use of special file formats such as AVI files. ActiveX Movie may eventually allow companies to provide online presentations that don't require a person's presence at a particular site for participation.

Animated GIF　(*See* GIF)

API (application programming interface)　A method of defining a standard set of function calls and other interface elements. It usually defines the interface between a high-level language and the lower-level elements used by a device driver or operating system. The ultimate goal is to provide some type of service to an application that requires access to the operating system or device feature set.

Application programming interface (*See* API)

AVI (audiovisual interface) file format A special file format that contains both audio and video in digital format. AVI is currently the most popular method for transmitting *multimedia files* across the Internet.

Binary values Refers to a base 2 data representation in the Windows registry. Normally used to hold status flags or other information that lends itself to a binary format.

BLOB (binary large object) A special field in a database table that accepts objects such as bitmaps, sounds, or text as input. This field is normally associated with the OLE capabilities of a DBMS, but some third-party products make it possible to add BLOB support to older database file formats such as Xbase DBF file format. BLOB fields always imply OLE client support by the DBMS.

BMP files Windows' standard bitmap graphics data format. This is a raster graphic data format that doesn't include any form of compression. It's normally used by Windows, but OS/2 (and various other operating systems) can also use this data format to hold graphics of various types.

Browse A special application interface element designed to show the user an overview of a database or other storage media (for example, the thumbnail sketches presented by some graphics applications). Think of a browse as the table of contents to the rest of the storage area. A browse normally contains partial views of several data storage elements (records or picture thumbnails in most cases) that a user can then zoom to see their entirety. A browse form normally contains scrollbars or other high-speed interface elements to make it easier for the user to move from one section of the overall storage media to the next.

Browser A special application normally used to display data downloaded from the Internet. The most common form of Internet data is the HTML (hypertext markup language) page. However, modern browsers can also display various types of graphics and even standard desktop application files such as Word for Windows documents directly. The actual capabilities provided by a browser vary widely depending on the software vendor and platform.

B

CAB (cabinet) file A compressed format file similar to the ZIP files used to transfer code and data from one location to another. The CAB format is normally used only by developers.

CCITT (Consultative Committee for International Telegraph and Telephony) This group is now the ITU. Please see ITU for details.

CGI (common gateway interface) One of the more common methods of transferring data from a client machine to a Web server on the Internet. CGI relies on scripts to define how the data should be interpreted. There are two basic data transfer types. The user can send new information to the server or can query data already existing on the server. For example, a data entry form asking for the user's name and address would be an example of the first type of transaction. A search engine page on the Internet (a page that helps the user find information on other sites) is an example of the second type of transaction. The Web server normally provides some type of feedback for the user by transmitting a new page of information once the CGI script is complete. This could be as simple as an acknowledgment for data entry or a list of Internet sites for a data query.

Class ID (*See* CLSID)

Client The recipient of data, services, or resources from a file or other server. This term can refer to a workstation or an application. The server can be another PC or an application.

CLSID (class ID or identifier) A method of assigning a unique identifier to each object in the registry. Also refers to various high-level language constructs. Every object must provide a unique CLSID. The identifier is generated locally on the machine where the object is created, using some type of special software. (For example, the Microsoft OLE 2 SDK provides a utility for generating CLSIDs.) High-level languages such as Visual Basic and most C compilers normally perform the CLSID generation sequence automatically for the programmer.

COM (component object model) A Microsoft specification for an object-oriented code and data encapsulation method and transference technique. It's the basis for technologies such as OLE (object linking and embedding) and ActiveX (the replacement name for OCXs—an object-oriented code library technology). COM is limited to local connections. DCOM (distributed component object model) is the technology used to allow data transfers and the use of OCXs within the Internet environment.

Common gateway interface (*See* CGI)

Component object model (*See* COM)

Container Part of the object-oriented terminology that has become part of OLE. A container is a drive, file, or other resource used to hold objects. The container is normally referenced as an object itself.

Cookie One or more special files used by an Internet browser to store site-specific settings or other information specific to Web pages. The purpose of this file is to store the value of one or more variables so that the Web page can restore them the next time the user visits a site. A Webmaster always saves and restores the cookie as part of some Web page programming task using a programming language such as JavaScript, Java, VBScript, or CGI. In most cases this is the only file that a Webmaster can access on the client site's hard drive. The cookie could appear in one or more files anywhere on the hard drive, depending on the browser currently in use. Microsoft Internet Explorer uses one file for each site storing a cookie and places them in the Cookies folder that normally appears under the main Windows directory. Netscape Navigator uses a single file named COOKIE.TXT to store all of the cookies from all sites. This file normally appears in the main Navigator folder.

CryptoAPI (*See* Cryptographic Application Programming Interface)

Cryptographic Application Programming Interface (CryptoAPI) The specification provided by Microsoft that enables software developers to add encryption technology to their applications. It uses a 128-bit encryption technology, which means that the developer can't export such applications outside the United States or Canada.

Cryptographic Service Provider (*See* CSP)

CSP (Cryptographic Service Provider) A specialty company that deals in certifying the identity of companies, developers, or individuals on the Internet. This identification check allows the company to issue an electronic certificate, which can then be used to conduct transactions securely. Several levels of certification are normally provided within a specific group. For example, there are three levels of individual certification. The lowest merely verifies the individual's identity through an Internet mail address. The highest level requires the individual to provide written proof along with a notarized statement. When you access a certified site or try to download a certified document such as an ActiveX control, the browser will display the electronic certificate onscreen, allowing you to make a security determination based on fact.

B

DACL (discretionary access control list) A Windows NT-specific security component. The DACL controls who can actually use the object. You can assign both groups and individual users to a specific object.

Database management system (*See* DBMS)

DBMS (database management system) A collection of tables, forms, queries, reports, and other data elements. It acts as a central processing point for data accessed by one or more users. Most DBMSs (except those that are free-form or text-based) rely on a system of tables for storing information. Each table contains records (rows) consisting of separate data fields (columns). Common DBMSs include Access, Paradox, dBASE, and Filemaker Pro.

DCOM (distributed component object model) The advanced form of the component object model (COM) used by the Internet. This particular format enables data transfers across the Internet or other nonlocal sources. It adds the capability to perform asynchronous as well as synchronous data transfers—which prevents the client application from becoming blocked as it waits for the server to respond. *See* COM for more details.

DDE (dynamic data exchange) The ability to cut data from one application and paste it into another application. For example, you could cut a graphic image created with a paint program and paste it into a word processing document. Once pasted, the data doesn't reflect the changes made to it by the originating application. DDE also provides a method for communicating with an application that supports it and for requesting data. For example, you could use an Excel macro to call Microsoft Word and request the contents of a document file. Some applications also use DDE to implement file association strategies. For example, Microsoft Word uses DDE in place of command line switches to gain added flexibility when a user needs to open or print a file.

DDF (Diamond Directive File) Similar to an INF (information) or BAT (batch) file, the DDF provides instructions to a CAB (cabinet) creation utility such as DIANTZ for compressing one or more files into a single storage file. CAB files are normally used to distribute data locally, using a CD-ROM or other similar type of media, or remotely, through an Internet or other server connection. The DDF can also list files needed for a complete installation, but stored in other locations. Normally these missing files will already appear on the user's computer, so downloading them again would waste time. The DDF makes it possible to download them only as needed.

Diamond Directive File (*See* DDF)

Digital Signatures Initiative (*See* DSI)

Discretionary access control list (*See* DACL)

Distributed component object model (*See* DCOM)

DLL (dynamic link library) A specific form of application code loaded into memory by request. It's not executable by itself. A DLL does contain one or more discrete routines that an application may use to provide specific features. For example, a DLL could provide a common set of file dialogs used to access information on the hard drive. More than one application can use the functions provided by a DLL, reducing overall memory requirements when more than one application is running.

Drag and drop A technique used in object-oriented operating systems to access data without actually opening the file using conventional methods. For example, this system allows the user to pick up a document file, drag it to the printer, and drop it. The printer will print the document using its default settings.

DSI (Digital Signatures Initiative) A standard originated by the W^3C (World Wide Web Consortium) to overcome some limitations of channel-level security. For example, channel-level security can't deal with documents and application semantics. A channel also doesn't use the Internet's bandwidth very efficiently because all the processing takes place on the Internet rather than the client or server. This standard defines a mathematical method for transferring signatures—essentially a unique representation of a specific individual or company. DSI also provides a new method for labeling security properties (PICS2) and a new format for assertions (PEP). This standard is also built on the PKCS #7 and X509.v3 standards.

Dynamic data exchange (*See* DDE)

Dynamic link library (*See* DLL)

Encryption (*See* Cryptographic Application Programming Interface)

Encryption level The amount of encryption a file receives. Normally, the size of the encryption key is the determining factor in the strength and level of encryption. Most Internet browsers and local applications use two sizes: 40-bit and 128-bit. A 40-bit key can provide up to 2^{40} key combinations and is considered moderately difficult to break. A 128-bit key can provide up to 2^{128} key combinations and is considered very difficult to break. Only the 40-bit key technology is currently approved by the United States government for transport outside the United States or Canada. *See* Cryptographic Application Programming Interface for additional information.

B

File Transfer Management System   (*See* FTMS)

File transfer protocol   (*See* FTP)

FTMS (File Transfer Management System)   The Proginet Corporation introduced this ActiveX technology, which brings mainframe data to the desktop. Their Fusion FTMS will work with any development language that supports OLE containers such as Delphi, Visual C++, and PowerBuilder. Essentially, you'll place an ActiveX control on a form, define where to find the data, and then rely on the control to make the connection. Using this control reduces the amount of labor required to implement and maintain a mainframe connection. A special transfer server on the mainframe completes the package by automating all transfer requests. No longer does an operator have to manually download a needed file to the company's Web site before a client can access it. Users can directly access the data on the mainframe and download it to their local hard drive.

FTP (file transfer protocol)   One of several common data transfer protocols for the Internet. This particular protocol specializes in data transfer in the form of a file download. The user is presented with a list of available files in a directory list format. An FTP site may choose DOS or UNIX formatting for the file listing, though the DOS format is extremely rare. Unlike HTTP sites, an FTP site provides a definite information hierarchy through the use of directories and subdirectories, much like the file directory structure used on most workstation hard drives.

GIF (graphics interchange format)   The standard file format used to transfer data over the Internet. There are several different standards for this file format—the latest of which is the GIF89a standard you'll find used on most Internet sites. The GIF standard was originally introduced by CompuServe as a method for reducing the time required to download a graphic and the impact of any single bit errors that might occur. A secondary form of the GIF is the animated GIF. It allows the developer to store several images within one file. Between each file is one or more control blocks that determine block boundaries, the display location of the next image in relation to the display area, and other display features. A browser or other specially designed application will display the graphic images one at a time in the order they appear within the file to create animation effects.

Gopher   One of several common Internet data transfer protocols. Like FTP, Gopher specializes in file transfers. However, the two protocols differ in that Gopher always uses the UNIX file-naming convention, and it provides a friendlier interface than FTP. Even though Gopher transfers tend to be more reliable than those provided by FTP, FTP sites are far more common.

Graphics interchange format   (*See* GIF)

HTML (hypertext markup language)   A scripting language for the Internet that depends on the use of tags (keywords within angle brackets <>) to display formatted information onscreen in a non-platform-specific manner. The non-platform-specific nature of this scripting language makes it difficult to perform some basic tasks such as placement of a screen element at a specific location. However, the language does provide for the use of fonts, color, and various other enhancements onscreen. There are also tags for displaying graphic images. Scripting tags for using more complex scripting languages such as VBScript and JavaScript were recently added, though not all browsers support this addition. The latest tag addition allows the use of ActiveX controls.

HTTP (hypertext transfer protocol)   One of several common data transfer protocols for the Internet. This particular protocol specializes in the display of onscreen information such as data entry forms or informational displays. HTTP relies on HTML as a scripting language for describing special screen display elements, though you can also use HTTP to display nonformatted text.

Hypertext markup language   (*See* HTML)

Hypertext transfer protocol   (*See* HTTP)

IDAPI (Independent Database Application Programming Interface)   A set of Windows function calls and other interface elements introduced by companies led by Borland. IDAPI is designed to improve access to information contained in database files through the use of a common interface and data-independent access methods.

IETF (Internet Engineering Task Force)   The standards group tasked with finding solutions to pressing technology problems on the Internet. This group can approve standards created both within the organization itself and outside the organization as part of other group efforts. For example, Microsoft has requested the approval of several new Internet technologies through this group. If approved, the technologies would become an Internet-wide standard for performing data transfer and other specific kinds of tasks.

IMTF (Internet Management Task Force)   The standards group responsible for implementing new technologies on the Internet. The problem is that this group is mainly composed of volunteers. The wheels of progress grind slowly for the IMTF, just like any other standards organization. It's so slow, in fact, that many companies have come up with

B

their own solutions for making the Internet a friendlier place to work. For example, Microsoft has developed ActiveX in response to specific Internet-related problems, while Netscape has developed Netscape ONE (Open Network Environment).

Independent Database Application Programming Interface (*See* IDAPI)

INF (information) file   A special form of device or application configuration. It contains all the parameters that Windows requires to install or configure the device or application. For example, an application INF file might contain the location of data files and the interdependencies of DLLs. Both application and device INF files contain the registry and INF file entries required to make Windows recognize the application or device.

International Telephony Union   (*See* ITU)

Internet Engineering Task Force   (*See* IETF)

Internet Management Task Force   (*See* IMTF)

Internet protocol   (*See* IP)

Internet Server Application Programming Interface   (*See* ISAPI)

IP (Internet protocol)   The information exchange portion of the TCP/IP protocol used by the Internet. IP is an actual data transfer protocol that defines how the information is placed into packets and sent from one place to another. TCP (transmission control protocol) is the protocol that defines how the actual data transfer takes place. One of the problems with IP that standards groups are addressing right now is that it doesn't encrypt the data packets—anyone can read a packet traveling on the Internet. Future versions of IP will address this need by using some form of encryption technology. In the meantime, some companies have coupled TCP with other technologies to provide encryption technology for the short term.

ISAPI (Internet Server Application Programming Interface)   A set of function calls and interface elements designed to make using Microsoft's Internet Information Server (IIS) and associated products such as Peer Web Server easier. Essentially this set of API calls provides the programmer with access to the server itself. Such access makes it easier to provide full server access to the Internet server through a series of ActiveX controls without the use of a scripting language.

ITU (International Telephony Union) Formerly the CCITT. This group is most famous for their standards concerning modem communications. However, in recent years, this group has also begun work with both FAX and Internet standards (among other concerns). All of the older ITU standards still use the CCITT moniker. Newer standards use the ITU moniker. Unlike many other standards groups, the ITU is multi-national and is staffed by representatives from many different countries.

Joint Pictures Entertainment Group file format (*See* JPEG file format)

JPEG file (*See* JPEG file format)

JPEG (Joint Pictures Entertainment Group) file format One of two graphics file formats used on the Internet. This is a vector file format normally used to render high-resolution images or pictures.

LAN (local area network) A combination of hardware and software used to connect a group of PCs to each other and/or to a mini or mainframe computer. Two main networking models are in use: peer-to-peer and client/server. The peer-to-peer model doesn't require a dedicated server. In addition, all the workstations in the group can share resources. The client/server model uses a central server for resource sharing, but some special methods are provided for using local resources in a limited way.

Local area network (*See* LAN)

Locally unique identifier (*See* LUID)

LUID (locally unique identifier) Essentially a pointer to an object, the LUID identifies each process and resource for security purposes. In other words, even if a user has two copies of precisely the same resource option (like a document), both copies would have a unique LUID. This method of identification prevents some types of security access violation under Windows NT.

Macro A form of programming that records keystrokes and other programming-related tasks to a file on disk or within the current document. Most applications provide a macro recorder that records the keystrokes and mouse clicks you make. This means that you don't even have to write them, in most cases. Macros are especially popular in spreadsheets. Most macros use some form of DDE to complete OLE-related tasks.

B

Mail Handling Service   (*See* MHS)

Mail Transfer System   (*See* MTS)

MFC (Microsoft Foundation Class) files   The set of DLLs required to make many Microsoft applications work. These files contain the shared classes used as a basis for creating the application. For example, a pushbutton is a separate class within these files. Normally, you'll find the MFC files in the Windows SYSTEM folder—they use MFC as the starting letters of the filename.

MHS (Mail Handling Service)   A method for encrypting and decrypting user mail and performing other mail management services. Most NOSs provide some type of MHS as part of the base system. Several standards are available on the Internet for providing MHS as part of a Web site. The two most notable specifications are IETF RFC1421from the IETF and X.400 from the ITU (formerly CCITT).

Microsoft Foundation Class files   (*See* MFC files)

MTS (Mail Transfer System)   A method of transferring mail from one location to another. In most cases this requires some form of encryption along with other transport-specific issues. Most NOSs provide some type of MTS as part of their base services. However, the Internet requires special transport mechanisms. Several standards are available on the Internet for providing MTS as part of a Web site. The two most notable specifications are IETF RFC1421 from the IETF and X.400 from the ITU (formerly CCITT).

Nested objects   Two or more objects that are coupled in some way. The objects normally appear within the confines of a container object. Object nesting allows multiple objects to define the properties of a higher-level object. It also allows the user to associate different types of objects with each other.

Netscape ONE (Open Network Environment)   A set of specialized application programming interfaces (APIs) and class libraries based on the Internet Inter-ORB Protocol (IIOP) and Common Object Request Broker Architecture (CORBA) specifications that enable a programmer to create customized Internet applications. One of the benefits of this customization is that the programmer could get by without using CGI or other scripting languages to access data on the server, a requirement using standard HTTP. ONE currently includes five Java-based foundation class libraries: User Interface Controls, User Interface Services, Security, Messaging, and Distributed Objects. Future plans include foundation classes for databases, and file server directory library access for Novell's NetWare Directory Services (NDS) and other products. This new technology also requires a JavaScript upgrade that Microsoft may or may not support.

Network interface card (*See* NIC)

NIC (network interface card)   The device responsible for allowing a workstation to communicate with a file server and other workstations. It provides the physical means of creating the connection. The card plugs into an expansion slot in the computer. A cable that attaches to the back of the card completes the communication path.

NOS (network operating system)   The operating system that runs on the file server or other centralized file/print sharing devices. This operating system normally provides multiuser access capability and user accounting software in addition to other network-specific utilities.

Object conversion   A method of changing the format and properties of an object created by one application to the format and properties used by another. Conversion moves the data from one application to another, usually without a loss in formatting, but always without a loss of content.

Object linking and embedding (*See* OLE)

OCX (OLE Control eXtension)   A special form of VBX designed to make adding OLE capabilities to an application easier for the programmer. Essentially, an OCX is a DLL with an added programmer and OLE interface.

ODBC (Open Database Connectivity)   A set of Windows function calls and other interface elements introduced by Microsoft. ODBC is designed to improve access to information contained in database files through the use of a common interface and data-independent access methods. Normally, ODBC relies on SQL to translate DBMS-specific commands from the client into a generic language. The ODBC agents on the server translate these SQL requests into server-specific commands.

OLE (object linking and embedding)   The process of packaging a filename and any required parameters into an object and then pasting this object into the file created by another application. For example, you could place a graphic object within a word processing document or spreadsheet. When you look at the object, it appears as if you simply pasted the data from the originating application into the current application (similar to DDE). When linked, the data provided by the object automatically changes as you change the data in the original object. When embedded, the data doesn't change unless you specifically edit it, but the data retains the original format and you still use the original application to edit the data. Often you can start the originating application and automatically load the required data by double-clicking on the object. The newer OLE 2 specification allows for in-place data editing as well as editing in a separate application window.

OLE Control eXtension   (*See* OCX)

ONE   (*See* Netscape ONE)

Open Database Connectivity   (*See* ODBC)

PCT (Private Communication Technology)   The IETF is working with Microsoft on this particular protocol. Like SSL, PCT is designed to provide a secure method of communication between a client and server at the low protocol level. It can work with any high-level protocol such as HTTP, FTP, or TELNET. PCT is designed to prevent hackers from eavesdropping on communications between a client and server through the use of encryption, authentication, and digital signatures. As with SSL, client authentication is optional. PCT also assumes that you have TCP or another reliable transport protocol in place. It corrects some inherent weaknesses in SSL by providing extended cryptographic negotiation and other added features.

PEM (Privacy Enhanced Mail)   A set of four approved IETF specifications (IETF RFC1421 through IETF RFC1424) that define the methods for sending and receiving mail on the Internet. Of prime importance are techniques for encrypting and decrypting mail in such a way that optimal privacy is assured with a minimal amount of user interaction. The specification also covers topics related to mail encryption, including the certification of vendors to perform the service and the use of CSPs.

Privacy Enhanced Mail   (*See* PEM)

Private Communication Technology   (*See* PCT)

Private key file   (*See* PVK)

PVK (private key file)   A file contained on either the client or server machine that allows full data encryption to take place. When the key in this file is combined with the public key provided with a file, the file becomes accessible. Since the PVK file never gets transmitted from one place to another, the level of data communication security is greatly increased. PVK files are used with all kinds of certificate-based communications. For example, getting a personal certificate from VeriSign or another organization involves creating a PVK on your computer. Developers also create a PVK for use with various types of Internet technologies such as ActiveX. The process of creating the private and public keys and assigning them to the actual component is called *signing*. In the same way, signed mail or other communications can greatly enhance security by making the author of the document known.

RAD (rapid application development) A tool that allows you to design your program's interface and then write the commands to make that user interface do something useful. Visual Basic and Delphi are both examples of RAD programs.

Rapid application development (*See* RAD)

Remote access The ability to use a remote resource as you would a local resource. In some cases, this also means downloading the remote resource to use as a local resource.

Remote procedure call (*See* RPC)

Rich Text Format (*See* RTF)

RPC (remote procedure call) The ability to use code or data on a machine as if it were local. This is an advanced capability that will eventually pave the way for decentralized applications.

RTF (Rich Text Format) A file format originally introduced by Microsoft that allows an application to store formatting information in plain ASCII text. All commands begin with a backslash. For example, the \cf command tells an RTF-capable editor which color to use from the color table when displaying a particular section of text.

SACL (security access control list) The SACL controls Windows' auditing feature. Every time a user or group accesses an object and the auditing feature for that object is turned on, Windows makes an entry in the audit log.

Secure Sockets Layer (*See* SSL)

Security access control list (*See* SACL)

Security identifier (*See* SID)

ShellX (Shell extension) A special application that gives some type of added values to the operating system interface. In most cases, the application must register itself with the registry before the operating system will recognize it.

SID (security identifier) The part of a user's access token that identifies the user throughout the network—it's like having an account number. The user token that the SID identifies tells what groups the user belongs to and what privileges the user has. Each group also has a SID, so the user's SID contains references to the various group SIDs that he or she belongs to, not a complete set of group access rights. You would normally use the User Manager utility under Windows NT to change the contents of this access token.

B

SQL (Structured Query Language)   Most DBMSs use this language to exchange information. Some also use it as a native language. SQL provides a method for requesting information from the DBMS. It defines which table or tables to use, what information to get from the table, and how to sort that information.

SSL (Secure Sockets Layer)   A W^{3}C standard originally proposed by Netscape for transferring encrypted information from the client to the server at the protocol layer. Sockets allow low-level encryption of transactions in higher-level protocols such as HTTP, NNTP, and FTP. The standard also specifies methods for server and client authentication (though client site authentication is optional).

Stickey Keys   One of several special features provided by Microsoft to help the physically challenged use computers better. This feature is provided as part of the Accessibility applet in Windows 95 and Windows NT 4.0.

Stream object   An encapsulated data container used to transfer information from one object to another. For example, a stream object could move data from application memory to a file on disk.

Structured Query Language   (*See* SQL)

TCP/IP (transmission control protocol/Internet protocol)   A standard communication line protocol developed by the U.S. Department of Defense. The protocol defines how two devices talk to each other. Think of the protocol as a type of language used by the two devices.

Token calls   Part of the Windows NT security API that deals with user access to a particular object. To gain access to an object, the requesting object must provide a token. In essence, a token is a ticket to gain entrance to the secured object. The security API compares the rights provided by the requesting object's token with those required to gain entry to the secured object. If the requesting object's rights are equal to or greater than those required to gain entry, then the operating system grants access. Tokens are a universal form of entry under Windows NT and aren't restricted to the user or external applications. Even the operating system must use them.

UNC (uniform naming convention)   A method for identifying network resources without using specific locations. In most cases this convention is used with drives and printers, but it can also be used with other types of resources. A UNC normally uses a device name in place of an identifier. For example, a disk drive on a remote machine might be referred to as "\\AUX\DRIVE-C". The advantage of using a UNC is that the resource name won't change even if the resource location does (as would happen if users changed drive mappings on their machine).

Uniform naming convention   (*See* UNC)

Uniform resource locator   (*See* URL)

URL (uniform resource locator)   The basic method of identifying a location on the Internet. A resource could be a file, a Web site, or anything else you can access through this media. The URL always contains three essential parts. The first part identifies the protocol used to access the resource. For example, the letters *http* at the beginning of an URL always signify that the site uses the hypertext transfer protocol and will present some type of visual information. The second part of the URL is the name of a host. For example, the most popular host name is *www*, which stands for World Wide Web. The third part of the URL is a domain. This is normally the name of the site machine and the kind of site you plan to access. (For example, *MyCompany.com* would tell you that the domain is a machine named MyCompany and that it's some kind of commercial site.) After the site information are directories, just like you have on your hard drive. So an URL like http://www.mycompany.com/mysite.html would point to a Web page that uses HTTP on the World Wide Web at mycompany.com.

VBA (Visual Basic for Applications)   A form of Microsoft Visual Basic used by applications. It provides more capabilities than VBScript, yet less than the full-fledged Visual Basic programming language. The basic tenet of this language is full machine access without a high learning curve. VBA was originally designed to allow users to create script-type macros and provide interapplication communication. It's been extended since that time to provide a higher-level programming language for times when VBScript doesn't provide enough capabilities to perform a specific task.

VBX (Visual Basic eXtension)   A special form of DLL that contains functions as well as a programmer interface. The DLL part of VBX accepts requests from an application for specific services, such as opening a file. The programmer interface portion appears on the toolbar of a program, such as Visual Basic, as a button. Clicking the button creates one instance of that particular type of control.

Virtual reality modeling language   (*See* VRML)

Visual Basic eXtension   (*See* VBX)

Visual Basic for Applications   (*See* VBA)

VRML (virtual reality modeling language)   A special scripting (scene description) language that allows a Web site to transfer vector graphic imaging information with a minimum of overhead. The value of this language is that it uses very little actual data to transfer the coordinate

B

information required. VRML is still very much in the experimental stage—transaction speeds are a major concern due to the relatively narrow bandwidth of current dial-up connections and the multitude of changes that take place during a VRML session. Even using minimized data transfer doesn't make VRML a fast performer with the current state of technology.

W^{3}C (World Wide Web Consortium)   A standards organization essentially devoted to Internet security issues, but also involved in other issues such as the special <OBJECT> tag required by Microsoft to implement ActiveX technology. The W^{3}C first appeared on the scene in December 1994 when they endorsed SSL (Secure Sockets Layer). In February 1995 they also endorsed application-level security for the Internet. Their current project is the Digital Signatures Initiative—W^{3}C presented it in May 1996 in Paris.

WAN (wide area network)   A grouping of two or more LANs in more than one physical location.

Wide area network   (*See* WAN)

World Wide Web Consortium   (*See* W^{3}C)

Index

A

<A HREF> tag, 113, 189, 451-453
About box, modifying, 30
Absolute security descriptor, 196
Access allowed ACE, explained, 197
Access control entries (ACEs), 197, 200
Access control lists (ACLs), 196-197, 200
Access denied ACE, explained, 197
Access tokens, Windows security, 193-196
ACE headers, 197
ACEs (access control entries), 197, 200
ACLs (access control lists), 196-197, 200
Acrobat ActiveX for Windows 95, 532-533
ActivDoc application, creating, 339-356
ActiveMovie control, 426, 498-508
ActiveX
    application integration, 22
    application updates, 23
    capabilities for users, 22
    component resources, 517-533
    history of, 6-15
    security of, 23
    user response time, 22
    user's perspective, 22-23
    what it is, 15-17
    what it will do, 17-18
ActiveX Accessibility API, 143
ActiveX connection, 15
ActiveX Control Cachefolder (Netscape
    Navigator), 218
ActiveX Control Pad controls, table of, 426-432
ActiveX Control Pad utility, 55-56, 426-432

ActiveX control-based browser plug-ins,
    531-533
ActiveX controls. *See* Controls (ActiveX)
ActiveX Document, 143-166
    architecture, 155-166
    converting an existing application, 352-356
    creating, 339-356
    creating a connection, 149-150
    object participation, 147-148
    OLE interface functions, 158
    server, 345-352
    testing, 352
    what it is, 145-155
ActiveX hyperlink interface, 289-294
ActiveX Movie, 143-144
ActiveX Scripting, 223-259
    establishing communications, 227-228
    interface elements, 226-227
    overview, 225-229
    scripting engine states, 228-229
ActiveX Template Library for Visual C++, 68
ActiveX VRML, 143-144
Adaptable links, 11
Add Event dialog, 319
Add Member Variable dialog, 36, 373
Add Method dialog, 308
Add Property dialog, 33
AddACE function, 199
Adding a Class dialog, 372
Additional Controls dialog, 60
AddRef function, 72
Advanced Options dialog, 341
Alchemy Mind Works, 277

ALLText HT/Pro TList Enhanced Outline,
    524-525
ALX (HTML layout) files, 477-480
Anchors, 113-114
Animated GIFs, 270-271, 276-285
Apex Data Bound Grid control, 482-488
Application launching, 307-314
Application integration, 22
Application updates, 23
Audio files, 496-498, 509-513
Authentication, client-side, 206
AVI video files, 498, 507

B

Backing up the registry, 77
Bells and whistles, 27
<BGSOUND> tag, 275
Blob key, explained, 212
Block cipher (Microsoft), 211, 213
Browser, testing ActiveX controls locally, 54-59
Browser plug-ins, 531-533
Business perspective of the Internet, 173-174

C

C++ versions, 26. *See also* Visual C++ 4.2
CAB files, building, 136-140
CalculateTotals(), 248
CALG_RC2 (block cipher), 211, 213
CALG_RC4 (stream cipher), 211
Case statements, 396-397
CCmdTarget class, 350-351
<CENTER> tag, 122, 124
Certificate-Based Key Management (PEM2), 183
CERT2SPC utility, 220
CheckBox control, 427
Class declarations (Visual C++ 4.2 and MFC),
    354
Class entries, capitalization of, 373
Class factory, explained, 134
Class Wizard dialog, 32
Classes, defining, 360-365
ClassWizard, 309, 318, 360-365, 376, 389
Client, defined, 8
Client-side authentication, 206

CLSID (class identifier) key, 82, 134-135
CODEBASE property, 466
Color changes, Web site, 314-327, 418
ComboBox control, 428
Command (application), 528
Command Button control, 428
Communications Library 3, 525-526
Compiler, 27
Component download (CAB) files, building,
    136-140
Component object instantiation, 69
Component Object Model (COM), 12, 65-69
Component resources (ActiveX), 517-533
    choosing, 518-522
    company support, 520
    cost, 521
    demo or shareware, 519-520
    efficiency, 521-522
    flexibility, 521
    money-back guarantee, 520
    recommendations, 519
    royalties, 518-519
    source code, 519
Compound documents, 7
    defined, 8
    Word for Windows, 74-75
Container, defined, 8
Context menu, 84
Control environment, 71
Control Pad controls, table of, 426-432
Control Pad utility, 55-56, 426-432
Control Properties dialog, 100
Control streams, OLE, 98-104
Controls (ActiveX)
    acquiring, 526-531
    activating, 310
    building basic, 25-62
    download size, 27
    vs. OCX controls, 18-19
    improvements in Visual C++ 4.2, 337-339
    layout, 256, 259
    with one object in each, 28
    signing, 219
    testing, 28, 49-62, 221
    testing a full Web page, 60-61
    testing locally within a browser, 54-59
    testing in a standard environment, 50-53

testing on an uncontaminated machine, 61-62
in the Toolbox, 59
unregistering, 219
using with JavaScript, 254-259
using with VBScript, 249-254
working with, 248-259
Cookies (JavaScript), 235, 436-441
CorelDRAW 5.0, 83-85
CPButtonCtrl class, implementing, 369-397
CryptAquireContext(), 210
CryptDestroyKey(), 212
CryptExportKey(), 212
CryptGenKey(), 211
CryptGetProvParam(), 210
CryptGetUserKey(), 211
CryptoAPI (Cryptography API), 208-213
Cryptographic Service Provider (CSP), 209
Cryptographic Service Provider Developer's Kit (CSPDK), 209
CUserInfoCtrl:CUserInfoCtrl(), 302
Cybercash, 188

D

DAO. *See* Data Access Objects
DAO example, 461-476
    ActiveX control settings, 466
    database field structure, 463
    program listing, 467-474
DASS, 180
DAO3032.DLL, 454
Data, as the object of protection, 175-176
Data access functions, DAO vs. ODBC, 457
Data access in an HTML layout, 476-480
Data Access Objects (DAO), 453-461
    data access functions, 457
    explained, 454-456
    within an HTML page, 476-480
    vs. ODBC, 456-459
Data binding, 487-488
Data entry, 423-447
Data entry form, 425-441
Data entry forms with scripts, 441-447
Data grid display, 482
Data protection, creating, 176-177
Data security. *See* Security

Data storage, 73-75
Data streaming, 508
Database connection, 449-488
Database field structure, 463
Date Select (application), 528
DCOM (distributed component object model), 14
DDE (dynamic data exchange), 6-7
Demo component resources, 519-520
DepictIt control, 397-421
    building, 397-415
    program listing, 400-411
    testing, 415-421
DFX_ functions, 457
Dialog editor, 31
DIANTZ.EXE, 136-140
DigiCash, 188
Digital certificate dialog, 207
Digital ID, classes of, 206
Digital signature, implementing, 205
Digital Signature Initiative, 179
Digital signatures, 204-208
Distributed Authentication Security Service (DASS), 180
distributed component object model (DCOM), 14
DLLs (dynamic link libraries), 67-68
Documents, ActiveX. *See* ActiveX Document
Documents, HTML. *See* HTML documents
DoPropExchange function, 46
DOS libraries, 67
Dot syntax reference, 234
Double buffering, 459
Downloading from the Internet, security of, 134-136, 190, 213-221
Drag and drop, 10
Drawing (simple), creating, 397-421
DSI (Digital Signatures Initiative), 181
dynamic data exchange (DDE), 6-7
dynamic link libraries (DLLs), 67-68

E

EarthTime, 530-531
<EMBED> tag, 499
Encryption algorithms, Microsoft, 211
Encryption (file), 191, 209-213

Extended Internet Tag SHTTP (EIT SHTTP), 181
External testing, 61-62

F

Fax Plus, 525-526
Fields (input), 424
File association area (registry), 83
File directories, obtaining, 172
Files, encrypting, 209-213
Firewalls, 176
First Virtual Accounts scheme, 187-188
Fonts property page, 390
<FORM> tag, 125, 128
Forms
    aesthetics of, 425, 432-435
    data entry, 425-441
    Microsoft Forms 2.0, 427-431
    usability consideration, 425, 432-435
Freeing memory used by object instances, 96

G

Generic Security Service Application Program
    Interface (GSS-APPI), 181-182
GetACE function, 199
GetColor(), 322
GetKernelObjectSecurity call, 198
GetSecurityDescriptorDACL call, 199
GetUserObjectSecurity call, 198
GIF Construction Set, using, 277-283
GIFs (animated), 270-271, 276-285
Glossary of terms, 535-552
Grabbing user information, 299-306
Graphics, 367-421
Graphics Server SDK, 523-524
Group SIDs, ordering of, 200
GSS-APPI, 181-182
GSS-APPI C-bindings, 182

H

<HEAD> tag, 111
History of ActiveX, 6-15
HKEY_CLASSES_ROOT | CLSID key, 82, 134-135

HKEY_CLASSES_ROOT display, 80
HotSpot control, 426
HREF anchor technique, 451-453
HTML documents
    adding graphics, 118-121
    adding headings, 111-113
    creating, 114-131
    creating tables in, 121-124
    unordered and ordered lists in, 116-119
HTML forms, 124-131
HTML (hypertext markup language), 107-140
HTML layout, data access in, 476-480
HTML layout files (ALX), 477-480
HTML links and anchors, 113-114
HTML overview, 109-114
HTML tags, twelve basic, 110-111
http:, 107
<Hx> tag, 111-113
Hyperlinking basics, 289-294

I

Icon and text button, implementing, 369-397
IETF FRC1423 (PEM3), 183
IETF informational sites, 179
IETF (Internet Engineering Task Force), 179-180
IETF RFC documents, 179
IETF RFC1421 (PEM1), 183
IETF RFC1422 (PEM2), 183
IETF RFC1424 (PEM4), 184
IETF RFC1507 (DASS), 180
IETF RFC1508 (GSS-APPI), 181
IETF RFC1508 (GSS-APPI) C-bindings, 182
IETF RFC1510 (Kerberos V5), 185
IETF RFC1630 (URI), 186
Image control, 427
ImageKnife, 527-528
<IMG> tag, 120
Indenting code for easy reading, 124
In-place editing, 145-146
<INPUT> tag, 125, 247, 313, 326
Insert OLE Control dialog, 99
Instantiating a component object, 69
Interface, creating, 71-72
Interface elements of ActiveX scripting, 226-227
Interlaced images, 285
Internal testing, 50-61

Internet, 261-294
   business perspective of, 173-174
   designing for, 263-266
   security standards, 178-188
   Wild West of computers, 172-178
Internet Component Download service,
   137-139, 189-190, 219
Internet downloads, 134-136, 213-221
Internet Explorer 3.0 (Microsoft), 71
   ActiveMovie example in, 506
   HTML tags in, 116
   in-place editing, 146
   sound files, 496-497
   Temporary Internet Files, 218
   use of OCCACHE folders, 218
Internet Protocol Security Protocol (IPSec), 182
IOleCommandTarget class, 162-164
IOleDocument class, 159-160
IOleDocumentView class, 160-162
IPrint class, 164-166
ISAPI Wizard (Visual C++ 4.2), 330
IUnknown interface, 71-72

J

JASC products, 277
JavaScript language, 19-21
   basic scripting, 243-248
   overview, 234-237
   security problems, 171-172
   using ActiveX controls with, 254-259
JEPI (Joint Electronic Payment Initiative), 182,
   186
Jittery script, 265

K

Kerberos Network Authentication Service (V5),
   185
Key Certification and Related Services (PEM4),
   184
Keys (registry), 78-82
   OLE 1, 82-87
   OLE 2, 87-92

L

Label control, 429
Launching a program, 307-314
LaunchIt control, 308-315
Layers of protection, CryptoAPI, 208-209
Library, DOS, 67
Library support, adding, 357-358
Light Lib, 529-530
Links, 113-114, 285-294
   adaptable, 11
   storage-independent, 10-11
ListBox control, 429
Locally unique identifier (LUID), 194

M

MAKECERT utility, 220
<MARQUEE> tag, 246
Masked Edit (application), 528
Media player (ActiveMovie control), 498-508
MediaKnife, 527-528
Memory used by object instances, freeing, 96
Message Encryption and Authentication
   Procedures (PEM1), 183
Message map, defining, 375-376
MFC class declarations, 354
MFC ClassWizard, 309, 318, 360-365, 376, 389
MFC (Microsoft Foundation Class), 136
Microsoft Access SQL commands, 484
Microsoft Developer Studio, 29
Microsoft encryption algorithms, 211
Microsoft Forms 2.0
   controls, 427-431
   Frame, 428
   Image, 429
   MultiPage, 429
Microsoft Internet Explorer. *See* Internet
   Explorer 3.0
Microsoft Office Binders. *See* ActiveX Document
Microsoft OLE 2 SDK, 72
Microsoft RemoteData control, 480-488
Microsoft Visual C++ 4.0, 29. *See also* Visual
   C++ 4.2
MIDI sound files, 497
MODALTYPE, 48
Money, standard methods of handling, 187-188

Money-back guarantee (component resources),
520
Monikers. *See* URL monikers
Multimedia, 491-513
    third-party solutions, 508-513
    Windows built-in, 493-498

N

Navigation stack, explained, 290
NCompass ActiveX Pro, 70
Nested objects, 10
Netscape Navigator
    ActiveMovie example in, 505
    ActiveX Control Cache folder, 218
    online transactions, 188
    sound files, 496
    and VBScript, 504
    video files, 498
Network OLE, 14
New Project Information dialog, 342
New Query dialog, 464
New technologies, 329-365

O

Object conversion, 11-12
Object Data Stream Tool, 98-103
object linking. *See* OLE
Object menu, 8
<OBJECT> tag, 100-104, 131-134, 257, 306,
    461-462
Objects, 8
    ActiveX Document, 147-148
    in Data Access Objects (DAO), 453-461
    freeing memory used by, 96
    one object in each control, 28
    Windows, 193
OCCACHE folders, 70, 218
OCXs (OLE Control eXtensions), 18, 65-66, 68.
    See also Controls (ActiveX)
ODBC, 455-459
ODBC data access functions, 457
ODS file, 102-104
ODS_Tool utility, 67, 98-104
OLE automation, 11

OLE Control Wizard, 29-30
OLE Control Wizard screens, 30
OLE Document Objects, 144
OLE (object linking and embedding), 7-9,
    65-104
    control hosting, 69-75
    control streams, 98-104
    Events page, 34
    interface functions for ActiveX Document,
      158
    from OLE 1 to OLE 2, 9-12
    programming, 13-14
    registry keys, 82-92
    terms, 8
OLE 1 registry keys, 82-87
OLE 2 registry keys, 87-92
OLEViewer utility, 67, 87, 92-98, 156-157
    ActivDoc application in, 343
    enhanced views, 96-98
    Expert Mode, 97-98
    freeing memory, 96
    interfaces, 94-95
OnClick() message handling function, 47
OnOnOffChanged function, 47
OnResetState function, 47
Optimized object storage, 12
OptionButton control, 430
Order entry form sample, 247
Out-process server, 149

P

Pages (Web). *See also* Web sites
    that download slowly, 266-269
    tricks for friendly but fast, 269-276
    viewing source code for, 108
<PARAM> tag, 133
parseFloat(), 248
parseInt(), 248
PButton control, 369-397
    adding custom icons, 394-397
    creating a test program, 388-391
    defining a message map, 375-376
    defining property pages, 371-375
    program listing, 377-386
    using on a Web page, 391-394

PCT (Private Communication Technology), 182, 201-204
   corrects problems with SSL, 202
   how it works, 204
   protocol connection, 204
   second version of, 203-204
Persistent data, 27
PKCS #7 signed data structure, 218
<PRE> tag, 275
Privacy Enhanced Mail
   Part I (PEM1), 183
   Part II (PEM2), 183
   Part III (PEM3), 183
   Part IV (PEM4), 184
Private Communication Technology. *See* PCT
Program, launching, 307-314
ProgramName property, 310
Properties, 30, 32-33
Properties dialog pages, 51-52
Property Inspector, 47
Property Page dialog, 35
Property pages, 33-37, 48, 371-375
Publishing (Web Publishing Wizard), 150-156
Pixel trap, 266-269
Pixels, explained, 266

Q

Query interface, 72
QueryServiceObjectSecurity call, 199

R

Radio Button Properties dialog, 35
Radio buttons, 34
RealAudio, 509-513
RegEdit utility, 76-77
RegEnumValue(), 302-303
RegGetKeySecurity call, 199
Registry keys, 78-92
Registry query, 301-304
Registry subkeys, 80-82
Registry values, 78-79
Registry (Windows), 75-87
   access basics, 299-306
   backing up, 77

   defined, 75
   file association area, 83
RegOpenKey(), 301
RegOpenKeyEx(), 301
RegSetKeySecurity call, 199
RegSvr32 program, 219
Release function, 72
RemoteData control, 480-488
RemoteData control properties, 483
Resource Symbols dialog, 31
Resources, creating, 358-360
RFX_ functions, 457
Royalties (component resources), 518-519
Running an application, 307-314

S

SACL (security access control list), 196
Safety Violation dialog, 58
Sandbox approach to security, 170
Save Content dialog, 102
<SCRIPT> tag, 504
Script Wizard, 128-131, 242-243, 250, 256, 417-419
Script Wizard dialog, displaying, 417
Scripting, 189, 223-259, 441-447
Scripting basics, 237-248
Scripting engine, 226
Scripting engine states, 228-229
Scripting host, 225
Scrollbar control, 430
Secure/Multipurpose Internet Mail Extensions, 184
Secure/Wide Area Network (S/WAN), 184
Security, 169-221
   Internet standards for, 178-188
   JavaScript, 171-172
   protecting the server, 201
   safe Internet downloads, 23, 134-136, 213-221
   scripting, 189
   secure environment solution, 177-178
   Windows NT, 189-213
   Windows NT built-in features, 191-201
Security access control list (SACL), 196
Security descriptors, 194, 196-199
Security identifiers (SIDs), 193, 200

<SELECT> tag, 125-126
Self-relative security descriptor, 196
Server, 8, 201
SetColor(), 322
SetKernelObjectSecurity call, 198
SetSecurityDescriptorSACL call, 199
SetServiceObjectSecurity call, 199
SetUserObjectSecurity call, 198
Shareware component resources, 519-520
ShellX (shell extension) key, 80-82
Shrink-wrap approach to security, 171
SHTTP (Secure Hypertext Transfer Protocol), 185
SIDs, 193, 200
SIGNCODE utility, 220-221
Signing your code, 219
Simple Query Wizard, 464
Sites (Web)
    improving with color changes, 314-327
    tracking visited, 172
Size property (window size), 311
SmartHelp, 529
S/MIME, 184
Sound files, 264-265, 496-497, 509-513
Source code (component resources), 519
Source code for Web pages, viewing, 108
Special extension registry subkeys, 80-82
SpinButton control, 430
SQL commands in Microsoft Access, 484
Square (sunken) with red "X", what it means, 306
SSL (Secure Sockets Layer), 179-180, 185, 202
Standard toolbar, 358
Sticky Keys, 143
Storage objects, 73-74
STORAGE.DLL, 73-74
Storage-independent links, 10-11
Storing data, 73-75
Stream cipher (Microsoft), 211
Stream objects, 73-74
S/WAN, 184
SysInfo (application), 528
System alarm ACE, 197
System audit ACE, 197

TabStrip control, 430
TCP, 202
TCP/IP, 202
Template Library for Visual C++, 68
Terminology, glossary of, 535-552
Test program, creating, 388-391
Testing a control (basics), 28, 49-62
    external, 61-62
    internal, 50-61
Text button and icon, implementing, 369-397
<TEXTAREA> tag, 126
TextBox control, 431
TList Enhanced Outline, 524-525
ToggleButton control, 431
Token calls (Windows), 195
Toolbar (standard), 358
Toolbox, new control in, 59
Tracking sites visited, 172
Trust provider, 215

U

UNC (Uniform Naming Convention), 154
Universal Resource Identifiers (URIs) in WWW, 186
Uploading a file, tricking the user into, 171
URL monikers, 286
    creating, 288-289
    interfaces, 287-288
    overview, 286-288
    working with, 356-365
URLs (Uniform Resource Locators), 286
User information, grabbing, 299-306
UserInfo ActiveX utility, 306
Users
    perspective of ActiveX, 22-23
    response time, 22
    tricking into uploading a file, 171
Utilites (utility programs), 297-327

V

VBA (Visual Basic for Applications), 229-233
VBScript (Visual Basic Script) language, 21-22
    basic scripting, 238-243
    and Netscape Navigator, 504

T

<TABLE> tag, 121-122, 326

overview, 229-233
   using ActiveX controls with, 249-254
VBXs (Visual Basic eXtensions), 68
VDOLive ActiveX for Windows 95, 531-532
Version management, 11
VFAT file system, 198
Video files, 498, 507
View menu, 97
Viewing source code for Web pages, 108
Visual Basic for Applications (VBA), 229-233
Visual Basic scripting. *See* VBScript
Visual C++ 4.0, 29
Visual C++ 4.2 (Microsoft)
   ActiveX control improvements, 337-339
   application enhancements, 337
   class declarations, 354
   ISAPI Wizard, 330-334
   new features of, 329-337
Visual editing, 10
VRML ActiveX for Windows 95, 532

W

WAV sound files, 264-265, 496
Web Publishing Wizard, 150-156
Web server security, 176
Web sites
   improving with color changes, 314-327
   tracking visited, 172

WebBrowser object, 432
Window.Document.Write(), 305
Windows access tokens, 193-196
Windows built-in multimedia capabilities, 493-498
Windows 95 registry, 76
Windows NT registry, 75
Windows NT security, 189-213
Windows objects, 193
Windows registry OLE, 75-87
Windows security descriptor, 193
Windows Software Publishing Trust Provider, 217-219
Windows token calls, 195
Windows trust verification API, 214-217
WinExec(), 307-314
WinVerifyTrust(), 135, 215-218
Word for Windows compound document, 74-75
World Wide Web Consortium (W3C), 19
Write() method, 305
W3C (World Wide Web Consortium), 179-180, 186-187

X

X.509 certificates, 218-219